*Matthew might be said to designate
Christ principally in terms of the mystery
of the Incarnation, and thus he is
depicted in the figure of a man....*

*Mark in terms of the victory of the
Resurrection, and thus he is depicted in
the figure of a lion....*

*Luke in terms of the mystery of the
Passion, and thus he is depicted in the
figure of a bull....*

*But John, who flies to the heights of his
divinity, is depicted as an eagle.*

ST. THOMAS AQUINAS

THE
WORD ON FIRE
BIBLE

ST. MATTHEW

ST. MARK

ST. LUKE

ST. JOHN

THE GOSPELS

General Editor: Brandon Vogt
Creative Director: Rozann Lee
Content Manager: Matthew Becklo
Content Assistant: Bert Ghezzi

Art direction, cover design, and layout by
Nicolas Fredrickson and Michael Stevens.

Art commentary entries written by Michael Stevens.

Scripture quotations are from the *New Revised Standard Version Bible: Catholic Edition* (copyright © 1989, 1993), National Council of the Churches of Christ in the United States of America. Used by permission. All rights reserved worldwide.

Text of the *New Revised Standard Version: Catholic Edition*:

Imprimatur:
Most Reverend Daniel E. Pilarczyk
President, National Conference of Catholic Bishops
Washington, DC, September 12, 1991

Imprimatur:
Canadian Conference of Catholic Bishops
Ottawa, October 15, 1991

Unless otherwise indicated, Church Father quotes from *Nicene and Post-Nicene Fathers, Second Series*, edited by Philip Schaff and Henry Wace (Buffalo, NY: Christian Literature Publishing Co., 1894). Revised and edited for *NewAdvent.org* by Kevin Knight. Used by permission. All rights reserved.

Excerpts from *The Priority of Christ: Toward a Postliberal Catholicism* by Robert Barron (copyright © 2007), *2 Samuel* by Robert Barron (copyright © 2015), *Exploring Catholic Theology: Essays on God, Liturgy, and Evangelization* by Robert Barron (copyright © 2015). Used by permission of Baker Academic, a division of Baker Publishing Group. All rights reserved.

Excerpts from *And Now I See: A Theology of Transformation* by Robert Barron (copyright © 1998), *Thomas Aquinas: Spiritual Master* by Robert Barron (copyright © 2008), *Word on Fire: Proclaiming the Power of Christ* by Robert Barron (copyright © 2008). Used by permission of The Crossroad Publishing Company, www.crossroadpublishing.com. All rights reserved.

Excerpts from *No Man Is an Island* by Thomas Merton (copyright © 1955 by The Abbey of Our Lady of Gethsemani and renewed in 1983 by the Trustees of the Merton Legacy Trust). Used by permission of Houghton Mifflin Harcourt Publishing Company. All rights reserved.

ISBN: 978-1-943243-55-6 (paperback)
ISBN: 978-1-943243-54-9 (hardcover)
ISBN: 978-1-943243-53-2 (leatherbound)

Library of Congress Control Number: 2020931212
Barron, Robert E., 1959–

Printed and bound in Italy

23 22 21 20   3 4

www.wordonfire.org

Contents

About Bishop Robert Barron

Bishop Robert Barron is Auxiliary Bishop in the Archdiocese of Los Angeles and founder of Word on Fire Catholic Ministries. He received a master's degree in philosophy from the Catholic University of America in 1982 and a doctorate in sacred theology from the Institut Catholique de Paris in 1992.

Bishop Barron was ordained a priest in 1986 in the Archdiocese of Chicago, and then appointed to the theological faculty of Mundelein Seminary in 1992. He has also served as a visiting professor at the University of Notre Dame and at the Pontifical University of St. Thomas Aquinas. He was twice scholar in residence at the Pontifical North American College at the Vatican.

He served as the Rector/President of Mundelein Seminary/ University of St. Mary of the Lake from 2012 until 2015.

On July 21, 2015, Pope Francis appointed Bishop Barron to be Auxiliary Bishop in the Archdiocese of Los Angeles. He was ordained bishop on September 8, 2015.

About Word on Fire

Word on Fire Catholic Ministries is a nonprofit global media apostolate that supports the work of Bishop Robert Barron and reaches millions of people to draw them into—or back to—the Catholic faith.

Word on Fire is evangelical; it proclaims Jesus Christ as the source of conversion and new life. Word on Fire is Catholic; it utilizes the tremendous resources of the Roman Catholic tradition—art, architecture, poetry, philosophy, theology, and the lives of the saints—in order to explain and interpret the event of Jesus Christ. Word on Fire is missionary; it uses media both old and new to spread the faith in the culture and share the gifts of the Church that Jesus wants his people to enjoy.

A Note About the Translation

The translation used for *The Word on Fire Bible* is the *New Revised Standard Version Bible: Catholic Edition* (NRSV-CE). It first appeared in 1989, and has received wide acclaim and broad support from academics and pastors as a Bible for all Christians.

The translation received the imprimatur of the United States Conference of Catholic Bishops and the Canadian Conference of Catholic Bishops in 1991, granting official approval for Catholic use in private study and devotional reading.

The NRSV-CE stands out among other translations because of its accuracy and readability. According to the translation committee, it is "as literal as possible" in adhering to the ancient texts and only "as free as necessary" to make the meaning clear in graceful, understandable English.

It's a wonderful translation—both for those who have never read the Bible and for those who have studied it for years.

About the Angelico Typeface

Quotations in *The Word on Fire Bible* are set in Angelico, a custom font drawn especially for this Bible. Its proportions were inspired by the designs of Renaissance typographer Erhard Ratdolt, and the font is named after Renaissance friar and fresco painter Blessed Fra Angelico, whose example of holiness and artistic mastery was a major inspiration for the visual style of this Bible.

"HE WHO WISHES TO PAINT CHRIST'S STORY MUST LIVE WITH CHRIST."

BLESSED FRA ANGELICO

About the Cover Design

Design by Nicolas Fredrickson and Michael Stevens | Essay by Nicolas Fredrickson

The cover design of *The Word on Fire Bible: The Gospels* is inspired by traditional Catholic altarpieces and iconography. Vertically through the middle you'll see the creaturely representations of the four Gospel writers, as identified throughout the Catholic tradition: a man, a lion, an ox, and an eagle.

The outer four quadrants highlight the Gospels in various ways. In the lower left you will find the serpent from Genesis—an image of the devil. The serpent tempts humanity and, through the fall of man, maintains dominion for a time as "the ruler of this world" (John 12:31). But there is hope for mankind in the midst of this tragedy. In Genesis 3:15, God tells the serpent that his reign will end and gives us the first hint of the Incarnation, which is why theologians describe this verse as the *protoevangelium*, or the first Gospel.

The upper left quadrant depicts the night of the Nativity, which Luke's Gospel presents as the fulfillment of Nathan's prophecy that God would raise up a son of David and "establish the throne of his kingdom forever" (2 Sam. 7:13). But the startling claim of the Gospels is that this newborn King is not only human but divine—the marriage of heaven and earth in person. As John tells us in the first chapter of his Gospel: "The Word became flesh and lived among us" (John 1:14).

The upper right quadrant depicts the Passion of Christ. His anticipated "hour" has come, fulfilling Isaiah's prophecy of the "suffering servant": "He was wounded for our transgressions, crushed for our iniquities; upon him was the punishment that made us whole, and by his bruises we are healed" (Isa. 53:5). This innocent man, as St. Paul tells us, "humbled himself and became obedient to the point of death—even death on a cross" (Phil. 2:8).

Finally, in the lower right quadrant, the story reaches its culmination. After the Crucifixion, Jesus was wrapped in burial cloths and laid in a tomb. A small but important detail tells us that this tomb was in a garden (John 19:41). This connects the passage to the Garden of Eden in a significant way. The empty tomb discovered by Jesus' followers shows that while death was introduced in the Garden of Eden, death was defeated in this new garden. The long-awaited "offspring" of the third chapter of Genesis has finally crushed the head of the serpent.

The letters toward the center are drawn from Christ identifying himself as "the Alpha and the Omega" (Rev. 22:13), representing his eternity. The four outermost symbols are ancient symbols of Christ: IHS is an abbreviation for "Jesus" in the Greek; INRI is an acronym for the Latin phrase *Iesus Nazarenus, Rex Iudaeorum* (Jesus of Nazareth, the King of the Jews), which was inscribed and hung on the cross above Jesus' head (John 19:19); the overlapping P and X in the upper left is called the Chi Rho, another abbreviation from the Greek for "Christ"; and the lower right is an abbreviation from the Greek for "Jesus Christ Conquers."

The Word on Fire Bible

A BIBLE FOR RESTLESS HEARTS

NON NISI TE DOMINE

by Bishop Robert Barron

WHEN I WAS A CHILD of eleven or twelve, my parents gave me a Bible as a Christmas present. Like many others before and since, I eagerly set out with the intention of reading my new treasure from cover to cover. I think I got through the tenth chapter of Genesis before giving up. Prompted by a suggestion of my father, I recommenced, this time with the New Testament. Somewhere in the first third of the Gospel of Matthew, I ran out of steam. Now, I realize I was only a young man at the time, but the fact remains: the Bible is a hard book. To say to someone "Just start reading it" is about as helpful as recommending to a novice who has never encountered a word of Shakespeare, "Just pick up a collection of the Bard's plays and enjoy." The Church has realized from the beginning that we need assistance if we are to read the Scriptures with profit. We require precisely the interpretive lens provided by the great scholars, saints, mystics, popes, and prophets who have gone before us—those who have, in the course of time, been recognized as masters of the sacred writings.

This realization informs the innumerable "study Bibles" that have emerged in recent years. By this I mean editions of the Scriptures that include, alongside the biblical texts themselves, commentaries, explanations, and prompts for further exploration. *The Word on Fire Bible* is in this genre, but it has several distinctive features that make it particularly relevant to our time.

First, it is specially geared toward those who, for a variety of reasons, are not affiliated with the Christian faith, or indeed with any organized religion. In the course of the last forty years or so, there has been a massive increase, at least in the Western countries, in the number of those who claim no religious identity. In the United States, the percentage of the unaffiliated has risen from 5% in the early 1970s to 26% in 2019. And if we focus on millennials, the figure rises to fully 40%. *The Word on Fire Bible* is designed to appeal to nonbelievers, searchers, and those with far more questions about religion than answers.

Secondly and relatedly, its commentaries hone in on two simple but fundamental questions: Who is God, and who is Jesus Christ? We understand that the religiously unaffiliated are unlikely to be interested in intra-ecclesial squabbles or the minutiae of theology. They want to get to the heart of the matter. And so this Bible sheds particular light on the peculiar, puzzling, unnerving, and endlessly fascinating figure that stands at the very heart of the biblical story—namely, the God of Israel—and on the one whom St. Paul characterized as the "image of the invisible God" (Col. 1:15), the first-century Jewish teacher and miracle worker who spoke and acted in the very person of God and who now, Christians claim, reigns as risen Lord of all creation.

Thirdly, *The Word on Fire Bible* brings in a chorus of voices from the great theological and spiritual tradition in order to sing the meaning of the Scriptures. The reader will hear from Augustine, Thomas Aquinas, John Henry Newman, Thérèse of Lisieux, John Paul II, and many, many other teachers in the way of the Spirit. And since it is a Word on Fire Bible, it also includes my own voice as well. For over thirty years, I have been preaching from the Bible as part of my ordinary work as a priest, and since about 2000, I have been sharing homilies on radio and podcasts in connection with my evangelical work. Excerpts from a wide variety of these sermons and other commentaries are featured in this text. Once again, the majority of these elaborations center on the sorts of questions that religious "outsiders" and spiritual inquirers are likely to ask.

A fourth and final distinctive element in this Bible is the focus on what Pope Francis calls the *via pulchritudinis* (the way of beauty). Catholicism is a very beautiful religion, and that beauty has the power to claim us. The beautiful does not merely entertain; rather, it invades, chooses, and changes the one to whom it deigns to appear. It opens the mind to a consideration of ever higher forms of the beautiful, conducing finally to the transcendent source of beauty itself. And so *The Word on Fire Bible* features many striking works of art as well as literary explanations of those pieces—all designed to introduce the seeker to Christ through the aesthetic splendor that he has inspired.

The Bible is indeed the greatest book ever written. It has shaped the cultures of the world in countless ways, and it contains the words of everlasting life. But for so many today, it is largely opaque, indecipherable—at best a puzzling text from a prescientific age. My fondest hope is that this Word on Fire edition of the Sacred Scriptures can bring God's Word to life in a fresh way, especially for those who, whether they fully know it or not, are restlessly seeking the Lord.

How to Approach the Bible

by Bishop Robert Barron

WHEN LEADERS OF THE CATHOLIC CHURCH gathered in the mid-twentieth century for the Second Vatican Council, they recognized the need for a renewal when it came to reading and appreciating the Bible. They called for greater study of the Bible among laypeople, placing the Scriptures more fully at the center of the liturgy, and making the sacred writings the "soul of theology." But that dream is still, I believe, largely unrealized.

In point of fact, when we consult the numerous studies of the ever-increasing army of the religiously unaffiliated, we discover that the Bible is often a prime reason why people, especially young people, are *alienated* from the Christian faith. We hear that it is nonsense written by prescientific people who knew nothing about the way the world works; that it is bronze-age mythology; that it encourages genocide, violence against women, slavery, and militaristic aggression; that its central character is, in the language of one atheist provocateur, like King Lear in Act Five, except more insane.

So how can we recover the depth and power of the Bible in the twenty-first century? How can we hold off the many charges made against it? In the course of this brief essay, I would like to propose five interpretive strategies.

A first one is this: always be critically attentive to the variety of genres on display in the Scriptures. The Bible is not so much a book as a library, a collection of books. One of the standard questions posed by inquirers today is whether the Bible should be taken literally. In a way, it's as pointless a question as whether one should take the library literally. It depends, of course, on which section you're in! If you find a book on a history shelf, you might indeed read it straightforwardly, but if you take a book off a poetry shelf or from the fiction department, you would be foolish to read either text literally. If in your wanderings through the library, you come across Richard Ellmann's celebrated biography of James Joyce, you would read it through entirely different lenses than you would to decipher Joyce's own *Finnegans Wake*. The library that is the Bible contains seventy-three books, written by a wide variety of different authors, addressed to various audiences at differing moments in history, concerning a myriad of themes, and employing a plethora of literary genres. Readily identifiable within the biblical corpus are legend, saga, tall tale, history, poetry, song, prophecy, biography, epistolary literature, and apocalypse, and each of these literary types requires a particular kind of interpretive approach. Very often, both critics and advocates of the Bible look for a univocal answer to the question of scriptural interpretation: it's all history; it's all mythology; it's all spiritual poetry; etc. But these easy answers are counterindicated. To give one example of the utility of attending to genre: much of the confusion—largely generated by various forms of twentieth-century fundamentalism—regarding the "scientific" interpretation of the first three chapters of the book of Genesis could be avoided by attending to the kind of literature we are dealing with in those astonishing passages. The four Gospels, too, call for their own distinct approach. While they are indeed historical accounts of a real person bearing a remarkable consensus in essentials, each Evangelist is focused on particular theological insights and interests, and they differ on certain secondary details such as chronology. We should not expect them to give us history in the modern journalistic sense, but rather four unique and stylized portraits of the life, death, and Resurrection of Jesus of Nazareth, handed down by the people who knew him.

Having clarified that the Bible is, in one sense, a library of books, I would also stress—and this constitutes the second interpretive strategy—that Scripture is, in another sense, one book. When I was coming of age in the university and seminary, the dominant form of scriptural analysis was the so-called historical-critical method. The stated purpose of this mode of interpretation is to use a variety of tools—linguistic, historical, archaeological, etc.—to determine the intentions of the human authors of the various biblical books. In other words, what was in the mind of Jeremiah or Isaiah or the author of second Samuel as he addressed his audience? There are virtues to this approach, to be sure, and a sound scriptural interpreter should never set it aside completely. But the historical-critical method also carries with it a shadow—namely, the tendency to lose the forest for the trees. As the historical critic focuses in on the intentions of the various authors writing to their disparate audiences at different historical moments, he can lose sight of the overall purpose of the Bible considered as a totality. He can overlook the fact that, despite all of its sometimes disconcerting variety, the Bible is finally telling one great story, or perhaps better, unfolding one great drama. This theo-dramatic consciousness makes the interpreter attentive to the themes, patterns, rhymes, and trajectories contained within the entire Bible. When, for example, the Church Fathers saw deep correspondences between Old Testament anticipations and New Testament fulfillments—what they called "types and antitypes"—they were operating out of this hermeneutical framework. Hans Urs von Balthasar taught that in a truly great work of art, each section of the whole relates harmonically to every other section and to the totality of the work. Think for example of the relationship between the parts and the whole in the Parthenon or in Chartres Cathedral or in Dante's *Divine Comedy*. The same dynamic obtains, Balthasar argued, within the Bible, every book of which speaks in some sense to every other and contributes to the sweep of the story as a whole.

And this segues neatly into the third of our interpretive strategies, which is to find a "canon within the canon" of Scripture. Some of our greatest biblical masters have held that one teaching or saying within the Bible can function as the key to opening the door of the entire Bible. In his seminal treatise *De doctrina Christiana*, St. Augustine proposed Jesus' command to love God above all things and our neighbor for the sake of God as the ultimate criterion of correct biblical reading. That is to say, every story, poem, doctrine, or saying in the Bible should be read as ultimately designed to inculcate love of God and neighbor. And if we turn the principle around, we find that any interpretation of a biblical passage that militates against the love of God and neighbor is necessarily a bad interpretation. The Church Father Origen of Alexandria, who was one of the finest biblical minds in the tradition, opined that the canon within the canon is the mysterious scene from the book of Revelation in which a Lamb, "standing as if it had been slaughtered" (Rev. 5:6), opens the seven seals of the sacred scroll in the heavenly court. The scroll, on Origen's reading, stands for the Scriptures, and the Lamb is the crucified and risen Jesus. The point is that Jesus alone truly explains the meaning of the Bible. Therefore, if we read a biblical passage in such a way that our interpretation is out of step with what was revealed in the dying and rising of the Lord, we have necessarily engaged in an inadequate reading. This strategy is precisely what enabled Origen and the tradition that followed him to read the violent passages of the Old Testament—so objectionable to people today—as allegories of the spiritual struggle against evil.

A fourth strategy is one that I learned from the theologian William Placher: to distinguish between what is in the Bible and what the Bible teaches. Written over a thousand years, from around 1000 BC to AD 100, but embodying traditions that go back much further, the biblical books carry with them an awful lot of cultural baggage from the ancient world. In the Bible we can find ideas about cosmology, medicine, disease control, and the weather that are clearly outmoded, and we can find cultural practices such as the denigration of women, the marginalization of children, slavery, etc. that are patently morally objectionable. These things are undoubtedly in the Bible, but they are not, I would argue, what the Bible is teaching. In order to discover the true doctrine of the Scriptures, we have to attend, as I stated earlier, not to particular passages taken out of context, but rather to the overarching themes and patterns within the Bible as a whole. And what allows us to intuit these central teachings is precisely the long and disciplined conversation across time, engaged in by the community formed by the biblical texts. This back-and-forth argument—exemplified, for instance, in the Jewish context by Talmudic scholars and in the Christian context by scholastic theologians—is the sifting process by which wheat and chaff are separated.

And this conduces to the fifth and final of my recommendations for correct interpretation: always remember that the Bible is the Church's book. The Scriptures as we know them were put in final canonical form sometime in the fourth century. This "canonization" represented the culmination of a centuries-long process—both Jewish and Christian—of analysis, debate, and judgment. Many books fell away in the course of time, since it was determined—again, by both Jewish and Christian authorities—that they did not adequately represent the faith of the community. Though skeptics today hold that certain books, the Gnostic Gospels for example, did not make it into the canon due to power struggles in the ancient Church, a much more satisfying explanation is that these texts were correctly judged not to be reliable witnesses to Christian revelation. The point is that the books of the Bible were assembled by the Church and for the Church. According to the practice in most universities in the West, it is indeed possible to read the Bible as a mildly interesting example of ancient near-Eastern literature, but this is to do terrible violence to the Scriptures, tearing them away from the only context in which they truly make sense. Their purpose, ultimately, is to tell the great story of Israel, which reaches its climax in the dying and rising of the Messiah, and to draw all people into communion with Jesus Christ. The proper framework for reading the Bible, therefore, is ecclesial and evangelical.

And this is the Christocentric orientation I should like you to have as you turn to the pages of *The Word on Fire Bible*. I invite you to read it with real thoughtfulness according to the strategies outlined above. I'm convinced this exercise will both call forth your critical attention and awaken your spiritual curiosity—and will lead you, I fondly hope, to the one who says, "I am the way, and the truth, and the life" (John 14:6).

Features of the Word on Fire Bible

St. John Chrysostom
(349–407)

———

Homilies on Matthew

Church Father Commentary

To enrich the reading of the Gospels, we have included commentary from the Church Fathers, the earliest Christian theologians. These quotations are identified by a beige background and gold Chi Rho, an ancient graphical symbol for Jesus made by superimposing the first two letters from the word "Christ" in Greek (ΧΡΙΣΤΟΣ). Because many of the Church Fathers lived during or shortly after the time of the Apostles, these commentaries represent some of the oldest Christian writings in existence aside from the New Testament itself.

G.K. Chesterton
(1874–1936)

———

The Everlasting Man

Recent Author Commentary

Writings by more recent saints and spiritual masters are found within a light gray background marked with the IHS Christogram. This icon was popularized in the fifteenth century and, similar to the Chi Rho, is a symbol made from the first letters of Jesus' name in Greek (ΙΗΣΟΥΣ). Between the Church Father and Recent Author excerpts, nearly two thousand years of spiritual wisdom surrounds the biblical text to enhance your study.

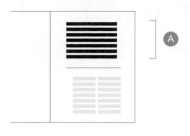

Single Column Bible Text

The single column format of the biblical text provides a legible and immersive reading experience inspired by the layout of a novel (A). This design encourages longer reading sessions and facilitates deeper study.

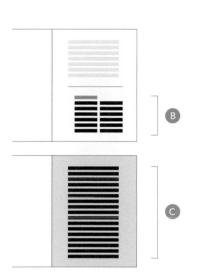

Bishop Barron Commentary

In addition to quotations from the Fathers and recent authors, this Bible also features a wealth of commentary by Bishop Robert Barron. Shorter commentaries appear in a two column layout above or below the Scripture text (B). Longer, more detailed commentaries appear in a single column on a gray background (C).

Word Study

μακάριος

MAKARIOS

Greek Word Studies

In his commentary, Bishop Barron often highlights terms from the original Greek. These words are called out using the format at left, allowing you to see each word as it appears in the original Greek New Testament.

Via Pulchritudinis Art Commentary

Throughout the Gospels, exquisite selections of art from across the centuries illuminate pertinent Scripture passages. Each piece of artwork is accompanied by an essay (written by Michael Stevens) to connect the work to the Scriptures. As you reflect, you are invited to draw nearer to Christ through what Pope Francis calls the *via pulchritudinis* (the way of beauty).

THE GOSPEL
ACCORDING
to MATTIIEW

Introduction to the Gospel of Matthew
by Brandon Vogt

I WAS ONCE TALKING WITH A YOUNG MAN who expressed interest in reading the Bible for the first time, and he asked where to begin. Should he start from Genesis and plow through the whole text? Or instead begin with the shortest book? Maybe the easiest book? I told him any of those approaches would work, but that I recommended he start with the four Gospels, which recount the life and teachings of Jesus. I explained that Jesus of Nazareth—this strange, beguiling Jewish carpenter who claimed to be the Son of God, performed miracles, and then rose from the dead— stands at the center of the Bible's entire story. Everything before the Gospels points to Jesus; everything after reflects on him. So there's no better place to start in the Bible than the Gospels.

But which of the four Gospels? Many people recommend commencing with the Gospel of Mark, because it's the shortest and liveliest. However, I prefer Matthew's Gospel. The first Christians favored it too, giving it a primacy of honor. For various reasons, it was the most widely shared Gospel in the early Church: it is the first Gospel written by one of Jesus' twelve Apostles; it contains a nice mix of Jesus' teachings, actions, and miracles; and it beautifully ties together the Old and New Covenants—which is to say, God's plan for Israel *before* Jesus and God's plan for the world *after* him. This is why, when the early Church wanted to reflect on Jesus' life and hear his voice, it usually turned first to the Gospel of Matthew. So that's what I recommended to the young man.

A while later, I followed up to ask how his reading was going. He hesitated, then admitted, "Well, to be honest, it didn't really go anywhere. I opened up Matthew, as you suggested, but I barely made it past the first page. It started with this long list of boring, ancient names that I couldn't even pronounce, and I just got stuck."

I commiserated. I remembered having the same experience when reading Matthew for the first time. While other biblical books get right into the action, the Gospel of Matthew confusingly begins with a long genealogy, listing dozens of Jesus' relatives all the way back to Abraham, who lived about two thousand years before Jesus. In addition, the rest of the Gospel is saturated with allusions to Jewish culture and religion, and nearly a hundred quotes from the Old Testament. It's easy to get bogged down in all of these ancient accoutrements and wonder why any of it matters to a twenty-first-century reader.

Yet after having read Matthew's Gospel several times since then, I'm convinced that the way the Gospel is structured, with its strongly Jewish flavor and its opening lineage, is not only important, but is the main interpretive key to the whole Gospel. For the major thrust of Matthew's Gospel is this: to fully understand Jesus, you have to understand Israel.

Suppose a friend of yours wanted to read *The Lord of the Rings* by J.R.R. Tolkien. It's unlikely you would tell him, "Just read the climactic chapter about Frodo scaling Mount Doom to destroy the Ring." Questions would immediately ensue: Who is Frodo? What is Mount Doom? What is the Ring? And why does it need to be destroyed? Of course, you might grasp *some* of the story by reading this one main chapter in isolation, but to fully understand its meaning and gravity, you must read it in light of its long backstory: the many battles, factions, and adventures; the forging of the One Ring; the evil Sauron's machinations and desire for power; the allure of the Ring, its history, and why the quest to destroy it is so difficult and necessary. In other words, you must read Frodo in light of the whole background of Middle-earth. In the same way, we must understand Jesus against the whole background of Israel.

This is where Matthew's Gospel shines. The author tells the story of Jesus, a first-century wandering preacher, but he constantly paints around the edges, filling in the narrative with the necessary Jewish milieu. The author is insistent, starting with the first words on the first page, that we understand Jesus as the climax to this long, sweeping narrative about Israel that has stretched across thousands of years and all the books of the Old Testament. We can almost hear him saying that the Old Testament is a story of a people drawn to God and drifting away, a tale of great heroes and disappointing failures (both of which are represented in Jesus' genealogy), an account of prophecies uttered and unfulfilled, until finally, we see the arrival of Jesus, who, according to Matthew, brings the whole story to its fruition.

Now, it's true that this volume of *The Word on Fire Bible* doesn't include the Old Testament, so from this volume alone you won't get the full backstory. However, the author of Matthew's Gospel does much of the work for you. He positions Jesus in his ancient Jewish context so he's less of an abstraction and more of the concrete pinnacle of Israel's story. Also, you'll find commentary and insights throughout this book to fill in the background, helping you to understand why this action or that statement from Jesus is so significant, and how first-century Israelites would have received it.

Much of what Jesus says and does throughout the Gospel of Matthew is coded. For example, he never comes out and explicitly says, "I am God, the second person of the Holy Trinity! Come worship me!" Instead, he reveals his divine identity slowly and mysteriously, using veiled allusions that first-century Jews would have understood but Roman enemies would have overlooked.

For example, consider Jesus' repeated references to "the kingdom." The word "kingdom" appears over fifty times in Matthew's Gospel, almost always on the lips of Jesus, marking it as central to his preaching. Jesus repeatedly proclaims "the kingdom of heaven" or "the kingdom of God." Now, to some listeners who are oblivious to the great story of Israel or who read this merely in political terms, it seems Jesus is announcing plans to inaugurate a new first-century monarchy. He's deeming himself King, a divinely appointed political ruler like Caesar Augustus, one who is perhaps planning to raise an army to help his fellow Jews escape the oppressive boot of Roman rule.

But as you'll notice throughout Matthew's Gospel, this isn't the type of kingdom Jesus has in mind. Reading his kingdom in light of the great story of Israel, you discover this kingdom is the one whispered about through Israel's history, one that has been glimpsed at different periods but never fully realized, from the kingdom Adam was supposed to grow and protect in Eden to the kingdom of David at its spiritual peak. In light of this great story, Jesus is less like Caesar and more like King David. Jesus the King is meant, above all, to guide his people toward right praise and worship of God.

However, Matthew gives us an added twist: Jesus' new kingdom is not limited to the Jews, like David's kingdom. It also stretches far beyond the petty categories of politics and temporal power. It's a kingdom not just for Israelites, but one extending across all creation, from earth to heaven, and even across time. In this new kingdom, humility, sacrifice, love, worship, and enemy-forgiveness are the defining features—not power, dominance, selfishness, fear, and vengeance.

This is the great proclamation and invitation of Matthew's Gospel: a new kingdom has arrived, led by Jesus Christ, a new and definitive King, and wherever you live on earth and whatever your background, you're invited to be part of it, to come under his glorious reign. David's kingdom was for the Jews; Jesus' kingdom is for the world.

But how do we enter this kingdom? Jesus tells us throughout Matthew's Gospel: turn away from sinful behavior and align your will to God's, so that you want what he wants (Matt. 4:17); pick up your cross—your unique difficulties and struggles—and carry it alongside Christ (Matt. 16:24), ask for the kingdom and seek it with vigor (Matt. 7:7–8); shed your ego and become childlike with humility (Matt. 18:2–4); become baptized and join the Church that Jesus established (Matt. 28:19–20, 16:15–19).

There's much more to reflect on in this magnificent book, but as with all great books, the best way to understand it is simply to read it yourself. Whether you're new to the Bible or have read it numerous times, brace yourself to meet the captivating figure of Jesus, who is unlike any character of history (or fiction, for that matter). This Gospel displays him with particular multivalence. Jesus paradoxically appears harsh yet merciful, authoritative yet humble, mercurial yet balanced and trusted. It's not that Jesus is self-contradictory; it's that he's beyond our normal human categories. There is an untamed electricity that courses through the wire of Jesus' life as it unfolds through Matthew's Gospel. It will shock and surprise you, perhaps even attract you. In any case, encountering it will never leave you the same.

Brandon Vogt is the Content Director for Word on Fire Catholic Ministries. He is the author of eight books, including Why I Am Catholic (And You Should Be Too).

THE GENEALOGY OF JESUS THE MESSIAH

1 An account of the genealogy of Jesus the Messiah, the son of David, the son of Abraham.

²Abraham was the father of Isaac, and Isaac the father of Jacob, and Jacob the father of Judah and his brothers, ³ and Judah the father of Perez and Zerah by Tamar, and Perez the father of Hezron, and Hezron the father of Aram, ⁴ and Aram the father of Aminadab, and Aminadab the father of Nahshon, and Nahshon the father of Salmon, ⁵ and Salmon the father of Boaz by Rahab, and Boaz the father of Obed by Ruth, and Obed the father of Jesse, ⁶ and Jesse the father of King David.

And David was the father of Solomon by the wife of Uriah, ⁷ and Solomon the father of Rehoboam, and Rehoboam the father of Abijah, and Abijah the father of Asaph, ⁸ and Asaph the father of Jehoshaphat, and Jehoshaphat the father of Joram, and Joram the father of Uzziah, ⁹ and Uzziah the father of Jotham, and Jotham the father of Ahaz, and Ahaz the

---

Why the Genealogy of Jesus Matters
Matthew 1:1–16 | Bishop Barron

Why does the Bible record the genealogy of Jesus? Because it was desperately important for Matthew to show that Jesus came out of a rich, densely textured history. St. Irenaeus tells us that the Incarnation, in a certain sense, had been taking place over a long period of time, God gradually accustoming himself to the human race.

Look at this long line of characters here in Jesus' lineage: saints, sinners, cheats, prostitutes, murderers, poets, kings, insiders and outsiders—all leading to the Christ.

Of course, King David is mentioned. He was, without doubt, a great figure, the king who united the nation. But he was also an adulterer and a murderer. (He slept with a married woman, Bathsheba, and had her husband killed in battle.) There's also Rahab, a former prostitute.

From this long line of great, not-so-great, prominent, obscure, saints, sinners, kings, and paupers came "Jesus . . . who is called the Messiah."

The point is clear: God became one of us, in all of our grace and embarrassment, in all of our beauty and ordinariness. God had a series of human ancestors, and like most families, they were something of a motley crew.

And what good news this is for us! It means that God can bring the Christ to birth even in people like us.

father of Hezekiah, [10] and Hezekiah the father of Manasseh, and Manasseh the father of Amos, and Amos the father of Josiah, [11] and Josiah the father of Jechoniah and his brothers, at the time of the deportation to Babylon.

[12] And after the deportation to Babylon: Jechoniah was the father of Salathiel, and Salathiel the father of Zerubbabel, [13] and Zerubbabel the father of Abiud, and Abiud the father of Eliakim, and Eliakim the father of Azor, [14] and Azor the father of Zadok, and Zadok the father of Achim, and Achim the father of Eliud, [15] and Eliud the father of Eleazar, and Eleazar the father of Matthan, and Matthan the father of Jacob, [16] and Jacob the father of Joseph the husband of Mary, of whom Jesus was born, who is called the Messiah.

[17] So all the generations from Abraham to David are fourteen generations; and from David to the deportation to Babylon, fourteen generations; and from the deportation to Babylon to the Messiah, fourteen generations.

THE BIRTH OF JESUS THE MESSIAH

[18] Now the birth of Jesus the Messiah took place in this way. When his mother Mary had been engaged to Joseph, but before they lived together, she was found to be with child from the Holy Spirit. [19] Her husband Joseph, being a righteous man and unwilling to expose her to public disgrace, planned to dismiss her quietly. [20] But just when he had resolved to do this, an angel of the Lord appeared to him in a dream and said, "Joseph, son of David, do not be afraid to take Mary as your wife, for the child conceived in her is from the Holy Spirit. [21] She will bear a son, and you are to name him Jesus, for he will save his people from their sins." [22] All this took place to fulfill what had been spoken by the Lord through the prophet:

> [23] *"Look, the virgin shall conceive and bear a son,*
> *and they shall name him Emmanuel,"*

which means, "God is with us." [24] When Joseph awoke from sleep, he did as the angel of the Lord commanded him; he took her as his wife, [25] but had no marital relations with her until she had borne a son; and he named him Jesus.

AND THEY SHALL *name him*

EMMANUEL. MATTHEW 1:23

St. John Chrysostom
(349–407)

———

Homilies on Matthew

Why Jesus and Not Emmanuel?

Matthew 1:23

How was it then that his name was not called Emmanuel, but Jesus Christ? Because the prophet did not say "You shall name him," but "They shall name him"—that is, the multitude and the events that follow. For here he puts the event as a name: and this is customary in Scripture, to substitute the events that take place for names.

G.K. Chesterton
(1874–1936)

———

The Everlasting Man

God, the Cave-Man

Matthew 1:18–25

The human story began in a cave; the cave which popular science associates with the cave-man and in which practical discovery has really found archaic drawings of animals. The second half of human history, which was like a new creation of the world, also begins in a cave....

It was here that a homeless couple had crept underground with the cattle when the doors of the crowded caravanserai had been shut in their faces; and it was here beneath the very feet of the passers-by, in a cellar under the very floor of the world, that Jesus Christ was born....

God also was a Cave-Man, and had also traced strange shapes of creatures, curiously colored, upon the wall of the world; but the pictures that he made had come to life.

THE VISIT OF THE WISE MEN

2 In the time of King Herod, after Jesus was born in Bethlehem of Judea, wise men from the East came to Jerusalem, ² asking, "Where is the child who has been born king of the Jews? For we observed his star at its rising, and have come to pay him homage." ³ When King Herod heard this, he was frightened, and all Jerusalem with him; ⁴ and calling together all the chief priests and scribes of the people, he inquired of them where the Messiah was to be born. ⁵ They told him, "In Bethlehem of Judea; for so it has been written by the prophet:

> ⁶'And you, Bethlehem, in the land of Judah,
> are by no means least among the rulers of Judah;
> for from you shall come a ruler
> who is to shepherd my people Israel.' "

⁷ Then Herod secretly called for the wise men and learned from them the exact time when the star had appeared. ⁸ Then he sent them to Bethlehem,

---

King Herod vs. the Magi

Matthew 2:1–12 | Bishop Barron

Matthew's account purposely juxtaposes King Herod and the mysterious Magi from the East. History tells us that Herod was the consummate political survivor, a canny realist who had, through threats, murder, and corruption, found his way to the top of the political ladder.

But while he was fussing around, desperately trying to maintain himself in power, figures from a distant country were blithely indifferent to politics and games of domination. Instead, they were intensely surveying the night sky, looking for signs from God.

And they found one. As these Magi crossed the border into Herod's country, they came onto Herod's radar screen. Who were they? Spies? And whom were they seeking? A newborn king? To Herod, that sounded like a threat; it sounded like treason.

So under the pretense of piety, he called the Magi to himself and inquired after the star's first appearance, getting the time coordinates, and then he asked them to go to Bethlehem and find the exact locale. Why? To stamp out this new baby king, this king who threatened to undermine Herod's tyrannical rule.

Herod was afraid of Jesus and responded with violence; the Magi were captivated by Jesus and responded with worship.

saying, "Go and search diligently for the child; and when you have found him, bring me word so that I may also go and pay him homage." ⁹ When they had heard the king, they set out; and there, ahead of them, went the star that they had seen at its rising, until it stopped over the place where the child was. ¹⁰ When they saw that the star had stopped, they were overwhelmed with joy. ¹¹ On entering the house, they saw the child with Mary his mother; and they knelt down and paid him homage. Then, opening their treasure chests, they offered him gifts of gold, frankincense, and myrrh. ¹² And having been warned in a dream not to return to Herod, they left for their own country by another road.

THE ESCAPE TO EGYPT

¹³ Now after they had left, an angel of the Lord appeared to Joseph in a dream and said, "Get up, take the child and his mother, and flee to Egypt, and remain there until I tell you; for Herod is about to search for the child, to destroy him." ¹⁴ Then Joseph got up, took the child and his mother by night, and went to Egypt, ¹⁵ and remained there until the death of Herod. This was to fulfill what had been spoken by the Lord through the prophet, "Out of Egypt I have called my son."

THE MASSACRE OF THE INFANTS

¹⁶ When Herod saw that he had been tricked by the wise men, he was infuriated, and he sent and killed all the children in and around Bethlehem who were two years old or under, according to the time that he had learned

---

St. Thomas Aquinas
(1225–1274)

Commentary on Matthew

The Three Gifts

Matthew 2:11

The Magi found three things in Christ—namely, royal dignity: "he shall reign as king and deal wisely" (Jer. 23:5); and therefore, they offered gold in tribute. The greatness of the priesthood: and, therefore, frankincense, as a sacrifice. Man's mortality: and therefore, myrrh.

from the wise men. ¹⁷ Then was fulfilled what had been spoken through the prophet Jeremiah:

> ¹⁸ *"A voice was heard in Ramah,*
> *wailing and loud lamentation,*
> *Rachel weeping for her children;*
> *she refused to be consoled, because they are no more."*

THE RETURN FROM EGYPT

¹⁹ When Herod died, an angel of the Lord suddenly appeared in a dream to Joseph in Egypt and said, ²⁰ "Get up, take the child and his mother, and go to the land of Israel, for those who were seeking the child's life are dead." ²¹ Then Joseph got up, took the child and his mother, and went to the land of Israel. ²² But when he heard that Archelaus was ruling over Judea in place of his father Herod, he was afraid to go there. And after being warned in a dream, he went away to the district of Galilee. ²³ There he made his home in a town called Nazareth, so that what had been spoken through the prophets might be fulfilled, "He will be called a Nazorean."

Who Were the Magi?

Matthew 2:1–12 | Bishop Barron

In this chapter, we're introduced to the "wise men," often described as Magi or astrologers, who are seeking out a foreign king. In many ways, this is a microcosm of God's plan for humanity.

The Old Testament reveals how God chose Israel to be especially his own, a priestly people, a holy nation. But the reason for this choice was not to glorify Israel over against the other nations; rather, it was to make of Israel a beacon to the world, so that through Israel all might be gathered to himself.

Similarly, the wise men are seeking a king, born for the Jews, but he wouldn't be for the Jews alone. This Messiah would be the King of kings, a light to all the nations.

How wonderful that the sign of this King's birth should be a star, something that can be clearly seen *by* every nation and *from* any nation. And when the Magi saw it, they were willing to leave their own country behind.

Then, after greeting the newborn King, they went back to their own country, but they went back by a different route. This is a biblical sign that they were changed. They would remain Babylonians, but they had become citizens of a higher country. They couldn't return by the same path.

Matthew 2:11

FOLLOWER OF GIOTTO | *c. 1340–1343*

The Adoration of the Magi

Essay by Michael Stevens

In this painting of the adoration of the Magi, the artist provides
a thoughtful meditation on the kingship of Jesus. Here we see
the Christ child sitting on Mary's lap, and a wise man kneeling in
worship. This may appear to be a straightforward exchange, but
the radical significance of this interaction is revealed by a pivotal
feature: the wise man's crown laid on the steps at the feet of Jesus.
Through this spare, elegant detail, the artist powerfully illustrates
one of the most controversial claims of Christianity: that Jesus
Christ is the supreme ruler of creation, and that every power on
earth—no matter how dignified—must bow before him.

The Magi's crown

The crown laid at the feet of Jesus
represents the Magi's recognition of Jesus'
authority and kingship. While Herod views
Jesus' birth as a threat to his secular rule,
the Magi welcome Jesus' coming with
open hearts.

Angels

The presence of the angels on the right
side of the composition reminds the
viewer that the newborn Christ is the ruler
of heaven as well as earth.

Background architecture

Contrary to common depictions of the
Magi around the manger on the night of
Jesus' birth, Matthew clearly reports this
story taking place some time after that.
This painting better reflects the scriptural
narrative, with Mary and Jesus greeting the
Magi not at the stable but at their home.

THE PROCLAMATION OF JOHN THE BAPTIST

3 In those days John the Baptist appeared in the wilderness of Judea, proclaiming, ² "Repent, for the kingdom of heaven has come near." ³ This is the one of whom the prophet Isaiah spoke when he said,

> "The voice of one crying out in the wilderness:
> 'Prepare the way of the Lord,
> make his paths straight.'"

⁴ Now John wore clothing of camel's hair with a leather belt around his waist, and his food was locusts and wild honey. ⁵ Then the people of Jerusalem and all Judea were going out to him, and all the region along the Jordan, ⁶ and they were baptized by him in the river Jordan, confessing their sins.

⁷ But when he saw many Pharisees and Sadducees coming for baptism, he said to them, "You brood of vipers! Who warned you to flee from the wrath to come? ⁸ Bear fruit worthy of repentance. ⁹ Do not presume to say to yourselves, 'We have Abraham as our ancestor'; for I tell you, God is able from these stones to raise up children to Abraham. ¹⁰ Even now the ax is lying at the root of the trees; every tree therefore that does not bear good fruit is cut down and thrown into the fire.

Who Was John the Baptist?

Matthew 3:11–12 | Bishop Barron

It's really impossible to grasp the significance of Jesus without passing through the cleansing bath of John the Baptist. He provides a lens through which Jesus is properly interpreted.

John, Matthew tells us, made his appearance as a preacher in the desert of Judea. Deserts are places of simplicity and poverty, places where distractions and attachments are eliminated—and hence where the voice of God can be heard. Wealth, pleasure, power, honor—and all of their avatars and priests—are shouting at us, luring us, tempting us. But what is God saying? We have to go to these silent and deserted places in order to hear.

What's the first word out of the prophet's mouth? "Repent." This might be a dirty word to many people today, but it cuts to the heart of every one of us, precisely because we all know that our lives are not where they are supposed to be. We have all fallen short of the glory of God; we have all fallen into patterns of self-absorption and addiction. So let us hear John's word today: "Repent." It's a command to turn around, to start moving in a new direction.

¹¹ "I baptize you with water for repentance, but one who is more powerful than I is coming after me; I am not worthy to carry his sandals. He will baptize you with the Holy Spirit and fire. ¹² His winnowing fork is in his hand, and he will clear his threshing floor and will gather his wheat into the granary; but the chaff he will burn with unquenchable fire."

THE BAPTISM OF JESUS

¹³ Then Jesus came from Galilee to John at the Jordan, to be baptized by him. ¹⁴ John would have prevented him, saying, "I need to be baptized by you, and do you come to me?" ¹⁵ But Jesus answered him, "Let it be so now; for it is proper for us in this way to fulfill all righteousness." Then he consented. ¹⁶ And when Jesus had been baptized, just as he came up from the water, suddenly the heavens were opened to him and he saw the Spirit of God descending like a dove and alighting on him. ¹⁷ And a voice from heaven said, "This is my Son, the Beloved, with whom I am well pleased."

The Reason Jesus Was Baptized

Matthew 3:13–17 | Bishop Barron

It seems strange that Jesus came to John the Baptist seeking baptism. Why? Because baptism washes away our sins, which means only sinners need baptism. Yet if Jesus was a sinner, then he would not be God, and all of Christian theology would be undermined. So it's a strange scene, and if the Gospel writers had any justification for dropping it out, they surely would have. But they all reference it in their accounts.

Interestingly, John the Baptist expresses this same confusion: "I need to be baptized by you, and do you come to me?" But Jesus replies, "Let it be so now; for it is proper for us in this way to fulfill all righteousness."

So there's the answer; but what does it mean? Fulfilling righteousness, in the Old Testament, meant something like "doing what God wants," or "getting right with God." In Old Testament times, this was our business, something we humans performed. But Jesus came to bring that to completion. From here on out, Jesus was intimating, God sets things right with us himself, bending down under our hand and submitting to us.

Many of the early Church Fathers understood that by allowing himself to be baptized, Jesus sanctified the waters of Baptism for all Christians who would come after him. He went into the waters so we could join him, arising as new creations. He raised Baptism from the level of cleansing rite to sacrament.

Fulton Sheen
(1895–1979)

Life of Christ

One with Sinners

Matthew 3:13–17

When he went down into the river Jordan to be baptized, he made himself one with sinners. The innocent can share the burdens of the guilty. If a husband is guilty of a crime, it is pointless to tell his wife not to worry about it, or that it is no concern of hers. It is equally absurd to say that our Lord should not have been baptized because he had no personal guilt. If he was to be identified with humanity, so much so as to call himself the "Son of Man," then he had to share the guilt of humanity. And this was the meaning of the baptism by John.

THE TEMPTATION OF JESUS

4 Then Jesus was led up by the Spirit into the wilderness to be tempted by the devil. [2] He fasted forty days and forty nights, and afterwards he was famished. [3] The tempter came and said to him, "If you are the Son of God, command these stones to become loaves of bread." [4] But he answered, "It is written,

> 'One does not live by bread alone,
> but by every word that comes from the mouth of God.'"

[5] Then the devil took him to the holy city and placed him on the pinnacle of the temple, [6] saying to him, "If you are the Son of God, throw yourself down; for it is written,

> 'He will command his angels concerning you,'

and

> 'On their hands they will bear you up,
> so that you will not dash your foot against a stone.'"

[7] Jesus said to him, "Again it is written, 'Do not put the Lord your God to the test.'"

⁸ Again, the devil took him to a very high mountain and showed him all the kingdoms of the world and their splendor; ⁹ and he said to him, "All these I will give you, if you will fall down and worship me." ¹⁰ Jesus said to him, "Away with you, Satan! for it is written,

> 'Worship the Lord your God,
> and serve only him.'"

¹¹ Then the devil left him, and suddenly angels came and waited on him.

JESUS BEGINS HIS MINISTRY IN GALILEE

¹² Now when Jesus heard that John had been arrested, he withdrew to Galilee. ¹³ He left Nazareth and made his home in Capernaum by the sea, in the territory of Zebulun and Naphtali, ¹⁴ so that what had been spoken through the prophet Isaiah might be fulfilled:

> ¹⁵ "Land of Zebulun, land of Naphtali,
> on the road by the sea, across the Jordan, Galilee of the Gentiles—
> ¹⁶ the people who sat in darkness
> have seen a great light,
> and for those who sat in the region and shadow of death
> light has dawned."

¹⁷ From that time Jesus began to proclaim, "Repent, for the kingdom of heaven has come near."

The Strategy of Jesus

Matthew 4:3–10 | Bishop Barron

One of the most elemental forms of spiritual dysfunction is to make the satisfaction of sensual desire the center of one's life. Thus Jesus enters, through psychological and spiritual identification, into the condition of the person lured by this sin, but then he manages to withstand the temptation and in fact to twist this perversion back to rectitude.

He does the same thing with Satan's temptations to glory and to power. If these perversions had been addressed only from a distance, only through divine fiat, they would not have been truly conquered; but when they are withstood by someone willing fully to submit to their lure, they are effectively exploded from within, undermined, defeated. This is the strategy of Jesus, the Lamb of God.

JESUS CALLS THE FIRST DISCIPLES

[18] As he walked by the Sea of Galilee, he saw two brothers, Simon, who is called Peter, and Andrew his brother, casting a net into the sea—for they were fishermen. [19] And he said to them, "Follow me, and I will make you fish for people." [20] Immediately they left their nets and followed him. [21] As he went from there, he saw two other brothers, James son of Zebedee and his brother John, in the boat with their father Zebedee, mending their nets, and he called them. [22] Immediately they left the boat and their father, and followed him.

JESUS MINISTERS TO CROWDS OF PEOPLE

[23] Jesus went throughout Galilee, teaching in their synagogues and proclaiming the good news of the kingdom and curing every disease and every sickness among the people. [24] So his fame spread throughout all Syria, and they brought to him all the sick, those who were afflicted with various diseases and pains, demoniacs, epileptics, and paralytics, and he cured them. [25] And great crowds followed him from Galilee, the Decapolis, Jerusalem, Judea, and from beyond the Jordan.

Fishers of Men

Matthew 4:18–22 | Bishop Barron

In this passage, Matthew tells of Jesus calling his first disciples. What is it about this scene that is so peaceful and right? Somehow it gets at the very heart of Jesus' life and work, revealing what he is about. He comes into the world as the second person of the Blessed Trinity, a representative from the community that is God—and thus his basic purpose is to draw the world into community around him.

Jesus says to Simon and Andrew, "Follow me, and I will make you fish for people." This tells us something about how God acts. He is direct and in-your-face; he does the choosing. "Follow me," Jesus says. He is not offering a doctrine, a theology, or a set of beliefs. He is offering himself. It's as if he's saying, "Walk in my path; walk in imitation of me."

Finally, Jesus explains, "I will make you fish for people." This is one of the best one-liners in Scripture. Notice the first part of the phrase: "I will make you." This is counter to the culture's prevailing view that we're self-made, that we invent and define our own reality. Jesus puts this lie to bed. We learn from him that it's God who acts, and if we give ourselves to his creative power, he will make us into something far better than we ever could.

THE BEATITUDES

5 When Jesus saw the crowds, he went up the mountain; and after he sat down, his disciples came to him. ² Then he began to speak, and taught them, saying:

³ "Blessed are the poor in spirit, for theirs is the kingdom of heaven.

⁴ "Blessed are those who mourn, for they will be comforted.

⁵ "Blessed are the meek, for they will inherit the earth.

⁶ "Blessed are those who hunger and thirst for righteousness, for they will be filled.

⁷ "Blessed are the merciful, for they will receive mercy.

⁸ "Blessed are the pure in heart, for they will see God.

⁹ "Blessed are the peacemakers, for they will be called children of God.

¹⁰ "Blessed are those who are persecuted for righteousness' sake, for theirs is the kingdom of heaven.

¹¹ "Blessed are you when people revile you and persecute you and utter all kinds of evil against you falsely on my account. ¹² Rejoice and be glad, for your reward is great in heaven, for in the same way they persecuted the prophets who were before you.

Becoming Salt and Light

Matthew 5:13–16 | Bishop Barron

In his Sermon on the Mount, Jesus compares his disciples to salt and light. Notice that these two realities exist not for themselves but for something else. In Jesus' time, salt was not valued for itself, but for the way it preserved meat and enhanced the flavor of other foods. Similarly, light isn't meant for itself; rather, we see things by it.

In our rather privatized culture, we tend to think of religion as something for ourselves; but on the biblical reading, religiosity is like salt and light: it is meant not for oneself but for others.

Perhaps we can bring these two images together by saying that we find salvation for ourselves precisely in the measure that we bring God's life to others. Followers of Jesus are meant to be salt, which effectively preserves what is best in the society around them. And they are also light by which people around them come to see what is worth seeing.

By the very quality and integrity of our lives, we shed light, illumining what is beautiful and revealing what is ugly. The implication is that, without vibrant Christians, the world is a much worse place.

SALT AND LIGHT

13 "You are the salt of the earth; but if salt has lost its taste, how can its saltiness be restored? It is no longer good for anything, but is thrown out and trampled under foot.

14 "You are the light of the world. A city built on a hill cannot be hid. 15 No one after lighting a lamp puts it under the bushel basket, but on the lampstand, and it gives light to all in the house. 16 In the same way, let your light shine before others, so that they may see your good works and give glory to your Father in heaven.

THE LAW AND THE PROPHETS

17 "Do not think that I have come to abolish the law or the prophets; I have come not to abolish but to fulfill. 18 For truly I tell you, until heaven and earth pass away, not one letter, not one stroke of a letter, will pass from the law until all is accomplished. 19 Therefore, whoever breaks one of the least of these commandments, and teaches others to do the same, will be called least in the kingdom of heaven; but whoever does them and teaches them will be called great in the kingdom of heaven. 20 For I tell you, unless your righteousness exceeds that of the scribes and Pharisees, you will never enter the kingdom of heaven.

CONCERNING ANGER

21 "You have heard that it was said to those of ancient times, 'You shall not murder'; and 'whoever murders shall be liable to judgment.' 22 But I say to you that if you are angry with a brother or sister, you will be liable

---

YOU ARE

THE LIGHT

of the

WORLD.

MATTHEW 5:14

to judgment; and if you insult a brother or sister, you will be liable to the council; and if you say, 'You fool,' you will be liable to the hell of fire. [23] So when you are offering your gift at the altar, if you remember that your brother or sister has something against you, [24] leave your gift there before the altar and go; first be reconciled to your brother or sister, and then come and offer your gift. [25] Come to terms quickly with your accuser while you are on the way to court with him, or your accuser may hand you over to the judge, and the judge to the guard, and you will be thrown into prison. [26] Truly I tell you, you will never get out until you have paid the last penny.

CONCERNING ADULTERY

[27] "You have heard that it was said, 'You shall not commit adultery.' [28] But I say to you that everyone who looks at a woman with lust has already committed adultery with her in his heart. [29] If your right eye causes you to sin, tear it out and throw it away; it is better for you to lose one of your members than for your whole body to be thrown into hell. [30] And if your right hand causes you to sin, cut it off and throw it away; it is better for you to lose one of your members than for your whole body to go into hell.

CONCERNING DIVORCE

[31] "It was also said, 'Whoever divorces his wife, let him give her a certificate of divorce.' [32] But I say to you that anyone who divorces his wife, except on the ground of unchastity, causes her to commit adultery; and whoever marries a divorced woman commits adultery.

CONCERNING OATHS

[33] "Again, you have heard that it was said to those of ancient times, 'You shall not swear falsely, but carry out the vows you have made to the Lord.' [34] But I say to you, Do not swear at all, either by heaven, for it is the throne of God, [35] or by the earth, for it is his footstool, or by Jerusalem, for it is the city of the great King. [36] And do not swear by your head, for you cannot make one hair white or black. [37] Let your word be 'Yes, Yes' or 'No, No'; anything more than this comes from the evil one.

CONCERNING RETALIATION

[38] "You have heard that it was said, 'An eye for an eye and a tooth for a tooth.' [39] But I say to you, Do not resist an evildoer. But if anyone strikes you on the right cheek, turn the other also; [40] and if anyone wants to sue you and take your coat, give your cloak as well; [41] and if anyone forces you to go one mile, go also the second mile. [42] Give to everyone who begs from you, and do not refuse anyone who wants to borrow from you.

The landscape

Jesus' sermon is full of vivid images of nature to illustrate humanity's relationship with God. It's fitting, then, that Ferenczy, a master of landscape, emphasizes the surrounding natural environment by placing the figures in the lower third of the composition and reserving the rest for lush greenery.

Jesus' followers

The painter portrays people of all ages and backgrounds in the scene, and the armored soldier who casually sits to Christ's right is especially striking. Through the inclusion of a varied range of people, the artist reminds us that Jesus' message is for all people and all times.

A mirrored posture

The man in the left foreground mirrors the posture of Jesus, creating a counterbalance to the figure of Christ and emphasizing his humble posture: relaxed and speaking eye to eye with his followers.

Matthew 5:1–48

KÁROLY FERENCZY | *1896*

The Sermon on the Mount

Essay by Michael Stevens

In his painting *The Sermon on the Mount*, Hungarian master
Károly Ferenczy offers an unconventional take on one of the most
universally beloved stories in the Bible. What's most striking about
this scene is its setting: instead of first-century Judea, the artist
portrays Christ among people from a variety of times and places,
including the artist's own nineteenth-century Hungary. It's likely
that the models for this painting were members of Ferenczy's own
family, and most in the scene appear to be wearing contemporized,
informal clothing. This creative interpretation highlights the
perennial power and wisdom of Jesus' greatest sermon, and by
positioning Jesus amid a relaxed and modernized crowd, we're
encouraged to listen along with them—right here and now.

Unpacking Jesus' Greatest Sermon
Matthew 5:1–48 | Bishop Barron

JESUS' SERMON ON THE MOUNT, recounted in Matthew 5–7, is perhaps the most famous sermon ever preached. We read in the first verse that, "when Jesus saw the crowds, he went up the mountain; and after he sat down, his disciples came to him." This is important. We might pass over these minor actions, but through them, Jesus is symbolically establishing himself as the new Moses.

In the Old Testament, we find Moses, the great teacher, going up a mountain to receive the Law, and then coming down to teach it. Similarly, Jesus goes up a mountain and sits down to teach. However, Jesus is not receiving a law; he is giving one. During his sermon, we hear, "You have heard that it was said…But I say…" which reveals that Jesus has authority even over the Torah, which Jews held, above all, as sacred.

To be clear, Jesus is not speaking as an anti-Moses, but as a new Moses. The Law is not being abrogated; it is being intensified, raised to a new pitch. The Old Testament Law was always meant to bring humanity in line with divinity. In the beginning, this alignment was at a fairly basic level. But now that the definitive Moses has appeared, the alignment is becoming absolute, radical, complete.

Jesus declares that he would not undermine the Law and the prophets but fulfill them. Jesus himself was an observant Jew, and the themes and images of the Holy Scriptures were elemental for him.

But what is he going to fulfill? Theologian N.T. Wright has pointed out that the Old Testament is essentially an unfinished symphony, a drama without a climax. It is the articulation of a hope, a dream, a longing—but without a realization of that hope, without a satisfaction of that longing.

Israel knew itself to be the people with the definite mission to become holy and thereby to render the world holy. But instead, Israel fell into greater and greater sins; and instead of being the catalyst for the conversion of the world, the world was continually overwhelming and enslaving Israel.

And then came Jesus, who turned out to be, in the most unexpected way, the fulfillment of the dream. From the beginning of his ministry, Jesus affected the gathering of the tribes of Israel through conversion and the forgiveness of sins.

Thus, as the fulfillment of Israel's entire story, he begins his primary teaching with the "Beatitudes" (Matt. 5:3–11), a title that stems from the Latin noun *beātitūdō*, meaning "happiness" or "blessedness." Through this series of paradoxes, surprises, and reversals, Jesus begins setting a topsy-turvy universe aright.

How should we understand them? A key is the Greek word *makarios*, rendered "blessed" or "happy" or perhaps even "lucky," which is used to start each of the Beatitudes.

"Blessed are the poor in spirit." We might say, "How lucky you are if you are not addicted to material things." Here Jesus is telling us how to realize our deepest desire, which is the desire for God, not for passing things that only bring temporary comfort.

"Blessed are those who mourn." We might interpret it this way: "How lucky you are if you are not addicted to good feelings." Doing the will of God sometimes involves the acceptance of enormous pain, but when you're free from dependence on good feelings, you're liberated for whatever life demands.

"Blessed are the meek." One of the world's greatest seductions is power. But what we ought to do is eschew worldly power, so that the power of the will of God might reign in us.

"Blessed are you when people revile you and persecute you and utter all kinds of evil against you falsely on my account." In other words, how lucky you are if you are not addicted to the approval of others.

Later in his sermon, Jesus teaches, "You have heard that it was said to those of ancient times, 'You shall not murder'; and 'whoever murders shall be liable to judgment.' But I say to you that if you are angry with a brother or sister, you will be liable to judgment." Killing is an action, but that action is rooted in a more fundamental dysfunction: a hateful attitude, a disordered soul, a basic misperception of reality. To be like God utterly, we obviously have to eliminate cruel and hateful actions, but we have to go deeper, eliminating cruel and hateful thoughts and attitudes as well, for God is love, right through.

Word Study

μακάριος

MAKARIOS

Adjective
Blessed, happy, lucky

LOVE FOR ENEMIES

[43] "You have heard that it was said, 'You shall love your neighbor and hate your enemy.' [44] But I say to you, Love your enemies and pray for those who persecute you, [45] so that you may be children of your Father in heaven; for he makes his sun rise on the evil and on the good, and sends rain on the righteous and on the unrighteous. [46] For if you love those who love you, what reward do you have? Do not even the tax collectors do the same? [47] And if you greet only your brothers and sisters, what more are you doing than others? Do not even the Gentiles do the same? [48] Be perfect, therefore, as your heavenly Father is perfect.

How to Love Your Enemies

Matthew 5:43–48 | Bishop Barron

The Sermon on the Mount is one of the most puzzling texts in the New Testament, especially the part about loving our enemies—not tolerating them, or vaguely accepting them, but loving them. This is one of Christianity's most distinctive teachings.

How do we make sense of it? When you love those who hate you, you confuse and confound them, taking away the very energy that feeds their hatred.

We want God to behave as we would—that is to say, to withdraw his love from those who don't deserve it and to give his love to those who do deserve it. But this is just not the way God operates.

Why should you pray for someone who is persecuting you? Why shouldn't you be allowed at least to answer him in kind—

an eye for an eye? Because God doesn't operate that way, and you are being drawn into the divine life.

Why should you turn the other cheek to someone who has struck you? Because it's practical? No—because that's the way God operates, and you're being called into the divine life.

Why should you go beyond simply loving those who love you? Because that's the way God operates: he loves the saints and he loves the worst of sinners.

Is any of this easy to do? No, of course not. Are we able to get to this state through willing it, through earnest practice? Of course not. That's why love is referred to as a theological virtue. It is the sheerest participation in the divine life, and it can only come from God. But God does offer this gift to us when we ask for it in prayer.

CONCERNING ALMSGIVING

6 "Beware of practicing your piety before others in order to be seen by them; for then you have no reward from your Father in heaven.

² "So whenever you give alms, do not sound a trumpet before you, as the hypocrites do in the synagogues and in the streets, so that they may be praised by others. Truly I tell you, they have received their reward. ³ But when you give alms, do not let your left hand know what your right hand is doing, ⁴ so that your alms may be done in secret; and your Father who sees in secret will reward you.

CONCERNING PRAYER

⁵ "And whenever you pray, do not be like the hypocrites; for they love to stand and pray in the synagogues and at the street corners, so that they may be seen by others. Truly I tell you, they have received their reward. ⁶ But whenever you pray, go into your room and shut the door and pray to your Father who is in secret; and your Father who sees in secret will reward you.

⁷ "When you are praying, do not heap up empty phrases as the Gentiles do; for they think that they will be heard because of their many words. ⁸ Do not be like them, for your Father knows what you need before you ask him.

⁹ "Pray then in this way:
Our Father in heaven,
hallowed be your name.
¹⁰ Your kingdom come.
Your will be done,
on earth as it is in heaven.
¹¹ Give us this day our daily bread.
¹² And forgive us our debts,
as we also have forgiven our debtors.
¹³ And do not bring us to the time of trial,
but rescue us from the evil one.

¹⁴ For if you forgive others their trespasses, your heavenly Father will also forgive you; ¹⁵ but if you do not forgive others, neither will your Father forgive your trespasses.

CONCERNING FASTING

¹⁶ "And whenever you fast, do not look dismal, like the hypocrites, for they disfigure their faces so as to show others that they are fasting. Truly I tell you, they have received their reward. ¹⁷ But when you fast, put oil on your head and wash your face, ¹⁸ so that your fasting may be seen not by others but by your Father who is in secret; and your Father who sees in secret will reward you.

The Prayer That Sets Us Right

Matthew 6:5–15 | Bishop Barron

This great prayer that Jesus taught us links us to all of the great figures in Christian history, from Peter and Paul to Augustine, Thomas Aquinas, Francis of Assisi, John Henry Newman, G.K. Chesterton, John Paul II, and right up to the present day.

A desire to pray is planted deep within us. It just means the desire to speak to God and to listen to him. Keep in mind that prayer is not designed to change God's mind or to tell God something he doesn't know. God isn't like a big city boss or a reluctant pasha whom we have to persuade. He is rather the one who wants nothing other than to give us good things—though they might not always be what we want.

Can you see how this prayer rightly orders us? We must put God's holy name first; we must strive to do his will in all things and at all times; we must be strengthened by spiritual food or we will fall; we must be agents of forgiveness; we must be able to withstand the dark powers.

CONCERNING TREASURES

[19] "Do not store up for yourselves treasures on earth, where moth and rust consume and where thieves break in and steal; [20] but store up for yourselves treasures in heaven, where neither moth nor rust consumes and where thieves do not break in and steal. [21] For where your treasure is, there your heart will be also.

St. John Chrysostom
(349–407)

Homilies on Matthew

Our Father, Not My Father

Matthew 6:9

He teaches us to make our prayer common, on behalf of our brothers and sisters. For he says not, "My Father in heaven," but, "Our Father," offering up his supplications for the body in common, and nowhere looking to his own but everywhere to his neighbor's good.

THE SOUND EYE

[22] "The eye is the lamp of the body. So, if your eye is healthy, your whole body will be full of light; [23] but if your eye is unhealthy, your whole body will be full of darkness. If then the light in you is darkness, how great is the darkness!

SERVING TWO MASTERS

[24] "No one can serve two masters; for a slave will either hate the one and love the other, or be devoted to the one and despise the other. You cannot serve God and wealth.

DO NOT WORRY

[25] "Therefore I tell you, do not worry about your life, what you will eat or what you will drink, or about your body, what you will wear. Is not life more than food, and the body more than clothing? [26] Look at the birds of the air; they neither sow nor reap nor gather into barns, and yet your heavenly Father feeds them. Are you not of more value than they? [27] And can any of you by worrying add a single hour to your span of life?

The Antidote for Worry

Matthew 6:25–34 | Bishop Barron

In his map of the Christian life, Jesus exhorts us not to worry. He calls us to entrust our lives completely to God. How often the Bible compels us to meditate on the meaning of faith! We might say that the Scriptures rest upon faith, that they remain inspired at every turn by the spirit of faith.

Paul Tillich said that "faith" is the most misunderstood word in the religious vocabulary, and I've always felt that he's right about that. What is faith? Faith is an attitude of trust in the presence of God. Faith is openness to what God will reveal, do, and invite. It should be obvious that in dealing with the infinite, all-powerful, personal God, we are never in control.

This is precisely what we see in the lives of the saints: Mother Teresa moving into the worst slum in the world in an attitude of trust; St. Francis of Assisi just abandoning everything and living for God; Rose Hawthorne deciding to take cancer sufferers into her own home; St. Anthony of Egypt leaving everything behind and going into the desert; Maximilian Kolbe saying, "I'm a Catholic priest; take me in his place." So do not worry, and depend on God for everything. Have faith!

[28] And why do you worry about clothing? Consider the lilies of the field, how they grow; they neither toil nor spin, [29] yet I tell you, even Solomon in all his glory was not clothed like one of these. [30] But if God so clothes the grass of the field, which is alive today and tomorrow is thrown into the oven, will he not much more clothe you—you of little faith? [31] Therefore do not worry, saying, 'What will we eat?' or 'What will we drink?' or 'What will we wear?' [32] For it is the Gentiles who strive for all these things; and indeed your heavenly Father knows that you need all these things. [33] But strive first for the kingdom of God and his righteousness, and all these things will be given to you as well.

[34] "So do not worry about tomorrow, for tomorrow will bring worries of its own. Today's trouble is enough for today.

Surrender First

Matthew 6:33 | Bishop Barron

Notice how Jesus does not dismiss the reality and importance of concrete concerns, but at the same time notice how radically he relativizes them in relation to the kingdom of God. What must always come first is our radical trust in the Lord, our surrender to his will and providential purpose. Within that context, we can indeed seek after the goods of the world, but spiritual sickness comes when we invert the relationship.

JUDGING OTHERS

7 "Do not judge, so that you may not be judged. [2] For with the judgment you make you will be judged, and the measure you give will be the measure you get. [3] Why do you see the speck in your neighbor's eye, but do not notice the log in your own eye? [4] Or how can you say to your neighbor, 'Let me take the speck out of your eye,' while the log is in your own eye? [5] You hypocrite, first take the log out of your own eye, and then you will see clearly to take the speck out of your neighbor's eye.

PROFANING THE HOLY

[6] "Do not give what is holy to dogs; and do not throw your pearls before swine, or they will trample them under foot and turn and maul you.

Enlarging Your Soul

Matthew 7:1–5 | Bishop Barron

Instead of projecting violence and negativity onto another, Jesus is teaching his listeners to turn to the difficult but ultimately soul-enlarging task of self-criticism and *metanoia* (going beyond the mind that you have). Rooted in the *magna anima* (the great soul), secure in the unconditional love of the divine, one has the requisite courage to face the inner darkness and one is liberated from the hopeless pattern of casting blame and inventing scapegoats. But it is Jesus the judge who makes this possible, who, through the power of his soul, illumines the dark and unveils the game.

ASK, SEARCH, KNOCK

⁷ "Ask, and it will be given you; search, and you will find; knock, and the door will be opened for you. ⁸ For everyone who asks receives, and everyone who searches finds, and for everyone who knocks, the door will be opened. ⁹ Is there anyone among you who, if your child asks for bread, will give a stone? ¹⁰ Or if the child asks for a fish, will give a snake? ¹¹ If you then, who are evil, know how to give good gifts to your children, how much more will your Father in heaven give good things to those who ask him!

THE GOLDEN RULE

¹² "In everything do to others as you would have them do to you; for this is the law and the prophets.

THE NARROW GATE

¹³ "Enter through the narrow gate; for the gate is wide and the road is easy that leads to destruction, and there are many who take it. ¹⁴ For the gate is narrow and the road is hard that leads to life, and there are few who find it.

A TREE AND ITS FRUIT

¹⁵ "Beware of false prophets, who come to you in sheep's clothing but inwardly are ravenous wolves. ¹⁶ You will know them by their fruits. Are grapes gathered from thorns, or figs from thistles? ¹⁷ In the same way, every good tree bears good fruit, but the bad tree bears bad fruit. ¹⁸ A good tree cannot bear bad fruit, nor can a bad tree bear good fruit. ¹⁹ Every tree that does not bear good fruit is cut down and thrown into the fire. ²⁰ Thus you will know them by their fruits.

CONCERNING SELF-DECEPTION

[21] "Not everyone who says to me, 'Lord, Lord,' will enter the kingdom of heaven, but only the one who does the will of my Father in heaven. [22] On that day many will say to me, 'Lord, Lord, did we not prophesy in your name, and cast out demons in your name, and do many deeds of power in your name?' [23] Then I will declare to them, 'I never knew you; go away from me, you evildoers.'

HEARERS AND DOERS

[24] "Everyone then who hears these words of mine and acts on them will be like a wise man who built his house on rock. [25] The rain fell, the floods came, and the winds blew and beat on that house, but it did not fall, because it had been founded on rock. [26] And everyone who hears these words of mine and does not act on them will be like a foolish man who built his house on sand. [27] The rain fell, and the floods came, and the winds blew and beat against that house, and it fell—and great was its fall!"

[28] Now when Jesus had finished saying these things, the crowds were astounded at his teaching, [29] for he taught them as one having authority, and not as their scribes.

Getting Answers from God

Matthew 7:7–11 | Bishop Barron

Faith is power, for it is a link to the reality of God, the power that made and sustains the cosmos. When we remain in the narrow confines of our perceptions, our thoughts, our hopes, we live in a very cramped way.

To have faith is to live outside of the box, risking, venturing, believing the impossible. Sometimes, the power of faith is manifested in spectacular and immediately obvious ways. There is a long tradition, stretching back to Jesus himself and including many of the saints, of faith healing. When someone consciously and confidently opens himself to God, acting as a kind of conduit, the divine energy can flow.

There is also the power of prayer. When some people ask in a spirit of trust, really believing that what they are asking for will happen, it happens.

**St. John
Chrysostom**
(349–407)

*Homilies on
Matthew*

They Were Astounded at His Teaching

Matthew 7:28

They were astonished most of all at his authority.
Unlike Moses or the prophets, he did not speak
always with reference to another; on the contrary, he
indicates everywhere that he himself has the power
of deciding. When setting forth his laws, for instance,
his pattern is "You have heard that it was said … But I
say to you…" (Matt. 5:27). And when he speaks of the
judgment day, he speaks of himself as the Judge, able
to bestow both punishments and honors…. Lest this
should be thought boastful or arrogant, he does his
works at the same time, showing his authority to heal,
so that the people might not be perplexed in seeing
him teach in this way.

JESUS CLEANSES A LEPER

8 When Jesus had come down from the mountain, great crowds followed
him; ² and there was a leper who came to him and knelt before him,
saying, "Lord, if you choose, you can make me clean." ³ He stretched out his
hand and touched him, saying, "I do choose. Be made clean!" Immediately
his leprosy was cleansed. ⁴ Then Jesus said to him, "See that you say nothing
to anyone; but go, show yourself to the priest, and offer the gift that Moses
commanded, as a testimony to them."

JESUS HEALS A CENTURION'S SERVANT

⁵ When he entered Capernaum, a centurion came to him, appealing to
him ⁶ and saying, "Lord, my servant is lying at home paralyzed, in terrible
distress." ⁷ And he said to him, "I will come and cure him." ⁸ The centurion
answered, "Lord, I am not worthy to have you come under my roof; but only
speak the word, and my servant will be healed. ⁹ For I also am a man under
authority, with soldiers under me; and I say to one, 'Go,' and he goes, and
to another, 'Come,' and he comes, and to my slave, 'Do this,' and the slave
does it." ¹⁰ When Jesus heard him, he was amazed and said to those who
followed him, "Truly I tell you, in no one in Israel have I found such faith.
¹¹ I tell you, many will come from east and west and will eat with Abraham
and Isaac and Jacob in the kingdom of heaven, ¹² while the heirs of the

St. Thomas Aquinas
(1225–1274)

Commentary on Saint Matthew's Gospel

Why Does Jesus Touch the Leper?
Matthew 8:1–4

When curing, Christ does three things: he stretches out his hand when he gives help; sometimes he stretches out his hand, but does not touch; and sometimes he touches, and this is when he produces a change.

But why does he touch [the leper], since this was forbidden in the Law? He did it to show that he is above the Law.... One who touches seems to break the Law. But in fact he did not break it, because it was forbidden on account of contagion. Therefore, because he could not be infected, he could touch.

Furthermore, he touched in order to show his humanity; because it is not enough for a sinner to be subjected to God with regard to his divinity, but also with respect to his humanity.

Again, he touched him in order to manifest the doctrine concerning the power in the sacraments; because both touch and words are required, for when the word is joined to the element, the sacrament comes to be.

kingdom will be thrown into the outer darkness, where there will be weeping and gnashing of teeth." [13] And to the centurion Jesus said, "Go; let it be done for you according to your faith." And the servant was healed in that hour.

JESUS HEALS MANY AT PETER'S HOUSE
[14] When Jesus entered Peter's house, he saw his mother-in-law lying in bed with a fever; [15] he touched her hand, and the fever left her, and she got up and began to serve him. [16] That evening they brought to him many who were possessed with demons; and he cast out the spirits with a word, and cured all who were sick. [17] This was to fulfill what had been spoken through the prophet Isaiah, "He took our infirmities and bore our diseases."

WOULD-BE FOLLOWERS OF JESUS

[18] Now when Jesus saw great crowds around him, he gave orders to go over to the other side. [19] A scribe then approached and said, "Teacher, I will follow you wherever you go." [20] And Jesus said to him, "Foxes have holes, and birds of the air have nests; but the Son of Man has nowhere to lay his head." [21] Another of his disciples said to him, "Lord, first let me go and bury my father." [22] But Jesus said to him, "Follow me, and let the dead bury their own dead."

JESUS STILLS THE STORM

[23] And when he got into the boat, his disciples followed him. [24] A windstorm arose on the sea, so great that the boat was being swamped by the waves; but he was asleep. [25] And they went and woke him up, saying, "Lord, save us! We are perishing!" [26] And he said to them, "Why are you afraid, you of little faith?" Then he got up and rebuked the winds and the sea; and there was a dead calm. [27] They were amazed, saying, "What sort of man is this, that even the winds and the sea obey him?"

JESUS HEALS THE GADARENE DEMONIACS

[28] When he came to the other side, to the country of the Gadarenes, two demoniacs coming out of the tombs met him. They were so fierce that no one could pass that way. [29] Suddenly they shouted, "What have you to do with us, Son of God? Have you come here to torment us before the

---

What Is Your Ultimate Concern?

Matthew 8:5–13 | Bishop Barron

The centurion who asked Jesus to heal his servant showed great trust in him. To trust is to have hope, to turn one's heart to God. It means to root one's life, to ground and center one's concerns, in God. And to trust and to turn one's heart to human beings means to root the whole of one's life, to ground and center one's concerns, in the things of this world: in wealth, fame, power, honor, or pleasure.

What is the center of gravity of your life? What is your "ultimate concern"? The Bible consistently presents this as an either/or. Think of the passage in the book of Joshua, when Joshua lays it on the line for the people of Israel: "Put away the foreign gods that are among you, and incline your hearts to the Lord" (Josh. 24:23).

Jesus tells his followers, "Whoever is not with me is against me" (Matt. 12:30). We each have to confront this either/or with great honesty and clarity.

time?" ³⁰ Now a large herd of swine was feeding at some distance from them. ³¹ The demons begged him, "If you cast us out, send us into the herd of swine." ³² And he said to them, "Go!" So they came out and entered the swine; and suddenly, the whole herd rushed down the steep bank into the sea and perished in the water. ³³ The swineherds ran off, and on going into the town, they told the whole story about what had happened to the demoniacs. ³⁴ Then the whole town came out to meet Jesus; and when they saw him, they begged him to leave their neighborhood.

In the Darkest Times, Pray

Matthew 8:23–27 | Bishop Barron

During the storm, Jesus' disciples cried out to their Master in desperation: "Lord, save us! We are perishing!" This is a *de profundis* prayer. It comes from Psalm 130: "Out of the depths I cry to you, O Lord. Lord, hear my voice! Let your ears be attentive to the voice of my supplications!" It is the prayer offered at the darkest times of life, when we feel utterly incapable of helping ourselves.

Perhaps you yourself are in this precise situation. Perhaps your life is sinking, or you're recovering from serious injury or emotional pain, or you've just received some devastating news. Perhaps you find yourself caught in a terrible, unrelenting depression. Maybe you've just lost a loved one, and you're awash in a sea of grief.

If that's you, then pray as the disciples did. Awaken someone who can help. Jesus sleeping in the midst of the storm is a very powerful symbol of God's sovereignty over even the darkest and most difficult trials that life throws at us.

JESUS HEALS A PARALYTIC

9 And after getting into a boat he crossed the sea and came to his own town. ² And just then some people were carrying a paralyzed man lying on a bed. When Jesus saw their faith, he said to the paralytic, "Take heart, son; your sins are forgiven." ³ Then some of the scribes said to themselves, "This man is blaspheming." ⁴ But Jesus, perceiving their thoughts, said, "Why do you think evil in your hearts? ⁵ For which is easier, to say, 'Your sins are forgiven,' or to say, 'Stand up and walk'? ⁶ But so that you may know that the Son of Man has authority on earth to forgive sins"—he then said to the paralytic—"Stand up, take your bed and go to your home." ⁷ And he stood up and went to his home. ⁸ When the crowds saw it, they were filled with awe, and they glorified God, who had given such authority to human beings.

THE CALL OF MATTHEW

⁹ As Jesus was walking along, he saw a man called Matthew sitting at the tax booth; and he said to him, "Follow me." And he got up and followed him.

¹⁰ And as he sat at dinner in the house, many tax collectors and sinners came and were sitting with him and his disciples. ¹¹ When the Pharisees saw this, they said to his disciples, "Why does your teacher eat with tax collectors and sinners?" ¹² But when he heard this, he said, "Those who are well have no need of a physician, but those who are sick. ¹³ Go and learn what this means, 'I desire mercy, not sacrifice.' For I have come to call not the righteous but sinners."

THE QUESTION ABOUT FASTING

¹⁴ Then the disciples of John came to him, saying, "Why do we and the Pharisees fast often, but your disciples do not fast?" ¹⁵ And Jesus said to them, "The wedding guests cannot mourn as long as the bridegroom is with them, can they? The days will come when the bridegroom is taken away from them, and then they will fast. ¹⁶ No one sews a piece of unshrunk cloth on an old cloak, for the patch pulls away from the cloak, and a worse tear is made. ¹⁷ Neither is new wine put into old wineskins; otherwise, the skins burst, and the wine is spilled, and the skins are destroyed; but new wine is put into fresh wineskins, and so both are preserved."

AND HE

SAID

TO HIM,

"FOLLOW

ME."

MATTHEW 9:9

The Calling of Matthew

Matthew 9:9–13 | Bishop Barron

I WISH TO GET AT THIS STORY of Matthew's conversion—penned by the convert himself—by looking at it through a lens provided by a sixteenth-century artist.

Near the Piazza Navona in Rome, there stands the splendid church of San Luigi dei Francesi, and on the wall of a dark corner chapel of that edifice there hangs an unforgettable canvas by the late Renaissance painter Caravaggio. Caravaggio's Matthew sits at his tax collector's table wearing all of the finery of a sixteenth-century Italian dandy: silk stockings, jaunty hat, sword at his side, a feathered cap on his head. (If the artist were alive today, he would most likely depict Matthew wearing an Armani suit, a Rolex watch on his wrist, and Gucci leather shoes on his feet.) Matthew is surrounded by a whole coterie of others who, like him, seem caught up in the superficialities of the high life, and the board at which they sit is piled high with the money that Matthew had extorted from his neighbors and fellow citizens.

Across from the tax collector stands the mysterious figure of Jesus wrapped in shadow. He stretches out his hand and indicates Matthew, who points a finger at his own chest and gazes incredulously at Jesus, as if to say, "You're calling *me*?" Just as the world comes into being through a sheer act of grace, so newness of spiritual life flows not from the worthiness of the one who receives it, but from the pure generosity of the one who gives it. And as Paul put it in his first letter to Timothy, God "desires everyone to be saved" (1 Tim. 2:4), even those who, like Matthew, find themselves deeply rooted in a lifestyle inimical to the divine will. If the spiritual life is construed as a game of meriting and deserving, achieving and rewarding, it becomes dysfunctional. It must be thought of as, first and last, a grace joyfully received.

CARAVAGGIO | *The Calling of Saint Matthew* | 1599–1600

Jesus' pointing finger

Jesus' pointing finger is modeled on Michelangelo's famous depiction of the creation of Adam on the ceiling of the Sistine Chapel. What's surprising is that Jesus' hand is not modeled on God's hand, but Adam's. This is meant to show that Christ is the New Adam who redeems us from the *first* Adam's sin.

Matthew's gestures

Matthew's left hand is posed similarly to Christ's, but is directed back at himself. The message he is conveying to Jesus is, "Really? You're choosing *me*?" In contrast to this is the positioning of his right hand, which reaches toward the money on the table. The two gestures appear to conflict with one another, and they reveal the struggle in Matthew's heart between his worldly attachments and the call of Jesus.

Ray of light

This painting is a spectacular example of Caravaggio's defining chiaroscuro: a technique in which extreme contrast between light and shadow is used to draw the eye to key areas of the composition. In this painting, the ray of light above Christ's hand emphasizes the power and authority with which he summons Matthew from a life of comfort and greed.

Now what, for us, is that creative and beckoning hand of Jesus? What does it look like? It might be that nagging sense of dissatisfaction, even when we are surrounded with all of the things we thought would make us happy. It might be the voice of a child saying, as a steeple looms into view through the car window, "Why don't we go to church?" It might be that strange and delicious tug we feel in the presence of holy things or holy people. It might be that line from the Scripture that, in an instant, rearranges the furniture of our minds. It might be a weeping willow tree so beautiful that it makes us weep. It might be the experience of hitting bottom, a humiliation so profound that our illusions of self-reliance permanently vanish. Although Jesus can call us in many ways, there is a privileged medium of this vocation, and Caravaggio subtly indicates it in his composition. Though his hand and face are arrestingly visible, Jesus is, for the most part, obscured by the body of Peter, who lurches in front of him, interposing himself, as it were, between Christ and the viewer. According to the standard iconography, Peter, the rock and the bearer of the keys, is symbolic of the Church. Therefore, Caravaggio is suggesting that it is primarily though the Church—the liturgy, the Eucharist, the proclamation of the Scriptures, the summons to moral excellence, the lives of the saints—that we experience the call of Jesus to conversion.

To return to the narrative in Matthew's Gospel, Jesus tells the tax collector, "Follow me." The call of Jesus addresses the mind, to be sure, but it is meant to move through the mind into the body, and through the body into the whole of one's life, into the most practical moves and decisions. "Follow me" has the sense of "Apprentice to me" or "Walk as I walk; think as I think; choose as I choose; see as I see." Discipleship entails an entire reworking of the self according to the pattern and manner of Jesus.

Upon hearing the address of the Lord, Matthew, we are told, "got up and followed him." The Greek word behind "got up" is *anastas*, the same word used to describe the Resurrection (*anastasis*) of Jesus from the dead. Following Jesus is indeed a kind of resurrection from the dead, since it involves the transition from a lower form of life to a higher, from a preoccupation with the ephemeral goods of the world to an immersion in the affairs of God. Those who have undergone a profound conversion tend to speak of their former life as a kind of illusion, something not entirely real.

Thus Paul can say, "It is no longer I who live, but it is Christ who lives in me" (Gal. 2:20); Thomas Merton can speak of the "false self" that has given way to the authentic self; and, perhaps most movingly, the father of the prodigal son can say, "This son of mine was dead and is alive again; he was lost and is found!" (Luke 15:24). So is conversion an *anastasis*, a rising from death.

Then the Gospel tells us what happened after Matthew's conversion: "And as he sat at dinner in the house, many tax collectors and sinners came and were sitting with him and his disciples." The first thing that Jesus does, once he calls the sinner to conversion, is invite him to a party! At the very heart of the spiritual life is the conviction that God stands in need of nothing. Our existence adds nothing to the perfection of God; rather, our existence, in its totality, is a free gift. Therefore, our moral excellence adds nothing to God, and our moral depravity takes nothing from God. What follows from this metaphysical insight is the saving knowledge that God is incapable of playing games of calculation with us. It is not as though we have to "make up for" years of misbehavior in order to be pleasing to God. It is not the case that we have to mollify the hurt feelings of a long-suffering God before he will draw us into his life. The Creator of the universe, the uncaused cause of all of finitude, is always ready to celebrate with us, because he is neither compromised by our sin nor enhanced by our virtue. He is nothing but love, right through, and therefore the party is permanently on. All we have to do is respond to the invitation. What sense, then, do we make of all the scriptural texts having to do with divine anger? Those biblical metaphors should be interpreted as expressions of God's passion to set things right. Following Thomas Aquinas, we might say that God is not so much angry for his own sake, but rather for ours. It just annoys him (so to speak) that so many of us are refusing his invitation, constantly extended, to join the fun.

And notice how magnetic the converted Matthew has become! To the party flock all of his fellow tax collectors and other sinners. The call of Jesus has summoned Matthew and through him a whole host of others similarly excluded, by their own self-absorption, from the thrill of the divine life. We can only imagine how rowdy, impolite, and socially questionable this gang of lowlifes is. But there they are, gathered, because of Matthew, around the shepherd of Israel. Whenever I read the account of Matthew's conversion, I'm reminded of the story of Charles Colson, the Watergate conspirator turned Christian evangelist. When he was working for Richard Nixon, Colson said that he would gladly have walked over his grandmother to get the president re-elected. By all accounts, Colson was one of the most ruthless, focused, and morally bankrupt people in the Nixon White House—and that was saying a lot! Then, while he was in prison, Colson experienced, to his infinite surprise, a radical conversion to Jesus Christ, and for decades after, conducted a remarkably successful ministry to prisoners. Christ called this one sinner, and through him, a bevy of others have joined the party.

So it goes in the order of grace.

A GIRL RESTORED TO LIFE AND A WOMAN HEALED

[18] While he was saying these things to them, suddenly a leader of the synagogue came in and knelt before him, saying, "My daughter has just died; but come and lay your hand on her, and she will live." [19] And Jesus got up and followed him, with his disciples. [20] Then suddenly a woman who had been suffering from hemorrhages for twelve years came up behind him and touched the fringe of his cloak, [21] for she said to herself, "If I only touch his cloak, I will be made well." [22] Jesus turned, and seeing her he said, "Take heart, daughter; your faith has made you well." And instantly the woman was made well. [23] When Jesus came to the leader's house and saw the flute players and the crowd making a commotion, [24] he said, "Go away; for the girl is not dead but sleeping." And they laughed at him. [25] But when the crowd had been put outside, he went in and took her by the hand, and the girl got up. [26] And the report of this spread throughout that district.

JESUS HEALS TWO BLIND MEN

[27] As Jesus went on from there, two blind men followed him, crying loudly, "Have mercy on us, Son of David!" [28] When he entered the house, the blind men came to him; and Jesus said to them, "Do you believe that I am able to do this?" They said to him, "Yes, Lord." [29] Then he touched their eyes and said,

"According to your faith let it be done to you." [30] And their eyes were opened. Then Jesus sternly ordered them, "See that no one knows of this." [31] But they went away and spread the news about him throughout that district.

JESUS HEALS ONE WHO WAS MUTE

[32] After they had gone away, a demoniac who was mute was brought to him. [33] And when the demon had been cast out, the one who had been mute spoke; and the crowds were amazed and said, "Never has anything like this been seen in Israel." [34] But the Pharisees said, "By the ruler of the demons he casts out the demons."

THE HARVEST IS GREAT, THE LABORERS FEW

[35] Then Jesus went about all the cities and villages, teaching in their synagogues, and proclaiming the good news of the kingdom, and curing every disease and every sickness. [36] When he saw the crowds, he had compassion for them, because they were harassed and helpless, like sheep without a shepherd. [37] Then he said to his disciples, "The harvest is plentiful, but the laborers are few; [38] therefore ask the Lord of the harvest to send out laborers into his harvest."

Announcing the Defeat of the Dark Powers

Matthew 9:38 | Bishop Barron

Jesus directs his disciples to "ask the Lord of the harvest to send out laborers into his harvest," to pray for evangelists to rescue the lost. But what precisely does it mean to evangelize?

Euangelion (glad tidings) was a familiar word in the culture of the New Testament authors. When the emperor or one of his generals won a battle, he would send evangelists ahead to announce the glad tidings.

The first Christians were being consciously edgy when they adapted this word to their purposes. They were saying that the definitive battle had indeed been won, but that it had nothing to do with Caesar and his armies. It had to do with the victory that God had won in Christ over sin and death.

Jesus went into the belly of the beast, into the heart of our dysfunction, to the limits of godforsakenness, and he defeated the dark powers. He demonstrated that the divine love is greater than our greatest enemies.

This evangelical message entails, too, that there is a new King, a new Emperor. Christ, the victor over sin and death, must be the center of your life.

THE TWELVE APOSTLES

10 Then Jesus summoned his twelve disciples and gave them authority over unclean spirits, to cast them out, and to cure every disease and every sickness. ² These are the names of the twelve apostles: first, Simon, also known as Peter, and his brother Andrew; James son of Zebedee, and his brother John; ³ Philip and Bartholomew; Thomas and Matthew the tax collector; James son of Alphaeus, and Thaddaeus; ⁴ Simon the Cananaean, and Judas Iscariot, the one who betrayed him.

THE MISSION OF THE TWELVE

⁵ These twelve Jesus sent out with the following instructions: "Go nowhere among the Gentiles, and enter no town of the Samaritans, ⁶ but go rather to the lost sheep of the house of Israel. ⁷ As you go, proclaim the good news, 'The kingdom of heaven has come near.' ⁸ Cure the sick, raise the dead, cleanse the lepers, cast out demons. You received without payment; give without payment. ⁹ Take no gold, or silver, or copper in your belts, ¹⁰ no bag for your journey, or two tunics, or sandals, or a staff; for laborers deserve their food. ¹¹ Whatever town or village you enter, find out who in it is worthy, and stay there until you leave. ¹² As you enter the house, greet it. ¹³ If the house is worthy, let your peace come upon it; but if it is not worthy, let your peace return to you. ¹⁴ If anyone will not welcome you or listen to your words, shake off the dust from your feet as you leave that house or town. ¹⁵ Truly I tell you, it will be more tolerable for the land of Sodom and Gomorrah on the day of judgment than for that town.

COMING PERSECUTIONS

¹⁶ "See, I am sending you out like sheep into the midst of wolves; so be wise as serpents and innocent as doves. ¹⁷ Beware of them, for they will hand you over to councils and flog you in their synagogues; ¹⁸ and you will be dragged before governors and kings because of me, as a testimony to them and the Gentiles. ¹⁹ When they hand you over, do not worry about how you are to speak or what you are to say; for what you are to say will be given to you at that time; ²⁰ for it is not you who speak, but the Spirit of your Father speaking through you. ²¹ Brother will betray brother to death, and a father his child, and children will rise against parents and have them put to death; ²² and you will be hated by all because of my name. But the one who endures to the end will be saved. ²³ When they persecute you in one town, flee to the next; for truly I tell you, you will not have gone through all the towns of Israel before the Son of Man comes.

²⁴ "A disciple is not above the teacher, nor a slave above the master; ²⁵ it is enough for the disciple to be like the teacher, and the slave like the master. If they have called the master of the house Beelzebul, how much more will they malign those of his household!

WHOM TO FEAR

26 "So have no fear of them; for nothing is covered up that will not be uncovered, and nothing secret that will not become known. 27 What I say to you in the dark, tell in the light; and what you hear whispered, proclaim from the housetops. 28 Do not fear those who kill the body but cannot kill the soul; rather fear him who can destroy both soul and body in hell. 29 Are not two sparrows sold for a penny? Yet not one of them will fall to the ground apart from your Father. 30 And even the hairs of your head are all counted. 31 So do not be afraid; you are of more value than many sparrows.

32 "Everyone therefore who acknowledges me before others, I also will acknowledge before my Father in heaven; 33 but whoever denies me before others, I also will deny before my Father in heaven.

Do Not Be Afraid

Matthew 10:26–33 | Bishop Barron

In this passage, Jesus gives us the biblical antidote for fear. What are you afraid of? What do you have to lose? Does it terrify you to think that you might lose your wealth? Your social status? The affection of others? Your health? Your power and influence? Your reputation and good name? Your life?

In the great film *A Man for All Seasons*, King Henry VIII is infinitely frustrated because he cannot manipulate Thomas More. The king wants his chancellor to approve his illegitimate second marriage and to sanction his authority over the Church in England. But his usual methods don't work, precisely because More is not afraid of the king.

In time, Henry takes away More's job, status, money, reputation, friends, family, freedom—each time hoping that he will give in—until finally the king takes away his life. Everyone else he could intimidate, but not More.

And Thomas More's last words are instructive here: "I die his majesty's good servant, but God's first." Thomas More did fear someone. He had that holy fear that the Bible speaks of often: the fear of the Lord. There was something he feared losing—and that was intimacy and friendship with God.

G.K. Chesterton
(1874–1936)

———

Orthodoxy

The Sword That Separates

Matthew 10:34–39

Love desires personality; therefore love desires division. It is the instinct of Christianity to be glad that God has broken the universe into little pieces, because they are living pieces. It is her instinct to say "little children love one another" rather than to tell one large person to love himself.

This is the intellectual abyss between Buddhism and Christianity; that for the Buddhist or Theosophist personality is the fall of man, for the Christian it is the purpose of God, the whole point of his cosmic idea. The world-soul of the Theosophists asks man to love it only in order that man may throw himself into it. But the divine center of Christianity actually threw man out of it in order that he might love it. The oriental deity is like a giant who should have lost his leg or hand and be always seeking to find it; but the Christian power is like some giant who in a strange generosity should cut off his right hand, so that it might of its own accord shake hands with him. We come back to the same tireless note touching the nature of Christianity; all modern philosophies are chains which connect and fetter; Christianity is a sword which separates and sets free.

No other philosophy makes God actually rejoice in the separation of the universe into living souls. But according to orthodox Christianity this separation between God and man is sacred, because this is eternal. That a man may love God it is necessary that there should be not only a God to be loved, but a man to love him. All those vague theosophical minds for whom the universe is an immense melting-pot are exactly the minds which shrink instinctively from that earthquake saying of our Gospels, which declare that the Son of God came not with peace but with a sundering sword. The saying rings entirely true even considered as what it obviously is; the statement that any man who preaches real love is bound to beget hate. It is as true of democratic fraternity as a divine love; sham love ends in compromise and common philosophy; but real love has always ended in bloodshed.

Yet there is another and yet more awful truth behind the obvious meaning of this utterance of our Lord. According to himself the Son was a sword separating brother and brother that they should for an æon hate each other. But the Father also was a sword, which in the black beginning separated brother and brother, so that they should love each other at last.

NOT PEACE, BUT A SWORD

[34] "Do not think that I have come to bring peace to the earth; I have not come to bring peace, but a sword.

> [35] *For I have come to set a man against his father,*
> *and a daughter against her mother,*
> *and a daughter-in-law against her mother-in-law;*
> [36] *and one's foes will be members of one's own household.*

[37] Whoever loves father or mother more than me is not worthy of me; and whoever loves son or daughter more than me is not worthy of me; [38] and whoever does not take up the cross and follow me is not worthy of me. [39] Those who find their life will lose it, and those who lose their life for my sake will find it.

REWARDS

[40] "Whoever welcomes you welcomes me, and whoever welcomes me welcomes the one who sent me. [41] Whoever welcomes a prophet in the

name of a prophet will receive a prophet's reward; and whoever welcomes a righteous person in the name of a righteous person will receive the reward of the righteous; ⁴² and whoever gives even a cup of cold water to one of these little ones in the name of a disciple—truly I tell you, none of these will lose their reward."

MESSENGERS FROM JOHN THE BAPTIST

11 Now when Jesus had finished instructing his twelve disciples, he went on from there to teach and proclaim his message in their cities.

² When John heard in prison what the Messiah was doing, he sent word by his disciples ³ and said to him, "Are you the one who is to come, or are we to wait for another?" ⁴ Jesus answered them, "Go and tell John what you hear and see: ⁵ the blind receive their sight, the lame walk, the lepers are cleansed, the deaf hear, the dead are raised, and the poor have good news brought to them. ⁶ And blessed is anyone who takes no offense at me."

JESUS PRAISES JOHN THE BAPTIST

⁷ As they went away, Jesus began to speak to the crowds about John: "What did you go out into the wilderness to look at? A reed shaken by the wind? ⁸ What then did you go out to see? Someone dressed in soft robes? Look, those who wear soft robes are in royal palaces. ⁹ What then did you go out to see? A prophet? Yes, I tell you, and more than a prophet. ¹⁰ This is the one about whom it is written,

'See, I am sending my messenger ahead of you,
who will prepare your way before you.'

¹¹ Truly I tell you, among those born of women no one has arisen greater than John the Baptist; yet the least in the kingdom of heaven is greater than he.

Flannery O'Connor
(1925–1964)

The Habit of Being

Pushing Hard Against the Age
Matthew 11:12

I'm still not sure about that title [*The Violent Bear It Away*] but it's something for me to lean on in my conception of the book. And more than ever now it seems that the kingdom of heaven has to be taken by violence, or not at all. You have to push as hard as the age that pushes against you.

LIPPO MEMMI | *c. 1325*

Saint John the Baptist

Essay by Michael Stevens

In this exquisite altarpiece panel by Lippo Memmi, we see John the Baptist as described in the Gospels: clothed in camel's hair with a leather belt around his waist. The style of this work is typical of the time period, with generous use of gold leaf and a flattened, simplified portrayal of the human body. However, as straightforward as the painting itself may be, the man it depicts was anything but conventional.

John the Baptist's clothes, beautifully rendered by the artist, are a sign of his total rejection of earthly comforts in favor of the message of God. They also have a deeper biblical significance: the attire of John is described as almost identical to that of the prophet Elijah's in 2 Kings 1:7–8. This parallel is very intentional. Both men preach a message of radical repentance, and their similarity in appearance points to their related prophetic roles.

Memmi also shows John carrying a scroll, inscribed with a message: "Here is the Lamb of God who takes away the sin of the world!" This quotation is from John 1:29, and represents the central message of John the Baptist: that the Messiah is here, and that we must acknowledge his presence by a sincere change of heart.

John's belt

John's leather belt refers back to the description of the prophet Elijah in 2 Kings 1:7–8.

Inscribed scroll

John's scroll reads "Here is the Lamb of God who takes away the sin of the world!" The lettering is in a traditional medieval style that mimics the calligraphic letterforms found in earlier Byzantine iconography.

Use of gold

In this style of Italian medieval painting, layers of gold leaf were carefully applied to the background to represent the holiness of the saint depicted and the glory of heaven.

The Violent Bear It Away

Matthew 11:12 | Bishop Barron

The title for Flannery O'Connor's irresistibly powerful second and final novel, The *Violent Bear It Away*, is taken from the Douay-Rheims translation of this Gospel passage: "From the days of John the Baptist until now, the kingdom of heaven suffereth violence, and the violent bear it away."

Matthew 11:12 is a famously ambiguous passage and has given rise to a variety of interpretations over the centuries. Many have taken it to mean that the kingdom of God is attacked by violent people (such as those who killed John the Baptist) and that they threaten to take it away. But others have interpreted it in the opposite direction, as a word of praise to the spiritually violent who manage to get into the kingdom. Flannery O'Connor herself sides with this latter group. In a letter from July 1959, she says, "St. Thomas's gloss on this verse is that the violent Christ is here talking about represent those ascetics who strain against mere nature. St. Augustine concurs." We must keep in mind that the "mere nature" that classical Christianity describes is a fallen nature, one that tends away from God and his demands. Thus the "violent," on this reading, are those spiritually heroic types who resist the promptings and tendencies of this nature and seek to discipline it in various ways in order to enter into the kingdom or order of God.

One of only two novels that O'Connor ever wrote, The *Violent Bear It Away* is, like so many of her stories, shocking, convoluted in plot, funny, violent, and filled with unforgettably strange characters. And the key to understanding the novel—and in particular, the character of Old Tarwater—is this Gospel passage. Old Tarwater is a fanatic who, with a spiritual ferociousness and sometimes with literal violence, opposes the ways of "mere nature." Like so many other of O'Connor's backwoods spiritual heroes, Old Tarwater has much in common with the ascetics of the ancient Church, those quasi-madmen who shut themselves up in desert caves or climbed on top of pillars or starved themselves nearly to death in order to signal to a complacent society the radicality of the Christian life. It is not egocentric moderns who bear the kingdom, but rather the "violent," those who realize that their lives are not about them.

¹² From the days of John the Baptist until now the kingdom of heaven has suffered violence, and the violent take it by force. ¹³ For all the prophets and the law prophesied until John came; ¹⁴ and if you are willing to accept it, he is Elijah who is to come. ¹⁵ Let anyone with ears listen!

¹⁶ "But to what will I compare this generation? It is like children sitting in the marketplaces and calling to one another,

¹⁷ 'We played the flute for you, and you did not dance;
we wailed, and you did not mourn.'

¹⁸ For John came neither eating nor drinking, and they say, 'He has a demon'; ¹⁹ the Son of Man came eating and drinking, and they say, 'Look, a glutton and a drunkard, a friend of tax collectors and sinners!' Yet wisdom is vindicated by her deeds."

WOES TO UNREPENTANT CITIES

²⁰ Then he began to reproach the cities in which most of his deeds of power had been done, because they did not repent. ²¹ "Woe to you, Chorazin! Woe to you, Bethsaida! For if the deeds of power done in you had been done in Tyre and Sidon, they would have repented long ago in sackcloth and ashes. ²² But I tell you, on the day of judgment it will be more tolerable for Tyre and Sidon than for you. ²³ And you, Capernaum, will you be exalted to heaven? No, you will be brought down to Hades. For if the deeds of power

---

The Inner Life of God

Matthew 11:25–30 | Bishop Barron

In the final lines of this chapter, we are being invited into profound mysteries. Jesus addresses his Father and thereby reveals his own deepest identity within the Holy Trinity. He says, "I thank you, Father, Lord of heaven and earth, because you have hidden these things from the wise and the intelligent and have revealed them to infants."

It is important we keep in mind that this is not simply a good and holy man addressing God, but rather the very Son of God addressing his Father. We are being given a share in the inner life of God, the conversation between the first two Trinitarian persons.

And what are the "things" (*tauta* in Greek) that have been concealed from the wise and revealed to the infants? Nothing other than the mystery of Jesus' relationship to his Father, the love that obtains between Father and Son, the inner life of God. From the beginning, this is what God wanted to give us.

done in you had been done in Sodom, it would have remained until this day. ²⁴ But I tell you that on the day of judgment it will be more tolerable for the land of Sodom than for you."

JESUS THANKS HIS FATHER

²⁵ At that time Jesus said, "I thank you, Father, Lord of heaven and earth, because you have hidden these things from the wise and the intelligent and have revealed them to infants; ²⁶ yes, Father, for such was your gracious will. ²⁷ All things have been handed over to me by my Father; and no one knows the Son except the Father, and no one knows the Father except the Son and anyone to whom the Son chooses to reveal him.

²⁸ "Come to me, all you that are weary and are carrying heavy burdens, and I will give you rest. ²⁹ Take my yoke upon you, and learn from me; for I am gentle and humble in heart, and you will find rest for your souls. ³⁰ For my yoke is easy, and my burden is light."

St. John Chrysostom
(349–407)

Homilies on Matthew

And I Will Give You Rest
Matthew 11:28

Not this or that person, but all that are in anxiety, in sorrows, in sins. Come, not that I may call you to account, but that I may do away with your sins; come, not because I want your honor, but because I want your salvation. "And I," says he, "will give you rest."

PLUCKING GRAIN ON THE SABBATH

12 At that time Jesus went through the grainfields on the sabbath; his disciples were hungry, and they began to pluck heads of grain and to eat. ² When the Pharisees saw it, they said to him, "Look, your disciples are doing what is not lawful to do on the sabbath." ³ He said to them, "Have you not read what David did when he and his companions were hungry? ⁴ He entered the house of God and ate the bread of the Presence, which it was not lawful for him or his companions to eat, but only for the priests. ⁵ Or have you not read in the law that on the sabbath the priests in the

temple break the sabbath and yet are guiltless? [6] I tell you, something greater than the temple is here. [7] But if you had known what this means, 'I desire mercy and not sacrifice,' you would not have condemned the guiltless. [8] For the Son of Man is lord of the sabbath."

THE MAN WITH A WITHERED HAND

[9] He left that place and entered their synagogue; [10] a man was there with a withered hand, and they asked him, "Is it lawful to cure on the sabbath?" so that they might accuse him. [11] He said to them, "Suppose one of you has only one sheep and it falls into a pit on the sabbath; will you not lay hold of it and lift it out? [12] How much more valuable is a human being than a sheep! So it is lawful to do good on the sabbath." [13] Then he said to the man, "Stretch out your hand." He stretched it out, and it was restored, as sound as the other. [14] But the Pharisees went out and conspired against him, how to destroy him.

GOD'S CHOSEN SERVANT

[15] When Jesus became aware of this, he departed. Many crowds followed him, and he cured all of them, [16] and he ordered them not to make him known.

A Breathtaking Claim

Matthew 12:1–8 | Bishop Barron

Again and again in the Gospels, Jesus is portrayed as violating the sacred command to rest on the seventh day. For example, he often cures on the Sabbath, much to the dismay of the protectors of Jewish law.

And then in this passage, after his disciples pick grain on the Sabbath, Jesus declares himself "lord of the sabbath." It's hard to express how breathtaking this claim would be for a first-century Jew to make. Yahweh alone could be assigned the title "lord of the sabbath," so what is Jesus implying?

In short, he is claiming that he is above their rituals, even perhaps the defining practice of pious Jews, because he is the Lord. Thus, the rules must be placed in subordination to the kingdom of God, the kingdom that the Lord Jesus is ushering in even here and now.

Even more, he says, "I tell you, something greater than the temple is here." The Jerusalem temple was, for first-century Jews, the dwelling place of Yahweh on earth and hence the most sacred place imaginable. The only one who could reasonably claim to be "greater" than the temple would be the one who was worshiped in the temple; therefore, Jesus is affirming unambiguously that he is divine.

Whoever Is Not with Me Is Against Me

Matthew 12:30 | Bishop Barron

Life is filled with ambiguities, and sometimes a certain psychological "pluralism" is permissible, even welcome; but what Jesus is saying here is that, in regard to one's ultimate concern and final allegiance, one has to be clear, unified, and unambiguous. Sometimes, despite strong counterarguments and very grave dangers, a definitive choice has to be made.

---

¹⁷ This was to fulfill what had been spoken through the prophet Isaiah:

> ¹⁸ *"Here is my servant, whom I have chosen,*
> *my beloved, with whom my soul is well pleased.*
> *I will put my Spirit upon him,*
> *and he will proclaim justice to the Gentiles.*
> ¹⁹ *He will not wrangle or cry aloud,*
> *nor will anyone hear his voice in the streets.*
> ²⁰ *He will not break a bruised reed*
> *or quench a smoldering wick*
> *until he brings justice to victory.*
> ²¹ *And in his name the Gentiles will hope."*

JESUS AND BEELZEBUL

²² Then they brought to him a demoniac who was blind and mute; and he cured him, so that the one who had been mute could speak and see. ²³ All the crowds were amazed and said, "Can this be the Son of David?" ²⁴ But when the Pharisees heard it, they said, "It is only by Beelzebul, the ruler of the demons, that this fellow casts out the demons." ²⁵ He knew what they were thinking and said to them, "Every kingdom divided against itself is laid waste, and no city or house divided against itself will stand. ²⁶ If Satan casts out Satan, he is divided against himself; how then will his kingdom stand? ²⁷ If I cast out demons by Beelzebul, by whom do your own exorcists cast them out? Therefore they will be your judges. ²⁸ But if it is by the Spirit of God that I cast out demons, then the kingdom of God has come to you. ²⁹ Or how can one enter a strong man's house and plunder his property, without first tying up the strong man? Then indeed the house can be plundered. ³⁰ Whoever is not with me is against me, and whoever does not gather with me scatters. ³¹ Therefore I tell you, people will be forgiven for every sin and blasphemy, but blasphemy against the Spirit will not be forgiven. ³² Whoever speaks a word against the Son of

Man will be forgiven, but whoever speaks against the Holy Spirit will not be forgiven, either in this age or in the age to come.

A TREE AND ITS FRUIT

[33] "Either make the tree good, and its fruit good; or make the tree bad, and its fruit bad; for the tree is known by its fruit. [34] You brood of vipers! How can you speak good things, when you are evil? For out of the abundance of the heart the mouth speaks. [35] The good person brings good things out of a good treasure, and the evil person brings evil things out of an evil treasure. [36] I tell you, on the day of judgment you will have to give an account for every careless word you utter; [37] for by your words you will be justified, and by your words you will be condemned."

THE SIGN OF JONAH

[38] Then some of the scribes and Pharisees said to him, "Teacher, we wish to see a sign from you." [39] But he answered them, "An evil and adulterous generation asks for a sign, but no sign will be given to it except the sign of the prophet Jonah. [40] For just as Jonah was three days and three nights in the belly of the sea monster, so for three days and three nights the Son of Man will be in the heart of the earth. [41] The people of Nineveh will rise up at the judgment with this generation and condemn it, because they repented at the proclamation of Jonah, and see, something greater than Jonah is here! [42] The queen of the South will rise up at the judgment with this generation and condemn it, because she came from the ends of the earth to listen to the wisdom of Solomon, and see, something greater than Solomon is here!

THE RETURN OF THE UNCLEAN SPIRIT

[43] "When the unclean spirit has gone out of a person, it wanders through waterless regions looking for a resting place, but it finds none. [44] Then it says, 'I will return to my house from which I came.' When it comes, it finds it empty, swept, and put in order. [45] Then it goes and brings along seven other spirits more evil than itself, and they enter and live there; and the last state of that person is worse than the first. So will it be also with this evil generation."

THE TRUE KINDRED OF JESUS

[46] While he was still speaking to the crowds, his mother and his brothers were standing outside, wanting to speak to him. [47] Someone told him, "Look, your mother and your brothers are standing outside, wanting to speak to you." [48] But to the one who had told him this, Jesus replied, "Who is my mother, and who are my brothers?" [49] And pointing to his disciples, he said, "Here are my mother and my brothers! [50] For whoever does the will of my Father in heaven is my brother and sister and mother."

THE PARABLE OF THE SOWER

13 That same day Jesus went out of the house and sat beside the sea. [2] Such great crowds gathered around him that he got into a boat and sat there, while the whole crowd stood on the beach. [3] And he told them many things in parables, saying: "Listen! A sower went out to sow. [4] And as he sowed, some seeds fell on the path, and the birds came and ate them up. [5] Other seeds fell on rocky ground, where they did not have much soil, and they sprang up quickly, since they had no depth of soil. [6] But when the sun rose, they were scorched; and since they had no root, they withered away. [7] Other seeds fell among thorns, and the thorns grew up and choked them. [8] Other seeds fell on good soil and brought forth grain, some a hundredfold, some sixty, some thirty. [9] Let anyone with ears listen!"

THE PURPOSE OF THE PARABLES

[10] Then the disciples came and asked him, "Why do you speak to them in parables?" [11] He answered, "To you it has been given to know the secrets of the kingdom of heaven, but to them it has not been given. [12] For to those who have, more will be given, and they will have an abundance; but from those who have nothing, even what they have will be taken away. [13] The reason I speak to them in parables is that 'seeing they do not perceive, and hearing they do not listen, nor do they understand.' [14] With them indeed is fulfilled the prophecy of Isaiah that says:

> 'You will indeed listen, but never understand,
> and you will indeed look, but never perceive.
> [15] For this people's heart has grown dull,
> and their ears are hard of hearing,
> and they have shut their eyes;
> so that they might not look with their eyes,
> and listen with their ears,
> and understand with their heart and turn—
> and I would heal them.'

[16] But blessed are your eyes, for they see, and your ears, for they hear. [17] Truly I tell you, many prophets and righteous people longed to see what you see, but did not see it, and to hear what you hear, but did not hear it.

FOR TO THOSE WHO HAVE,
more WILL BE GIVEN. MATTHEW 13:12

The Parable of the Sower and You

Matthew 13:1–23 | Bishop Barron

AT THE BEGINNING OF THIS CHAPTER, we see that Jesus "went out of the house and sat beside the sea" and that large crowds gathered around him. This is Jesus speaking to the whole world, having come out from the seclusion of his "house."

Sitting down, he is in the attitude of the ancient teacher and judge. And he speaks the parable of the sower. The sower sows far and wide, some of the seed landing on the path, where the birds eat it up; some falling on rocky ground, where the life is choked off; some is sown among thorns; and some is sown on rich soil, where it bears thirty, sixty, or a hundredfold.

We have a rare privilege in that Jesus himself gives a direct explanation of the meaning of this parable. It would be unwise in the extreme to venture down some other interpretive path. Keep in mind that Jesus himself in person is the seed sown. Jesus is the seed that wants to take root in us. This seed is sown far and wide, through all sorts of means. It is destined for the whole world.

The seed sown on the path, says the Lord, refers to the one who "hears the word of the kingdom and does not understand it, [so] the evil one comes and snatches away what is sown in the heart."

One of the blocks to receiving the word is lack of understanding, lack of education in the ways of the Spirit. Israel was the extensive and complex preparation for the reception of the word. The fundamentals have to be in place before the word can be accepted. What a prophetic word to our time!

A recent poll concerning religious attitudes in America showed that most Americans favor a radical tolerance in regard to religious beliefs. It also showed that there was a shocking ignorance in regard to belief systems, dogmas, and the history of one's religion.

There's nothing in the world wrong with tolerance, but it can sometimes be a cover for indifference, a conviction that one belief is as good as another. Do we accept that kind of thinking in regard to politics? Religious education programs are falling far behind what they should be.

The seed sown on rocky ground is "the one who hears the word and immediately receives it with joy; yet such a person has no root, but endures only for a while." When difficulties and persecutions arrive, he loses confidence.

This too happens all the time. People can be fascinated by the spiritual and the religious, drawn in by a charismatic personality, or an intense experience, or a trauma. But then they lack the discipline of a religious tradition, becoming in time vaguely spiritual. But nothing in life that is taken seriously subsists without discipline and perseverance.

The third problem is laid out as such: "As for what was sown among thorns, this is the one who hears the word, but the cares of the world and the lure of wealth choke the word, and it yields nothing." Some people hear the word and take it in, but then they are unable to maintain their focus and sense of priority.

The word of God is the central and defining dynamic of life. To know the will of God, to know the mind of God, to understand his purpose and path is all-important. Without it, you lose your way amidst all of the conflicting voices and inclinations of the world.

Jesus refers to these as "the cares of the world and the lure of wealth." How much time do you spend worrying about the particular concerns of home and family, fame and work, money-making and saving? There's nothing wrong with these preoccupations in right proportion. But if they take on a dominating significance, something is off. Does the lure of riches obscure your deeper desires?

So from this we can construe the nature of good soil. When we understand the faith; when we take the time to read theology, to study the Scriptures, to feel with the Church; when we have perseverance;

when we are disciplined and enter into the practice of the faith; when we have our priorities straight—then the seed will take root in us. And it will bear fruit thirty, sixty, or a hundredfold.

The Point of Parables

Matthew 13:10–17 | Bishop Barron

The disciples ask Jesus why he speaks to the crowds in parables. Jesus is explaining the kingdom of God in these provocative and puzzling stories and images that seem to be his preferred way of preaching. And he replies to his disciples, "The reason I speak to them in parables is that 'seeing they do not perceive, and hearing they do not listen, nor do they understand.'" In other words, he tells parables because the crowds refuse to believe in him and what he has to say.

Many parables are strange and initially off-putting and puzzling. Of course, that is the point of parables: to bother us, throw us off base, confuse us a bit. How characteristic this was of Jesus' preaching! He rarely lays things out in doctrinal form: he prefers to tell these puzzling, funny stories. Why? Because in many cases stories reveal truth that arguments can't quite capture.

THE PARABLE OF THE SOWER EXPLAINED

18 "Hear then the parable of the sower. 19 When anyone hears the word of the kingdom and does not understand it, the evil one comes and snatches away what is sown in the heart; this is what was sown on the path. 20 As for what was sown on rocky ground, this is the one who hears the word and immediately receives it with joy; 21 yet such a person has no root, but endures only for a while, and when trouble or persecution arises on account of the word, that person immediately falls away. 22 As for what was sown among thorns, this is the one who hears the word, but the cares of the world and the lure of wealth choke the word, and it yields nothing.

²³ But as for what was sown on good soil, this is the one who hears the word and understands it, who indeed bears fruit and yields, in one case a hundredfold, in another sixty, and in another thirty."

THE PARABLE OF WEEDS AMONG THE WHEAT

²⁴ He put before them another parable: "The kingdom of heaven may be compared to someone who sowed good seed in his field; ²⁵ but while everybody was asleep, an enemy came and sowed weeds among the wheat, and then went away. ²⁶ So when the plants came up and bore grain, then the weeds appeared as well. ²⁷ And the slaves of the householder came and said to him, 'Master, did you not sow good seed in your field? Where, then, did these weeds come from?' ²⁸ He answered, 'An enemy has done this.' The slaves said to him, 'Then do you want us to go and gather them?' ²⁹ But he replied, 'No; for in gathering the weeds you would uproot the wheat along with them. ³⁰ Let both of them grow together until the harvest; and at harvest time I will tell the reapers, Collect the weeds first and bind them in bundles to be burned, but gather the wheat into my barn.'"

THE PARABLE OF THE MUSTARD SEED

³¹ He put before them another parable: "The kingdom of heaven is like a mustard seed that someone took and sowed in his field; ³² it is the smallest of all the seeds, but when it has grown it is the greatest of shrubs and becomes a tree, so that the birds of the air come and make nests in its branches."

THE PARABLE OF THE YEAST

³³ He told them another parable: "The kingdom of heaven is like yeast that a woman took and mixed in with three measures of flour until all of it was leavened."

THE USE OF PARABLES

³⁴ Jesus told the crowds all these things in parables; without a parable he told them nothing. ³⁵ This was to fulfill what had been spoken through the prophet:

> *"I will open my mouth to speak in parables;*
> *I will proclaim what has been hidden from the foundation of the world."*

JESUS EXPLAINS THE PARABLE OF THE WEEDS

³⁶ Then he left the crowds and went into the house. And his disciples approached him, saying, "Explain to us the parable of the weeds of the field." ³⁷ He answered, "The one who sows the good seed is the Son of Man; ³⁸ the field is the world, and the good seed are the children of the kingdom; the weeds are the children of the evil one, ³⁹ and the enemy who sowed them is the devil; the harvest is the end of the age, and the reapers are angels.

Parasitic Evil

Matthew 13:24–30 | Bishop Barron

God sows his good seed, his word, his love and compassion, but his project is met with opposition. Thus, Jesus told the parable of the wheat and the weeds, which indicates that evil always insinuates itself into the very fabric of the good.

In classical theology, we speak of evil as a *privatio boni*, a "privation of the good," meaning that evil is always and everywhere parasitic on the good. Just as a parasite is living off of the healthy body (and thereby weakening it), so moral evil lives off of the good soul, the good society, the good Church (and thereby weakens them).

What is the result? That it is exceptionally difficult to extricate the evil from the good without damaging the good. To be sure, there are certain evils that simply have to be addressed—right now, no questions, no hesitations. But there are other evils (and they really are evil) that are best left alone for the time being, lest more damage is done in the process of extricating them.

---

[40] Just as the weeds are collected and burned up with fire, so will it be at the end of the age. [41] The Son of Man will send his angels, and they will collect out of his kingdom all causes of sin and all evildoers, [42] and they will throw them into the furnace of fire, where there will be weeping and gnashing of teeth. [43] Then the righteous will shine like the sun in the kingdom of their Father. Let anyone with ears listen!

THREE PARABLES

[44] "The kingdom of heaven is like treasure hidden in a field, which someone found and hid; then in his joy he goes and sells all that he has and buys that field.

[45] "Again, the kingdom of heaven is like a merchant in search of fine pearls; [46] on finding one pearl of great value, he went and sold all that he had and bought it.

[47] "Again, the kingdom of heaven is like a net that was thrown into the sea and caught fish of every kind; [48] when it was full, they drew it ashore, sat down, and put the good into baskets but threw out the bad. [49] So it will be at the end of the age. The angels will come out and separate the evil from the righteous [50] and throw them into the furnace of fire, where there will be weeping and gnashing of teeth.

Impasto texture

One of the primary elements in Van Gogh's painting is the use of impasto: the technique of applying thick layers of paint to create a rough, raised surface on the canvas. This helped to produce the movement and texture that his paintings became known for.

Cypress tree

The cypress tree is a common theme in Van Gogh's landscapes, and some critics interpret them as an allegory for death and new life, with their vertical orientation bridging heaven and earth.

Cloudscape

Van Gogh's clouds are famous for their powerful sense of motion. In this painting, the beautiful blue-green tones of the sky are a vibrant complement to the amber yellow of the wheat, and the color palette accentuates the tense interplay between earth and sky.

Matthew 13:1–23

VINCENT VAN GOGH | *1889*

Wheat Field with Cypresses

Essay by Michael Stevens

This masterpiece depicting a wheat field beneath a tumultuous sky was considered by Van Gogh to be one of his finest landscapes. In it, we sense the deep reverence the artist had for the fierce and dynamic beauty of nature. While Van Gogh was a man of faith who created many explicitly Christian works over his lifetime, in landscape paintings such as this one we sense his awareness of spiritual realities more implicitly—through elements such as his persistent interest in the dramatic relationship of the sky to the earth. The clouds above are wild and turbulent, and the landscape below responds to this energy with a similar churning motion. In this unstable balance of elements, we can see Van Gogh's appreciation of both the verdant beauty of nature and its untamable power.

In the Gospel, Jesus uses a similar image from nature to represent his message and the many forces that oppose it. He tells of a sower scattering seed across varied terrain in hopes of a bountiful harvest. While the ruthless elements choke and destroy much of what is sown, some falls on good soil—symbolizing the hearts of those who are open to Christ's word.

Van Gogh recognized God's hand in his creation, and the beauty that grows and unfolds in the hearts and minds of those open to receiving his word. In fact, Van Gogh was so acutely aware of this interplay between creation and new life, he described it as an act of divine artistry: "Christ is more of an artist than the artists; he works in the living spirit and the living flesh. He makes men instead of statues."

The Pearl of Great Price

Matthew 13:44–46 | Bishop Barron

The Christian tradition says that we are all created "through Christ." This means that, at the very root of our being, from our "beginning," we are meant to realize a Christomorphic destiny, playing out, in a unique manner, the form of Jesus. This *imago* is in us, whether we like it or not, and the drama of our lives is nothing but the discovery and unfolding of it.

Jesus speaks here of the treasure buried in a field that a man stumbles upon. And when he finds it, he sells everything he has in order to buy that field. Could the field be the human heart, and the treasure the *imago* of Christ? Could the selling of everything be the surrendering of all for the sake of the mission?

And he speaks of the merchant's search for a pearl of great price; when the pearl is found, the merchant sells everything in order to acquire it. Could this pearl be his Christoform identity, the one thing worth looking for? And could the selling of everything else be the discovery of a rightly ordered life?

Joseph Campbell says that the greatest tragedy in life is not so much failure, but rather climbing the ladder of success and finding out that it is up against the wrong wall! Bob Dylan was reflecting ruefully on the same phenomenon when he said, "You find out when you reach the top / you're on the bottom." We can spend our entire life in pursuit of goals that are worthless, or even goals that are objectively good but not *ours*, or better, Christ's for us.

TREASURES NEW AND OLD

[51] "Have you understood all this?" They answered, "Yes." [52] And he said to them, "Therefore every scribe who has been trained for the kingdom of heaven is like the master of a household who brings out of his treasure what is new and what is old." [53] When Jesus had finished these parables, he left that place.

THE REJECTION OF JESUS AT NAZARETH

[54] He came to his hometown and began to teach the people in their synagogue, so that they were astounded and said, "Where did this man get this wisdom and these deeds of power? [55] Is not this the carpenter's son? Is not his mother called Mary? And are not his brothers James and Joseph and Simon and Judas? [56] And are not all his sisters with us? Where then did this man get all this?" [57] And they took offense at him. But Jesus said to them, "Prophets are not without honor except in their own country and in their own house." [58] And he did not do many deeds of power there, because of their unbelief.

THE DEATH OF JOHN THE BAPTIST

14 At that time Herod the ruler heard reports about Jesus; [2] and he said to his servants, "This is John the Baptist; he has been raised from the dead, and for this reason these powers are at work in him." [3] For Herod had arrested John, bound him, and put him in prison on account of Herodias, his brother Philip's wife, [4] because John had been telling him, "It is not lawful for you to have her." [5] Though Herod wanted to put him to death, he feared the crowd, because they regarded him as a prophet. [6] But when Herod's birthday came, the daughter of Herodias danced before the company, and she pleased Herod [7] so much that he promised on oath to grant her whatever she might ask. [8] Prompted by her mother, she said, "Give me the head of John the Baptist here on a platter." [9] The king was grieved, yet out of regard for his oaths and for the guests, he commanded it to be given; [10] he sent and had John beheaded in the prison. [11] The head was brought on a platter and given to the girl, who brought it to her mother. [12] His disciples came and took the body and buried it; then they went and told Jesus.

Mastering God's Opponents

Matthew 14:22–33 | Bishop Barron

Jesus comes to his disciples walking on the sea. And he comes at the darkest time of the night, when they are isolated and in danger.

God's mastery of the sea is a biblical commonplace. The Spirit of the Lord hovers over the surface of the waters in Genesis (Gen. 1:2); in Exodus, God splits the Red Sea in two (Exod. 14:21); in the book of the prophet Isaiah, God is described as having conquered the monsters of the deep (Isa. 27:1).

The water—especially the stormy water—represents all of the cosmic powers that oppose themselves to God, all those spiritual and physical forces that threaten us, most especially death itself.

In walking on the water, Jesus shows that he is the master of all of these forces, that his power and authority are greater.

Paul says, "For I am convinced that neither death, nor life, nor angels, nor rulers, nor things present, nor things to come, nor powers, nor height, nor depth, nor anything else in all creation, will be able to separate us from the love of God in Christ Jesus our Lord" (Rom. 8:38–39). Jesus says in the Gospel of John, "I have conquered the world!" (John 16:33).

And so Christ comes to his Church precisely when it is threatened. "And remember, I am with you always, to the end of the age" (Matt. 28:20). The Lord accompanies his Church, coming to it and subduing the stormy forces that surround it.

FEEDING THE FIVE THOUSAND

¹³ Now when Jesus heard this, he withdrew from there in a boat to a deserted place by himself. But when the crowds heard it, they followed him on foot from the towns. ¹⁴ When he went ashore, he saw a great crowd; and he had compassion for them and cured their sick. ¹⁵ When it was evening, the disciples came to him and said, "This is a deserted place, and the hour is now late; send the crowds away so that they may go into the villages and buy food for themselves." ¹⁶ Jesus said to them, "They need not go away; you give them something to eat." ¹⁷ They replied, "We have nothing here but five loaves and two fish." ¹⁸ And he said, "Bring them here to me." ¹⁹ Then he ordered the crowds to sit down on the grass. Taking the five loaves and the two fish, he looked up to heaven, and blessed and broke the loaves, and gave them to the disciples, and the disciples gave them to the crowds. ²⁰ And all ate and were filled; and they took up what was left over of the broken pieces, twelve baskets full. ²¹ And those who ate were about five thousand men, besides women and children.

JESUS WALKS ON THE WATER

²² Immediately he made the disciples get into the boat and go on ahead to the other side, while he dismissed the crowds. ²³ And after he had dismissed the crowds, he went up the mountain by himself to pray. When evening came, he was there alone, ²⁴ but by this time the boat, battered by the waves, was far from the land, for the wind was against them. ²⁵ And early in the morning he came walking toward them on the sea. ²⁶ But when the

St. John Chrysostom
(349–407)

Homilies on Matthew

The Mother of Quiet

Matthew 14:23

For what purpose does Jesus go up into the mountain? To teach us that loneliness and retirement are good when we pray to God. He is continually withdrawing into the wilderness, and there he often spends the whole night in prayer, teaching us earnestly to seek such quietness in our prayers, as time and place may confer. For the wilderness is the mother of quiet; it is a calm and a harbor, delivering us from all turmoils.

disciples saw him walking on the sea, they were terrified, saying, "It is a ghost!" And they cried out in fear. [27] But immediately Jesus spoke to them and said, "Take heart, it is I; do not be afraid."

[28] Peter answered him, "Lord, if it is you, command me to come to you on the water." [29] He said, "Come." So Peter got out of the boat, started walking on the water, and came toward Jesus. [30] But when he noticed the strong wind, he became frightened, and beginning to sink, he cried out, "Lord, save me!" [31] Jesus immediately reached out his hand and caught

Fulton Sheen
(1895–1979)

———

Life of Christ

Why Did Peter Sink?

Matthew 14:30–31

The Lord bade Peter come; but after a few moments Peter began to sink. Why? Because he took account of the winds; because he concentrated on natural difficulties; because he trusted not in the power of the Master and failed to keep his eyes on him. "But when he noticed the strong wind, he became frightened, and [began] to sink."

He finally cried out to the Lord for help: "'Lord, save me!' Jesus immediately reached out his hand and caught him, saying to him, 'You of little faith, why did you doubt?'" The deliverance was first; then the gentle rebuke; and that probably with a smile on his face and love in his voice.

But this was not the only time that poor Peter would doubt the Master whom he loved so well. He who then asked to walk upon the waters in order to come quickly to the Lord was the one who would later swear that he was ready to go to prison and even to death for him. Courageous in the boat but timid in the waters, he would later on be bold at the Last Supper, but cowardly the night of the trial. The scene at the lake was a rehearsal for another fall of Peter.

him, saying to him, "You of little faith, why did you doubt?" ³² When they got into the boat, the wind ceased. ³³ And those in the boat worshiped him, saying, "Truly you are the Son of God."

JESUS HEALS THE SICK IN GENNESARET

³⁴ When they had crossed over, they came to land at Gennesaret. ³⁵ After the people of that place recognized him, they sent word throughout the region and brought all who were sick to him, ³⁶ and begged him that they might touch even the fringe of his cloak; and all who touched it were healed.

THE TRADITION OF THE ELDERS

15 Then Pharisees and scribes came to Jesus from Jerusalem and said, ² "Why do your disciples break the tradition of the elders? For they do not wash their hands before they eat." ³ He answered them, "And why do you break the commandment of God for the sake of your tradition? ⁴ For God said, 'Honor your father and your mother,' and, 'Whoever speaks evil of father or mother must surely die.' ⁵ But you say that whoever tells father or mother, 'Whatever support you might have had from me is given to God,' then that person need not honor the father. ⁶ So, for the sake of your tradition, you make void the word of God. ⁷ You hypocrites! Isaiah prophesied rightly about you when he said:

> ⁸ *'This people honors me with their lips,*
> *but their hearts are far from me;*
> ⁹ *in vain do they worship me,*
> *teaching human precepts as doctrines.' "*

THINGS THAT DEFILE

¹⁰ Then he called the crowd to him and said to them, "Listen and understand: ¹¹ it is not what goes into the mouth that defiles a person, but it is what comes out of the mouth that defiles." ¹² Then the disciples approached and said to him, "Do you know that the Pharisees took offense when they heard what you said?" ¹³ He answered, "Every plant that my heavenly Father has not planted will be uprooted. ¹⁴ Let them alone; they are blind guides of the blind. And if one blind person guides another, both will fall into a pit." ¹⁵ But Peter said to him, "Explain this parable to us." ¹⁶ Then he said, "Are you also still without understanding? ¹⁷ Do you not see that whatever goes into the mouth enters the stomach, and goes out into the sewer? ¹⁸ But what comes out of the mouth proceeds from the heart, and this is what defiles. ¹⁹ For out of the heart come evil intentions, murder, adultery, fornication, theft, false witness, slander. ²⁰ These are what defile a person, but to eat with unwashed hands does not defile."

Thomas Merton
(1915–1968)

———

No Man Is an Island

Why Sincerity Is Critical to Prayer

Matthew 15:7–8

Sincerity is, perhaps, the most vitally important quality of true prayer. It is the only valid test of our faith, our hope, and our love of God. No matter how deep our meditations, nor how severe our penances, how grand our liturgy, how pure our chant, how noble our thoughts about the mysteries of God; they are all useless if we do not really mean what we say. What is the good of bringing down upon ourselves the curses uttered by the ancient prophets and taken up again by Christ himself: "You hypocrites! Isaiah prophesied rightly about you when he said: 'This people honors me with their lips, but their hearts are far from me'" (cf. Isa. 29:13).

Since the monk is a man of prayer and a man of God, his most important obligation is sincerity. Everywhere in St. Benedict's *Rule* we are reminded of this. Those who are not true monks "lie to God by their tonsure," he says (*Rule*, chapter 1). The first thing to be sought in a candidate for the monastic life is sincerity in seeking God—*si vere Deum quaerit*. One of the instruments of good works, by which the monk becomes a saint, is to "utter truth from his heart and from his lips," and another is that he should not desire to be called a saint without being one, but become a saint in all truth. In order that the truth of his virtue might be more certain, he must desire to manifest it in deeds rather than words. But above all in his prayer, his thoughts must agree with what he sings: *mens concordet voci* [let the heart be in accord with the voice]. Like Jesus himself, St. Benedict prefers that prayer should be short and pure, rather than that the monk should multiply empty words or meditations without meaning.

The most important thing in prayer is that we present ourselves as we are before God as he is. This cannot be done without a generous effort of recollection and self-searching. But if we are sincere, our prayer will never be fruitless. Our sincerity itself establishes an instant contact with the God of all truth.

THE CANAANITE WOMAN'S FAITH

[21] Jesus left that place and went away to the district of Tyre and Sidon. [22] Just then a Canaanite woman from that region came out and started shouting, "Have mercy on me, Lord, Son of David; my daughter is tormented by a demon." [23] But he did not answer her at all. And his disciples came and urged him, saying, "Send her away, for she keeps shouting after us." [24] He answered, "I was sent only to the lost sheep of the house of Israel." [25] But she came and knelt before him, saying, "Lord, help me." [26] He answered, "It is not fair to take the children's food and throw it to the dogs." [27] She said, "Yes, Lord, yet even the dogs eat the crumbs that fall from their masters' table." [28] Then Jesus answered her, "Woman, great is your faith! Let it be done for you as you wish." And her daughter was healed instantly.

JESUS CURES MANY PEOPLE

[29] After Jesus had left that place, he passed along the Sea of Galilee, and he went up the mountain, where he sat down. [30] Great crowds came to him, bringing with them the lame, the maimed, the blind, the mute, and many others. They put them at his feet, and he cured them, [31] so that the crowd was amazed when they saw the mute speaking, the maimed whole, the lame walking, and the blind seeing. And they praised the God of Israel.

FEEDING THE FOUR THOUSAND

[32] Then Jesus called his disciples to him and said, "I have compassion for the crowd, because they have been with me now for three days and have nothing to eat; and I do not want to send them away hungry, for they might faint on the way." [33] The disciples said to him, "Where are we to get enough bread in the desert to feed so great a crowd?" [34] Jesus asked them, "How many loaves have you?" They said, "Seven, and a few small fish." [35] Then ordering the crowd to sit down on the ground, [36] he took the seven loaves

Even the Dogs Eat the Crumbs

Matthew 15:21–28 | Bishop Barron

A key spiritual principle is that grace is sheer gift. And when you cling to a gift, hoarding it for yourself, you undermine its nature as gift. The whole point of receiving the divine life is to give it away in turn. If you hoard it and make it your private prerogative, you undermine it; it turns to ashes. But when you give it away, it is renewed within you.

We see this dynamic in the controversial and puzzling story of Jesus' conversation with the Canaanite woman. The foreign woman comes to Jesus seeking a favor, but he protests that he has been sent only to the lost sheep of the house of Israel. He seems to be operating out of an exclusivist understanding of Israel's privileges. When she presses the matter, the Lord comes back harshly enough: "It is not fair to take the children's food and throw it to the dogs." At which point, the petitioner utters one of the great comebacks recorded in the Bible: "Yes, Lord, yet even the dogs eat the crumbs that fall from their masters' table."

Delighted not only by her cleverness and pluck but by the depth of her faith, Jesus says, "Woman, great is your faith! Let it be done for you as you wish." Yes, the table of grace was set for the children of Israel, but the food from that table was not meant for Israelites alone, but for all those who would come to that table, by hook or by crook. Israel was chosen, yes—but for the sake of the world.

---

and the fish; and after giving thanks he broke them and gave them to the disciples, and the disciples gave them to the crowds. [37] And all of them ate and were filled; and they took up the broken pieces left over, seven baskets full. [38] Those who had eaten were four thousand men, besides women and children. [39] After sending away the crowds, he got into the boat and went to the region of Magadan.

THE DEMAND FOR A SIGN

16 The Pharisees and Sadducees came, and to test Jesus they asked him to show them a sign from heaven. [2] He answered them, "When it is evening, you say, 'It will be fair weather, for the sky is red.' [3] And in the morning, 'It will be stormy today, for the sky is red and threatening.' You know how to interpret the appearance of the sky, but you cannot interpret the signs of the times. [4] An evil and adulterous generation asks for a sign, but no sign will be given to it except the sign of Jonah." Then he left them and went away.

Who Do You Say That I Am?

Matthew 16:13–18 | Bishop Barron

Who do people say that the Son of Man is? The disciples said, "Some say John the Baptist, but others Elijah, and still others Jeremiah or one of the prophets." We can easily imagine that Jesus, like any celebrity, had excited a buzz of interest and that there must have been many such opinions and interpretations bandied about. But what all of those readings—reflective of the popular consensus—had in common was that they were wrong.

Having heard the results of this popular opinion survey, Jesus turned to his inner circle, the Twelve, and asked, "But who do you say that I am?" Peter alone spoke: "You are the Messiah, the Son of the living God." He would have said *Mashiach*, "the anointed," the one who would gather the tribes and cleanse the temple and defeat Israel's enemies; but then he added that startling phrase, "Son of the living God." Somehow, even at this relatively early stage in Jesus' ministry, Peter intuited that Jesus was much more than a prophet or rabbi or seer, however significant. He knew that there was something qualitatively different about his Master.

Jesus responded to this confession of Peter with some of the most extraordinary language in the New Testament: "Blessed are you, Simon son of Jonah! For flesh and blood has not revealed this to you, but my Father in heaven. And I tell you, you are Peter, and on this rock I will build my church, and the gates of Hades will not prevail against it." Neither the crowds nor the aristocratic circle around Jesus knew who he was—only Peter knew. And this knowledge did not come from Peter's intelligence or from an extraordinary education (he didn't have one) or from his skill at assessing popular opinion. It came as a gift from God, a special charism of the Holy Spirit. Because of this gift, given only to the head of the Twelve, Jesus called Simon by a new name: in Aramaic *Cephas* (rock or rocky), rendered in Greek as *Petros* and in English as Peter. On the foundation of this rock, Jesus declared that he would build his *ekklesia*, his Church. Though it was fashionable some years ago for scholars to deny that Jesus ever intended to found a Church, now most analysts hold that it would be hard to imagine a Messiah without a messianic community—that is to say, without a renewed Israel. And Jesus insists that this society, grounded in Peter's confession, would constitute an army so powerful that not even the fortified capital of the dark kingdom itself could withstand it. It is fascinating to me how often we construe this saying of Jesus in precisely the opposite direction, as though the Church is guaranteed safety against the onslaughts of hell. In point of fact, Jesus is suggesting a much more aggressive image: his Church will lay successful siege upon the kingdom of evil, knocking down its gate and breaching its walls. And notice, too, how Jesus uses the future tense—"I will build my church." Therefore he cannot be speaking simply of Peter personally but of all those who would participate in his charism throughout the centuries. The integrity of this *ekklesia* will be guaranteed up and down the centuries—not through appeal to popular opinion (as instructive as that might be), nor through the ministrations of an institutional or theological elite (as necessary as those might be), but rather through the pope's charismatic knowledge of who Jesus is.

Word Study

ἐκκλησία

EKKLÉSIA

Noun
Church, assembly, called out from

THE YEAST OF THE PHARISEES AND SADDUCEES

[5] When the disciples reached the other side, they had forgotten to bring any bread. [6] Jesus said to them, "Watch out, and beware of the yeast of the Pharisees and Sadducees." [7] They said to one another, "It is because we have brought no bread." [8] And becoming aware of it, Jesus said, "You of little faith, why are you talking about having no bread? [9] Do you still not perceive? Do you not remember the five loaves for the five thousand, and how many baskets you gathered? [10] Or the seven loaves for the four thousand, and how many baskets you gathered? [11] How could you fail to perceive that I was not speaking about bread? Beware of the yeast of the Pharisees and Sadducees!" [12] Then they understood that he had not told them to beware of the yeast of bread, but of the teaching of the Pharisees and Sadducees.

PETER'S DECLARATION ABOUT JESUS

[13] Now when Jesus came into the district of Caesarea Philippi, he asked his disciples, "Who do people say that the Son of Man is?" [14] And they said, "Some say John the Baptist, but others Elijah, and still others Jeremiah or one of the prophets." [15] He said to them, "But who do you say that I am?" [16] Simon Peter answered, "You are the Messiah, the Son of the living God." [17] And Jesus answered him, "Blessed are you, Simon son of Jonah! For flesh and blood has not revealed this to you, but my Father in heaven. [18] And I tell you, you are Peter, and on this rock I will build my church, and the gates of Hades will not prevail against it. [19] I will give you the keys of the kingdom of heaven, and whatever you bind on earth will be bound in heaven, and whatever you loose on earth will be loosed in heaven." [20] Then he sternly ordered the disciples not to tell anyone that he was the Messiah.

MICHELANGELO AND GIACOMO DELLA PORTA | *1547–1590*

The Dome of St. Peter's Basilica

Essay by Michael Stevens

In the sixteenth chapter of Matthew, the Apostle Peter is appointed as head of the Church by Jesus, beginning an unbroken succession of popes that continues to the present day. This story is powerfully commemorated inside the dome of St. Peter's Basilica in Vatican City, and the Latin inscription quotes directly from Matthew's Gospel:

TU ES PETRUS ET SUPER HANC PETRAM AEDIFICABO ECCLESIAM MEAM ET TIBI DABO CLAVES REGNI CAELORUM. ("You are Peter, and on this rock I will build my church, and . . . I will give you the keys of the kingdom of heaven.")

What's most amazing is that this dome and inscription actually encircle the original gravesite of St. Peter, whose bones lie only a few hundred feet below. This allows for the words of Christ—"You are Peter, and on this rock I will build my church"—to take on a completely new and literal meaning. Not only did Peter become the figurative "rock" upon which the succession of popes was founded, his tomb became the literal bedrock and foundation upon which the massive church of St. Peter's Basilica was built.

The height of the dome

Standing 448.1 feet tall from the floor of the church to the tip of the cross at its apex, the scale of Michelangelo's design for St. Peter's dome was famously ambitious. It remains the tallest dome in the world and continues to dominate the modern-day skyline of Rome.

The shell of the dome

While appearing to be made of solid stone from the exterior, the dome is actually partially hollow and built in layers of wood and bricks. Because of its massive scale, makeshift reinforcements have been required to prevent its collapse over time, including the tying of chains around its circumference to bind the structure together.

JESUS FORETELLS HIS DEATH AND RESURRECTION

²¹ From that time on, Jesus began to show his disciples that he must go to Jerusalem and undergo great suffering at the hands of the elders and chief priests and scribes, and be killed, and on the third day be raised. ²² And Peter took him aside and began to rebuke him, saying, "God forbid it, Lord! This must never happen to you." ²³ But he turned and said to Peter, "Get behind me, Satan! You are a stumbling block to me; for you are setting your mind not on divine things but on human things."

G.K. Chesterton
(1874–1936)
—
Heretics

Why the Church Is Indestructible

Matthew 16:18

When Christ at a symbolic moment was establishing his great society, he chose for its corner-stone neither the brilliant Paul nor the mystic John, but a shuffler, a snob, a coward—in a word, a man. And upon this rock he has built his Church, and the gates of hell have not prevailed against it. All the empires and the kingdoms have failed, because of this inherent and continual weakness, that they were founded by strong men and upon strong men. But this one thing, the historic Christian Church, was founded on a weak man, and for that reason it is indestructible. For no chain is stronger than its weakest link.

THE CROSS AND SELF-DENIAL

²⁴ Then Jesus told his disciples, "If any want to become my followers, let them deny themselves and take up their cross and follow me. ²⁵ For those who want to save their life will lose it, and those who lose their life for my sake will find it. ²⁶ For what will it profit them if they gain the whole world but forfeit their life? Or what will they give in return for their life?

²⁷ "For the Son of Man is to come with his angels in the glory of his Father, and then he will repay everyone for what has been done. ²⁸ Truly I tell you, there are some standing here who will not taste death before they see the Son of Man coming in his kingdom."

**St. Cyprian
of Carthage**
(200–258)

———

Treatises

On This Rock I Will Build My Church
Matthew 16:18–19

"I tell you," [Jesus] says, "you are Peter, and on this rock I will build my church, and the gates of Hades will not prevail against it. I will give you the keys of the kingdom of heaven, and whatever you bind on earth will be bound in heaven, and whatever you loose on earth will be loosed in heaven." ... On [Peter] he builds the Church, and to him he gives the command to feed the sheep [John 21:17], and although he assigns a like power to all the Apostles, yet he founded a single chair [*cathedra*], and he established by his own authority a source and an intrinsic reason for that unity. Indeed, the others were also what Peter was [i.e., Apostles], but a primacy is given to Peter, whereby it is made clear that there is but one Church and one chair. So too, all [the Apostles] are shepherds, and the flock is shown to be one, fed by all the Apostles in single-minded accord. If someone does not hold fast to this unity of Peter, can he imagine that he still holds the faith? If he [should] desert the chair of Peter upon whom the Church was built, can he still be confident that he is in the Church?

THE TRANSFIGURATION

17 Six days later, Jesus took with him Peter and James and his brother John and led them up a high mountain, by themselves. ² And he was transfigured before them, and his face shone like the sun, and his clothes became dazzling white. ³ Suddenly there appeared to them Moses and

Elijah, talking with him. 4 Then Peter said to Jesus, "Lord, it is good for us to be here; if you wish, I will make three dwellings here, one for you, one for Moses, and one for Elijah." 5 While he was still speaking, suddenly a bright cloud overshadowed them, and from the cloud a voice said, "This is my Son, the Beloved; with him I am well pleased; listen to him!" 6 When the disciples heard this, they fell to the ground and were overcome by fear. 7 But Jesus came and touched them, saying, "Get up and do not be afraid." 8 And when they looked up, they saw no one except Jesus himself alone.

The Strange Light

Matthew 17:1–8 | Bishop Barron

Frequently in the course of the liturgical year the Church invites us to reflect on this strange story of the Transfiguration of the Lord. In all three of the synoptic Gospels we hear that Jesus went up to a high mountain—that place of contact with God—and was there transfigured in the presence of three of his disciples. "His face," Matthew tells us, "shone like the sun, and his clothes became dazzling white." This luminous transformation of Jesus has bedazzled mystics and inspired artists and poets throughout the Christian centuries. There is a terrific depiction of the scene in one of the stained glass windows of the façade of Chartres Cathedral. When, at the close of the day, the setting sun shines directly on this particular window, the figure of Jesus does indeed become incandescent, glowing like a jewel.

What does this event mean, and why does the Church ask us to meditate upon it so regularly? Thomas Aquinas devotes an entire question in the third part of the Summa theologiae to a consideration of the Transfiguration, and his treatment sums up much of the wisdom of the Church Fathers on this matter. So let us attend with some care to his interpretation. Aquinas says that it was fitting for Christ to be manifested in his glory to his select Apostles, because those who walk an arduous path need a clear sense of the goal of their journey. The arduous path that Thomas speaks of is this life, with all of its attendant sufferings, failures, setbacks, disappointments, anxieties, and injustices. Beset by all of this negativity, a pilgrim on life's way can easily succumb to despair unless he is granted a glimpse of the glory that comes at the end of his striving. And this is why, Aquinas argues, Jesus, while on his way to the cross, for a brief moment allows the light to shine through him. This is why he permits the end of the journey to appear, however fleetingly, in the midst of the journey. Though we live and move within the confines of this world of space and time, we are not meant, finally, for this dimensional system; we are summoned to life on high with God, in a transformed state of existence. The Transfiguration, therefore, awakens our sense of wonder and steels our courage to face the darkness here below.

Next, Aquinas inquires more precisely after the light (*claritas*, in his Latin) that is said to have shone from the face and figure of Christ. A resurrected body, Thomas says, has four distinctive qualities: impassibility (it is beyond suffering), agility (it can move freely), subtlety (it is not obstructed by material obstacles), and clarity (it shines). Why have people, through history and across cultures, associated holiness with light? Why are the saints, in our tradition, pictured with luminous halos around their heads? Why have some people, even in our own time, seen a sort of glow emanating from particularly spiritual figures such as St. Teresa of Kolkata or Padre Pio? One reason, Thomas suggests, is that light is the quality by which we see. Holy people provide a sort of interpretive grid to our experience; their form of life turns on the light that allows us to perceive the truth of things more clearly. But the most fundamental reason that we associate holiness with light is that light is beautiful and sanctity is beautiful above all. Aquinas says that Jesus, at the Transfiguration, began to shine with the radiance of heaven so as to entrance us with the prospect of our own beautiful transfiguration.

After considering Jesus himself, Thomas turns to the "witnesses" of the event. Two are figures from Israelite history (Moses and Elijah), and three are contemporaries of Jesus (Peter, James, and John). This juxtaposition of past and present is important, Aquinas maintains, because the salvation won by Christ properly transcends time, drawing into its power those who came before and those who would come after. Moses and Elijah symbolize the past; the Apostles, who would carry the Gospel to the world, signify the future. All dimensions of time are drawn toward the magnetic point of the cross and Resurrection. This same collapsing of the distinctions between the modalities of time occurs at the Mass, when the past is brought to the present and the present is carried to the eschatological fulfillment at the end of time. Moses, Elijah, Peter, James, and John are therefore a kind of prototype of the Eucharistic community.

But we can also speak of each of these characters more specifically. Moses stands for the Law, the Torah. Jesus is consistently presented in the Gospels as the fulfillment of the Torah and as the new Moses. Thus, even as a child, he is, like Moses, hunted down; and when he gives the Sermon on the Mount, he appears as the Mosaic lawgiver par excellence. The Gospels imply that what was presented to Moses on tablets of stone has been offered perfectly through Jesus. The order and logic of God— visible truly but inadequately through the commands, prohibitions, and practices of the Old Law—are now fully, personally, and compellingly present in Jesus himself. This is why he can say, "Do not think that I have come to abolish the law or the prophets" (Matt. 5:17). He is not so much a better lawgiver than Moses as he is the Law made flesh. The correlation between these two revelations of the divine order is elegantly expressed in the conversation between Moses and Jesus.

And Elijah stands for prophecy, for he was generally perceived as the greatest of the prophets. Elijah, Elisha, Amos, Hosea, Isaiah, Jeremiah, Ezekiel, Daniel, and all of their prophetic confreres spoke the truth about God to varying degrees of intensity and in relation to various circumstances. But Jesus is not simply one more speaker of divine truth, not merely the greatest of the prophets. He is the divine Word; he is in person and in its entirety what all the prophets witnessed to from the outside and in fragmentary ways. It is this analogical relationship between Truth and truth-telling that is on display in the conversation between Jesus and Elijah. Both Moses and Elijah evanesce in the presence of Jesus, finding themselves by losing themselves, saying with John the Baptist, "He must increase, but I must decrease" (John 3:30).

Finally, Thomas turns to the contemporary witnesses. Why is Peter there? Because, says Aquinas, he loved the Lord the most. After the Resurrection, Jesus asks Peter, "Simon son of John, do you love me more than these?" (John 21:15). When he receives a positive answer, he commands Peter to feed his sheep. Why is John there? Because he is the one whom the Lord loved the most. We know that throughout the Gospel that bears his name, John is referred to indirectly as "the disciple whom Jesus loved" (John 21:20). What is implied here is something that the theologian Hans Urs von Balthasar intuited—that those who understand Jesus are those who enter into a relationship of love with him. "Getting" him is not so much a matter of clarity of mind as intensity of affection. Conversely, those who don't understand him—the Pharisees, the rich young man, Judas, and Pilate come readily to mind—are those who refused his friendship. Therefore, Peter and John saw the Transfiguration, not because they were the cleverest or most powerful among the Apostles, but because they had fallen in love with the Lord.

Now, why was James permitted to see the vision? Because, Thomas says, James was the first of Jesus' intimate followers to prove the intensity of his love for Christ by giving his life: he would become the first martyr among the Apostles. Love is desiring the good of the other as other. Therefore, there is no greater test of love than one's willingness to die for the object of one's love. This is the test that James would endure; and this is why James was privileged to see.

The meaning of the Old Testament revelation, the goal of the spiritual journey, the nature of the resurrected life, the condition for the possibility of seeing the Lord—all of it is illumined in the strange light of the Transfiguration.

⁹ As they were coming down the mountain, Jesus ordered them, "Tell no one about the vision until after the Son of Man has been raised from the dead." ¹⁰ And the disciples asked him, "Why, then, do the scribes say that Elijah must come first?" ¹¹ He replied, "Elijah is indeed coming and will restore all things; ¹² but I tell you that Elijah has already come, and they did not recognize him, but they did to him whatever they pleased. So also the Son of Man is about to suffer at their hands." ¹³ Then the disciples understood that he was speaking to them about John the Baptist.

JESUS CURES A BOY WITH A DEMON

¹⁴ When they came to the crowd, a man came to him, knelt before him, ¹⁵ and said, "Lord, have mercy on my son, for he is an epileptic and he suffers terribly; he often falls into the fire and often into the water. ¹⁶ And I brought him to your disciples, but they could not cure him." ¹⁷ Jesus answered, "You faithless and perverse generation, how much longer must I be with you? How much longer must I put up with you? Bring him here to me." ¹⁸ And Jesus rebuked the demon, and it came out of him, and the boy was cured instantly. ¹⁹ Then the disciples came to Jesus privately and said, "Why could we not cast it out?" ²⁰ He said to them, "Because of your little faith. For truly I tell you, if you have faith the size of a mustard seed, you will say to this mountain, 'Move from here to there,' and it will move; and nothing will be impossible for you."

Do You Have Enough Faith?

Matthew 17:14–20 | Bishop Barron

Here we meet a boy with a demon whom the disciples could not heal. They asked Jesus why they had failed, and he said: "Because of your little faith. For truly I tell you, if you have faith the size of a mustard seed, you will say to this mountain, 'Move from here to there,' and it will move; and nothing will be impossible for you."

In all circumstances, you have to pray with faith. Jesus says before working one miracle, "Do you believe that I am able to do this?" (Matt. 9:28).

And once, Matthew tells us, he was unable to perform many miracles because he met with so little faith among the people (Matt. 13:58).

Many people today, especially in the healing ministry, seem able to reproduce what Jesus did, precisely because of the purity of their faith. Is part of our problem simply a lack of faith? Perhaps. We allow our skepticism to get the better of us. We're just a little embarrassed by asking God for things, or we're convinced that he is a distant power only vaguely connected to our lives. But God is far greater than that.

The Transfiguration panel

This panel illustrates the Transfiguration
of Christ, portraying his face as a pure,
luminous white. The true whiteness
of Christ's face and vivid colors of the
surrounding panes are only revealed
when activated by bright sunlight. The
panel is shown within the full chronology
of events leading up to Christ's death and
Resurrection, highlighting the relationships
between different stories in the narrative.

THE BUILDERS OF CHARTRES CATHEDRAL | *Twelfth century*

The Passion Window

Essay by Michael Stevens

Chartres Cathedral is one of the most significant architectural accomplishments in the Catholic tradition of church construction, and one of the finest examples of the Gothic style ever constructed. The cathedral is impressive in every way and features two skyscraping towers, magnificent stone portals, and a dizzyingly high ceiling supported by a complex web of flying buttresses.

For all its splendorous features, perhaps the most exquisite treasure of the cathedral is its vast array of stained glass windows, which remain remarkably well preserved in spite of fires, military conflicts, and harsh weather conditions over the centuries. The windows illustrate a wide variety of theological ideas and spiritual narratives, mostly from the Bible, but also depict secular figures and political events relevant to the region. The piece at left details the account of Christ's Passion using a series of narrative panels. Among these panels is the story of Jesus' Transfiguration, in which Christ's face, surrounded by rich blue and red panes, blazes a dazzling white.

Lancet arch shape

The pointed arch shape, known as a lancet arch, is one of the defining elements in Gothic architecture. It serves as not only the foundational shape for the windows but nearly every other type of arched construction in the church as well, including the ceiling. The point at the top of the arch directs weight directly downwards, preventing the collapse of the arch's sides and allowing architects to build much taller. This innovation in arch building, combined with the use of flying buttresses—huge, leg-shaped supports that brace the church walls from the outside— allowed Gothic cathedrals like Chartres to be built to incredible heights, with every aspect of the church's design directing the eye upward to heaven and contemplation of God.

Crafting stained glass

Stained glass of the medieval era was colored by the mixing of metal oxides with molten glass. After coloring and cooling, details on the glass could then be painted by hand. The glass would then be heated once again to permanently fuse the painted design to the surface. The craftsmen of Chartres became known for their mastery of this tedious process, which established the city as a major producer of stained glass.

Fulton Sheen
(1895–1979)

———

Life of Christ

Why Did Jesus Pay the Temple Tax?

Matthew 17:24–27

The question about our Lord paying the temple tax was not a simple one. He had said that he was the Temple of God, and had exercised his divine rights over the material temple by purging it of buyers and sellers. Would he who said that he was a Temple of God because divinity was dwelling in his human nature now pay the temple tribute? To pay the temple tax after his clear affirmation at the festival of Booths that he was the Son of God would have given rise to some serious misunderstandings. The point at issue was not the poverty of the Master; it was whether or not he who is the living Temple of God would subordinate himself to the symbol and sign of himself....

After having affirmed that as the King of heaven he was immune from earthly tributes, he turned to Peter and said, "However, so that we do not give offense to them, go to the sea and cast a hook; take the first fish that comes up; and when you open its mouth, you will find a coin; take that and give it to them for you and me."

The king's son is free. But he who is the Son of God became the Son of Man sharing the poverty, trials, the labors, and the homelessness of men. Later on, he would subject himself to arrest, the crown of thorns, and to the cross. Presently, as the Son of Man, he would not stand on his dignity as the Son of God, nor claim immunity from servile obligations, but would voluntarily concede to a tax in order to avoid scandal. It is not a mark of greatness always to affirm one's right, but often to suffer an indignity.

There might be scandal if he showed contempt for the temple. As he submitted himself to John's baptism to fulfill all righteousness; as his mother offered doves, though she needed no purification from his birth; so he would submit himself to the tax to sanctify the human bonds he wore.

JESUS AGAIN FORETELLS HIS DEATH AND RESURRECTION

[22] As they were gathering in Galilee, Jesus said to them, "The Son of Man is going to be betrayed into human hands, [23] and they will kill him, and on the third day he will be raised." And they were greatly distressed.

JESUS AND THE TEMPLE TAX

[24] When they reached Capernaum, the collectors of the temple tax came to Peter and said, "Does your teacher not pay the temple tax?" [25] He said, "Yes, he does." And when he came home, Jesus spoke of it first, asking, "What do you think, Simon? From whom do kings of the earth take toll or tribute? From their children or from others?" [26] When Peter said, "From others," Jesus said to him, "Then the children are free. [27] However, so that we do not give offense to them, go to the sea and cast a hook; take the first fish that comes up; and when you open its mouth, you will find a coin; take that and give it to them for you and me."

TRUE GREATNESS

18 At that time the disciples came to Jesus and asked, "Who is the greatest in the kingdom of heaven?" [2] He called a child, whom he put among them, [3] and said, "Truly I tell you, unless you change and become like children, you will never enter the kingdom of heaven. [4] Whoever becomes humble like this child is the greatest in the kingdom of heaven. [5] Whoever welcomes one such child in my name welcomes me.

TEMPTATIONS TO SIN

[6] "If any of you put a stumbling block before one of these little ones who believe in me, it would be better for you if a great millstone were fastened around your neck and you were drowned in the depth of the sea.

Welcoming One Such Child

Matthew 18:5 | Bishop Barron

After completing her novitiate in Darjeeling, Mother Teresa made temporary vows and began teaching in the convent school there and working part-time as an aide to the nursing staff at a small hospital.

Once a man arrived at the hospital with a bundle out of which protruded what appeared to be twigs. When Teresa looked more closely, she saw that they were the impossibly emaciated legs of a child, blind and at the point of death. The man told the young sister that if she didn't take the boy, he would throw him to the jackals.

Teresa's journal takes up the story: "With much pity and love I take the little one into my arms, and fold him in my apron. The child has found a second mother." And then this passage dawned upon her: "Whoever welcomes one such child in my name welcomes me." This is the key to the mature practical spirituality of Mother Teresa: in serving the suffering and the poorest of the poor, one is serving Christ.

---

[7] Woe to the world because of stumbling blocks! Occasions for stumbling are bound to come, but woe to the one by whom the stumbling block comes!

[8] "If your hand or your foot causes you to stumble, cut it off and throw it away; it is better for you to enter life maimed or lame than to have two hands or two feet and to be thrown into the eternal fire. [9] And if your eye causes you to stumble, tear it out and throw it away; it is better for you to enter life with one eye than to have two eyes and to be thrown into the hell of fire.

THE PARABLE OF THE LOST SHEEP

[10] "Take care that you do not despise one of these little ones; for, I tell you, in heaven their angels continually see the face of my Father in heaven. [12] What do you think? If a shepherd has a hundred sheep, and one of them has gone astray, does he not leave the ninety-nine on the mountains and go in search of the one that went astray? [13] And if he finds it, truly I tell you, he rejoices over it more than over the ninety-nine that never went astray. [14] So it is not the will of your Father in heaven that one of these little ones should be lost.

REPROVING ANOTHER WHO SINS

[15] "If another member of the church sins against you, go and point out the fault when the two of you are alone. If the member listens to you, you have regained that one. [16] But if you are not listened to, take one or two others along with you, so that every word may be confirmed by the evidence of

two or three witnesses. ¹⁷ If the member refuses to listen to them, tell it to the church; and if the offender refuses to listen even to the church, let such a one be to you as a Gentile and a tax collector. ¹⁸ Truly I tell you, whatever you bind on earth will be bound in heaven, and whatever you

The Right Way to Correct Someone

Matthew 18:15–17 | Bishop Barron

In this passage, Jesus is instructing his community in the difficult task of correcting an errant brother or sister. He tells them to avoid the practice of gossiping and complaining to others about a grievance; rather, they should confront the person who has offended them directly and courageously. That way, the difficulty is addressed, the loving concern of the complainant is evident, and the process of rumor, attack, counter-attack, innuendo, and scapegoating is arrested.

Now, if the person does not respond to this loving intervention, "take one or two others along with you, so that every word may be confirmed by the evidence of two or three witnesses." Thus, the wider community is involved, but only minimally—enough to bring the offender to repentance. Only if this small circle of the Church is ignored should one bring the complaint to the whole community.

What is so rich here is the pursuit of the issue (since speaking the truth, even when it is dangerous, is essential), coupled with a deep care for the person in question and also for the entire family of the Church (since love is our constant call). And then the wonderful conclusion: "If the member refuses to listen to them, tell it to the church; and if the offender refuses to listen even to the church, let such a one be to you as a Gentile and a tax collector."

This sounds, at first, like a total rejection, but then we recall how Jesus treated the Gentiles and tax collectors—eating with them, pursuing them, drawing them into the circle. There might be a moment of rejection and expulsion in the process of fraternal correction (as we can see, for example, in the Pauline epistles), but it is only provisional and only for the sake of eventual reconciliation.

St. Augustine, who was never afraid to speak the hard truth when necessary, followed the recommendations of Matthew 18 very concretely. Over the table in his episcopal residence where he dined with the priests of his diocese hung a sign that read: "If you speak ill of your brother here, you are not welcome at this table." And it is said that the Bishop of Hippo would enforce the rule, pointing to the sign when one of his charges began complaining or gossiping.

loose on earth will be loosed in heaven. ¹⁹ Again, truly I tell you, if two of you agree on earth about anything you ask, it will be done for you by my Father in heaven. ²⁰ For where two or three are gathered in my name, I am there among them."

FORGIVENESS

²¹ Then Peter came and said to him, "Lord, if another member of the church sins against me, how often should I forgive? As many as seven times?" ²² Jesus said to him, "Not seven times, but, I tell you, seventy-seven times.

THE PARABLE OF THE UNFORGIVING SERVANT

²³ "For this reason the kingdom of heaven may be compared to a king who wished to settle accounts with his slaves. ²⁴ When he began the reckoning, one who owed him ten thousand talents was brought to him; ²⁵ and, as he could not pay, his lord ordered him to be sold, together with his wife and children and all his possessions, and payment to be made. ²⁶ So the slave fell on his knees before him, saying, 'Have patience with me, and I will pay you everything.' ²⁷ And out of pity for him, the lord of that slave released him and forgave him the debt. ²⁸ But that same slave, as he went out, came upon one of his fellow slaves who owed him a hundred denarii; and seizing

---

Become a Better Forgiver

Matthew 18:21–35 | Bishop Barron

Peter asked Jesus, how often should we forgive our neighbor? Seven times? Jesus answered, "Not seven times, but, I tell you, seventy-seven times." In other words, endlessly, constantly, without calculation.

This is precisely why the Gospel makes the link between God's forgiveness of us and our forgiveness of one another. The latter flows directly from the former. Note the correlation between the two modes of forgiveness in the Lord's Prayer:

"Forgive us our trespasses as we forgive those who trespass against us."

How do you become a better forgiver? Perhaps I can offer four practical suggestions. First, keep your own sins frequently before your mind's eye. Second, go to confession more regularly. Third, forgive offenses quickly. Don't give them time to settle deeply into your psyche; seek reconciliation right away. Finally, forgive through a concrete act or a concrete sign. Write a note, make a phone call, give a gift, offer your own presence. Forgiveness is most effective when it becomes concrete.

him by the throat, he said, 'Pay what you owe.' ²⁹ Then his fellow slave fell down and pleaded with him, 'Have patience with me, and I will pay you.' ³⁰ But he refused; then he went and threw him into prison until he would pay the debt. ³¹ When his fellow slaves saw what had happened, they were greatly distressed, and they went and reported to their lord all that had taken place. ³² Then his lord summoned him and said to him, 'You wicked slave! I forgave you all that debt because you pleaded with me. ³³ Should you not have had mercy on your fellow slave, as I had mercy on you?' ³⁴ And in anger his lord handed him over to be tortured until he would pay his entire debt. ³⁵ So my heavenly Father will also do to every one of you, if you do not forgive your brother or sister from your heart."

TEACHING ABOUT DIVORCE

19 When Jesus had finished saying these things, he left Galilee and went to the region of Judea beyond the Jordan. ² Large crowds followed him, and he cured them there.

³ Some Pharisees came to him, and to test him they asked, "Is it lawful for a man to divorce his wife for any cause?" ⁴ He answered, "Have you not read that the one who made them at the beginning 'made them male and female,' ⁵ and said, 'For this reason a man shall leave his father and mother and be joined to his wife, and the two shall become one flesh'? ⁶ So they are no longer two, but one flesh. Therefore what God has joined together, let no one separate." ⁷ They said to him, "Why then did Moses command us to give a certificate of dismissal and to divorce her?" ⁸ He said to them, "It was because you were so hard-hearted that Moses allowed you to divorce your wives, but from the beginning it was not so. ⁹ And I say to you, whoever divorces his wife, except for unchastity, and marries another commits adultery."

¹⁰ His disciples said to him, "If such is the case of a man with his wife, it is better not to marry." ¹¹ But he said to them, "Not everyone can accept this teaching, but only those to whom it is given. ¹² For there are eunuchs who have been so from birth, and there are eunuchs who have been made eunuchs by others, and there are eunuchs who have made themselves eunuchs for the sake of the kingdom of heaven. Let anyone accept this who can."

JESUS BLESSES LITTLE CHILDREN

¹³ Then little children were being brought to him in order that he might lay his hands on them and pray. The disciples spoke sternly to those who brought them; ¹⁴ but Jesus said, "Let the little children come to me, and do not stop them; for it is to such as these that the kingdom of heaven belongs." ¹⁵ And he laid his hands on them and went on his way.

God the Son

Christ sits in the middle and wears two contrasting garments—one an earthy red, and the other blue. The red represents Christ's human nature and ministry on earth as well as his blood poured out for sinners. Like the Father's inner robe, the blue portion of Christ's clothing also signifies his divinity. The two garments' colors are harmonious and pithily capture the two natures of Jesus. Finally, the gold stripe on Christ's shoulder symbolizes his sharing in the kingship of God the Father.

Circular composition

The three persons are arranged inside a perfect circle, which symbolizes their Trinitarian oneness and perfection. The circle also helps to guide the viewer's eye around the painting, creating a focal point in the space between the conversing figures.

Overlapping wings

The Father and the Son's wings overlap one another, signifying their familial relationship.

God the Holy Spirit

The Holy Spirit also wears the same divine blue as the others, showing his nature as God, but outside he wears a robe of lush green, representing his role in the creation of the world. This harkens back to Genesis, where we are told that the Spirit "swept over the face of the waters" (Gen. 1:2) before the creation of the universe and living things.

God the Father

The Father is shown on the left. His outer garment appears to shimmer elusively in the light, somewhere between gold and violet. This symbolizes his incorporeal (immaterial) nature, as well as his majesty over creation. Under this is a robe of blue, symbolizing his divinity. Across from him, the Son and the Holy Spirit bow their heads in acknowledgment that the Father is the unbegotten source of the Trinitarian processions.

Background elements

The three primary background elements are borrowed from the biblical story of the angels' visit to Abraham's house, and each symbolizes a person of the Trinity. The house of Abraham behind God the Father represents his patriarchal authority by linking him to the character of Abraham, who was the father of the Hebrew people. The tree behind God the Son represents the cross of Jesus and new life offered by his Resurrection. The mountain behind the Holy Spirit (faintly seen) represents the soul's journey to holiness, which is possible only through his divine power.

See *Marriage Mimics the Trinity's Love* (commentary on Matthew 19:3–12)

ANDREI RUBLEV | *c. 1425*

The Trinity

Essay by Michael Stevens

This depiction of the three persons of the Trinity is considered to be one of the finest works ever produced in the ancient tradition of Eastern iconography. Its creator, Andrei Rublev, is widely considered to be the greatest iconographer of all time, and this is one of the few panels of his that has been verified beyond doubt as his original work. Within this panel is contained a world of theological insight—a complex network of symbolism that is easily overlooked without careful study.

Rublev's representation of the Trinity is strikingly different from the typical Western Christian's visualization of the Trinity, with God the Father as an elderly man, God the Son as a young man, and God the Holy Spirit as a dove. Here the artist uses the image of three conversing angelic figures to illustrate the relationship of the persons of the Trinity. The figures are drawn directly from Genesis 18, wherein three mysterious angelic figures visit the house of Abraham and receive his hospitality. While this biblical account from the Old Testament was written long before the Christian doctrine of the Trinity was understood, it has been interpreted as a Trinitarian foreshadowing by many of the Church Fathers. Flowing from this interpretation, Rublev gives us many clues that the three figures in his icon are not meant to represent mere angels, but are in fact the three persons of the Holy Trinity.

THE RICH YOUNG MAN

¹⁶ Then someone came to him and said, "Teacher, what good deed must I do to have eternal life?" ¹⁷ And he said to him, "Why do you ask me about what is good? There is only one who is good. If you wish to enter into life, keep the commandments." ¹⁸ He said to him, "Which ones?" And Jesus said, "You shall not murder; You shall not commit adultery; You shall not steal; You shall not bear false witness; ¹⁹ Honor your father and mother; also, You shall love your neighbor as yourself." ²⁰ The young man said to him, "I have kept all these; what do I still lack?" ²¹ Jesus said to him, "If you wish to be perfect, go, sell your possessions, and give the money to the poor, and you will have treasure in heaven; then come, follow me." ²² When the young man heard this word, he went away grieving, for he had many possessions.

²³ Then Jesus said to his disciples, "Truly I tell you, it will be hard for a rich person to enter the kingdom of heaven. ²⁴ Again I tell you, it is easier for a camel to go through the eye of a needle than for someone who is rich to enter the kingdom of God." ²⁵ When the disciples heard this, they were greatly astounded and said, "Then who can be saved?" ²⁶ But Jesus looked at them and said, "For mortals it is impossible, but for God all things are possible."

Marriage Mimics the Trinity's Love

Matthew 19:3–12 | Bishop Barron

As Jesus teaches about the sanctity and permanence of marriage, we begin to see why the love of a husband and wife is a sacrament of God's love. The Father and the Son—while remaining distinct—give themselves utterly to each other, and this mutual giving is the Holy Spirit.

So when two people come together in love and form one flesh, they mimic the love between the Father and the Son. And when their love gives rise to a child, this mimics sacramentally the spiration of the Holy Spirit. Father, mother, and children are evocative of the divine Father, Son, and Holy Spirit.

And this is why Jesus speaks so forcefully about marriage, and why his Church, at its best, has echoed him up and down the centuries. It is because marriage is such a sacred sign that the Church has sought so assiduously to protect it.

I know that the Church is often criticized for surrounding marriage and sexuality with so many rules. I realize that libertarians through the ages have fought against the supposed uptight moralism of the Church. But human beings always surround precious things with laws, restrictions, and prohibitions.

²⁷ Then Peter said in reply, "Look, we have left everything and followed you. What then will we have?" ²⁸ Jesus said to them, "Truly I tell you, at the renewal of all things, when the Son of Man is seated on the throne of his glory, you who have followed me will also sit on twelve thrones, judging the twelve tribes of Israel. ²⁹ And everyone who has left houses or brothers or sisters or father or mother or children or fields, for my name's sake, will receive a hundredfold, and will inherit eternal life. ³⁰ But many who are first will be last, and the last will be first.

Finding True Freedom

Matthew 19:16–30 | Bishop Barron

The opening chapter of John Paul II's 1993 encyclical *Veritatis Splendor* is an analysis of this account of the conversation between Jesus and the rich young man in Matthew. Found in all three of the synoptic Gospels, this scene has been identified by N.T. Wright as a turning point and hinge in the Gospel narrative, and for John Paul as well, it is a key text. For the pope, to grasp the meaning of this story is to understand the central dynamic of the New Testament, the free response to Jesus' offer of eternal life. Stanley Hauerwas has exulted that this major statement of Catholic moral theology commences not with philosophical abstractions but with Jesus. The truth to which subjective freedom is oriented has always been ultimately the truth who is the person of Christ.

In Matthew's telling, a young man comes to Jesus and asks, "Teacher, what good deed must I do to have eternal life?" For the pope, this honest and searching question symbolizes the universal longing of the human being for moral integrity. As such, it is not primarily a question regarding rules, commandments, and prohibitions, but a quest for "the full meaning of life." Jesus' initial response is somewhat enigmatic: "Why do you ask me about what is good? There is only one who is good." In fact, it cuts to the heart of the matter. The greatest mistake that the moral searcher can make is to presume that the goal of his quest can be found in any good or truth other than God. One of the most insistently repeated themes of the Bible is that, since we are made according to God's image, we will not find fulfillment in anything other than God. And this insight is repeated by practically every major figure in our tradition, most famously and poetically by Augustine ("Our hearts are restless till they rest in Thee"), and more rationally but just as clearly by Thomas Aquinas in the opening questions of the *Prima secundae*.

How is this prime objective value to be sought? Jesus asks the rich young man whether he has followed the commandments, and the young man responds affirmatively. Here we are at the first stage of moral development, but the distinctive mark of biblical ethics is already visible. Since the one we seek is himself an act of self-forgetting love, we attain him only to the degree that we become internally conformed to his way of being. Hence all of those egregious violations of love—murder, adultery, hatred of one's neighbor, and so on—must be eliminated in the seeker after God.

But the real drama of this story begins precisely at the point where one might be tempted to say that ethical reflection ends. Somewhat plaintively, the young man says, "I have kept all these; what do I still lack?" Though we may suspect that it is only someone very young who could claim that he has kept all of the commandments, we still notice something of great importance in his intuition and question. Because the human being is made in God's image, his soul has a kind of infinite *capax*, an expansiveness that corresponds, however imperfectly, to the fullness of the divine reality. Therefore, the simple keeping of the fundamental commandments—most of which are negative in character—can never be enough to satisfy the spirit. Once the soul has been shaped in the direction of love through the discipline of the commandments, it is now ready for a more complete and dramatic self-emptying. It is ready for the *sequela Christi*, the following of Christ on the path of discipleship. And this is a matter not only of external imitation but of the deepest inner conformity to Christ, a walking with him in the manner of an apprentice shaping his life in accord with his master's. It goes beyond the commandments, because it involves a total gift of self, even to the point of death; for Christ leads the disciple in one direction: the cross. This "law of the gift," as George Weigel describes it, comes to more explicit expression at the end of *Veritatis Splendor* when the pope analyzes the limit case of Christian martyrdom. Though he doesn't court death, the disciple of Jesus accepts death when circumstances are such that there is no other way to bear witness to the holiness of God and the dignity of human life.

A first theme to which we should attend in the story of the rich young man is that of freedom. Of his own free will, the man comes up to Jesus and poses his question; Jesus answers him and then stands open to further dialogue; finally, he invites him to the deepest form of life. At no point in this conversation is there a hint of violence or coercion. Even at the end, when the young man walks away sad, unable to respond to Jesus' demand, the Lord lets him go. The true God does not compete with freedom; rather, he awakens it and directs it.

Second, we notice a dovetailing of the inner and outer, of the objective and the subjective. The choice of the proper object for freedom—God—corresponds at every stage to the choice to be conformed unto Christ. The *sequela Christi* is hence freedom's objective and subjective norm. In choosing Christ, the person opts for his proper end (because Jesus *is* the God he seeks), and he creates his proper self (for Jesus *is* the paradigm of a renewed humanity). When Paul says, "It is no longer I who live, but it is Christ who lives in me" (Gal. 2:20), he implies that the fully gathered self is the self that is conformed to the point of identity with the thoughts and desires of Jesus.

What John Paul II saw was that human freedom is realized in a surrender to the truth of God, and that that truth is none other than a God who hands over his life to us. The most authentic humanism, therefore, consists in a meeting of two ecstasies, divine and human, a dovetailing of two freedoms, a coming together of an infinite and finite mode of being-for-the-other. In a word, authentic humanism *is* Jesus Christ.

THE LABORERS IN THE VINEYARD

20 "For the kingdom of heaven is like a landowner who went out early in the morning to hire laborers for his vineyard. ² After agreeing with the laborers for the usual daily wage, he sent them into his vineyard. ³ When he went out about nine o'clock, he saw others standing idle in the marketplace; ⁴ and he said to them, 'You also go into the vineyard, and I will pay you whatever is right.' So they went. ⁵ When he went out again about noon and about three o'clock, he did the same. ⁶ And about five o'clock he went out and found others standing around; and he said to them, 'Why are you standing here idle all day?' ⁷ They said to him, 'Because no one has hired us.' He said to them, 'You also go into the vineyard.' ⁸ When evening came, the owner of the vineyard said to his manager, 'Call the laborers and give them their pay, beginning with the last and then going to the first.' ⁹ When those hired about five o'clock came, each of them received the usual daily wage. ¹⁰ Now when the first came, they thought they would receive more; but each of them also received the usual daily wage. ¹¹ And when they received it, they grumbled against the landowner, ¹² saying, 'These last worked only one hour, and you have made them equal to us who have borne the burden of the day and the scorching heat.' ¹³ But he replied to one of them, 'Friend, I am doing you no wrong; did you not agree with me for the usual daily wage? ¹⁴ Take what belongs to you and go; I choose to give to this last the same as I give to you. ¹⁵ Am I not allowed to

Fussing about Rewards

Matthew 20:1–16 | Bishop Barron

A landowner goes out to hire workers for his field, hiring some the first thing in the morning and then others at different times during the day. Then he pays each the same wage. Why should those who have worked only an hour be paid the same as those who have slaved in the hot sun all day? Is the landowner really being unfair?

Perhaps he saw something the first workers didn't see. Perhaps he saw, in his compassion, that their day spent waiting for work, in order to feed their families, was a terrible one, marked by anxiety and a sense of failure. Or perhaps he knew they were poorer, more desperate, or less gifted. Maybe he knew they needed a bit more encouragement.

Here's a second perspective on this mysterious story. We sinners are very susceptible to a reward-centered understanding of our relationship to God. Tit for tat; I do this, then you better do that. But this is very juvenile.

We've been invited to work in the vineyard of the Lord. That is the greatest privilege imaginable, to participate in the Lord's work of saving the world. Why are we fussing about rewards? And how liberating this is! I don't have to spend my life fussing and spying and worrying and comparing.

---

do what I choose with what belongs to me? Or are you envious because I am generous?' ¹⁶ So the last will be first, and the first will be last."

A THIRD TIME JESUS FORETELLS HIS DEATH AND RESURRECTION

¹⁷ While Jesus was going up to Jerusalem, he took the twelve disciples aside by themselves, and said to them on the way, ¹⁸ "See, we are going up to Jerusalem, and the Son of Man will be handed over to the chief priests and scribes, and they will condemn him to death; ¹⁹ then they will hand him over to the Gentiles to be mocked and flogged and crucified; and on the third day he will be raised."

THE REQUEST OF THE MOTHER OF JAMES AND JOHN

²⁰ Then the mother of the sons of Zebedee came to him with her sons, and kneeling before him, she asked a favor of him. ²¹ And he said to her, "What do you want?" She said to him, "Declare that these two sons of mine will sit, one at your right hand and one at your left, in your kingdom." ²² But Jesus answered, "You do not know what you are asking. Are you able to drink the cup that I am about to drink?" They said to him, "We are able." ²³ He said to them, "You will indeed drink my cup, but to sit at my right

hand and at my left, this is not mine to grant, but it is for those for whom it has been prepared by my Father."

²⁴ When the ten heard it, they were angry with the two brothers. ²⁵ But Jesus called them to him and said, "You know that the rulers of the Gentiles lord it over them, and their great ones are tyrants over them. ²⁶ It will not be so among you; but whoever wishes to be great among you must be your servant, ²⁷ and whoever wishes to be first among you must be your slave; ²⁸ just as the Son of Man came not to be served but to serve, and to give his life a ransom for many."

JESUS HEALS TWO BLIND MEN

²⁹ As they were leaving Jericho, a large crowd followed him. ³⁰ There were two blind men sitting by the roadside. When they heard that Jesus was passing by, they shouted, "Lord, have mercy on us, Son of David!" ³¹ The crowd sternly ordered them to be quiet; but they shouted even more loudly, "Have mercy on us, Lord, Son of David!" ³² Jesus stood still and called them, saying, "What do you want me to do for you?" ³³ They said to him, "Lord, let our eyes be opened." ³⁴ Moved with compassion, Jesus touched their eyes. Immediately they regained their sight and followed him.

Wanting Substitutes for God

Matthew 20:20–28 | Bishop Barron

The mother of James and John asks Jesus on their behalf to place them in high places in his kingdom. There are four classic substitutes for God: wealth, pleasure, power, and honor. The two brothers specifically want the last two.

Power is not, in itself, a bad thing. And the same is true of honor. Thomas Aquinas said that honor is the flag of virtue. It's a way of signaling to others something that's worth noticing.

So then what's the problem? The problem is that they are asking for these two things in the wrong spirit. The ego will want to use power not for God's purposes or in service of truth, beauty, and goodness, but for its own aggrandizement and defense. When honor is sought for its own sake or in order to puff up the ego, it becomes dangerous as well.

What's the way out? Jesus tells us: "Whoever wishes to be great among you must be your servant, and whoever wishes to be first among you must be your slave." When you serve others, when you become the least, you are accessing the power of God and seeking the honor of God.

St. John Chrysostom
(349–407)

Homilies on Matthew

Two Blind Men

Matthew 20:29–34

Let us listen to these blind men, who saw better than many. They were not able to see the Lord when he came near, nor had they anyone to guide them. Nevertheless, they strove to approach, crying out in a loud voice, and when reproved for this cried out all the more. For such is the nature of a persevering soul—it is borne up by the very things that hinder it.

JESUS' TRIUMPHAL ENTRY INTO JERUSALEM

21 When they had come near Jerusalem and had reached Bethphage, at the Mount of Olives, Jesus sent two disciples, ² saying to them, "Go into the village ahead of you, and immediately you will find a donkey tied, and a colt with her; untie them and bring them to me. ³ If anyone says anything to you, just say this, 'The Lord needs them.' And he will send them immediately." ⁴ This took place to fulfill what had been spoken through the prophet, saying,

> ⁵ *"Tell the daughter of Zion,*
> *Look, your king is coming to you,*
> *humble, and mounted on a donkey,*
> *and on a colt, the foal of a donkey."*

⁶ The disciples went and did as Jesus had directed them; ⁷ they brought the donkey and the colt, and put their cloaks on them, and he sat on them. ⁸ A very large crowd spread their cloaks on the road, and others cut branches from the trees and spread them on the road. ⁹ The crowds that went ahead of him and that followed were shouting,

"Hosanna to the Son of David!
Blessed is the one who comes in the name of the Lord!
Hosanna in the highest heaven!"

¹⁰ When he entered Jerusalem, the whole city was in turmoil, asking, "Who is this?" ¹¹ The crowds were saying, "This is the prophet Jesus from Nazareth in Galilee."

Fulton Sheen
(1895–1979)

———

Life of Christ

Riding on a Donkey
Matthew 21:5

The prophecy came from God through a prophet, and now God himself was bringing it to fulfillment. The prophecy of Zechariah was meant to contrast the majesty and the humility of the Savior.

As one looks at the ancient sculptured slabs of Assyria and Babylon, the murals of Egypt, the tombs of the Persians, and the scrolls of the Roman columns, one is struck by the majesty of kings riding in triumph on horses or in chariots, and sometimes over the prostrate bodies of their foes.

In contrast to this, here is one who comes triumphant upon an ass. How Pilate, if he was looking out of his fortress that Sunday, must have been amused by the ridiculous spectacle of a man being proclaimed as a King, and yet seated on the beast that was the symbol of the outcast—a fitting vehicle for one riding into the jaws of death!

If he had entered into the city with regal pomp in the manner of conquerors, he would have given occasion to believe that he was a political Messiah. But the circumstance he chose validated his claim that his kingdom was not of this world. There is no suggestion that this pauper King was a rival of Caesar.

DUCCIO | *1308–1311*

Christ Entering Jerusalem

Essay by Michael Stevens

This painting of Jesus' entrance into Jerusalem is one of twenty-six narrative panels in the monumental Maestà altarpiece by the Italian painter Duccio. At the time of its completion circa 1311, the Maestà was the largest panel painting ever made, and it has become famous for its innovative, three-dimensional, and highly detailed style. Besides its technical contributions, it is also a moving reflection on the beginning of Jesus' Passion.

In this scene, Christ is seated on a donkey, as described in the Gospel, and is approaching the fortified architecture of Jerusalem. He is surrounded by a dense crowd who fill the streets, laying freshly cut tree branches in the road to adorn Christ's path. This gesture, from which "Palm Sunday" gets its name, represents the crowd's recognition of Jesus' kingship. In the background, people climb the trees, both to cut new branches and to catch a better view of Jesus as he enters the city.

For all the excitement and celebration in this scene, though, there is a somber undercurrent. In this story, we anticipate how quickly those who worshiped Christ upon his arrival to Jerusalem were to then hand him over for crucifixion in the days immediately following. We sense the betrayal and bitter Passion to come for our Lord, and in turn sense our own tendency to turn our backs on Jesus when the cost of following him is great.

Architecture of Jerusalem

Duccio was innovative in his evolution of the flatness of medieval painting toward three-dimensional illusionism—a shift that marked the transition into a new, Renaissance style. This is evident in his treatment of the buildings in the background, as well as the archway in the middleground, each of which employs complex perspective and seems to leap off the panel.

Christ's donkey

The artist depicts Jesus as he is described in the Gospel: riding on a donkey. But given this story is referred to as Christ's triumphal entry, why a donkey and not something more impressive, like a magnificent war horse? The answer lies in Zechariah 9:9, which contains a prophecy of a coming king who brings peace and victory to Jerusalem. He is described by the prophet as "humble and riding on a donkey."

JESUS CLEANSES THE TEMPLE

[12] Then Jesus entered the temple and drove out all who were selling and buying in the temple, and he overturned the tables of the money changers and the seats of those who sold doves. [13] He said to them, "It is written,

'My house shall be called a house of prayer';
but you are making it a den of robbers.'"

[14] The blind and the lame came to him in the temple, and he cured them. [15] But when the chief priests and the scribes saw the amazing things that he did, and heard the children crying out in the temple, "Hosanna to the Son of David," they became angry [16] and said to him, "Do you hear what these are saying?" Jesus said to them, "Yes; have you never read,

'Out of the mouths of infants and nursing babies
you have prepared praise for yourself'?"

[17] He left them, went out of the city to Bethany, and spent the night there.

JESUS CURSES THE FIG TREE

[18] In the morning, when he returned to the city, he was hungry. [19] And seeing a fig tree by the side of the road, he went to it and found nothing at all on it but leaves. Then he said to it, "May no fruit ever come from you again!" And the fig tree withered at once. [20] When the disciples saw it, they were amazed, saying, "How did the fig tree wither at once?" [21] Jesus answered them, "Truly I tell you, if you have faith and do not doubt, not only will you do what has been done to the fig tree, but even if you say to this mountain, 'Be lifted up and thrown into the sea,' it will be done. [22] Whatever you ask for in prayer with faith, you will receive."

Getting to the Roots of Our Sin

Matthew 21:28–32 | Bishop Barron

This passage highlights the repentance of a son who changed his mind and obeyed his father. This is the way of Jesus. He wants a total renovation of our lives. He wants us to get to the roots of our sin and dysfunction, addressing not just the symptoms but the deep causes.

Perhaps your relational life or sexual life are dysfunctional; Jesus wants to root out the problem, not just change the behavior. Perhaps your professional life has become tainted by sin; Jesus wants to cut to the roots of it, in your pride or your fear or your ambition. Perhaps there is a pattern of violence in your behavior; Christ wants to get to the envy or the greed that lies behind it. Change your heart and turn to God.

THE AUTHORITY OF JESUS QUESTIONED

²³ When he entered the temple, the chief priests and the elders of the people came to him as he was teaching, and said, "By what authority are you doing these things, and who gave you this authority?" ²⁴ Jesus said to them, "I will also ask you one question; if you tell me the answer, then I will also tell you by what authority I do these things. ²⁵ Did the baptism of John come from heaven, or was it of human origin?" And they argued with one another, "If we say, 'From heaven,' he will say to us, 'Why then did you not believe him?' ²⁶ But if we say, 'Of human origin,' we are afraid of the crowd; for all regard John as a prophet." ²⁷ So they answered Jesus, "We do not know." And he said to them, "Neither will I tell you by what authority I am doing these things.

THE PARABLE OF THE TWO SONS

²⁸ "What do you think? A man had two sons; he went to the first and said, 'Son, go and work in the vineyard today.' ²⁹ He answered, 'I will not'; but later he changed his mind and went. ³⁰ The father went to the second and said the same; and he answered, 'I go, sir'; but he did not go. ³¹ Which of the two did the will of his father?" They said, "The first." Jesus said to them, "Truly I tell you, the tax collectors and the prostitutes are going into the kingdom of God ahead of you. ³² For John came to you in the way of righteousness and you did not believe him, but the tax collectors and the prostitutes believed him; and even after you saw it, you did not change your minds and believe him.

Our Lives Are Not about Us

Matthew 21:33–43 | Bishop Barron

Just before his Passion and death, Jesus tells the striking story of the landowner who planted a vineyard. The fertile vineyard stands for Israel, his chosen people. But it could be broadened out to include the world. What do we learn from this beautiful image? That God has made for his people a place where they can find rest, enjoyment, and good work.

We—Israel, the Church, the world—are not the owners of this vineyard; we are tenants. One of the most fundamental spiritual mistakes we can make is to think that we own the world. We are tenants, entrusted with the responsibility of caring for it, but everything that we have and are is on loan. Our lives are not about us.

Christ is God's judgment. We are all under his judgment. In the measure that we reject him or refuse to listen to him, we place our tenancy in jeopardy. And so the great question that arises from this reading: How am I using the gifts that God gave me for God's purposes? My money? My time? My talents? My creativity? My relationships? All is for God, and thus all is under God's judgment.

THE PARABLE OF THE WICKED TENANTS

33 "Listen to another parable. There was a landowner who planted a vineyard, put a fence around it, dug a wine press in it, and built a watchtower. Then he leased it to tenants and went to another country. 34 When the harvest time had come, he sent his slaves to the tenants to collect his produce. 35 But the tenants seized his slaves and beat one, killed another, and stoned another. 36 Again he sent other slaves, more than the first; and they treated them in the same way. 37 Finally he sent his son to them, saying, 'They will respect my son.' 38 But when the tenants saw the son, they said to themselves, 'This is the heir; come, let us kill him and get his inheritance.' 39 So they seized him, threw him out of the vineyard, and killed him. 40 Now when the owner of the vineyard comes, what will he do to those tenants?" 41 They said to him, "He will put those wretches to a miserable death, and lease the vineyard to other tenants who will give him the produce at the harvest time."

42 Jesus said to them, "Have you never read in the scriptures:

> 'The stone that the builders rejected
> has become the cornerstone;
> this was the Lord's doing,
> and it is amazing in our eyes'?

43 Therefore I tell you, the kingdom of God will be taken away from you and given to a people that produces the fruits of the kingdom. 44 The one who falls on this stone will be broken to pieces; and it will crush anyone on whom it falls."

45 When the chief priests and the Pharisees heard his parables, they realized that he was speaking about them. 46 They wanted to arrest him, but they feared the crowds, because they regarded him as a prophet.

THE PARABLE OF THE WEDDING BANQUET

22 Once more Jesus spoke to them in parables, saying: 2 "The kingdom of heaven may be compared to a king who gave a wedding banquet for his son. 3 He sent his slaves to call those who had been invited to the wedding banquet, but they would not come. 4 Again he sent other slaves, saying, 'Tell those who have been invited: Look, I have prepared my dinner, my oxen and my fat calves have been slaughtered, and everything is ready; come to the wedding banquet.' 5 But they made light of it and went away, one to his farm, another to his business, 6 while the rest seized his slaves, mistreated them, and killed them. 7 The king was enraged. He sent his troops, destroyed those murderers, and burned their city. 8 Then he said to his slaves, 'The wedding is ready, but those invited were not worthy.

You're Invited to a Wedding

Matthew 22:1–14 | Bishop Barron

Jesus likened the kingdom of heaven to a king who gave a wedding feast for his son. Notice that the father (God the Father) is giving a banquet for his son (God the Son) and bride (the Church). Jesus is the marriage of divinity and humanity—and we his followers are invited to join in the joy of this union.

The joyful intimacy of the Father and Son is now offered to us to be shared. Listen to Isaiah to learn the details of this banquet: "On this mountain the Lord of hosts will make for all peoples a feast of rich food, a feast of well-aged wines, of rich food filled with marrow, of well-aged wines strained clear" (Isa. 25:6).

Now, there is an edge to all of this. For it is the king who is doing the inviting and it is a wedding banquet for his son. We can see how terribly important it is to respond to the invitation of the King of kings.

We have heard the invitation of God to enter into intimacy with him, to make him the center of our lives, to be married to him in Christ—and often we find the most pathetic excuses not to respond.

---

⁹ Go therefore into the main streets, and invite everyone you find to the wedding banquet.' ¹⁰ Those slaves went out into the streets and gathered all whom they found, both good and bad; so the wedding hall was filled with guests.

¹¹ "But when the king came in to see the guests, he noticed a man there who was not wearing a wedding robe, ¹² and he said to him, 'Friend, how did you get in here without a wedding robe?' And he was speechless. ¹³ Then the king said to the attendants, 'Bind him hand and foot, and throw him into the outer darkness, where there will be weeping and gnashing of teeth.' ¹⁴ For many are called, but few are chosen."

THE QUESTION ABOUT PAYING TAXES

¹⁵ Then the Pharisees went and plotted to entrap him in what he said. ¹⁶ So they sent their disciples to him, along with the Herodians, saying, "Teacher, we know that you are sincere, and teach the way of God in accordance with truth, and show deference to no one; for you do not regard people with partiality. ¹⁷ Tell us, then, what you think. Is it lawful to pay taxes to the emperor, or not?" ¹⁸ But Jesus, aware of their malice, said, "Why are you putting me to the test, you hypocrites? ¹⁹ Show me the coin used for the tax." And they brought him a denarius. ²⁰ Then he said to them, "Whose head is this, and whose title?" ²¹ They answered, "The emperor's."

Everything Belongs to God

Matthew 22:15–22 | Bishop Barron

The Pharisees try to catch Jesus on the horns of a dilemma: "Is it lawful to pay taxes to the emperor, or not?" If he says yes, he will anger the crowds. If no, he will anger Rome.

Jesus deftly escapes from the trap with one of his famous one-liners: "Give therefore to the emperor the things that are the emperor's, and to God the things that are God's." Clever, but much more than merely clever. In some ways, it is the implicit resolution of this very vexing problem.

We should not read this one-liner as though there is a clearly demarcated political realm that belongs to the Caesars of the world and a clearly demarcated spiritual realm that belongs to God. And we certainly shouldn't read it in the modern mode—that the public arena belongs to politics, while religion is relegated to the private dimension.

No; this won't do, precisely because God is God, not a being in or above the world, not one reality among many. God is the sheer act of being itself, which necessarily pervades, influences, grounds, and has to do with everything, even as he transcends everything in creation.

God is the deepest source and inspiration for everything in life, from sports to law to the arts to science and medicine. God is love itself. Everything comes from God and returns to God.

Then he said to them, "Give therefore to the emperor the things that are the emperor's, and to God the things that are God's." ²² When they heard this, they were amazed; and they left him and went away.

THE QUESTION ABOUT THE RESURRECTION

²³ The same day some Sadducees came to him, saying there is no resurrection; and they asked him a question, saying, ²⁴ "Teacher, Moses said, 'If a man dies childless, his brother shall marry the widow, and raise up children for his brother.' ²⁵ Now there were seven brothers among us; the first married, and died childless, leaving the widow to his brother. ²⁶ The second did the same, so also the third, down to the seventh. ²⁷ Last of all, the woman herself died. ²⁸ In the resurrection, then, whose wife of the seven will she be? For all of them had married her."

²⁹ Jesus answered them, "You are wrong, because you know neither the scriptures nor the power of God. ³⁰ For in the resurrection they neither marry nor are given in marriage, but are like angels in heaven. ³¹ And as

for the resurrection of the dead, have you not read what was said to you by God, ³² 'I am the God of Abraham, the God of Isaac, and the God of Jacob'? He is God not of the dead, but of the living." ³³ And when the crowd heard it, they were astounded at his teaching.

THE GREATEST COMMANDMENT

³⁴ When the Pharisees heard that he had silenced the Sadducees, they gathered together, ³⁵ and one of them, a lawyer, asked him a question to test him. ³⁶ "Teacher, which commandment in the law is the greatest?" ³⁷ He said to him, "'You shall love the Lord your God with all your heart, and with all your soul, and with all your mind.' ³⁸ This is the greatest and first

Thomas Merton
(1915–1968)
———
No Man Is an Island

The God of Abraham, Isaac, and Jacob
Matthew 22:32

The god of the philosophers lives in the mind that knows him, receives life by the fact that he is known, lives as long as he is known, and dies when he is denied. But the true God (whom the philosophers can truly find through their abstractions if they remember their vocation to pass beyond abstractions) gives life to the mind that is known by him. . . .

Therefore Jesus said: "The God of Abraham, the God of Isaac, and the God of Jacob . . . is God not of the dead, but of the living." So true is it that the Lord is the "living God" that all those whose God he is will live forever, because he is their God.

Such was the argument that Jesus gave to the Sadducees, who did not believe in the resurrection of the dead. If God was the "God of Abraham" then Abraham must rise from the dead: no one who has the living God for his Lord can stay dead. He is our God only if we belong entirely to him. To belong entirely to life is to have passed from death to life.

commandment. [39] And a second is like it: 'You shall love your neighbor as yourself.' [40] On these two commandments hang all the law and the prophets."

THE QUESTION ABOUT DAVID'S SON

[41] Now while the Pharisees were gathered together, Jesus asked them this question: [42] "What do you think of the Messiah? Whose son is he?" They said to him, "The son of David." [43] He said to them, "How is it then that David by the Spirit calls him Lord, saying,

> [44] 'The Lord said to my Lord,
> "Sit at my right hand,
> until I put your enemies under your feet" '?

[45] If David thus calls him Lord, how can he be his son?" [46] No one was able to give him an answer, nor from that day did anyone dare to ask him any more questions.

JESUS DENOUNCES SCRIBES AND PHARISEES

23 Then Jesus said to the crowds and to his disciples, [2] "The scribes and the Pharisees sit on Moses' seat; [3] therefore, do whatever they teach you and follow it; but do not do as they do, for they do not practice what they teach. [4] They tie up heavy burdens, hard to bear, and lay them on the shoulders of others; but they themselves are unwilling to lift a finger to move them. [5] They do all their deeds to be seen by others; for they make their phylacteries broad and their fringes long. [6] They love to have the place of honor at banquets and the best seats in the synagogues, [7] and to be greeted with respect in the marketplaces, and to have people call them rabbi. [8] But you are not to be called rabbi, for you have one teacher, and you are all students. [9] And call no one your father on earth, for you have one Father—the one in heaven. [10] Nor are you to be called instructors, for you have one instructor, the Messiah. [11] The greatest among you will be your servant. [12] All who exalt themselves will be humbled, and all who humble themselves will be exalted.

[13] "But woe to you, scribes and Pharisees, hypocrites! For you lock people out of the kingdom of heaven. For you do not go in yourselves, and when others are going in, you stop them. [15] Woe to you, scribes and Pharisees, hypocrites! For you cross sea and land to make a single convert, and you make the new convert twice as much a child of hell as yourselves.

[16] "Woe to you, blind guides, who say, 'Whoever swears by the sanctuary is bound by nothing, but whoever swears by the gold of the sanctuary is bound by the oath.' [17] You blind fools! For which is greater, the gold or the sanctuary that has made the gold sacred? [18] And you say, 'Whoever

Correcting Bad Religion

Matthew 23:1–12 | Bishop Barron

In this passage, Jesus launches a blistering attack on the scribes and Pharisees. What are the underlying problems that bother Jesus?

First, "They tie up heavy burdens, hard to bear, and lay them on the shoulders of others; but they themselves are unwilling to lift a finger to move them." Some religious leaders burden people, making demands that are terrible, exulting in their own moral superiority.

Second, "They do all their deeds to be seen by others." They use the law and morality as a means of inflating the ego. A pious Jew would wear phylacteries as a sign of devotion. Well, they think, why not widen them, drawing attention to them and showing people how pious they are?

Third, "They love to have the place of honor at banquets and the best seats in the synagogues, and to be greeted with respect in the marketplaces, and to have people call them rabbi." Titles, privileges, places of honor, marks of respect—like any drug, these provide a rush. The trouble is that this drug wears off rather quickly, and then we want more of it: a greater title, more respect, more recognition.

What is Jesus' recommendation for those caught in this dilemma? Be satisfied with doing your work on behalf of God's kingdom, whatever it is. To be great is to be a servant: lowly, simple, often forgotten. Eschew marks of respect; don't seek them.

---

swears by the altar is bound by nothing, but whoever swears by the gift that is on the altar is bound by the oath.' 19 How blind you are! For which is greater, the gift or the altar that makes the gift sacred? 20 So whoever swears by the altar, swears by it and by everything on it; 21 and whoever swears by the sanctuary, swears by it and by the one who dwells in it; 22 and whoever swears by heaven, swears by the throne of God and by the one who is seated upon it.

23 "Woe to you, scribes and Pharisees, hypocrites! For you tithe mint, dill, and cummin, and have neglected the weightier matters of the law: justice and mercy and faith. It is these you ought to have practiced without neglecting the others. 24 You blind guides! You strain out a gnat but swallow a camel!

25 "Woe to you, scribes and Pharisees, hypocrites! For you clean the outside of the cup and of the plate, but inside they are full of greed and self-indulgence. 26 You blind Pharisee! First clean the inside of the cup, so that the outside also may become clean.

²⁷ "Woe to you, scribes and Pharisees, hypocrites! For you are like whitewashed tombs, which on the outside look beautiful, but inside they are full of the bones of the dead and of all kinds of filth. ²⁸ So you also on the outside look righteous to others, but inside you are full of hypocrisy and lawlessness.

²⁹ "Woe to you, scribes and Pharisees, hypocrites! For you build the tombs of the prophets and decorate the graves of the righteous, ³⁰ and you say, 'If we had lived in the days of our ancestors, we would not have taken part with them in shedding the blood of the prophets.' ³¹ Thus you testify against yourselves that you are descendants of those who murdered the prophets. ³² Fill up, then, the measure of your ancestors. ³³ You snakes, you brood of vipers! How can you escape being sentenced to hell? ³⁴ Therefore I send you prophets, sages, and scribes, some of whom you will kill and crucify, and some you will flog in your synagogues and pursue from town to town, ³⁵ so that upon you may come all the righteous blood shed on earth, from the blood of righteous Abel to the blood of Zechariah son of Barachiah, whom you murdered between the sanctuary and the altar. ³⁶ Truly I tell you, all this will come upon this generation.

THE LAMENT OVER JERUSALEM

³⁷ "Jerusalem, Jerusalem, the city that kills the prophets and stones those who are sent to it! How often have I desired to gather your children together as a hen gathers her brood under her wings, and you were not willing! ³⁸ See, your house is left to you, desolate. ³⁹ For I tell you, you will not see me again until you say, 'Blessed is the one who comes in the name of the Lord.'"

St. Cyril of Jerusalem
(313–386)

Catechetical Lectures

Clean the Inside of Your Cup
Matthew 23:26

Cleanse your cup, that you may receive grace more abundantly. For though remission of sins is given equally to all, the communion of the Holy Spirit is given in proportion to each man's faith. If you have labored little, you receive little; but if you have done much, the reward is great. You are running for yourself; see to your own interest.

THE DESTRUCTION OF THE TEMPLE FORETOLD

24 As Jesus came out of the temple and was going away, his disciples came to point out to him the buildings of the temple. [2] Then he asked them, "You see all these, do you not? Truly I tell you, not one stone will be left here upon another; all will be thrown down."

SIGNS OF THE END OF THE AGE

[3] When he was sitting on the Mount of Olives, the disciples came to him privately, saying, "Tell us, when will this be, and what will be the sign of your coming and of the end of the age?" [4] Jesus answered them, "Beware that no one leads you astray. [5] For many will come in my name, saying, 'I am the Messiah!' and they will lead many astray. [6] And you will hear of wars and rumors of wars; see that you are not alarmed; for this must take place, but the end is not yet. [7] For nation will rise against nation, and kingdom against kingdom, and there will be famines and earthquakes in various places: [8] all this is but the beginning of the birth pangs.

PERSECUTIONS FORETOLD

[9] "Then they will hand you over to be tortured and will put you to death, and you will be hated by all nations because of my name. [10] Then many will fall away, and they will betray one another and hate one another. [11] And many false prophets will arise and lead many astray. [12] And because of the increase of lawlessness, the love of many will grow cold. [13] But the one who endures to the end will be saved. [14] And this good news of the kingdom will be proclaimed throughout the world, as a testimony to all the nations; and then the end will come.

THE DESOLATING SACRILEGE

[15] "So when you see the desolating sacrilege standing in the holy place, as was spoken of by the prophet Daniel (let the reader understand), [16] then those in Judea must flee to the mountains; [17] the one on the housetop must not go down to take what is in the house; [18] the one in the field must not turn back to get a coat. [19] Woe to those who are pregnant and to those who are nursing infants in those days! [20] Pray that your flight may not be in winter or on a sabbath. [21] For at that time there will be great suffering, such as has not been from the beginning of the world until now, no, and never will be. [22] And if those days had not been cut short, no one would be saved; but for the sake of the elect those days will be cut short. [23] Then if anyone says to you, 'Look! Here is the Messiah!' or 'There he is!'—do not believe it. [24] For false messiahs and false prophets will appear and produce great signs and omens, to lead astray, if possible, even the elect. [25] Take note, I have told you beforehand. [26] So, if they say to you, 'Look! He is in the wilderness,' do not go out. If they say, 'Look! He is in the inner rooms,'

do not believe it. ²⁷ For as the lightning comes from the east and flashes as far as the west, so will be the coming of the Son of Man. ²⁸ Wherever the corpse is, there the vultures will gather.

THE COMING OF THE SON OF MAN

²⁹ "Immediately after the suffering of those days

> the sun will be darkened,
> and the moon will not give its light;
> the stars will fall from heaven,
> and the powers of heaven will be shaken.

³⁰ Then the sign of the Son of Man will appear in heaven, and then all the tribes of the earth will mourn, and they will see 'the Son of Man coming on the clouds of heaven' with power and great glory. ³¹ And he will send out his angels with a loud trumpet call, and they will gather his elect from the four winds, from one end of heaven to the other.

THE LESSON OF THE FIG TREE

³² "From the fig tree learn its lesson: as soon as its branch becomes tender and puts forth its leaves, you know that summer is near. ³³ So also, when you see all these things, you know that he is near, at the very gates. ³⁴ Truly I tell you, this generation will not pass away until all these things have taken place. ³⁵ Heaven and earth will pass away, but my words will not pass away.

St. John Chrysostom
(349–407)

Homilies on Matthew

This Generation?

Matthew 24:34

What does Jesus mean when he says "this generation"? He is not speaking of the generation then living but of the age of believers. . . . The faithful will not be destroyed by any of the things cited. . . . Over this generation—the faithful, that is—nothing shall prevail, not famine, nor pestilence, nor earthquake, nor wars, nor false Christs, nor false prophets, nor deceivers, nor traitors, nor those that bring temptation, nor false brethren, nor any other temptations.

THE NECESSITY FOR WATCHFULNESS

[36] "But about that day and hour no one knows, neither the angels of heaven, nor the Son, but only the Father. [37] For as the days of Noah were, so will be the coming of the Son of Man. [38] For as in those days before the flood they were eating and drinking, marrying and giving in marriage, until the day Noah entered the ark, [39] and they knew nothing until the flood came and swept them all away, so too will be the coming of the Son of Man. [40] Then two will be in the field; one will be taken and one will be left. [41] Two women will be grinding meal together; one will be taken and one will be left. [42] Keep awake therefore, for you do not know on what day your Lord is coming. [43] But understand this: if the owner of the house had known in what part of the night the thief was coming, he would have stayed awake and would not have let his house be broken into. [44] Therefore you also must be ready, for the Son of Man is coming at an unexpected hour.

THE FAITHFUL OR THE UNFAITHFUL SLAVE

[45] "Who then is the faithful and wise slave, whom his master has put in charge of his household, to give the other slaves their allowance of food at the proper time? [46] Blessed is that slave whom his master will find at work when he arrives. [47] Truly I tell you, he will put that one in charge of all his possessions. [48] But if that wicked slave says to himself, 'My master is delayed,' [49] and he begins to beat his fellow slaves, and eats and drinks with drunkards, [50] the master of that slave will come on a day when he does not expect him and at an hour that he does not know. [51] He will cut him in pieces and put him with the hypocrites, where there will be weeping and gnashing of teeth.

Christ Will Come Again

Matthew 24:37–44 | Bishop Barron

Jesus compares the terror of the end times with that of the flood that destroyed the earth in Noah's time. Why should the coming of the Son of Man strike fear in us? Because if he is the Son of God, then he will break into our sinful world like a cleansing fire, a wild storm, or a violent revolution.

Since he is the Life, that life which is opposed to him has to give way. Since he is the Truth, then false claimants to truth must cede to him. And since he is the Way, then the false ways have to be abandoned. And all of this will hurt. The best way to prepare is to watch, pray, and renounce our sins.

Linework

The overall impression of da Vinci's linework is one of chaos and energy, but upon closer inspection, the individual marks that make up the shockwaves and clouds are revealed as surprisingly precise and lyrical curves.

Handwriting

Leonardo's handwritten notes, seen in this work across the upper lefthand side, are composed in his own shorthand version of Italian. He wrote from right to left using horizontally flipped letter shapes, a technique known as mirror cursive. Leonardo did this partially because of the simple fact that he was left handed, and writing from right to left was faster and easier for him.

In this handwriting excerpt, da Vinci notes his technique for accurately rendering falling rain.

Matthew 24:1–51

LEONARDO DA VINCI | *1517–1518*

A Deluge

Essay by Michael Stevens

In Matthew 24, Jesus' words are urgent as he speaks of his coming at the end of the age. Here Jesus describes a scene full of earthquakes, lightning flashes, famines, and wars. He even invokes the narrative of Noah's flood, comparing the return of the Son of Man to a sudden rush of water, sweeping away the unprepared.

There is a similar sense of calamity in this mysterious drawing by Leonardo da Vinci, which depicts an apocalyptic scene similar to the one described by Christ in the Gospel. In the last decade of his life, da Vinci became consumed by a fascination with apocalyptic destruction. This is evidenced by a fixation on the subject in his personal writings, along with the creation of this strange series of black ink and chalk drawings, all of which feature images of natural disaster and explosive energy.

In this particular composition, jets of water appear to blast outward across the surrounding terrain, razing the landscape to the ground. The lines that compose the drawing build up to create dense layers of abstracted movement, as if the artist were working and reworking the drawing in a frenzied panic. Although da Vinci did not explicitly base these drawings on narratives from the Bible, they likely represented a personal investigation into the themes of death and the end of time—concepts that became increasingly troubling for da Vinci as he neared the end of his life.

Thomas Merton
(1915–1968)

―――

No Man Is an Island

Here Is the Bridegroom

Matthew 25:6

God our Creator and Savior has given us a language in which he can be talked about, since faith comes by hearing and our tongues are the keys that open heaven to others.

But when the Lord comes as a Bridegroom there remains nothing to be said except that he is coming, and that we must go out to meet him. *Ecce Sponsus venit! Exite obviam ei!* [Here is the bridegroom! Come out to meet him.]

After that we go forth to find him in solitude. There we communicate with him alone, without words, without discursive thoughts, in the silence of our whole being.

When what we say is meant for no one else but him, it can hardly be said in language. What is not meant to be related is not even experienced on a level that can be clearly analyzed. We know that it must not be told, because it cannot.

But before we come to that which is unspeakable and unthinkable, the Spirit hovers on the frontiers of language, wondering whether or not to stay on its own side of the border, in order to have something to bring back to other men. This is the test of those who wish to cross the frontier. If they are not ready to leave their own ideas and their own words behind them, they cannot travel further.

THE PARABLE OF THE TEN BRIDESMAIDS

25 "Then the kingdom of heaven will be like this. Ten bridesmaids took their lamps and went to meet the bridegroom. [2] Five of them were foolish, and five were wise. [3] When the foolish took their lamps, they took no oil with them; [4] but the wise took flasks of oil with their lamps. [5] As the bridegroom was delayed, all of them became drowsy and slept. [6] But at midnight there was a shout, 'Look! Here is the bridegroom! Come out to meet him.' [7] Then all those bridesmaids got up and trimmed their lamps. [8] The foolish said to the wise, 'Give us some of your oil, for our lamps are going out.' [9] But the wise replied, 'No! there will not be enough for you and for us; you had better go to the dealers and buy some for yourselves.' [10] And while they went to buy it, the bridegroom came, and those who were ready went with him into the wedding banquet; and the door was shut. [11] Later the other bridesmaids came also, saying, 'Lord, lord, open to us.' [12] But he replied, 'Truly I tell you, I do not know you.' [13] Keep awake therefore, for you know neither the day nor the hour.

THE PARABLE OF THE TALENTS

[14] "For it is as if a man, going on a journey, summoned his slaves and entrusted his property to them; [15] to one he gave five talents, to another two, to another one, to each according to his ability. Then he went away.

God in Gift Form

Matthew 25:14–30 | Bishop Barron

Here Jesus gives us the challenging parable of the talents. A man goes on a journey, but before leaving he entrusts his money to three of his servants. To one he gives five talents, to a second, two, and to a third, one.

The first man trades with the five talents. The second does the same, and both receive a rich return on their investment. The third man cautiously buries his talent.

When the owner returns, he praises the first two servants and gives them greater responsibilities, but the third man he upbraids.

Think of the talents as everything that we've received from God—life, breath, being, and powers. Because they come from God, they are meant to become gifts. If you cling to them, in the manner of the third servant, they don't grow; in fact, they wither away.

¹⁶ The one who had received the five talents went off at once and traded with them, and made five more talents. ¹⁷ In the same way, the one who had the two talents made two more talents. ¹⁸ But the one who had received the one talent went off and dug a hole in the ground and hid his master's money. ¹⁹ After a long time the master of those slaves came and settled accounts with them. ²⁰ Then the one who had received the five talents came forward, bringing five more talents, saying, 'Master, you handed over to me five talents; see, I have made five more talents.' ²¹ His master said to him, 'Well done, good and trustworthy slave; you have been trustworthy in a few things, I will put you in charge of many things; enter into the joy of your master.' ²² And the one with the two talents also came forward, saying, 'Master, you handed over to me two talents; see, I have made two more talents.' ²³ His master said to him, 'Well done, good and trustworthy slave; you have been trustworthy in a few things, I will put you in charge of many things; enter into the joy of your master.' ²⁴ Then the one who had received the one talent also came forward, saying, 'Master, I knew that you were a harsh man, reaping where you did not sow, and gathering where

What Is the Quality of Your Love?

Matthew 25:31–46 | Bishop Barron

At the end of Matthew 25, we encounter the scene of the Last Judgment. We hear that the specifics are a matter of love concretely expressed: "For I was hungry and you gave me food, I was thirsty and you gave me something to drink, I was a stranger and you welcomed me, I was naked and you gave me clothing, I was sick and you took care of me, I was in prison and you visited me." And we know the famous connection that Jesus makes: "Truly I tell you, just as you did it to one of the least of these who are members of my family, you did it to me."

There is something awful about the specificity of these demands. This is not love in the abstract, having affection for "humanity." It is caring for *that person* who is homeless, for *that person* who is ill, for *that person* who is in prison.

We do not take our money, our social status, or our worldly power into the next world; but we do take the quality of our love. You might consider doing an examination of conscience at the end of each day, and use as your criterion this passage. Perhaps put it up on your wall or post it next to your bed so that you see it before you go to sleep.

you did not scatter seed; ²⁵ so I was afraid, and I went and hid your talent in the ground. Here you have what is yours.' ²⁶ But his master replied, 'You wicked and lazy slave! You knew, did you, that I reap where I did not sow, and gather where I did not scatter? ²⁷ Then you ought to have invested my money with the bankers, and on my return I would have received what was my own with interest. ²⁸ So take the talent from him, and give it to the one with the ten talents. ²⁹ For to all those who have, more will be given, and they will have an abundance; but from those who have nothing, even what they have will be taken away. ³⁰ As for this worthless slave, throw him into the outer darkness, where there will be weeping and gnashing of teeth.'

THE JUDGMENT OF THE NATIONS

³¹ "When the Son of Man comes in his glory, and all the angels with him, then he will sit on the throne of his glory. ³² All the nations will be gathered before him, and he will separate people one from another as a shepherd separates the sheep from the goats, ³³ and he will put the sheep at his right hand and the goats at the left. ³⁴ Then the king will say to those at his right hand, 'Come, you that are blessed by my Father, inherit the kingdom prepared for you from the foundation of the world; ³⁵ for I was hungry and you gave me food, I was thirsty and you gave me something to drink, I was a stranger and you welcomed me, ³⁶ I was naked and you gave me clothing, I was sick and you took care of me, I was in prison and you visited me.' ³⁷ Then the righteous will answer him, 'Lord, when was it that we saw you hungry and gave you food, or thirsty and gave you something to drink? ³⁸ And when was it that we saw you a stranger and welcomed you, or naked and gave you clothing? ³⁹ And when was it that we saw you sick or in prison and visited you?' ⁴⁰ And the king will answer them, 'Truly I tell you, just as you did it to one of the least of these who are members of my family, you did it to me.' ⁴¹ Then he will say to those at his left hand, 'You that are accursed, depart from me into the eternal fire prepared for the devil and his angels; ⁴² for I was hungry and you gave me no food, I was thirsty and you gave me nothing to drink, ⁴³ I was a stranger and you did not welcome me, naked and you did not give me clothing, sick and in prison and you did not visit me.' ⁴⁴ Then they also will answer, 'Lord, when was it that we saw you hungry or thirsty or a stranger or naked or sick or in prison, and did not take care of you?' ⁴⁵ Then he will answer them, 'Truly I tell you, just as you did not do it to one of the least of these, you did not do it to me.' ⁴⁶ And these will go away into eternal punishment, but the righteous into eternal life."

JUST AS YOU DID IT TO ONE *of the* LEAST OF THESE, YOU DID IT TO ME.

MATTHEW 25:40

You Did It to Me

Matthew 25:31–46 | Bishop Barron

Once a rabbi inquired of Jesus which of the many laws (there were over six hundred) that governed Jewish life was the most important. With disarming simplicity and directness, Jesus responded: "You shall love the Lord your God with all your heart, and with all your soul, and with all your mind. This is the greatest and the first commandment. And a second is like it: You shall love your neighbor as yourself" (Matt. 22:37–39). The mutuality of these two loves is implicit in the entire teaching of Jesus. The absolute love for God is not in competition with a radical commitment in love to our fellow human beings, precisely because God is not one being among many, but the very ground of the existence of the finite world. Thomas Aquinas would state it this way: to love God is to love, necessarily, whatever participates in God, and this is to say the entire world.

Perhaps the most powerful evocation of this principle in the teaching of Jesus is the haunting parable of the sheep and the goats in chapter 25 of Matthew's Gospel. Jesus tells the crowd that when the Son of Man comes in his glory to judge the living and the dead, "he will separate people one from another as a shepherd separates the sheep from the goats." To those on his right, he will say, "Come, you that are blessed by my Father, inherit the kingdom prepared for you from the foundation of the world; for I was hungry and you gave me food, I was thirsty and you gave me something to drink, I was a stranger and you welcomed me, I was naked and you gave me clothing, I was sick and you took care of me, I was in prison and you visited me." In their puzzlement, the righteous will ask when they performed all of these acts of love for the Lord, and he will reply, "Truly I tell you, just as you did it to one of the least of these who are members of my family, you did it to me." Then comes the reversal. To those on his left, the King will say, "You that are accursed, depart from me into the eternal fire prepared for the devil and his angels; for I was hungry and you gave me no food, I was thirsty and you gave me nothing

to drink, I was a stranger and you did not welcome me, naked and you did not give me clothing, sick and in prison and you did not visit me." As puzzled as their counterparts, these people wonder when they neglected the Lord so thoroughly. Then comes the answer: "Truly I tell you, just as you did not do it to one of the least of these, you did not do it to me." To love Christ is to love the ones whom Christ loves. The very drama of the parable is intended to stir us out of any complacency and beguile us out of any confusion on this score.

A man who understood the theology and ethics of Matthew 25 in his bones was Peter Maurin, the co-founder of the Catholic Worker Movement. Maurin was born in France in 1877, one of twenty-four children. In the course of his early education, which was supervised by the Christian Brothers, he became deeply inspired by the example of St. Francis of Assisi. In 1909, when the French government turned aggressively against the Church, Peter left his native country and eventually began to live a radical sort of Franciscan life, embracing poverty out of love for the Gospel, working as a simple laborer during the day and sleeping in skid-row shelters at night. During those vagabond years, he was struggling to develop a coherent Catholic social philosophy, a theory of economics and politics thoroughly informed by Matthew 25. He knew that the Church had codified that section of

Matthew as "the corporal and spiritual works of mercy," among which were feeding the hungry, clothing the naked, visiting the imprisoned, burying the dead, counseling the doubtful, and praying for the living and the dead. He wondered what society would look like if those ideals were the foundation of the political and social order. He also read with great care the social teaching of the Church, especially as it was articulated in Pope Leo XIII's *Rerum Novarum* of 1891 and Pope Pius XI's *Quadragesimo Anno* of 1931. In Pope Leo's text, he discovered the principle that the pope had borrowed from Thomas Aquinas—namely, that while the ownership of private property is allowed, a use of private property should always be for the common good. In Pope Pius' encyclical, he discovered what has been characterized as the structuring element of all of Catholic social teaching, the principle of subsidiarity, which stipulates that in matters political and economic there ought always to be a preferential option for the most local level of authority and operation. The unambiguous application of this principle, Maurin saw, would prevent individuals and communities from abdicating their direct responsibility for practicing the corporal works of mercy. He wanted to build a society in which, in his words, "it would be easier for men to be good."

Maurin recognized Matthew 25 as "dynamite," from the Greek *dynamis* (power)—a favorite word of St. Paul, by the way. But he worried that "we have taken the dynamite of the Church, placed it in hermetically sealed containers, and sat on the lids." We have tended, in other words, to see the Gospel commands as a matter of private spirituality and not as society-transforming power. It is time, he concluded, "to blow up the dynamite of the Church!" As a non-native speaker of English, he was sensitive to peculiar turns of phrase that Anglophones would take for granted. He delighted in the term "go-getter," but he wanted, at the same time, to undermine it: "We should turn a nation of go-getters into a nation of go-givers!"

In 1932, just as the Great Depression was getting underway, Peter Maurin arrived in New York City. There he met a young social activist and spiritual seeker, recently converted to Catholicism. Her name was Dorothy Day. Dorothy had been a radical and a friend to some of the leaders in the cultural and political avant-garde of the 1920s, including the playwright Eugene O'Neill and the political agitator John Reed. But she had become fascinated with the Catholic Church, especially after the birth of her first child, when she said that she felt a gratitude so great that it corresponded to nothing in this world. When she met Peter Maurin, she was looking for a way to combine her radical political commitment to her newfound Catholic faith. The vagabond philosopher was the answer to her prayers. When they met, Peter spoke, uninterrupted, for seven hours! Despite this overwhelming loquaciousness, Dorothy was entranced by Peter's vision for a renewal of American society and his recommendation that the revolution should start with the founding of a newspaper that would present Catholic social teaching, and the establishment of "houses of hospitality" where the poor would be welcomed and where the corporal and spiritual works of mercy would be practiced. On May 1, 1933, Dorothy Day came to Washington Square Park in Greenwich Village and distributed the first edition of *The Catholic Worker* newspaper, selling it for one penny a copy (still the price today). Not long afterward, she and Maurin set up the first Catholic Worker House of Hospitality on the Lower East Side of Manhattan and commenced to take care of the poor. Today, there are such houses all over the country and indeed around the world. It is most important to see that neither of these figures could be blandly described as a "social worker." Throughout their lives, they attended Mass, assisted at Benedictions, participated in retreats, prayed the rosary, etc., for they saw their radical devotion to the poor in inescapable correlation to their even more radical love of Christ.

Someone who operated very much in the spirit of Dorothy Day was St. Teresa of Kolkata. Much of Mother Teresa's day was taken up with prayer, meditation, Mass, Eucharistic Adoration, and the rosary, but the rest of her time, as we well know, was spent in the grittiest work among the poorest of the poor, practicing the corporal and spiritual works of mercy, blowing up the dynamite of the Church. Father Paul Murray, the Irish Dominican spiritual writer and sometime advisor to Mother Teresa, relates the following story. He was one day in deep conversation with Mother, searching out the sources of her spirituality and mission. At the end of their long talk, she asked him to spread his hand out on the table, and touching his fingers one by one as she spoke the words, she said, "You did it to me."

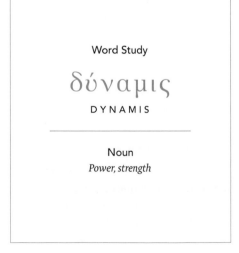

Word Study

δύναμις

DYNAMIS

Noun
Power, strength

THE PLOT TO KILL JESUS

26 When Jesus had finished saying all these things, he said to his disciples, ² "You know that after two days the Passover is coming, and the Son of Man will be handed over to be crucified."

³ Then the chief priests and the elders of the people gathered in the palace of the high priest, who was called Caiaphas, ⁴ and they conspired to arrest Jesus by stealth and kill him. ⁵ But they said, "Not during the festival, or there may be a riot among the people."

THE ANOINTING AT BETHANY

⁶ Now while Jesus was at Bethany in the house of Simon the leper, ⁷ a woman came to him with an alabaster jar of very costly ointment, and she poured it on his head as he sat at the table. ⁸ But when the disciples saw it, they were angry and said, "Why this waste? ⁹ For this ointment could have been sold for a large sum, and the money given to the poor." ¹⁰ But Jesus, aware of this, said to them, "Why do you trouble the woman? She has performed a good service for me. ¹¹ For you always have the poor with you, but you will not always have me. ¹² By pouring this ointment on my body she has prepared me for burial. ¹³ Truly I tell you, wherever this good news is proclaimed in the whole world, what she has done will be told in remembrance of her."

JUDAS AGREES TO BETRAY JESUS

¹⁴ Then one of the twelve, who was called Judas Iscariot, went to the chief priests ¹⁵ and said, "What will you give me if I betray him to you?" They paid him thirty pieces of silver. ¹⁶ And from that moment he began to look for an opportunity to betray him.

The Good News of Judas

Matthew 26:14–25 | Bishop Barron

The Last Supper takes place during Passover, the day when the paschal lambs were slaughtered. Why is this important? Because Christ is himself the Paschal Lamb who will be slaughtered for the salvation of the world, and this sacrifice is made sacramentally present at every Mass.

Interestingly, Judas is present there at the Last Supper, the root of the Mass. This is startlingly good news. Why? It means Jesus associates with all of us sinners, in all of our dysfunction. He entered into the darkness in all of its power in order to bring the light. If even Judas was invited into the Lord's presence, so are you.

THE PASSOVER WITH THE DISCIPLES

¹⁷ On the first day of Unleavened Bread the disciples came to Jesus, saying, "Where do you want us to make the preparations for you to eat the Passover?" ¹⁸ He said, "Go into the city to a certain man, and say to him, 'The Teacher says, My time is near; I will keep the Passover at your house with my disciples.' " ¹⁹ So the disciples did as Jesus had directed them, and they prepared the Passover meal.

²⁰ When it was evening, he took his place with the twelve; ²¹ and while they were eating, he said, "Truly I tell you, one of you will betray me." ²² And they became greatly distressed and began to say to him one after another, "Surely not I, Lord?" ²³ He answered, "The one who has dipped his hand into the bowl with me will betray me. ²⁴ The Son of Man goes as it is written of him, but woe to that one by whom the Son of Man is betrayed! It would have been better for that one not to have been born." ²⁵ Judas, who betrayed him, said, "Surely not I, Rabbi?" He replied, "You have said so."

THE INSTITUTION OF THE LORD'S SUPPER

²⁶ While they were eating, Jesus took a loaf of bread, and after blessing it he broke it, gave it to the disciples, and said, "Take, eat; this is my body." ²⁷ Then he took a cup, and after giving thanks he gave it to them, saying, "Drink from it, all of you; ²⁸ for this is my blood of the covenant, which is poured out for many for the forgiveness of sins. ²⁹ I tell you, I will never again drink of this fruit of the vine until that day when I drink it new with you in my Father's kingdom."

³⁰ When they had sung the hymn, they went out to the Mount of Olives.

PETER'S DENIAL FORETOLD

³¹ Then Jesus said to them, "You will all become deserters because of me this night; for it is written,

> 'I will strike the shepherd,
> and the sheep of the flock will be scattered.'

³² But after I am raised up, I will go ahead of you to Galilee." ³³ Peter said to him, "Though all become deserters because of you, I will never desert you." ³⁴ Jesus said to him, "Truly I tell you, this very night, before the cock crows, you will deny me three times." ³⁵ Peter said to him, "Even though I must die with you, I will not deny you." And so said all the disciples.

The Words with Power

Matthew 26:26–28 | Bishop Barron

If Jesus were an ordinary prophet or teacher, these powerful words, spoken the night before his death, would have burned themselves into the consciousness of his followers and carried enormous symbolic resonance. They might even have changed his disciples profoundly at the spiritual and psychological level.

But Jesus was not one prophet among many; he was the incarnate Word of God. Therefore, his words had the power to create, to affect reality at the deepest possible level. Since what he says *is*, the words "This is my body" and "This is my blood" effectively change the bread and wine into his Body and Blood. Like all divine utterances, they *produce* what they say. The same Word that spoke the elements of bread and wine into existence in the first place now speaks them into a new mode of being, changing them into the bearers of Christ's sacramental presence.

For Catholic theology, this efficacious word of Christ has not passed out of existence or evanesced into a vague historical memory. Rather, it endures in the Church: in its preaching, its teaching, its sacraments, and above all in the Eucharistic liturgy.

JESUS PRAYS IN GETHSEMANE

³⁶ Then Jesus went with them to a place called Gethsemane; and he said to his disciples, "Sit here while I go over there and pray." ³⁷ He took with him Peter and the two sons of Zebedee, and began to be grieved and agitated. ³⁸ Then he said to them, "I am deeply grieved, even to death; remain here, and stay awake with me." ³⁹ And going a little farther, he threw himself on the ground and prayed, "My Father, if it is possible, let this cup pass from me; yet not what I want but what you want." ⁴⁰ Then he came to the disciples and found them sleeping; and he said to Peter, "So, could you not stay awake with me one hour? ⁴¹ Stay awake and pray that you may not come into the time of trial; the spirit indeed is willing, but the flesh is weak." ⁴² Again he went away for the second time and prayed, "My Father, if this cannot pass unless I drink it, your will be done." ⁴³ Again he came and found them sleeping, for their eyes were heavy. ⁴⁴ So leaving them again, he went away and prayed for the third time, saying the same words. ⁴⁵ Then he came to the disciples and said to them, "Are you still sleeping and taking your rest? See, the hour is at hand, and the Son of Man is betrayed into the hands of sinners. ⁴⁶ Get up, let us be going. See, my betrayer is at hand."

THE BETRAYAL AND ARREST OF JESUS

[47] While he was still speaking, Judas, one of the twelve, arrived; with him was a large crowd with swords and clubs, from the chief priests and the elders of the people. [48] Now the betrayer had given them a sign, saying, "The one I will kiss is the man; arrest him." [49] At once he came up to Jesus and said, "Greetings, Rabbi!" and kissed him. [50] Jesus said to him, "Friend, do what you are here to do." Then they came and laid hands on Jesus and arrested him. [51] Suddenly, one of those with Jesus put his hand on his sword, drew it, and struck the slave of the high priest, cutting off his ear. [52] Then Jesus said to him, "Put your sword back into its place; for all who take the sword will perish by the sword. [53] Do you think that I cannot appeal to my Father, and he will at once send me more than twelve legions of angels? [54] But how then would the scriptures be fulfilled, which say it must happen in this way?" [55] At that hour Jesus said to the crowds, "Have you come out with swords and clubs to arrest me as though I were a bandit? Day after day I sat in the temple teaching, and you did not arrest me. [56] But all this has taken place, so that the scriptures of the prophets may be fulfilled." Then all the disciples deserted him and fled.

JESUS BEFORE THE HIGH PRIEST

[57] Those who had arrested Jesus took him to Caiaphas the high priest, in whose house the scribes and the elders had gathered. [58] But Peter was following him at a distance, as far as the courtyard of the high priest; and going inside, he sat with the guards in order to see how this would end. [59] Now the chief priests and the whole council were looking for false testimony against Jesus so that they might put him to death, [60] but they found none, though many false witnesses came forward. At last two came forward [61] and said, "This fellow said, 'I am able to destroy the temple of God and to build it in three days.' "

St. Hilary of Poitiers
(310–368)

On Matthew

Cutting Off the Ear
Matthew 26:50–51

The Apostle cuts the ear off the high priest's servant—that is, a disciple of Christ cuts off a disobedient ear.... What was once incapable of hearing truth is now cut off.

Christ's hand raised in blessing

In this mosaic, Jesus is shown at the center of the table, blessing the bread and the wine with his disciples gathered on each side. This gesture is directly paralleled by the actions of the priest in the Mass as he acts *in persona Christi*—"in the person of Christ." At Mass, we as Catholics are invited to come and witness this same mystery of the Last Supper, and to receive Jesus' true Body and Blood just as the disciples did.

Triptych arrangement

This three-paneled arrangement is very common in Christian art across the centuries, and is known as a triptych. Triptychs were typically hinged together, and were associated with altarpieces and the celebration of the Mass. Their "three-in-one" construction is symbolic of the unity of the Trinity.

Latin inscription

Inscribed at the center of this piece in precisely cut featherwork are the words of the Eucharistic Prayer offered by the priest during the Mass at the moment of the consecration of the bread and the wine. These words are based directly on the words of Jesus in Matthew 26:26 and following, in which he tell his disciples, "Take, eat; this is my body."

Matthew 26:26–30

UNKNOWN ARTIST | *Sixteenth century*

The Last Supper

Essay by Michael Stevens

At first glance, this piece may look like an ordinary painting.
Its detailed lettering and meticulously shaded figures give every
impression of careful color mixing and precise brushwork. But
it is not a painting at all. This image is actually a feather mosaic
made from thousands of carefully glued feather slices.

The technique of feather mosaic was developed in pre-Hispanic
Mesoamerica, but was adopted as a vehicle for Christian imagery
as European influence grew in the New World. This piece, made
in the region that is now Mexico, includes features that were
sourced from a wide variety of indigenous birds, which combine
to form an intricate arrangement of images and lettering.

The scene in the central panel is of the Last Supper. It shows
Christ seated with the twelve Apostles with his hand raised in
blessing over the meal. The Latin inscription reads:

hoc est enim corpus meum	(This is my body
hic est enim calix sanguinis	This is the cup of my blood
mei novi et aeterni testamenti	The blood of the new and
qui pro vobis et pro multis	eternal covenant
effundetur in remissionem	It will be shed for you and for
peccatorum	many for the forgiveness of sins)

This deceptively simple mosaic is much more than meets the eye—
and so is the Last Supper story it depicts. On the surface, we see
what looks like an ordinary meal unfolding: a group of men, seated
at a table, eating a meal of what appears to be simple bread and
wine. But through Jesus' words, "This is my body," a profound
transformation is unfolding: Christ is changing ordinary food into
his very Body, Blood, Soul, and Divinity.

⁶² The high priest stood up and said, "Have you no answer? What is it that they testify against you?" ⁶³ But Jesus was silent. Then the high priest said to him, "I put you under oath before the living God, tell us if you are the Messiah, the Son of God." ⁶⁴ Jesus said to him, "You have said so. But I tell you,

> From now on you will see the Son of Man
>
> seated at the right hand of Power
>
> and coming on the clouds of heaven."

⁶⁵ Then the high priest tore his clothes and said, "He has blasphemed! Why do we still need witnesses? You have now heard his blasphemy. ⁶⁶ What is your verdict?" They answered, "He deserves death." ⁶⁷ Then they spat in his face and struck him; and some slapped him, ⁶⁸ saying, "Prophesy to us, you Messiah! Who is it that struck you?"

PETER'S DENIAL OF JESUS

⁶⁹ Now Peter was sitting outside in the courtyard. A servant-girl came to him and said, "You also were with Jesus the Galilean." ⁷⁰ But he denied it before all of them, saying, "I do not know what you are talking about." ⁷¹ When he went out to the porch, another servant-girl saw him, and she said to the bystanders, "This man was with Jesus of Nazareth." ⁷² Again he denied it with an oath, "I do not know the man." ⁷³ After a little while the bystanders came up and said to Peter, "Certainly you are also one of them, for your accent betrays you." ⁷⁴ Then he began to curse, and he swore an oath, "I do not know the man!" At that moment the cock crowed. ⁷⁵ Then Peter remembered what Jesus had said: "Before the cock crows, you will deny me three times." And he went out and wept bitterly.

JESUS BROUGHT BEFORE PILATE

27 When morning came, all the chief priests and the elders of the people conferred together against Jesus in order to bring about his death. ² They bound him, led him away, and handed him over to Pilate the governor.

THE SUICIDE OF JUDAS

³ When Judas, his betrayer, saw that Jesus was condemned, he repented and brought back the thirty pieces of silver to the chief priests and the elders. ⁴ He said, "I have sinned by betraying innocent blood." But they said, "What is that to us? See to it yourself." ⁵ Throwing down the pieces of silver in the temple, he departed; and he went and hanged himself. ⁶ But the chief priests, taking the pieces of silver, said, "It is not lawful to put them into the treasury, since they are blood money." ⁷ After conferring together, they used them to buy the potter's field as a place to bury foreigners. ⁸ For this reason that field has been called the Field of Blood to this day. ⁹ Then was fulfilled what had been spoken through the prophet Jeremiah, "And they

took the thirty pieces of silver, the price of the one on whom a price had been set, on whom some of the people of Israel had set a price, [10] and they gave them for the potter's field, as the Lord commanded me."

PILATE QUESTIONS JESUS

[11] Now Jesus stood before the governor; and the governor asked him, "Are you the King of the Jews?" Jesus said, "You say so." [12] But when he was accused by the chief priests and elders, he did not answer. [13] Then Pilate said to him, "Do you not hear how many accusations they make against you?" [14] But he gave him no answer, not even to a single charge, so that the governor was greatly amazed.

BARABBAS OR JESUS?

[15] Now at the festival the governor was accustomed to release a prisoner for the crowd, anyone whom they wanted. [16] At that time they had a notorious prisoner, called Jesus Barabbas. [17] So after they had gathered, Pilate said to them, "Whom do you want me to release for you, Jesus Barabbas or Jesus who is called the Messiah?" [18] For he realized that it was out of jealousy that they had handed him over. [19] While he was sitting on the judgment seat, his wife sent word to him, "Have nothing to do with that innocent man, for today I have suffered a great deal because of a dream about him." [20] Now the chief priests and the elders persuaded the crowds to ask for Barabbas and to have Jesus killed. [21] The governor again said to them, "Which of the two do you want me to release for you?" And they said, "Barabbas." [22] Pilate said to them, "Then what should I do with Jesus who is called the Messiah?" All of them said, "Let him be crucified!" [23] Then he asked, "Why, what evil has he done?" But they shouted all the more, "Let him be crucified!"

PILATE HANDS JESUS OVER TO BE CRUCIFIED

[24] So when Pilate saw that he could do nothing, but rather that a riot was beginning, he took some water and washed his hands before the crowd, saying, "I am innocent of this man's blood; see to it yourselves." [25] Then the people as a whole answered, "His blood be on us and on our children!" [26] So he released Barabbas for them; and after flogging Jesus, he handed him over to be crucified.

THE SOLDIERS MOCK JESUS

[27] Then the soldiers of the governor took Jesus into the governor's headquarters, and they gathered the whole cohort around him. [28] They stripped him and put a scarlet robe on him, [29] and after twisting some thorns into a crown, they put it on his head. They put a reed in his right hand and knelt before him and mocked him, saying, "Hail, King of the Jews!" [30] They spat on him, and took the reed and struck him on the head. [31] After mocking him, they stripped him of the robe and put his own clothes on him. Then they led him away to crucify him.

Christ's head

Christ's head, which is the focal point of this image, is placed directly at the center of the composition. The instruments with which the soldiers press his crown deeper create dramatic diagonal lines that compel the eye toward the face of our Lord, while forming a Trinitarian triangle above his head. The armored guard to the left has turned his back and gazes passively at Jesus. Whether animate or inanimate, every object in the scene exists to draw us toward Christ and into his experience of suffering.

Royal garments

Matthew 27:28 tells us that the soldiers "stripped him and put a scarlet robe on him." This robe, combined with the crown of thorns, was meant to be a mockery of Jesus' kingship—a humiliating caricature of royal garments.

Reed in Christ's hand

The reed in Christ's hand is meant to mockingly recall the scepter of a king—yet Christ carries it with dignity and gentleness. This creates a sharp contrast with the white-knuckled force with which the soldiers clutch their instruments of torture. The way Christ's reed extends three-dimensionally from the scene shows the influence of Caravaggio, who often painted objects to appear as if they were breaking out from the window of the canvas into the world of the viewer.

Matthew 27:27–31

DIRCK VAN BABUREN | *1621–1622*

Christ Crowned with Thorns

Essay by Michael Stevens

In this gripping painting by Dirck van Baburen, we see Jesus
being crowned with thorns by a crowd of jeering Roman
guards. Faced with excruciating pain, Christ appears serene and
composed—his body bowed low as if to signify his willingness
to endure the torment. His expression is one of selfless
perseverance, and we are reminded that the long journey to
Calvary is just beginning.

Van Baburen was a lesser-known Baroque painter, and few of his
artworks are presently identified. He was raised in Utrecht, but his
travels to Rome exposed him to the work of Caravaggio early in
his career, whose style became a primary influence in his work.
In this painting, we see many of the same techniques Caravaggio
used to create a sense of realism and depth: dramatic use of
chiaroscuro to highlight key details in the scene, an emphasis on
three-dimensionality in elements such as the reed in Jesus' hand,
and the use of powerful facial expressions to provide insight into
the psychology of the figures depicted. The overall effect is one
of tender sensitivity combined with technical precision and clarity.

THE CRUCIFIXION OF JESUS

³² As they went out, they came upon a man from Cyrene named Simon; they compelled this man to carry his cross. ³³ And when they came to a place called Golgotha (which means Place of a Skull), ³⁴ they offered him wine to drink, mixed with gall; but when he tasted it, he would not drink it. ³⁵ And when they had crucified him, they divided his clothes among themselves by casting lots; ³⁶ then they sat down there and kept watch over him. ³⁷ Over his head they put the charge against him, which read, "This is Jesus, the King of the Jews."

³⁸ Then two bandits were crucified with him, one on his right and one on his left. ³⁹ Those who passed by derided him, shaking their heads ⁴⁰ and saying, "You who would destroy the temple and build it in three days, save yourself! If you are the Son of God, come down from the cross." ⁴¹ In the same way the chief priests also, along with the scribes and elders, were mocking him, saying, ⁴² "He saved others; he cannot save himself. He is the King of Israel; let him come down from the cross now, and we will believe in him. ⁴³ He trusts in God; let God deliver him now, if he wants to; for he said, 'I am God's Son.'" ⁴⁴ The bandits who were crucified with him also taunted him in the same way.

Why Is the Cross Good News?

Matthew 27:34–54 | Bishop Barron

At the Crucifixion, Jesus is presented as the divine presence that has journeyed into sin in order to save us. Accordingly, all forms of human dysfunction are on display in the Passion narrative. During those terrible hours, Jesus' mission came to its fulfillment. What commenced at Bethlehem and continued at the Jordan River now comes to completion.

In contrast to the rock-hard attitude of Jesus, conforming himself to the will of his Father, we find almost all the ways that we flee the will of God: betrayal, indifference, spiritual sloth, violence, cowardice, untruth, scapegoating, self-destruction, abuse of authority, and wanton cruelty. No wonder that "darkness came over the whole land until three in the afternoon." At the beginning of creation, God said, "Let there be light" (Gen. 1:3). But his world had become darkened in every way through sin.

Yet what is the simple and powerful good news? That Jesus associates with all of us sinners, in all of our dysfunction. He entered into the darkness in all of its power in order to bring the light.

THE DEATH OF JESUS

⁴⁵ From noon on, darkness came over the whole land until three in the afternoon. ⁴⁶ And about three o'clock Jesus cried with a loud voice, "Eli, Eli, lema sabachthani?" that is, "My God, my God, why have you forsaken me?" ⁴⁷ When some of the bystanders heard it, they said, "This man is calling for Elijah." ⁴⁸ At once one of them ran and got a sponge, filled it with sour wine, put it on a stick, and gave it to him to drink. ⁴⁹ But the others said, "Wait, let us see whether Elijah will come to save him." ⁵⁰ Then Jesus cried again with a loud voice and breathed his last. ⁵¹ At that moment the curtain of the temple was torn in two, from top to bottom. The earth shook, and the rocks were split. ⁵² The tombs also were opened, and many bodies of the saints who had fallen asleep were raised. ⁵³ After his resurrection they came out of the tombs and entered the holy city and appeared to many. ⁵⁴ Now when the centurion and those with him, who were keeping watch over Jesus, saw the earthquake and what took place, they were terrified and said, "Truly this man was God's Son!"

⁵⁵ Many women were also there, looking on from a distance; they had followed Jesus from Galilee and had provided for him. ⁵⁶ Among them were Mary Magdalene, and Mary the mother of James and Joseph, and the mother of the sons of Zebedee.

St. John Chrysostom
(349–407)

———

Homilies on Matthew

My God, My God, Why Have You Forsaken Me?
Matthew 27:46

Why does Jesus speak this way, crying out, "Eli, Eli, lema sabachthani" [My God, my God, why have you forsaken me]? He does it so that they might see that to his very last gasp he is honoring God as his Father and is no enemy of God. His own voice is the voice of Scripture, quoting a cry from the psalm [Ps. 22]. Even in his last moments he is found bearing witness to the sacred writings.

G.K. Chesterton
(1874–1936)
—
The Everlasting Man

Burying the Old Cultures,
Rising of the New

Matthew 27:32–66

The mob went along with the Sadducees and the Pharisees, the philosophers and the moralists. It went along with the imperial magistrates and the sacred priests, the scribes and the soldiers, that the one universal human spirit might suffer a universal condemnation; that there might be one deep, unanimous chorus of approval and harmony when Man was rejected of men.

There were solitudes beyond where none shall follow. There were secrets in the inmost and invisible part of that drama that have no symbol in speech; or in any severance of a man from men. Nor is it easy for any words less stark and single-minded than those of the naked narrative even to hint at the horror of exaltation that lifted itself above the hill. Endless expositions have not come to the end of it, or even to the beginning. And if there be any sound that can produce a silence, we may surely be silent about the end and the extremity; when a cry was driven out of that darkness in words dreadfully distinct and dreadfully unintelligible, which man shall never understand in all the eternity they have purchased for him; and for one annihilating instant an abyss that is not for our thoughts had opened even in the unity of the absolute; and God had been forsaken of God.

They took the body down from the cross and one of the few rich men among the first Christians obtained permission to bury it in a rock tomb in his garden; the Romans setting a military guard lest there should be some riot and attempt to recover the body.

There was once more a natural symbolism in these natural proceedings; it was well that the tomb should be sealed with all the secrecy of ancient eastern sepulture and guarded by the authority of the Caesars. For in that second cavern the whole of that great and glorious humanity which we call antiquity was gathered up and covered over; and in that place it was buried. It was the end of a very great thing called human history; the history that was merely human. The mythologies and the philosophies were buried there, the gods and the heroes and the sages. In the great Roman phrase, they had lived. But as they could only live, so they could only die; and they were dead.

THE BURIAL OF JESUS

⁵⁷ When it was evening, there came a rich man from Arimathea, named Joseph, who was also a disciple of Jesus. ⁵⁸ He went to Pilate and asked for the body of Jesus; then Pilate ordered it to be given to him. ⁵⁹ So Joseph took the body and wrapped it in a clean linen cloth ⁶⁰ and laid it in his own new tomb, which he had hewn in the rock. He then rolled a great stone to the door of the tomb and went away. ⁶¹ Mary Magdalene and the other Mary were there, sitting opposite the tomb.

THE GUARD AT THE TOMB

⁶² The next day, that is, after the day of Preparation, the chief priests and the Pharisees gathered before Pilate ⁶³ and said, "Sir, we remember what that impostor said while he was still alive, 'After three days I will rise again.' ⁶⁴ Therefore command the tomb to be made secure until the third day; otherwise his disciples may go and steal him away, and tell the people, 'He has been raised from the dead,' and the last deception would be worse than the first." ⁶⁵ Pilate said to them, "You have a guard of soldiers; go, make it as secure as you can." ⁶⁶ So they went with the guard and made the tomb secure by sealing the stone.

THE RESURRECTION OF JESUS

28 After the sabbath, as the first day of the week was dawning, Mary Magdalene and the other Mary went to see the tomb. ² And suddenly there was a great earthquake; for an angel of the Lord, descending from heaven, came and rolled back the stone and sat on it. ³ His appearance was like lightning, and his clothing white as snow. ⁴ For fear of him the guards shook and became like dead men. ⁵ But the angel said to the women, "Do not be afraid; I know that you are looking for Jesus who was crucified. ⁶ He is not here; for he has been raised, as he said. Come, see the place where he lay. ⁷ Then go quickly and tell his disciples, 'He has been raised from the dead, and indeed he is going ahead of you to Galilee; there you will see him.' This is my message for you." ⁸ So they left the tomb quickly with fear and great joy, and ran to tell his disciples. ⁹ Suddenly Jesus met them and said, "Greetings!" And they came to him, took hold of his feet, and worshiped him. ¹⁰ Then Jesus said to them, "Do not be afraid; go and tell my brothers to go to Galilee; there they will see me."

THE REPORT OF THE GUARD

¹¹ While they were going, some of the guard went into the city and told the chief priests everything that had happened. ¹² After the priests had assembled with the elders, they devised a plan to give a large sum of money to the soldiers, ¹³ telling them, "You must say, 'His disciples came

---

No Resurrection, No Christianity

Matthew 28:1–10 | Bishop Barron

The Resurrection of Jesus from the dead is the be-all and end-all of the Christian faith. If Jesus didn't rise from the dead, all bishops, priests, and Christian ministers should go home and get honest jobs, and all the Christian faithful should leave their churches immediately.

As Paul himself put it: "If Christ has not been raised, then our proclamation has been in vain and your faith has been in vain" (1 Cor. 15:14). It's no good, of course, trying to explain the Resurrection away or rationalize it as a myth, a symbol, or an inner subjective experience. None of that does justice to the novelty and sheer strangeness of the biblical message.

It comes down finally to this: if Jesus was not raised from death, Christianity is a fraud and a joke. But if he did rise from death, then Christianity is the fullness of God's revelation, and Jesus must be the absolute center of our lives. There is no third option.

St. Jerome
(347–420)

———

*Commentary
on Matthew*

Undoing Eve's Curse

Matthew 28:8–10

Two different emotions filled the minds of these women: fear and joy. The fear came from the scale of the miracle they had witnessed, the joy from seeing their longings for the resurrection fulfilled. Both feelings drove them forward. They continued till they met the Apostles in order that the seed of faith would be sown abroad.... Thus it happened that Eve's curse was undone by these women.

Fulton Sheen
(1895–1979)

———

Life of Christ

Bribery of the Guards

Matthew 28:11–15

The "large sum of money" contrasted rather strongly with the meager thirty pieces of silver which Judas received. The Sanhedrin did not deny the Resurrection; in fact, they bore their own unbiased testimony to its truth. And that same testimony they carried to the Gentiles through Pilate. They even gave the money of the temple to the Roman soldiers whom they despised; for they had found a greater hate. The money Judas had returned they would not touch because it was "blood money" (Matt. 27:6). But now they would buy a lie to escape the purifying Blood of the Lamb.

The bribery of the guard was really a stupid way to escape the fact of the Resurrection. First of all, there was the problem of what would be done with his body after the disciples had possession of it. All that the enemies of our Lord would have had to do to disprove the Resurrection would be to produce the body. Quite apart from the fact that it was very unlikely that a whole guard of Roman soldiers slept while they were on duty, it was absurd for them to say that what had happened, happened when they were asleep. The soldiers were advised to say they were asleep; and yet they were so awake as to have seen thieves and to know that they were disciples. If all of the soldiers were asleep, they could never have discovered the thieves; if a few of them were awake, they should have prevented the theft. It is equally improbable that a few timid disciples should attempt to steal their master's body from a grave closed by stone, officially sealed, and guarded by soldiers without awakening the sleeping guards. The orderly arrangement of the burial cloths afforded further proof that the body was not removed by his disciples.

The secret removal of the body would have been to no purpose so far as the disciples were concerned, nor had any of them even thought of it; for the moment, the life of their master was a failure and a defeat. The crime was certainly greater in the bribers than in the bribed; for, the council was educated and religious; the soldiers were untutored and simple. The Resurrection of Christ was officially proclaimed to the civil authorities; the Sanhedrin believed in the Resurrection before the Apostles. It had bought the kiss of Judas; now it hoped it could buy the silence of the guards.

by night and stole him away while we were asleep.' [14] If this comes to the governor's ears, we will satisfy him and keep you out of trouble." [15] So they took the money and did as they were directed. And this story is still told among the Jews to this day.

THE COMMISSIONING OF THE DISCIPLES

[16] Now the eleven disciples went to Galilee, to the mountain to which Jesus had directed them. [17] When they saw him, they worshiped him; but some doubted. [18] And Jesus came and said to them, "All authority in heaven and on earth has been given to me. [19] Go therefore and make disciples of all nations, baptizing them in the name of the Father and of the Son and of the Holy Spirit, [20] and teaching them to obey everything that I have commanded you. And remember, I am with you always, to the end of the age."

Walking the Way of Holiness

Matthew 28:19–20 | Bishop Barron

Matthew brings his Gospel to completion with Jesus' great commission. This passage tells us that there is Another who will tie us up and take us where we never imagined we could or would go (John 21:18); there is a Power that is operative in us and accompanies us whether we know it or not and that will accomplish what we, by our own power, could never accomplish (Eph. 3:20). To allow ourselves to be tied up and taken, to surrender to the greater authority, is to walk the most dramatic of the ways of holiness: coming to terms with the fact that our lives are not about us. When we do, we are then sent to do the work of Jesus.

HE IS NOT HERE;

for HE HAS

BEEN RAISED,

AS HE SAID.

MATTHEW 28:6

GIULIO BONASONE | *1561*

The Resurrection

Essay by Michael Stevens

In this masterfully crafted etching by Giulio Bonasone, the pivotal scene in salvation history is portrayed with stunning power and clarity. We feel the energy and significance of this moment, and sense the fear in the eyes of the tomb guards who cower in terror before the risen, victorious Christ. Jesus stands in a halo of blinding light, and beneath his feet are the powers of darkness: his tomb, which is trampled underfoot, and his foes, who are thrown down to the ground.

Giulio Bonasone was famous for his single-color etched copies of famous full-color paintings of the Italian masters, and most of his work is, like this example, black and white. The process of translating full color painted images into black and white etched prints was no easy task, and forced the artist to rely on intricate linework alone to render the subtleties of colorful frescoes and vivid panel paintings. What is intriguing about this Resurrection piece, however, is that it is not a copy, but the artist's original composition. Here we see what Bonasone—steeped in the work of the masters—is capable of when given complete creative freedom.

Converging lines

Whether intentionally or not, the artist's use of converging, radial lines create a composition that parallels a theological reality: that Jesus' Resurrection is at the center of everything, and that all other aspects of Christian life flow from and return to this singular claim.

Christ's sarcophagus

Christ is shown standing in triumph over his burial sarcophagus in the ultimate posture of victory. In his right hand he is waving a banner high overhead, symbolizing his triumph over evil once and for all.

Inscription at lower right

Bonasone became famous for his etched copies of the Renaissance masters. However, in this piece, Bonasone has inscribed I. BONASONE / IN.VENTOR at the bottom right. This signifies that this print is not a copy of another artist's work but is indeed his own original design.

THE GOSPEL
ACCORDING
to MARK

Introduction to the Gospel of Mark

Rev. Stephen Grunow

IN THE FOURTH CHAPTER of the Gospel of Mark there is testimony to an incident that provoked awe and fear in the followers of Jesus—an incident that reveals how to best approach reading, and understanding, this Gospel. In the course of their travels, Christ and his disciples are making their way in a boat when a storm overtakes them. Fearing for their lives, the disciples wake up Jesus (who is, inexplicably, asleep during all the turmoil). Christ rises from his slumber and commands the winds to cease and the sea to be calm—and, much to the amazement and fear of his companions, this is precisely what happens!

This memorable vignette that is placed near to the beginning of the Gospel of Mark indicates that Jesus is much more than who he appears to be. It raises the question, even to his followers: Who is this Jesus? The incident also shows that Jesus will position our answers rather than be positioned by them. The one whom the winds and the seas obey will resist our categories of understanding. And yet Mark's Gospel will also present the category through which we can come to understand the mystery of Christ's identity, and that category is God—and not just any divinity of our choosing, but the God of the Israelites.

The incident of Jesus commanding and calming the wind and the sea is but one occasion in the Gospel of Mark where he speaks and acts in the person of the God of Israel. Testimony to this particular event evokes the opening of the Old Testament book of Genesis, which describes the God of Israel presiding over the primordial watery abyss, and through his command—that is, through his Word—manifesting his power to create. The similarity between the description of the God of Israel in the book of Genesis and the account of Christ acting to command the wind and the waves likely would not have been missed by those Israelites who heard this account from Mark's Gospel, and it would likely have provoked the same amazement and fear experienced by the disciples of the Lord Jesus. The claim being made about Jesus is extraordinary and upsetting, and Mark intends that we understand this and what is at stake.

As such, the testimony of Mark is testimony about the God who, in Christ, has done something shocking, something that he should not be able or willing to do: God has revealed himself in the particularity of an individual man named Jesus, a revelation that the Church would come to articulate as the Incarnation. This revelation happens in history, situated in a particular place and particular time and witnessed by particular people who shared their experience of this revelation with others. The witnesses to this revelation are convinced that God is not just manifesting his presence and power in the words of Jesus in the manner of a prophet, but is appearing in person, meeting humanity face to face. This is Mark's answer to the question of Christ's mysterious identity, and it is the answer indicated time and time again in the Gospel as Jesus speaks and acts.

The other question explored in the text is why God presents himself in such an unexpected way. The answer to this question can be discerned in the many occasions in which God, in Christ, places himself in situations of opposition or in circumstances that are deeply troubling. Embedded in a volatile political and religious environment; surrounded by potential enemies; immersed in the midst of a humanity afflicted by illness, ignorance, and death; opposed by fallen spiritual powers—in all this, Jesus makes his way in the world. God has entered into his creation because things have gone terribly wrong, and it is this state of affairs that helps us to understand what necessitated God's extraordinary intervention. God, in Christ, has come to set right a world gone wrong. But how? What the Gospel of Mark presents as Christ's mission is as mysterious as Christ's identity.

The worldly approach to the human predicament would be to attempt to fix things through our own self-striving, adjustments in political or economic realities, the reformation of religion, or advances in standards of living. Yet all these attempts have always had a mixed result, and our best efforts seem so easily undermined. The raw facts of being human and the oftentimes perilous state of the world are apparently intractable. Thus, when God reveals himself in Christ, he resists the reduction of his mission to fixing the world by using the very things that have brought us to such an impasse. God instead confronts the realities that are driving the world to the great unraveling of God's original purposes: sin, death, and the devil. These are the realities that bring us time and time again to the precipice of destruction and despair, subverting even the best among us, provoking the fear that leads to all manner of tyranny, and enticing us with promises that inevitably prove to be false and empty. It is these dark powers that God has come to expose and undermine, and in doing so, signal their ultimate defeat.

Christ's confrontation with sin, death, and the devil will reach its stark culmination when God seemingly places himself in their clutches and apparently succumbs to their power. Yet Mark insists this is precisely what Christ has come to do, and represents the undoing of the very powers that insist they have defeated him. It is this stunning reversal of our expectations that is meant to leave the reader of Mark amazed and afraid, compelled to tease out the personal implications of such a strange and off-putting revelation.

In the end, Mark wants us to understand that we are situated vis-à-vis Christ in the same manner as Christ's disciples when faced with a storm at sea. We will inevitably find ourselves calling out to the one who has placed himself in the midst of the howling winds and ferocious waves that beset so much of human experience. These winds and waves are not merely meteorological phenomena, but are ingredient to our experience of being frail and finite in a fallen world. We long for the rescue that only comes from the one whom the winds and the seas obey. And this one does not remain nameless and unknown to us; it is Jesus, the God of Israel, who is the one, true God.

Rev. Stephen Grunow is the CEO of Word on Fire Catholic Ministries.

WHO THEN IS THIS,
THAT EVEN THE
WIND AND THE SEA
OBEY HIM?

—— MARK 4:41 ——

THE PROCLAMATION OF JOHN THE BAPTIST

1 The beginning of the good news of Jesus Christ, the Son of God.
² As it is written in the prophet Isaiah,

> *"See, I am sending my messenger ahead of you,*
> *who will prepare your way;*
> ³ *the voice of one crying out in the wilderness:*
> *'Prepare the way of the Lord,*
> *make his paths straight,'"*

Fighting Words

Mark 1:1 | Bishop Barron

The opening line of Mark's Gospel—"The beginning of the good news of Jesus Christ, the Son of God"—can sound anodyne and harmlessly pious to us, but in the first century, those were fighting words.

Mark's Greek term, *euangelion*, which we render as "good news," was a word that was typically used to describe an imperial victory. When the emperor won a battle or quelled a rebellion, he sent evangelists ahead with the good news.

Do you see now how subversive Mark's words were? He was writing from Rome, from the belly of the beast, from the heart of the empire whose leaders had killed his friends Peter and Paul just a few years before, and he was declaring that the true victory didn't have a thing to do with Caesar, but rather with someone whom Caesar had put to death and whom God raised up.

And just to rub it in, he refers to this resurrected Lord as "Son of God." Ever since the time of Augustus, "Son of God" was a title claimed by the Roman emperor.

Not so, says Mark. The authentic Son of God is the one who is more powerful than Caesar. The opening line of the Gospel of Mark is a direct challenge to Rome: Jesus Christ, not Caesar or any of his descendants, is Lord. Jesus Christ, the God-man risen from the dead, the one who gathered the tribes, cleansed the temple, and fought with the enemies of the human race—he is the one to whom final allegiance is due.

The fact that this story is *news* indicates that we are not to look under, around, or over it in order to get the point. Rather, the story itself—the narrative of Jesus as the Christ, in all of its peculiarity, surprise, and novelty—is the point.

[4] John the baptizer appeared in the wilderness, proclaiming a baptism of repentance for the forgiveness of sins. [5] And people from the whole Judean countryside and all the people of Jerusalem were going out to him, and were baptized by him in the river Jordan, confessing their sins. [6] Now John was clothed with camel's hair, with a leather belt around his waist, and he ate locusts and wild honey. [7] He proclaimed, "The one who is more powerful than I is coming after me; I am not worthy to stoop down and untie the thong of his sandals. [8] I have baptized you with water; but he will baptize you with the Holy Spirit."

THE BAPTISM OF JESUS

[9] In those days Jesus came from Nazareth of Galilee and was baptized by John in the Jordan. [10] And just as he was coming up out of the water, he saw the heavens torn apart and the Spirit descending like a dove on him. [11] And a voice came from heaven, "You are my Son, the Beloved; with you I am well pleased."

THE TEMPTATION OF JESUS

[12] And the Spirit immediately drove him out into the wilderness. [13] He was in the wilderness forty days, tempted by Satan; and he was with the wild beasts; and the angels waited on him.

Joining Our Sinfulness

Mark 1:9–11 | Bishop Barron

The first thing we must keep in mind about the baptism of Jesus was that it was embarrassing. The first Christians maintained that this was the Son of God, the sinless Lamb who takes away the sins of the world, the Word made flesh. So why is he seeking a baptism of repentance?

John the Baptist was working in the country north of Jerusalem, along the banks of the Jordan River, and his theme was unambiguous: repent. Those who came to him were coming to have their sins dealt with; they were admitting their guilt. So why Jesus?

As is usually the case with the Bible, there is an irony in the fire. Before ever a word passes Jesus' lips, he is teaching, in fact communicating the heart of the faith, by this stunning reversal. In this gesture, God lays aside his glory and humbly joins us in our sinfulness, standing with us, assuming our burden, even if he himself had no sin.

MARTIN SCHONGAUER | *c. 1490*

The Four Evangelists

Essay by Michael Stevens

This engraving by Gothic printmaker and painter Martin Schongauer depicts the traditional symbols of the four Gospel writers. This arrangement of creatures, known as the Tetramorph, recurs across the tradition of Christian art and is associated with the reading and writing of the four Gospels—often adorning the pages of illuminated manuscripts.

In the Tetramorph, Matthew is represented by a man, Mark by a lion, Luke by an ox, and John by an eagle. They are based on the four creatures described first in Ezekiel 1, and again in Revelation 4. Although these scriptural passages do not explicitly identify them as representations of the Gospel writers, ancient Christians began to associate these creatures with the four Evangelists as early as the second century.

Matthew

St. Jerome offers the most succinct rationale for the symbolism behind each evangelist's creature by linking each to the opening passage of its corresponding Gospel. In his model, the man represents Matthew because his Gospel begins with the genealogy of Christ: a device that emphasizes Jesus' humanity.

Mark

St. Jerome's scheme identifies the lion as Mark, comparing its opening passage—John the Baptist's urgent proclamation in the desert—to the roar of a wild lion.

Luke

In St. Jerome's analysis, the ox symbolizes Luke, whose Gospel narrative begins with the story of the temple priest Zechariah. Through this lens, the ox represents the sacrificial animals that were associated with priestly duties.

John

St. Jerome links the eagle to John's Gospel, which begins by "flying upward" to the heights of the theological realm in its spectacular prologue: "In the beginning was the Word…"

St. Gregory of Nazianzus
(329–390)

Orations

The Paradoxes of Christ

Mark 1:9–13

He was baptized as man, but he remitted sins as God—not because he needed purifying rites himself, but that he might sanctify the element of water. He was tempted as man, but he conquered as God.... He hungered, but he fed thousands.... He thirsted, but he cried, "Let anyone who is thirsty come to me" (John 7:37).... He was wearied, but he is the rest of them that are weary and heavy laden.... He prays, but he hears prayer.

THE BEGINNING OF THE GALILEAN MINISTRY

[14] Now after John was arrested, Jesus came to Galilee, proclaiming the good news of God, [15] and saying, "The time is fulfilled, and the kingdom of God has come near; repent, and believe in the good news."

JESUS CALLS THE FIRST DISCIPLES

[16] As Jesus passed along the Sea of Galilee, he saw Simon and his brother Andrew casting a net into the sea—for they were fishermen. [17] And Jesus said to them, "Follow me and I will make you fish for people." [18] And immediately they left their nets and followed him. [19] As he went a little farther, he saw James son of Zebedee and his brother John, who were in their boat mending the nets. [20] Immediately he called them; and they left their father Zebedee in the boat with the hired men, and followed him.

THE MAN WITH AN UNCLEAN SPIRIT

[21] They went to Capernaum; and when the sabbath came, he entered the synagogue and taught. [22] They were astounded at his teaching, for he taught them as one having authority, and not as the scribes. [23] Just then there was in their synagogue a man with an unclean spirit, [24] and he cried out, "What have you to do with us, Jesus of Nazareth? Have you come to destroy us? I know who you are, the Holy One of God." [25] But Jesus rebuked him, saying, "Be silent, and come out of him!" [26] And the unclean spirit, convulsing him and crying with a loud voice, came out of him. [27] They were all amazed, and they kept on asking one another, "What is this? A new teaching—with authority! He commands even the unclean spirits, and they obey him." [28] At once his fame began to spread throughout the surrounding region of Galilee.

A New Way of Seeing

Mark 1:14–15 | Bishop Barron

CHRISTIANITY IS, above all, a way of *seeing*. Everything else in Christian life flows from and circles around the transformation of vision. Christians see differently, and that is why their prayer, their worship, their action, their whole way of being in the world have a distinctive accent and flavor. What united figures as diverse as James Joyce, Caravaggio, John Milton, the architect of Chartres, Dorothy Day, Dietrich Bonhoeffer, and the later Bob Dylan is a peculiar and distinctive take on things, a style, a way, which flow finally from Jesus of Nazareth.

But what is it that Christians see, and how do they come to see it? What is the "mystical" sense that stands stubbornly at the heart of all Christian experience? This passage from the earliest Gospel, that of Mark, can help us answer these questions.

After his baptism and temptation in the desert, Jesus goes into Galilee and begins to preach. The first words out of his mouth, as Mark reports them, serve as a sort of summary statement of his life and work: "The time is fulfilled, and the kingdom of God has come near; repent, and believe in the good news."

The moment has arrived, the privileged time, the *kairos*; something that human beings have been longing for and striving after and hoping to see has appeared, and the time is now for a decision, for action. Jesus' very first words are a wake-up call, a warning bell in the night, a summons to attention. This is not the time to be asleep, not the time to be languishing in complacency and self-satisfaction, not the time for delaying tactics, for procrastination and second-guessing. In the Byzantine liturgy, we find the oft-repeated call to "be attentive," and in the Buddhist tradition, there is a great emphasis placed on wakefulness.

In the fiction of James Joyce, we often find that moments of spiritual insight are preceded by a great thunderclap, the cosmic alarm shocking the characters (and the reader) into wide-awakeness. The initial words of Jesus' first sermon are a similar invitation to psychological and spiritual awareness: there is something to be seen, so open your eyes!

But what is it that he wants us to notice? What is this astonishing state of affairs that must not be missed? "The kingdom of God has come near." Now, there have been libraries of books written on the subject of the "kingdom," some suggesting that it refers to a political realignment of Jewish society, others that it signals a purely spiritual condition beyond the world, still others that it points to a change of heart in the individual. To my mind, the metaphor of the kingdom, in its poetic richness, is legitimately open to all of those interpretations, but it has a primary referent in the person of *Jesus himself*. Jesus wants us to open our eyes and see *him*—more to the point, to see what God is doing in and through him. He himself *is* the kingdom of God coming into the world with transformative power.

In Jesus of Nazareth, the divine and human have come together in a salvific way, and this reconciliation is the long-awaited kingdom of God. Though there are many themes that run through the Hebrew Scriptures, there is one motif that is consistent and persistent: the passionate and aching desire for deliverance, the cry of the heart toward the God from whom the people feel alienated. If only the power of rebellion and sin were ended and the friendship of God and human beings reestablished, peace, *shalom*, all-pervasive well-being would reign. What Jesus announces in his first sermon in the hills of Galilee, and what he demonstrates throughout his life and ministry, is that this wild desire of his ancestors, this hope against hope, this intimate union of God and humanity, is an accomplished fact, something that can be seen and heard and touched.

We have been summoned to attentiveness, and we have heard the word announcing the coming together of the divine and human. But what is it that enables us truly to hear and respond? How can we see the light that has been so unexpectedly and suddenly turned on? Again we consult Jesus' opening speech in Mark's Gospel: "Repent." The word so often and so misleadingly translated as "repent" is *metanoeite*. This Greek term is based upon two words, *meta* (beyond) and *nous* (mind or spirit), and thus, in its most basic form, it means something like "go beyond the mind that you have." The English word "repent" has a moralizing overtone, suggesting a change in behavior or action, whereas Jesus' term seems to be hinting at a change at a far more fundamental level of one's being. Jesus urges his listeners to change their way of knowing, their way of perceiving and grasping reality, their perspective, their mode of seeing. What Jesus implies is this: the new state of affairs has arrived, the divine and human have met, but the way you customarily see is going to blind you to this novelty. In the Gnostic Gospel of Thomas, Jesus expresses the same concern: "The kingdom of God is spread out on the earth, *but people do not see it.*" Minds, eyes, ears, senses, perceptions—all have to be opened up, turned around, revitalized. *Metanoia*, soul transformation, is Jesus' first recommendation.

Word Study

μετάνοια

METANOIA

Noun
Change of mind or purpose

But what exactly is the problem with the way we think and see? To give an adequate answer to that question we would have to work our way through the whole of the Bible and the Christian tradition, for the attempt to name and heal spiritual blindness is one of the most basic motifs of our religion. But perhaps a simple answer can be given in these terms: we see and know and perceive with a mind of fear rather than a mind of trust. When we fear, we cling to who we are and what we have; when we are afraid, we see ourselves as the threatened center of a hostile universe, and thus we violently defend ourselves and lash out at potential adversaries. And fear—according to so many of the biblical authors and so many of the mystics and theologians of our tradition—is a function of living our lives at the surface level, a result of forgetting our deepest identity. At the root and ground of our being, at the "center" of who we are, there is what Christianity calls "the image and likeness of God." This means that at the foundation of our existence, we are one with the divine power that continually creates and sustains the universe; we are held and cherished by the infinite love of God. When we rest in this center and realize its power, we know that, in an ultimate sense, we are safe, or in more classical religious language, "saved." And therefore we can let go of fear and begin to live in radical trust. But when we lose sight of this rootedness in God, we live exclusively on the tiny island of the ego, and our lives become dominated by fear. Fear is the "original sin" of which the Church Fathers speak; fear is the poison that was injected into human consciousness and human society from the beginning; fear is the debilitating and life-denying element that upsets the "chemical balance" of both psyche and society.

To overcome fear is to move from the *pusilla anima* (the small soul) to the *magna anima* (the great soul). When we are dominated by our egos, we live in a very narrow space, in the *angustiae* (the straits) between this fear and that, between this attachment and that. But when we surrender in trust to the bearing power of God, our souls become great, roomy, expansive. We realize that we are connected to all things and to the creative energy of the whole cosmos. Interestingly, the term *magna anima* shares a Sanskrit root with the word *mahatma*, and both mean "great soul." What Jesus calls for in *metanoia* is the transformation from the terrified and self-regarding small soul to the confident and soaring great soul. The seeing of the kingdom, in short, is not for the pusillanimous but for the magnanimous.

So far, Jesus' programmatic opening homily reveals the following: open your eyes; see the coming together of the divine and the human; learn to live in the power of that Incarnation (the kingdom) through *metanoia*, through the changing of your attitude, your orientation, your way of seeing. But Jesus' great speech does not end with the call to *metanoia*; rather, it explicitly names the state of being in the kingdom of God, the goal and end point of the change of heart: "Believe in the good news." Now, like the word *metanoiete*, the term *pisteute* (believe) has been terribly misunderstood over the centuries, coming, unfortunately, to mean the dry assent to religious propositions for which there is little or no evidence. Since the Enlightenment and its altogether legitimate insistence on rational responsibility, faith, in the sense just described, has come into disrepute. It seems to be the last refuge of uncritical people, those desperate to find some assurance with regard to the ultimate things and thus willing to swallow even the most far-fetched theories and beliefs. Happily, "belief" in the biblical and traditional sense of the term has nothing to do with this truncated and irresponsible rationality. "To believe," as Jesus uses the term, signals not so much a way of knowing as a way of *being known*. To have faith is to allow oneself to be overwhelmed by the power of God, to permit the divine energy to reign at all levels of one's being. As such, it is not primarily a matter of understanding and assenting to propositions as it is surrendering to the God who wants to become incarnate in us. In Paul Tillich's language, "faith" is being grasped by ultimate concern, permitting oneself to be shaken and turned by the in-breaking of God.

Hence when Jesus urges his listeners to believe, he is inviting them, not so much to adhere to a new set of propositions, but rather to let go of the dominating and fearful ego and learn once more to live in the confidence of the *magna anima*. He is calling them to find the new center of their lives where *he finds his own*, in the unconditional love of God. One of the tragic ironies of the tradition is that Jesus' "faith," interpreted along rationalist lines, serves only to boost up the ego, confirming it in its grasping and its fear: "I *have* the faith, and you don't"; or "Do I *really* understand the statements I claim to believe?" The state of mind designed to quell the ego has been, more often than not, transformed into one more ego game. "Believe in the good news" has nothing to do with these games of the mind. It has everything to do with radical change of life and vision, with the simple (and dreadfully complex) process of allowing oneself to swim in the divine sea, to find the true self by letting go of the old center.

JESUS HEALS MANY AT SIMON'S HOUSE

²⁹ As soon as they left the synagogue, they entered the house of Simon and Andrew, with James and John. ³⁰ Now Simon's mother-in-law was in bed with a fever, and they told him about her at once. ³¹ He came and took her by the hand and lifted her up. Then the fever left her, and she began to serve them.

³² That evening, at sundown, they brought to him all who were sick or possessed with demons. ³³ And the whole city was gathered around the door. ³⁴ And he cured many who were sick with various diseases, and cast out many demons; and he would not permit the demons to speak, because they knew him.

A PREACHING TOUR IN GALILEE

³⁵ In the morning, while it was still very dark, he got up and went out to a deserted place, and there he prayed. ³⁶ And Simon and his companions hunted for him. ³⁷ When they found him, they said to him, "Everyone is searching for you." ³⁸ He answered, "Let us go on to the neighboring towns, so that I may proclaim the message there also; for that is what I came out to do." ³⁹ And he went throughout Galilee, proclaiming the message in their synagogues and casting out demons.

JESUS CLEANSES A LEPER

⁴⁰ A leper came to him begging him, and kneeling he said to him, "If you choose, you can make me clean." ⁴¹ Moved with pity, Jesus stretched out his hand and touched him, and said to him, "I do choose. Be made clean!" ⁴² Immediately the leprosy left him, and he was made clean. ⁴³ After sternly

---

Restored to Health and Worship

Mark 1:40–45 | Bishop Barron

Leprosy frightened people in ancient times—as contagious and mysterious diseases frighten people up through modern times. But more than this, leprosy rendered someone unclean and therefore incapable of engaging in the act of worship. It is not accidental that a priest would be the one to examine someone suffering from leprosy.

The man who knelt before Jesus and begged for a cure was not simply concerned about his medical condition; he was an Israelite in exile from the temple—and hence he was a very apt symbol of the general condition of scattered, exiled, wandering Israel. In curing him, Jesus was, symbolically speaking, gathering the tribes and bringing them back to the worship of the true God.

warning him he sent him away at once, ⁴⁴ saying to him, "See that you say nothing to anyone; but go, show yourself to the priest, and offer for your cleansing what Moses commanded, as a testimony to them." ⁴⁵But he went out and began to proclaim it freely, and to spread the word, so that Jesus could no longer go into a town openly, but stayed out in the country; and people came to him from every quarter.

JESUS HEALS A PARALYTIC

2 When he returned to Capernaum after some days, it was reported that he was at home. ² So many gathered around that there was no longer room for them, not even in front of the door; and he was speaking the word to them. ³ Then some people came, bringing to him a paralyzed man, carried by four of them. ⁴ And when they could not bring him to Jesus because of the crowd, they removed the roof above him; and after having dug through it, they let down the mat on which the paralytic lay. ⁵ When Jesus saw their faith, he said to the paralytic, "Son, your sins are forgiven." ⁶ Now some of the scribes were sitting there, questioning in their hearts, ⁷ "Why does this fellow speak in this way? It is blasphemy! Who can forgive sins but God alone?" ⁸ At once Jesus perceived in his spirit that they were discussing these questions among themselves; and he said to them, "Why do you raise such questions in your hearts? ⁹ Which is easier, to say to the paralytic, 'Your sins are forgiven,' or to say, 'Stand up and take your mat and walk'? ¹⁰ But so that you may know that the Son of Man has authority

St. Irenaeus
(130–202)
———
Against Heresies

Why Jesus Could Forgive Sin
Mark 2:5–7

The Word rightly says to man, "Your sins are forgiven"; he, being the same we sinned against in the beginning, grants forgiveness of sins in the end. If we had disobeyed the command of any other, and some different being were to say, "Your sins are forgiven," he would be neither good, nor true, nor just. For how could he be good, who presumes to give from what does not belong to himself? Or how can he be just, who snatches away the goods of another?

How Do We Truly Forgive?

Mark 2:7 | Bishop Barron

Forgiveness is one of the most vital and most misunderstood practices of the Christian path. Its importance should be obvious from the Gospels themselves, where it is centrally featured in both the preaching and praxis of Jesus. The forgiveness even of enemies is insisted upon in the Sermon on the Mount, and the pardoning of those who trespass against us is at the heart of the prayer that Jesus taught his Church. But more to the point, Jesus' own startling practice of forgiving the sins of others emerges as one of the distinctive and most controversial elements in his ministry: "Why does this fellow speak in this way? It is blasphemy! Who can forgive sins but God alone?" And both rhetoric and practice reach their fullest expression when the crucified Jesus asks the Father to forgive those who are torturing him to death, and when the risen Jesus says "Shalom" to those who had abandoned him. We speak the truth because Jesus is the Truth; we forgive because he forgave.

But what exactly is forgiveness? We must not, despite our typically modern tendency to do so, subjectivize and interiorize forgiveness, as though it amounted to little more than a conviction or a resolution. To say, "I have put that offense out of my mind and have resolved to move on" is not forgiveness; even to feel no further anger at someone who has hurt me and to refrain from harming that person is not tantamount to real forgiveness. Forgiveness, in the full New Testament sense of the term, is an act and not an attitude. It is the active and embodied repairing of a broken relationship, even in the face of opposition, violence, or indifference. When a relationship is severed, each party should, in justice, do his part to reestablish the bond. Forgiveness— which of necessity transcends justice—is the bearing of the other person's burden, moving toward her, even when she refuses to move an inch toward you. There is something relentless, even aggressive, about forgiveness, since it amounts to a refusal ever to give up on a relationship.

---

on earth to forgive sins"—he said to the paralytic—¹¹"I say to you, stand up, take your mat and go to your home." ¹²And he stood up, and immediately took the mat and went out before all of them; so that they were all amazed and glorified God, saying, "We have never seen anything like this!"

JESUS CALLS LEVI

¹³ Jesus went out again beside the sea; the whole crowd gathered around him, and he taught them. ¹⁴ As he was walking along, he saw Levi son of

Alphaeus sitting at the tax booth, and he said to him, "Follow me." And he got up and followed him.

¹⁵ And as he sat at dinner in Levi's house, many tax collectors and sinners were also sitting with Jesus and his disciples—for there were many who followed him. ¹⁶ When the scribes of the Pharisees saw that he was eating with sinners and tax collectors, they said to his disciples, "Why does he eat with tax collectors and sinners?" ¹⁷ When Jesus heard this, he said to them, "Those who are well have no need of a physician, but those who are sick; I have come to call not the righteous but sinners."

THE QUESTION ABOUT FASTING

¹⁸ Now John's disciples and the Pharisees were fasting; and people came and said to him, "Why do John's disciples and the disciples of the Pharisees fast, but your disciples do not fast?" ¹⁹ Jesus said to them, "The wedding guests cannot fast while the bridegroom is with them, can they? As long as they have the bridegroom with them, they cannot fast. ²⁰ The days will come when the bridegroom is taken away from them, and then they will fast on that day.

²¹ "No one sews a piece of unshrunk cloth on an old cloak; otherwise, the patch pulls away from it, the new from the old, and a worse tear is made.

Bread and Water at a Wedding?

Mark 2:18–22 | Bishop Barron

People came and said to Jesus, "Why do John's disciples and the disciples of the Pharisees fast, but your disciples do not fast?" Jesus' answer is wonderful: "The wedding guests cannot fast while the bridegroom is with them, can they?" (That's a typically Jewish style, by the way—answering a question with another question.)

This great image of the wedding feast comes up frequently in the New Testament, most obviously in the narrative of the wedding feast at Cana.

And it is echoed in the tradition. Jesus is the wedding of heaven and earth, the marriage of divinity and humanity; he is the Bridegroom and the Church is the Bride. In him, the most intimate union is achieved between God and the world.

Could you imagine people fasting at a wedding banquet? Could you imagine going into an elegant room with your fellow guests and being served bread and water? It would be ridiculous! So, says Jesus: "As long as they have the bridegroom with them, they cannot fast." The mark of the Christian dispensation is joy, exuberance, and delight. God and the world have come together. What could be better news?

²² And no one puts new wine into old wineskins; otherwise, the wine will burst the skins, and the wine is lost, and so are the skins; but one puts new wine into fresh wineskins."

PRONOUNCEMENT ABOUT THE SABBATH

²³ One sabbath he was going through the grainfields; and as they made their way his disciples began to pluck heads of grain. ²⁴ The Pharisees said to him, "Look, why are they doing what is not lawful on the sabbath?" ²⁵ And he said to them, "Have you never read what David did when he and his companions were hungry and in need of food? ²⁶ He entered the house of God, when Abiathar was high priest, and ate the bread of the Presence, which it is not lawful for any but the priests to eat, and he gave some to his companions." ²⁷ Then he said to them, "The sabbath was made for humankind, and not humankind for the sabbath; ²⁸ so the Son of Man is lord even of the sabbath."

THE MAN WITH A WITHERED HAND

3 Again he entered the synagogue, and a man was there who had a withered hand. ² They watched him to see whether he would cure him on the sabbath, so that they might accuse him. ³ And he said to the man who had the withered hand, "Come forward." ⁴ Then he said to them, "Is it lawful to do good or to do harm on the sabbath, to save life or to kill?" But they were silent. ⁵ He looked around at them with anger; he was grieved at their hardness of heart and said to the man, "Stretch out your hand." He stretched it out, and his hand was restored. ⁶ The Pharisees went out and immediately conspired with the Herodians against him, how to destroy him.

A MULTITUDE AT THE SEASIDE

⁷ Jesus departed with his disciples to the sea, and a great multitude from Galilee followed him; ⁸ hearing all that he was doing, they came to him in great numbers from Judea, Jerusalem, Idumea, beyond the Jordan, and the region around Tyre and Sidon. ⁹ He told his disciples to have a boat ready for him because of the crowd, so that they would not crush him; ¹⁰ for he had cured many, so that all who had diseases pressed upon him to touch him. ¹¹ Whenever the unclean spirits saw him, they fell down before him and shouted, "You are the Son of God!" ¹² But he sternly ordered them not to make him known.

JESUS APPOINTS THE TWELVE

¹³ He went up the mountain and called to him those whom he wanted, and they came to him. ¹⁴ And he appointed twelve, whom he also named apostles, to be with him, and to be sent out to proclaim the message,

Healing Sin-Sick Souls

Mark 3:7–12 | Bishop Barron

Crowds come to Jesus for healing and deliverance from unclean spirits. We hear that people brought the sick from all over the region, as well as those troubled by unclean spirits—and all of them were cured.

Now, I realize that we today might be a bit skeptical of such miraculous healings. But it's hard to deny that Jesus was known as a healer and a miracle worker. And there is abundant evidence that the performance of miracles was a major reason why the first preachers were taken seriously.

Have there been miracle workers and miraculous places up and down the centuries? Yes indeed. But the Church has customarily done this work through its hospitals and clinics, through figures such as John of God, Catherine of Siena, and Teresa of Kolkata. But the Church also serves through its sacraments, which heal sin-sick souls.

This is the apostolic dimension of the Church's life, and without it, it would no longer be the Church. Parishes, parish priests, missionaries, servants of the poor and sick—the whole apostolic life of the Church is represented here.

He Called Those Whom He Wanted

Mark 3:13 | Bishop Barron

St. Thérèse of Lisieux tells us that she endeavored to write down her spiritual memoir at the prompting of her sister, who was also her religious superior to whom she was bound in obedience. After praying that she say nothing displeasing to Christ, she took up the Gospel of Mark, and her eyes fell on these words: "He went up the mountain and called to him those whom he wanted, and they came to him."

This verse, she says, is the interpretive key to her life, for it describes the way Christ has worked in her soul: "He does not call those who are worthy, but those whom he pleases." Hers was a story of a divine love, graciously willing the good of the other, that awakens an imitative reaction in the one who is loved. It is not a narrative of economic exchange— rewards for worthiness—but of the loop of grace, unmerited love engendering disinterested love, the divine life propagating itself in what is other.

Joseph Ratzinger (Pope Benedict XVI) (1927–)

Jesus of Nazareth: From the Baptism to the Transfiguration

You Cannot Make Yourself a Disciple

Mark 3:13

The calling of the disciples is a prayer event; it is as if they were begotten in prayer, in intimacy with the Father. The calling of the Twelve, far from being purely functional, takes on a deeply theological meaning: their calling emerges from the Son's dialogue with the Father and is anchored there. This is also the necessary starting point for understanding Jesus' words, "Ask the Lord of the harvest to send out laborers into his harvest" (Matt. 9:38).

We cannot simply pick the laborers in God's harvest in the same way that an employer seeks his employees. God must always be asked for them and he himself must choose them for this service. This theological character is reinforced in Mark's phrase: "[Jesus] called to him those whom he wanted." You cannot make yourself a disciple—it is an event of election, a free decision of the Lord's will, which in its turn is anchored in his communion of will with the Father.

[15] and to have authority to cast out demons. [16] So he appointed the twelve: Simon (to whom he gave the name Peter); [17] James son of Zebedee and John the brother of James (to whom he gave the name Boanerges, that is, Sons of Thunder); [18] and Andrew, and Philip, and Bartholomew, and Matthew, and Thomas, and James son of Alphaeus, and Thaddaeus, and Simon the Cananaean, [19] and Judas Iscariot, who betrayed him.

JESUS AND BEELZEBUL

Then he went home; [20] and the crowd came together again, so that they could not even eat. [21] When his family heard it, they went out to restrain him, for people were saying, "He has gone out of his mind." [22] And the scribes who came down from Jerusalem said, "He has Beelzebul, and by the ruler of the demons he casts out demons." ²³ And he called them to him, and spoke to them in parables, "How can Satan cast out Satan? ²⁴ If a kingdom is divided against itself, that kingdom cannot stand. ²⁵ And if a house is divided against itself, that house will not be able to stand. ²⁶ And if Satan has risen up against himself and is divided, he cannot stand, but his end has come. ²⁷ But no one can enter a strong man's house and plunder his property without first tying up the strong man; then indeed the house can be plundered.

²⁸ "Truly I tell you, people will be forgiven for their sins and whatever blasphemies they utter; ²⁹ but whoever blasphemes against the Holy Spirit can never have forgiveness, but is guilty of an eternal sin"—³⁰ for they had said, "He has an unclean spirit."

THE TRUE KINDRED OF JESUS

³¹ Then his mother and his brothers came; and standing outside, they sent to him and called him. ³² A crowd was sitting around him; and they said to him, "Your mother and your brothers and sisters are outside, asking for you." ³³ And he replied, "Who are my mother and my brothers?" ³⁴ And looking at those who sat around him, he said, "Here are my mother and my brothers! ³⁵ Whoever does the will of God is my brother and sister and mother."

St. Augustine
(354–430)

___

*Tractates on the
Gospel of John*

Brothers of Christ?

Mark 3:31

The Scripture must be understood as it speaks. It has its own language; one who does not know this language is perplexed and says, "How did the Lord have brothers? For surely Mary did not give birth a second time?" Far from it! With her begins the dignity of virgins.... How do we prove this? From Scripture itself. Lot is called Abraham's brother; he was his brother's son. Read, and you will find that Abraham was Lot's uncle on the father's side, and yet they are called brothers. Why, but because they were kinsmen? When you have known this rule, you will find that all the blood relations of Mary are the brothers of Christ.

THE PARABLE OF THE SOWER

4 Again he began to teach beside the sea. Such a very large crowd gathered around him that he got into a boat on the sea and sat there, while the whole crowd was beside the sea on the land. ² He began to teach them many things in parables, and in his teaching he said to them: ³ "Listen! A sower went out to sow. ⁴ And as he sowed, some seed fell on the path, and the birds came and ate it up. ⁵ Other seed fell on rocky ground, where it did not have much soil, and it sprang up quickly, since it had no depth of soil. ⁶ And when the sun rose, it was scorched; and since it had no root, it withered away. ⁷ Other seed fell among thorns, and the thorns grew up and choked it, and it yielded no grain. ⁸ Other seed fell into good soil and brought forth grain, growing up and increasing and yielding thirty and sixty and a hundredfold." ⁹ And he said, "Let anyone with ears to hear listen!"

THE PURPOSE OF THE PARABLES

¹⁰ When he was alone, those who were around him along with the twelve asked him about the parables. ¹¹ And he said to them, "To you has been given the secret of the kingdom of God, but for those outside, everything comes in parables; ¹² in order that

> 'they may indeed look, but not perceive,
> and may indeed listen, but not understand;
> so that they may not turn again and be forgiven.' "

¹³ And he said to them, "Do you not understand this parable? Then how will you understand all the parables? ¹⁴ The sower sows the word. ¹⁵ These are the ones on the path where the word is sown: when they hear, Satan immediately comes and takes away the word that is sown in them. ¹⁶ And these are the ones sown on rocky ground: when they hear the word, they immediately receive it with joy. ¹⁷ But they have no root, and endure only for a while; then, when trouble or persecution arises on account of the word, immediately they fall away. ¹⁸ And others are those sown among the thorns: these are the ones who hear the word, ¹⁹ but the cares of the world, and the lure of wealth, and the desire for other things come in and choke the word, and it yields nothing. ²⁰ And these are the ones sown on the good soil: they hear the word and accept it and bear fruit, thirty and sixty and a hundredfold."

A LAMP UNDER A BUSHEL BASKET

²¹ He said to them, "Is a lamp brought in to be put under the bushel basket, or under the bed, and not on the lampstand? ²² For there is nothing hidden, except to be disclosed; nor is anything secret, except to come to light.

Lighting Up Dark Corners

Mark 4:21–25 | Bishop Barron

Jesus said: "Is a lamp brought in to be put under the bushel basket, or under the bed, and not on the lampstand?" Well, light is wonderful in the measure that it illumines and brightens and delights. But light can also be disconcerting. Think of how bad most of us look in direct light! I much prefer the indirect light that you can produce indoors over the full glare of the sun, which reveals every flaw, imperfection, and peculiarity of your face.

Think of what happens when you suddenly shine a light into a dark corner in your basement or down a lonely alley. The bugs and the vermin reveal themselves. Unsavory things scurry about for cover, afraid of the light.

When you invite Jesus into your life, you are inviting the light into your life. Again, this is wonderful, but it is also frightening. Jesus will shine his light in every corner of your life, in every room of your house. Things that look presentable in the dark or in the indirect light will suddenly stand out in all of their unpleasantness.

Why God Starts Small

Mark 4:26–34 | Bishop Barron

The growth of God's kingdom is like the mustard seed, the smallest of all seeds, which springs up and becomes the largest of plants. It is a law of the spiritual life that God wants good things to start small and grow over time.

But why would God work the way he does? Well, it is a commonplace of the Bible that God rejoices in our cooperation. He wants us to participate, through freedom, intelligence, and creativity, in what he is doing. And so he plants seeds, and he wants us to cultivate them.

God told St. Francis of Assisi, in a vision, "Francis, rebuild my Church." Of course, God could have rebuilt his Church miraculously, in an instant, but he wanted Francis to get involved. Similarly, God could have renewed the spiritual life of Christianity in the third century through a great infusion of grace, but he inspired St. Anthony to leave everything behind and go live alone in the desert.

When things start small, they can fly under the radar while they gain strength and heft and seriousness. Also, those involved can be tested and tried. Suppose you want to do something great and you pray and God gives you massively what you want. You might not be ready, and your project will fizzle out. So be patient and embrace the small invitations.

²³ Let anyone with ears to hear listen!" ²⁴ And he said to them, "Pay attention to what you hear; the measure you give will be the measure you get, and still more will be given you. ²⁵ For to those who have, more will be given; and from those who have nothing, even what they have will be taken away."

THE PARABLE OF THE GROWING SEED

²⁶ He also said, "The kingdom of God is as if someone would scatter seed on the ground, ²⁷ and would sleep and rise night and day, and the seed would sprout and grow, he does not know how. ²⁸ The earth produces of itself, first

---

Seeing at a Deeper Level

Mark 4:35–41 | Bishop Barron

In this wonderful story of the calming of the storm at sea, we witness some of the spiritual dynamics of fear and trust. Making their way across the lake in their tiny boat, the disciples stand symbolically for all of us journeying through life within the confines of the fearful *pusilla anima* (small soul). When they confront the storm and the mighty waves, they are immediately filled with terror, convinced that they are going to drown. Similarly, when the trials and anxieties of life confront the ego, the first reaction is fear, since the ego is fundamentally persuaded that there is nothing "under" it or "behind" it, no power beyond itself upon which it can rely.

In the midst of this terrible *Sturm und Drang*, this inner and outer tension, Jesus, Mark tells us, is "asleep on the cushion"—that is, utterly at peace, centered, at rest. Jesus stands here for the divine power that is "asleep" within all of us, indeed within the very confines of the ego. He symbolizes that divine energy that remains unaffected by the fear-storms generated by the grasping ego.

Continuing to read the story at a spiritual level, we see that it is none other than this divine power that successfully stills the storm and calms the waves: "He woke up and rebuked the wind, and said to the sea, 'Peace! Be still!'"

This beautiful narrative seems to suggest that if we but awaken to the presence of Christ within us, if we learn to live and to see at a deeper level, if we live in basic trust rather than fear, then we can withstand even the most frightening storms. When, at the close of the story, Jesus asked the bewildered and exhausted disciples, "Why are you afraid? Have you still no faith?" he is wondering why they have not yet let go of the ego mind, the mind of fear, why they have not yet experienced the change of heart necessary for living in the kingdom of God.

the stalk, then the head, then the full grain in the head. ²⁹ But when the grain is ripe, at once he goes in with his sickle, because the harvest has come."

THE PARABLE OF THE MUSTARD SEED

³⁰ He also said, "With what can we compare the kingdom of God, or what parable will we use for it? ³¹ It is like a mustard seed, which, when sown upon the ground, is the smallest of all the seeds on earth; ³² yet when it is sown it grows up and becomes the greatest of all shrubs, and puts forth large branches, so that the birds of the air can make nests in its shade."

THE USE OF PARABLES

³³ With many such parables he spoke the word to them, as they were able to hear it; ³⁴ he did not speak to them except in parables, but he explained everything in private to his disciples.

JESUS STILLS A STORM

³⁵ On that day, when evening had come, he said to them, "Let us go across to the other side." ³⁶ And leaving the crowd behind, they took him with them in the boat, just as he was. Other boats were with him. ³⁷ A great windstorm arose, and the waves beat into the boat, so that the boat was already being swamped. ³⁸ But he was in the stern, asleep on the cushion, and they woke him up and said to him, "Teacher, do you not care that we are perishing?" ³⁹ He woke up and rebuked the wind, and said to the sea, "Peace! Be still!" Then the wind ceased, and there was a dead calm. ⁴⁰ He said to them, "Why are you afraid? Have you still no faith?" ⁴¹ And they were filled with great awe and said to one another, "Who then is this, that even the wind and the sea obey him?"

JESUS HEALS THE GERASENE DEMONIAC

5 They came to the other side of the sea, to the country of the Gerasenes. ² And when he had stepped out of the boat, immediately a man out of the tombs with an unclean spirit met him. ³ He lived among the tombs; and no one could restrain him any more, even with a chain; ⁴ for he had often been restrained with shackles and chains, but the chains he wrenched apart, and the shackles he broke in pieces; and no one had the strength to subdue him. ⁵ Night and day among the tombs and on the mountains he was always howling and bruising himself with stones. ⁶ When he saw Jesus from a distance, he ran and bowed down before him; ⁷ and he shouted at the top of his voice, "What have you to do with me, Jesus, Son of the Most High God? I adjure you by God, do not torment me." ⁸ For he had said to him, "Come out of the man, you unclean spirit!" ⁹ Then Jesus asked him, "What is your name?" He replied, "My name is Legion; for we are many." ¹⁰ He begged him earnestly not to send them out of the country. ¹¹ Now

there on the hillside a great herd of swine was feeding; [12] and the unclean spirits begged him, "Send us into the swine; let us enter them." [13] So he gave them permission. And the unclean spirits came out and entered the swine; and the herd, numbering about two thousand, rushed down the steep bank into the sea, and were drowned in the sea.

[14] The swineherds ran off and told it in the city and in the country. Then people came to see what it was that had happened. [15] They came to Jesus and saw the demoniac sitting there, clothed and in his right mind, the very man who had had the legion; and they were afraid. [16] Those who had seen what had happened to the demoniac and to the swine reported it. [17] Then they began to beg Jesus to leave their neighborhood. [18] As he was getting into the boat, the man who had been possessed by demons begged him that he might be with him. [19] But Jesus refused, and said to him, "Go home to your friends, and tell them how much the Lord has done for you, and what mercy he has shown you." [20] And he went away and began to proclaim in the Decapolis how much Jesus had done for him; and everyone was amazed.

Restoring the Scapegoat

Mark 5:1–20 | Bishop Barron

Jesus makes his way into the country of the Gerasenes and is confronted by another man with an unclean spirit, this one living among the tombs. Mark tells us that this unfortunate was chained and fettered, though he often broke these bonds, and that he spent his days howling among the tombs and bruising himself with rocks. Like the Capernaum demoniac he knows that Jesus represents a threat to his twisted *ordo*: "What have you to do with me, Jesus, Son of the Most High God? I adjure you by God, do not torment me." When Jesus asks his name, the man replies awfully: "My name is Legion; for we are many"—or, in another even more vivid rendering, "for there are hundreds

of us." This is a single person, but he speaks in the voice of the many, for the demonic consciousness is split, riven, uncentered. Like a tempest, it is all wind and confusion.

But there is something else at work here. One wonders why the man has been chained. Is it for his own protection or is it perhaps because someone wants to keep him there? Is this agonized and self-mutilating man, in a curious sense, serving a purpose? Is he there among the tombs on the outskirts of the town for a reason? Theorists as diverse as René Girard, Carl Jung, and Walter Wink have written persuasively on the theme of scapegoating violence. All three agree that scapegoats perform a decisively important function in the development and maintenance of human societies, effectively channeling away the rivalry, competition, fear, and violence that would otherwise tear a community apart. A certain strained peacefulness reigns when warring factions in a society can discharge the tension between them onto a scapegoat—usually a person or group that is already threatening in its otherness. Jung speaks in this context of "shadow projection," the tendency of individuals and collectives to project onto a convenient scapegoat all of those qualities that remain problematic and unintegrated in themselves. This discharges the negativity of the shadow but in a way that is, obviously, nonproductive to the projector and damaging to the scapegoat. Nevertheless, there is a short-term benefit to the process, and this explains the *necessity* of keeping the marginalized scapegoat, so to speak, within view. The one who neutralizes the unbearable tensions of a community is, to some degree, cast out, but he is also clung to desperately, since without him the group would revert to self-destructive violence.

Thus we find the psychologically and culturally complex scapegoating of Jews in Christian Europe and of African Americans in the United States. In each case the hated "other" effectively united the warring factions in the majority culture by providing them with a common enemy, and thus both Jews and African Americans were, while ostracized and persecuted, curiously admired, even lionized, by their persecutors. (Think here

of the wonderful and horrifying scene in *Schindler's List* where the Nazi camp commandant seeks intimacy with his Jewish housekeeper and then, moments later, savagely beats her.) The hated were, to be sure, on the margins, but they were prevented from wandering too far.

And thus is the Gerasene demoniac—precisely as a scapegoat—chained to keep him close? Can we not imagine the citizens of the town coming out to gawk at the poor soul, much as the children in *To Kill a Mockingbird* watched and taunted Boo Radley, their fearsome, fascinating bogeyman? In the context of this discussion, the tortured man's name takes on new resonance. He calls himself Legion for there are "many" in him. Could the many in question be each of the citizens of the town who have, to one degree or another, projected their shadows onto him? Could his name designate the crowd because it was the crowd, in its collective hatred and violence, who created him? René Girard makes the intriguing suggestion that the demoniac's bruising of himself with stones recalls the original stoning by which he was driven from the town by the mob. It is furthermore interesting that Jesus casts the legion of demons into a herd of pigs, since the pig was, for the Jews, unclean, a sort of scapegoated animal. Finally, we note what is, at first glance, the surprising reaction of the townspeople upon learning of the man's cure. Instead of rejoicing in his good fortune, they are disconcerted and beg Jesus to leave their region. In light of the reading we have been offering, this reaction is entirely understandable, for the last thing the Gerasenes want is the restoration to sanity and sociability of their scapegoat. Without him and his hatred-channeling role, the town might revert to the chaos of factional violence. Begging Jesus to leave the area is an indirect admission on their part that his intervention and presence have thrown off the subtle balance upon which the survival of the town depends.

The Gospel writers consistently reveal to us how impatient Jesus is with the demonic whenever he confronts it, whether on the personal or, in this case, on the societal level. The kingdom of God is opposed to the *pusilla anima* (small soul) and the proclamation of the kingdom disrupts and unveils the games, structures, social expressions, and strategies of that little mind. By curing the Gerasene demoniac, Jesus announces his intention to break the pattern of scapegoating, thus showing the people of the village a new way of being in community.

The Miracle Worker

Mark 5:1–20 | Bishop Barron

When he drove the unclean spirit from the Gerasene demoniac, we see Jesus the miracle worker on vivid display.

Modern thinkers tend to be wary of this dimension. For instance, Thomas Jefferson took a straight razor to the pages of the Gospels and cut out everything that smacked of the supernatural—miracles, exorcisms, and so on. The problem, of course, is that he had to make an absolute mess of Mark's Gospel, which is positively chock-a-block with such things.

Jefferson's contemporary, the great modern philosopher David Hume, wrote a powerfully influential text against miracles. He claimed that since the laws of nature were set, miracles were, strictly speaking, impossible. Accounts of them, he concluded, were the result of the foggy or wishful thinking of primitive people.

But though God typically lets the universe run according to its natural rhythms and patterns, what is to prevent God from shaping it and influencing it occasionally in remarkable ways, in order to signal his purpose and presence?

A GIRL RESTORED TO LIFE AND A WOMAN HEALED

[21] When Jesus had crossed again in the boat to the other side, a great crowd gathered around him; and he was by the sea. [22] Then one of the leaders of the synagogue named Jairus came and, when he saw him, fell at his feet [23] and begged him repeatedly, "My little daughter is at the point of death. Come and lay your hands on her, so that she may be made well, and live." [24] So he went with him.

And a large crowd followed him and pressed in on him. [25] Now there was a woman who had been suffering from hemorrhages for twelve years. [26] She had endured much under many physicians, and had spent all that she had; and she was no better, but rather grew worse. [27] She had heard about Jesus, and came up behind him in the crowd and touched his cloak, [28] for she said, "If I but touch his clothes, I will be made well." [29] Immediately her hemorrhage stopped; and she felt in her body that she was healed of her disease. [30] Immediately aware that power had gone forth from him, Jesus turned about in the crowd and said, "Who touched my clothes?" [31] And his disciples said to him, "You see the crowd pressing in on you; how can you say, 'Who touched me?'" [32] He looked all around to see who had done it. [33] But the woman, knowing what had happened to her, came in fear and trembling, fell down before him, and told him the whole truth. [34] He said to her, "Daughter, your faith has made you well; go in peace, and be healed of your disease."

[35] While he was still speaking, some people came from the leader's house to say, "Your daughter is dead. Why trouble the teacher any further?" [36] But overhearing what they said, Jesus said to the leader of the synagogue, "Do not fear, only believe." [37] He allowed no one to follow him except Peter, James, and John, the brother of James. [38] When they came to the house of the leader of the synagogue, he saw a commotion, people weeping and wailing loudly. [39] When he had entered, he said to them, "Why do you make a commotion and weep? The child is not dead but sleeping." [40] And they laughed at him. Then he put them all outside, and took the child's father and mother and those who were with him, and went in where the child was. [41] He took her by the hand and said to her, "Talitha cum," which means, "Little girl, get up!" [42] And immediately the girl got up and began to walk about (she was twelve years of age). At this they were overcome with amazement. [43] He strictly ordered them that no one should know this, and told them to give her something to eat.

Christ's halo

The halo adorning the head of Christ appears to glow against the stormy skies. With this detail, Pencz uses simple linework combined with the white of the page to create the impression of intense light.

Swirling waters

The swirling waters surrounding the boat appear to tumble and undulate with terrifying force, underscoring the cause of the disciples' distress.

The ship as a symbol of the Church

The Church is often symbolized by the image of a ship. This is because of the role the Church plays in guiding souls safely to the shores of heaven. While the image of a ship is typically invoked purely as an allegory, in this engraving we see the key figures of the early Church aboard a literal sea vessel.

Mark 4:35–41

GEORG PENCZ | *1534–1535*

Christ Sleeping During the Storm on Lake Tiberias

Essay by Michael Stevens

Georg Pencz was a German engraver and painter who worked in the atelier of the master Albrecht Dürer. He visited Italy early in his career, where he absorbed many of the stylistic features of Italian Renaissance painting—features that he then applied to his printmaking.

In this work—a print from a series known as *The Story of Christ*—the Apostles are shown in a boat on stormy waters, desperately rowing in an attempt to seize control of their vessel. In the midst of this chaos, Christ is shown fast asleep. The irony in this scene, though, is that Jesus is sleeping not because he is ignorant of the situation or apathetic, but rather because his supreme power over nature provides him with perfect peace of mind.

A Radical and Dangerous Healing

Mark 5:25–34 | Bishop Barron

A centerpiece of Mark 5 is Jesus healing the hemorrhaging woman. Having a flow of blood for twelve years meant that anyone with whom she came in contact would be considered unclean. She couldn't, in any meaningful sense, participate in the ordinary life of her society.

The woman touches Jesus—and how radical and dangerous an act this was, since it should have rendered Jesus unclean. But so great is her faith that her touch, instead, renders *her* clean.

Jesus effectively restores her to full participation in her community.

But what is perhaps most important is this: Jesus implicitly puts an end to the ritual code of the book of Leviticus. What he implies is that the identity of the new Israel, the Church, would not be through ritual behaviors but through imitation of him. Notice how central this is in the New Testament. We hear elsewhere in the Gospels that Jesus declares all foods clean, and throughout the letters of Paul we hear a steady polemic against the Law. All of this is meant to show that Jesus is at the center of the new community.

THE REJECTION OF JESUS AT NAZARETH

6 He left that place and came to his hometown, and his disciples followed him. ² On the sabbath he began to teach in the synagogue, and many who heard him were astounded. They said, "Where did this man get all this? What is this wisdom that has been given to him? What deeds of power are being done by his hands! ³ Is not this the carpenter, the son of Mary and brother of James and Joses and Judas and Simon, and are not his sisters here with us?" And they took offense at him. ⁴ Then Jesus said to them, "Prophets are not without honor, except in their hometown, and among their own kin, and in their own house." ⁵ And he could do no deed of power there, except that he laid his hands on a few sick people and cured them. ⁶ And he was amazed at their unbelief.

THE MISSION OF THE TWELVE

Then he went about among the villages teaching. ⁷ He called the twelve and began to send them out two by two, and gave them authority over the unclean spirits. ⁸ He ordered them to take nothing for their journey except a staff; no bread, no bag, no money in their belts; ⁹ but to wear sandals and not to put on two tunics. ¹⁰ He said to them, "Wherever you enter a house, stay there until you leave the place. ¹¹ If any place will not welcome you

St. Justin Martyr
(100–165)

Dialogue with Trypho

You Are My Son

Mark 6:3

When Jesus came to the Jordan, he was thought to be simply the son of Joseph the carpenter … and was deemed a carpenter himself (for he was in the habit of working as a carpenter when among men, making ploughs and yokes by which he taught the symbols of righteousness and an active life); but then the Holy Spirit, for man's sake, lighted on him in the form of a dove, and there came from the heavens a voice: "You are my Son" (Mark 1:11).

Battling the Devil

Mark 6:6–13 | Bishop Barron

In this passage from Mark's Gospel, we find the account of Jesus sending out the Twelve, two by two, on mission. The first thing he gave them, Mark tells us, was "authority over the unclean spirits." And the first pastoral act that they performed was to "cast out many demons."

In the 1960s and 1970s, it was common, even in seminaries, to dismiss such talk as primitive superstition—or perhaps to modernize it and make it a literary device, using symbolic language evocative of the struggle with evil in the abstract. But the problem with that approach is that it just does not do justice to the Bible. The biblical authors knew all about evil in both its personal and institutional expressions, but they also knew about a level of spiritual dysfunction that lies underneath both

of those more ordinary dimensions. They knew about the world of fallen or morally compromised spirits. Jesus indeed battled sin in individual hearts as well as the sin that dwelt in institutional structures, but he also struggled with a dark power more fundamental and more dangerous than those.

What—or, better, who—is this threatening spiritual force? It is a devil, a fallen or morally compromised angel. Imagine a truly wicked person who is also very smart, very talented, and very enterprising. Now raise that person to a far higher pitch of ontological perfection, and you will have some idea of what a devil is like. Very rarely, devils intervene in human affairs in vividly frightening and dramatic ways. But typically devils act more indirectly and clandestinely, through temptation, influence, and suggestion. One of the most terrifying religious paintings in the world is in the Cathedral of Orvieto in Italy. It is a depiction of the Antichrist by the great early Renaissance painter Luca Signorelli. The artist shows the devil whispering into the ear of the Antichrist, and also working his arm through the vesture of his victim in such a way that it appears to be the Antichrist's own arm, thereby beautifully symbolizing how the dark power acts precisely with us and through us.

What are his usual effects? We can answer that question quite well by examining the names that the Bible gives to this figure. He is often called *diabolos* in the Greek of the New Testament, a word derived from *dia-balein* (to throw apart, to scatter). God is a great gathering force, for by his very nature he is love; but the devil's work is to sunder, to set one against the other. Whenever communities, families, nations, or churches are divided, we sniff out the diabolic. The other great New Testament name for the devil is *ho Satanas*, which means "the accuser." Perform a little experiment: gauge how often in the course of the day you accuse another person of something or find yourself accused. It's easy enough to notice how often dysfunctional families and societies finally collapse into an orgy of mutual blaming. That's satanic work.

An extraordinarily important aspect of the Good News of Christianity is that Jesus, through his death and Resurrection, has won victory over these dark forces. And Jesus has entrusted to his Church the means to apply this victory—the weapons, if you will, to win the spiritual war. These are the sacraments (especially the Eucharist and Confession), the Bible, personal prayer, the rosary, etc.

Jesus sent out the Twelve to battle dark spirits. He still empowers his Church to do the same. Don't be reluctant to use the weapons—and the healing balms—that he has given.

---

and they refuse to hear you, as you leave, shake off the dust that is on your feet as a testimony against them." [12] So they went out and proclaimed that all should repent. [13] They cast out many demons, and anointed with oil many who were sick and cured them.

THE DEATH OF JOHN THE BAPTIST

[14] King Herod heard of it, for Jesus' name had become known. Some were saying, "John the baptizer has been raised from the dead; and for this reason these powers are at work in him." [15] But others said, "It is Elijah." And others said, "It is a prophet, like one of the prophets of old." [16] But when Herod heard of it, he said, "John, whom I beheaded, has been raised."

John's Death and Jesus' Mission

Mark 6:17–29 | Bishop Barron

Herod had arrested John, from whom Jesus had sought baptism, and put him to death. The arrest and death of John the Baptist were signals for Jesus.

We must remember that Jesus, like any Jew of his time, would have read the world through the lens of the Sacred Scriptures. They were the interpretive framework for everything. It was a commonplace of the prophets and the Psalms and parts of the Torah that the era of the Messiah would be preceded by a time of tribulation, when the opponents of God would rise up to counter God's purposes.

Jesus saw this in the arrest of John. This great national figure, this prophet to Israel, was arrested and eventually killed by the enemies of God—and he took it as a signal that the time for his own messianic work had now come.

---

¹⁷ For Herod himself had sent men who arrested John, bound him, and put him in prison on account of Herodias, his brother Philip's wife, because Herod had married her. ¹⁸ For John had been telling Herod, "It is not lawful for you to have your brother's wife." ¹⁹ And Herodias had a grudge against him, and wanted to kill him. But she could not, ²⁰ for Herod feared John, knowing that he was a righteous and holy man, and he protected him. When he heard him, he was greatly perplexed; and yet he liked to listen to him. ²¹ But an opportunity came when Herod on his birthday gave a banquet for his courtiers and officers and for the leaders of Galilee. ²² When his daughter Herodias came in and danced, she pleased Herod and his guests; and the king said to the girl, "Ask me for whatever you wish, and I will give it." ²³ And he solemnly swore to her, "Whatever you ask me, I will give you, even half of my kingdom." ²⁴ She went out and said to her mother, "What should I ask for?" She replied, "The head of John the baptizer." ²⁵ Immediately she rushed back to the king and requested, "I want you to give me at once the head of John the Baptist on a platter." ²⁶ The king was deeply grieved; yet out of regard for his oaths and for the guests, he did not want to refuse her. ²⁷ Immediately the king sent a soldier of the guard with orders to bring John's head. He went and beheaded him in the prison,

²⁸ brought his head on a platter, and gave it to the girl. Then the girl gave it to her mother. ²⁹ When his disciples heard about it, they came and took his body, and laid it in a tomb.

FEEDING THE FIVE THOUSAND

³⁰ The apostles gathered around Jesus, and told him all that they had done and taught. ³¹ He said to them, "Come away to a deserted place all by yourselves and rest a while." For many were coming and going, and they had no leisure even to eat. ³² And they went away in the boat to a deserted place by themselves. ³³ Now many saw them going and recognized them, and they hurried there on foot from all the towns and arrived ahead of them. ³⁴ As he went ashore, he saw a great crowd; and he had compassion for them, because they were like sheep without a shepherd; and he began to teach them many things. ³⁵ When it grew late, his disciples came to him and said, "This is a deserted place, and the hour is now very late; ³⁶ send them away so that they may go into the surrounding country and villages and buy something for themselves to eat." ³⁷ But he answered them, "You give them something to eat." They said to him, "Are we to go and buy two hundred denarii worth of bread, and give it to them to eat?" ³⁸ And he said to them, "How many loaves have you? Go and see." When they had found out, they said, "Five, and two fish." ³⁹ Then he ordered them to get all the people to sit down in groups on the green grass. ⁴⁰ So they sat down in groups of hundreds and of fifties. ⁴¹ Taking the five loaves and the two fish, he looked up to heaven, and blessed and broke the loaves, and gave them to his disciples to set before the people; and he divided the two fish among them all. ⁴² And all ate and were filled; ⁴³ and they took up twelve baskets full of broken pieces and of the fish. ⁴⁴ Those who had eaten the loaves numbered five thousand men.

JESUS WALKS ON THE WATER

⁴⁵ Immediately he made his disciples get into the boat and go on ahead to the other side, to Bethsaida, while he dismissed the crowd. ⁴⁶ After saying farewell to them, he went up on the mountain to pray.

⁴⁷ When evening came, the boat was out on the sea, and he was alone on the land. ⁴⁸ When he saw that they were straining at the oars against an adverse wind, he came towards them early in the morning, walking on the sea. He intended to pass them by. ⁴⁹ But when they saw him walking on the sea, they thought it was a ghost and cried out; ⁵⁰ for they all saw him and were terrified. But immediately he spoke to them and said, "Take heart, it is I; do not be afraid." ⁵¹ Then he got into the boat with them and the wind ceased. And they were utterly astounded, ⁵² for they did not understand about the loaves, but their hearts were hardened.

Fulton Sheen
(1895–1979)

———

Life of Christ

The New Moses

Mark 6:30–44

As a grain of wheat slowly multiples in the ground, so the bread and fishes, by a divinely hastened process, were multiplied until everyone had his fill. If he had given money, no one would have had his fill. Nature was to go as far as it could, then God supplied the rest. He ordered that the fragments be gathered up; they filled twelve baskets. In the reckoning of men there is always a deficit; in the arithmetic of God, there is always a surplus.

The effect of the miracle on the multitude was stupendous. There was no denying the fact that Christ had divine power; he showed it in multiplying the bread. It brought their minds back immediately to Moses, who had given their forefathers manna in the desert. And had not Moses said that he was the prefigure of Christ or the Messiah?

"The Lord your God will raise up for you a prophet like me from among your own people; you shall heed such a prophet" (Deut. 18:15).

If Moses had not authenticated or sealed himself by bread in the desert, was not this the one to whom Moses had pointed, since he too gave bread miraculously? Who, then, could be a better King for them to throw off the yoke of the Romans and make them free? Here was a Deliverer, greater than Joshua, and here were five thousand men ready to take up arms; here was a King greater than David or Solomon, who could rebel against the tyrants and set the people free. They had already acknowledged him as Prophet and Teacher; now they would proclaim him as King.

HEALING THE SICK IN GENNESARET

[53] When they had crossed over, they came to land at Gennesaret and moored the boat. [54] When they got out of the boat, people at once recognized him, [55] and rushed about that whole region and began to bring the sick on mats to wherever they heard he was. [56] And wherever he went, into villages or cities or farms, they laid the sick in the marketplaces, and begged him that they might touch even the fringe of his cloak; and all who touched it were healed.

THE TRADITION OF THE ELDERS

7 Now when the Pharisees and some of the scribes who had come from Jerusalem gathered around him, [2] they noticed that some of his disciples were eating with defiled hands, that is, without washing them. [3] (For the Pharisees, and all the Jews, do not eat unless they thoroughly wash their hands, thus observing the tradition of the elders; [4] and they do not eat anything from the market unless they wash it; and there are also many other traditions that they observe, the washing of cups, pots, and bronze kettles.) [5] So the Pharisees and the scribes asked him, "Why do your disciples not live according to the tradition of the elders, but eat with defiled hands?" [6] He said to them, "Isaiah prophesied rightly about you hypocrites, as it is written,

> 'This people honors me with their lips,
> but their hearts are far from me;
> [7] in vain do they worship me,
> teaching human precepts as doctrines.'

[8] You abandon the commandment of God and hold to human tradition."

[9] Then he said to them, "You have a fine way of rejecting the commandment of God in order to keep your tradition! [10] For Moses said, 'Honor your father and your mother'; and, 'Whoever speaks evil of father or mother must surely die.' [11] But you say that if anyone tells father or mother, 'Whatever support you might have had from me is Corban' (that is, an offering to God)— [12] then you no longer permit doing anything for a father or mother, [13] thus making void the word of God through your tradition that you have handed on. And you do many things like this."

[14] Then he called the crowd again and said to them, "Listen to me, all of you, and understand: [15] there is nothing outside a person that by going in can defile, but the things that come out are what defile."

**Joseph Ratzinger
(Pope Benedict XVI)**
(1927–)

_Jesus of Nazareth:
Holy Week_

From Ritual to Encounter

Mark 7:1–23

In the cultic ordering of all religions, purification regulations play a major part: they give man a sense of the holiness of God and of his own darkness, from which he must be liberated if he is to be able to approach God. The system of cultic purifications dominated the whole of life in observant Judaism at the time of Jesus. In chapter 7 of Mark's Gospel, we encounter Jesus' fundamental challenge to this concept of cultic purity obtained through ritual actions; and in Paul's letters, the question of "purity" before God is repeatedly debated.

In Mark's Gospel we see the radical transformation that Jesus brought to the concept of purity before God: it is not ritual actions that make us pure. Purity and impurity arise within man's heart and depend on the condition of his heart.

Yet the question immediately presents itself: How does the heart become pure? Who are the pure in heart, those who can see God (Matt. 5:8)? Liberal exegesis has claimed that Jesus replaced the ritual concept of purity with a moral concept: in place of the cult and all that went with it, we have morality. In this view, Christianity is considered to be essentially about morality, a kind of moral "rearmament." But this does not do justice to the radically new dimension of the New Testament....

In place of ritual purity, what we have now is not merely morality, but the gift of encounter with God in Jesus Christ.... It is the incarnate God who makes us truly pure and draws creation into unity with God.

The Darkness of the Heart

Mark 7:14–23 | Bishop Barron

Jesus explains that sinful behavior flows from within our hearts. The Bible often speaks of the "heart," by which it means the core of the self, the deepest center of who we are, that place from which our thoughts and actions arise. God wants to penetrate that heart, so that he becomes the center of our souls. But there is something terribly dark in the human heart. We are made in the image and likeness of God, but that image can be so distorted by sin as to be barely recognizable.

Christianity clearly teaches the awful truth of the fall, and we see the evidence of it in the mystery of sin, which is not to be ignored, not to be trifled with, not to be rationalized away. We are all capable of dark and evil acts. I'm not okay and neither are you. We see the tangled web that is sin. It grows like a fungus or like a cancer.

Have our hearts become hardened, so that God cannot get in? Is there a deep resistance in us to grace?

---

¹⁷ When he had left the crowd and entered the house, his disciples asked him about the parable. ¹⁸ He said to them, "Then do you also fail to understand? Do you not see that whatever goes into a person from outside cannot defile, ¹⁹ since it enters, not the heart but the stomach, and goes out into the sewer?" (Thus he declared all foods clean.) ²⁰ And he said, "It is what comes out of a person that defiles. ²¹ For it is from within, from the human heart, that evil intentions come: fornication, theft, murder, ²² adultery, avarice, wickedness, deceit, licentiousness, envy, slander, pride, folly. ²³ All these evil things come from within, and they defile a person."

THE SYROPHOENICIAN WOMAN'S FAITH

²⁴ From there he set out and went away to the region of Tyre. He entered a house and did not want anyone to know he was there. Yet he could not escape notice, ²⁵ but a woman whose little daughter had an unclean spirit immediately heard about him, and she came and bowed down at his feet. ²⁶ Now the woman was a Gentile, of Syrophoenician origin. She begged him to cast the demon out of her daughter. ²⁷ He said to her, "Let the

children be fed first, for it is not fair to take the children's food and throw it to the dogs." ²⁸ But she answered him, "Sir, even the dogs under the table eat the children's crumbs." ²⁹ Then he said to her, "For saying that, you may go—the demon has left your daughter." ³⁰ So she went home, found the child lying on the bed, and the demon gone.

JESUS CURES A DEAF MAN

³¹ Then he returned from the region of Tyre, and went by way of Sidon towards the Sea of Galilee, in the region of the Decapolis. ³² They brought to him a deaf man who had an impediment in his speech; and they begged him to lay his hand on him. ³³ He took him aside in private, away from the crowd, and put his fingers into his ears, and he spat and touched his tongue. ³⁴ Then looking up to heaven, he sighed and said to him, "Ephphatha," that is, "Be opened." ³⁵ And immediately his ears were opened, his tongue was released, and he spoke plainly. ³⁶ Then Jesus ordered them to tell no one; but the more he ordered them, the more zealously they proclaimed it. ³⁷ They were astounded beyond measure, saying, "He has done everything well; he even makes the deaf to hear and the mute to speak."

Talking Back to Jesus

Mark 7:24–30 | Bishop Barron

The story of Jesus' conversation with the Syrophoenician woman is one of those famously problematic passages in the New Testament. This poor woman, a Canaanite, a foreigner, comes forward and tells Jesus of her daughter who is troubled by a demon, and the Lord just ignores her. When she persists, Jesus says, "I was sent only to the lost sheep of the house of Israel" (Matt. 15:24). When she prostrates herself at his feet, Jesus says, "Let the children be fed first, for it is not fair to take the children's food and throw it to the dogs."

Of course, the woman gets off one of the best one-liners in the Scriptures, almost all of which otherwise belong to Jesus himself: "Sir, even the dogs under the table eat the children's crumbs." At this point, Jesus praises her for her faith and cures her daughter.

What's going on here is really interesting and provocative. The Syrophoenician woman is being invited into a life of discipleship, into the following of Jesus. She is resisted—not because Jesus is having a bad day but because he wants the strength of her faith to show itself. And it does.

Be Opened

Mark 7:31–37 | Bishop Barron

IN THIS PASSAGE from the Gospel of Mark, we find the moving account of Jesus' healing of a man who is unable to speak or to hear. As is always the case with these narratives of miraculous cures, we have to look at both the surface meaning and the deeper meaning. One of the relatively few things that even the most skeptical of New Testament critics agree upon is that Jesus had a reputation as a healer and wonder worker. Certainly a major reason why crowds followed him and bothered to listen to his teaching was that they were attracted by the prospect of a miracle. Thus it is safe to say that this story—so marked by psychological perception and attention to curious detail—concerns a real event in the ministry of Jesus. But since, as Augustine pointed out, Jesus is the Word made flesh, every one of his actions is also a word—that is to say, a revelation of some abiding and universal spiritual truth. So let us endeavor to decipher some of the symbolic meanings hidden in the story.

As the narrative commences, Jesus is making his way into the Decapolis, the region of the "ten cities" on the southeastern side of the Sea of Galilee. These ten towns were very much under Hellenistic influence and therefore marked by a certain religious syncretism, blendings of Jewish and Gentile beliefs. A deaf man is brought to the Lord. Is it surprising, if we pursue our symbolic reading, that in this religiously mixed area there would be someone deaf to the Word of God? Hearing is, of course, a major scriptural motif, for the God of the Bible speaks, and his speech goes out to a people who are meant to hearken to his voice. The young Samuel, at the prompting of Eli the priest, says in response to the inviting voice of Yahweh, "Speak, for your servant is listening" (1 Sam. 3:10). The prophets are channels of the divine word, and they continually urge Israel not to be dull and inattentive. The central statement of Israelite faith, the interpretive key to the entire Old Testament, is the *shema*: "Hear, O Israel: The Lord is our God, the Lord alone" (Deut. 6:4). And St. Paul tells the Christian church at

Rome that "faith comes from what is heard" (Rom. 10:17). Therefore, this deaf man, brought before Jesus, stands for all of us who do not or cannot hear the word of God, all of us who have grown oblivious to it or lost the capacity to discern it with clarity.

What makes someone today unable to hear God's word? Consider, first, the incredible variety of voices and sounds competing for our attention. Technology has made readily available to us voices from TVs, iPhones, radios, movies, and computers; and from these various media, we hear, in their infinite variety, politicians, pop stars, advertisers, preachers, musicians, commentators, clowns, and fools. Elijah experienced Yahweh as a "sound of sheer silence" (1 Kings 19:12), and John the Baptist heard the Lord's voice in the stillness of the desert. How can we be anything but deaf to divine speech, surrounded as we are by such a relentless cacophony?

Moreover, more and more of us are staying away from church and growing, consequently, increasingly ignorant of the Bible. Years ago, I was a visiting professor at a major Catholic university. In the course of my lecturing, I would regularly refer to biblical passages—Job, the woman at the well, the parables of Jesus—and I was continually amazed how often these very bright young people, almost all of whom were from a Catholic background, were oblivious to the Scripture. And this is by no means a problem unique to Catholics. The biblical literacy that could be assumed in the nineteenth and early twentieth century is no longer present in the popular culture. Just think how blithely Melville, Hawthorne, Faulkner, and Hemingway could assume that their audience was conversant with the Bible; now their biblical allusions have to be carefully explained even to an alert reader.

A third problem is, if I can put it this way, a kind of tone deafness in regard to the word of God. Some people can hear musical notes, but they are incapable of discriminating clearly and consistently between a melody that is in tune with the accompaniment and one that is off-key. They hear "music," but they can't discern between relatively good and bad tones. Something similar obtains in regard to the things of the spirit. There is an awful lot of "religious" speech on offer in the culture today, but too many of us are tin-eared when it comes to telling the difference between authentic biblical religion and other varieties. The pronouncements of the pope, the speeches of the Dalai Lama, the cultural assessments offered by television evangelists, and the psychological truisms presented by avatars of the New Age can all sound vaguely "religious" or "spiritual" to those tone deaf to the nuances of religious speech.

Now, the man brought to Jesus suffers not only from deafness but from the inevitable concomitant of deafness: the inability to speak clearly. If a person is unable properly to hear sounds, she remains incapable, obviously, of reproducing those sounds in her own speech. This physical dynamic is precisely reproduced in the spiritual order: deafness to the word of God results in a severe incapacity to speak that word articulately and with any convincing power. How many Catholics today can speak the word of God with clarity and confidence? How many of us become tongue-tied when people ask us what we believe or pose a pointed question about the faith? Many Catholics complain that they feel incapable of effectively evangelizing, because they simply don't know enough about the Scripture, theology, and the teachings of the Church. This awkwardness of speech flows from the deafness we just explored.

So what does Jesus do with the deaf and dumb man? Mark tells us that "he took him aside in private, away from the crowd." We see something very similar in the story of the healing of a blind man in the eighth chapter of Mark's Gospel: Jesus leads the man away from the village, and when he has cured him, he tells him not to return to the town. The crowd is a large part of the problem. The raucous voices of so many, the prevalence of the received wisdom, the insistent bray of the advertising culture, the confusing Babel of competing spiritualities—all of it makes us deaf to God's word. And therefore, we have to be moved away, to a place of silence and communion. Jesus draws us, accordingly, into his space, the space of the Church. There, away from the crowd, we can immerse ourselves in the rhythm of the liturgy, listen avidly to the Scripture, study the theological tradition, watch at close quarters the moves of holy people, take in the beauty of sacred art and architecture. There we can hear.

Here is how Mark describes the actual cure: Jesus "put his fingers into his ears, and he spat and touched his tongue. Then looking up to heaven, he sighed and said to him, 'Ephphatha,' that is, 'Be opened.'" Scholars tell us that spitting and touching of the tongue were gestures typically employed by healers in Jesus' day. But I find the other details most intriguing. Looking up to his Father and inserting his fingers into the man's ears, Jesus establishes, as it were, an electrical current, running from the Father, through the Son, into the suffering man. He literally plugs him in to the divine energy, compelling him to hear the word. And how wonderful is that groaning "Ephphatha," one of only a handful of times that the Gospel writers preserve Jesus' original Aramaic speech. Once the man is opened to the divine word, he begins to speak clearly. So would we, away from the cacophonous crowd and plugged into the dynamism of Jesus Christ and his Church. If you want to speak the word persuasively, listen attentively!

FEEDING THE FOUR THOUSAND

8 In those days when there was again a great crowd without anything to eat, he called his disciples and said to them, 2 "I have compassion for the crowd, because they have been with me now for three days and have nothing to eat. 3 If I send them away hungry to their homes, they will faint on the way—and some of them have come from a great distance." 4 His disciples replied, "How can one feed these people with bread here in the desert?" 5 He asked them, "How many loaves do you have?" They said, "Seven." 6 Then he ordered the crowd to sit down on the ground; and he took the seven loaves, and after giving thanks he broke them and gave them to his disciples to distribute; and they distributed them to the crowd. 7 They had also a few small fish; and after blessing them, he ordered that these too should be distributed. 8 They ate and were filled; and they took up the broken pieces left over, seven baskets full. 9 Now there were about four thousand people. And he sent them away. 10 And immediately he got into the boat with his disciples and went to the district of Dalmanutha.

THE DEMAND FOR A SIGN

[11] The Pharisees came and began to argue with him, asking him for a sign from heaven, to test him. [12] And he sighed deeply in his spirit and said, "Why does this generation ask for a sign? Truly I tell you, no sign will be given to this generation." [13] And he left them, and getting into the boat again, he went across to the other side.

THE YEAST OF THE PHARISEES AND OF HEROD

[14] Now the disciples had forgotten to bring any bread; and they had only one loaf with them in the boat. [15] And he cautioned them, saying, "Watch out—beware of the yeast of the Pharisees and the yeast of Herod." [16] They said to one another, "It is because we have no bread." [17] And becoming aware of it, Jesus said to them, "Why are you talking about having no bread? Do you still not perceive or understand? Are your hearts hardened? [18] Do you have eyes, and fail to see? Do you have ears, and fail to hear? And do you not remember? [19] When I broke the five loaves for the five thousand, how many baskets full of broken pieces did you collect?" They said to him, "Twelve." [20] "And the seven for the four thousand, how many baskets full of broken pieces did you collect?" And they said to him, "Seven." [21] Then he said to them, "Do you not yet understand?"

THEY ATE

and were

FILLED.

MARK 8:8

Healing the Blind

Mark 8:22–26 | Bishop Barron

In this somewhat comical account of Jesus' healing of the blind man at Bethsaida, the sightless man comes to Jesus seeking a cure, and the first thing that Christ does is to lead him out of the village. Then after putting spittle on the man's eyes and imposing hands on him, he asks, "Can you see anything?" The man, who was beginning to see, replied, "I can see people, but they look like trees, walking." Laying hands on him a second time, Jesus effects a total cure and finally the man sees "clearly." Dismissing the man, Jesus says emphatically, "Do not even go into the village."

Now, blindness is a rich biblical image for lack of spiritual sight, the inability to see things as they are. One of the effects of the fall was a loss of holiness—that is to say, seeing with the eyes of Christ, appreciating the world as a participation in the creative energy of God. All of us sinners, to varying degrees, are blind to this metaphysics of creation and tend to see the world from the standpoint of the self-elevating ego. What this tightly packed Markan narrative discloses is one of the origins of this spiritual debility: too much time in the village. It is most significant that the account of the healing is bracketed by two distanciations from the city. Jesus leads him away from the village and then sternly warns him not to return. Is it possible that the soul blindness of this man had been caused by too much time in the city? Had he been immersed too completely in the attitudes, prejudices, and conventional viewpoints of the town? Martin Heidegger speaks of the tyranny of *was man sagt*, of "what everybody says," and Carl Jung knows the dangers of surrendering to the collective consciousness, to the mass movements and general attitudes that surround us.

The village evokes all those ways that we are, unconsciously for the most part, influenced and shaped by the sinfulness of our society. The shared and mutually justified attitudes of hatred, violence, division, and ostracization—all the effluvia of the small mind—are like a blinding sand storm. Sin is passed on *propagatione et non imitatione* (by propagation and not simply by imitation). The sinful "city" has us; our minds are, willy-nilly, shaped by it, and therefore it is impossible for us to extricate ourselves from it. In the striking symbolism of the Markan story, Jesus the healer and judge has to lead us blind people out of the city and give us sight—and then strictly enjoin us not to return to the blinding ways of the village. We unfortunate village dwellers must, through the power of Christ, put on the mind of Christ. And then we must live in a new town: the community of love and justice that is the Church. It is this city of vision that effectively challenges (and judges) the enduring power of the blinding society.

**Hans Urs
von Balthasar**
(1905–1988)

———

*Explorations in
Theology IV: Spirit
and Institution*

A Place Apart

Mark 8:22–26

The blind man in Mark is brought to Jesus by his
fellow villagers; Jesus then takes him by the hand and
leads him outside the village to be healed. Then he
sends him back to his people.

Here the personalizing of the encounter is done by
an act of geographical distancing, but note how the
man is being led by the hand: it is a walk into solitude,
led by Jesus (compare with Mark 7:33), but it is not
so far away that observers could not follow and
describe the procedure.

From time to time, Jesus will lead the disciples to a
"place apart," away from the street, from unbelief,
from activity and bustle—it might be the Cenacle, the
Garden of Olives, the "deserted place" mentioned
in Mark (6:32)—but the crowd always overtakes
them. Being singled out by Jesus never means
becoming isolated.

JESUS CURES A BLIND MAN AT BETHSAIDA

²² They came to Bethsaida. Some people brought a blind man to him and
begged him to touch him. ²³ He took the blind man by the hand and led
him out of the village; and when he had put saliva on his eyes and laid
his hands on him, he asked him, "Can you see anything?" ²⁴ And the man
looked up and said, "I can see people, but they look like trees, walking."
²⁵ Then Jesus laid his hands on his eyes again; and he looked intently and
his sight was restored, and he saw everything clearly. ²⁶ Then he sent him
away to his home, saying, "Do not even go into the village."

PETER'S DECLARATION ABOUT JESUS

²⁷ Jesus went on with his disciples to the villages of Caesarea Philippi; and
on the way he asked his disciples, "Who do people say that I am?" ²⁸ And they

answered him, "John the Baptist; and others, Elijah; and still others, one of the prophets." ²⁹ He asked them, "But who do you say that I am?" Peter answered him, "You are the Messiah." ³⁰ And he sternly ordered them not to tell anyone about him.

JESUS FORETELLS HIS DEATH AND RESURRECTION

³¹ Then he began to teach them that the Son of Man must undergo great suffering, and be rejected by the elders, the chief priests, and the scribes, and be killed, and after three days rise again. ³² He said all this quite openly. And Peter took him aside and began to rebuke him. ³³ But turning and looking at his disciples, he rebuked Peter and said, "Get behind me, Satan! For you are setting your mind not on divine things but on human things."

³⁴ He called the crowd with his disciples, and said to them, "If any want to become my followers, let them deny themselves and take up their cross and follow me. ³⁵ For those who want to save their life will lose it, and those who lose their life for my sake, and for the sake of the gospel, will save it. ³⁶ For what will it profit them to gain the whole world and forfeit their life? ³⁷ Indeed, what can they give in return for their life? ³⁸ Those who are ashamed of me and of my words in this adulterous and sinful generation, of them the Son of Man will also be ashamed when he comes in the glory of his Father with the holy angels."

The Cost of Following Christ

Mark 8:34–9:1 | Bishop Barron

Jesus says that those who wish to come after him must "deny themselves and take up their cross and follow me." Notice that this is not simply a question of accepting suffering that happens to befall us. This is not simply a Stoic resignation. Jesus is telling those who follow him to actively take up their crosses, to seek them out, to carry them as Jesus willingly carried his.

What Jesus did on the cross was to bear the burden of the world's sin. He bore others' burdens in love. And this is what we must do too, actively seeking out ways to lighten other people's loads.

And then the great paradox: "For those who want to save their life will lose it, and those who lose their life for my sake, and for the sake of the gospel, will save it." When we cling and grasp, we lose; when we let go in radical love, we find. Close your fist on your life and it crumbles to the dust; open your hand and let it go, and it grows tenfold.

Elijah's chariot of fire

Elijah is drawn into heaven by a blazing chariot of fire
in a scene that recalls the poetry of Psalm 104:

*"You set the beams of your chambers on the waters,
you make the clouds your chariot,
you ride on the wings of the wind,
you make the winds your messengers,
fire and flame your ministers."*

Striking the Jordan's waters

This story from the second chapter of 2 Kings
involves both the prophet Elijah and his
spiritual son Elisha striking the surface of the
Jordan River to part its waters. This gesture,
captured in Valck's depiction of Elisha, harkens
back to Moses and his parting of the Red Sea.

GERARD VALCK | *c. 1680*

The Translation of Elijah

Essay by Michael Stevens

This engraving, which shows the translation of the prophet Elijah into heaven, was created by the Dutch artist Gerard Valck. In this scene from the Old Testament, Elijah is assumed into heaven in bodily form, drawn by a chariot of fire. On the ground below is the prophet Elisha, who witnesses the scene in amazement. The artist captures the movement and momentum of Elijah's translation to heaven with amazing clarity and precision. He uses a black and white color palette combined with fine linework to convincingly render a vast array of textured surfaces and visual effects: from sunlight, flames, and clouds, to musculature, water, and windswept fabrics.

Elijah's life was a foreshadowing of the prophetic role of John the Baptist, and even more importantly, the ministry of Jesus himself. Elijah, John, and Jesus all practiced forms of asceticism and spread a similar message of repentance, and between the three there are significant overlaps in words and deeds. These similarities, however, were often a source of confusion in Jesus' day, and at different moments in the Gospel we hear the crowds mistake Jesus for the return of Elijah. These misidentifications were largely due to the widespread expectation that Elijah was to return from heaven according to a literal (and incorrect) reading of Old Testament prophecy. In the eighth chapter of Mark, we see an example of this: when Jesus asks his disciples, "Who do people say that I am?" they respond, "John the Baptist; and others, Elijah; and still others, one of the prophets."

Peter is the voice in the Gospel story who cuts through the confusion to identify Jesus as who he really is: not merely a prophet or a wise teacher but the Messiah himself.

THIS IS MY SON,
THE BELOVED;

—

LISTEN

— *to* —

HIM!

MARK 9:7

9 And he said to them, "Truly I tell you, there are some standing here who will not taste death until they see that the kingdom of God has come with power."

THE TRANSFIGURATION

² Six days later, Jesus took with him Peter and James and John, and led them up a high mountain apart, by themselves. And he was transfigured before them, ³ and his clothes became dazzling white, such as no one on earth could bleach them. ⁴ And there appeared to them Elijah with Moses, who were talking with Jesus. ⁵ Then Peter said to Jesus, "Rabbi, it is good for us to be here; let us make three dwellings, one for you, one for Moses, and one for Elijah." ⁶ He did not know what to say, for they were terrified. ⁷ Then a cloud overshadowed them, and from the cloud there came a voice, "This is my Son, the Beloved; listen to him!" ⁸ Suddenly when they looked around, they saw no one with them any more, but only Jesus.

THE COMING OF ELIJAH

⁹ As they were coming down the mountain, he ordered them to tell no one about what they had seen, until after the Son of Man had risen from the dead. ¹⁰ So they kept the matter to themselves, questioning what this rising from the dead could mean. ¹¹ Then they asked him, "Why do the scribes say that Elijah must come first?" ¹² He said to them, "Elijah is indeed coming first to restore all things. How then is it written about the Son of Man, that he is to go through many sufferings and be treated with contempt? ¹³ But I tell you that Elijah has come, and they did to him whatever they pleased, as it is written about him."

St. Augustine
(354–430)

Sermons on Selected Lessons of the New Testament

White as Snow

Mark 9:3

Jesus himself shone as the sun, signifying that he was "the true light, which enlightens everyone... coming into the world" [John 1:9]. What this sun is to the eyes of the flesh, that is the Lord to the eyes of the heart. His clothing now is his Church....What wonder then if membership in the Church is signified [at Baptism] by white clothing, when you hear the prophet Isaiah saying, "Though your sins are like scarlet, they shall be like snow" (Isa. 1:18)?

The Dazzling and Terrifying Light

Mark 9:2–8 | Bishop Barron

In his later texts, the philosopher Jean-Luc Marion speaks of the "saturated phenomenon," an appearance that is so filled with givenness and meaning that it overwhelms the one who would attempt to take it in. Whatever comes to manifestation in any way is given, but certain appearances are filled to overflowing with givenness, so much so that they dazzle the gaze and the mind that would perceive them.

The New Testament account of the Transfiguration of Jesus displays brilliantly the dynamics of the saturated phenomenon. The Christ whom Peter, James, and John had come to know through ordinary perception became, on the mountain of Transfiguration, dazzlingly white, and Moses and Elijah appeared alongside him. The brightness signals a kind of surplus of visibility, a flooding of the eyes, and the presence of the two great Old Testament figures hints at the new dimensions and profiles of meaning opening up. The reaction of Peter and the other disciples is altogether understandable. "Rabbi," says Peter, "it is good for us to be here; let us make three dwellings, one for you, one for Moses, and one for Elijah." In the presence of the icon, that which awakens and lures the gaze beyond what it can see, one feels oneself in the presence of that which is extraordinarily good.

Therefore, when Peter stands before the hyperdonation of the super-saturated phenomenon of the transfigured Jesus, he properly remarks at the goodness of what is happening to him.

Then comes the odd comment about the dwellings, a remark that has been interpreted in a variety of ways throughout the tradition. The best reading is, I would maintain, suggested by Mark himself: "He did not know what to say, for they were terrified." Peter is not so much trying to cling to the moment or to control these sacred figures; he is babbling. When the faculties are flooded, as they are in extraordinary experiences, we often say things that make no sense. The "terror" of which Mark speaks is precisely this fear born of the incapacity to control or take in what is happening.

Then there is the final detail concerning the cloud and the voice. The cloud bespeaks the overshadowing of the perceptive powers associated with the hyperluminosity of the Transfiguration. The disciples are thrown into the dark—not for want of light but from surplus of light. And the voice—the divine proclamation regarding the identity of Jesus—evokes the sacred nonvisibility that saturates the visibility of the icon. The transfigured Christ is so filled with the givenness of the divine presence that that presence can only be heard and not seen. More to the point, the voice carries an instruction—"Listen to him!"—suggesting that an icon is never controlled or measured by the gaze of the looker, but rather vice versa. Peter, James, and John are not so much seeing and measuring God as being seen and being measured by God.

THE HEALING OF A BOY WITH A SPIRIT

[14] When they came to the disciples, they saw a great crowd around them, and some scribes arguing with them. [15] When the whole crowd saw him, they were immediately overcome with awe, and they ran forward to greet him. [16] He asked them, "What are you arguing about with them?" [17] Someone from the crowd answered him, "Teacher, I brought you my son; he has a spirit that makes him unable to speak; [18] and whenever it seizes him, it dashes him down; and he foams and grinds his teeth and becomes rigid; and I asked your disciples to cast it out, but they could not do so." [19] He answered them, "You faithless generation, how much longer must I be among you? How much longer must I put up with you? Bring him to me." [20] And they brought the boy to him. When the spirit saw him, immediately it convulsed the boy, and he fell on the ground and rolled about, foaming at the mouth. [21] Jesus asked the father, "How long has this been happening to him?" And he said, "From childhood. [22] It has often cast him into the fire and into the water, to destroy him; but if you are able to do anything, have pity on us and help us." [23] Jesus said to him, "If you are able!—All things can be done for the one who believes." [24] Immediately the father of the child cried out, "I believe; help my unbelief!" [25] When Jesus saw that a crowd came running together, he rebuked the unclean spirit, saying to it, "You spirit that keeps this boy from speaking and hearing, I command you, come out of him, and never enter him again!" [26] After crying out and convulsing him terribly, it came out, and the boy was like a corpse, so that most of them said, "He is dead." [27] But Jesus took him by the hand and lifted him up, and he was able to stand. [28] When he had entered the house, his disciples asked him privately, "Why could we not cast it out?" [29] He said to them, "This kind can come out only through prayer."

JESUS AGAIN FORETELLS HIS DEATH AND RESURRECTION

[30] They went on from there and passed through Galilee. He did not want anyone to know it; [31] for he was teaching his disciples, saying to them, "The Son of Man is to be betrayed into human hands, and they will kill him, and three days after being killed, he will rise again." [32] But they did not understand what he was saying and were afraid to ask him.

**Hans Urs
von Balthasar**
(1905–1988)

———

*Explorations in
Theology IV: Spirit
and Institution*

Rise to Faith

Mark 9:22–24

Being confronted by Jesus rouses man from his anonymity and self-absorption into self-awareness, as the many healing and forgiving events in the Gospels illustrate. For it is only when he is truly present to himself that man can accept the word meant for him by God and the work that God wishes to accomplish in him. Those who have fallen asleep spiritually are awakened, the ones scattered are gathered, and the alienated are given back their identity. Each individual, as an individual, must rise to faith, to wakeful readiness for God, mediated and accomplished in the encounter with Jesus. One hears this happening in the following dialogue:

"'But if you are able to do anything, have pity on us and help us.' Jesus said to him, 'If you are able!— All things can be done for the one who believes.' Immediately the father of the child cried out, 'I believe; help my unbelief!'"

The central act in all conversion is this dawning awareness of one's own reality, which, however, is called into being only in the encounter with Jesus. Here all the disguises and subterfuges in which the ego has cloaked and alienated itself are stripped away, and the soul stands naked before God. But it is not by her own effort that the soul has divested herself of her garments. It is given to her as a gift.

WHO IS THE GREATEST?

[33] Then they came to Capernaum; and when he was in the house he asked them, "What were you arguing about on the way?" [34] But they were silent, for on the way they had argued with one another who was the greatest. [35] He sat down, called the twelve, and said to them, "Whoever wants to be first must be last of all and servant of all." [36] Then he took a little child and put it among them; and taking it in his arms, he said to them, [37] "Whoever welcomes one such child in my name welcomes me, and whoever welcomes me welcomes not me but the one who sent me."

ANOTHER EXORCIST

[38] John said to him, "Teacher, we saw someone casting out demons in your name, and we tried to stop him, because he was not following us." [39] But Jesus said, "Do not stop him; for no one who does a deed of power in my name will be able soon afterward to speak evil of me. [40] Whoever is not against us is for us. [41] For truly I tell you, whoever gives you a cup of water to drink because you bear the name of Christ will by no means lose the reward.

TEMPTATIONS TO SIN

[42] "If any of you put a stumbling block before one of these little ones who believe in me, it would be better for you if a great millstone were hung around your neck and you were thrown into the sea. [43] If your hand causes you to stumble, cut it off; it is better for you to enter life maimed than to have two hands and to go to hell, to the unquenchable fire. [45] And if your foot causes you to stumble, cut it off; it is better for you to enter life lame than to have two feet and to be thrown into hell. [47] And if your eye causes you to stumble, tear it out; it is better for you to enter the kingdom of God with one eye than to have two eyes and to be thrown into hell, [48] where their worm never dies, and the fire is never quenched.

[49] "For everyone will be salted with fire. [50] Salt is good; but if salt has lost its saltiness, how can you season it? Have salt in yourselves, and be at peace with one another."

Cutting Off Hands and Feet

Mark 9:42–48 | Bishop Barron

Jesus speaks, with incredible bluntness, about cutting off one's hand and foot and plucking out one's own eye. If these things are a block to your salvation, get rid of them, for it is better to enter life maimed than to enter hell with all of your limbs and members.

The hand is the organ by which we reach out and grasp things. The soul is meant for union with God, but we have, instead, reached out to creatures, all of our energies grasping at finite things.

The Lord also speaks of the foot. The foot is the organ by which we set ourselves on a definite path. We are meant to walk on the path that is Christ. Do we? Or have we set out down a hundred errant paths, leading to wealth, honor, power, or pleasure?

We are designed to seek after and look for God. Have we spent much of our lives looking in all the wrong places, beguiled by the beauties and enticements of this world? And are we willing to pluck out our eye spiritually, to abandon many of the preoccupations that have given us pleasure?

TEACHING ABOUT DIVORCE

10 He left that place and went to the region of Judea and beyond the Jordan. And crowds again gathered around him; and, as was his custom, he again taught them.

² Some Pharisees came, and to test him they asked, "Is it lawful for a man to divorce his wife?" ³ He answered them, "What did Moses command you?" ⁴ They said, "Moses allowed a man to write a certificate of dismissal and to divorce her." ⁵ But Jesus said to them, "Because of your hardness of heart he wrote this commandment for you. ⁶ But from the beginning of creation, 'God made them male and female.' ⁷ 'For this reason a man shall leave his father and mother and be joined to his wife, ⁸ and the two shall become one flesh.' So they are no longer two, but one flesh. ⁹ Therefore what God has joined together, let no one separate."

¹⁰ Then in the house the disciples asked him again about this matter. ¹¹ He said to them, "Whoever divorces his wife and marries another commits adultery against her; ¹² and if she divorces her husband and marries another, she commits adultery."

JESUS BLESSES LITTLE CHILDREN

¹³ People were bringing little children to him in order that he might touch them; and the disciples spoke sternly to them. ¹⁴ But when Jesus saw this, he was indignant and said to them, "Let the little children come to me; do not stop them; for it is to such as these that the kingdom of God belongs. ¹⁵ Truly I tell you, whoever does not receive the kingdom of God as a little child will never enter it." ¹⁶ And he took them up in his arms, laid his hands on them, and blessed them.

Becoming One Flesh

Mark 10:6–8 | Bishop Barron

Throughout the history of religion and philosophy, a puritanical strain is apparent. Whether it manifests itself as Manichaeism, Gnosticism, or Platonic dualism, the puritanical philosophy teaches that spirit is good and matter is evil or fallen. In most such schemas, the whole purpose of life is to escape from matter, especially from sexuality, which so ties us to the material realm.

But authentic biblical Christianity is not puritanical. The Creator God described in the book of Genesis made the entire panoply of things physical—planets, stars, the moon and sun, animals, fish, and even things that creep and crawl upon the earth—and found all of it good, even very good. Accordingly, there is nothing perverse or morally questionable about bodies, sex, sexual longing, or the sexual act. In fact, it's just the contrary. When Jesus himself is asked about marriage and sexuality, he hearkens back to the book of Genesis and the story of creation: "But from the beginning of creation, 'God made them male and female.' 'For this reason a man shall leave his father and mother and be joined to his wife, and the two shall become one flesh.'" That last sentence is inescapably sexual. Plato might have been a puritan, and perhaps John Calvin too, but Jesus most certainly was not.

THE RICH MAN

[17] As he was setting out on a journey, a man ran up and knelt before him, and asked him, "Good Teacher, what must I do to inherit eternal life?" [18] Jesus said to him, "Why do you call me good? No one is good but God alone. [19] You know the commandments: 'You shall not murder; You shall not commit adultery; You shall not steal; You shall not bear false witness; You shall not defraud; Honor your father and mother.'" [20] He said to him, "Teacher, I have kept all these since my youth." [21] Jesus, looking at him, loved him and said, "You lack one thing; go, sell what you own, and give the money to the poor, and you will have treasure in heaven; then come, follow me." [22] When he heard this, he was shocked and went away grieving, for he had many possessions.

[23] Then Jesus looked around and said to his disciples, "How hard it will be for those who have wealth to enter the kingdom of God!" [24] And the disciples were perplexed at these words. But Jesus said to them again, "Children, how hard it is to enter the kingdom of God! [25] It is easier for a

The High Adventure of the Spiritual Life

Mark 10:17–27 | Bishop Barron

A rich young man stops Jesus and asks what he must do to inherit eternal life. There is something absolutely right about the young man, something spiritually alive, and that is his deep desire to share in everlasting life. He knows what he wants, and he knows where to find it.

Jesus responds to his wonderful question by enumerating many of the commandments. The young man takes this in, and replies, "Teacher, I have kept all these since my youth." So Jesus looks at him with love and says, "Go, sell what you own, and give the money to the poor, and you will have treasure in heaven; then come, follow me."

God is nothing but love, straight through, and therefore the life of friendship with him, in the richest sense, is a life of total love, self-forgetting love. Jesus senses that this young man is ready for the high adventure of the spiritual life; he is asking the right question and he is properly prepared.

But at this point, the young man tragically balks. The spiritual life, at the highest pitch, is about giving your life away, and this is why having many possessions is a problem.

---

camel to go through the eye of a needle than for someone who is rich to enter the kingdom of God." 26 They were greatly astounded and said to one another, "Then who can be saved?" 27 Jesus looked at them and said, "For mortals it is impossible, but not for God; for God all things are possible."

28 Peter began to say to him, "Look, we have left everything and followed you." 29 Jesus said, "Truly I tell you, there is no one who has left house or brothers or sisters or mother or father or children or fields, for my sake and for the sake of the good news, 30 who will not receive a hundredfold now in this age—houses, brothers and sisters, mothers and children, and fields, with persecutions—and in the age to come eternal life. 31 But many who are first will be last, and the last will be first."

A THIRD TIME JESUS FORETELLS HIS DEATH AND RESURRECTION
32 They were on the road, going up to Jerusalem, and Jesus was walking ahead of them; they were amazed, and those who followed were afraid. He took the twelve aside again and began to tell them what was to happen to him, 33 saying, "See, we are going up to Jerusalem, and the Son of Man will be handed over to the chief priests and the scribes, and they will condemn

Amazed and Afraid

Mark 10:32 | Bishop Barron

This strange passage from the tenth chapter of Mark's Gospel is rarely commented upon, but in its peculiarity, it is very telling.

Jesus is in the company of his disciples, and they are making their way from Galilee in the north to Judea in the south. Mark reports: "They were on the road, going up to Jerusalem, and Jesus was walking ahead of them; they were amazed, and those who followed were afraid." They were simply walking along the road with Jesus, and they found him overwhelming and frightening. Why they should have had such a response remains inexplicable until we remember that awe and fear are, in the Old Testament tradition, two standard reactions to God. The twentieth-century philosopher of religion Rudolf Otto famously characterized the transcendent God as the *mysterium tremendum et fascinans*—the mystery that fascinates us even as it causes us to tremble with fear,

in whose presence we are amazed and afraid. In his sly, understated way, Mark is telling us that this Jesus is also the God of Israel.

Once we grasp that Jesus was no ordinary teacher and healer but Yahweh moving among his people, we can begin to understand his words and actions more clearly. If we survey the texts of the Old Testament—and the first Christians relentlessly read Jesus in light of these writings—we see that Yahweh was expected to do four great things. He would gather the scattered tribes of Israel; he would cleanse the temple of Jerusalem; he would definitively deal with the enemies of the nation; and finally, he would reign as Lord of heaven and earth. The eschatological hope expressed especially in the prophets and the Psalms was that through these actions, Yahweh would purify Israel and through the purified Israel bring salvation to all. What startled the first followers of Jesus was that he accomplished these four tasks in the most unexpected way.

---

him to death; then they will hand him over to the Gentiles; [34] they will mock him, and spit upon him, and flog him, and kill him; and after three days he will rise again."

THE REQUEST OF JAMES AND JOHN

[35] James and John, the sons of Zebedee, came forward to him and said to him, "Teacher, we want you to do for us whatever we ask of you." [36] And he said to them, "What is it you want me to do for you?" [37] And they said to him, "Grant us to sit, one at your right hand and one at your left, in your glory." [38] But Jesus said to them, "You do not know what you are asking. Are you

able to drink the cup that I drink, or be baptized with the baptism that I am baptized with?" [39] They replied, "We are able." Then Jesus said to them, "The cup that I drink you will drink; and with the baptism with which I am baptized, you will be baptized; [40] but to sit at my right hand or at my left is not mine to grant, but it is for those for whom it has been prepared."

[41] When the ten heard this, they began to be angry with James and John. [42] So Jesus called them and said to them, "You know that among the Gentiles those whom they recognize as their rulers lord it over them, and their great ones are tyrants over them. [43] But it is not so among you; but whoever wishes to become great among you must be your servant, [44] and whoever wishes to be first among you must be slave of all. [45] For the Son of Man came not to be served but to serve, and to give his life a ransom for many."

THE HEALING OF BLIND BARTIMAEUS

[46] They came to Jericho. As he and his disciples and a large crowd were leaving Jericho, Bartimaeus son of Timaeus, a blind beggar, was sitting by the roadside. [47] When he heard that it was Jesus of Nazareth, he began to shout out and say, "Jesus, Son of David, have mercy on me!" [48] Many sternly ordered him to be quiet, but he cried out even more loudly, "Son of David, have mercy on me!" [49] Jesus stood still and said, "Call him here." And they called the blind man, saying to him, "Take heart; get up, he is calling you." [50] So throwing off his cloak, he sprang up and came to Jesus. [51] Then Jesus said to him, "What do you want me to do for you?" The blind man said to him, "My teacher, let me see again." [52] Jesus said to him, "Go; your faith has made you well." Immediately he regained his sight and followed him on the way.

Let Me See Again

Mark 10:46–52 | Bishop Barron

Physical blindness is an evocative symbol of the terrible blindness of the soul that all of us sinners experience. When the *pusilla anima* (small soul) reigns, when the *imago Dei* (image of God) is covered over, we see within the narrow spectrum of our fearful desires. Blind Bartimaeus, sitting helplessly by the road outside of Jericho begging for alms and attention, expresses this hopeless and darkened-over state of soul. When he hears that Jesus of Nazareth is in the vicinity, he begins to cry out, "Son of David, have mercy on me!" The original Greek here is *eleēson me*, beautifully reflective of the liturgical cry of the Church, *Kyrie eleison*, "Lord have mercy." Bartimaeus gives voice to the prayerful groaning of the whole people of God for release from the imprisonment of the small soul. Though he is reprimanded by the crowd, Bartimaeus continues to shout, until finally Jesus calls out to him. This is the summons that echoes from the very depths of one's own being, the call of the *magna anima* (great soul), the invitation to rebirth and reconfiguration.

Inspired by this voice, convinced that he has discovered the pearl of great price, the *unum necessarium* (Luke 10:42), Bartimaeus jumps up, throws off his cloak, and comes to Jesus. In the early centuries of the Church, those about to be baptized were invited to strip themselves of their clothes, symbolizing thereby their renunciation of their old way of life. In Mark's story, the blind man prepares for inner transformation by throwing off the cloak of his old consciousness, his old pattern of desire, the lifestyle that has rendered him spiritually blind.

Then, at the feet of Jesus, Bartimaeus hears the question that all of us hear in the stillness of the heart, the question that comes from the divine power within and that subtly but firmly invites us to transformation: "What do you want me to do for you?" God beckons us, but God never compels us. Then, in one of the simplest and most poignant lines in the Scripture, Bartimaeus says, "My teacher, let me see again." Desperately in the dark, hounded by the demons of desire, caught in the narrow passage of ego-consciousness, Bartimaeus wants to see with a deeper, broader, and clearer vision. In his pain, and also in his confidence, Bartimaeus stands for all of us spiritual seekers, all who hope against hope that there might be a way to live outside the tyranny of the ego. He wants a new attitude, a new perspective—the great soul. And what saves the blind man is the repentance that culminates in faith, the shift in consciousness from ego-dominance to surrender. What restores the vision of the spiritual seeker is the throwing off of the old mind and the adoption, through God's grace, of a divine mind.

Of course, at the end of the story we hear that Bartimaeus "followed him on the way." It ends, in a word, with discipleship. Once the soul has been transfigured, the only path that seems appealing is the one walked by Christ— that is to say, the path of radical self-offering, self-surrender. Fired by the God-consciousness, in touch with the divine source within us, drinking from the well of eternal life, we are inspired simply to pour ourselves out in love.

Word Study

έλέησον

ELEĒSON

Verb
To have pity or mercy

Mark 10:46–52

CLAUDE MONET | *1890s*

The Rouen Cathedral Series

Essay by Michael Stevens

Claude Monet was the leader of the Impressionist movement in French painting, and pioneered a style that emphasized, above all, the act of *seeing*. Rather than emphasizing the objects in his landscapes and cityscapes in themselves, Monet's artwork focuses on more ephemeral aspects, such as the interplay of sunlight, time of day, and weather. In order to capture such specific, fleeting details accurately, Monet would paint outdoors in an attempt to translate the optical effects of his environment in a more immediate way.

This series of paintings of Rouen Cathedral was created as a study of the effects of light on the church's facade across a wide range of beautifully varied conditions. Within this series we sense Monet's obsession with optics and perception, as he tests his powers of observation across over thirty canvases.

In the Gospel, we also encounter the theme of eyesight in the story of Bartimaeus, whose blindness is healed by Jesus. We are only given a short account of the event. While this may seem like an abrupt ending to the narrative, for Bartimaeus, the story is only beginning. By restoring his eyesight, Christ has opened not only his field of vision but his very mind to an entirely new mode of understanding. From this moment on, every scene before him— from sunsets, to starry skies, to the faces of his loved ones—is now grasped by his intellect in a qualitatively different way than before. Bartimaeus can now experience firsthand the nuanced sensations that only eyesight can effect in the psyche—sensations that are inexhaustibly specific and infinitely beautiful.

JESUS' TRIUMPHAL ENTRY INTO JERUSALEM

11 When they were approaching Jerusalem, at Bethphage and Bethany, near the Mount of Olives, he sent two of his disciples ² and said to them, "Go into the village ahead of you, and immediately as you enter it, you will find tied there a colt that has never been ridden; untie it and bring it. ³ If anyone says to you, 'Why are you doing this?' just say this, 'The Lord needs it and will send it back here immediately.' " ⁴ They went away and found a colt tied near a door, outside in the street. As they were untying it, ⁵ some of the bystanders said to them, "What are you doing, untying the colt?" ⁶ They told them what Jesus had said; and they allowed them to take it. ⁷ Then they brought the colt to Jesus and threw their cloaks on it; and he sat on it. ⁸ Many people spread their cloaks on the road, and others spread leafy branches that they had cut in the fields. ⁹ Then those who went ahead and those who followed were shouting,

"Hosanna!

Blessed is the one who comes in the name of the Lord!

¹⁰ Blessed is the coming kingdom of our ancestor David!

Hosanna in the highest heaven!"

¹¹ Then he entered Jerusalem and went into the temple; and when he had looked around at everything, as it was already late, he went out to Bethany with the twelve.

JESUS CURSES THE FIG TREE

¹² On the following day, when they came from Bethany, he was hungry. ¹³ Seeing in the distance a fig tree in leaf, he went to see whether perhaps he would find anything on it. When he came to it, he found nothing but leaves, for it was not the season for figs. ¹⁴ He said to it, "May no one ever eat fruit from you again." And his disciples heard it.

JESUS CLEANSES THE TEMPLE

¹⁵ Then they came to Jerusalem. And he entered the temple and began to drive out those who were selling and those who were buying in the temple, and he overturned the tables of the money changers and the seats of those who sold doves; ¹⁶ and he would not allow anyone to carry anything through the temple. ¹⁷ He was teaching and saying, "Is it not written,

'My house shall be called a house of prayer for all the nations'?

But you have made it a den of robbers."

¹⁸ And when the chief priests and the scribes heard it, they kept looking for a way to kill him; for they were afraid of him, because the whole crowd was spellbound by his teaching. ¹⁹ And when evening came, Jesus and his disciples went out of the city.

The New Temple

Mark 11:1 | Bishop Barron

No first-century Jew would have missed the excitement and danger implicit in the coded language of the accounts describing Jesus' entry into Jerusalem just a few days before his death.

We hear that Jesus and his disciples "were approaching Jerusalem, at Bethphage and Bethany, near the Mount of Olives." A bit of trivial geographical detail, we might be tempted to conclude. But we have to remember that pious Jews of Jesus' time were immersed in the infinitely complex world of the Hebrew Scriptures and stubbornly read everything through the lens provided by those writings.

About five hundred years before Jesus' time, the prophet Ezekiel had relayed a vision of the *Shekinah* (the glory) of Yahweh leaving the temple due to its corruption: "Then the glory of the Lord went out from the threshold of the house [the temple] and stopped above the cherubim. The cherubim ... rose up from the earth in my sight as they went out.... They stopped at the entrance of the east gate of the house of the Lord; and the glory of the God of Israel was above them" (Ezek. 10:18–19). This was one of the most devastating texts in the Old Testament. The temple of the Lord was seen as, in almost a literal sense, the dwelling place of God, the meeting place of heaven and earth. Thus even to imagine that the glory of the Lord had quit his temple was shocking in the extreme. However, Ezekiel also prophesied that one day the glory of God would return to the temple, and precisely from the same direction in which it had left: "Then he brought me to the gate, the gate facing east. And there, the glory of the God of Israel was coming from the east; the sound was like the sound of mighty waters; and the earth shone with his glory" (Ezek. 43:1–2). Furthermore, upon the return of the Lord's glory, Ezekiel predicted, the corrupt temple would be cleansed, restored, and rebuilt.

Now let's return to Jesus, who, during his public ministry, consistently spoke and acted in the very person of God and who said, in reference to himself, "Something greater than the temple is here" (Matt. 12:6). As the Jews of Jesus' day saw him approaching Jerusalem from the east, they would have remembered Ezekiel's vision and would have begun to entertain the wild but thrilling idea that perhaps this Jesus was, in person, the glory of Yahweh returning to his dwelling place on earth. And, in light of this, they would have understood the bewildering acts that Jesus performed in the temple. He was, in fact, another Ezekiel, pronouncing judgment on the old temple and then announcing a magnificent rebuilding campaign: "Destroy this temple, and in three days I will raise it up" (John 2:19). Jesus, they came to understand, was the new and definitive Temple, the meeting place of heaven and earth.

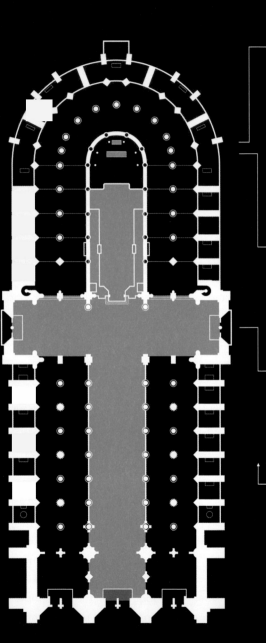

The drawing above is based on the floor plan of Notre-Dame de Paris.

The tabernacle

The tabernacle of the church is where the Eucharist is kept, and it directly parallels the Holy of Holies of the temple—the innermost tabernacle where God made his dwelling place. In every Catholic tabernacle, Jesus is really present under the appearance of bread. This recalls the unleavened bread of the Passover meal, as well as the heavenly "manna" (Exod. 16:31), which was stored in the ark of the covenant within the Holy of Holies.

The altar

In the Mass, shortly after the prayer of consecration, we hear the priest proclaim from the altar, "Behold, the Lamb of God." This reflects the reality that Jesus is the definitive sacrifice that completes all former sacrifices.

Cruciform floor plan

Traditionally, the floor plan of a cathedral is in the shape of a cross. With this architectural scheme, not only does the ritual of the Mass partake in the pattern of Christ's sacrifice—the architecture is shaped after it as well.

Orientation

Cathedrals are typically oriented to the east—a term that comes from the Latin *oriens,* which means "east." This practice of church-building has scriptural roots in Matthew 24:27, which anticipates the Second Coming of Christ: "For as the lightning comes from the east and flashes as far as the west, so will the coming of the Son of Man."

The Cathedral as a New Temple

Essay by Michael Stevens

Throughout the Gospels, we continually see Jesus fulfilling the patterns set forth in ancient Hebrew customs and rituals. In Mark 11, we read of two events that, beneath the surface, signify Jesus' fulfillment of the Old Covenant—which is to say, the practice of ancient temple sacrifice.

In Mark 11:1–11, Jesus enters Jerusalem, beginning the sequence that will eventually lead to his death on the cross. The timing of this event during the week of Passover is significant: it corresponds to the ancient practice of leading the paschal lambs into Jerusalem in preparation for the Passover sacrifice. By processing into Jerusalem and going to the temple immediately after, Jesus is positioning himself as a new type of Paschal Lamb: the ultimate sacrifice that will take away the sins of the world. After this, just a few verses later, we encounter yet another story that carries a similar significance: Jesus' cleansing of the temple. By cleansing the Jewish place of animal sacrifices, Jesus prepares the world for an entirely new kind of Temple, one that will be much greater than anything that has come before.

Over the centuries, the tradition of Christian cathedral-building has developed to reflect Jesus' role as the new Passover sacrifice and the definitive Temple. As a place set aside for the celebration of the Eucharist, cathedral architecture is meant to highlight the many parallels between ancient temple rituals and the Mass. It reflects the Catholic understanding that a church is not merely a place for preaching and collective singing, but is in fact a place of sacrifice and the very dwelling place of God.

Cleansing Your Temple

Mark 11:15–19 | Bishop Barron

JESUS ENTERED THE GREAT TEMPLE in Jerusalem—which meant everything to a Jew of Jesus' time—and began to tear the place apart. Precisely because the temple was supposed to be so holy, Jesus was flabbergasted at what had happened to it, at how the trading of merchants had come to dominate.

From the earliest days, Christian writers and spiritual teachers saw the temple as symbolic of the human person. In fact, didn't St. Paul himself refer to the body as a "temple of the Holy Spirit" (1 Cor. 6:19)? Your very self is meant to be a temple, where God's spirit dwells and where prayer—communion with God—is central.

But what happens to us sinners? The money changers and the merchants enter in. What is supposed to be a place of prayer becomes a den of thieves. And so the Lord must do in us now what he did in the temple then: a little house-cleaning.

One of the best ways that we can cooperate with this process is to attend to the Ten Commandments. Let's go back to basics.

The first three commandments have to do with the question of our fundamental spiritual orientation: Who or what, precisely, is the object of your worship? What do you hold to be spiritually basic? If we're honest, a lot of us would say something like sex, pleasure, money, power, status, or to sum all of this up, our own egos. And so we need to hear the very first commandment: "I am the Lord your God.... You shall have no other gods before me" (Exod. 20:2–3).

Relatedly, you shall not disrespect God with your speech, for this leads rather quickly to a denigration of God. And thirdly, you must worship this God on a regular basis. There is no place for the attitude of "I'm alright with God, and I just have no time for going to Mass"; or "I get nothing out of the Mass." So what? You're obliged to concretize your worship. "Remember the sabbath day, and keep it holy" (Exod. 20:8).

And then, following from this basic form of worship, there comes a whole series of commandments dealing with our relations to other people. "Honor your father and your mother" (Exod. 20:12). What is the quality of your relationship with those who are nearest and dearest to you? If things are off there, they are probably off everywhere else.

"You shall not murder" (Exod. 20:13). Now, I suppose that very few murderers are reading this right now. Very few of you have actually killed another person. But what is the role that violence plays in your life? What is the quality of your temper? Have you effectively killed people—that is to say, rendered them lifeless? Do you enhance the lives of those around you, or are people less alive after they've been with you?

"You shall not commit adultery" (Exod. 20:14). The Bible is not obsessed with sex, but it does recognize the importance of our sexuality in the moral sphere. Much of our popular culture wants to teach us that sex is basically amoral—a matter, finally, of indifference. As long as you're not hurting anyone, anything goes.

But sex, like everything else in us, is meant to serve love, to become a gift. Is your sex life self-indulgent, simply for the sake of your pleasure? Do you use other people for your sexual satisfaction? Are you the victim of lust? Do you practice forms of sex that are simply perverse?

"You shall not steal" (Exod. 20:15). Do you steal other's property, even very small things, little amounts of money? Do you perhaps steal on a grand scale? How dispiriting the Enron and related corporate scandals are. White collar crime, negotiated through computers, is no less a crime.

"You shall not bear false witness against your neighbor" (Exod. 20:16). Do you steal someone's good name and reputation through gossip? What is the quality of your speech? How much time do you spend inveighing against your neighbor, even making things up to make him look bad? How much time do you spend scapegoating, blaming, accusing?

"You shall not covet your neighbor's house; you shall not covet your neighbor's wife" (Exod. 20:17). Coveting—or desiring, in relation to Girard's theory of mimetic desire—is our tendency to want things because other people want them, which leads to conflict. Don't play these games of conflict.

What shape is the temple of your soul in? Suppose that Jesus has made a whip of cords, knotted with the Ten Commandments. What would he clear out of you?

THE LESSON FROM THE WITHERED FIG TREE

20 In the morning as they passed by, they saw the fig tree withered away to its roots. 21 Then Peter remembered and said to him, "Rabbi, look! The fig tree that you cursed has withered." 22 Jesus answered them, "Have faith in God. 23 Truly I tell you, if you say to this mountain, 'Be taken up and thrown into the sea,' and if you do not doubt in your heart, but believe that what you say will come to pass, it will be done for you. 24 So I tell you, whatever you ask for in prayer, believe that you have received it, and it will be yours.

25 "Whenever you stand praying, forgive, if you have anything against anyone; so that your Father in heaven may also forgive you your trespasses."

JESUS' AUTHORITY IS QUESTIONED

27 Again they came to Jerusalem. As he was walking in the temple, the chief priests, the scribes, and the elders came to him 28 and said, "By what authority are you doing these things? Who gave you this authority to do them?" 29 Jesus said to them, "I will ask you one question; answer me, and I will tell you by what authority I do these things. 30 Did the baptism of John come from heaven, or was it of human origin? Answer me." 31 They argued with one another, "If we say, 'From heaven,' he will say, 'Why then did you not believe him?' 32 But shall we say, 'Of human origin'?"—they were afraid of the crowd, for all regarded John as truly a prophet. 33 So they answered Jesus, "We do not know." And Jesus said to them, "Neither will I tell you by what authority I am doing these things."

THE PARABLE OF THE WICKED TENANTS

12 Then he began to speak to them in parables. "A man planted a vineyard, put a fence around it, dug a pit for the wine press, and built a watchtower; then he leased it to tenants and went to another country. 2 When the season came, he sent a slave to the tenants to collect from them his share of the produce of the vineyard. 3 But they seized him, and beat him, and sent him away empty-handed. 4 And again he sent another

slave to them; this one they beat over the head and insulted. [5] Then he sent another, and that one they killed. And so it was with many others; some they beat, and others they killed. [6] He had still one other, a beloved son. Finally he sent him to them, saying, 'They will respect my son.' [7] But those tenants said to one another, 'This is the heir; come, let us kill him, and the inheritance will be ours.' [8] So they seized him, killed him, and threw him out of the vineyard. [9] What then will the owner of the vineyard do? He will come and destroy the tenants and give the vineyard to others. [10] Have you not read this scripture:

> 'The stone that the builders rejected
> has become the cornerstone;
> [11] this was the Lord's doing,
> and it is amazing in our eyes'?"

[12] When they realized that he had told this parable against them, they wanted to arrest him, but they feared the crowd. So they left him and went away.

THE QUESTION ABOUT PAYING TAXES

[13] Then they sent to him some Pharisees and some Herodians to trap him in what he said. [14] And they came and said to him, "Teacher, we know that you are sincere, and show deference to no one; for you do not regard people with partiality, but teach the way of God in accordance with truth. Is it lawful to pay taxes to the emperor, or not? [15] Should we pay them, or should we not?" But knowing their hypocrisy, he said to them, "Why are you putting me to the test? Bring me a denarius and let me see it." [16] And they brought one. Then he said to them, "Whose head is this, and whose title?" They answered, "The emperor's." [17] Jesus said to them, "Give to the emperor the things that are the emperor's, and to God the things that are God's." And they were utterly amazed at him.

THE QUESTION ABOUT THE RESURRECTION

[18] Some Sadducees, who say there is no resurrection, came to him and asked him a question, saying, [19] "Teacher, Moses wrote for us that if a man's brother dies, leaving a wife but no child, the man shall marry the widow and raise up children for his brother. [20] There were seven brothers; the first married and, when he died, left no children; [21] and the second married the widow and died, leaving no children; and the third likewise; [22] none of the seven left children. Last of all the woman herself died. [23] In the resurrection whose wife will she be? For the seven had married her."

[24] Jesus said to them, "Is not this the reason you are wrong, that you know neither the scriptures nor the power of God? [25] For when they rise

Intimacy in Heaven

Mark 12:18–27 | Bishop Barron

Jesus debated the materialists of his day, the Sadducees, who denied the resurrection. They put forward an almost comical case of seven brothers who died, leaving no descendants for the woman that each had married in turn. They ask, "In the resurrection whose wife will she be?" Jesus brushes aside this bit of facile casuistry.

The body is a means of communication. The most intense personal communication possible is that which happens between two married people—sexual, psychological, personal intimacy. Given the limitations and restrictions of our bodies here below, this type of intimacy is possible only with one other person.

The heavenly state involves a body too, but a transformed, transfigured, elevated body, what Paul called a "spiritual body" (1 Cor. 15:44). It is still a means of communication, but now it is so intense and spiritualized that it can mediate an intimate communion with all those who love the Lord. We are not less than bodily in heaven; we are super-bodily. We communicate more extensively and more intimately, and with everyone. Hence, in heaven we are not given to one person in marriage, but to all. All of this becomes plain in the Resurrection of Jesus from the dead.

---

from the dead, they neither marry nor are given in marriage, but are like angels in heaven. [26] And as for the dead being raised, have you not read in the book of Moses, in the story about the bush, how God said to him, 'I am the God of Abraham, the God of Isaac, and the God of Jacob'? [27] He is God not of the dead, but of the living; you are quite wrong."

THE FIRST COMMANDMENT

[28] One of the scribes came near and heard them disputing with one another, and seeing that he answered them well, he asked him, "Which commandment is the first of all?" [29] Jesus answered, "The first is, 'Hear, O Israel: the Lord our God, the Lord is one; [30] you shall love the Lord your God with all your heart, and with all your soul, and with all your mind, and with all your strength.' [31] The second is this, 'You shall love your neighbor as yourself.' There is no other commandment greater than these." [32] Then the scribe said to him, "You are right, Teacher; you have truly said that 'he is one, and besides him there is no other'; [33] and 'to love him with all the heart, and with all the understanding, and with all the strength,' and 'to love one's neighbor as oneself,'—this is much more important than all whole burnt offerings and sacrifices." [34] When Jesus saw that he answered wisely,

The Logic of Love

Mark 12:28–34 | Bishop Barron

When a scribe asked Jesus to identify the first commandment, he answered with what the ancient Israelites referred to as the *shema*: "Hear, O Israel: the Lord our God, the Lord is one." This invites an examination of conscience: Is God the one Lord of your life? Who or what are his rivals for your attention, for your ultimate concern? Or to turn the question around: Does absolutely everything in your life belong to God?

You might ask, "But how do I give myself to a reality that I cannot see?" This is where the second command of Jesus comes into play. When asked which is the first of all the commandments, Jesus responded with the *shema*, but then he placed a second command alongside it—namely, "You shall love your neighbor as yourself."

There is a strict logic at work here. When you really love someone, you tend to love, as well, what they love. Well, what does God love? He loves everything and everyone that he has made. So, if you want to love God, and you find this move difficult because God seems so distant, love everyone you come across for the sake of God.

---

he said to him, "You are not far from the kingdom of God." After that no one dared to ask him any question.

THE QUESTION ABOUT DAVID'S SON

[35] While Jesus was teaching in the temple, he said, "How can the scribes say that the Messiah is the son of David? [36] David himself, by the Holy Spirit, declared,

> 'The Lord said to my Lord,
> "Sit at my right hand,
>   until I put your enemies under your feet." '

[37] David himself calls him Lord; so how can he be his son?" And the large crowd was listening to him with delight.

JESUS DENOUNCES THE SCRIBES

[38] As he taught, he said, "Beware of the scribes, who like to walk around in long robes, and to be greeted with respect in the marketplaces, [39] and to have the best seats in the synagogues and places of honor at banquets! [40] They devour widows' houses and for the sake of appearance say long prayers. They will receive the greater condemnation."

St. John Henry Newman
(1801–1890)

Parochial and Plain Sermons

You Are Not Far from the Kingdom

Mark 12:34

In these words ["You are not far from the kingdom of God"], then, we are taught, first, that the Christian's faith and obedience are not the same religion as that of natural conscience, as being some way beyond it; secondly, that this way is "not far," not far in the case of those who try to act up to their conscience; in other words, that obedience to conscience leads to obedience to the Gospel, which, instead of being something different altogether, is but the completion and perfection of that religion which natural conscience teaches....

There are, in other words, not two ways of pleasing God; what conscience suggests, Christ has sanctioned and explained.

THE WIDOW'S OFFERING

41 He sat down opposite the treasury, and watched the crowd putting money into the treasury. Many rich people put in large sums. 42 A poor widow came and put in two small copper coins, which are worth a penny. 43 Then he called his disciples and said to them, "Truly I tell you, this poor widow has put in more than all those who are contributing to the treasury. 44 For all of them have contributed out of their abundance; but she out of her poverty has put in everything she had, all she had to live on."

THE DESTRUCTION OF THE TEMPLE FORETOLD

13 As he came out of the temple, one of his disciples said to him, "Look, Teacher, what large stones and what large buildings!" 2 Then Jesus asked him, "Do you see these great buildings? Not one stone will be left here upon another; all will be thrown down."

3 When he was sitting on the Mount of Olives opposite the temple, Peter, James, John, and Andrew asked him privately, 4 "Tell us, when will this be, and what will be the sign that all these things are about to be accomplished?" 5 Then Jesus began to say to them, "Beware that no one leads you astray.

[6] Many will come in my name and say, 'I am he!' and they will lead many astray. [7] When you hear of wars and rumors of wars, do not be alarmed; this must take place, but the end is still to come. [8] For nation will rise against nation, and kingdom against kingdom; there will be earthquakes in various places; there will be famines. This is but the beginning of the birth pangs.

PERSECUTION FORETOLD

[9] "As for yourselves, beware; for they will hand you over to councils; and you will be beaten in synagogues; and you will stand before governors and kings because of me, as a testimony to them. [10] And the good news must first be proclaimed to all nations. [11] When they bring you to trial and hand you over, do not worry beforehand about what you are to say; but say whatever is given you at that time, for it is not you who speak, but the Holy Spirit. [12] Brother will betray brother to death, and a father his child, and children will rise against parents and have them put to death; [13] and you will be hated by all because of my name. But the one who endures to the end will be saved.

St. Hilary of Poitiers (310–368)

On the Trinity

The End

Mark 13:13

Therefore the Lord exhorts us to wait with patient and reverent faith until the end comes....It is not a blessed dissolution that awaits us, nor is nonexistence the fruit, nor annihilation the appointed reward of faith. Instead, the end is the final attainment of the promised blessedness, in which the goal of perfect happiness is reached, with no further goal beyond. For these, "the end" is to abide in the condition of uninterrupted rest toward which they are pressing.

THE DESOLATING SACRILEGE

[14] "But when you see the desolating sacrilege set up where it ought not to be (let the reader understand), then those in Judea must flee to the mountains; [15] the one on the housetop must not go down or enter the house to take

anything away; ¹⁶ the one in the field must not turn back to get a coat. ¹⁷ Woe to those who are pregnant and to those who are nursing infants in those days! ¹⁸ Pray that it may not be in winter. ¹⁹ For in those days there will be suffering, such as has not been from the beginning of the creation that God created until now, no, and never will be. ²⁰ And if the Lord had not cut short those days, no one would be saved; but for the sake of the elect, whom he chose, he has cut short those days. ²¹ And if anyone says to you at that time, 'Look! Here is the Messiah!' or 'Look! There he is!'—do not believe it. ²² False messiahs and false prophets will appear and produce signs and omens, to lead astray, if possible, the elect. ²³ But be alert; I have already told you everything.

THE COMING OF THE SON OF MAN

²⁴ "But in those days, after that suffering, the sun will be darkened, and the moon will not give its light, ²⁵ and the stars will be falling from heaven, and the powers in the heavens will be shaken. ²⁶ Then they will see 'the Son of Man coming in clouds' with great power and glory. ²⁷ Then he will send out the angels, and gather his elect from the four winds, from the ends of the earth to the ends of heaven.

Looking Even Now for Christ's Coming

Mark 13:24–32 | Bishop Barron

The whole of Mark 13 features apocalyptic musings. The word "apocalypse" means unveiling, a revelation. And Jesus uses here language from the seventh chapter of the prophet Daniel: "The powers in the heavens will be shaken. Then they will see 'the Son of Man coming in clouds' with great power and glory."

Daniel spoke of a succession of four kingdoms, which would be followed by the arrival of God's definitive kingdom. This is the fulfillment of Nathan's prophecy that a son of David would reign forever (2 Sam. 7:12–17).

I realize how strange all of this can sound, but there is a spiritual point of enormous significance behind all of it. We should not trust in any of the powers of the world to give us security and peace. Such peace will come only with the arrival of God's kingdom.

What you should look to is the Son of Man coming on the clouds of heaven. This is meant in an ultimate sense. The Second Coming signals the end of the world as we know it. But the Son of Man is coming on the clouds of heaven even now, in the life of the Church.

THE LESSON OF THE FIG TREE

²⁸ "From the fig tree learn its lesson: as soon as its branch becomes tender and puts forth its leaves, you know that summer is near. ²⁹ So also, when you see these things taking place, you know that he is near, at the very gates. ³⁰ Truly I tell you, this generation will not pass away until all these things have taken place. ³¹ Heaven and earth will pass away, but my words will not pass away.

THE NECESSITY FOR WATCHFULNESS

³² "But about that day or hour no one knows, neither the angels in heaven, nor the Son, but only the Father. ³³ Beware, keep alert; for you do not know when the time will come. ³⁴ It is like a man going on a journey, when he leaves home and puts his slaves in charge, each with his work, and commands the doorkeeper to be on the watch. ³⁵ Therefore, keep awake—for you do not know when the master of the house will come, in the evening, or at midnight, or at cockcrow, or at dawn, ³⁶ or else he may find you asleep when he comes suddenly. ³⁷ And what I say to you I say to all: Keep awake."

St. John Henry Newman
(1801–1890)

Parochial and Plain Sermons

Watch and Pray

Mark 13:33

Our Savior gave this warning when he was leaving this world—leaving it, that is, as far as his visible presence is concerned. He looked forward to the many hundred years which were to pass before he came again. He knew his own purpose and his Father's purpose gradually to leave the world to itself, gradually to withdraw from it the tokens of his gracious presence.... In this text, he mercifully whispers into our ears, not to trust in what we see, not to share in the general unbelief [around us], not to be carried away by the world, but to "beware, keep alert," and look out for his coming.

THE PLOT TO KILL JESUS

14 It was two days before the Passover and the festival of Unleavened Bread. The chief priests and the scribes were looking for a way to arrest Jesus by stealth and kill him; [2] for they said, "Not during the festival, or there may be a riot among the people."

THE ANOINTING AT BETHANY

[3] While he was at Bethany in the house of Simon the leper, as he sat at the table, a woman came with an alabaster jar of very costly ointment of nard, and she broke open the jar and poured the ointment on his head. [4] But some were there who said to one another in anger, "Why was the ointment wasted in this way? [5] For this ointment could have been sold for more than three hundred denarii, and the money given to the poor." And they scolded her. [6] But Jesus said, "Let her alone; why do you trouble her? She has performed a good service for me. [7] For you always have the poor with you, and you can show kindness to them whenever you wish; but you will not always have me. [8] She has done what she could; she has anointed my body beforehand for its burial. [9] Truly I tell you, wherever the good news is proclaimed in the whole world, what she has done will be told in remembrance of her."

JUDAS AGREES TO BETRAY JESUS

[10] Then Judas Iscariot, who was one of the twelve, went to the chief priests in order to betray him to them. [11] When they heard it, they were greatly pleased, and promised to give him money. So he began to look for an opportunity to betray him.

THE PASSOVER WITH THE DISCIPLES

[12] On the first day of Unleavened Bread, when the Passover lamb is sacrificed, his disciples said to him, "Where do you want us to go and make the preparations for you to eat the Passover?" [13] So he sent two of his disciples, saying to them, "Go into the city, and a man carrying a jar of water will meet you; follow him, [14] and wherever he enters, say to the owner of the house, 'The Teacher asks, Where is my guest room where I may eat the Passover with my disciples?' [15] He will show you a large room upstairs, furnished and ready. Make preparations for us there." [16] So the disciples set out and went to the city, and found everything as he had told them; and they prepared the Passover meal.

[17] When it was evening, he came with the twelve. [18] And when they had taken their places and were eating, Jesus said, "Truly I tell you, one of you will betray me, one who is eating with me." [19] They began to be distressed and to say to him one after another, "Surely, not I?" [20] He said to them, "It

is one of the twelve, one who is dipping bread into the bowl with me.[21] For the Son of Man goes as it is written of him, but woe to that one by whom the Son of Man is betrayed! It would have been better for that one not to have been born."

Fulton Sheen
(1895–1979)

Life of Christ

Not Readers, But Actors

Mark 14:22–25

By that communion they were made one with Christ, to be offered with him, in him, and by him. All love craves unity. As the highest peak of love in the human order is the unity of husband and wife in the flesh, so the highest unity in the divine order is the unity of the soul and Christ in Communion. When the Apostles, and the Church later on, would obey our Lord's words to renew the memorial and to eat and drink of him, the Body and Blood would not be that of the physical Christ then before them, but that of the glorified Christ in heaven who continually makes intercession for sinners. The salvation of the cross, being sovereign and eternal, is thus applied and actualized in the course of time by the heavenly Christ.

When our Lord, after he changed the bread and wine to his Body and Blood, told his Apostles to eat and drink, he was doing for the soul of man what food and drink do for the body. Unless the plants sacrifice themselves to being plucked up from the roots, they cannot nourish or commune with man. The sacrifice of what is lowest must precede communion with what is higher. First his death was mystically represented; then communion followed. The lower is transformed into the higher; chemical into plants; plants into animals; chemicals, plants, and animals into man; and man into Christ by Communion. The followers of Buddha derive no strength from his life but only from his writings. The writings of Christianity are not as important as the life of Christ, who living in glory, now pours forth on his followers the benefits of his sacrifice.

The one note that kept ringing through his life was his death and glory. It was for that that he came primarily. Hence the night before his death, he gave to his Apostles something which on dying no one else could ever give—namely, himself. Only divine wisdom could have conceived such a memorial! Humans, left to themselves, might have spoiled the drama of his redemption. They might have done two things with his death which would have fallen so short of the way of divinity. They might have regarded his redemptive death as a drama presented once in history like the assassination of Lincoln. In that case, it would have been only an incident, not a redemption—the tragic end of a man, not the salvation of humanity. Regrettably, this is the way so many look upon the cross of Christ, forgetting his Resurrection and the pouring-out of the merits of his cross in the memorial action he ordered and commanded. In such a case, his death would be only like a national Memorial Day and nothing more.

Or they might have regarded it as a drama which was played only once, but one which ought often to be recalled only through meditating on its details. In this case, they would go back and read the accounts of the drama critics who lived at the time—namely, Matthew, Mark, Luke, and John. This would be only a literary recall of his death, as Plato records the death of Socrates, and would have made the death of our Lord no different from the death of any man.

Our Lord never told anyone to write about his redemption, but he did tell his Apostles to renew it, apply it, commemorate it, prolong it by obeying his orders given at the Last Supper. He wanted the great drama of Calvary to be played not once, but for every age of his own choosing. He wanted men not to be readers about his redemption, but actors in it, offering up their body and blood with his in the re-enactment of Calvary, saying with him, "This is my body and this is my blood"; dying to their lower natures to live to grace; saying that they cared not for the appearance or species of their lives such as their family relationships, jobs, duties, physical appearance, or talents, but that their intellects, their wills, their substance—all that they truly were—would be changed into Christ; that the heavenly Father looking down on them would see them in his Son, see their sacrifices massed in his sacrifice, their mortification incorporated with his death, so that eventually they might share in his glory.

THE INSTITUTION OF THE LORD'S SUPPER

²² While they were eating, he took a loaf of bread, and after blessing it he broke it, gave it to them, and said, "Take; this is my body." ²³ Then he took a cup, and after giving thanks he gave it to them, and all of them drank from it. ²⁴ He said to them, "This is my blood of the covenant, which is poured out for many. ²⁵ Truly I tell you, I will never again drink of the fruit of the vine until that day when I drink it new in the kingdom of God."

PETER'S DENIAL FORETOLD

²⁶ When they had sung the hymn, they went out to the Mount of Olives. ²⁷ And Jesus said to them, "You will all become deserters; for it is written,

> 'I will strike the shepherd,
>   and the sheep will be scattered.'

²⁸ But after I am raised up, I will go before you to Galilee." ²⁹ Peter said to him, "Even though all become deserters, I will not." ³⁰ Jesus said to him,

"Truly I tell you, this day, this very night, before the cock crows twice, you will deny me three times."[31] But he said vehemently, "Even though I must die with you, I will not deny you." And all of them said the same.

JESUS PRAYS IN GETHSEMANE

[32] They went to a place called Gethsemane; and he said to his disciples, "Sit here while I pray."[33] He took with him Peter and James and John, and began to be distressed and agitated.[34] And he said to them, "I am deeply grieved, even to death; remain here, and keep awake."[35] And going a little farther,

---

Joseph Ratzinger (Pope Benedict XVI) (1927–)

Introduction to Christianity

Being For One Another

Mark 14:24

Because Christian faith demands the individual but wants him for the whole and not for himself, the real basic law of Christian existence is expressed in the preposition "for."... That is why in the chief Christian sacrament, which forms the center of Christian worship, the existence of Jesus Christ is explained as existence "for many," "for you," as an open existence that makes possible and creates the communication of all with one another through communication in him....

Being a Christian means essentially changing over from being for oneself to being for one another. This also explains what is really meant by the often rather odd-seeming concept of election ("being chosen"). It means, not a preference that leaves the individual undisturbed in himself and divides him from the others, but embarking on the common task.... Accordingly, the basic Christian decision signifies the assent to being a Christian, the abandonment of self-centeredness and accession to Jesus Christ's existence with its concentration on the whole.

he threw himself on the ground and prayed that, if it were possible, the hour might pass from him. ³⁶ He said, "Abba, Father, for you all things are possible; remove this cup from me; yet, not what I want, but what you want." ³⁷ He came and found them sleeping; and he said to Peter, "Simon, are you asleep? Could you not keep awake one hour? ³⁸ Keep awake and pray that you may not come into the time of trial; the spirit indeed is willing, but the flesh is weak." ³⁹ And again he went away and prayed, saying the same words. ⁴⁰ And once more he came and found them sleeping, for their eyes were very heavy; and they did not know what to say to him. ⁴¹ He came a third time and said to them, "Are you still sleeping and taking your rest? Enough! The hour has come; the Son of Man is betrayed into the hands of sinners. ⁴² Get up, let us be going. See, my betrayer is at hand."

THE BETRAYAL AND ARREST OF JESUS

⁴³ Immediately, while he was still speaking, Judas, one of the twelve, arrived; and with him there was a crowd with swords and clubs, from the chief priests, the scribes, and the elders. ⁴⁴ Now the betrayer had given them a sign, saying, "The one I will kiss is the man; arrest him and lead him away under guard." ⁴⁵ So when he came, he went up to him at once and said, "Rabbi!" and kissed him. ⁴⁶ Then they laid hands on him and arrested him. ⁴⁷ But one of those who stood near drew his sword and struck the slave of the high priest, cutting off his ear. ⁴⁸ Then Jesus said to them, "Have you come out with swords and clubs to arrest me as though I were a bandit? ⁴⁹ Day after day I was with you in the temple teaching, and you did not arrest me. But let the scriptures be fulfilled." ⁵⁰ All of them deserted him and fled.

⁵¹ A certain young man was following him, wearing nothing but a linen cloth. They caught hold of him, ⁵² but he left the linen cloth and ran off naked.

JESUS BEFORE THE COUNCIL

⁵³ They took Jesus to the high priest; and all the chief priests, the elders, and the scribes were assembled. ⁵⁴ Peter had followed him at a distance, right into the courtyard of the high priest; and he was sitting with the guards, warming himself at the fire. ⁵⁵ Now the chief priests and the whole council were looking for testimony against Jesus to put him to death; but they found none. ⁵⁶ For many gave false testimony against him, and their testimony did not agree. ⁵⁷ Some stood up and gave false testimony against him, saying, ⁵⁸ "We heard him say, 'I will destroy this temple that is made with hands, and in three days I will build another, not made with hands.'" ⁵⁹ But even on this point their testimony did not agree. ⁶⁰ Then the high priest stood up before them and asked Jesus, "Have you no answer?

What is it that they testify against you?" ⁶¹ But he was silent and did not answer. Again the high priest asked him, "Are you the Messiah, the Son of the Blessed One?" ⁶² Jesus said, "I am; and

> *'you will see the Son of Man*
> *seated at the right hand of the Power,'*
> *and 'coming with the clouds of heaven.'"*

⁶³ Then the high priest tore his clothes and said, "Why do we still need witnesses? ⁶⁴ You have heard his blasphemy! What is your decision?" All of them condemned him as deserving death. ⁶⁵ Some began to spit on him, to blindfold him, and to strike him, saying to him, "Prophesy!" The guards also took him over and beat him.

PETER DENIES JESUS

⁶⁶ While Peter was below in the courtyard, one of the servant-girls of the high priest came by. ⁶⁷ When she saw Peter warming himself, she stared at him and said, "You also were with Jesus, the man from Nazareth." ⁶⁸ But he denied it, saying, "I do not know or understand what you are talking about." And he went out into the forecourt. Then the cock crowed. ⁶⁹ And the servant-girl, on seeing him, began again to say to the bystanders, "This man is one of them." ⁷⁰ But again he denied it. Then after a little while the bystanders again said to Peter, "Certainly you are one of them; for you are a Galilean." ⁷¹ But he began to curse, and he swore an oath, "I do not know this man you are talking about." ⁷² At that moment the cock crowed for the second time. Then Peter remembered that Jesus had said to him, "Before the cock crows twice, you will deny me three times." And he broke down and wept.

JESUS SAID,
"I AM; AND
'YOU WILL SEE
THE SON OF MAN
SEATED AT THE
RIGHT HAND OF
THE POWER,' AND
'COMING WITH
THE CLOUDS OF
HEAVEN.'"

MARK 14:62

Peter's body language

Caravaggio was a master of facial expression and gesture, which provides clear insight into the emotional experiences of the characters in his scenes. Here, we see the shame in Peter's eyes as he denies Jesus, and his closed posture appears defensive and weak.

Light and shadow

The interplay of light and shadow within the scene draws focus to the face of the girl in the middle, who accuses Peter of being a friend of Christ's. This is contrasted by the shadowy profile of the man with the helmet, who leans in menacingly with a hostile finger pointing toward Peter.

Mark 14:66–72

CARAVAGGIO | *1610*

The Denial of Saint Peter

Essay by Michael Stevens

The Italian Baroque master Caravaggio was one of the most admired artists of his time, and his innovative and daring techniques were emulated by generations of painters after him. Known for his candid, realistic portrayals of biblical stories, he rejected the hyper-idealized style of painting that was in vogue during the Baroque period in favor of a rugged, naturalistic approach. Instead of winged cherubs and visions of heaven, Caravaggio focuses on accurate representation of the human body, facial expressions, perspective, light, and shadow.

While he was well respected by many of his peers for his innovative and meticulous technique, he was also sharply criticized by some for his unvarnished, unidealized depictions of sacred narratives. Some viewed his style as too visually raw, given the significance and sacredness of the subject matter.

While it's true that his approach as a painter was a radical departure from what had come before, those who reprimanded Caravaggio for his naturalistic style sadly overlooked a brilliant theological truth embedded in his artwork: that Jesus came to us not as some elevated, grandiose, immaterial being, but in flesh and blood—as a human being. Furthermore, during Christ's time on earth, he deliberately sought out a rugged group of ordinary, flawed individuals to become his closest disciples. The painting exemplifies this fact, as Peter—the chief of the twelve Apostles—denies even knowing Christ, turning his back on his friend and Savior.

Odd Details in the Passion Account

Mark 14:3–52 | Bishop Barron

THERE IS NO STORY BETTER KNOWN to Western people than the narrative of Christ's Passion and death. Whether we believe it or not, whether or not it plays a role in shaping our religious lives, this story is in our blood and our bones. Ernest Hemingway once related a story about a cabin boy on one of his boats who was reading a book with rapt attention. Hemingway asked the young man what he was studying so carefully, and he responded, "The Gospel of Mark." "Well, why," he continued, "are you so wrapped up in it?" And the boy said, "I'm dying to see how it ends!" The anecdote is funny, of course, because it's so anomalous: Who, in the Western world, doesn't know how that most familiar of stories ends? But this very familiarity can block our appreciation for the dynamics of the Passion narrative. Once this best-known of all stories gets underway, it can swim effortlessly through our minds, unfolding without really being noticed. What I wish to do therefore is to defamiliarize the account a bit by drawing your attention to three odd details in Mark's version of the Passion, each one of which, precisely in its quirkiness, sheds light on the meaning of the text.

On Mark's telling, the Passion narrative commences with the account of a woman who performs an extravagant act: "While he was at Bethany in the house of Simon the leper, as he sat at the table, a woman came with an alabaster jar of very costly ointment of nard, and she broke open the jar and poured the ointment on his head." This gesture—wasting something as expensive as an entire jar of perfume—is sniffed at by the bystanders, who complain that, at the very least, the nard could have been sold and the money given to the poor. But Jesus is having none of it: "Let her alone; why do you trouble her? She has performed a good service for me." Why does Mark use this tale to preface his telling of the Passion? Why does he allow the odor of this woman's perfume to waft, as it were, over the whole of the story? It is because, I believe, this extravagant gesture shows the meaning of what Jesus is about to do: the absolutely radical giving away of self. There is nothing calculating, careful, or conservative about the woman's action; she offers everything, breaking open the jar as a symbol of the breaking open of her heart in love. Giving voice to the austere rationalism of the Enlightenment, Immanuel Kant spoke of "religion within the limits of reason alone"; but as Paul Tillich commented, authentic religion, ultimate concern, can never be hemmed in by reason alone. Flowing from the deepest place in the heart, religion resists the strictures set for it by a fussily moralizing reason (on full display in those who complain about the woman's extravagance). At the climax of his life, Jesus will give himself away totally, lavishly, unreasonably—and this is why the woman's beautiful gesture is a sort of overture to the opera that will follow.

A second peculiar detail in Mark's account concerns the Last Supper and its immediate aftermath. Jesus has gathered with his intimate friends on the night before his death. He knows that the next day he shall be tortured and publicly executed. In the course of the supper, Jesus identifies himself so radically with the Passover bread and wine that they are now properly called his Body and his Blood. Like broken bread, the Lord says, his body will be given away in love; and like spilled wine, his blood will be poured out on behalf of many. The sadness and portentousness in that room must have been unbearable, much like the mood in the prison cell where a condemned man sits with his family while he awaits his execution. How does this terrible gathering come to a close? They sing! "When they had sung the hymn, they went out to the Mount of Olives." Can you imagine a condemned criminal singing on the eve of his execution? Wouldn't there be something odd, even macabre, about such a display? But Jesus knows—and his Church knows with him—that this joyful outburst, precisely at that awful time, is altogether appropriate. This is not to deny for a moment the terror of that night nor the seriousness of what will follow the next day; but it is to acknowledge that an act of total love is the passage to fullness of life. Therefore, as you give your life away, sing! Every Mass is a remembrance of that somber night: during the Eucharistic Prayer, we explicitly recall what Jesus did the night before he died. But immediately after the consecration, as Christ in his sacrificial death becomes really present to us, we sing an acclamation of praise. The strange juxtaposition of terror and exuberant joy mimics the dynamics of the Last Supper.

A third peculiarity of Mark's version of the Passion is the curious appearance of a naked man in the Garden of Gethsemane. In the confusion following the betrayal and arrest of Jesus, as the disciples flee their master, an unnamed youth finds himself in an awkward predicament: "A certain young man was following him, wearing nothing but a linen cloth. They caught hold of him, but he left the linen cloth and ran off naked." Scholars suggest that, like a Renaissance painter who places contemporary figures anachronistically into a depiction of a biblical scene, Mark is symbolically situating all of us in the Garden of Gethsemane in the figure of this man running off into the night. The principal clue to his symbolic identity is in the simple description of him as someone "following" Jesus, which makes him evocative of all disciples of the Lord from that day to the present. Another clue is his manner of dress. The Greek term here is *sindona*, which designates the kind of garment worn in the early Church by the newly baptized. The point is this: following Jesus, being a baptized member of his Church, is a dangerous business. Participating in Jesus' kingdom puts you, necessarily, in harm's way, for Jesus' way of ordering things is massively opposed to the world's way of doing so. The shame of this young man—running away from the Lord at the moment of crisis—is the shame of all of us fearful disciples of Jesus who, more often than not, leave behind, in the hands of our enemies, our baptismal identity. The naked young man, escaping into the night, therefore poses a question: What do we do at the moment of truth?

This mysterious figure makes a comeback before the Gospel of Mark closes, and in his return all of us sinners can find hope. On the morning of the Resurrection, the Marys come to the tomb, carrying their spices and fretting about the massive stone covering the mouth of the grave.

They find the stone rolled away and, upon entering the sepulcher, they see "a young man, dressed in a white robe, sitting on the right side." The words used for "young man" and "white robe" are the same that Mark used to describe the disciple in the Gethsemane scene. This confident figure announces the Resurrection to the startled women. "Do not be alarmed; you are looking for Jesus of Nazareth who was crucified. He has been raised; he is not here." Exegetes suggest that this angelic presence in the empty tomb of Jesus is evocative of all of us disciples of Jesus at our best. Wearing once more our white baptismal garments, which we had abandoned during times of persecution, we announce to the world the Good News that the crucified one is alive. Having recovered our courage, our voice, and our identity, we function as angels (the word *angelos* simply means "messenger") of the Resurrection.

An alabaster jar broken open and the smell of perfume filling the house; a songburst on the eve of execution; a humiliated man now become an angel—three peculiar Markan lenses for reading the greatest story ever told.

Word Study

σινδών

SINDŌN

Noun
A linen cloth

JESUS BEFORE PILATE

15 As soon as it was morning, the chief priests held a consultation with the elders and scribes and the whole council. They bound Jesus, led him away, and handed him over to Pilate. ² Pilate asked him, "Are you the King of the Jews?" He answered him, "You say so." ³ Then the chief priests accused him of many things. ⁴ Pilate asked him again, "Have you no answer? See how many charges they bring against you." ⁵ But Jesus made no further reply, so that Pilate was amazed.

ARE YOU

THE KING

of the JEWS?

MARK 15:2

PILATE HANDS JESUS OVER TO BE CRUCIFIED

⁶ Now at the festival he used to release a prisoner for them, anyone for whom they asked. ⁷ Now a man called Barabbas was in prison with the rebels who had committed murder during the insurrection. ⁸ So the crowd came and began to ask Pilate to do for them according to his custom. ⁹ Then he answered them, "Do you want me to release for you the King of the Jews?" ¹⁰ For he realized that it was out of jealousy that the chief priests had handed him over. ¹¹ But the chief priests stirred up the crowd to have him release Barabbas for them instead. ¹² Pilate spoke to them again, "Then what do you wish me to do with the man you call the King of the Jews?" ¹³ They shouted back, "Crucify him!" ¹⁴ Pilate asked them, "Why, what evil has he done?" But they shouted all the more, "Crucify him!" ¹⁵ So Pilate, wishing to satisfy the crowd, released Barabbas for them; and after flogging Jesus, he handed him over to be crucified.

THE SOLDIERS MOCK JESUS

¹⁶ Then the soldiers led him into the courtyard of the palace (that is, the governor's headquarters); and they called together the whole cohort. ¹⁷ And they clothed him in a purple cloak; and after twisting some thorns into a crown, they put it on him. ¹⁸ And they began saluting him, "Hail,

---

Are You the King?

Mark 14:61–15:20 | Bishop Barron

The kingship of Jesus emerges with greatest clarity and irony when he enters into his Passion. Upon being brought before the Sanhedrin, Jesus is asked whether he is the "Messiah, the Son of the Blessed One" (Mark 14:61). Any reference to the *Mashiach*, the "anointed one," is at least implicitly a reference to David, whom Samuel anointed as king. When Jesus calmly responds, "I am" (Mark 14:62), the high priest tears his robes, for how could a shackled criminal possibly be the kingly descendant of David? Mark is insinuating that Jesus is a King, but a strange and deeply puzzling version of a King.

Upon being presented to Pilate, Jesus is asked the functionally equivalent question: "Are you the King of the Jews?" Again a blandly affirmative answer comes: "You say so." This leads the soldiers to mock him, placing a purple cloak on his shoulders and a crown of thorns on his head and shouting, "Hail, King of the Jews!" (Mark 15:18). Mark does not want us to miss the irony that, precisely as the King of the Jews and the Son of David, Jesus is implicitly King to those soldiers, for the mission of the Davidic King is the unification not only of the tribes of Israel but also of the tribes of the world.

Into the Darkness

Mark 15:1–15, 26–32 | Bishop Barron

Jesus came before Pontius Pilate and the Roman governor quickly discerned that this man was innocent, yet he caved in to the crowd calling for his blood. In that decision we see cowardice, yes, but also abuse of power, misuse of office—sin that is not only personal but institutional.

And then we see the mockery of Jesus. Here is a man hanging from an instrument of torture, struggling for his life—and people mock him. We see envy, anger, hitting someone when he's down.

All of our dysfunction is revealed on that cross. St. Peter put it with disquieting laconicism: "You killed the Author of life" (Acts 3:15). In the light of the cross, all of the vermin are revealed. In the light of the cross, no one can say, "I'm okay and you're okay." This is why we speak of the cross as God's judgment on the world.

But Jesus doesn't abandon us in our dysfunction. He confronts it, enters into its darkness, but then heals it through the light of his sacrificial death and Resurrection.

St. Augustine
(354–430)

———

Tractates on the Gospel of John

The Judge on the Cross

Mark 15:15

The thief escaped; Christ was condemned. He who was guilty of many crimes received pardon; he who pardoned every criminal willing to confess was condemned. Yet the very cross itself, if you will stop to consider, was a judgment seat, with the Judge set up in the middle between a thief to be pardoned and a thief to be condemned. Here the final judgment is prefigured, with defendants separated left and right. Even while being judged himself, he acted the part of a judge.

King of the Jews!" ¹⁹ They struck his head with a reed, spat upon him, and knelt down in homage to him. ²⁰ After mocking him, they stripped him of the purple cloak and put his own clothes on him. Then they led him out to crucify him.

THE CRUCIFIXION OF JESUS

²¹ They compelled a passer-by, who was coming in from the country, to carry his cross; it was Simon of Cyrene, the father of Alexander and Rufus. ²² Then they brought Jesus to the place called Golgotha (which means the place of a skull). ²³ And they offered him wine mixed with myrrh; but he did not take it. ²⁴ And they crucified him, and divided his clothes among them, casting lots to decide what each should take.

²⁵ It was nine o'clock in the morning when they crucified him. ²⁶ The inscription of the charge against him read, "The King of the Jews." ²⁷ And with him they crucified two bandits, one on his right and one on his left. ²⁹ Those who passed by derided him, shaking their heads and saying, "Aha! You who would destroy the temple and build it in three days, ³⁰ save yourself, and come down from the cross!" ³¹ In the same way the chief priests, along with the scribes, were also mocking him among themselves and saying, "He saved others; he cannot save himself. ³² Let the Messiah, the King of Israel, come down from the cross now, so that we may see and believe." Those who were crucified with him also taunted him.

The One Voice Not Silenced

Mark 15:39 | Bishop Barron

Jesus had consistently forbidden anyone to identify him as the Messiah, fearing, the Gospel seems to insinuate, that any such proclamation would be misconstrued in a political or triumphalist direction. It is ironically fitting that the only witness whose voice is not silenced is the one who speaks in the presence of the dead Christ. He can give witness freely precisely because it is in death that Jesus' messianic identity is properly and unambiguously revealed. He is the one who had been sent to do the will of the Father, and that will was that he go to the darkness of godforsakenness out of love. Only in his death, only in the practically infinite tension between the Father's command and the Son's obedience, is the person and mission of Christ visible: he is the justice that throws everything off.

Christ's triumphal entry

The story begins at the top left of the composition with Christ's triumphal entry into Jerusalem. This sets the Passion sequence in motion, which unfolds in a linear progression that winds through the city from top to bottom, left to right.

Dark region of the painting

The left third of the painting appears much darker than the surrounding area—as if a cloud were casting a shadow down on the cityscape. This represents the section of the narrative that occurred at night, including the scenes of the downfall of Judas, the Last Supper, the agony in the garden, and Jesus' arrest.

Calvary

Calvary, the site of the Crucifixion itself, is placed at the very top of the composition, and is wreathed in an ominous cover of storm clouds. This helps to establish the death of Jesus as the moment of highest narrative tension, after which the composition flows downward and resolves with the story of Jesus' Resurrection.

HANS MEMLING | *1470–1471*

Scenes from the Passion of Christ

Essay by Michael Stevens

Across human history there is no story that seems to grip the mind more powerfully than the Passion of Jesus. From the time of the early Church right up to the present day, images of Christ crucified have permeated every artistic medium imaginable: from painting and sculpture, to music, film, and literature. Within the contours of the Passion story, artists have found endless viewpoints for reflection on the bitter betrayal, suffering, and desolation surrounding the events of Jesus' death, as well as the boundless hope, joy, and triumph in the reality of his Resurrection.

These manifold vantage points are given a cinematic scale in Flemish artist Hans Memling's epic painting *Scenes from the Passion of Christ*. Through a labyrinthine composition of daunting complexity, the artist weaves together a bird's eye view of the entire Passion story. The sequence begins with the triumphal entry at top left and culminates in the Resurrection at middle right. Between these points, an astonishing amount of narrative content is developed and elaborated upon, including the cleansing of the temple, the downfall of Judas, the Last Supper, the agony in the garden, the trial before the Sanhedrin, the scourging at the pillar, the crowning with thorns, the handing over of Jesus to be crucified, the carrying of the cross, the Crucifixion, the deposition from the cross, and the burial of Jesus.

THE DEATH OF JESUS

[33] When it was noon, darkness came over the whole land until three in the afternoon. [34] At three o'clock Jesus cried out with a loud voice, "Eloi, Eloi, lema sabachthani?" which means, "My God, my God, why have you forsaken me?" [35] When some of the bystanders heard it, they said, "Listen, he is calling for Elijah." [36] And someone ran, filled a sponge with sour wine, put it on a stick, and gave it to him to drink, saying, "Wait, let us see whether Elijah will come to take him down." [37] Then Jesus gave a loud cry and breathed his last. [38] And the curtain of the temple was torn in two, from top to bottom. [39] Now when the centurion, who stood facing him, saw that in this way he breathed his last, he said, "Truly this man was God's Son!"

[40] There were also women looking on from a distance; among them were Mary Magdalene, and Mary the mother of James the younger and of Joses, and Salome. [41] These used to follow him and provided for him when he was in Galilee; and there were many other women who had come up with him to Jerusalem.

THE BURIAL OF JESUS

[42] When evening had come, and since it was the day of Preparation, that is, the day before the sabbath, [43] Joseph of Arimathea, a respected member of the council, who was also himself waiting expectantly for the kingdom of

---

G.K. Chesterton
(1874–1936)
———
Orthodoxy

When God Seemed to Be an Atheist

Mark 15:34

Christianity alone has felt that God, to be wholly God, must have been a rebel as well as a king. Alone of all creeds, Christianity has added courage to the virtues of the Creator. For the only courage worth calling courage must necessarily mean that the soul passes a breaking point—and does not break. In this indeed I approach a matter more dark and awful than it is easy to discuss; and I apologize in advance if any of my phrases fall wrong or seem irreverent touching a matter which the greatest saints and thinkers have justly feared to approach.

But in that terrific tale of the Passion there is a distinct emotional suggestion that the author of all things (in some unthinkable way) went not only through agony, but through doubt. It is written, "Thou shalt not tempt the Lord thy God." No; but the Lord thy God may tempt himself; and it seems as if this was what happened in Gethsemane. In a garden Satan tempted man: and in a garden God tempted God. He passed in some superhuman manner through our human horror of pessimism.

When the world shook and the sun was wiped out of heaven, it was not at the Crucifixion, but at the cry from the cross: the cry which confessed that God was forsaken of God. And now let the revolutionists choose a creed from all the creeds and a god from all the gods of the world, carefully weighing all the gods of inevitable recurrence and of unalterable power. They will not find another god who has himself been in revolt. Nay (the matter grows too difficult for human speech), but let the atheists themselves choose a god. They will find only one divinity who ever uttered their isolation; only one religion in which God seemed for an instant to be an atheist.

God, went boldly to Pilate and asked for the body of Jesus. [44] Then Pilate wondered if he were already dead; and summoning the centurion, he asked him whether he had been dead for some time. [45] When he learned from the centurion that he was dead, he granted the body to Joseph. [46] Then Joseph bought a linen cloth, and taking down the body, wrapped it in the linen cloth, and laid it in a tomb that had been hewn out of the rock. He then rolled a stone against the door of the tomb. [47] Mary Magdalene and Mary the mother of Joses saw where the body was laid.

The Disturbing Message of the Resurrection

Mark 16:9–15 | Bishop Barron

Jesus' commission to his disciples shows that he wants to save all. And a great lesson of the Resurrection is that the path of salvation has been opened to everyone. Paul told us that "though he was in the form of God, [Jesus] did not regard equality with God as something to be exploited, but emptied himself, taking the form of a slave … [becoming] obedient to the point of death—even death on a cross" (Phil. 2:6–8).

In a word, Jesus went all the way down, journeying into pain, despair, alienation, even godforsakenness. Why? In order to reach all of those who had wandered from God. Then, in light of the Resurrection, the first Christians came to know that, even as we run as fast as we can away from the Father, all the way to godforsakenness, we are running into the arms of the Son. The Resurrection shows that Christ can gather back to the Father everyone whom he has embraced through his suffering love.

THE RESURRECTION OF JESUS

16 When the sabbath was over, Mary Magdalene, and Mary the mother of James, and Salome bought spices, so that they might go and anoint him. ² And very early on the first day of the week, when the sun had risen, they went to the tomb. ³ They had been saying to one another, "Who will roll away the stone for us from the entrance to the tomb?" ⁴ When they looked up, they saw that the stone, which was very large, had already been rolled back. ⁵ As they entered the tomb, they saw a young man, dressed in a white robe, sitting on the right side; and they were alarmed. ⁶ But he said to them, "Do not be alarmed; you are looking for Jesus of Nazareth, who was crucified. He has been raised; he is not here. Look, there is the place they laid him. ⁷ But go, tell his disciples and Peter that he is going ahead of you to Galilee; there you will see him, just as he told you." ⁸ So they went out and fled from the tomb, for terror and amazement had seized them; and they said nothing to anyone, for they were afraid.

[THE SHORTER ENDING OF MARK]

And all that had been commanded them they told briefly to those around Peter. And afterward Jesus himself sent out through them, from east to west, the sacred and imperishable proclamation of eternal salvation.

Why Did Jesus Leave?

Mark 16:15–20 | Bishop Barron

Jesus commissioned his disciples (and us) to proclaim the Gospel to the whole world. Then he was taken up to heaven, where he took his place at God's right hand, as the disciples went forth and preached everywhere.

The Ascension of Jesus signals the beginning of the era of the Church. As Jesus leaves the scene (at least in the most obvious sense), he opens the stage for us. What if Caesar, Lincoln, Roosevelt, and Churchill were still striding the world stage? No one would have the courage to enter the game. So Jesus leaves, that we might act in his name and in accord with his Spirit.

[THE LONGER ENDING OF MARK]

JESUS APPEARS TO MARY MAGDALENE

⁹ Now after he rose early on the first day of the week, he appeared first to Mary Magdalene, from whom he had cast out seven demons. ¹⁰ She went out and told those who had been with him, while they were mourning and weeping. ¹¹ But when they heard that he was alive and had been seen by her, they would not believe it.

JESUS APPEARS TO TWO DISCIPLES

¹² After this he appeared in another form to two of them, as they were walking into the country. ¹³ And they went back and told the rest, but they did not believe them.

JESUS COMMISSIONS THE DISCIPLES

¹⁴ Later he appeared to the eleven themselves as they were sitting at the table; and he upbraided them for their lack of faith and stubbornness, because they had not believed those who saw him after he had risen. ¹⁵ And he said to them, "Go into all the world and proclaim the good news to the whole creation. ¹⁶ The one who believes and is baptized will be saved; but the one who does not believe will be condemned. ¹⁷ And these signs will accompany those who believe: by using my name they will cast out demons; they will speak in new tongues; ¹⁸ they will pick up snakes in their hands, and if they drink any deadly thing, it will not hurt them; they will lay their hands on the sick, and they will recover."

THE ASCENSION OF JESUS

¹⁹ So then the Lord Jesus, after he had spoken to them, was taken up into heaven and sat down at the right hand of God. ²⁰ And they went out and proclaimed the good news everywhere, while the Lord worked with them and confirmed the message by the signs that accompanied it.

What Does the Resurrection Mean?

Mark 16:1–8 | Bishop Barron

THE RESURRECTION is the be-all and end-all of Christian faith. It is the still point around which everything Christian turns. It is the great non-negotiable at the heart of our system of beliefs and practices. The four Gospels, the epistles of Paul and John, the writings of Augustine, Jerome, and Chrysostom, the poetry of Dante, the *Summa theologiae* of Thomas Aquinas, Michelangelo's Sistine Ceiling, Chartres Cathedral, the sermons of John Henry Newman, the mysticism of Teresa of Avila, the radical witness of Mother Teresa—all of it flows from the event of the Resurrection, and without the Resurrection, none of it makes a bit of sense. Paul stated this truth as succinctly and clearly as you could wish: "If Christ has not been raised, your faith is futile" (1 Cor. 15:17). The Resurrection of Jesus from the dead is the Gospel, the *euangelion*, the Good News. Everything else is commentary.

But what precisely do Christians mean when we speak of Christ's Resurrection? Let me get at it indirectly, by specifying what we don't mean. Despite the suggestions of far too many theologians in recent years, we don't mean that "resurrection" is a literary conceit, a symbolic way of expressing the truth that Jesus' "spirit" or "cause" survives his physical demise. In the 1970s, Edward Schillebeeckx speculated that, after Jesus' terrible death, his disciples gathered together in their fear and pain for mutual support. What they discovered in time, largely through the suggestions of Peter, was that, despite their cowardly abandonment of Jesus at his hour of need, they "felt forgiven" by their departed Lord. They expressed this subjective experience through evocative narratives about an empty tomb and appearances of the risen Jesus. Only naïve readers, then and now, would take such stories as straightforward history, Schillebeeckx concluded. We find something very similar in the recent Christology proposed by Roger Haight. Haight speculates that the disciples came together after the death of Jesus and recalled, over time, his words, deeds, and gestures, and how Jesus had been for them a privileged symbol of the presence of God. This survival of the provocative memory of Jesus in their midst they expressed in the pictorial language of the biblical Resurrection stories.

If that's all the Church means by the Resurrection of Jesus, I say, "Why bother?" Were this approach correct, the language of resurrection from the dead could be applied, with equal validity, to practically any great religious or spiritual figure in history. Didn't the followers of the Buddha fondly remember him and his cause after his death? Couldn't the disciples of Confucius have sat in a memory circle and recalled how he had radically changed their lives? Couldn't the friends of Zoroaster have felt forgiven by him after he had passed from the scene? Indeed, couldn't the members of the Abraham Lincoln Society manage to generate many of the convictions and feelings about Lincoln that Schillebeeckx and Haight claim the Apostles generated about Jesus? And would any of these demythologizing explanations begin to make sense of that excitement, that sense of novelty, surprise, and eschatological breakthrough that runs right through the four Gospels, through every one of the epistles, to the book of Revelation? Can we really imagine St. Paul tearing into Corinth with the earth-shaking message that a dead man was found to be quite inspiring? Can we really imagine St. Peter enduring his upside-down crucifixion because he and the other disciples had "felt forgiven"?

More to it, these painfully reductive readings of the Resurrection stories actually betray a thin and unsophisticated grasp of the biblical authors. Here the magisterial work of the New Testament scholar N.T. Wright is particularly illuminating. Wright says that the composers of the New Testament were aware of a whole range of options in regard to the status of those who had died. From their Jewish heritage, they knew of the shadowy realm of Sheol and the sad figures that dwell therein. They knew further that people could return from Sheol in ghostly form. (Think of the prophet Samuel called up from the dead by the witch of Endor in the twenty-eighth chapter of the first book of Samuel.) They even had a sense of reincarnation, evident in widespread convictions about the return of Elijah in advance of the Messiah or in the popular report that Jesus himself was John the Baptist or one of the prophets returned from death. From the Hellenistic and Roman cultural matrix, furthermore, the New Testament authors would have inherited the Platonic theory that the soul at death escapes from the body as from a prison in order to move into a higher spiritual arena. They also were aware of a perspective, combining both Greek and Hebrew elements, according to which the souls of the dead abide for a time with God in a quasi-disembodied state, while they await the general resurrection at the *eschaton*. This view is on clear display in the famous passage from the book of Wisdom that says, "The souls of the righteous are in the hand of God, and no torment will ever touch them" (Wis. 3:1). Finally, they knew all about hallucinations, illusions, and projections (though they wouldn't have used those terms), as is clear from the first reactions of the disciples upon hearing the reports of Jesus' post-Resurrection appearances.

The point is that they used *none of these categories* when speaking of the Resurrection of Jesus. They didn't say that Jesus had gone to Sheol and was languishing there; nor did they claim that he had returned from that realm à la Samuel. They certainly did not think that Jesus' soul had escaped from his body or that he was vaguely "with God" like any other of the righteous dead. They did not think that the general resurrection of the dead had taken place. And most certainly, they did not think that the Resurrection was a symbolic way of talking about something that had happened to them. Again and again, they emphasize how discouraged, worn down, and confused they were after the Crucifixion. That this dejected band would spontaneously generate the faith that would send them careering around the world with the message of Resurrection strains credulity.

What is undeniably clear is that something had happened to Jesus— something so strange that those who witnessed it had no category apt to describe it. Perhaps we would get closest to it if we were to say that what was expected of all of the righteous dead at the *eschaton*—the bodily resurrection—had come true in time for this one man, Jesus of Nazareth, the same Jesus whom they knew, with whom they had shared meals and fellowship. This Jesus, who had died and had been buried, appeared alive to them, bodily present, though transformed, no longer conditioned by the limitations of space and time. This is what rendered them speechless at first, and then, especially after the event of Pentecost, prepared to go to the ends of the earth, enduring every hardship, even to the point of martyrdom, in order to proclaim the Good News.

The women came to the tomb early on Easter Sunday morning in order to anoint the body of Jesus and pay their respects. As they made their way to the sepulcher, they probably shared stories of Jesus and repeated his words, recalling to one another how profoundly he had influenced them. They undoubtedly expected to linger at the tomb after their task was completed, continuing to reflect wistfully and sadly on this great man. This is, more or less, what any mourners would do at the tomb of a fondly remembered friend. But there is nothing peaceful about the tomb of Jesus. When the women arrived, they noticed that the stone had been rolled away. Suspecting that someone had broken in and stolen the body, they approached the open grave, only—to their infinite surprise—to spy a man in a white garment who said, "He is not here." It is at that moment that they began to suspect that someone, in fact, had broken *out* of the tomb. So overwhelmed, so disoriented were they that they ran from the spot—"seized," Mark tells us, by "terror and amazement." Gathered round the tomb of a friend or hero, one might feel nostalgic, sad, inspired, but one would not, I suggest, be frightened and amazed. The point is this: something so new happened at Easter that the tame category of wistful remembrance is ludicrously inadequate as an explanation.

Jesus is risen; it is true. And that makes all the difference.

The feet of Christ

Dürer portrays the feet of Jesus moments before they leave the frame. The vertical direction of Christ's movement is counterbalanced by the horizontal marks in the sky, and the stable mass of figures who watch from below.

Footprints

Footprints have been left on the rock from which Christ rises, calling attention to the empty space left behind. While he is leaving for a time, we know that he will return again.

Mark 16:19–20

ALBRECHT DÜRER | *Sixteenth century*

The Ascension

Essay by Michael Stevens

In this scene, we see the Ascension of Christ into heaven as envisioned by the German Renaissance artist Albrecht Dürer. Dürer was prolific during his career and established a reputation early in life as a master of woodcut, engraving, and drawing. In addition to his output as a printmaker, he was also an accomplished art theorist and mathematician and was keenly interested in the use of scientific and geometrical tools within the realm of art.

What is most striking about this scene is the verticality with which Christ leaves the composition—straight up into the clouds. The inclusion of only his feet, which barely remain in view, makes for a surreal effect and provides a stark contrast to the firmly grounded disciples who stand beneath. As one looks at the faces of the disciples, they appear to be overwhelmed with sadness at the sight of Jesus' departure. The open space on the rock, with its two footprints, emphasizes the vacant place that Jesus leaves behind as he rises to heaven.

But in spite of the disciples' grief, we know this is not the end of the story. Jesus' followers will soon experience the joy and renewal of Pentecost and witness the birth of the Church. Besides this, they have also been given the Eucharist: the fulfillment of Jesus' promise to his friends to always remain with them. So while this may appear on the surface to be a scene of abandonment, we know that the Church has received a new form of his continued presence until his promised return to earth.

THE GOSPEL
ACCORDING
to LUKE

Introduction to the Gospel of Luke

Elizabeth Scalia

WHAT ARE WE TO MAKE of the Gospel of Luke—a Gospel traditionally believed to have come from the hand of a Greek physician (the same man who wrote the Acts of the Apostles) and whose words comprise nearly a quarter of the New Testament? We could do the usual research and access plenty of information about how and where it is sourced, but if we approach Luke and his "Good News" simply as curious readers and thinkers, then it is self-evident that the writer is intelligent. It is also clear that he is deeply read, because what Luke delivers is the sort of highly engaging and lasting chronicle that can only come from someone who understands how to build a story and sustain interest; someone who knows what a strong narrative requires: background, compelling details, a steady and reasonable build-up within time frames, logic (where mystery does not confound it), and most emphatically, the human element through which generations of readers can envision, imagine, and identify.

The great strength of Luke's Gospel, as with Acts, is how accessibly, rationally, and convincingly he presents a narrative that must necessarily challenge, even defy, reason. In comparison with the other Gospel writers, Luke is the one who gives us a distinct, richly detailed account of the ongoing interplay between God and humanity, heaven and earth—one that we can and do believe because, in this Gospel in particular, belief is grounded in plausible and subtle human reactions and responses.

A mere four verses into Luke's first chapter, he sets the stage and shows us the first instance of earthbound reason responding to heavenly mystery. The archangel Gabriel brings some surprising news to the aged priest Zechariah: "Your wife Elizabeth will bear you a son, and you will name him John" (Luke 1:13). He responds, "How will I know that this is so? For I am an old man, and my wife is getting on in years" (Luke 1:18). Zechariah's question to Gabriel seems like one we ourselves might ask in the same situation. In today's parlance, we might say, "Get out! That's impossible!"

Meanwhile, in the very same chapter, we read of Gabriel making another visit, this time to Nazareth, where he greets an adolescent virgin, Mary, with similarly shocking news (Luke 1:26–37). On first consideration, Mary's reply to Gabriel's news doesn't seem so different from Zechariah's, and yet she is not "punished" as we perceive the priest to be. Both asked an apparently rational question of the heavenly messenger—"How?"—yet one questioner is struck dumb for the asking, but the other is not. That seems confusing. How could God seem so inconsistent, or Gabriel so capricious?

All of these details are meant to give us a sense not of God's duality but of the justice that heaven applies to each of us individually. The questions Zechariah and Mary ask seem similar, and yet they are very different, particularly when one takes experience and youth into consideration, which justice would demand. Zechariah was a priest; he'd served within the holy place for many years. And yet, in the face of an angel's proclamation, his first reaction is a skeptical one. "How will I *know*?" he asks, which is the same as saying, "How can I believe this? How can I *trust* this?" Mary too asks a rational question, but it is really quite different from her elder cousin's. "How can this be," she asks, "since I am a virgin?" (Luke 1:34). She is not asking "How can I trust this?" but rather, "By what *means*?" It's a perfectly reasonable question for any woman to ask, at any age. And because Mary's question is constructively curious rather than skeptical, she is given the answer her openness deserves—one that is still mysterious but, because her faith is strong, that allows her to give her *fiat* (her assent in Luke 1:38), and thus begin our ongoing pageant of salvation. She may not understand, but Mary knows that God's "got this"—and that is enough for her.

Zechariah is struck mute, but far from being a punishment, it should be perceived as a gift. This lifelong priest from an exalted class has been given a chance to still his too-ready, too-presumptuous tongue in order to re-engage mind, heart, and soul toward God. He is given time to feed his interior life—to rediscover and resubmerge himself into the fathomless depths of faith that first called to him—and thus prepare for the new life about to be thrust into his care.

Mary, meanwhile, who never doubted what she'd been told, found her way to Elizabeth and Zechariah. What might Zechariah have thought when she arrived at their house, telling her relatives the unthinkable news (even as Elizabeth intuited it)? We imagine the old priest—who should have known better than to doubt—watching this girl serenely consenting to it all. Zechariah had to have recognized how short he had fallen in the face of a heavenly outreach, and been humbled by it. No wonder that when his tongue was finally loosed, Zechariah's first prayer evidenced the fruit of his silence, contemplation, and discernment: "Blessed be the Lord God of Israel" (Luke 1:68).

The two great and praise-filled offerings of Mary (Luke 1:46–55) and Zechariah (Luke 1:68–79) have, for more than sixteen hundred years, formed the backbone of the liturgical offices of Lauds and Vespers—the morning and evening praise the Church offers to the Creator. Although by two different people, of two different sexes and generations, and with two different personal experiences of an encounter with heaven, their words ultimately echo each other in a shared understanding that God is holy, and that God is faithful.

And Luke is just getting started!

Another important aspect of the Gospel writer and how to read him is this: a good writer is a good *reader*; a good storyteller is a good *observer*; and a good doctor is a good *listener*. We find all of this in Luke, who not only relates events as they have been shared with him but always brings us a lesson as well. As a doctor he may have told his patients to pay attention to every little clue their body gives them so as to sustain homeostasis—to observe the rapidity of their breathing, the moisture of eye and mouth, or the smell of their breath for signs of dehydration. In a similar way, his Gospel writing encourages us not just to take an overview of his words but to pay attention to every line. In Scripture, everything matters, and not a single line is set in place for mere dressing. What we learn from Luke is how to listen, attend, observe, and even use our imaginations in order to—like Zechariah—internalize a lesson meant distinctly for us.

To offer just one example, in Jesus' telling of the parable of the prodigal son, we read: "So he set off and went to his father. But while he was still far off, his father saw him and was filled with compassion; he ran and put his arms around him and kissed him" (Luke 15:20). It's a wonderful and reassuring description of how God waits for us to return to him in order to shower us with his mercy and forgiveness. And yet there are six words within the message that bring us further into that mystery of mercy, and give us an additional—and instructive—reason to hope: "While he was still far off . . ."

If there is a particular Christian message that sometimes skews our understanding, or dashes our hope for salvation, it is the notion that faith is an instant event and an all-in proposition—one is either converted immediately and accepts every doctrine instantly and without question, or one is "doing it wrong." But as we see with Zechariah and Mary, it is human to wonder, and not everyone is at all times emotionally, intellectually, or spiritually in the perfect place for insta-conversion. Nevertheless, God is eagerly looking for us—so eagerly that he will, like the father of the prodigal, run toward us with open arms, even when we are "still far off." What a hopeful and helpful reality this is to contemplate! All of our conversions are ongoing—we are always "still far off" in one respect or another—and yet God is so anxious for our reunion with him that he will come to us, even when we are mere specks on his horizon.

There are no unimportant parts in Scripture, no "skippable" verses not worth reading. Read Luke's words with a careful eye, an open heart, and a soul begging to be informed. And keep a notebook handy, because this physician is telling stories within the stories, providing medicine within the medicine—all "to make ready a people prepared for the Lord" (Luke 1:17).

Elizabeth Scalia is the Editor-at-Large for Word on Fire Catholic Ministries. She is author of several books, including the award-winning Strange Gods, *and is a Benedictine Oblate.*

DEDICATION TO THEOPHILUS

1 Since many have undertaken to set down an orderly account of the events that have been fulfilled among us, [2] just as they were handed on to us by those who from the beginning were eyewitnesses and servants of the word, [3] I too decided, after investigating everything carefully from the very first, to write an orderly account for you, most excellent Theophilus, [4] so that you may know the truth concerning the things about which you have been instructed.

THE BIRTH OF JOHN THE BAPTIST FORETOLD

[5] In the days of King Herod of Judea, there was a priest named Zechariah, who belonged to the priestly order of Abijah. His wife was a descendant of Aaron, and her name was Elizabeth. [6] Both of them were righteous before God, living blamelessly according to all the commandments and regulations of the Lord. [7] But they had no children, because Elizabeth was barren, and both were getting on in years.

[8] Once when he was serving as priest before God and his section was on duty, [9] he was chosen by lot, according to the custom of the priesthood, to enter the sanctuary of the Lord and offer incense. [10] Now at the time of the incense offering, the whole assembly of the people was praying outside. [11] Then there appeared to him an angel of the Lord, standing at the right side of the altar of incense. [12] When Zechariah saw him, he was terrified; and fear overwhelmed him. [13] But the angel said to him, "Do not be afraid, Zechariah, for your prayer has been heard. Your wife Elizabeth will bear you a son, and you will name him John. [14] You will have joy and gladness, and many will rejoice at his birth, [15] for he will be great in the sight of the Lord. He must never drink wine or strong drink; even before his birth he will be filled with the Holy Spirit. [16] He will turn many of the people of Israel to the Lord their God. [17] With the spirit and power of Elijah he will go before him, to turn the hearts of parents to their children, and the disobedient to the wisdom of the righteous, to make ready a people prepared for the Lord." [18] Zechariah said to the angel, "How will I know that this is so? For I am an old man, and my wife is getting on in years." [19] The angel replied, "I am Gabriel. I stand in the presence of God, and I have been sent to speak to you and to bring you this good news. [20] But now, because you did not believe my words, which will be fulfilled in their time, you will become mute, unable to speak, until the day these things occur."

[21] Meanwhile the people were waiting for Zechariah, and wondered at his delay in the sanctuary. [22] When he did come out, he could not speak to them, and they realized that he had seen a vision in the sanctuary. He

Finding Your Role in the Theo-drama

Luke 1:30–45 | Bishop Barron

Upon hearing the message of Gabriel concerning her own pregnancy and that of her cousin, Mary "went with haste to a Judean town in the hill country" to see Elizabeth.

Why did she go with such speed and purpose? Because she had found her mission, her role in the theo-drama. We are dominated today by the ego-drama in all of its ramifications and implications. The ego-drama is the play that I'm writing, I'm producing, I'm directing, and I'm starring in. We see this absolutely everywhere in our culture. Freedom of choice reigns supreme: I become the person that I choose to be.

The theo-drama is the great story being told by God, the great play being directed by God. What makes life thrilling is to discover your role in it. This is precisely what has happened to Mary. She has found her role—indeed a climactic role—in the theo-drama, and she wants to conspire with Elizabeth, who has also discovered her role in the same drama. And, like Mary, we have to find our place in God's story.

St. Irenaeus
(130–202)
——
Against Heresies

Mary Undoing Eve

Luke 1:26–38

Just as Eve was led astray by the word of an angel … so did the Virgin Mary by the word of an angel receive the glad tidings that she should bear God, through obedience to his word. If the former disobeyed God, the latter was persuaded to obey God and thus became Eve's advocate. Just as the human race was subjected to death by means of a virgin, so it is rescued by a virgin; the scales were rebalanced when a virginal obedience redressed a virginal disobedience. The coming of the serpent is conquered by the harmlessness of the dove, and the bonds that firmly bound us to death were cut.

kept motioning to them and remained unable to speak. ²³ When his time of service was ended, he went to his home.

²⁴ After those days his wife Elizabeth conceived, and for five months she remained in seclusion. She said, ²⁵ "This is what the Lord has done for me when he looked favorably on me and took away the disgrace I have endured among my people."

Joseph Ratzinger (Pope Benedict XVI) (1927–)

Jesus of Nazareth: The Infancy Narratives

Heaven Holding Its Breath
Luke 1:36–38

In one of his Advent homilies, Bernard of Clairvaux offers a stirring presentation of the drama of this moment. After the error of our first parents, the whole world was shrouded in darkness, under the dominion of death. Now God seeks to enter the world anew. He knocks at Mary's door. He needs human freedom. The only way he can redeem man, who was created free, is by means of a free "yes" to his will. In creating freedom, he made himself in a certain sense dependent upon man. His power is tied to the unenforceable "yes" of a human being. So Bernard portrays heaven and earth as it were holding its breath at this moment of the question addressed to Mary. Will she say yes? She hesitates … will her humility hold her back? Just this once—Bernard tells her—do not be humble but daring! Give us your "yes"! This is the crucial moment when, from her lips, from her heart, the answer comes: "Let it be with me according to your word." It is the moment of free, humble, yet magnanimous obedience in which the loftiest choice of human freedom is made.

Mary becomes a mother through her "yes." The Church Fathers sometimes expressed this by saying that Mary conceived through her ear—that is to say: through her hearing. Through her obedience, the

Word entered into her and became fruitful in her. In this connection, the Fathers developed the idea of God's birth in us through faith and Baptism, in which the *Lógos* comes to us ever anew, making us God's children. For example, we may recall the words of Saint Irenaeus: "How shall man pass into God, unless God has first passed into man? How was mankind to escape this birth into death, unless he were born again through faith, by that new birth from the Virgin, the sign of salvation that is God's wonderful and unmistakable gift?"

THE BIRTH OF JESUS FORETOLD

26 In the sixth month the angel Gabriel was sent by God to a town in Galilee called Nazareth, 27 to a virgin engaged to a man whose name was Joseph, of the house of David. The virgin's name was Mary. 28 And he came to her and said, "Greetings, favored one! The Lord is with you." 29 But she was much perplexed by his words and pondered what sort of greeting this might be. 30 The angel said to her, "Do not be afraid, Mary, for you have found favor with God. 31 And now, you will conceive in your womb and bear a son, and you will name him Jesus. 32 He will be great, and will be called the Son of the Most High, and the Lord God will give to him the throne of his ancestor David. 33 He will reign over the house of Jacob forever, and of his kingdom there will be no end." 34 Mary said to the angel, "How can this be, since I am a virgin?" 35 The angel said to her, "The Holy Spirit will come upon you, and the power of the Most High will overshadow you; therefore the child to be born will be holy; he will be called Son of God. 36 And now, your relative Elizabeth in her old age has also conceived a son; and this is the sixth month for her who was said to be barren. 37 For nothing will be impossible with God." 38 Then Mary said, "Here am I, the servant of the Lord; let it be with me according to your word." Then the angel departed from her.

MARY VISITS ELIZABETH

39 In those days Mary set out and went with haste to a Judean town in the hill country, 40 where she entered the house of Zechariah and greeted Elizabeth. 41 When Elizabeth heard Mary's greeting, the child leaped in her womb. And Elizabeth was filled with the Holy Spirit 42 and exclaimed with a loud cry, "Blessed are you among women, and blessed is the fruit of your

womb. ⁴³ And why has this happened to me, that the mother of my Lord comes to me? ⁴⁴ For as soon as I heard the sound of your greeting, the child in my womb leaped for joy. ⁴⁵ And blessed is she who believed that there would be a fulfillment of what was spoken to her by the Lord."

MARY'S SONG OF PRAISE

⁴⁶ And Mary said,

"My soul magnifies the Lord,
⁴⁷ and my spirit rejoices in God my Savior,
⁴⁸ for he has looked with favor on the lowliness of his servant.
Surely, from now on all generations will call me blessed;
⁴⁹ for the Mighty One has done great things for me,
and holy is his name.
⁵⁰ His mercy is for those who fear him
from generation to generation.
⁵¹ He has shown strength with his arm;
he has scattered the proud in the thoughts of their hearts.
⁵² He has brought down the powerful from their thrones,
and lifted up the lowly;
⁵³ he has filled the hungry with good things,
and sent the rich away empty.
⁵⁴ He has helped his servant Israel,
in remembrance of his mercy,
⁵⁵ according to the promise he made to our ancestors,
to Abraham and to his descendants forever."

⁵⁶ And Mary remained with her about three months and then returned to her home.

THE BIRTH OF JOHN THE BAPTIST

⁵⁷ Now the time came for Elizabeth to give birth, and she bore a son. ⁵⁸ Her neighbors and relatives heard that the Lord had shown his great mercy to her, and they rejoiced with her.

⁵⁹ On the eighth day they came to circumcise the child, and they were going to name him Zechariah after his father. ⁶⁰ But his mother said, "No; he is to be called John." ⁶¹ They said to her, "None of your relatives has this name." ⁶² Then they began motioning to his father to find out what name he wanted to give him. ⁶³ He asked for a writing tablet and wrote, "His name is John." And all of them were amazed. ⁶⁴ Immediately his mouth was opened and his tongue freed, and he began to speak, praising God. ⁶⁵ Fear came over all their neighbors, and all these things were talked

My Soul Magnifies the Lord

Luke 1:46–56 | Bishop Barron

Mary's great hymn of praise to Yahweh commences with the simple declaration, "My soul magnifies the Lord." Mary announces here that her whole being is ordered to the glorification of God. Her ego wants nothing for itself; it wants only to be an occasion for giving honor to God. But since God needs nothing, whatever glory Mary gives to him returns to her benefit so that she is magnified in the very act of magnifying him. In giving herself away fully to God, Mary becomes a superabundant source of life; indeed, she becomes pregnant with God. This odd and wonderful rhythm of magnifying and being magnified is the key to understanding everything about Mary, from her divine motherhood, to her Assumption and Immaculate Conception, to her mission in the life of the Church.

The great nineteenth-century Jesuit poet Gerard Manley Hopkins caught this in his ballad "The May Magnificat." He wonders aloud in the first few stanzas why May should be a month dedicated to Mary, and he provides Mary's own answer:

Ask of her, the mighty mother:
Her reply puts this other
Question: What is Spring?
Growth in every thing—

Then, with typical verbal dexterity and spiritual enthusiasm, Hopkins delineates the modes of growth in springtime:

Flesh and fleece, fur and feather,
Grass and greenworld all together;
Star-eyed strawberry-breasted
Throstle above her nested
Cluster of bugle blue eggs thin
Forms and warms the life within;
And bird and blossom swell
In sod or sheath or shell.

And he imagines Mary the Mother of God surveying all of this life with limitless pleasure:

All things rising, all things sizing
Mary sees, sympathising
With that world of good
Nature's motherhood.

Mary's utter willingness to magnify the Lord made of her a matrix of life. The spring itself, in all of its wild fecundity, is but a hint at the vitality that she unleashes.

---

about throughout the entire hill country of Judea. [66] All who heard them pondered them and said, "What then will this child become?" For, indeed, the hand of the Lord was with him.

Luke 1:26–38

FRA ANGELICO | *1440–1441*

Annunciation

Essay by Michael Stevens

In this fresco by Fra Angelico, we see one of the pivotal moments in salvation history unfolding: the Annunciation. In this scene, Mary responds to the angel Gabriel with her *fiat:* her resounding "yes" to God's will that she be the mother of Jesus.

Fra Angelico ("the Angelic Brother") was a Dominican monk revered for both his breathtaking talent as a painter, as well as his prayerfulness and deep devotion. His frescoes display both medieval and Renaissance characteristics, and merge the spare, serene simplicity found in early Italian style with the spatial depth and three-dimensionality that would go on to define the Italian painting of the High Renaissance.

This painting was commissioned for the Convent of San Marco in Florence, and adorns the wall of one of the friar's cells. By placing frescoes such as these directly within the living quarters of the monks, residents were encouraged to pray and reflect upon their mysteries continuously.

Gabriel's shadowless form

While Mary's shadow is visible on the wall behind her, the angel Gabriel's body casts no shadow. This represents the angel's immaterial nature.

St. Peter Martyr in prayer

St. Peter Martyr, one of the most celebrated Dominican martyr-saints, is pictured at the left edge of the composition, and watches the spectacle unfold in quiet reflection. By placing a Dominican hero in the story, we are invited to join St. Peter Martyr and watch the Gospel story unfold beside him.

The Convent of San Marco

The architecture within the Annunciation scene—with its luminous, bare walls and vaulted ceilings—is directly modeled after the monastery's cloister, as if to suggest that this event could have taken place in the immediate vicinity of the viewer.

ZECHARIAH'S PROPHECY

⁶⁷ Then his father Zechariah was filled with the Holy Spirit and spoke this prophecy:

⁶⁸ "Blessed be the Lord God of Israel,
for he has looked favorably on his people and redeemed them.
⁶⁹ He has raised up a mighty savior for us
in the house of his servant David,
⁷⁰ as he spoke through the mouth of his holy prophets from of old,
⁷¹ that we would be saved from our enemies and from the hand of all
who hate us.
⁷² Thus he has shown the mercy promised to our ancestors,
and has remembered his holy covenant,
⁷³ the oath that he swore to our ancestor Abraham,
to grant us ⁷⁴ that we, being rescued from the hands of our enemies,
might serve him without fear, ⁷⁵ in holiness and righteousness
before him all our days.
⁷⁶ And you, child, will be called the prophet of the Most High;
for you will go before the Lord to prepare his ways,
⁷⁷ to give knowledge of salvation to his people
by the forgiveness of their sins.
⁷⁸ By the tender mercy of our God,
the dawn from on high will break upon us,
⁷⁹ to give light to those who sit in darkness and in the shadow of death,
to guide our feet into the way of peace."

⁸⁰ The child grew and became strong in spirit, and he was in the wilderness until the day he appeared publicly to Israel.

BLESSED *be the*

LORD

GOD OF ISRAEL.

LUKE 1:68

Mary and the New David

Luke 1:5–45 | Bishop Barron

THE FIRST CHAPTER of the Gospel of Luke is thoroughly drenched in Davidic themes from the Old Testament. Once this association with David is seen, we can understand the rest of Luke's Gospel about the work and ministry of Jesus with much greater clarity.

Luke's narrative begins with two "temple" persons: Zechariah, "who belonged to the priestly order of Abijah," and his wife Elizabeth, who is characterized as a "descendant of Aaron" and hence of priestly stock. The first thing we hear about Zechariah is that he serves as priest in the Jerusalem temple, offering incense in the sanctuary. David's dream was to build the temple in which Zechariah serves, and Zechariah's gestures are a ritualized mimicking of the moves of the king who danced before the ark. While in the sanctuary, we are told, Zechariah is visited by the angel Gabriel, who tells him that Elizabeth, despite her advanced years, will give birth to a son who will, like Elijah, prepare the way for the Messiah. The temple locale and the announcement of the birth of a child against all expectations brings us back to the beginning of 1 Samuel and Hannah's pregnancy, which resulted in the birth of Samuel, who would serve as forerunner to David. Indeed, Elizabeth's words upon conceiving ("This is what the Lord has done for me when he looked favorably on me and took away the disgrace I have endured among my people") powerfully evoke Hannah's frame of mind when she, after many tears and much prayer, finally became pregnant.

That same angel Gabriel made a subsequent appearance to Mary, a virgin residing in Nazareth and betrothed to Joseph, "of the house of David." Gabriel announced that this young woman would give birth to a son to whom she must give the name "Jesus." When Mary voiced her perplexity, the angel offered this further clarification: "He will be great, and will be called the Son of the Most High, and the Lord God will give to him the throne of his ancestor David. He will reign over the house of Jacob forever, and of his kingdom there will be no end." The Davidic line, which had come to an end politically with the death of Zedekiah, had gone, as it were, underground, continuing through Zerubbabel, a Davidide at the time of the return from exile, and then through a series of unknown figures for over five hundred years until it surfaced with Joseph and Jesus. Only with the angel's clarification that this Jesus would be "Son of the Most High" can one begin to understand something about the prophet Nathan's promise (2 Sam. 7:12–17) that has always been puzzling: the eternal quality of the reign of the son of David. Did this mean that the line would continue, temporally, forever, or that one member of that line would somehow sit on the throne forever? If the descendant of David referred to by Gabriel is in fact a figure not only human but also divine, his reign can be seen as properly transtemporal.

Upon declaring herself "the servant of the Lord" and acquiescing to the angel's request, Mary became the definitive Ark of the Covenant, the bearer of Yahweh's presence. A connection that the Church Fathers make with particular enthusiasm is between the ark of the covenant, which bore the divine law, and Mary of Nazareth, who bore the divine presence in the fullest possible sense. Maximus of Turin says, "But what would we say the ark was if not holy Mary, since the ark carried within it the tables of the covenant, while Mary bore the master of the same covenant?" One of the many artistic depictions of this patristic association is the relief of a juxtaposed Mary and the ark, which was carved in stone over the left portal at Notre Dame Cathedral in Paris. A number of symbolic echoes can be heard. David arose and went to get the ark, which was in the house of Abinadab, situated on "the hill" (probably a shrine) in the country of Judah. In the Gospel of Luke we are told that just after the angel Gabriel's annunciation to Mary, "Mary set out and went with haste to a Judean town in the hill country, where she entered the house of Zechariah and greeted Elizabeth." In other words, the supreme Ark, like its prototype, situates itself on a hilltop shrine in Judea. I do not say "shrine" casually here, for Zechariah is a temple priest and Elizabeth a descendant of Aaron, the first priest. Further, after the death of Uzzah, David asks, "How can the ark of the Lord come into my care?" (2 Sam. 6:9). Upon receiving her cousin, Elizabeth asks, "And why has this happened to me, that the mother of my Lord comes to me?" Both David and Elizabeth are unworthy to be in the presence of the bearer of the Lord. The king danced with all his might before the ark, and "when Elizabeth heard Mary's greeting, the child leaped in her womb"—the unborn John the Baptist performing an infant's dance in the presence of the true Ark.

Mary then delivers an exultant prayer reminiscent in almost every detail of the prayer uttered centuries before by Hannah upon the birth of Samuel (1 Sam. 2:1–10). Surely Luke is thereby bolstering his claim that Jesus is the long-awaited Son of David, the fulfillment of Nathan's prophecy. Finally, an intriguing detail: after the Uzzah incident, David sent the ark to the home of Obed-edom, where it stayed for three months. After proclaiming her great song, the Magnificat, "Mary remained with [Elizabeth] about three months and then returned to her home." There can be little doubt that Luke is consciously echoing these stories of the ark in order to highlight Mary's identity as *Theotokos*, the "God-bearer."

What does all of this mean for the life of Jesus? From the beginning to the end of his preaching career, Jesus' central theme was the arrival of the kingdom of God. What his original audience would have understood by this phrase was, doubtless, the ingathering of the scattered tribes of Israel, and what becomes eminently clear in all of the Gospels is that this coming together would happen in and through Jesus himself, much as the knitting together of ancient Israel happened in the person of David. In the accounts of the woman at the well, Zacchaeus, the man born blind, and the Syrophoenician woman, and in offering open table fellowship to saints, sinners, prostitutes, and Pharisees alike, Jesus undertook the kingly task. It is most important to grasp that he was not simply exemplifying the virtue of "inclusivity" in the contemporary sense; he was doing what the Davidic Messiah was expected to do. Jesus definitively fulfills what David himself left incomplete and unfinished.

The pomegranate

The pomegranate in Christ's left hand symbolizes his Passion, with the red seeds evoking the blood that was shed on the cross for our salvation.

Mary's clothing

Mary's clothing is modeled after the fashionable garments worn by noblewomen of Florence at the time this painting was created. By depicting Mary as a royal lady of the fifteenth century, Botticelli points to Mary's queenship in a way that his audience would have immediately understood.

Luke 1:46–56

SANDRO BOTTICELLI | *1481*

The Madonna of the Magnificat

Essay by Michael Stevens

This sublime image by Sandro Botticelli, known as *The Madonna of the Magnificat*, portrays Mary as she composes the Magnificat— her great prayer of thanksgiving and praise to God after the Annunciation and the Visitation.

At the bottom left, a group of angels (depicted without wings) holds up a small book, in which Mary writes. On the facing page of the book is the Canticle of Zechariah—the second proclamation of gratitude featured in Luke 1, and one that directly parallels Mary's.

Botticelli treats the face of Mary with incredible sensitivity and grace, and embellishes her radiant, flowing hair with layers of fine metallic gold. She looks down tenderly as she dips her quill into the inkwell, reflecting on what she will write next.

Jesus is framed on the lap of Mary by a diagonal part in her blue clothing, which reveals a beautiful field of red that surrounds him. The shape of these draperies around Christ recall the Hebrew tabernacle—the tent of meeting where God's presence dwelt in the Old Testament. Through this detail, Botticelli positions Mary as the New Tabernacle, in which God—incarnate in her womb—finds a new dwelling place.

THE BIRTH OF JESUS

2 In those days a decree went out from Emperor Augustus that all the world should be registered. ² This was the first registration and was taken while Quirinius was governor of Syria. ³ All went to their own towns to be registered. ⁴ Joseph also went from the town of Nazareth in Galilee to Judea, to the city of David called Bethlehem, because he was descended from the house and family of David. ⁵ He went to be registered with Mary, to whom he was engaged and who was expecting a child. ⁶ While they were there, the time came for her to deliver her child. ⁷ And she gave birth to her firstborn son and wrapped him in bands of cloth, and laid him in a manger, because there was no place for them in the inn.

G.K. Chesterton
(1874–1936)

—

Collected Poems

The House of Christmas

Luke 2:7

There fared a mother driven forth
Out of an inn to roam;
In the place where she was homeless
All men are at home.
The crazy stable close at hand,
With shaking timber and shifting sand,
Grew a stronger thing to abide and stand
Than the square stones of Rome.

For men are homesick in their homes,
And strangers under the sun,
And they lay on their heads in a foreign land
Whenever the day is done.
Here we have battle and blazing eyes,
And chance and honor and high surprise,
But our homes are under miraculous skies
Where the yule tale was begun.

A Child in a foul stable,
Where the beasts feed and foam;
Only where He was homeless
Are you and I at home;

We have hands that fashion and heads that know,
But our hearts we lost—how long ago!
In a place no chart nor ship can show
Under the sky's dome.

This world is wild as an old wives' tale,
And strange the plain things are,
The earth is enough and the air is enough
For our wonder and our war;
But our rest is as far as the fire-drake swings
And our peace is put in impossible things
Where clashed and thundered unthinkable wings
Round an incredible star.

To an open house in the evening
Home shall men come,
To an older place than Eden
And a taller town than Rome.
To the end of the way of the wandering star,
To the things that cannot be and that are,
To the place where God was homeless
And all men are at home.

**Joseph Ratzinger
(Pope Benedict XVI)**
(1927–)

*Jesus of Nazareth:
The Infancy
Narratives*

No Place for Them in the Inn
Luke 2:7

"There was no place for them in the inn." Prayerful reflection over these words has highlighted an inner parallel between this saying and the profoundly moving verse from Saint John's prologue: "He came to what was his own, and his own people did not accept him" (John 1:11). For the Savior of the world, for him in whom all things were created (see Col. 1:16), there was no room.... He who was crucified outside the city (see Heb. 13:12) also came into the world outside the city.

This should cause us to reflect—it points toward the reversal of values found in the figure of Jesus Christ and his message. From the moment of his birth, he belongs outside the realm of what is important and powerful in worldly terms. Yet it is this unimportant and powerless child that proves to be the truly powerful one, the one on whom ultimately everything depends. So one aspect of becoming a Christian is having to leave behind what everyone else thinks and wants, the prevailing standards, in order to enter the light of the truth of our being, and aided by that light to find the right path.

THE SHEPHERDS AND THE ANGELS

⁸ In that region there were shepherds living in the fields, keeping watch over their flock by night. ⁹ Then an angel of the Lord stood before them, and the glory of the Lord shone around them, and they were terrified. ¹⁰ But the angel said to them, "Do not be afraid; for see—I am bringing you good news of great joy for all the people: ¹¹ to you is born this day in the city of David a Savior, who is the Messiah, the Lord. ¹² This will be a sign for you: you will find a child wrapped in bands of cloth and lying in a manger." ¹³ And suddenly there was with the angel a multitude of the heavenly host, praising God and saying,

¹⁴ "Glory to God in the highest heaven,
    and on earth peace among those whom he favors!"

¹⁵ When the angels had left them and gone into heaven, the shepherds said to one another, "Let us go now to Bethlehem and see this thing that has taken place, which the Lord has made known to us." ¹⁶ So they went with haste and found Mary and Joseph, and the child lying in the manger. ¹⁷ When they saw this, they made known what had been told them about this child; ¹⁸ and all who heard it were amazed at what the shepherds told them. ¹⁹ But Mary treasured all these words and pondered them in her heart. ²⁰ The shepherds returned, glorifying and praising God for all they had heard and seen, as it had been told them.

Jesus vs. Caesar

Luke 2:1–14 | Bishop Barron

JESUS ENTERED THE WORLD, notes C.S. Lewis, so anonymously and clandestinely—as a baby born to insignificant parents in an out-of-the-way corner of the Roman Empire—because he was a warrior compelled to slip quietly behind enemy lines. Though there is truth to Teilhard de Chardin's claim that God entered his world like an artist entering his studio—which is to say, with utter confidence and familiarity—there is also something quite importantly right about Lewis' observation. The universe that God entered in Christ was not alien to God, but it was, by the same token, hardly friendly to the Creator; rather, it was "enemy-occupied territory," or to adapt Teilhard's metaphor, it was indeed the artist's studio, but it was filled with trashed, broken, and half-finished pieces. Raymond Brown reminds us that the Christmas stories are not charming tales that we tell to children; despite their undoubted charms, they are harsh and terrible, for the shadow of the cross falls over them.

The second chapter of the Gospel of Luke opens with an invocation of two of the weightiest political potentates of the time: "In those days a decree went out from Emperor Augustus that all the world should be registered. This was the first registration and was taken while Quirinius was governor of Syria." Caesar Augustus was the *kyrios* (lord) of the civilized world, and Quirinius was his satrap, charged with the task of implementing Augustus' will in the eastern corner of the empire. In mentioning those names, Luke is drawing our attention to the domination system, the power establishment, of the Roman authority. With the help of Quirinius, Caesar is performing an act uniquely characteristic of one who wields political power—the taking of a census. An emperor would count his people in order to tax them more judiciously or to draft them more efficiently into his armies or to enable his underlings in the chain of command to manage them more thoroughly. The manipulative and overbearing quality of census taking becomes clear in the Old Testament, when David's desire to take a census of his people is met with the sternest divine disapproval.

In commencing his story this way, calling to mind the mighty and powerful, Luke was in line with the best traditions of his day. Poems, narratives, and encomia in the ancient world centered almost invariably on the exploits of the best and brightest. If ordinary persons found their way into such literary accounts, they functioned as, at best, comic relief and more typically as foils to the heroic protagonists. But Luke effects a great reversal, because it becomes clear as the narrative unfolds that this story is not about Augustus and Quirinius at all, but rather about two very ordinary people making their way from one shabby village to another. And in point of fact, Augustus and his aide function in the narrative precisely as a foil to them. Because of the census, "Joseph also went from the town of Nazareth in Galilee to Judea, to the city of David called Bethlehem, because he was descended from the house and family of David." The decree, which Augustus took to be indicative of his lordship of the world, in fact serves the purpose of moving Joseph and his wife to the city of David so that the Messiah may be born in the place that God had declared. Real divine power, we are being told, is above worldly power and uses it for its ends, and hence we ought not concentrate on the negligible authority of Augustus. Rather, we must look to this couple.

"While they were there, the time came for her to deliver her child," but she was compelled to give birth in a primitive place, a shelter for animals, because "there was no place for them in the inn." We are meant to meditate on the contrast between this unspeakably primitive setting—baser even than the traveler's hostel at tiny Bethlehem—and the palace of Augustus on the Palatine Hill in Rome, the site from which the census decree undoubtedly went out. Quite naturally we associate power with luxury and the possession of fine things, but in light of this unsettling narrative, we realize that such an association would be mistaken. The power that animates the cosmos has much more to do with the emptying of self than with the pampering of self. Augustus' home, in the heart of the capital city of a world-spanning empire, would be the safest and most comfortable place imaginable, while a stable or a cave outside Bethlehem would be just about the most vulnerable, least protected space that we could imagine. Real power comes not from the protection of the ego from danger but rather from willingness to expose the ego to danger for the sake of love. *Kyrios* Jesus has begun his battle, in short, with *kyrios* Augustus; a tale of competing kingdoms, competing conceptions of power, is being told.

"And she gave birth to her firstborn son and wrapped him in bands of cloth." Augustus was certainly considered the freest man in the world of the first century. Wielding absolute political power, commanding an unchallenged army, he could do practically whatever he wanted; there were no restrictions placed on the ranginess of his will. But the son born to Joseph and Mary is, from the first moment, wrapped up, tied, confined. Bound by no one, Augustus seems to be utterly free; but real freedom, Luke is telling us, is enjoyed by the child totally bound by his Father's will and hence tied to the good of the world he has come to serve. Once he has decided to create, God cannot remain indifferent to the world and its needs; on the contrary, he is bound by a fiercely parental love to everything that participates in his being. Authentic divine freedom therefore has nothing to do with a capricious voluntarism, whereby God groundlessly and arbitrarily decides how or whether he will act. The Christ child—wrapped up in swaddling clothes—is the icon of this God of bound freedom, a God who faces down the ersatz divinity on the Palatine Hill.

Luke then tells us that this humble and bound child is "laid … in a manger." In his imperial splendor, Caesar Augustus would have been undoubtedly the best-provided-for person in the ancient world. Any material need he had—for food, drink, sex, bodily pleasure—would have been met easily and fully. In common conceptions of the good life, this kind of access to physical satisfaction would play an important role. Once more, the Lukan infancy narrative turns things upside down. The baby King is not fed; rather, laid in the place where the animals eat, he is offered as food for the world. This act anticipates the dynamism of his public life, during which he will be given over and again for the feeding of others. At the climax of his career, Jesus will present himself as bread to be eaten and wine to be drunk, giving himself away rather than drawing fame, protection, honor, and sustenance to himself. When he is pierced on the cross, blood and water flow from his side, signaling that, to the very end, life goes out from him for the good of the Church. Here the law of the gift is on iconic display: being increases in the measure that it is given away; life is enhanced in the measure that one participates in the loop of grace.

"In that region there were shepherds living in the fields, keeping watch over their flock by night." We ought not to be romantic about shepherds, imagining them as winsomely bucolic figures. In New Testament times, shepherds were considered rather shady characters, ne'er-do-wells unable to hold down a steady job, unreliable and dishonest. So questionable was their reputation that their testimony was inadmissible in a court of law. They would be the last people with whom Quirinius or Caesar Augustus were likely to have dealings, the most removed from the corridors of power, responsibility, and respectability. Yet it is to them that a messenger from the heavenly court appears: "Then an angel of the Lord stood before them, and the glory of the Lord shone around them, and they were terrified." Jesus commenced his public life standing in the muddy waters of the Jordan shoulder to shoulder with sinners, seeking a baptism of repentance. The deep embarrassment that this association caused can be sensed in the defensiveness of both Matthew and John in their recounting of the incident. He scandalized his coreligionists by consistently eating and drinking with known sinners, in clear violation of well-established purity codes. At the end of his life, he hung on a cross between two criminals, a writ of condemnation over his head. So here, the announcers of the Incarnation find their way precisely to the ordinary, the lowly, the unsavory. The divine life is not kept behind a metaphysical *cordon sanitaire* but rather expresses itself in the act by which it goes in love into what is opposed to it. Augustus would meet his enemy through some form of violence, but Christ meets his enemy with engagement and invitation.

Because they are in the presence of the numinous, the shepherds are naturally afraid, but the emissary from God's circle is not interested in perpetuating their fear: "Do not be afraid; for see—I am bringing you good news of great joy for all the people: to you is born this day in the city of David a Savior, who is the Messiah, the Lord." Worldly powers are deeply concerned with the inculcation of fear. Every system of domination, every political or cultural tyranny, is predicated upon the fear of punishment, ostracization, torture, or death. Because the relatively weak can be cowed by the relatively strong, the latter stay in power and a sort of dysfunctional equilibrium is maintained. But the divine lordship is predicated not on the domination born of terror but rather on the inclusivity born of love. Augustus' empire, as Augustine argued so persuasively in *The City of God*, was held together by violence and the threat of violence, and its order was therefore a pseudo-justice, the kind of order that holds sway in a band of thieves. What the angel proposes to the shepherds is another *Kyrios*, the Messiah Jesus, whose rule will constitute a true justice because it is conditioned not by fear but by love and forgiveness, and oriented not to maintenance of the tyrant's power but toward the production of "joy for all the people." That this is not simply an idle dream or a vague abstraction becomes clear in the course of the Gospels as Jesus' kingdom is pitted in a desperate struggle against the established order, coming to a climax on the battle of the cross. In the contrast between Augustus and the child king in the second chapter of Luke, this contest is quietly adumbrated.

The political dimension of the angel's message emerges with even greater clarity when Luke tells us, "Suddenly there was with the angel a multitude of the heavenly host, praising God and saying, 'Glory to God in the highest heaven, and on earth peace among those whom he favors!'" Again, we shouldn't be overly romantic or sentimental here. The customary reaction to an angel is terror, and now there is a host of these terrifying beings. Moreover, the word employed, *stratias* (host), has a definite military overtone: there emerges on Christmas night, Luke is telling us, an entire army of angels arrayed for battle.

The contrast between Augustus, the *kyrios* of the most impressive fighting force on the earth, and Jesus, the *Kyrios* of a heavenly host, couldn't be clearer or more telling. These soldiers—more powerful by far than Caesar's—don't brandish swords and utter battle cries; they sing the praise of God. What gives them harmonic cohesiveness is precisely their common devotion to the divine power that transcends them. What has led to violent divisions on earth—giving rise to the need for armies like Caesar's—is none other than a loss of this common praise of God among human beings. When God is no longer acknowledged as primary, when he is no longer glorified, the ego quickly emerges as the center of the soul's preoccupations, and this in turn leads inevitably to the war of all against all. And this is why the liturgical song of the angels is correlated to peace on earth: when our voices—as the Roman liturgy has it—blend with those of the celestial choir (when we assume the same properly ordered psychological and spiritual stance as they), order follows here below. Once more the conflict is on display: the emperor's *ordo* maintained through fear and violence versus the Christ's *ordo* maintained through the praise of God.

Word Study

κύριος

KYRIOS

Noun
Lord, master

JESUS IS NAMED

²¹ After eight days had passed, it was time to circumcise the child; and he was called Jesus, the name given by the angel before he was conceived in the womb.

JESUS IS PRESENTED IN THE TEMPLE

²² When the time came for their purification according to the law of Moses, they brought him up to Jerusalem to present him to the Lord ²³ (as it is written in the law of the Lord, "Every firstborn male shall be designated as holy to the Lord"), ²⁴ and they offered a sacrifice according to what is stated in the law of the Lord, "a pair of turtledoves or two young pigeons."

²⁵ Now there was a man in Jerusalem whose name was Simeon; this man was righteous and devout, looking forward to the consolation of Israel, and the Holy Spirit rested on him. ²⁶ It had been revealed to him by the Holy Spirit that he would not see death before he had seen the Lord's Messiah. ²⁷ Guided by the Spirit, Simeon came into the temple; and when

---

Setting the Human Race Right

Luke 2:22–35 | Bishop Barron

What is the significance of the Presentation of Jesus in the temple? The temple was, in practically a literal sense, the dwelling place of the Lord. In the temple, divinity and humanity embraced, and the human race was brought back in line with God.

But the sins of the nation had, according to the prophet Ezekiel, caused the glory of the Lord to depart from the temple (Ezek. 10:18–19). Therefore, one of the deepest aspirations of Israel was to reestablish the temple as the place of right praise so that the glory of the Lord might return. When Joseph and Mary bring the infant Jesus into the temple, therefore, we are meant to appreciate that the prophecy of Ezekiel is being fulfilled (Ezek. 43). The glory of Yahweh is returning to his favorite dwelling. And this is precisely what Simeon sees.

The old seer is a symbol of ancient Israel, watching and waiting for the coming of the Messiah. Simeon knew all of the old prophecies; he embodied the expectation of the nation; and the Holy Spirit had given him the revelation that he would not die until he had laid eyes on his Savior.

But there is more to the Presentation story than the return of the Lord to his temple, for he comes to his temple precisely in human form, indeed in the form of a little baby. The Son of God, having taken to himself a human nature, is presented to the Father as a sacrifice, and thereby the human race is set right.

the parents brought in the child Jesus, to do for him what was customary under the law, ²⁸ Simeon took him in his arms and praised God, saying,

²⁹ "Master, now you are dismissing your servant in peace,
according to your word;

³⁰ for my eyes have seen your salvation,

³¹ which you have prepared in the presence of all peoples,

³² a light for revelation to the Gentiles
and for glory to your people Israel."

³³ And the child's father and mother were amazed at what was being said about him. ³⁴ Then Simeon blessed them and said to his mother Mary, "This child is destined for the falling and the rising of many in Israel, and to be a sign that will be opposed ³⁵ so that the inner thoughts of many will be revealed—and a sword will pierce your own soul too."

³⁶ There was also a prophet, Anna the daughter of Phanuel, of the tribe of Asher. She was of a great age, having lived with her husband seven years after her marriage, ³⁷ then as a widow to the age of eighty-four. She never left the temple but worshiped there with fasting and prayer night and day. ³⁸ At that moment she came, and began to praise God and to speak about the child to all who were looking for the redemption of Jerusalem.

THE RETURN TO NAZARETH

³⁹ When they had finished everything required by the law of the Lord, they returned to Galilee, to their own town of Nazareth. ⁴⁰ The child grew and became strong, filled with wisdom; and the favor of God was upon him.

THE BOY JESUS IN THE TEMPLE

⁴¹ Now every year his parents went to Jerusalem for the festival of the Passover. ⁴² And when he was twelve years old, they went up as usual for the festival. ⁴³ When the festival was ended and they started to return, the boy Jesus stayed behind in Jerusalem, but his parents did not know it. ⁴⁴ Assuming that he was in the group of travelers, they went a day's journey. Then they started to look for him among their relatives and friends. ⁴⁵ When they did not find him, they returned to Jerusalem to search for him. ⁴⁶ After three days they found him in the temple, sitting among the teachers, listening to them and asking them questions. ⁴⁷ And all who heard him were amazed at his understanding and his answers. ⁴⁸ When his parents saw him they were astonished; and his mother said to him, "Child, why have you treated us like this? Look, your father and I have been searching for you in great anxiety." ⁴⁹ He said to them, "Why were you searching for me? Did you not know that I must be in my Father's house?" ⁵⁰ But they did not understand what he said to them. ⁵¹ Then he went down with them

and came to Nazareth, and was obedient to them. His mother treasured all these things in her heart.

⁵² And Jesus increased in wisdom and in years, and in divine and human favor.

Mission Supersedes Family

Luke 2:41–52 | Bishop Barron

When Mary and Joseph find twelve-year-old Jesus in the temple, they, with understandable exasperation, upbraid him: "Child, why have you treated us like this?" But Jesus responds, "Did you not know that I must be in my Father's house?"

The story conveys a truth that runs sharply counter to our sensibilities: even the most powerful familial emotions must, in the end, give way to mission. Though she felt an enormous pull in the opposite direction, Mary let her son go, allowing him to find his vocation in the temple. Legitimate sentiment devolves into sentimentality precisely when it comes to supersede the call of God.

On a biblical reading, the family is, above all, the forum in which both parents and children are able to discern their missions. It is perfectly good, of course, if deep bonds and rich emotions are cultivated within the family, but those relationships and passions must cede to something that is more fundamental, more enduring, more spiritually focused.

The paradox is this: precisely in the measure that everyone in the family focuses on God's call for one another, the family becomes more loving and peaceful.

DID YOU NOT KNOW THAT

I MUST *be in*

MY FATHER'S

HOUSE?

LUKE 2:49

THE PROCLAMATION OF JOHN THE BAPTIST

3 In the fifteenth year of the reign of Emperor Tiberius, when Pontius Pilate was governor of Judea, and Herod was ruler of Galilee, and his brother Philip ruler of the region of Ituraea and Trachonitis, and Lysanias ruler of Abilene, ² during the high priesthood of Annas and Caiaphas, the word of God came to John son of Zechariah in the wilderness. ³ He went into all the region around the Jordan, proclaiming a baptism of repentance for the forgiveness of sins, ⁴ as it is written in the book of the words of the prophet Isaiah,

> "The voice of one crying out in the wilderness:
> 'Prepare the way of the Lord,
>   make his paths straight.
> ⁵ Every valley shall be filled,
>   and every mountain and hill shall be made low,
>   and the crooked shall be made straight,
>   and the rough ways made smooth;
> ⁶ and all flesh shall see the salvation of God.'"

⁷ John said to the crowds that came out to be baptized by him, "You brood of vipers! Who warned you to flee from the wrath to come? ⁸ Bear fruits worthy of repentance. Do not begin to say to yourselves, 'We have Abraham as our ancestor'; for I tell you, God is able from these stones to raise up children

---

Change Your Behavior

Luke 3:10–14 | Bishop Barron

John the Baptist comes to the Judean desert preaching repentance. And so people with great enthusiasm, asking as though their lives depended on it, inquire of John: "What then should we do?" This question, of course, tells us something about repentance: that it has to do with action.

One's life has gone off the rails in different ways, and one wants to get it back on track. This is possible only through certain things that one does. The spiritual life is therefore a set of behaviors.

And what does John tell them? He mentions very specific and very concrete acts of justice. Here he stands in the long line of Hebrew prophets: Amos, Isaiah, Jeremiah, Ezekiel, Joel, Zechariah—all of whom, in various ways, tell the Israelite people to be just.

to Abraham. [9] Even now the ax is lying at the root of the trees; every tree therefore that does not bear good fruit is cut down and thrown into the fire."

[10] And the crowds asked him, "What then should we do?" [11] In reply he said to them, "Whoever has two coats must share with anyone who has none; and whoever has food must do likewise." [12] Even tax collectors came to be baptized, and they asked him, "Teacher, what should we do?" [13] He said to them, "Collect no more than the amount prescribed for you." [14] Soldiers also asked him, "And we, what should we do?" He said to them, "Do not extort money from anyone by threats or false accusation, and be satisfied with your wages."

[15] As the people were filled with expectation, and all were questioning in their hearts concerning John, whether he might be the Messiah, [16] John answered all of them by saying, "I baptize you with water; but one who is more powerful than I is coming; I am not worthy to untie the thong of his sandals. He will baptize you with the Holy Spirit and fire. [17] His winnowing fork is in his hand, to clear his threshing floor and to gather the wheat into his granary; but the chaff he will burn with unquenchable fire."

Drawn Into the Inner Life of God
Luke 3:21–22 | Bishop Barron

Jesus' baptism by John demonstrates the importance of our receiving the sacrament of Baptism. One of the earliest descriptions of Baptism is *vitae spiritualis ianua*, which means "the door to the spiritual life."

To grasp the full meaning of this is to understand something decisive about Christianity. For Christianity is not primarily about "becoming a good person" or "doing the right thing." Let's face it: anyone—pagan, Muslim, Jew, nonbeliever—can be any of those things.

To be a Christian is to be grafted onto Christ and hence drawn into the very dynamics of the inner life of God. We don't speak simply of following or imitating Jesus. We speak of becoming a member of his Mystical Body.

Do you see why it is so important that we are baptized "in the name of the Father, and of the Son, and of the Holy Spirit"? For Baptism draws us into the relationship between the Father and the Son—which is to say, in the Holy Spirit. Baptism, therefore, is all about our incorporation, through the power of God's love, into God's own life.

¹⁸ So, with many other exhortations, he proclaimed the good news to the people. ¹⁹ But Herod the ruler, who had been rebuked by him because of Herodias, his brother's wife, and because of all the evil things that Herod had done, ²⁰ added to them all by shutting up John in prison.

THE BAPTISM OF JESUS

²¹ Now when all the people were baptized, and when Jesus also had been baptized and was praying, the heaven was opened, ²² and the Holy Spirit descended upon him in bodily form like a dove. And a voice came from heaven, "You are my Son, the Beloved; with you I am well pleased."

THE ANCESTORS OF JESUS

²³ Jesus was about thirty years old when he began his work. He was the son (as was thought) of Joseph son of Heli, ²⁴ son of Matthat, son of Levi, son of Melchi, son of Jannai, son of Joseph, ²⁵ son of Mattathias, son of Amos, son of Nahum, son of Esli, son of Naggai, ²⁶ son of Maath, son of Mattathias, son of Semein, son of Josech, son of Joda, ²⁷ son of Joanan, son of Rhesa, son of Zerubbabel, son of Shealtiel, son of Neri, ²⁸ son of Melchi, son of Addi, son of Cosam, son of Elmadam, son of Er, ²⁹ son of Joshua, son of Eliezer, son of Jorim, son of Matthat, son of Levi, ³⁰ son of Simeon, son of Judah, son of Joseph, son of Jonam, son of Eliakim, ³¹ son of Melea, son of Menna, son of Mattatha, son of Nathan, son of David, ³² son of Jesse, son of Obed, son of Boaz, son of Sala, son of Nahshon, ³³ son of Amminadab, son of Admin, son of Arni, son of Hezron, son of Perez, son of Judah, ³⁴ son of Jacob, son of Isaac, son of Abraham, son of Terah, son of Nahor, ³⁵ son of Serug, son of Reu, son of Peleg, son of Eber, son of Shelah, ³⁶ son of Cainan, son of Arphaxad, son of Shem, son of Noah, son of Lamech, ³⁷ son of Methuselah, son of Enoch, son of Jared, son of Mahalaleel, son of Cainan, ³⁸ son of Enos, son of Seth, son of Adam, son of God.

HE WILL BAPTIZE YOU WITH THE

HOLY SPIRIT

and FIRE.

LUKE 3:16

The Play Between Nature and Grace

Luke 3:10–17 | Bishop Barron

THIS PASSAGE speaks to one of the most significant themes in Catholic theology—namely, the play between nature and grace. Luke tells us that people came to John the Baptist, asking what they should do to reform their lives. John responds with good and very pointed moral advice. To the tax collectors he says, "Collect no more than the amount prescribed for you," and to the soldiers he urges, "Do not extort money from anyone by threats or false accusation, and be satisfied with your wages." In so saying, he was addressing very common practices of that time and place. Tax collectors regularly demanded more money than was just and skimmed the surplus for themselves—which helps to explain why they were so unpopular. And soldiers—young men with weapons and too much time on their hands—predictably acted as bully-boys, extorting money through threats of violence.

John the Baptist is, quite sensibly, calling such people to decency and justice. As such, he stands with great philosophers, poets, social reformers, and religious figures. Plato, Aristotle, Cicero, Thomas Jefferson, and Martin Luther King, Jr. all summoned people to be just, "to render to each his due," in Plato's pithy formula. John was also often called the last of the prophets, and he echoes his forebears.

So far, so natural. But then John adds something that should take our breath away: "One who is more powerful than I is coming; I am not worthy to untie the thong of his sandals"—that is to say, perform a task that was considered too demeaning even for a slave. We just couldn't imagine Isaiah saying such a thing about Jeremiah, or Amos about Hosea, or Plato about Aristotle. What John the Baptist is signaling is the qualitative difference between himself (and the entire prophetic tradition that he represents) and the coming Christ Jesus. John was baptizing with water, but the one he announces will baptize with fire and the Holy Spirit.

Notice how the emphasis has shifted from the active to the passive. John told his audience that there were certain very definite things that they could do. But the one who is coming will not so much call for action on our part; rather, he will accomplish something that we, even in principle, could never accomplish for ourselves. He will dip us (*baptizein*) in the Holy Spirit, which is precisely the love that obtains between the Father and the Son, the love that God is. It is with this very love that he will set us on fire.

This passivity is signaled as well in the second great image that John employs, one that might be opaque to us but that was eminently clear to the Baptist's first-century audience: "His winnowing fork is in his hand, to clear his threshing floor." When farmers in the ancient world wanted to separate wheat from chaff, they would place stalks of wheat on a flat surface and then, using a kind of rake or pitchfork (the winnowing fan), toss the grain in the air and allow the wind to blow the light and insubstantial chaff away. The one whom John heralds will in a similar way separate out what is life-enhancing in us from what is life-denying. Again, he will not so much expect us to accomplish this work; he will do it in us and for us.

None of this, of course, is to gainsay the significance of John's own teaching; but it is indeed to say that that teaching is inadequate. To put this in terms of the Church's classical theology, nature is not negated by grace but is rather completed and perfected by grace. Grace (*gratia* in Latin, *charis* in Greek) is, quite simply, gift, something offered and freely accepted. At the end of all our striving, we surrender to a power that, as Paul said, "is able to accomplish abundantly far more than all we can ask or imagine" (Eph. 3:20). After many years of tying our own belts and going where we want to go, someone else (the Holy Spirit) will tie us up and take us where we could never go on our own (John 21:18).

Now, what does this look like on the ground? What, to use William James' language, is its "cash value"? If, as we saw, this new life is an immersion in the very essence of God, it will look like love in the truly radical sense. Since God has no need whatsoever, he can never operate in a self-interested way. Hence, authentic love, the love that is the nature of God, is not indirect egotism: I will be kind to you that you might be kind to me. Rather, it is willing the good of the other as other, acting for the benefit of another, even when such action is in no way beneficial to us. Now think of Mother Teresa caring for the poorest of the poor in the worst slum in the world; now think of Junipero Serra going to the ends of the world to share the Gospel; now think of Rose Hawthorne taking cancer patients into her own apartment to care for them when no one else would.

Such love is a consequence of grace, of the coming of Christ, of being dipped into the fire of the Holy Spirit.

Word Study

βαπτίζω

BAPTIZÓ

Verb
To dip, sink

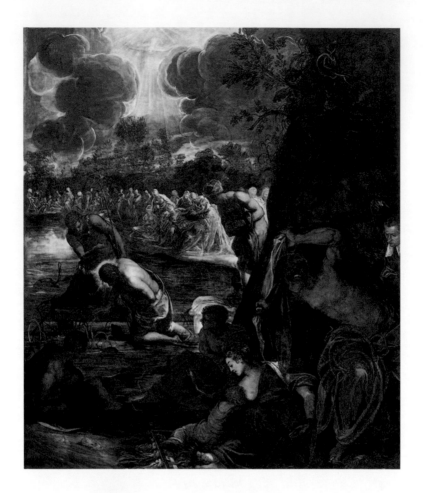

Red drapery

Tintoretto aimed to combine the muscular anatomy that defined southern Italian painting with the rich colorism of northern Italian painting. In his studio, Tintoretto had his motto inscribed on the wall: "The drawing of Michelangelo and the color of Titian." This careful attention to color is evident in the sumptuous drapery of the foreground figure.

Clouds

The thin, roughly formed clouds are typical of Tintoretto's style and attest to the speed with which he worked. This hallmark roughness gives his paintings a sense of cataclysmic energy and power.

Luke 3:21–22

JACOPO TINTORETTO | *Sixteenth century*

The Baptism of Christ

Essay by Michael Stevens

Jacopo Tintoretto was an unconventional painter in every way. He was almost entirely self-taught, and his bold and energetic visual style was known for its fast brushwork and unapologetic rawness. While he was harshly criticized by some, he managed to overcome his lack of formal training to become one of the most successful artists of his time in Venice, securing some of the most prestigious commissions in the city over his career.

The Baptism of Christ exhibits many of the stylistic features that Tintoretto was widely known for: energy, explosive light, movement, and a generally more dramatic take on Bible scenes—even those that were typically depicted as static and peaceful.

In this work, the artist has placed the viewer at a distance from Christ and John the Baptist, right in the middle of the crowd of witnesses who surround them. In the foreground, people of all kinds have gathered and inhabit a shadowy embankment—some watching with rapt attention, others unengaged or distracted. On the far bank, crowds of people are lined up to be baptized.

Cutting through the top of the composition is the Holy Spirit, who enters the scene accompanied by a blaze of light. The rays from this burst of energy point toward Jesus, whose head—mostly in shadow—eclipses a fiery halo: one of the only details that distinguishes Christ from the surrounding figures.

While Tintoretto's focus on the peripheral elements of the scene may seem odd at first, they serve to remind us that Jesus was baptized not for his own sake but in solidarity with sinners. By placing us on the outskirts of the scene, we're invited to watch carefully alongside the followers of John the Baptist as Jesus lowers himself into the muddy waters of our sin and sets the first example of sacramental life for his future Church.

THE TEMPTATION OF JESUS

4 Jesus, full of the Holy Spirit, returned from the Jordan and was led by the Spirit in the wilderness, [2] where for forty days he was tempted by the devil. He ate nothing at all during those days, and when they were over, he was famished. [3] The devil said to him, "If you are the Son of God, command this stone to become a loaf of bread." [4] Jesus answered him, "It is written, 'One does not live by bread alone.'"

[5] Then the devil led him up and showed him in an instant all the kingdoms of the world. [6] And the devil said to him, "To you I will give their glory and all this authority; for it has been given over to me, and I give it to anyone I please. [7] If you, then, will worship me, it will all be yours." [8] Jesus answered him, "It is written,

> *'Worship the Lord your God,*
> *and serve only him.'"*

God, Power, and Politics

Luke 4:5–8 | Bishop Barron

What is most interesting about this second temptation is that the devil couldn't offer all of the kingdoms of the world to Jesus unless he, the devil, owned them. All the kingdoms of the world, Luke is telling us, belong to a fallen spiritual force. I don't know a passage in any of the literature of the world that is as critical of political power as this one!

Whereas many (if not most) cultures both ancient and modern tend to apotheosize their political leaders, the Bible sees right through politics and politicians. One of the most important contributions of the Scriptures to contemporary politics, at least in the West, is this deep suspicion that power tends to corrupt.

The institutionalization of this suspicion in complex systems of checks and balances is a healthy outgrowth of the biblical view.

To be sure, scripturally minded people should not allow their suspicion to give way to a complete cynicism regarding politics. Since God is powerful, power in itself cannot be construed as something evil, and indeed the Bible frequently states that legitimate political authority participates in God's own governance of the cosmos. But given the general human tendency toward self-absorption and violence—about which the Bible is remarkably clear-eyed—one should never put one's total trust in political systems, leaders, or programs. And one should be ever aware of the fact that human legal arrangements are under the judgment and authority of God.

⁹ Then the devil took him to Jerusalem, and placed him on the pinnacle of the temple, saying to him, "If you are the Son of God, throw yourself down from here, ¹⁰ for it is written,

> 'He will command his angels concerning you,
>   to protect you,'

¹¹ and

> 'On their hands they will bear you up,
>   so that you will not dash your foot against a stone.'"

¹² Jesus answered him, "It is said, 'Do not put the Lord your God to the test.'" ¹³ When the devil had finished every test, he departed from him until an opportune time.

THE BEGINNING OF THE GALILEAN MINISTRY

¹⁴ Then Jesus, filled with the power of the Spirit, returned to Galilee, and a report about him spread through all the surrounding country. ¹⁵ He began to teach in their synagogues and was praised by everyone.

Tempted Like Jesus

Luke 4:1–13 | Bishop Barron

Just after his baptism, the Spirit leads Jesus into the desert to be tempted by the devil. At every point in the Gospels, we are meant to identify with Jesus. God became man that man might become God. We participate in him and thereby learn what a godly life is like.

Jesus has just learned his deepest identity and mission. And now he confronts—as we all must—the great temptations. What precisely is entailed in being the beloved Son of God?

First, the tempter urges him to use his divine power to satisfy his bodily desires, which Jesus dismisses with a word.

Having failed at his first attempt, the devil shifts to perhaps the greatest of the temptations: power. Power is extremely seductive. Many would gladly eschew material things or attention or fame in order to get it. Jesus' great answer in Matthew's account of this story is "Away with you, Satan!" (Matt 4:10). To seek power is to serve Satan—it is stated that bluntly.

Finally, the devil plays a subtler game— he tempts Jesus to manipulate his Father, encouraging him to jump from the temple and let angels save him. It is the temptation faced by Adam and Eve in the garden: deciding how and when God will act.

THE REJECTION OF JESUS AT NAZARETH

¹⁶ When he came to Nazareth, where he had been brought up, he went to the synagogue on the sabbath day, as was his custom. He stood up to read, ¹⁷ and the scroll of the prophet Isaiah was given to him. He unrolled the scroll and found the place where it was written:

¹⁸ *"The Spirit of the Lord is upon me,*
because he has anointed me
to bring good news to the poor.
He has sent me to proclaim release to the captives
and recovery of sight to the blind,
to let the oppressed go free,
¹⁹ *to proclaim the year of the Lord's favor."*

Fulton Sheen
(1895–1979)
———
Life of Christ

The Prophecy Fulfilled

Luke 4:16–21

In the synagogue, he was given the book of Isaiah. The particular prophecy which he read dealt with the suffering servant of God (Isa. 61:1–2).

> *"The Spirit of the Lord is upon me,*
> *because he has anointed me*
> *to bring good news to the poor.*
> *He has sent me to proclaim release to the captives*
> *and recovery of sight to the blind,*
> *to let the oppressed go free,*
> *to proclaim the year of the Lord's favor."*

This passage was familiar to the Jews. It was an Old Testament prophecy concerning the release of the Jews from the Babylonian captivity. But he did something unusual; he took this text woven out of the Exile, and wrapped it around himself. He changed the meaning of the "poor," the "captives," and the "blind." The "poor" were those who had no grace and lacked union with God; the "blind" were those who had not yet seen the Light; the "captives" were those who had not yet purchased true freedom from sin. He then proclaimed that all these centered in himself.

But above all, he declared the Jubilee. The Mosaic code made provision for every fiftieth year to be one of special grace and restoration. All debts were remitted; family inheritances which had, by the pressure of time, been alienated, were restored to their original owners; those who had mortgaged their liberty were restored to freedom. It was a divine safeguard against monopolies; and it kept family life intact. The Jubilee year was to him a symbol of his messianic appearance which he proclaimed because he had been anointed with the Spirit to do so. There were to be new spiritual riches, a new spiritual light, a new spiritual liberty, all centering in him—the Evangelist, the Healer, the Emancipator. All who were in the synagogue had their eyes fixed on him. Then came the startling, explosive words: "Today this scripture has been fulfilled in your hearing."

He knew they were expecting a political king who would throw off Roman domination. But he proclaimed redemption from sin, not from military dictatorship. In this way alone they must expect the prophecy of Isaiah to be fulfilled.

[20] And he rolled up the scroll, gave it back to the attendant, and sat down. The eyes of all in the synagogue were fixed on him. [21] Then he began to say to them, "Today this scripture has been fulfilled in your hearing." [22] All spoke well of him and were amazed at the gracious words that came from his mouth. They said, "Is not this Joseph's son?" [23] He said to them, "Doubtless you will quote to me this proverb, 'Doctor, cure yourself!' And you will say, 'Do here also in your hometown the things that we have heard you did at Capernaum.'" [24] And he said, "Truly I tell you, no prophet

is accepted in the prophet's hometown. ²⁵ But the truth is, there were many widows in Israel in the time of Elijah, when the heaven was shut up three years and six months, and there was a severe famine over all the land; ²⁶ yet Elijah was sent to none of them except to a widow at Zarephath in Sidon. ²⁷ There were also many lepers in Israel in the time of the prophet Elisha, and none of them was cleansed except Naaman the Syrian." ²⁸ When they heard this, all in the synagogue were filled with rage. ²⁹ They got up, drove him out of the town, and led him to the brow of the hill on which their town was built, so that they might hurl him off the cliff. ³⁰ But he passed through the midst of them and went on his way.

THE MAN WITH AN UNCLEAN SPIRIT

³¹ He went down to Capernaum, a city in Galilee, and was teaching them on the sabbath. ³² They were astounded at his teaching, because he spoke with authority. ³³ In the synagogue there was a man who had the spirit of an unclean demon, and he cried out with a loud voice, ³⁴ "Let us alone! What have you to do with us, Jesus of Nazareth? Have you come to destroy us? I know who you are, the Holy One of God." ³⁵ But Jesus rebuked him, saying, "Be silent, and come out of him!" When the demon had thrown him down before them, he came out of him without having done him any harm. ³⁶ They were all amazed and kept saying to one another, "What kind of utterance is this? For with authority and power he commands the unclean spirits, and out they come!" ³⁷ And a report about him began to reach every place in the region.

HEALINGS AT SIMON'S HOUSE

³⁸ After leaving the synagogue he entered Simon's house. Now Simon's mother-in-law was suffering from a high fever, and they asked him about her. ³⁹ Then he stood over her and rebuked the fever, and it left her. Immediately she got up and began to serve them.

⁴⁰ As the sun was setting, all those who had any who were sick with various kinds of diseases brought them to him; and he laid his hands on each of them and cured them. ⁴¹ Demons also came out of many, shouting, "You are the Son of God!" But he rebuked them and would not allow them to speak, because they knew that he was the Messiah.

JESUS PREACHES IN THE SYNAGOGUES

⁴² At daybreak he departed and went into a deserted place. And the crowds were looking for him; and when they reached him, they wanted to prevent him from leaving them. ⁴³ But he said to them, "I must proclaim the good news of the kingdom of God to the other cities also; for I was sent for this purpose." ⁴⁴ So he continued proclaiming the message in the synagogues of Judea.

A Day in the Life of Jesus

Luke 4:38–44 | Bishop Barron

Jesus is always hurrying from place to place, on the go, and Luke gives us a sort of "day in the life" of Jesus. And it is quite a day! The story begins just after the dramatic expulsion of a demon in the Capernaum synagogue. And after entering the house of Simon, Jesus cures Peter's mother-in-law, and then the entire town comes to his door. He spends the whole evening curing presumably hundreds who were variously afflicted.

In the eighteenth, nineteenth, and twentieth centuries, in an attempt to make Jesus more palatable to rationalists and "realists," theologians put great stress on Jesus' preaching, especially his ethical teaching.

But this is not the Jesus that Luke presents. Rather, he is a healer or *Soter*, rendered in Latin as *Salvator*, which just means "the bearer of the *salus*" or health. Jesus is portrayed as a healer, a Savior. In him, divinity and humanity have come together; in him, the divine life and divine power are breaking through. God's deepest intentions for his beloved creatures appear—what God plans for us in the kingdom to come is now historically anticipated.

JESUS CALLS THE FIRST DISCIPLES

5 Once while Jesus was standing beside the lake of Gennesaret, and the crowd was pressing in on him to hear the word of God, ² he saw two boats there at the shore of the lake; the fishermen had gone out of them and were washing their nets. ³ He got into one of the boats, the one belonging to Simon, and asked him to put out a little way from the shore. Then he sat down and taught the crowds from the boat. ⁴ When he had finished speaking, he said to Simon, "Put out into the deep water and let down your nets for a catch." ⁵ Simon answered, "Master, we have worked all night long but have caught nothing. Yet if you say so, I will let down the nets." ⁶ When they had done this, they caught so many fish that their nets were beginning to break. ⁷ So they signaled their partners in the other boat to come and help them. And they came and filled both boats, so that they began to sink. ⁸ But when Simon Peter saw it, he fell down at Jesus' knees, saying, "Go away from me, Lord, for I am a sinful man!" ⁹ For he and all who were with him were amazed at the catch of fish that they had taken; ¹⁰ and so also were James and John, sons of Zebedee, who were

partners with Simon. Then Jesus said to Simon, "Do not be afraid; from now on you will be catching people." ¹¹ When they had brought their boats to shore, they left everything and followed him.

Jesus Getting Into Your Boat

Luke 5:1–11 | Bishop Barron

What should we make of this odd story about Jesus and Peter in the fifth chapter of Luke's Gospel?

As the eager crowds press in on him, Jesus spies two boats moored by the shore of the lake. Without asking permission, he gets into the one belonging to Peter and asks the fisherman to put out a short distance from shore. After teaching the crowds a while, he turns to Peter and says, "Put out into the deep water and let down your nets for a catch." Though Simon Peter protests a bit—"Master, we have worked all night long but have caught nothing"—he acquiesces, and they manage to bring in such a great number of fish that their nets are in danger of tearing. This miraculous draught of fishes convicts Peter of his unworthiness, and he falls at the feet of the Lord to protest: "Go away from me, Lord, for I am a sinful man!" There are overtones of the call of Isaiah in this passage. The Old Testament prophet saw the glory of the Lord in the temple but then admitted his profound imperfection: "I am a man of unclean lips, and I live among a people of unclean lips" (Isa. 6:5). The proximity

of the divine light does not diminish our sense of sin; it enhances it. Once Isaiah admitted his sin, God cleansed him and then sent him on mission. In the very same way, the penitent Simon was forgiven and commissioned: "Do not be afraid; from now on you will be catching people."

This seemingly simple account is another of those subtle and religiously rich icons that the Evangelists were so deft at writing. It is a picture of discipleship and mission; Simon emerges as the archetype of the Church, which will always be a community of forgiven and empowered sinners. But it is also a depiction of the central dynamic in Christian ethics.

Let us examine the symbolic significance of the boat. For a Galilean fisherman, his boat was everything. It was his livelihood, his work, the means by which he supported his family and put food on the table. Recent archaeological and anthropological research has shown that first-century Galilean fishermen sent their product not only around the towns of Palestine but also to distant cities within the Roman Empire. So Peter's humble vessel represented his contact with the wider world and functioned, if I may put it this way, as an instrument of his professional creativity. As such, it serves as a symbol of all that Peter can accomplish spiritually and morally through his own power, using his gifts, energy, and creativity.

And Jesus just gets into his boat. He doesn't seek Peter's approval, nor does he solicit his permission. He simply commandeers this vessel that is central to the fisherman's life and commences to give orders. This represents something of enormous moment: the invasion of grace. Though God respects our relative independence and smiles on the work that we can accomplish on our own, he is not the least bit content to leave us in a "natural" state. Instead, he wants to live in us, to become the Lord of our lives, moving into our minds, wills, bodies, imaginations, nerves, and bones.

This commandeering of nature by grace does not involve the compromising of nature but rather its perfection and elevation. Peter, one presumes, had been successful enough as a fisherman, but now, under Jesus' direction, he goes out into the deep and brings in more than he could ever have imagined possible. When Jesus moves into the house of the soul, the powers of the soul are heightened and properly directed; when Jesus commands the boat of the natural human life, that life is preserved, strengthened, and given a new orientation. This is signaled symbolically by the Lord's directive to put out into the deep water. On our own, we can know and will within a very narrow range, seeking those goods and truths that appear within the horizon of our natural consciousness, but when grace invades us, we are enticed into far deeper waters.

JESUS CLEANSES A LEPER

[12] Once, when he was in one of the cities, there was a man covered with leprosy. When he saw Jesus, he bowed with his face to the ground and begged him, "Lord, if you choose, you can make me clean." [13] Then Jesus stretched out his hand, touched him, and said, "I do choose. Be made clean." Immediately the leprosy left him. [14] And he ordered him to tell no one. "Go," he said, "and show yourself to the priest, and, as Moses commanded, make an offering for your cleansing, for a testimony to them." [15] But now more than ever the word about Jesus spread abroad; many crowds would gather to hear him and to be cured of their diseases. [16] But he would withdraw to deserted places and pray.

Sinners Who Know It

Luke 5:8 | Bishop Barron

G.K. Chesterton once said, "There are saints indeed in my religion: but a saint only means a man who really knows that he is a sinner." As far as Chesterton is concerned, the relevant distinction is not between sinners and non-sinners, but rather between sinners who know it and those who don't. But this clarification is of tremendous moment, for sin is known only through contrast with grace, just as shadow is appreciated only in contradistinction to light. And thus people who can acknowledge their sins are, at least to some degree, participating in the center; they are, in a word, saints.

Chesterton's principle is confirmed by the peculiar fact that it is precisely the great saints who seem most acutely aware of their imperfections. Even Thérèse of Lisieux, the beloved and innocent "Little Flower," claimed that she was the worst of sinners. When we hear such protestations from the holiest of people, we are tempted to write them off as so much false modesty, but this would be a serious spiritual mistake.

In many northern cities, during the wintertime, tons of salt are dumped on the roadways to keep them clear of ice and snow, but then that salt is kicked up onto cars and windshields. When one is driving at night, away from direct lighting, one can see fairly well, even through a salt-caked windshield. But come the next morning, when one is driving straight toward the rising sun, that same windshield is suddenly opaque. John of the Cross said that the soul is like a pane of glass and God's love is like the sun. It is, accordingly, when God's love is shining most directly on the soul that its smudges and imperfections are most apparent. We sinners spend our time riding away from the divine light, our lives focused on money, sex, power, and our own egos; and thus it is not the least bit surprising that we remain relatively unaware of our sinfulness. But the saints, the ones who have directed their lives toward the light and heat of God, are most cognizant of all that still remains incomplete in their souls.

JESUS HEALS A PARALYTIC

17 One day, while he was teaching, Pharisees and teachers of the law were sitting near by (they had come from every village of Galilee and Judea and from Jerusalem); and the power of the Lord was with him to heal.

¹⁸ Just then some men came, carrying a paralyzed man on a bed. They were trying to bring him in and lay him before Jesus; ¹⁹ but finding no way to bring him in because of the crowd, they went up on the roof and let him down with his bed through the tiles into the middle of the crowd in front of Jesus. ²⁰ When he saw their faith, he said, "Friend, your sins are forgiven you." ²¹ Then the scribes and the Pharisees began to question, "Who is this who is speaking blasphemies? Who can forgive sins but God alone?" ²² When Jesus perceived their questionings, he answered them, "Why do you raise such questions in your hearts? ²³ Which is easier, to say, 'Your sins are forgiven you,' or to say, 'Stand up and walk'? ²⁴ But so that you may know that the Son of Man has authority on earth to forgive sins"—he said to the one who was paralyzed—"I say to you, stand up and take your bed and go to your home." ²⁵ Immediately he stood up before them, took what he had been lying on, and went to his home, glorifying God. ²⁶ Amazement seized all of them, and they glorified God and were filled with awe, saying, "We have seen strange things today."

JESUS CALLS LEVI

²⁷ After this he went out and saw a tax collector named Levi, sitting at the tax booth; and he said to him, "Follow me." ²⁸ And he got up, left everything, and followed him.

²⁹ Then Levi gave a great banquet for him in his house; and there was a large crowd of tax collectors and others sitting at the table with them. ³⁰ The Pharisees and their scribes were complaining to his disciples, saying, "Why do you eat and drink with tax collectors and sinners?" ³¹ Jesus answered, "Those who are well have no need of a physician, but those who are sick; ³² I have come to call not the righteous but sinners to repentance."

THE QUESTION ABOUT FASTING

³³ Then they said to him, "John's disciples, like the disciples of the Pharisees, frequently fast and pray, but your disciples eat and drink." ³⁴ Jesus said to them, "You cannot make wedding guests fast while the bridegroom is with them, can you? ³⁵ The days will come when the bridegroom will be taken away from them, and then they will fast in those days." ³⁶ He also told them a parable: "No one tears a piece from a new garment and sews it on an old garment; otherwise the new will be torn, and the piece from the new will not match the old. ³⁷ And no one puts new wine into old wineskins; otherwise the new wine will burst the skins and will be spilled, and the skins will be destroyed. ³⁸ But new wine must be put into fresh wineskins. ³⁹ And no one after drinking old wine desires new wine, but says, 'The old is good.'"

THE QUESTION ABOUT THE SABBATH

6 One sabbath while Jesus was going through the grainfields, his disciples plucked some heads of grain, rubbed them in their hands, and ate them. ² But some of the Pharisees said, "Why are you doing what is not lawful on the sabbath?" ³ Jesus answered, "Have you not read what David did when he and his companions were hungry? ⁴ He entered the house of God and took and ate the bread of the Presence, which it is not lawful for any but the priests to eat, and gave some to his companions?" ⁵ Then he said to them, "The Son of Man is lord of the sabbath."

THE MAN WITH A WITHERED HAND

⁶ On another sabbath he entered the synagogue and taught, and there was a man there whose right hand was withered. ⁷ The scribes and the Pharisees watched him to see whether he would cure on the sabbath, so that they might find an accusation against him. ⁸ Even though he knew what they were thinking, he said to the man who had the withered hand, "Come and stand here." He got up and stood there. ⁹ Then Jesus said to them, "I ask you, is it lawful to do good or to do harm on the sabbath, to save life or to destroy it?" ¹⁰ After looking around at all of them, he said to him, "Stretch out your hand." He did so, and his hand was restored. ¹¹ But they were filled with fury and discussed with one another what they might do to Jesus.

JESUS CHOOSES THE TWELVE APOSTLES

¹² Now during those days he went out to the mountain to pray; and he spent the night in prayer to God. ¹³ And when day came, he called his disciples and chose twelve of them, whom he also named apostles: ¹⁴ Simon, whom he named Peter, and his brother Andrew, and James, and John, and Philip, and Bartholomew, ¹⁵ and Matthew, and Thomas, and James son of Alphaeus, and Simon, who was called the Zealot, ¹⁶ and Judas son of James, and Judas Iscariot, who became a traitor.

JESUS TEACHES AND HEALS

¹⁷ He came down with them and stood on a level place, with a great crowd of his disciples and a great multitude of people from all Judea, Jerusalem, and the coast of Tyre and Sidon. ¹⁸ They had come to hear him and to be healed of their diseases; and those who were troubled with unclean spirits were cured. ¹⁹ And all in the crowd were trying to touch him, for power came out from him and healed all of them.

BLESSINGS AND WOES

²⁰ Then he looked up at his disciples and said:

"Blessed are you who are poor,

for yours is the kingdom of God.

²¹ "Blessed are you who are hungry now,

for you will be filled.

"Blessed are you who weep now,

for you will laugh.

²² "Blessed are you when people hate you, and when they exclude you, revile you, and defame you on account of the Son of Man. ²³ Rejoice in that day and leap for joy, for surely your reward is great in heaven; for that is what their ancestors did to the prophets.

²⁴ "But woe to you who are rich,

for you have received your consolation.

²⁵ "Woe to you who are full now,

for you will be hungry.

"Woe to you who are laughing now,

for you will mourn and weep.

²⁶ "Woe to you when all speak well of you, for that is what their ancestors did to the false prophets.

St. John Henry Newman
(1801–1890)

Parochial and Plain Sermons

The Danger of Riches

Luke 6:24

The most obvious danger which worldly possessions present to our spiritual welfare is that they become practically a substitute in our hearts for that one object to which our supreme devotion is due. They are present; God is unseen. They are means at hand of effecting what we want: whether God will hear our petitions [or not]…they minister to the corrupt inclinations of our nature; they promise and are able to be gods to us, and such gods too as require no service, but, like dumb idols, exalt the worshiper, impressing him with a notion of his own power and security.

Complete piece

St. Bartholomew

According to tradition, St. Bartholomew was flayed alive. Because of this, he is typically portrayed holding a knife.

Detail of the Apostles

St. Andrew

St. Andrew was martyred by crucifixion, and is often shown carrying an X-shaped cross. In this depiction, his cross is similar to Christ's.

St. James the Greater

St. James the Greater was known for his missionary journeys to foreign lands, and is shown with a walking staff to symbolize his evangelical travels.

St. Peter

St. Peter was given the keys of the kingdom in the Gospels, and is traditionally shown holding a pair of large keys.

Luke 6:12–16

TADDEO DI BARTOLO | *c. 1400*

Christ and the Twelve Apostles

Essay by Michael Stevens

This painting by Taddeo di Bartolo shows the twelve Apostles surrounding the figure of Jesus. While not all of the Apostles can be identified with certainty, some are painted carrying their traditional iconographic symbols, linking them to a specific character.

In traditional depictions of the Twelve such as this one, the symbol for a given Apostle corresponds to their unique means of martyrdom. By placing the instrument of death in the hands of the saint, the artist is celebrating their bravery in proclaiming Jesus—even to the point of death.

As inspiring as the examples of the martyr-saints are, it can be tempting to shy away from them at the same time—as if they are in a different category of holiness we cannot begin to approach. The reality, however, is that we are all called not only to sainthood but to be disciples of Jesus in the world, continuing the missionary work they began two thousand years ago—even to the point of persecution or death.

The Freedom of Detachment
Luke 6:20–26

IN LUKE'S VERSION OF THE BEATITUDES, we find a pithy presentation of what the view from the center is like. First we are told, "Blessed [*makarios*] are you who are poor." We notice that there is none of the softening offered by Matthew ("poor in spirit"), but a simple and straightforward statement of the blessedness of being poor. How do we interpret what seems prima facie to be a glorification of economic poverty? Let me propose the following reading: "How lucky you are if you are not addicted to material things." One of the classic substitutes for God is material wealth, the accumulating of "things." Like any drug, houses, cars, and property provide a "rush" when they first enter the system, but then in time, the thrill that they provide wears off, and more of the drug must be acquired. This rhythm continues inexorably and tragically until the addict is broken by it. Once, on a Sunday afternoon, a knock came to the door of the rectory where I was staying. When I answered, I found a man neatly dressed in expensive clothes and exuding confidence and self-possession. We sat down to talk, and he said, "Father, I've realized all of my dreams." "Well, that's wonderful," I responded benignly. "There's only one problem," he continued, "I'm perfectly miserable." It turned out that his dreams had to do almost exclusively with the accumulation of homes and the maintenance of an impressive stock portfolio. His education, his friendships, his social and professional life circled around and served that addictive and finally insatiable desire. The result, according to the predictable physics of the soul, is the crash into the misery that had taken possession of him. How "unlucky" for him to be tied up in such a net—and how necessary that he find detachment.

Luke's Beatitudes continue with "Blessed are you who weep now." Again, we are struck by the oddness of the claim: how fortunate you are if you display the outward sign of greatest anxiety and depression. Might we translate it as follows: "How lucky you are if you are not addicted to good feelings." We live in a culture that puts a premium on good feelings and attempts to deny or medicate depression. But *feeling happy* is just as much a false god as wealth or power. It is, in itself, only an emotional state, a fleeting and insubstantial psychological condition that cannot possibly satisfy the deepest yearning of the soul; yet it is sought with as much compulsive frenzy as any other drug. We feel the "rush" of pleasure and then, when the thrill fades, we try at all costs to reproduce it at a higher pitch. It is in this context that the addictive use of drugs, alcohol, and artificial stimulants, as well as the hedonistic pursuit of pleasure in sex and at the table, are to be understood. The person who lives in the center, the place of detachment, escapes (fortunately enough) this trap.

Luke's Jesus continues: "Blessed are you when people hate you, and when they exclude you, revile you, and defame you on account of the Son of Man." What could be stranger than this seemingly masochistic dictum? Again, some light might be shed if we translate it in terms of our hermeneutic of detachment: "How lucky you are if you are not addicted to the approval of others." Status, attention, and fame are among the most powerful and insinuating of the false gods who lure us. When I was a child, I reveled in the praise that my father offered me because of my schoolwork. But in time the thrill of that esteem wore off and I sought greater approval—first from my high school teachers, then from my college professors, then from graduate school instructors, and finally from my doctoral director. Each time I heard a word of praise, I felt the rush of the drug, but it was never enough. My life had become an unceasing quest for applause; I was trapped in the familiar pattern, needing approval as desperately as my body needed food and water. Jesus told his disciples: "Woe to you when all speak well of you," and Winston Churchill said, "Never trust a man who has no enemies." The one whom everyone loves is in spiritual distress, since the goodwill of the crowd has undoubtedly become that person's idol. As so many of the saints—and Jesus himself—witness, the path of spiritual freedom brings one almost inevitably into conflict with those who are still in chains. Those who have placed themselves in the Christ-center rest secure even as the approval of the fickle crowd waxes and wanes.

The freedom and fullness of detachment is probably no better expressed than in John of the Cross' beautiful mantra: "To reach satisfaction in all, desire satisfaction in nothing; to come to the knowledge of all, desire the knowledge of nothing; to come to possess all, desire the possession of nothing; to arrive at being all, desire to be nothing." This fourfold *nada* is not a negation but the deepest affirmation, since it is a "no" to a "no." Desiring to possess all, desiring to be all, is the nonbeing of attachment, the misery of addiction; desiring to possess nothing, desiring to be nothing, is accordingly freedom and being. It is finally to see the world as it is, and not through the distorting lens of cupidity and egotism. It is the view from the center.

LOVE FOR ENEMIES

[27] "But I say to you that listen, Love your enemies, do good to those who hate you, [28] bless those who curse you, pray for those who abuse you. [29] If anyone strikes you on the cheek, offer the other also; and from anyone who takes away your coat do not withhold even your shirt. [30] Give to everyone who begs from you; and if anyone takes away your goods, do not ask for them again. [31] Do to others as you would have them do to you.

[32] "If you love those who love you, what credit is that to you? For even sinners love those who love them. [33] If you do good to those who do good to you, what credit is that to you? For even sinners do the same. [34] If you lend to those from whom you hope to receive, what credit is that to you? Even sinners lend to sinners, to receive as much again. [35] But love your enemies, do good, and lend, expecting nothing in return. Your reward will be great, and you will be children of the Most High; for he is kind to the ungrateful and the wicked. [36] Be merciful, just as your Father is merciful.

JUDGING OTHERS

[37] "Do not judge, and you will not be judged; do not condemn, and you will not be condemned. Forgive, and you will be forgiven; [38] give, and

Absorb Your Opponent's Aggression

Luke 6:27–36 | Bishop Barron

Christ's teaching about love of enemies is one of the more the puzzling texts in the New Testament. He says we must love our enemies—not tolerate them, or vaguely accept them, but love them.

There is a form of oriental martial arts called aikido. The idea of aikido is to absorb the aggressive energy of your opponent, moving with it, continually frustrating him until he comes to the point of realizing that fighting is useless.

There is a great deal of this in Jesus' strategy of nonviolence and love of the enemy. You creatively absorb the aggression of your opponent, using it against him to show him the futility of violence. So when someone insults you, send back a compliment instead of an insult.

---

it will be given to you. A good measure, pressed down, shaken together, running over, will be put into your lap; for the measure you give will be the measure you get back."

³⁹ He also told them a parable: "Can a blind person guide a blind person? Will not both fall into a pit? ⁴⁰ A disciple is not above the teacher, but everyone who is fully qualified will be like the teacher. ⁴¹ Why do you see the speck in your neighbor's eye, but do not notice the log in your own eye? ⁴² Or how can you say to your neighbor, 'Friend, let me take out the speck in your eye,' when you yourself do not see the log in your own eye? You hypocrite, first take the log out of your own eye, and then you will see clearly to take the speck out of your neighbor's eye.

A TREE AND ITS FRUIT

⁴³ "No good tree bears bad fruit, nor again does a bad tree bear good fruit; ⁴⁴ for each tree is known by its own fruit. Figs are not gathered from thorns, nor are grapes picked from a bramble bush. ⁴⁵ The good person out of the good treasure of the heart produces good, and the evil person out of evil treasure produces evil; for it is out of the abundance of the heart that the mouth speaks.

THE TWO FOUNDATIONS

⁴⁶ "Why do you call me 'Lord, Lord,' and do not do what I tell you? ⁴⁷ I will show you what someone is like who comes to me, hears my words, and acts on them. ⁴⁸ That one is like a man building a house, who dug deeply and

laid the foundation on rock; when a flood arose, the river burst against that house but could not shake it, because it had been well built. ⁴⁹ But the one who hears and does not act is like a man who built a house on the ground without a foundation. When the river burst against it, immediately it fell, and great was the ruin of that house."

The Foundation of Your Life

Luke 6:46–49 | Bishop Barron

The one who comes to Jesus, hears his words, and acts on them, Jesus says, "is like a man building a house, who dug deeply and laid the foundation on rock; when a flood arose, the river burst against that house but could not shake it, because it had been well built."

This is the heart of it: if you are rooted in God, then you can withstand anything, precisely because you are linked to that power that is creating the cosmos. You will be blessed at that deepest place, and nothing can finally touch you.

But the one who does not take Jesus' words to heart "is like a man who built a house on the ground without a foundation. When the river burst against it, immediately it fell, and great was the ruin of that house."

When the inevitable trials come, the life built on pleasure, money, power, or fame will give way.

So the question is a simple one: Where do you stand? How goes it with your heart? On what, precisely, is the whole of your life built?

JESUS HEALS A CENTURION'S SERVANT

7 After Jesus had finished all his sayings in the hearing of the people, he entered Capernaum. ² A centurion there had a slave whom he valued highly, and who was ill and close to death. ³ When he heard about Jesus, he sent some Jewish elders to him, asking him to come and heal his slave. ⁴ When they came to Jesus, they appealed to him earnestly, saying, "He is worthy of having you do this for him, ⁵ for he loves our people, and it is he who built our synagogue for us." ⁶ And Jesus went with them, but when he was not far from the house, the centurion sent friends to say to him, "Lord, do not trouble yourself, for I am not worthy to have you come under my roof; ⁷ therefore I did not presume to come to you. But only speak the word, and let my servant be healed. ⁸ For I also am a man set under

authority, with soldiers under me; and I say to one, 'Go,' and he goes, and to another, 'Come,' and he comes, and to my slave, 'Do this,' and the slave does it." ⁹ When Jesus heard this he was amazed at him, and turning to the crowd that followed him, he said, "I tell you, not even in Israel have I found such faith." ¹⁰ When those who had been sent returned to the house, they found the slave in good health.

JESUS RAISES THE WIDOW'S SON AT NAIN

¹¹ Soon afterwards he went to a town called Nain, and his disciples and a large crowd went with him. ¹² As he approached the gate of the town, a man who had died was being carried out. He was his mother's only son, and she was a widow; and with her was a large crowd from the town. ¹³ When the Lord saw her, he had compassion for her and said to her, "Do not weep." ¹⁴ Then he came forward and touched the bier, and the bearers stood still. And he said, "Young man, I say to you, rise!" ¹⁵ The dead man sat up and began to speak, and Jesus gave him to his mother. ¹⁶ Fear seized all of them; and they glorified God, saying, "A great prophet has risen among us!" and "God has looked favorably on his people!" ¹⁷ This word about him spread throughout Judea and all the surrounding country.

MESSENGERS FROM JOHN THE BAPTIST

¹⁸ The disciples of John reported all these things to him. So John summoned two of his disciples ¹⁹ and sent them to the Lord to ask, "Are you the one who is to come, or are we to wait for another?" ²⁰ When the men had come to him, they said, "John the Baptist has sent us to you to ask, 'Are you the one who is to come, or are we to wait for another?' " ²¹ Jesus had just then cured many people of diseases, plagues, and evil spirits, and had given sight to many who were blind. ²² And he answered them, "Go and tell John what you have seen and heard: the blind receive their sight, the lame walk, the lepers are cleansed, the deaf hear, the dead are raised, the poor have good news brought to them. ²³ And blessed is anyone who takes no offense at me."

²⁴ When John's messengers had gone, Jesus began to speak to the crowds about John: "What did you go out into the wilderness to look at? A reed shaken by the wind? ²⁵ What then did you go out to see? Someone dressed in soft robes? Look, those who put on fine clothing and live in luxury are in royal palaces. ²⁶ What then did you go out to see? A prophet? Yes, I tell you, and more than a prophet. ²⁷ This is the one about whom it is written,

> 'See, I am sending my messenger ahead of you,
> who will prepare your way before you.'

²⁸ I tell you, among those born of women no one is greater than John; yet the least in the kingdom of God is greater than he." ²⁹ (And all the people

who heard this, including the tax collectors, acknowledged the justice of God, because they had been baptized with John's baptism. [30] But by refusing to be baptized by him, the Pharisees and the lawyers rejected God's purpose for themselves.)

[31] "To what then will I compare the people of this generation, and what are they like? [32] They are like children sitting in the marketplace and calling to one another,

'We played the flute for you, and you did not dance;

we wailed, and you did not weep.'

[33] For John the Baptist has come eating no bread and drinking no wine, and you say, 'He has a demon'; [34] the Son of Man has come eating and drinking, and you say, 'Look, a glutton and a drunkard, a friend of tax collectors and sinners!' [35] Nevertheless, wisdom is vindicated by all her children."

God Never Gives Up

Luke 7:31–35 | Bishop Barron

The Pharisees compared the eating habits of John the Baptist, who fasted, and Jesus, who dined with sinners. In the carefully stratified society of Jesus' time, a righteous person would never associate with the unrighteous for fear of becoming unclean.

But here is Jesus, scandalizing everyone because he does indeed break down these barriers. How would you feel if you saw me socializing with prostitutes and drug dealers, eating and drinking with terrorists? Would it shock you, dismay you, disappoint you? But this is what Jesus did, precisely because he is the Incarnation of the God who aggressively seeks out the lost.

God looks for us, comes running after us, never lets go, never relents, never gives up. The more we run, the more he runs after; the more we hide, the more he looks; the more we resist, the more he persists. God loves sinners and associates with them.

A SINFUL WOMAN FORGIVEN

[36] One of the Pharisees asked Jesus to eat with him, and he went into the Pharisee's house and took his place at the table. [37] And a woman in the city, who was a sinner, having learned that he was eating in the Pharisee's

house, brought an alabaster jar of ointment. [38] She stood behind him at his feet, weeping, and began to bathe his feet with her tears and to dry them with her hair. Then she continued kissing his feet and anointing them with the ointment. [39] Now when the Pharisee who had invited him saw it, he said to himself, "If this man were a prophet, he would have known who and what kind of woman this is who is touching him—that she is a sinner." [40] Jesus spoke up and said to him, "Simon, I have something to say to you." "Teacher," he replied, "speak." [41] "A certain creditor had two debtors; one owed five hundred denarii, and the other fifty. [42] When they could not pay, he canceled the debts for both of them. Now which of them will love him more?" [43] Simon answered, "I suppose the one for whom he canceled the greater debt." And Jesus said to him, "You have judged rightly." [44] Then turning toward the woman, he said to Simon, "Do you see this woman? I entered your house; you gave me no water for my feet, but she has bathed my feet with her tears and dried them with her hair. [45] You gave me no kiss, but from the time I came in she has not stopped kissing my feet. [46] You did not anoint my head with oil, but she has anointed my feet with ointment. [47] Therefore, I tell you, her sins, which were many, have been forgiven; hence she has shown great love. But the one to whom little is forgiven, loves little." [48] Then he said to her, "Your sins are forgiven." [49] But those who were at the table with him began to say among themselves, "Who is this who even forgives sins?" [50] And he said to the woman, "Your faith has saved you; go in peace."

St. Gregory the Great
(540–604)

Homilies on the Gospels

The Symbol of the Woman
Luke 7:36–50

The sinful woman, following the footsteps of the Lord, covering his feet with her tears, symbolizes the Church converted from heathenism. And this woman can symbolize us too when, having sinned, we turn back wholeheartedly to the Lord.

The Pharisee and the Sinful Woman
Luke 7:36–50

WE CAN SEE THROUGHOUT THE GOSPELS how, with a sort of awful power, Jesus judges religion itself. There are numerous accounts of Jesus' confrontation with religion and its official proponents—the scribes, elders, and Pharisees—including Luke's rich and paradigmatic narrative of the woman in the house of Simon the Pharisee.

Luke tells us that Simon had invited Jesus to a meal. It is most important to note that eating etiquette and behavior are of tremendous symbolic importance in the Gospels, for they bespeak one's attitude toward the kingdom of God. Jesus is at table with Simon, presumably in an elegant house and in a relatively formalized setting, and in walks a woman "who was a sinner." We can easily imagine the shock and discomfiture that her arrival precipitated, this intrusion of an uninvited and unwanted guest into a proper and carefully planned dinner party. Then the woman intensifies the unease in the room when she stands behind Jesus, weeping onto his feet, drying them with her hair, and then anointing them with oil. Insulted and moved to self-righteous indignation, Simon thinks to himself, "If this man were a prophet, he would have known who and what kind of woman this is who is touching him—that she is a sinner." There are several aspects to Simon's reaction, each one reflective of a dimension of the religiously toned *pusilla anima* (small soul). Simon is, first of all, dismayed at the social upset this woman's appearance has caused. His party was carefully designed to be only for the best, only those who met his probably exacting standards of social and religious behavior. When the woman with a bad reputation crashes his dinner party, she throws into sharp relief the exclusiveness and snobbishness that characterize the host. Her presence sullies the "cleanness" and distinctiveness that mean so much to Simon precisely as a Pharisee. The sinful woman's intrusion into his sanitized world—and Jesus' obvious acceptance of her—dramatically judge the violent exclusiveness of Simon's religiosity.

Secondly, Simon's attitude toward Jesus is revealing. He notices—and undoubtedly rejoices in—Jesus' apparent inability to read the heart of the intruder. Simon had invited this new spiritual phenom to supper in order to size him up, to determine whether he belongs in the inner circle of correct believers, and he is watching this scene unfold with great interest. It is clear that Jesus is not as discriminating as Simon himself, not as insightful in his assessments, not as religiously careful. Once more, ranking, ordering, and excluding are paramount in Simon's mind. But Jesus the judge decisively intervenes at this point: "Simon, I have something to say to you."

He then proposes to the Pharisee the parable of the creditor who forgave two debtors, one who owed him five hundred denarii and the other who owed him only fifty. "Now which of them," Jesus asks, "will love him more?" And Simon correctly responds, "I suppose the one for whom he canceled the greater debt." Then Jesus turns to the woman who, we recall, is standing behind him, and says, "Do you see this woman?" The "topography" here is not incidental. Jesus is between the Pharisee and the woman and thus, when he invites Simon to look at her, he forces him to see her "through" Jesus. Simon has seen her in a conventional way, in the manner dictated by his religious consciousness, and thus he has appreciated her only as an unwelcome troublemaker, a hopeless sinner. Jesus compels him to look again, but this time with new eyes, with the vision of holiness. And what is disclosed from this privileged point of view? "I entered your house; you gave me no water for my feet, but she has bathed my feet with her tears and dried them with her hair. You gave me no kiss, but from the time I came in she has not stopped kissing my feet. You did not anoint my head with oil, but she has anointed my feet with ointment." She is filled with a love for Christ that overflows in acts of self-offering and service; she breaks open her own heart in gratitude. But Simon has shown scant hospitality to his guest, offering little if anything of himself to Christ. The abundance of the woman's love discloses something to Jesus that had obviously been invisible to Simon: she has been forgiven much. "Therefore, I tell you, her sins, which were many, have been forgiven; hence she has shown great love." It is most important to note that Jesus does not, strictly speaking, forgive her sins; rather, he notices that she has been forgiven. And the evidence for it is her self-forgetting love. She loves so passionately and so courageously (risking the disapproval of Simon's elegant guests) precisely because she has been so graciously and abundantly forgiven. It is decidedly not the case, Jesus implies, that love precedes divine forgiveness as a sort of prerequisite; on the contrary, forgiveness precedes love as the condition for its possibility. It is not the case that one's moral life must be upright in order to win divine favor; rather, the sheer gift of God's favor tends to produce an upright moral life, a life of love.

How does all of this constitute a judgment on Simon's religiosity? The Pharisee is so concerned with propriety, cultic purity, and moral excellence that *he simply doesn't see* the presence of grace around him. Among the presuppositions of Simon's religion is the fundamentally egotistic conviction that divine favor is won through human achievement. It is this illusion of the *pusilla anima* that Jesus punctures. As long as divine love is appreciated as something that flows from ethical excellence, the sinful ego remains regnant, and the freedom and sovereignty of God are denied. The ethical component of religion is, for Simon and like-minded people, a tool by which the unconditioned ego grasps and manipulates the divine. The Pharisee's blindness to the implications of the woman's excessive love is tantamount to his blindness to the authentic workings of the God who is really God.

There is still another demonic component to Simon's religion. Unlike the woman, Simon is not rich in love and therefore he is not aware of the workings of God's forgiveness in him. In Jesus' language, he has been forgiven little. Now, is this because there is little in him that needs forgiveness? Simon's behavior as described in this brief narrative would suggest not. But it is the Pharisee's religion—his carrying out of the moral law in strict detail—that convinces him of his own self-righteousness and thus renders him indifferent to the divine forgiveness, at least in his case. His own cultic purity brushes forgiveness off the stage and thus produces what we see disclosed in the story: a man weak in love. Simon's pharisaical religiosity has blinded him to the need for repentance. He is desperately in the grip of the *pusilla anima*, but the defenses around the little mind are so powerful that the divine grace cannot penetrate in a healing way. What he is tragically unable to see—and this is the heart of the matter—is the joyful and grace-filled process of repentance that unfolds before his very eyes in the gestures of the forgiven woman. It is Jesus the judge who shines light into the darkness of Simon's religion itself, into its exclusiveness, violence, self-righteousness, and egotism.

SOME WOMEN ACCOMPANY JESUS

8 Soon afterwards he went on through cities and villages, proclaiming and bringing the good news of the kingdom of God. The twelve were with him, ² as well as some women who had been cured of evil spirits and infirmities: Mary, called Magdalene, from whom seven demons had gone out, ³ and Joanna, the wife of Herod's steward Chuza, and Susanna, and many others, who provided for them out of their resources.

No More Divisions

Luke 8:1–3 | Bishop Barron

One of the principal marks of Jesus' teaching is the overturning of social conventions. In service of what he calls the kingdom of God, God's way of ordering the world, Jesus says and does all sorts of outrageous things.

And one of the most striking and surprising of Jesus' moves is a radical inclusion of women. He allows women into his inner circle (practically unheard of for a rabbi). He speaks publicly to the woman at the well. He engages with the Syrophoenician woman. He forgives the woman caught in adultery. And the first witnesses of the Resurrection are women.

Luke was a companion of Paul, and his Gospel reflects many of Paul's themes. Paul famously says, "There is no longer Jew or Greek, there is no longer slave or free, there is no longer male and female; for all of you are one in Christ Jesus" (Gal. 3:28). This was a very radical claim in those times, for these were some of the most basic social divisions of the ancient world. Free men were a lot better off than slaves, Jews had huge advantages over Greeks, and males were seen as superior to females. But not anymore—not in light of the kingdom of God that Jesus announces.

THE PARABLE OF THE SOWER

⁴ When a great crowd gathered and people from town after town came to him, he said in a parable: ⁵ "A sower went out to sow his seed; and as he sowed, some fell on the path and was trampled on, and the birds of the air ate it up. ⁶ Some fell on the rock; and as it grew up, it withered for lack of moisture. ⁷ Some fell among thorns, and the thorns grew with it and choked it. ⁸ Some fell into good soil, and when it grew, it produced a hundredfold." As he said this, he called out, "Let anyone with ears to hear listen!"

THE PURPOSE OF THE PARABLES

⁹ Then his disciples asked him what this parable meant. ¹⁰ He said, "To you it has been given to know the secrets of the kingdom of God; but to others I speak in parables, so that

> 'looking they may not perceive,
> and listening they may not understand.'

THE PARABLE OF THE SOWER EXPLAINED

¹¹ "Now the parable is this: The seed is the word of God. ¹² The ones on the path are those who have heard; then the devil comes and takes away the word from their hearts, so that they may not believe and be saved. ¹³ The ones on the rock are those who, when they hear the word, receive it with joy. But these have no root; they believe only for a while and in a time of testing fall away. ¹⁴ As for what fell among the thorns, these are the ones who hear; but as they go on their way, they are choked by the cares and riches and pleasures of life, and their fruit does not mature. ¹⁵ But as for that in the good soil, these are the ones who, when they hear the word, hold it fast in an honest and good heart, and bear fruit with patient endurance.

A LAMP UNDER A JAR

¹⁶ "No one after lighting a lamp hides it under a jar, or puts it under a bed, but puts it on a lampstand, so that those who enter may see the light. ¹⁷ For nothing is hidden that will not be disclosed, nor is anything secret that will not become known and come to light. ¹⁸ Then pay attention to how you listen; for to those who have, more will be given; and from those who do not have, even what they seem to have will be taken away."

THE TRUE KINDRED OF JESUS

¹⁹ Then his mother and his brothers came to him, but they could not reach him because of the crowd. ²⁰ And he was told, "Your mother and your brothers are standing outside, wanting to see you." ²¹ But he said to them, "My mother and my brothers are those who hear the word of God and do it."

Fulton Sheen
(1895–1979)

———

Life of Christ

The Demons and the Pigs

Luke 8:26–39

A man possessed of an unclean spirit came out of the tombs to meet him. The actual scene was Decapolis, a predominantly Gentile region. Josephus strongly implied that Gerasa was a Greek city. The very fact that the people there were swineherds would seem to indicate further that they were not Jews. It is conceivable that they were Jews defying the Mosaic Law.

Considerable symbolism may be attached to the fact that in this pagan land, our Blessed Lord came face to face with discords and forces far worse than those which disturb the winds and waves and the bodies of men. Here there was something wilder, and more fearful, than the natural elements, which could bring confusion, anarchy, and ruin to the inner man. There had been a wholesome faith in the centurion and in the Syrophoenician woman. But there was nothing in this young man but the dominion of the devil. The other two pagans had spoken from their own hearts in tribute to our Savior. Here, however, it was an alien's spirit, a fallen spirit, that made the young man affirm the divinity: "What have you to do with me, Jesus, Son of the Most High God? I beg you, do not torment me."

When the Savior released the young man from the evil spirit and permitted it to enter into the swine instead, the townspeople ordered our Lord to depart from their coast. The spirit of capitalism, in its most evil form, made them feel that the restoring of a soul to the friendship of God, was nothing compared to the loss of a few pigs. While the respectable Gerasenes bade him depart, the Samaritans, who were sinners, wanted our Lord to stay with them.

JESUS CALMS A STORM

²² One day he got into a boat with his disciples, and he said to them, "Let us go across to the other side of the lake." So they put out, ²³ and while they were sailing he fell asleep. A windstorm swept down on the lake, and the boat was filling with water, and they were in danger. ²⁴ They went to him and woke him up, shouting, "Master, Master, we are perishing!" And he woke up and rebuked the wind and the raging waves; they ceased, and there was a calm. ²⁵ He said to them, "Where is your faith?" They were afraid and amazed, and said to one another, "Who then is this, that he commands even the winds and the water, and they obey him?"

JESUS HEALS THE GERASENE DEMONIAC

²⁶ Then they arrived at the country of the Gerasenes, which is opposite Galilee. ²⁷ As he stepped out on land, a man of the city who had demons met him. For a long time he had worn no clothes, and he did not live in a house but in the tombs. ²⁸ When he saw Jesus, he fell down before him and shouted at the top of his voice, "What have you to do with me, Jesus, Son of the Most High God? I beg you, do not torment me"—²⁹ for Jesus had commanded the unclean spirit to come out of the man. (For many times it had seized him; he was kept under guard and bound with chains and shackles, but he would break the bonds and be driven by the demon into the wilds.) ³⁰ Jesus then asked him, "What is your name?" He said, "Legion"; for many demons had entered him. ³¹ They begged him not to order them to go back into the abyss.

³² Now there on the hillside a large herd of swine was feeding; and the demons begged Jesus to let them enter these. So he gave them permission. ³³ Then the demons came out of the man and entered the swine, and the herd rushed down the steep bank into the lake and was drowned.

³⁴ When the swineherds saw what had happened, they ran off and told it in the city and in the country. ³⁵ Then people came out to see what had happened, and when they came to Jesus, they found the man from whom the demons had gone sitting at the feet of Jesus, clothed and in his right mind. And they were afraid. ³⁶ Those who had seen it told them how the one who had been possessed by demons had been healed. ³⁷ Then all the people of the surrounding country of the Gerasenes asked Jesus to leave them; for they were seized with great fear. So he got into the boat and returned. ³⁸ The man from whom the demons had gone begged that he might be with him; but Jesus sent him away, saying, ³⁹ "Return to your home, and declare how much God has done for you." So he went away, proclaiming throughout the city how much Jesus had done for him.

A GIRL RESTORED TO LIFE AND A WOMAN HEALED

[40] Now when Jesus returned, the crowd welcomed him, for they were all waiting for him. [41] Just then there came a man named Jairus, a leader of the synagogue. He fell at Jesus' feet and begged him to come to his house, [42] for he had an only daughter, about twelve years old, who was dying.

As he went, the crowds pressed in on him. [43] Now there was a woman who had been suffering from hemorrhages for twelve years; and though she had spent all she had on physicians, no one could cure her. [44] She came up behind him and touched the fringe of his clothes, and immediately her hemorrhage stopped. [45] Then Jesus asked, "Who touched me?" When all denied it, Peter said, "Master, the crowds surround you and press in on you." [46] But Jesus said, "Someone touched me; for I noticed that power had gone out from me." [47] When the woman saw that she could not remain hidden, she came trembling; and falling down before him, she declared in the presence of all the people why she had touched him, and how she had been immediately healed. [48] He said to her, "Daughter, your faith has made you well; go in peace."

Pope Francis
(1936–)

———

Lumen Fidei

Touching Jesus with Our Hearts
Luke 8:45–46

By his taking flesh and coming among us, Jesus has touched us, and through the sacraments he continues to touch us even today; transforming our hearts, he unceasingly enables us to acknowledge and acclaim him as the Son of God. In faith, we can touch him and receive the power of his grace. Saint Augustine, commenting on the account of the woman suffering from haemorrhages who touched Jesus and was cured, says: "To touch him with our hearts: that is what it means to believe." The crowd presses in on Jesus, but they do not reach him with the personal touch of faith, which apprehends the mystery that he is the Son who reveals the Father. Only when we are configured to Jesus do we receive the eyes needed to see him.

⁴⁹ While he was still speaking, someone came from the leader's house to say, "Your daughter is dead; do not trouble the teacher any longer." ⁵⁰ When Jesus heard this, he replied, "Do not fear. Only believe, and she will be saved." ⁵¹ When he came to the house, he did not allow anyone to enter with him, except Peter, John, and James, and the child's father and mother. ⁵² They were all weeping and wailing for her; but he said, "Do not weep; for she is not dead but sleeping." ⁵³ And they laughed at him, knowing that she was dead. ⁵⁴ But he took her by the hand and called out, "Child, get up!" ⁵⁵ Her spirit returned, and she got up at once. Then he directed them to give her something to eat. ⁵⁶ Her parents were astounded; but he ordered them to tell no one what had happened.

St. Cyril of Alexandria
(378–444)

Commentary on Luke

Not Dead, But Sleeping

Luke 8:52

Notice how skillfully [Jesus] manages this event. Although he knew very well that the girl was dead, he says, "She is not dead but sleeping." Why? So that by their laughter the crowd might establish clearly that the girl really was dead.... Let no man say that Christ spoke untruly. For to him, being Life by nature, there is nothing dead. And this is why we [his followers], having a firm hope of the resurrection of the dead, call them "those that sleep." For in Christ they will arise.

THE MISSION OF THE TWELVE

9 Then Jesus called the twelve together and gave them power and authority over all demons and to cure diseases, ² and he sent them out to proclaim the kingdom of God and to heal. ³ He said to them, "Take nothing for your journey, no staff, nor bag, nor bread, nor money—not even an extra tunic. ⁴ Whatever house you enter, stay there, and leave from there. ⁵ Wherever they do not welcome you, as you are leaving that town shake the dust off your feet as a testimony against them." ⁶ They departed and went through the villages, bringing the good news and curing diseases everywhere.

HEROD'S PERPLEXITY

⁷ Now Herod the ruler heard about all that had taken place, and he was perplexed, because it was said by some that John had been raised from the dead, ⁸ by some that Elijah had appeared, and by others that one of the ancient prophets had arisen. ⁹ Herod said, "John I beheaded; but who is this about whom I hear such things?" And he tried to see him.

FEEDING THE FIVE THOUSAND

¹⁰ On their return the apostles told Jesus all they had done. He took them with him and withdrew privately to a city called Bethsaida. ¹¹ When the crowds found out about it, they followed him; and he welcomed them, and spoke to them about the kingdom of God, and healed those who needed to be cured.

¹² The day was drawing to a close, and the twelve came to him and said, "Send the crowd away, so that they may go into the surrounding villages and countryside, to lodge and get provisions; for we are here in a deserted place." ¹³ But he said to them, "You give them something to eat." They said, "We have no more than five loaves and two fish—unless we are to go and buy food for all these people." ¹⁴ For there were about five thousand men. And he said to his disciples, "Make them sit down in groups of about fifty each." ¹⁵ They did so and made them all sit down. ¹⁶ And taking the five loaves and the two fish, he looked up to heaven, and blessed and broke them, and gave them to the disciples to set before the crowd. ¹⁷ And all ate and were filled. What was left over was gathered up, twelve baskets of broken pieces.

The Loop of Grace

Luke 9:10–17 | Bishop Barron

The miracle of the feeding of the thousands with a few loaves and fishes must have haunted the imaginations of the early Christian communities, for accounts of it can be found in all four Gospels.

In Luke's version, crowds began to gather around Jesus when they heard that he had retired to Bethsaida. Moved with pity, Jesus taught them and cured their sick, but as the day was drawing to a close, the disciples worried about what this enormous crowd would eat. "The twelve came to him and said, 'Send the crowd away, so that they may go into the surrounding villages and countryside, to lodge and get provisions; for we are here in a deserted place.'" The Twelve, symbolic of the gathered tribes of Israel, act here in contradiction to their own deepest identity, for they want to scatter those whom Jesus has drawn magnetically to himself. So Jesus challenges them: "You give them something to eat." But they protest: "We have no more than five loaves and two fish—unless we are to go and buy food for all these people." Oblivious to their complaint, Jesus instructs them to gather the crowd in groups of fifty or so. Then, taking the loaves and fish, Jesus said a blessing over them, broke them, and then gave them to the disciples for distribution. Everyone in the crowd of five thousand ate until they were satisfied.

There is no better exemplification in the Scriptures of the loop of grace. God offers, as a sheer grace, the gift of being, but if we try to cling to that gift and make it our own (in the manner of Eve and Adam), we lose it. The constant command of the Bible is this: what you have received as a gift, give as a gift—and you will find the original gift multiplied and enhanced. God's grace, precisely because it is grace, cannot be held on to; rather, it is had only in the measure that it remains grace—that is to say, a gift given away. God's life, in a word, is had only on the fly. One realizes this truth when one enters willingly into the loop of grace, giving away that which one is receiving. The hungry people who gather around Jesus in this scene are symbolic of the hungry human race, starving from the time of Adam and Eve for what will satisfy. In imitation of our first parents, we have tried to fill up the emptiness with wealth, pleasure, power, honor, the sheer love of domination—

but none of it works, precisely because we have all been wired for God and God is nothing but love. It is only when we conform ourselves to the way of love, only when, in a high paradox, we contrive to empty out the ego, that we are filled. Thus the five loaves and two fish symbolize that which has been given to us, all that we have received as a grace from God. If we appropriate it, we lose it. But if we turn it over to Christ, then we will find it transfigured and multiplied, even unto the feeding of the world.

But notice too that Jesus hands the loaves to the disciples, who in turn give them to the people. At the climax of the narrative, the disciples become themselves the instruments of nourishment, setting the loaves and fish before the people. The Body of Christ is not an amorphous, egalitarian collectivity but rather a structured society, governed and ordered hierarchically. To be fully in Christ's Body, therefore, is to be integrated into the complex system of an apostolic *ordo*. It is insufficient evangelically simply to proclaim Christ without at the same time inviting people to participate in the structured life of the Church. The lifeblood of the ecclesial body is grace, and the ordinary means by which that grace becomes available are the sacraments, visible signs of an invisible power. The divine life of Jesus is always, therefore, either directly or indirectly, mediated through the sacraments.

PETER'S DECLARATION ABOUT JESUS

[18] Once when Jesus was praying alone, with only the disciples near him, he asked them, "Who do the crowds say that I am?" [19] They answered, "John the Baptist; but others, Elijah; and still others, that one of the ancient prophets has arisen." [20] He said to them, "But who do you say that I am?" Peter answered, "The Messiah of God."

JESUS FORETELLS HIS DEATH AND RESURRECTION

[21] He sternly ordered and commanded them not to tell anyone, [22] saying, "The Son of Man must undergo great suffering, and be rejected by the elders, chief priests, and scribes, and be killed, and on the third day be raised."

[23] Then he said to them all, "If any want to become my followers, let them deny themselves and take up their cross daily and follow me. [24] For those who want to save their life will lose it, and those who lose their life for my sake will save it. [25] What does it profit them if they gain the whole world, but lose or forfeit themselves? [26] Those who are ashamed of me and of my words, of them the Son of Man will be ashamed when he comes in his glory and the glory of the Father and of the holy angels. [27] But truly I tell you, there are some standing here who will not taste death before they see the kingdom of God."

Crucifying Your Ego

Luke 9:22–25 | Bishop Barron

Jesus lays out his conditions for discipleship. For all of us sinners, to varying degrees, our own lives have become god—that is to say, we see the universe turning around our ego, our needs, our projects and our plans, our likes and dislikes.

True conversion—the *metanoia* that Jesus talks about—is so much more than moral reform, though it includes that. It has to do with a complete shift in consciousness, a whole new way of looking at one's life.

Jesus offered a teaching that must have been gut-wrenching to his first-century audience: "If any want to become my followers, let them deny themselves and take up their cross daily and follow me." His listeners knew what the cross meant: a death in utter agony, nakedness, and humiliation. They didn't think of the cross automatically in religious terms, as we do. They knew it in all of its awful power.

Unless you crucify your ego, you cannot be my follower, Jesus says. This move—this terrible move—has to be the foundation of the spiritual life.

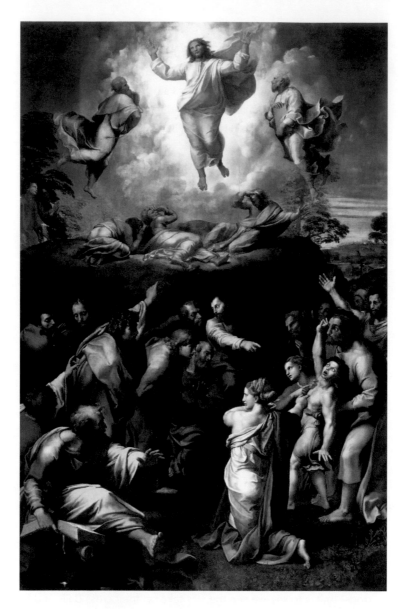

Moses and Elijah

In the Gospel, Moses and Elijah accompany Jesus as he is transfigured. In the painting, Raphael arranges their bodies to gently lean toward Christ, forming a triangle that converges on his head. In the Renaissance, triangles were symbols of perfection, and by using this compositional structure, Raphael shows how Jesus brings the Law and prophecy of the Old Testament—symbolized here by Moses and Elijah—to perfect fulfillment.

The figures on the left

Emerging from the trees are Sts. Justus and Pastor, who share their feast day with the Feast of the Transfiguration.

Luke 9:28–36

RAPHAEL | *1516–1520*

Transfiguration

Essay by Michael Stevens

Raphael is considered to be one of the greatest painters of the Renaissance, along with Michelangelo—his great rival—and Leonardo da Vinci. His work epitomizes the style of the High Renaissance, with its structured and stable composition.

This painting—the last piece Raphael worked on before he died— shows the Transfiguration, where Jesus revealed his glory to his disciples. At the top of the composition, the figure of Jesus blazes a cool, bright white. Directly below are his disciples, who lie on the ground in awe, and shield their faces from the blinding light. At the bottom a demoniac is brought before Jesus, forming a companion narrative to the Transfiguration and creatively collapsing the sequence of events in Luke's account into a single moment in time. Together, the two stories provide a contrast between the powers of light and dark, good and evil.

Raphael, a brilliant colorist, uses every instance of drapery on the figures to bring forth subtle tones of blue, green, red, and gold. All of the figures appear to be lit by the same surreal and otherworldly light of Christ, which illumines the entire scene and provides the source of all the hues' richness. Rather than homogenizing the color palette, the light of Jesus instead makes each character more distinct and vibrant. By creating this dynamic of light and color in the middle of terrifying darkness—both optical and spiritual— Raphael reminds us that as Christ's radiance casts out evil, it also makes those close to him more and more uniquely themselves.

THE TRANSFIGURATION

28 Now about eight days after these sayings Jesus took with him Peter and John and James, and went up on the mountain to pray. 29 And while he was praying, the appearance of his face changed, and his clothes became dazzling white. 30 Suddenly they saw two men, Moses and Elijah, talking to him. 31 They appeared in glory and were speaking of his departure, which he was about to accomplish at Jerusalem. 32 Now Peter and his companions were weighed down with sleep; but since they had stayed awake, they saw his glory and the two men who stood with him. 33 Just as they were leaving him, Peter said to Jesus, "Master, it is good for us to be here; let us make three dwellings, one for you, one for Moses, and one for Elijah"—not knowing what he said. 34 While he was saying this, a cloud came and overshadowed them; and they were terrified as they entered the cloud. 35 Then from the cloud came a voice that said, "This is my Son, my Chosen; listen to him!" 36 When the voice had spoken, Jesus was found alone. And they kept silent and in those days told no one any of the things they had seen.

JESUS HEALS A BOY WITH A DEMON

37 On the next day, when they had come down from the mountain, a great crowd met him. 38 Just then a man from the crowd shouted, "Teacher, I beg you to look at my son; he is my only child. 39 Suddenly a spirit seizes him, and all at once he shrieks. It convulses him until he foams at the mouth; it mauls him and will scarcely leave him. 40 I begged your disciples to cast it out, but they could not." 41 Jesus answered, "You faithless and perverse generation, how much longer must I be with you and bear with you? Bring your son here." 42 While he was coming, the demon dashed him to the ground in convulsions. But Jesus rebuked the unclean spirit, healed the boy, and gave him back to his father. 43 And all were astounded at the greatness of God.

JESUS AGAIN FORETELLS HIS DEATH

While everyone was amazed at all that he was doing, he said to his disciples, 44 "Let these words sink into your ears: The Son of Man is going to be betrayed into human hands." 45 But they did not understand this saying; its meaning was concealed from them, so that they could not perceive it. And they were afraid to ask him about this saying.

TRUE GREATNESS

46 An argument arose among them as to which one of them was the greatest. 47 But Jesus, aware of their inner thoughts, took a little child and put it by his side, 48 and said to them, "Whoever welcomes this child in my name welcomes me, and whoever welcomes me welcomes the one who sent me; for the least among all of you is the greatest."

ANOTHER EXORCIST

⁴⁹ John answered, "Master, we saw someone casting out demons in your name, and we tried to stop him, because he does not follow with us." ⁵⁰ But Jesus said to him, "Do not stop him; for whoever is not against you is for you."

A SAMARITAN VILLAGE REFUSES TO RECEIVE JESUS

⁵¹ When the days drew near for him to be taken up, he set his face to go to Jerusalem. ⁵² And he sent messengers ahead of him. On their way they entered a village of the Samaritans to make ready for him; ⁵³ but they did not receive him, because his face was set toward Jerusalem. ⁵⁴ When his disciples James and John saw it, they said, "Lord, do you want us to command fire to come down from heaven and consume them?" ⁵⁵ But he turned and rebuked them. ⁵⁶ Then they went on to another village.

WOULD-BE FOLLOWERS OF JESUS

⁵⁷ As they were going along the road, someone said to him, "I will follow you wherever you go." ⁵⁸ And Jesus said to him, "Foxes have holes, and birds of the air have nests; but the Son of Man has nowhere to lay his head." ⁵⁹ To another he said, "Follow me." But he said, "Lord, first let me go and bury my father." ⁶⁰ But Jesus said to him, "Let the dead bury their own dead; but as for you, go and proclaim the kingdom of God." ⁶¹ Another said, "I will follow you, Lord; but let me first say farewell to those at my home." ⁶² Jesus said to him, "No one who puts a hand to the plow and looks back is fit for the kingdom of God."

THE MISSION OF THE SEVENTY

10 After this the Lord appointed seventy others and sent them on ahead of him in pairs to every town and place where he himself intended to go. ² He said to them, "The harvest is plentiful, but the laborers are few; therefore ask the Lord of the harvest to send out laborers into his harvest. ³ Go on your way. See, I am sending you out like lambs into the midst of wolves. ⁴ Carry no purse, no bag, no sandals; and greet no one on the road. ⁵ Whatever house you enter, first say, 'Peace to this house!' ⁶ And if anyone is there who shares in peace, your peace will rest on that person; but if not, it will return to you. ⁷ Remain in the same house, eating and drinking whatever they provide, for the laborer deserves to be paid. Do not move about from house to house. ⁸ Whenever you enter a town and its people welcome you, eat what is set before you; ⁹ cure the sick who are there, and say to them, 'The kingdom of God has come near to you.' ¹⁰ But whenever you enter a town and they do not welcome you, go out into its streets and say, ¹¹ 'Even the dust of your town that clings to our feet, we wipe off in

protest against you. Yet know this: the kingdom of God has come near.' ¹² I tell you, on that day it will be more tolerable for Sodom than for that town.

WOES TO UNREPENTANT CITIES

¹³ "Woe to you, Chorazin! Woe to you, Bethsaida! For if the deeds of power done in you had been done in Tyre and Sidon, they would have repented long ago, sitting in sackcloth and ashes. ¹⁴ But at the judgment it will be more tolerable for Tyre and Sidon than for you. ¹⁵ And you, Capernaum,

will you be exalted to heaven?

No, you will be brought down to Hades.

¹⁶ "Whoever listens to you listens to me, and whoever rejects you rejects me, and whoever rejects me rejects the one who sent me."

THE RETURN OF THE SEVENTY

¹⁷ The seventy returned with joy, saying, "Lord, in your name even the demons submit to us!" ¹⁸ He said to them, "I watched Satan fall from heaven like a flash of lightning. ¹⁹ See, I have given you authority to tread on snakes and scorpions, and over all the power of the enemy; and nothing will hurt you. ²⁰ Nevertheless, do not rejoice at this, that the spirits submit to you, but rejoice that your names are written in heaven."

JESUS REJOICES

²¹ At that same hour Jesus rejoiced in the Holy Spirit and said, "I thank you, Father, Lord of heaven and earth, because you have hidden these things from the wise and the intelligent and have revealed them to infants; yes, Father, for such was your gracious will. ²² All things have been handed over to me by my Father; and no one knows who the Son is except the Father, or who the Father is except the Son and anyone to whom the Son chooses to reveal him."

²³ Then turning to the disciples, Jesus said to them privately, "Blessed are the eyes that see what you see! ²⁴ For I tell you that many prophets and kings desired to see what you see, but did not see it, and to hear what you hear, but did not hear it."

THE PARABLE OF THE GOOD SAMARITAN

²⁵ Just then a lawyer stood up to test Jesus. "Teacher," he said, "what must I do to inherit eternal life?" ²⁶ He said to him, "What is written in the law? What do you read there?" ²⁷ He answered, "You shall love the Lord your God with all your heart, and with all your soul, and with all your strength, and with all your mind; and your neighbor as yourself." ²⁸ And he said to him, "You have given the right answer; do this, and you will live."

The Greatest Commandment

Luke 10:25–28 | Bishop Barron

IT WAS A COMMON PRACTICE in Jesus' time to ask a rabbi to identify the central precept among the hundreds of laws that governed Jewish life, to specify the canon within the canon that would serve to interpret the whole of the Torah. Sometimes, to assure succinctness and brevity, a rabbi was compelled to offer this summary while standing on one foot. Thus Jesus, in accord with this custom, is asked, "Teacher, what must I do to inherit eternal life?" Jesus answers: "What is written in the law? What do you read there?" The man replies: "You shall love the Lord your God with all your heart, and with all your soul, and with all your strength, and with all your mind; and your neighbor as yourself." And Jesus concludes: "You have given the right answer; do this, and you will live."

All of religion is finally about awakening the deepest desire of the heart and directing it toward God; it is about the ordering of love toward that which is most worthy of love. But, Jesus says, a necessary implication of this love of God is compassion for one's fellow human beings. Why are the two commandments so tightly linked? There are many different ways to answer that question, but the best response is the simplest: because of who Jesus is. Christ is not simply a human being, and he is not simply God; rather, he is the God-man, the one in whose person divinity and humanity meet. Therefore, it is finally impossible to love him as God without loving the humanity that he has, in his own person, embraced. Therefore, the greatest commandment is an indirect Christology.

What does this entwined love of God and neighbor look like? To answer this question, we might turn not first to the theologians but to the saints. Rose Hawthorne was the third child of the great American writer Nathaniel Hawthorne, the author of *The Scarlet Letter*, *The House of the Seven Gables*, and some of the best short stories of the nineteenth century. Rose was born in 1851, when her father was at the height of his creative powers and enjoying a worldwide reputation. In the mid-1850s, Hawthorne, at the instigation of his friend President Franklin Pierce, was appointed US consul to Liverpool, and the writer took his family with him to England. There Rose came of age in quite sophisticated surroundings. She studied with private tutors and governesses; she mixed and mingled with the leaders of British society; and she traveled with her father to London, Paris, and Rome, where she even managed to charm Pope Pius IX.

But this idyllic existence ended rather quickly. Nathaniel Hawthorne died in 1864, just before Rose turned thirteen, and her mother died not long after that, leaving the girl bereft and adrift. When she was twenty, she married a man named John Lathrop, and a few years later she gave birth to a son, whom she deeply loved. Her child died at the age of five, however, leaving his mother saddened, as she put it, "beyond words." At this time, her husband's alcoholism began to manifest itself, and their marriage fell on hard times. In her deep depression, Rose Hawthorne began a spiritual search that eventually led to an interest in Catholicism. Despite her family's rather entrenched Protestantism, she entered the Catholic Church.

A turning point in her life occurred when she read in the paper the story of a young seamstress of some means who had been diagnosed with cancer, operated upon unsuccessfully, and then told that her case was hopeless. Squandering her entire fortune on a vain attempt to find a cure, the woman found herself utterly destitute and confined to a squalid shelter for cancer patients. The story broke Rose's heart. Getting down on her knees, she asked God to allow her to do something to help such people. In her prayer, the dynamics of the greatest commandment were operative. Her compassion for suffering humanity led her to God, and the confrontation with God led her to act on behalf of suffering humanity, the two loves joined as inextricably as the divine and human natures in Christ. And God answered her prayer. Rose enrolled herself in a nursing course and began to work at a hospital specializing in the treatment of cancer victims. On her first day at the hospital, she met Mary Watson, a woman with an advanced case of facial cancer, which rendered her so physically repulsive that even experienced nurses and doctors balked at caring for her. But Rose didn't flinch. She helped to change Mary Watson's dressing, and from that day they became friends.

Rose rented a small flat on the Lower East Side of Manhattan, living among the crowds of immigrant poor who were flooding into New York at the time. (She and her husband had separated, John having never been able to get his alcoholism under control.) She simply opened the doors of her apartment to cancer patients who had nowhere else to go, and she cared for them. Mary Watson, cruelly discharged from the hospital by doctors who considered her incurable, moved in with Rose. In time, people came from all over New York to stay with her and to find comfort in their dying days. And in accord with a basic law of the spiritual life, people began to present themselves as volunteers to help in Rose's work. We remember that when Francis of Assisi commenced to rebuild a crumbling church, he was soon joined by eleven helpers, and that when Mother Teresa of Kolkata went into the slums to aid the poor, she was joined by many of her former students. When people embrace God's work in a spirit of joy, others are drawn to them magnetically. Given the influx of patients and volunteers, Rose and her colleagues were obliged to rent larger space, which became possible because donations had begun to arrive.

At this point, Rose's husband, John, after a long and unsuccessful struggle with alcoholism, passed away, sending Rose into another bout of deep sadness. But his death also made possible what the Spirit was prompting her to do: to become a religious. She entered the Dominican Order and took the name Sr. Mary Alphonsa. As a Dominican nun, she continued her work with cancer patients and in time managed to supervise the building of a large hospital in the country. Finally, with a number of other sisters, she formed a new branch of the Dominican Order, dedicated specially to this much-needed and challenging work. This community of nursing sisters—now called the Hawthorne Dominicans—exists to this day and continues, with joyful devotion, to care for those suffering from incurable cancer.

Rose Hawthorne died in 1926. At the time of her death, her life story was published in a New York newspaper, where it was read by a young intellectual named Dorothy Day. Day was living on the Lower East

Side and struggling to eke out a career as a journalist. She was also a spiritual seeker, and the encounter with Rose's story helped focus her energies and prompt her in the direction of a more radical love. Just a few years later, she founded the Catholic Worker Movement, an organization dedicated to the intertwining of the love of God and the love of the poor, the hungry, the ignorant, and those forced to the margins of society. A seed sown by Rose Hawthorne took root in the receptive soil of Dorothy Day's soul.

Those who know Christ Jesus, fully divine and fully human, realize that the love of God necessarily draws us to a love for the human race. They grasp the logical consistency and spiritual integrity of the greatest commandment.

[29] But wanting to justify himself, he asked Jesus, "And who is my neighbor?" [30] Jesus replied, "A man was going down from Jerusalem to Jericho, and fell into the hands of robbers, who stripped him, beat him, and went away, leaving him half dead. [31] Now by chance a priest was going down that road; and when he saw him, he passed by on the other side. [32] So likewise a Levite, when he came to the place and saw him, passed by on the other side. [33] But a Samaritan while traveling came near him; and when he saw him, he was moved with pity. [34] He went to him and bandaged his wounds, having poured oil and wine on them. Then he put him on his own animal, brought him to an inn, and took care of him. [35] The next day he took out two denarii, gave them to the innkeeper, and said, 'Take care of him; and when I come back, I will repay you whatever more you spend.' [36] Which of these three, do you think, was a neighbor to the man who fell into the hands of the robbers?" [37] He said, "The one who showed him mercy." Jesus said to him, "Go and do likewise."

JESUS VISITS MARTHA AND MARY

[38] Now as they went on their way, he entered a certain village, where a woman named Martha welcomed him into her home. [39] She had a sister named Mary, who sat at the Lord's feet and listened to what he was saying.

Becoming Other Christs

Luke 10:25–37 | Bishop Barron

In one of the great windows of Chartres Cathedral, near Paris, France, there is an intertwining of two stories: the account of the fall of mankind and the parable of the Good Samaritan. This reflects a connection that was made by the Church Fathers. The Good Samaritan is a symbol of Jesus himself, in his role as Savior of the world.

Now our task is to be other Christs, which is why Jesus asks, "Which of these three, do you think, was a neighbor to the man who fell into the hands of the robbers?" His listener answered, "The one who showed him mercy." Jesus says to him, "Go and do likewise."

Becoming like Christ means we spend our lives looking for those people stranded by the road, victimized by sin. We don't walk by, indifferent to them, but rather we do what Jesus did. Even those who are our natural enemies, even those who frighten us. And we bring the Church's power to bear, pouring on the oil and wine of compassion, communicating the power of Christ's cross.

St. John Chrysostom
(349–407)

Homilies on Luke

The Inn of the Church

Luke 10:34–35

The inn is the Church, which receives travelers who are tired with their journey through the world and oppressed with the load of their sins; where the wearied traveler discarding the burden of his sins is relieved, and after being refreshed is restored with wholesome food. And this is what is said here. For outside the Inn is everything that is conflicting, hurtful, and evil, while within the Inn is contained all rest and health.

⁴⁰ But Martha was distracted by her many tasks; so she came to him and asked, "Lord, do you not care that my sister has left me to do all the work by myself? Tell her then to help me." ⁴¹ But the Lord answered her, "Martha, Martha, you are worried and distracted by many things; ⁴² there is need of only one thing. Mary has chosen the better part, which will not be taken away from her."

The One Necessary Thing

Luke 10:38–42 | Bishop Barron

This story of the conflict between Martha and Mary has often been interpreted as an account of the play between the active and the contemplative life, Jesus signaling his preference for the latter over the former. But I don't think that reading gets to the heart of it. It is rather a narrative concerning the spiritual problem of the one and the many.

Martha complains that her sister is not helping her with the numerous and time-consuming tasks of hospitality and tells Jesus to do something about it. The Lord responds, "Martha, Martha, you are worried and distracted by many things; there is need of only one thing. Mary has chosen the better part, which will not be taken away from her."

Martha's problem is not that she is busy or that she is engaging in the "active" life; her problem is that she is uncentered. Her mind, quite obviously, is divided, drifting from this concern to that, from one anxiety to another; there are *many things* that preoccupy her.

What Mary has chosen is not so much the contemplative life, but the focused life. She is anchored, rooted in the *unum necessarium* (one necessary thing), as the Vulgate renders this phrase. The implication seems to be that, were Mary to help with the many household tasks, she would not be "worried and distracted" by them, since she could relate them to the center, and that, were Martha to sit at the feet of Jesus, she would still squirm with impatience, since her spirit is divided.

As is so often the case in the spiritual life, the issue is not what they're doing, but how they're doing it. Indeed, the surest sign that something is off in Martha's soul is that she even tells God what to do!

There is a cacophony of voices calling out to you; there are a thousand influences pulling you this way and that. What's the one necessary thing? It is to listen to the voice of Jesus as he tells you of his love and as he tells you who you are.

THE LORD'S PRAYER

11 He was praying in a certain place, and after he had finished, one of his disciples said to him, "Lord, teach us to pray, as John taught his disciples." ² He said to them, "When you pray, say:

Father, hallowed be your name.

Your kingdom come.

³ Give us each day our daily bread.

⁴ And forgive us our sins,

for we ourselves forgive everyone indebted to us.

And do not bring us to the time of trial."

PERSEVERANCE IN PRAYER

⁵ And he said to them, "Suppose one of you has a friend, and you go to him at midnight and say to him, 'Friend, lend me three loaves of bread; ⁶ for a friend of mine has arrived, and I have nothing to set before him.' ⁷ And he answers from within, 'Do not bother me; the door has already been locked, and my children are with me in bed; I cannot get up and give you anything.' ⁸ I tell you, even though he will not get up and give him anything because he is his friend, at least because of his persistence he will get up and give him whatever he needs.

⁹ "So I say to you, Ask, and it will be given you; search, and you will find; knock, and the door will be opened for you. ¹⁰ For everyone who asks

---

Conversing with God

Luke 11:1–13 | Bishop Barron

What is prayer, and how should we pray? Prayer is intimate communion and conversation with God. Judging from Jesus' own life, prayer is something that we ought to do often, especially at key moments of our lives.

But how should we pray? What does it look like? Well, according to Jesus' model, you have to pray with forgiveness. The efficacy of prayer seems to depend on the reconciliation of differences.

You also have to pray with persistence. One reason that we don't receive what we want through prayer is that we give up too easily. Augustine said that God sometimes delays in giving us what we want because he wants our hearts to expand to be able to receive it.

Finally, we have to pray in Jesus' name. In doing so we are relying on his influence with the Father, trusting that the Father will listen to him.

receives, and everyone who searches finds, and for everyone who knocks, the door will be opened. [11] Is there anyone among you who, if your child asks for a fish, will give a snake instead of a fish? [12] Or if the child asks for an egg, will give a scorpion? [13] If you then, who are evil, know how to give good gifts to your children, how much more will the heavenly Father give the Holy Spirit to those who ask him!"

JESUS AND BEELZEBUL

[14] Now he was casting out a demon that was mute; when the demon had gone out, the one who had been mute spoke, and the crowds were amazed. [15] But some of them said, "He casts out demons by Beelzebul, the ruler of the demons." [16] Others, to test him, kept demanding from him a sign from heaven. [17] But he knew what they were thinking and said to them, "Every kingdom divided against itself becomes a desert, and house falls on house. [18] If Satan also is divided against himself, how will his kingdom stand?—for you say that I cast out the demons by Beelzebul. [19] Now if I cast out the demons by Beelzebul, by whom do your exorcists cast them out? Therefore they will be your judges. [20] But if it is by the finger of God that I cast out the demons, then the kingdom of God has come to you. [21] When a strong

Thomas Merton
(1915–1968)
———
No Man Is an Island

The One Gift Never Refused
Luke 11:13

Once we have the Spirit dwelling in our hearts, the measure of the giving of Christ corresponds to our own desire. For in teaching us of the indwelling of his Spirit of charity, Jesus always reminds us to ask, in order that we may receive. The Holy Spirit is the most perfect gift of the Father to men, and yet he is the one gift which the Father gives most easily. There are many lesser things that, if we ask for them, may still have to be refused us. But the Holy Spirit will never be refused. "If you then, who are evil, know how to give good gifts to your children, how much more will the heavenly Father give the Holy Spirit to those who ask him!"

man, fully armed, guards his castle, his property is safe. ²² But when one stronger than he attacks him and overpowers him, he takes away his armor in which he trusted and divides his plunder. ²³ Whoever is not with me is against me, and whoever does not gather with me scatters.

THE RETURN OF THE UNCLEAN SPIRIT

²⁴ "When the unclean spirit has gone out of a person, it wanders through waterless regions looking for a resting place, but not finding any, it says, 'I will return to my house from which I came.' ²⁵ When it comes, it finds it swept and put in order. ²⁶ Then it goes and brings seven other spirits more evil than itself, and they enter and live there; and the last state of that person is worse than the first."

TRUE BLESSEDNESS

²⁷ While he was saying this, a woman in the crowd raised her voice and said to him, "Blessed is the womb that bore you and the breasts that nursed you!" ²⁸ But he said, "Blessed rather are those who hear the word of God and obey it!"

THE SIGN OF JONAH

²⁹ When the crowds were increasing, he began to say, "This generation is an evil generation; it asks for a sign, but no sign will be given to it except the sign of Jonah. ³⁰ For just as Jonah became a sign to the people of Nineveh, so the Son of Man will be to this generation. ³¹ The queen of the South

---

The New Community

Luke 11:27–28 | Bishop Barron

Jesus turned upside-down many of the social conventions of his time and place precisely because he was so concerned to place the instantiation of the kingdom of God first in the minds of his followers. Among first-century Jews, the family was of paramount social and cultural importance. One's existence was largely defined by one's tribal affiliations and familial obligations. An enthusiastic disciple of Jesus took this for granted when she shouted out, "Blessed is the womb that bore you and the breasts that nursed you!" But Jesus dramatically relativized the family in responding, "Blessed rather are those who hear the word of God and obey it!"

He was insisting that the new community of the kingdom is more important than even the most revered social and religious system. Indeed, when we give the family a disproportionate importance, it becomes in short order dysfunctional, as is evidenced in the fact that much violent crime, even to this day, takes place within families.

Luke 11:1–13

REMBRANDT | *1652*

David in Prayer

Essay by Michael Stevens

Rembrandt is an artist known primarily for his paintings today, but in his own lifetime, he was equally revered for his etchings: ink prints made through the tedious process of carving fine line work into a metal plate.

In this piece, David is shown in prayer, kneeling at the side of his bed. The scene is so personal and informal that one is tempted to forget who this figure is: the sovereign king of Israel and the master poet-musician who penned the Psalms. There is a sense of spontaneity in this moment as well—as if David were interrupting his normal routine to take a moment before the Lord.

In the Gospel, Jesus teaches us to address God in this same way: sincerely and intimately. However, he takes it a step further by teaching us to call God "our Father." This was a radically new way of approaching God, and reveals what Jesus uniquely offers us: a completely new identity as children of God, wherein we can come to know him more intimately than we ever thought possible.

Crosshatch marks

These marks were designed to create the impression of paint rather than drawing, with groups of hatch marks coming together to form what appear to be brushstrokes.

David's harp

As the writer of the Psalms—prayers that were originally set to music—David was a skilled harpist and songwriter. In this etching, David's instrument has been set aside, emphasizing the silence in which he prays.

Fulton Sheen
(1895–1979)

———

*Three to
Get Married*

Blessed Be the Mother

Luke 11:27–28

Mary holds an important place in Christianity—not because men put her there, but because her own Son put her there.... So devoted was he to her that when a woman in the crowd lifted up her voice in praise of his mother—"Blessed is the womb that bore you and the breasts that nursed you"—he reminded that woman that his mother's glory was greater still: "Blessed rather are those who hear the word of God and obey it!" He was harkening back then to Mary's humble answer to God's Word as announced by the angel: "Let it be with me according to your word" (Luke 1:38)....

Devotion to the mother of our Lord in no way detracts from the adoration of her divine Son. The brightness of the moon does not detract from the brilliance of the sun, but rather bespeaks its brilliance.... Never has it been known that anyone who loved Mary denied the divinity of her Son. But it very often happens that those who show no love for Mary have no regard for the divinity of her Son. Every objection against devotion to Mary grows in the soil of an imperfect belief in the Son. It is a historical fact that, as the world lost the Mother, it also lost the Son. It may well be that, as the world returns to love of Mary, it will also return to a belief in the divinity of Christ.

will rise at the judgment with the people of this generation and condemn them, because she came from the ends of the earth to listen to the wisdom of Solomon, and see, something greater than Solomon is here! 32 The people of Nineveh will rise up at the judgment with this generation and condemn it, because they repented at the proclamation of Jonah, and see, something greater than Jonah is here!

What Jesus Hates

Luke 11:29–32 | Bishop Barron

Jesus tells the crowd that they will receive no sign except the sign of Jonah, which was a prophetic code for his death and Resurrection.

Everything Jesus said and did, in one way or another, is an anticipation of his Resurrection. The God of Israel, the God of Jesus Christ, is a God of life, a God of the living. He hates death and the ways of death.

He hates sin, which brings about spiritual death; he hates physical illness, which brings about bodily death; he hates corruption, which brings about societal death. And so he battles all these things all the way. Jesus heals blind eyes and deaf ears and crippled limbs; he illuminates darkened minds; he liberates imprisoned souls. His ministry is a ministry of life, of the triumph of life over death.

THE LIGHT OF THE BODY

³³ "No one after lighting a lamp puts it in a cellar, but on the lampstand so that those who enter may see the light. ³⁴ Your eye is the lamp of your body. If your eye is healthy, your whole body is full of light; but if it is not healthy, your body is full of darkness. ³⁵ Therefore consider whether the light in you is not darkness. ³⁶ If then your whole body is full of light, with no part of it in darkness, it will be as full of light as when a lamp gives you light with its rays."

JESUS DENOUNCES PHARISEES AND LAWYERS

³⁷ While he was speaking, a Pharisee invited him to dine with him; so he went in and took his place at the table. ³⁸ The Pharisee was amazed to see that he did not first wash before dinner. ³⁹ Then the Lord said to him, "Now you Pharisees clean the outside of the cup and of the dish, but inside you are full of greed and wickedness. ⁴⁰ You fools! Did not the one who made the outside make the inside also? ⁴¹ So give for alms those things that are within; and see, everything will be clean for you.

⁴² "But woe to you Pharisees! For you tithe mint and rue and herbs of all kinds, and neglect justice and the love of God; it is these you ought to have practiced, without neglecting the others. ⁴³ Woe to you Pharisees! For you love to have the seat of honor in the synagogues and to be greeted with respect in the marketplaces. ⁴⁴ Woe to you! For you are like unmarked graves, and people walk over them without realizing it."

⁴⁵ One of the lawyers answered him, "Teacher, when you say these things, you insult us too." ⁴⁶ And he said, "Woe also to you lawyers! For you load people with burdens hard to bear, and you yourselves do not lift a finger to ease them. ⁴⁷ Woe to you! For you build the tombs of the prophets whom your ancestors killed. ⁴⁸ So you are witnesses and approve of the deeds of your ancestors; for they killed them, and you build their tombs. ⁴⁹ Therefore also the Wisdom of God said, 'I will send them prophets and apostles, some of whom they will kill and persecute,' ⁵⁰ so that this generation may be charged with the blood of all the prophets shed since the foundation of the world, ⁵¹ from the blood of Abel to the blood of Zechariah, who perished between the altar and the sanctuary. Yes, I tell you, it will be charged against this generation. ⁵² Woe to you lawyers! For you have taken away the key of knowledge; you did not enter yourselves, and you hindered those who were entering."

⁵³ When he went outside, the scribes and the Pharisees began to be very hostile toward him and to cross-examine him about many things, ⁵⁴ lying in wait for him, to catch him in something he might say.

A WARNING AGAINST HYPOCRISY

12 Meanwhile, when the crowd gathered by the thousands, so that they trampled on one another, he began to speak first to his disciples, "Beware of the yeast of the Pharisees, that is, their hypocrisy. ² Nothing is covered up that will not be uncovered, and nothing secret that will not become known. ³ Therefore whatever you have said in the dark will be heard in the light, and what you have whispered behind closed doors will be proclaimed from the housetops.

EXHORTATION TO FEARLESS CONFESSION

⁴ "I tell you, my friends, do not fear those who kill the body, and after that can do nothing more. ⁵ But I will warn you whom to fear: fear him who, after he has killed, has authority to cast into hell. Yes, I tell you, fear him! ⁶ Are not five sparrows sold for two pennies? Yet not one of them is forgotten in God's sight. ⁷ But even the hairs of your head are all counted. Do not be afraid; you are of more value than many sparrows.

⁸ "And I tell you, everyone who acknowledges me before others, the Son of Man also will acknowledge before the angels of God; ⁹ but whoever denies me before others will be denied before the angels of God. ¹⁰ And everyone who speaks a word against the Son of Man will be forgiven; but whoever blasphemes against the Holy Spirit will not be forgiven. ¹¹ When they bring you before the synagogues, the rulers, and the authorities, do not worry about how you are to defend yourselves or what you are to say; ¹² for the Holy Spirit will teach you at that very hour what you ought to say."

Haunted by Nonbeing

Luke 12:13–21 | Bishop Barron

A rich man has been so successful that he doesn't have space enough to store his harvest, so he tears down his barns and builds bigger ones. But that very night, he dies—and all of it comes to naught. "So it is with those who store up treasures for themselves but are not rich toward God."

No matter how good, how beautiful a state of affairs is here below, it is destined to pass into nonbeing. That sunset that I enjoyed last night—that radiantly beautiful display—is now forever gone. It lasted only a while. That beautiful person—attractive, young, full of life, creative, joyful—will eventually age, get sick, break down, and die.

An image that always comes to mind when I think of these things is the gorgeous firework that bursts open like a giant flower and then, in the twinkling of an eye, is gone forever. Everything is haunted by nonbeing. Everything, finally, is a firework.

But this is not meant to depress us; it is meant to redirect our attention precisely to the things that are "above," to the eternity of God.

THE PARABLE OF THE RICH FOOL

[13] Someone in the crowd said to him, "Teacher, tell my brother to divide the family inheritance with me." [14] But he said to him, "Friend, who set me to be a judge or arbitrator over you?" [15] And he said to them, "Take care! Be on your guard against all kinds of greed; for one's life does not consist in the abundance of possessions." [16] Then he told them a parable: "The land of a rich man produced abundantly. [17] And he thought to himself, 'What should I do, for I have no place to store my crops?' [18] Then he said, 'I will do this: I will pull down my barns and build larger ones, and there I will store all my grain and my goods. [19] And I will say to my soul, Soul, you have ample goods laid up for many years; relax, eat, drink, be merry.' [20] But God said to him, 'You fool! This very night your life is being demanded of you. And the things you have prepared, whose will they be?' [21] So it is with those who store up treasures for themselves but are not rich toward God."

DO NOT WORRY

[22] He said to his disciples, "Therefore I tell you, do not worry about your life, what you will eat, or about your body, what you will wear. [23] For life is more than food, and the body more than clothing. [24] Consider the ravens: they neither sow nor reap, they have neither storehouse nor barn, and yet God feeds them. Of how much more value are you than the birds! [25] And can any of you by worrying add a single hour to your span of life? [26] If then you

are not able to do so small a thing as that, why do you worry about the rest? [27] Consider the lilies, how they grow: they neither toil nor spin; yet I tell you, even Solomon in all his glory was not clothed like one of these. [28] But if God so clothes the grass of the field, which is alive today and tomorrow is thrown into the oven, how much more will he clothe you—you of little faith! [29] And do not keep striving for what you are to eat and what you are to drink, and do not keep worrying. [30] For it is the nations of the world that strive after all these things, and your Father knows that you need them. [31] Instead, strive for his kingdom, and these things will be given to you as well.

[32] "Do not be afraid, little flock, for it is your Father's good pleasure to give you the kingdom. [33] Sell your possessions, and give alms. Make purses for yourselves that do not wear out, an unfailing treasure in heaven, where no thief comes near and no moth destroys. [34] For where your treasure is, there your heart will be also.

St. Cyril of Alexandria
(378–444)

Commentary on Luke

The Truly Rich

Luke 12:13–21, 33–34

Who is the one that is rich towards God? Clearly it is the one who loves virtue instead of wealth, for whom a few things are sufficient. It is the one whose hand is open to the needs of the poor, comforting the sorrows of those in poverty as fully as he is able. It is the one who gathers in the storehouses above, and lays up his treasures in heaven. Such a person will find that his investments have gained interest, a reward for his upright and blameless life.

WATCHFUL SLAVES

[35] "Be dressed for action and have your lamps lit; [36] be like those who are waiting for their master to return from the wedding banquet, so that they may open the door for him as soon as he comes and knocks. [37] Blessed are those slaves whom the master finds alert when he comes; truly I tell you, he will fasten his belt and have them sit down to eat, and he will come and

Purses That Don't Wear Out

Luke 12:33 | Bishop Barron

Faith, in a scriptural context, means ultimate trust. To pose the question about faith is to wonder where we finally anchor our lives; where we, in the last analysis, "stand"; where we, at the end of the day, orient our lives. When the ego's works are shaken, turned upside down, we tend to lose "faith" in them, and this, from a biblical standpoint, is all to the good, for we are not designed to root ourselves in something as vacillating and tiny as the ego. We are meant to put our final trust in that strange, awesome, and enticing power that infinitely transcends who we are and what we can do.

Jesus says: "Make purses for yourselves that do not wear out, an unfailing treasure in heaven, where no thief comes near and no moth destroys." Any "purse" or treasure of this world—any ideal, movement, institution, or person here below—will wear out, will prove unworthy of our final confidence. Rejoice that in God's providence you are not liable to succumb to the subtlest of temptations: faith in this world.

---

serve them. ³⁸ If he comes during the middle of the night, or near dawn, and finds them so, blessed are those slaves.

³⁹ "But know this: if the owner of the house had known at what hour the thief was coming, he would not have let his house be broken into. ⁴⁰ You also must be ready, for the Son of Man is coming at an unexpected hour."

THE FAITHFUL OR THE UNFAITHFUL SLAVE

⁴¹ Peter said, "Lord, are you telling this parable for us or for everyone?" ⁴² And the Lord said, "Who then is the faithful and prudent manager whom his master will put in charge of his slaves, to give them their allowance of food at the proper time? ⁴³ Blessed is that slave whom his master will find at work when he arrives. ⁴⁴ Truly I tell you, he will put that one in charge of all his possessions. ⁴⁵ But if that slave says to himself, 'My master is delayed in coming,' and if he begins to beat the other slaves, men and women, and to eat and drink and get drunk, ⁴⁶ the master of that slave will come on a day when he does not expect him and at an hour that he does not know, and will cut him in pieces, and put him with the unfaithful. ⁴⁷ That slave who knew what his master wanted, but did not prepare himself or do what was wanted, will receive a severe beating. ⁴⁸ But the one who did not know and did what deserved a beating will receive a light beating. From everyone to whom much has been given, much will be required; and from the one to whom much has been entrusted, even more will be demanded.

JESUS THE CAUSE OF DIVISION

⁴⁹ "I came to bring fire to the earth, and how I wish it were already kindled! ⁵⁰ I have a baptism with which to be baptized, and what stress I am under until it is completed! ⁵¹ Do you think that I have come to bring peace to the earth? No, I tell you, but rather division! ⁵² From now on five in one household will be divided, three against two and two against three; ⁵³ they will be divided:

> father against son
> and son against father,
> mother against daughter
> and daughter against mother,
> mother-in-law against her daughter-in-law
> and daughter-in-law against mother-in-law."

INTERPRETING THE TIME

⁵⁴ He also said to the crowds, "When you see a cloud rising in the west, you immediately say, 'It is going to rain'; and so it happens. ⁵⁵ And when you see the south wind blowing, you say, 'There will be scorching heat'; and it happens. ⁵⁶ You hypocrites! You know how to interpret the appearance of earth and sky, but why do you not know how to interpret the present time?

SETTLING WITH YOUR OPPONENT

⁵⁷ "And why do you not judge for yourselves what is right? ⁵⁸ Thus, when you go with your accuser before a magistrate, on the way make an effort to settle the case, or you may be dragged before the judge, and the judge

---

Fire on the Earth

Luke 12:49 | Bishop Barron

Jesus said, "I came to bring fire to the earth, and how I wish it were already kindled!" What is that fire? His forerunner, John, gave us a clue: "I baptize you with water; but one who is more powerful than I is coming; I am not worthy to untie the thong of his sandals. He will baptize you with the Holy Spirit and fire" (Luke 3:16).

Jesus came in order to torch the world with the heat and light of the divine Spirit, which is none other than the love shared by the Father and the Son, the very inner life of God. Jesus is a prophet because he teaches; he is a king because he leads and shepherds; but he is a priest because he is the spreader of the sacred fire.

hand you over to the officer, and the officer throw you in prison. [59] I tell you, you will never get out until you have paid the very last penny."

REPENT OR PERISH

13

At that very time there were some present who told him about the Galileans whose blood Pilate had mingled with their sacrifices. [2] He asked them, "Do you think that because these Galileans suffered in this way they were worse sinners than all other Galileans? [3] No, I tell you; but unless you repent, you will all perish as they did. [4] Or those eighteen who were killed when the tower of Siloam fell on them—do you think that they were worse offenders than all the others living in Jerusalem? [5] No, I tell you; but unless you repent, you will all perish just as they did."

THE PARABLE OF THE BARREN FIG TREE

[6] Then he told this parable: "A man had a fig tree planted in his vineyard; and he came looking for fruit on it and found none. [7] So he said to the gardener, 'See here! For three years I have come looking for fruit on this fig tree, and still I find none. Cut it down! Why should it be wasting the soil?' [8] He replied, 'Sir, let it alone for one more year, until I dig around it and put manure on it. [9] If it bears fruit next year, well and good; but if not, you can cut it down.'"

JESUS HEALS A CRIPPLED WOMAN

[10] Now he was teaching in one of the synagogues on the sabbath. [11] And just then there appeared a woman with a spirit that had crippled her for eighteen years. She was bent over and was quite unable to stand up straight. [12] When Jesus saw her, he called her over and said, "Woman, you are set free from your ailment." [13] When he laid his hands on her, immediately she stood up straight and began praising God. [14] But the leader of the synagogue, indignant because Jesus had cured on the sabbath, kept saying to the crowd, "There are six days on which work ought to be done; come on those days and be cured, and not on the sabbath day." [15] But the Lord answered him and said, "You hypocrites! Does not each of you on the sabbath untie his ox or his donkey from the manger, and lead it away to give it water? [16] And ought not this woman, a daughter of Abraham whom Satan bound for eighteen long years, be set free from this bondage on the sabbath day?" [17] When he said this, all his opponents were put to shame; and the entire crowd was rejoicing at all the wonderful things that he was doing.

THE PARABLE OF THE MUSTARD SEED

[18] He said therefore, "What is the kingdom of God like? And to what should I compare it? [19] It is like a mustard seed that someone took and sowed in the garden; it grew and became a tree, and the birds of the air made nests in its branches."

THE PARABLE OF THE YEAST

²⁰ And again he said, "To what should I compare the kingdom of God? ²¹ It is like yeast that a woman took and mixed in with three measures of flour until all of it was leavened."

THE NARROW DOOR

²² Jesus went through one town and village after another, teaching as he made his way to Jerusalem. ²³ Someone asked him, "Lord, will only a few be saved?" He said to them, ²⁴ "Strive to enter through the narrow door; for many, I tell you, will try to enter and will not be able. ²⁵ When once the owner of the house has got up and shut the door, and you begin to stand outside and to knock at the door, saying, 'Lord, open to us,' then in reply he will say to you, 'I do not know where you come from.' ²⁶ Then you will begin to say, 'We ate and drank with you, and you taught in our streets.' ²⁷ But he will say, 'I do not know where you come from; go away from me, all you evildoers!' ²⁸ There will be weeping and gnashing of teeth when

---

Will Only a Few Be Saved?

Luke 13:22–30 | Bishop Barron

People have been asking this question from time immemorial and they still ask it today: "Lord, will only a few be saved?" Heaven, hell, salvation, damnation— who will be in and who will be out? We have remained fascinated with these questions for a long time.

How should we approach this issue? The doctrine concerning hell is a corollary of two more fundamental truths—namely, that God is love and that we are free. Love (willing the good of the other) is all that God is. He doesn't go in and out of love; he doesn't change his mind; he's not loving to some, and not to others. He is indeed like the sun that shines on the good and bad alike, in the words of Jesus. No act of ours can possibly make him stop loving us. In this regard, he is like the best of parents.

However, we are also free. We are not God's marionettes, and hence we can say yes or we can say no to his love. If we turn toward it, we open like a sunflower; if we turn from it, we get burned.

Notice how Jesus ultimately answers the question though. He says to them, "Strive to enter through the narrow door." In other words, stop bickering over how many or few other people will be saved and, in the words of St. Paul, "work out your own salvation with fear and trembling" (Phil. 2:12).

you see Abraham and Isaac and Jacob and all the prophets in the kingdom of God, and you yourselves thrown out. ²⁹ Then people will come from east and west, from north and south, and will eat in the kingdom of God. ³⁰ Indeed, some are last who will be first, and some are first who will be last."

THE LAMENT OVER JERUSALEM

³¹ At that very hour some Pharisees came and said to him, "Get away from here, for Herod wants to kill you." ³² He said to them, "Go and tell that fox for me, 'Listen, I am casting out demons and performing cures today and tomorrow, and on the third day I finish my work. ³³ Yet today, tomorrow, and the next day I must be on my way, because it is impossible for a prophet to be killed outside of Jerusalem.' ³⁴ Jerusalem, Jerusalem, the city that kills the prophets and stones those who are sent to it! How often have I desired to gather your children together as a hen gathers her brood under her wings, and you were not willing! ³⁵ See, your house is left to you. And I tell you, you will not see me until the time comes when you say, 'Blessed is the one who comes in the name of the Lord.'"

As a Hen Gathers Her Chicks

Luke 13:34 | Bishop Barron

Jesus compares himself to a mother hen who longs to gather her chicks under her wing. As the theologian N.T. Wright points out, this is much more than a sentimental image. It refers to the gesture of a hen when fire is sweeping through the barn. In order to protect her chicks, she will sacrifice herself, gathering them under her wing and using her own body as a shield.

On the cross, Jesus used, as it were, his own sacrificed body as a shield, taking the full force of the world's hatred and violence. He entered into close quarters with sin (because that's where we sinners are found) and allowed the heat and fury of sin to destroy him, even as he protected us.

With this metaphor in mind, we can see, with special clarity, why the first Christians associated the crucified Jesus with the suffering servant of Isaiah. By enduring the pain of the cross, Jesus did indeed bear our sins; by his wounds we were indeed healed.

JESUS HEALS THE MAN WITH DROPSY

14 On one occasion when Jesus was going to the house of a leader of the Pharisees to eat a meal on the sabbath, they were watching him closely. ² Just then, in front of him, there was a man who had dropsy. ³ And Jesus asked the lawyers and Pharisees, "Is it lawful to cure people on the sabbath, or not?" ⁴ But they were silent. So Jesus took him and healed him, and sent him away. ⁵ Then he said to them, "If one of you has a child or an ox that has fallen into a well, will you not immediately pull it out on a sabbath day?" ⁶ And they could not reply to this.

HUMILITY AND HOSPITALITY

⁷ When he noticed how the guests chose the places of honor, he told them a parable. ⁸ "When you are invited by someone to a wedding banquet, do not sit down at the place of honor, in case someone more distinguished than you has been invited by your host; ⁹ and the host who invited both of you may come and say to you, 'Give this person your place,' and then in disgrace you would start to take the lowest place. ¹⁰ But when you are invited, go and sit down at the lowest place, so that when your host comes, he may say to you, 'Friend, move up higher'; then you will be honored in the presence of all who sit at the table with you. ¹¹ For all who exalt themselves will be humbled, and those who humble themselves will be exalted."

¹² He said also to the one who had invited him, "When you give a luncheon or a dinner, do not invite your friends or your brothers or your relatives

---

Stop Playing the Game

Luke 14:11–14 | Bishop Barron

Jesus has been invited to the home of a prominent person, a "leader of the Pharisees," and he notices how people jockey carefully for position, status, and prominence. They're likely thinking, who will notice me? Whom can I impress?

Jesus puts his finger on the most desperate scenario for an egotist. He tells them a parable about a man trying as hard as he can to be noticed. But he gets noticed for all the wrong reasons! His egotistic games backfire dreadfully, as everyone sees him reduced to embarrassment.

So what's the solution? Stop playing the game. Take the lowest place on purpose. Opt out. Invite people to a party who have no capacity whatsoever to invite you in return: "Invite the poor, the crippled, the lame, and the blind. And you will be blessed, because they cannot repay you, for you will be repaid at the resurrection of the righteous."

or rich neighbors, in case they may invite you in return, and you would be repaid. ¹³ But when you give a banquet, invite the poor, the crippled, the lame, and the blind. ¹⁴ And you will be blessed, because they cannot repay you, for you will be repaid at the resurrection of the righteous."

THE PARABLE OF THE GREAT DINNER

¹⁵ One of the dinner guests, on hearing this, said to him, "Blessed is anyone who will eat bread in the kingdom of God!" ¹⁶ Then Jesus said to him, "Someone gave a great dinner and invited many. ¹⁷ At the time for the dinner he sent his slave to say to those who had been invited, 'Come; for everything is ready now.' ¹⁸ But they all alike began to make excuses. The first said to him, 'I have bought a piece of land, and I must go out and see it; please accept my regrets.' ¹⁹ Another said, 'I have bought five yoke of oxen, and I am going to try them out; please accept my regrets.' ²⁰ Another said, 'I have just been married, and therefore I cannot come.' ²¹ So the slave returned and reported this to his master. Then the owner of the house became angry and said to his slave, 'Go out at once into the streets and lanes of the town and bring in the poor, the crippled, the blind, and the lame.' ²² And the slave said, 'Sir, what you ordered has been done, and there is still room.' ²³ Then the master said to the slave, 'Go out into the roads and lanes, and compel people to come in, so that my house may be filled. ²⁴ For I tell you, none of those who were invited will taste my dinner.'"

THE COST OF DISCIPLESHIP

²⁵ Now large crowds were traveling with him; and he turned and said to them, ²⁶ "Whoever comes to me and does not hate father and mother, wife and children, brothers and sisters, yes, and even life itself, cannot be my disciple. ²⁷ Whoever does not carry the cross and follow me cannot be my disciple. ²⁸ For which of you, intending to build a tower, does not first sit down and estimate the cost, to see whether he has enough to complete it? ²⁹ Otherwise, when he has laid a foundation and is not able to finish, all who see it will begin to ridicule him, ³⁰ saying, 'This fellow began to build and was not able to finish.' ³¹ Or what king, going out to wage war against another king, will not sit down first and consider whether he is able with ten thousand to oppose the one who comes against him with twenty thousand? ³² If he cannot, then, while the other is still far away, he sends a delegation and asks for the terms of peace. ³³ So therefore, none of you can become my disciple if you do not give up all your possessions.

ABOUT SALT

³⁴ "Salt is good; but if salt has lost its taste, how can its saltiness be restored? ³⁵ It is fit neither for the soil nor for the manure pile; they throw it away. Let anyone with ears to hear listen!"

The Trap of Creature Before Creator

Luke 14:26 | Bishop Barron

It's one of the most challenging things Jesus ever says: "Whoever comes to me and does not hate father and mother, wife and children, brothers and sisters, yes, and even life itself, cannot be my disciple."

There is the great spiritual principle that undergirds the entire Gospel: detachment. The heart of the spiritual life is to love God and then to love everything else for the sake of God. But we sinners, as St. Augustine said, fall into the trap of loving the creature and forgetting the Creator. That's when we get off the rails.

We treat something less than God as God, and trouble ensues. This is why Jesus tells his fair-weather fans that they have a very stark choice to make. Jesus must be loved first and last—and everything else in their lives has to find its meaning in relation to him.

In typical Semitic fashion, he makes this point through a stark exaggeration: "Whoever comes to me and does not hate father and mother, wife and children, brothers and sisters …" Well yes, hate them in the measure that they have become gods to you. For precisely in that measure are they dangerous.

St. Gregory of Nyssa
(335–394)

On Virginity

Build the Foundation of Virtue

Luke 14:28–30

What else do we learn from the parable of the tower but to strive to bring all our good resolutions to completion, finishing a complex edifice of virtue rooted in God's commandments? A single stone does not make a tower, any more than keeping one commandment will raise a soul's perfection to its required height. The foundation must by all means be built first, but laid over it, as the Apostle [Paul] says, must be "gold, silver, precious stones" (1 Cor. 3:12)—just as when the prophet cried, "Truly I love your commandments more than gold, more than fine gold" (Ps. 119:127).

THE PARABLE OF THE LOST SHEEP

15 Now all the tax collectors and sinners were coming near to listen to him. ² And the Pharisees and the scribes were grumbling and saying, "This fellow welcomes sinners and eats with them."

³ So he told them this parable: ⁴ "Which one of you, having a hundred sheep and losing one of them, does not leave the ninety-nine in the wilderness and go after the one that is lost until he finds it? ⁵ When he has found it, he lays it on his shoulders and rejoices. ⁶ And when he comes home, he calls together his friends and neighbors, saying to them, 'Rejoice with me, for I have found my sheep that was lost.' ⁷ Just so, I tell you, there will be more joy in heaven over one sinner who repents than over ninety-nine righteous persons who need no repentance.

THE PARABLE OF THE LOST COIN

⁸ "Or what woman having ten silver coins, if she loses one of them, does not light a lamp, sweep the house, and search carefully until she finds it? ⁹ When she has found it, she calls together her friends and neighbors, saying, 'Rejoice with me, for I have found the coin that I had lost.' ¹⁰ Just so, I tell you, there is joy in the presence of the angels of God over one sinner who repents."

Going After the One

Luke 15:1–10 | Bishop Barron

Consider the craziness of the shepherd: "Which one of you, having a hundred sheep and losing one of them, does not leave the ninety-nine in the wilderness and go after the one that is lost until he finds it?" Well, the implied answer is "No one." Who would take that great a risk, putting the ninety-nine in danger to find the one? It's just bad economics. Why would God fret over one little soul?

Because it's his nature; it's what he does. As St. Catherine of Siena put it, he is *pazzo d'amore* (crazy in love). God is as crazy for you as if you were the only one in the world.

And let's look at that lost sheep. A sheep is something more than a lost coin—which is to say, it has mobility, sense, appetites, and so on. There are souls who are like the lost sheep. Spiritually compromised, fundamentally unable to help themselves, they are at least aware that they are in a mess. They are like people who commence the Alcoholics Anonymous process by admitting that they have hit bottom and are out of control. They bleat, they cry for help.

And God finds them—and when he finds them, he carries them back, for they are unable to move on their own.

THE PARABLE OF THE PRODIGAL AND HIS BROTHER

[11] Then Jesus said, "There was a man who had two sons. [12] The younger of them said to his father, 'Father, give me the share of the property that will belong to me.' So he divided his property between them. [13] A few days later the younger son gathered all he had and traveled to a distant country, and there he squandered his property in dissolute living. [14] When he had spent everything, a severe famine took place throughout that country, and he began to be in need. [15] So he went and hired himself out to one of the citizens of that country, who sent him to his fields to feed the pigs. [16] He would gladly have filled himself with the pods that the pigs were eating; and no one gave him anything. [17] But when he came to himself he said, 'How many of my father's hired hands have bread enough and to spare, but here I am dying of hunger! [18] I will get up and go to my father, and I will say to him, "Father, I have sinned against heaven and before you; [19] I am no longer worthy to be called your son; treat me like one of your hired hands."' [20] So he set off and went to his father. But while he was still far off, his father saw him and was filled with compassion; he ran and put his arms around him and kissed him. [21] Then the son said to him, 'Father, I have sinned against heaven and before you; I am no longer worthy to be called your son.' [22] But the father said to his slaves, 'Quickly, bring out a robe—the best one—and put it on him; put a ring on his finger and sandals on his feet. [23] And get the fatted calf and kill it, and let us eat and celebrate; [24] for this son of mine was dead and is alive again; he was lost and is found!' And they began to celebrate.

[25] "Now his elder son was in the field; and when he came and approached the house, he heard music and dancing. [26] He called one of the slaves and asked what was going on. [27] He replied, 'Your brother has come, and your father has killed the fatted calf, because he has got him back safe and sound.' [28] Then he became angry and refused to go in. His father came out and began to plead with him. [29] But he answered his father, 'Listen! For all these years I have been working like a slave for you, and I have never disobeyed your command; yet you have never given me even a young goat so that I might celebrate with my friends. [30] But when this son of yours came back, who has devoured your property with prostitutes, you killed the fatted calf for him!' [31] Then the father said to him, 'Son, you are always with me, and all that is mine is yours. [32] But we had to celebrate and rejoice, because this brother of yours was dead and has come to life; he was lost and has been found.'"

Pope St. John Paul II
(1920–2005)

———

Dives in Misericordia

Mercy of the Father

Luke 15:11–32

Mercy—as Christ has presented it in the parable of the prodigal son—has the interior form of the love that in the New Testament is called *agape*. This love is able to reach down to every prodigal son, to every human misery, and above all to every form of moral misery, to sin. When this happens, the person who is the object of mercy does not feel humiliated, but rather found again and restored to value.

The father first and foremost expresses to him his joy that he has been found again and that he has returned to life. This joy indicates a good that has remained intact: even if he is a prodigal, a son does not cease to be truly his father's son; it also indicates a good that has been found again, which in the case of the prodigal son was his return to the truth about himself. . . .

The parable of the prodigal son expresses in a simple but profound way the reality of conversion. Conversion is the most concrete expression of the working of love and of the presence of mercy in the human world. The true and proper meaning of mercy does not consist only in looking, however penetratingly and compassionately, at moral, physical, or material evil: mercy is manifested in its true and proper aspect when it restores to value, promotes, and draws good from all the forms of evil existing in the world and in man. Understood in this way, mercy constitutes the fundamental content of the messianic message of Christ and the constitutive power of his mission.

The prodigal son's missing shoe

The prodigal son's shoe has slipped off his foot as he kneels at the feet of his father, and we can see that his feet are dirty and worn down. It is clear that the son's wanderings have taken an exhausting toll. This is contrasted by the fine garments the father wears—garments that, as the Gospel tells us, will soon be lavished upon the son.

The face of the elder son

In the Scriptures, we read that the elder son is baffled by his father's decision to slaughter the best of his livestock to celebrate his son's return. In the painting, we can sense this same disapproval of his younger brother and the mercy his father is showing him.

Luke 15:11–32

REMBRANDT | *1663–1669*

The Return of the Prodigal Son

Essay by Michael Stevens

In this painting by Rembrandt, considered one of the great masterpieces in all of European art, we see a moment of profound forgiveness: the Gospel account of the return of the prodigal son. Few paintings seem to capture the sweetness of God's forgiveness more powerfully than this image, and it exemplifies the tender empathy that permeates Rembrandt's wide array of biblically inspired works.

In *The Return of the Prodigal Son*, the artist deploys all of the techniques that define his painting style, including warm and inviting use of light; raw, bold brushwork; deep, intense, earthy colors; and facial expressions that seem to defy their lack of detail to communicate intense and specific emotions.

In the foreground we see the younger son, who collapses in exhausted relief into the embrace of his father, whose fortune he has squandered on a life of recklessness and selfishness. The father lays his hands on the back of his long-awaited son in a gesture that conveys both a sense of welcome as well as spiritual absolution. Several figures surrounding the scene—including the elder brother to the right, who observes with a somber expression on his face, as well as two servants who watch thoughtfully—are moved by what unfolds before them. From the depth of the darkness on the upper left, the mother emerges, whose reaction remains a mystery. But for all these observers, the dynamic between the father and the son is so powerfully reassuring as to completely overpower any sense of audience. For the father and the son, this is a moment of life-changing reconciliation, and any judgment on the part of the others has no bearing on the full restoration that has taken place.

The Prodigal Son

Luke 15:11–32 | Bishop Barron

IN CONSIDERING JESUS' PARABLE of the prodigal son, we are on interesting ground, for we are dealing with an icon of the Father told by the one who is himself the Icon of the Father. Thus we have Jesus indirectly crafting a subtle self-portrait. The gathering technique of the father in the story mirrors that of the heavenly Father, which in turn is iconically represented in that of Jesus. In the course of this narrative, we will see who the father/God/Jesus is and how he brings to himself an Israel that had, in a double sense, wandered into exile.

A man, Jesus tells us, had two sons, and "the younger of them said to his father, 'Father, give me the share of the property that will belong to me.'" As many have commented, this demand is presumptuous and highly insulting, for normally a son would not receive his inheritance until after his father had died. Thus, in claiming his money now, the younger son is none too subtly suggesting that he wishes his father would hurry up and die. Especially in Jesus' time and culture, a more stinging remark could scarcely be imagined. The parable opens, then, with the declaration of a clear break in the communion and coinherence that one would expect to hold between a father and his son. And if we attend closely to the language of the parable, we will sense further dimensions of this rupture. The boy doesn't ask his father, he tells him: "Give me the share of the property that will belong to me." By definition, a gift cannot be demanded; it can only be received graciously and as a sort of surprise. In making his demand, therefore, the younger son is precluding the possibility of a gifted relationship between himself and his father; he is cutting off the flow of grace.

Second, in asking for *property* that is coming to him, he emphatically confirms the gracelessness of the exchange. Property is what is "proper" to a person, what is uniquely his, what he can claim in at least a quasi-legal sense. In common usage, the word indicates what is to be held on to and defended against counter-claimants: we might hear someone say, "Get off my property," or set up a sign that defiantly declares "Private property." Jean-Luc Marion has helpfully drawn attention to the Greek term that undergirds "property" in this story: *ousia*. This is the only time in the New Testament that this famously controversial and theologically charged term is employed. In this context it obviously doesn't have the fully developed metaphysical sense that it has, for instance, in Aristotle, but it does have at least an overtone of the philosophical usage. The more ordinary meaning of *ousia* (displayed here) is money, property, or what is "presently disposable," ready to hand for use. Thus there is a link to the metaphysical "substance," which could be construed as that which a thing possesses as its own, that which it has ready to hand—as opposed to its more fleetingly possessed accidents. In demanding this *ousia*, then, the younger son is asking emphatically for something to have and hold as his own, free of any merely accidental link to either the source or the possible destination of his possession. He expects the gift (in a substantive sense) apart from giving, and this is precisely what he receives when his father "divided his property between them."

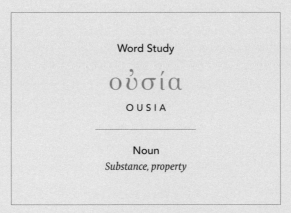

Word Study

οὐσία

OUSIA

Noun
Substance, property

Here is a portrait in miniature of God in relation to sin. In the Garden of Eden, Adam and Eve sought to eat of the tree of the knowledge of good and evil, taking God's place and seizing his prerogatives. At the prompting of the tempter, they wanted to take for themselves a life that can only be received as a gift. Prior to the fall, God and Adam had walked together in the cool of the evening as friends, giving and receiving in a circle of grace, and the original sin is nothing but the rupture of this friendship through the desire to possess *ousia*. The true God can be "had" only when one disposes oneself to receive the divine life as a grace and to give that life away in turn as a gift. Grace is "possessed" only in the measure that it is received and offered and never held on to.

A key implication of this analysis is that God is himself not an *ousia*, not a substance, not a supreme being in solemn possession of an infinite range of perfections. Rather, God is a supreme letting-be, a being-for-another, his perfections fluid and generously given. Consequently, in the measure that a human person endeavors to be a supreme being, she falls out of right relation with this God.

As the story unfolds, we hear what happens to "substance," so possessed. We are told that after a few days, the young man "gathered all he had and traveled to a distant country." We notice the frenzy of possessiveness implied in that "gathering" to himself all that was uniquely his, and we remark the thoroughness of the relational rupture with his father in his journey to a far country. The Greek here is instructive: the young man sets out to a *choran makran*, literally a great open space, a place without borders or points of reference. In Plato, the *chora* is the space in between the forms and physical objects, the realm of nonbeing and nonvisibility. The implication of the parable seems to be that this ontological emptiness is the consequence of the younger

---

Word Study

χώρα

CHŌRA

Adverb
Separately, separate from

son's severing of relation to his father. This is made explicit in the next phrase, "and there he squandered his property in dissolute living."

He had made bold to seize *ousia* from his father and claim it as his own, and now he sees what inevitably occurs when a gift becomes a possession. It is a basic biblical intuition that as long as one is receiving being as a grace and resolving to pass it on as a grace, one paradoxically keeps it. But if one endeavors to interrupt the flow and seize what is received, then that possession quickly withers away, dissipates. When the young man had spent everything, "a severe famine took place throughout that country, and he began to be in need." Read symbolically, this famine is not merely an unhappy accident that happens to intensify the young man's suffering; rather, it is the natural condition of the *chora makra*. Cut off from relationality and the giving and receiving of gifts, one necessarily experiences famine, a starvation of the soul.

So great became the young man's need that "he went and hired himself out to one of the citizens of that country, who sent him to his fields to feed the pigs." In these few laconic phrases, Jesus describes the spiritual dynamics of the "distant country." The only relationship that a citizen of the *chora makra* could envision is a professional one involving hiring and the paying of salaries. There it cannot be a question of giving and gratefully receiving, but only of the paying out and possessing of *ousia*, the hardened detritus of gracious exchange. Second, the feeding of pigs (animals particularly repugnant to pious Jews) indicates the dehumanization that characterizes the distant country: grubbing for what is one's own reduces one to the level of competitive and self-absorbed beasts. So pathetic is the younger son's situation that he "would gladly have filled himself with the pods that the pigs were eating," but—and here we come to the heart of it—"no one gave him anything." This is *the* mark of the distant country: it is the place where there is no giving. It is the country whose citizens only hire, pay, and receive what is strictly agreed to, and thus it is the polar opposite of the land where the young man's father is lord.

The younger son wandering in a distant land is evocative of the human race—all the descendants of Adam and Eve—who have lost contact with the flow of the divine life. Living in the land of hiring, taking, paying, and possessing, they starve spiritually. They are like the sad guests at the wedding feast of Cana who have run out of wine; they are like Israel in the land of exile, pining for Zion; or they are like the Psalmist's deer yearning for flowing streams. How appropriate, by the way, is that last image. The divine life flows because it is a process of giving and receiving; sin is substantive and fixed, "hard" currency. The only solution is a return to a graced mode of being.

And this is precisely what the prodigal realizes in a moment of clarity: "But when he came to himself he said, 'How many of my father's hired hands have bread enough and to spare, but here I am dying of hunger!'" Even those whom his father has hired—even those only professionally related to him—have enough and more than enough, with superabundance indicating that they are in the circle of grace. Were they merely possessing what their employer paid them, they would be psychologically and spiritually in the distant country and would soon enough run out. And this is why the younger son resolves, in the carefully rehearsed speech that we overhear, to ask his father to treat him as one of his hired hands: even the least in the country of grace have more than enough. Then, full of contrition, he sets out to return to his father.

While he is still a long way off (still to some degree in the land of exile), his father catches sight of him (he had obviously been looking for him) and is "filled with compassion; he ran and put his arms around him and kissed him." The word used in the Greek here for the feeling of compassion is *esplagnisthe*, meaning literally that the father's guts are moved, the visceral connection to his child stirred up. This same term is applied in the New Testament to the feelings of Jesus himself: "When he saw the crowds, he had compassion for them, because they were harassed and helpless, like sheep without a shepherd" (Matt. 9:36). This powerful feeling leads to an extraordinary gesture. As many have pointed out, in ancient Jewish society, it was considered terribly unseemly for an elderly man to run to meet someone; rather, he was the one to whom others would come in a spirit of respect and obeisance. So the father's running, throwing caution and respectability to the wind, is an act of almost shocking condescension and orientation to the other.

When they meet, the father embraces his son and kisses him; then the boy speaks: "Father, I have sinned against heaven and before you; I am no longer worthy to be called your son." The embrace of the father is one of the most powerful biblical symbols of the gathering: exiled Israel has returned, and the Father-God takes him to himself, drawing him back into the circle of light. How evocatively Rembrandt van Rijn depicted this inclusion-enlightenment in his late-career painting of the return of the prodigal: the penitent son is embraced by his father and participates thereby in a light that does not so much come from without as radiate from within the father himself.

The saint, remarked G.K. Chesterton, is someone who knows he is a sinner. Whenever characters in the Bible come close to the divine grace, they experience a heightened sense of their own unworthiness: Isaiah in the temple, Jeremiah at the moment of his call, Peter at the miraculous draught of fishes. This is the dynamic at work in the case of the prodigal son. Precisely in the measure that he is reconnected to the graciousness of God and the flow of his mercy, he knows unambiguously his sorry spiritual state. His cruel leavetaking and subsequent sojourn in the *chora makra* had perverted his relationship to his father, and it is in the embrace of his father that he truly senses this.

However, his worthiness to be called son has nothing to do with his own moral achievement or lack thereof. His father ignores his carefully rehearsed speech, and with an eagerness bordering on impatience, he instructs his servants: "Quickly, bring out a robe—the best one—and put it on him; put a ring on his finger and sandals on his feet. And get the fatted calf and kill it, and let us eat and celebrate." Our participation in the flow of the divine life is, necessarily, a gift—not so much because God arbitrarily chooses those who should receive it, but because it is itself nothing but the giving and receiving of gifts. It cannot, in principle, be earned or merited, but only accepted. We can only be embraced by it.

The father's comment on the reason for the celebration—"for this son of mine was dead and is alive again"—is theologically accurate. When the divine life hardens into a possession, it is, as we've seen, effectively lost; when one wanders away from the living stream of God, one necessarily dries up, and one's "life" is merely biological. Like the Gerasene demoniac—living among the tombs—the prodigal son had been one of the living dead. Authentic spiritual life is had only when one enters into the flow of grace, when one can accept robe, ring, and fatted calf.

With that the narrative of the parable turns to the elder brother, a man superficially quite unlike the prodigal son, but practically identical to him at the spiritual level. The strategy that the father employs to gather him in should be the focus of our attention. While the father was attentively waiting for the return of the younger son, the older brother was "in the field," a somewhat more subtle version of the *chora makra*, obviously indifferent to his brother's fate. Hearing the sounds of celebration, he approaches the house, and when he discovers the reason for the festivities, he is filled with indignation: "Then he became angry and refused to go in." In accord with his relentlessly inclusive character, the father comes out to this second exile and pleads with him to join the circle of celebration.

Then we hear the words that reveal the spiritual state of the older son: "Listen! For all these years I have been working like a slave for you, and I have never disobeyed your command; yet you have never given me even a young goat so that I might celebrate with my friends." Though he has remained physically close to his father, his exile is just as dramatic as his younger brother's, for he too has allowed his relationship to his father to harden into possessiveness. The harshly economic vocabulary gives away the game: working like a slave, obeying commands, getting something of *his* own, *his* friends. Just like his brother, this man wants to claim the father's love as his own possession and use it as he sees fit. Whereas the younger brother demanded it in a presumptuous way ("Give me the share of the property that will belong to me"), the elder brother "slaves" for it, working in a calculating way in order to earn it.

The problem is that, as we have already seen, the divine love—which is a flow of grace—cannot be received in this manner. The economic exchange model just cannot work, so slaving is every bit as ineffectual as hoarding. Rebellion against God and resentful obedience to his "commands" are equally hopeless strategies, since both attempt to transform the flow of grace into *ousia* that can be made one's own.

The gatherer-father then speaks to his older son: "Son, you are always with me, and all that is mine is yours." From the father's perspective, his son is connected to him, with him in such an intimate way that the life of the father flows to the son. The economic language of the son is therefore metaphysically and spiritually inappropriate, the result of a basic misperception. The Creator God relates to creation in just this ontologically intimate fashion, giving being every moment to whatever exists in the realm of finitude. Though a creature could imagine itself as existing in an extrinsic relation to God, this would be an incorrect, distorted view. The redeemer God wants nothing more than to give his own inner life away to the human race—"all that is mine is yours." The problem is that the sinner persists in misperceiving along competitive lines—"I have been working like a slave for you"—and thus fails to receive the gift.

The prophetic motif of the return of the exile applies, according to N.T. Wright, not only to those who are physically distant from Judea and Jerusalem, but also to those who are in a kind of internal exile, spiritually alienated from what Zion symbolizes. The prodigal son and his brother are perfect evocations of both types: while the younger son goes literally into a distant country, the older son retreats into an interior *chora makra*. They are co-equally far from the flow of grace. In Rembrandt's picture, the older brother resembles the father physically, and like him, he wears a sumptuous red cape, but he stands outside the circle of light that envelops his father and brother. The resemblance hints at the superficial similarity to the father that comes from physical proximity and mimicking the father's behavior (obeying his commands), but the darkness points to the spiritual exile that the older son endures.

The father, with equal vehemence and devotion, reaches out to both wanderers and seeks to bring them into the celebration. Here we can see how this parable is an icon of the Icon of God. In his work of gathering the scattered tribes of Israel—in both external and internal exile—Jesus is the living Icon of the Father, whose whole purpose is to gather his alienated creation back to himself. The embrace of the father and his words "all that is mine is yours" are representations of Jesus' ministry of gathering Israel into his circle of influence, which in turn is the Icon of the Father's noncompetitive and life-enhancing proximity to his creation.

The fundamental problem for both sons is their deep conviction that their relationship to their father is competitive and promethean. In order for them to be fully alive, they must wrest what is "their own" from him. So it goes when one stands in relation to a god who is only other, and not otherly other. Human beings will always resent a supreme being, because they will be locked, necessarily, in a terrible zero-sum game with him. And their rapport with such a god will devolve, accordingly, into the mercenary and the calculating, as we see clearly in Jesus' story. The spiritual strategy of the father is to convince his sons that they are not in competition with him, that in fact their own being and life will increase inasmuch as they accept the gift of his life.

THE PARABLE OF THE DISHONEST MANAGER

16 Then Jesus said to the disciples, "There was a rich man who had a manager, and charges were brought to him that this man was squandering his property. [2] So he summoned him and said to him, 'What is this that I hear about you? Give me an accounting of your management, because you cannot be my manager any longer.' [3] Then the manager said to himself, 'What will I do, now that my master is taking the position away from me? I am not strong enough to dig, and I am ashamed to beg. [4] I have decided what to do so that, when I am dismissed as manager, people may welcome me into their homes.' [5] So, summoning his master's debtors one by one, he asked the first, 'How much do you owe my master?' [6] He answered, 'A hundred jugs of olive oil.' He said to him, 'Take your bill, sit down quickly, and make it fifty.' [7] Then he asked another, 'And how much do you owe?'

He replied, 'A hundred containers of wheat.' He said to him, 'Take your bill and make it eighty.' [8] And his master commended the dishonest manager because he had acted shrewdly; for the children of this age are more shrewd in dealing with their own generation than are the children of light. [9] And I tell you, make friends for yourselves by means of dishonest wealth so that when it is gone, they may welcome you into the eternal homes.

[10] "Whoever is faithful in a very little is faithful also in much; and whoever is dishonest in a very little is dishonest also in much. [11] If then you have not been faithful with the dishonest wealth, who will entrust to you the true riches? [12] And if you have not been faithful with what belongs to another, who will give you what is your own? [13] No slave can serve two masters; for a slave will either hate the one and love the other, or be devoted to the one and despise the other. You cannot serve God and wealth."

THE LAW AND THE KINGDOM OF GOD

[14] The Pharisees, who were lovers of money, heard all this, and they ridiculed him. [15] So he said to them, "You are those who justify yourselves in the sight of others; but God knows your hearts; for what is prized by human beings is an abomination in the sight of God.

[16] "The law and the prophets were in effect until John came; since then the good news of the kingdom of God is proclaimed, and everyone tries to enter it by force. [17] But it is easier for heaven and earth to pass away, than for one stroke of a letter in the law to be dropped.

[18] "Anyone who divorces his wife and marries another commits adultery, and whoever marries a woman divorced from her husband commits adultery.

St. Augustine
(354–430)

———

Sermons

Freed from the Shackles

Luke 16:13

The little ones of Christ are those who have forsaken all that belonged to them and followed him. They gave whatever they had to the poor, that they might serve God without earthly shackles, so that by freeing their shoulders from the burdens of the world, they might raise them aloft as with wings.

THE RICH MAN AND LAZARUS

[19] "There was a rich man who was dressed in purple and fine linen and who feasted sumptuously every day. [20] And at his gate lay a poor man named Lazarus, covered with sores, [21] who longed to satisfy his hunger with what fell from the rich man's table; even the dogs would come and lick his sores. [22] The poor man died and was carried away by the angels to be with Abraham. The rich man also died and was buried. [23] In Hades, where he was being tormented, he looked up and saw Abraham far away with Lazarus by his side. [24] He called out, 'Father Abraham, have mercy on me, and send Lazarus to dip the tip of his finger in water and cool my tongue; for I am in agony in these flames.' [25] But Abraham said, 'Child, remember that during your lifetime you received your good things, and Lazarus in like manner evil things; but now he is comforted here, and you are in agony. [26] Besides all this, between you and us a great chasm has been fixed, so that those who might want to pass from here to you cannot do so, and no one can cross from there to us.' [27] He said, 'Then, father, I beg you to send him to my father's house— [28] for I have five brothers—that he may warn them, so

---

Gone, But Still Connected

Luke 16:19–31 | Bishop Barron

The story of the rich man and Lazarus focuses on the enduring existence of those who have gone before us into death. To say that we are nothing but "bodies" that flourish briefly and then fade away is to miss this dimension of our existence. Though we are tempted to see death as the end, something in us rebels against this.

And this is why Jesus speaks so readily of eternal life. There was a great debate in Jesus' time within Judaism in regard to the question of resurrection. Many, including the Sadducees, denied the idea of life after death; but others,

including the Pharisees, affirmed it. Jesus clearly sides with those who affirm it, and his own Resurrection from the dead affirmed this belief as emphatically as possible.

This story also has an enormously important practical consequence: we are related still to those who have gone before us. They are, in a very real sense, gone. But they have not disappeared. They are connected to God, and therefore to everything that God loves. They are not so much some*where* else as some*how* else, and thus they can relate to us in perhaps very intimate ways.

that they will not also come into this place of torment.' ²⁹ Abraham replied, 'They have Moses and the prophets; they should listen to them.' ³⁰ He said, 'No, father Abraham; but if someone goes to them from the dead, they will repent.' ³¹ He said to him, 'If they do not listen to Moses and the prophets, neither will they be convinced even if someone rises from the dead.' "

SOME SAYINGS OF JESUS

17 Jesus said to his disciples, "Occasions for stumbling are bound to come, but woe to anyone by whom they come! ² It would be better for you if a millstone were hung around your neck and you were thrown into the sea than for you to cause one of these little ones to stumble. ³ Be on your guard! If another disciple sins, you must rebuke the offender, and if there is repentance, you must forgive. ⁴ And if the same person sins against you seven times a day, and turns back to you seven times and says, 'I repent,' you must forgive."

⁵ The apostles said to the Lord, "Increase our faith!" ⁶ The Lord replied, "If you had faith the size of a mustard seed, you could say to this mulberry tree, 'Be uprooted and planted in the sea,' and it would obey you.

⁷ "Who among you would say to your slave who has just come in from plowing or tending sheep in the field, 'Come here at once and take your place at the table'? ⁸ Would you not rather say to him, 'Prepare supper for me, put on your apron and serve me while I eat and drink; later you may eat and drink'? ⁹ Do you thank the slave for doing what was commanded? ¹⁰ So you also, when you have done all that you were ordered to do, say, 'We are worthless slaves; we have done only what we ought to have done!' "

JESUS CLEANSES TEN LEPERS

¹¹ On the way to Jerusalem Jesus was going through the region between Samaria and Galilee. ¹² As he entered a village, ten lepers approached him. Keeping their distance, ¹³ they called out, saying, "Jesus, Master, have mercy on us!" ¹⁴ When he saw them, he said to them, "Go and show yourselves to the priests." And as they went, they were made clean. ¹⁵ Then one of them, when he saw that he was healed, turned back, praising God with a loud voice. ¹⁶ He prostrated himself at Jesus' feet and thanked him. And he was a Samaritan. ¹⁷ Then Jesus asked, "Were not ten made clean? But the other nine, where are they? ¹⁸ Was none of them found to return and give praise to God except this foreigner?" ¹⁹ Then he said to him, "Get up and go on your way; your faith has made you well."

THE COMING OF THE KINGDOM

²⁰ Once Jesus was asked by the Pharisees when the kingdom of God was coming, and he answered, "The kingdom of God is not coming with things

that can be observed; ²¹ nor will they say, 'Look, here it is!' or 'There it is!' For, in fact, the kingdom of God is among you."

²² Then he said to the disciples, "The days are coming when you will long to see one of the days of the Son of Man, and you will not see it. ²³ They will say to you, 'Look there!' or 'Look here!' Do not go, do not set off in pursuit. ²⁴ For as the lightning flashes and lights up the sky from one side to the other, so will the Son of Man be in his day. ²⁵ But first he must endure much suffering and be rejected by this generation. ²⁶ Just as it was in the days of Noah, so too it will be in the days of the Son of Man. ²⁷ They were eating and drinking, and marrying and being given in marriage,

G.K. Chesterton
(1874–1936)

What I Saw In America

Looking for the Kingdom

Luke 17:21

The devil can quote Scripture for his purpose; and the text of Scripture which he now most commonly quotes is, "The kingdom of God is within [among] you." That text has been the stay and support of more Pharisees and prigs and self-righteous spiritual bullies than all the dogmas in creation; it has served to identify self-satisfaction with the peace that passes all understanding.

And the text to be quoted in answer to it is that which declares that no man can receive the kingdom except as a little child [Luke 18:17]. What we are to have inside is the childlike spirit; but the childlike spirit is not entirely concerned about what is inside. It is the first mark of possessing it that one is interested in what is outside. The most childlike thing about a child is his curiosity and his appetite and his power of wonder at the world. We might almost say that the whole advantage of having the kingdom within is that we look for it somewhere else.

until the day Noah entered the ark, and the flood came and destroyed all of them. [28] Likewise, just as it was in the days of Lot: they were eating and drinking, buying and selling, planting and building, [29] but on the day that Lot left Sodom, it rained fire and sulfur from heaven and destroyed all of them [30] —it will be like that on the day that the Son of Man is revealed. [31] On that day, anyone on the housetop who has belongings in the house must not come down to take them away; and likewise anyone in the field must not turn back. [32] Remember Lot's wife. [33] Those who try to make their life secure will lose it, but those who lose their life will keep it. [34] I tell you, on that night there will be two in one bed; one will be taken and the other left. [35] There will be two women grinding meal together; one will be taken and the other left." [37] Then they asked him, "Where, Lord?" He said to them, "Where the corpse is, there the vultures will gather."

Our Clueless Behavior

Luke 17.26-37 | Bishop Barron

The Lord compares the clueless behavior of our time with that of the time of Noah. Listen to his warning: "Just as it was in the days of Noah, so too it will be in the days of the Son of Man." Those aren't very reassuring words.

Then he specifies: people were eating and drinking, marrying and being given in marriage, right up to the time of the flood, and then, when it came with shocking suddenness, they were destroyed. The end of an old world had arrived, but the inhabitants of that world were clueless. A new world was coming, but the prospective citizens of it had no idea how to prepare for it.

Our version of Noah's world-destroying flood might be the crashing of a huge comet into the earth. What if we knew that a comet was coming, but we did nothing about it, we adjusted in no way to it? This was the situation of those in Noah's time and, Jesus suggests, those in his own time. And it's our situation too. We must prepare for the Lord's coming by patterning our lives on the Gospel.

THE PARABLE OF THE WIDOW AND THE UNJUST JUDGE

18 Then Jesus told them a parable about their need to pray always and not to lose heart. [2] He said, "In a certain city there was a judge who neither feared God nor had respect for people. [3] In that city there was a widow who kept coming to him and saying, 'Grant me justice against my

opponent.' ⁴ For a while he refused; but later he said to himself, 'Though I have no fear of God and no respect for anyone, ⁵ yet because this widow keeps bothering me, I will grant her justice, so that she may not wear me out by continually coming.'" ⁶ And the Lord said, "Listen to what the unjust judge says. ⁷ And will not God grant justice to his chosen ones who cry to him day and night? Will he delay long in helping them? ⁸ I tell you, he will quickly grant justice to them. And yet, when the Son of Man comes, will he find faith on earth?"

THE PARABLE OF THE PHARISEE AND THE TAX COLLECTOR

⁹ He also told this parable to some who trusted in themselves that they were righteous and regarded others with contempt: ¹⁰ "Two men went up to the temple to pray, one a Pharisee and the other a tax collector. ¹¹ The Pharisee, standing by himself, was praying thus, 'God, I thank you that I am not like other people: thieves, rogues, adulterers, or even like this tax collector. ¹² I fast twice a week; I give a tenth of all my income.' ¹³ But the tax collector, standing far off, would not even look up to heaven, but was beating his breast and saying, 'God, be merciful to me, a sinner!' ¹⁴ I tell you, this man went down to his home justified rather than the other; for all who exalt themselves will be humbled, but all who humble themselves will be exalted."

JESUS BLESSES LITTLE CHILDREN

¹⁵ People were bringing even infants to him that he might touch them; and when the disciples saw it, they sternly ordered them not to do it.

WHOEVER DOES NOT RECEIVE THE KINGDOM OF GOD AS A LITTLE CHILD WILL NEVER ENTER IT.

LUKE 18:17

¹⁶ But Jesus called for them and said, "Let the little children come to me, and do not stop them; for it is to such as these that the kingdom of God belongs. ¹⁷ Truly I tell you, whoever does not receive the kingdom of God as a little child will never enter it."

Persistent Prayer

Luke 18:1–8 | Bishop Barron

The command to pray with persistence is everywhere in the Bible. We see it in Abraham's steady petition on behalf of the people of Sodom (Gen. 18:22–33). We hear it in Jesus' extraordinary teaching: "Ask, and it will be given you; search, and you will find; knock, and the door will be opened for you" (Luke 11:9). And we see it in the account of the persistent widow.

One reason that we don't receive what we want through prayer is that we give up too easily. What could be behind this rule of prayer? Augustine said that God sometimes delays in giving us what we want because he wants our hearts to expand. The more ardently we desire something, the more ready we are when it comes, the more we treasure it. The very act of asking persistently is accomplishing something spiritually important. So when the Lord seems slow to answer your prayer, never give up.

St. Augustine
(354–430)

———

Our Lord's Sermon on the Mount

Unceasing Petitions

Luke 18:1–8

These parables are not to be treated as strict allegories.... They stand here, in order that important truths may be suggested from smaller matters. A good example is the story of the judge who neither feared God nor regarded man, and yet yielded to the widow—not from piety or humanity, but merely to be spared some annoyance. The unjust judge himself does not in any way allegorically represent the person of God.... Yet the story does show how even an unworthy man, acting from petty motives, cannot disregard those who assail him with unceasing petitions.

The Entire Point of Religion

Luke 18:9–14 | Bishop Barron

A Pharisee and a tax collector—a stereotypically righteous and unrighteous person—both enter the temple to pray. But what a world of difference in their manner of praying!

The entire point of religion is to make us humble before God and to open us to the path of love. Everything else is more or less a footnote. Liturgy, prayer, the precepts of the Church, the Commandments, sacraments, sacramentals—all of it is finally meant to conform us to the way of love. When they instead turn us away from that path, they have been undermined.

Both St. Paul and the Gospel writers—as well as Jesus himself, of course—are intensely aware of this danger. This is precisely why Paul speaks of the dangers of the Law. He knew that people often use the Law as a weapon of aggression: since I know what is right and wrong in some detail, then I am uniquely positioned to point out your flaws. And when I point out your flaws, I elevate myself. In short, the Law, which is a gift from God, has been co-opted for the purposes of the ego. And when that happens, we're entirely missing the point of religion.

St. Francis de Sales
(1567–1622)

———

Introduction to the Devout Life

Yesterday a Sinner, Today a Saint

Luke 18:9–14

The vain Pharisee held the humble tax collector to be a great sinner, or even perhaps an unjust man, an adulterer, or an extortioner. But he was greatly deceived, for at that very time the tax collector was justified.

Alas! Since the goodness of God is so immense that one moment suffices to obtain and receive his grace, what assurance can we have, that he who was yesterday a sinner is not a saint today?

The day that is past ought not to judge the present day, nor the present day judge that which is past: it is only the last day that judges all.

THE RICH RULER

[18] A certain ruler asked him, "Good Teacher, what must I do to inherit eternal life?" [19] Jesus said to him, "Why do you call me good? No one is good but God alone. [20] You know the commandments: 'You shall not commit adultery; You shall not murder; You shall not steal; You shall not bear false witness; Honor your father and mother.'" [21] He replied, "I have kept all these since my youth." [22] When Jesus heard this, he said to him, "There is still one thing lacking. Sell all that you own and distribute the money to the poor, and you will have treasure in heaven; then come, follow me." [23] But when he heard this, he became sad; for he was very rich. [24] Jesus looked at him and said, "How hard it is for those who have wealth to enter the kingdom of God! [25] Indeed, it is easier for a camel to go through the eye of a needle than for someone who is rich to enter the kingdom of God."

[26] Those who heard it said, "Then who can be saved?" [27] He replied, "What is impossible for mortals is possible for God."

[28] Then Peter said, "Look, we have left our homes and followed you." [29] And he said to them, "Truly I tell you, there is no one who has left house or wife or brothers or parents or children, for the sake of the kingdom of God, [30] who will not get back very much more in this age, and in the age to come eternal life."

A THIRD TIME JESUS FORETELLS HIS DEATH AND RESURRECTION

[31] Then he took the twelve aside and said to them, "See, we are going up to Jerusalem, and everything that is written about the Son of Man by the prophets will be accomplished. [32] For he will be handed over to the Gentiles; and he will be mocked and insulted and spat upon. [33] After they have flogged him, they will kill him, and on the third day he will rise again." [34] But they understood nothing about all these things; in fact, what he said was hidden from them, and they did not grasp what was said.

JESUS HEALS A BLIND BEGGAR NEAR JERICHO

[35] As he approached Jericho, a blind man was sitting by the roadside begging. [36] When he heard a crowd going by, he asked what was happening. [37] They told him, "Jesus of Nazareth is passing by." [38] Then he shouted, "Jesus, Son of David, have mercy on me!" [39] Those who were in front sternly ordered him to be quiet; but he shouted even more loudly, "Son of David, have mercy on me!" [40] Jesus stood still and ordered the man to be brought to him; and when he came near, he asked him, [41] "What do you want me to do for you?" He said, "Lord, let me see again." [42] Jesus said to him, "Receive your sight; your faith has saved you." [43] Immediately he regained his sight and followed him, glorifying God; and all the people, when they saw it, praised God.

JESUS AND ZACCHAEUS

19 He entered Jericho and was passing through it. [2] A man was there named Zacchaeus; he was a chief tax collector and was rich. [3] He was trying to see who Jesus was, but on account of the crowd he could not, because he was short in stature. [4] So he ran ahead and climbed a sycamore tree to see him, because he was going to pass that way. [5] When Jesus came to the place, he looked up and said to him, "Zacchaeus, hurry and come down; for I must stay at your house today." [6] So he hurried down and was happy to welcome him. [7] All who saw it began to grumble and said, "He has gone to be the guest of one who is a sinner." [8] Zacchaeus stood there and said to the Lord, "Look, half of my possessions, Lord, I will give to the poor; and if I have defrauded anyone of anything, I will pay back four times as much." [9] Then Jesus said to him, "Today salvation has come to this house, because he too is a son of Abraham. [10] For the Son of Man came to seek out and to save the lost."

THE PARABLE OF THE TEN POUNDS

[11] As they were listening to this, he went on to tell a parable, because he was near Jerusalem, and because they supposed that the kingdom of God

---

God Does Not Play Hard to Get

Luke 19:1–10 | Bishop Barron

Notice in the story of Zacchaeus how quickly God responds to any sign of faith. Zacchaeus' climbing the sycamore tree shows he had more than a passing interest in seeing Jesus. He had a deep hunger of the spirit. His principal virtue was his willingness to go to great extremes.

This is what we do when we know that something of tremendous moment is at stake. When our health is endangered, we move, we act; when our job is threatened, we go to almost any extreme to keep it.

When Jesus spotted him he said, "Zacchaeus, hurry and come down; for I must stay at your house today." God responds to us readily when we show the least interest in him. He doesn't play hard to get; he is not coy with us. When we seek him, he responds, because loving us is his entire game.

Finally, notice how Jesus tells Zacchaeus to hurry. It's a good spiritual principle: don't wait, don't hesitate. Seize the moment of conversion when it comes.

Thomas Merton
(1915–1968)
——
No Man Is an Island

To Save the Lost
Luke 19:10

Only the lost are saved. Only the sinner is justified. Only the dead can rise from the dead, and Jesus said "the Son of Man came to seek out and to save the lost."

was to appear immediately. ¹² So he said, "A nobleman went to a distant country to get royal power for himself and then return. ¹³ He summoned ten of his slaves, and gave them ten pounds, and said to them, 'Do business with these until I come back.' ¹⁴ But the citizens of his country hated him and sent a delegation after him, saying, 'We do not want this man to rule over us.' ¹⁵ When he returned, having received royal power, he ordered these slaves, to whom he had given the money, to be summoned so that he might find out what they had gained by trading. ¹⁶ The first came forward and said, 'Lord, your pound has made ten more pounds.' ¹⁷ He said to him, 'Well done, good slave! Because you have been trustworthy in a very small thing, take charge of ten cities.' ¹⁸ Then the second came, saying, 'Lord, your pound has made five pounds.' ¹⁹ He said to him, 'And you, rule over five cities.' ²⁰ Then the other came, saying, 'Lord, here is your pound. I wrapped it up in a piece of cloth, ²¹ for I was afraid of you, because you are a harsh man; you take what you did not deposit, and reap what you did not sow.' ²² He said to him, 'I will judge you by your own words, you wicked slave! You knew, did you, that I was a harsh man, taking what I did not deposit and reaping what I did not sow? ²³ Why then did you not put my money into the bank? Then when I returned, I could have collected it with interest.' ²⁴ He said to the bystanders, 'Take the pound from him and give it to the one who has ten pounds.' ²⁵ (And they said to him, 'Lord, he has ten pounds!') ²⁶ 'I tell you, to all those who have, more will be given; but from those who have nothing, even what they have will be taken away. ²⁷ But as for these enemies of mine who did not want me to be king over them—bring them here and slaughter them in my presence.' "

Investing in the Spiritual Life

Luke 19:11–27 | Bishop Barron

Jesus uses images drawn from the world of business to instruct us in Christian living. And he especially liked the dynamic of investment, risk, and return as a model of the spiritual life. The reason is clear: God exists in gift form. Therefore, if you want his life in you, you have to learn to give it away.

Notice that the first two servants increased their wealth precisely in the measure that they risked it. This means that the one who truly has the divine life knows how to make it a gift, and that in turn will make the original gift increase. And the opposite holds true: "From those who have nothing, even what they have will be taken away." This means that if you try to cling to the divine life, you will, in short order, lose it.

JESUS' TRIUMPHAL ENTRY INTO JERUSALEM

[28] After he had said this, he went on ahead, going up to Jerusalem.

[29] When he had come near Bethphage and Bethany, at the place called the Mount of Olives, he sent two of the disciples, [30] saying, "Go into the village ahead of you, and as you enter it you will find tied there a colt that has never been ridden. Untie it and bring it here. [31] If anyone asks you, 'Why are you untying it?' just say this, 'The Lord needs it.'" [32] So those who were sent departed and found it as he had told them. [33] As they were untying the colt, its owners asked them, "Why are you untying the colt?" [34] They said, "The Lord needs it." [35] Then they brought it to Jesus; and after throwing their cloaks on the colt, they set Jesus on it. [36] As he rode along, people kept spreading their cloaks on the road. [37] As he was now approaching the path down from the Mount of Olives, the whole multitude of the disciples began to praise God joyfully with a loud voice for all the deeds of power that they had seen, [38] saying,

"Blessed is the king
who comes in the name of the Lord!
Peace in heaven,
and glory in the highest heaven!"

[39] Some of the Pharisees in the crowd said to him, "Teacher, order your disciples to stop." [40] He answered, "I tell you, if these were silent, the stones would shout out."

JESUS WEEPS OVER JERUSALEM

[41] As he came near and saw the city, he wept over it, [42] saying, "If you, even you, had only recognized on this day the things that make for peace! But now they are hidden from your eyes. [43] Indeed, the days will come upon you, when your enemies will set up ramparts around you and surround you, and hem you in on every side. [44] They will crush you to the ground, you and your children within you, and they will not leave within you one stone upon another; because you did not recognize the time of your visitation from God."

JESUS CLEANSES THE TEMPLE

[45] Then he entered the temple and began to drive out those who were selling things there; [46] and he said, "It is written,

> 'My house shall be a house of prayer';
> but you have made it a den of robbers.'"

[47] Every day he was teaching in the temple. The chief priests, the scribes, and the leaders of the people kept looking for a way to kill him; [48] but they did not find anything they could do, for all the people were spellbound by what they heard.

G.K. Chesterton
(1874–1936)
———
Orthodoxy

The Stones Cry Out

Luke 19:40

The following propositions have been urged: First, that some faith in our life is required even to improve it; second, that some dissatisfaction with things as they are is necessary even in order to be satisfied; third, that to have this necessary content and necessary discontent it is not sufficient to have the obvious equilibrium of the Stoic.

For mere resignation has neither the gigantic levity of pleasure nor the superb intolerance of pain. There is a vital objection to the advice merely to grin and bear it. The objection is that if you merely bear it, you do not grin. Greek heroes do not grin: but gargoyles do—because they are Christian. And when a Christian is pleased, he is (in the most exact sense) frightfully pleased; his pleasure is frightful.

Christ prophesied the whole of Gothic architecture in that hour when nervous and respectable people (such people as now object to barrel organs) objected to the shouting of the gutter-snipes of Jerusalem. He said, "If these were silent, the stones would shout out." Under the impulse of his spirit arose like a clamorous chorus the façades of the mediæval cathedrals, thronged with shouting faces and open mouths. The prophecy has fulfilled itself: the very stones cry out.

THE AUTHORITY OF JESUS QUESTIONED

20 One day, as he was teaching the people in the temple and telling the good news, the chief priests and the scribes came with the elders ² and said to him, "Tell us, by what authority are you doing these things? Who is it who gave you this authority?" ³ He answered them, "I will also ask you a question, and you tell me: ⁴ Did the baptism of John come from heaven, or was it of human origin?" ⁵ They discussed it with one another, saying, "If we say, 'From heaven,' he will say, 'Why did you not believe him?' ⁶ But if we say, 'Of human origin,' all the people will stone us; for they are convinced that John was a prophet." ⁷ So they answered that they did not know where it came from. ⁸ Then Jesus said to them, "Neither will I tell you by what authority I am doing these things."

THE PARABLE OF THE WICKED TENANTS

⁹ He began to tell the people this parable: "A man planted a vineyard, and leased it to tenants, and went to another country for a long time. ¹⁰ When the season came, he sent a slave to the tenants in order that they might give him his share of the produce of the vineyard; but the tenants beat him and sent him away empty-handed. ¹¹ Next he sent another slave; that one

Fulton Sheen
(1895–1979)

———

Life of Christ

No One Can Remain Indifferent

Luke 20:17–19

There are two figures in Luke 20: one is of a man dashing himself against the stone that is laid passively on earth. Our Lord here meant rejecting him during this time of his humiliation. The other figure is of the stone actively considered as when it falls, for example, from a cliff. By this he meant himself as glorified and crushing all earthly opposition.

The first would refer to Israel in the present moment when it rejected him, and for which Jerusalem, he said, would be desolate. The other would refer to those who rejected him after his glorious Resurrection, Ascension, and the progress of his kingdom on earth.

Every man, he claimed, had some contact with him. He is free to reject his influence, but the rejection is the stone which crushes him. No one can remain indifferent once he has met him. He remains the perpetual element in the character of every hearer. No teacher in the world ever claimed that rejecting [the teacher] would harden one's heart and make a man worse. But here is one who, within three days of going to his death, said that the very rejection of him would decay the heart.

Whether one believes or disbelieves him, one is never the same afterward. Christ said that he was either the rock on which men would build the foundation of life, or the rock which would crush them. Never did men just simply pass him by; he is the abiding Presence. Some may think that they allow him to pass by without receiving him, but this he called fatal neglect. A fatal crushing would follow not only neglect or indifference, but also when there was formal opposition.

also they beat and insulted and sent away empty-handed. ¹² And he sent still a third; this one also they wounded and threw out. ¹³ Then the owner of the vineyard said, 'What shall I do? I will send my beloved son; perhaps they will respect him.' ¹⁴ But when the tenants saw him, they discussed it among themselves and said, 'This is the heir; let us kill him so that the inheritance may be ours.' ¹⁵ So they threw him out of the vineyard and killed him. What then will the owner of the vineyard do to them? ¹⁶ He will come and destroy those tenants and give the vineyard to others." When they heard this, they said, "Heaven forbid!" ¹⁷ But he looked at them and said, "What then does this text mean:

> 'The stone that the builders rejected
> has become the cornerstone'?

¹⁸ Everyone who falls on that stone will be broken to pieces; and it will crush anyone on whom it falls." ¹⁹ When the scribes and chief priests realized that he had told this parable against them, they wanted to lay hands on him at that very hour, but they feared the people.

THE QUESTION ABOUT PAYING TAXES

²⁰ So they watched him and sent spies who pretended to be honest, in order to trap him by what he said, so as to hand him over to the jurisdiction and authority of the governor. ²¹ So they asked him, "Teacher, we know that you are right in what you say and teach, and you show deference to no one, but teach the way of God in accordance with truth. ²² Is it lawful for us to pay taxes to the emperor, or not?" ²³ But he perceived their craftiness and said to them, ²⁴ "Show me a denarius. Whose head and whose title does it bear?" They said, "The emperor's." ²⁵ He said to them, "Then give to the emperor the things that are the emperor's, and to God the things that are God's." ²⁶ And they were not able in the presence of the people to trap him by what he said; and being amazed by his answer, they became silent.

THE QUESTION ABOUT THE RESURRECTION

²⁷ Some Sadducees, those who say there is no resurrection, came to him ²⁸ and asked him a question, "Teacher, Moses wrote for us that if a man's brother dies, leaving a wife but no children, the man shall marry the widow and raise up children for his brother. ²⁹ Now there were seven brothers; the first married, and died childless; ³⁰ then the second ³¹ and the third married her, and so in the same way all seven died childless. ³² Finally the woman also died. ³³ In the resurrection, therefore, whose wife will the woman be? For the seven had married her."

³⁴ Jesus said to them, "Those who belong to this age marry and are given in marriage; ³⁵ but those who are considered worthy of a place in

that age and in the resurrection from the dead neither marry nor are given in marriage. ³⁶ Indeed they cannot die anymore, because they are like angels and are children of God, being children of the resurrection. ³⁷ And the fact that the dead are raised Moses himself showed, in the story about the bush, where he speaks of the Lord as the God of Abraham, the God of Isaac, and the God of Jacob. ³⁸ Now he is God not of the dead, but of the living; for to him all of them are alive." ³⁹ Then some of the scribes answered, "Teacher, you have spoken well." ⁴⁰ For they no longer dared to ask him another question.

THE QUESTION ABOUT DAVID'S SON

⁴¹ Then he said to them, "How can they say that the Messiah is David's son? ⁴² For David himself says in the book of Psalms,

> 'The Lord said to my Lord,
> "Sit at my right hand,
> ⁴³ until I make your enemies your footstool." '

⁴⁴ David thus calls him Lord; so how can he be his son?"

JESUS DENOUNCES THE SCRIBES

⁴⁵ In the hearing of all the people he said to the disciples, ⁴⁶ "Beware of the scribes, who like to walk around in long robes, and love to be greeted with respect in the marketplaces, and to have the best seats in the synagogues and places of honor at banquets. ⁴⁷ They devour widows' houses and for the sake of appearance say long prayers. They will receive the greater condemnation."

The Resurrection of the Dead

Luke 20:27–40 | Bishop Barron

Jesus sparred with some Sadducees about the general resurrection of the dead. They held that there is no life after death. We could practically hear their speech on the lips of skeptics today. But Jesus is having none of it. The dead shall indeed rise, he says; otherwise, how could Moses have spoken of God as "the God of Abraham, the God of Isaac, and the God of Jacob," all of whom were long dead by Moses' time? But their risen existence, though in continuity, even bodily continuity, with what has gone before, will be transformed, transfigured, raised up.

If you are a complete materialist and secularist, you hold that everything and everybody, in the end, just fades away. But if you believe in the resurrection of the body, then everything in this world has the possibility of redemption.

THE WIDOW'S OFFERING

21 He looked up and saw rich people putting their gifts into the treasury; [2] he also saw a poor widow put in two small copper coins. [3] He said, "Truly I tell you, this poor widow has put in more than all of them; [4] for all of them have contributed out of their abundance, but she out of her poverty has put in all she had to live on."

THE DESTRUCTION OF THE TEMPLE FORETOLD

[5] When some were speaking about the temple, how it was adorned with beautiful stones and gifts dedicated to God, he said, [6] "As for these things that you see, the days will come when not one stone will be left upon another; all will be thrown down."

SIGNS AND PERSECUTIONS

[7] They asked him, "Teacher, when will this be, and what will be the sign that this is about to take place?" [8] And he said, "Beware that you are not led astray; for many will come in my name and say, 'I am he!' and, 'The time is near!' Do not go after them.

[9] "When you hear of wars and insurrections, do not be terrified; for these things must take place first, but the end will not follow immediately." [10] Then he said to them, "Nation will rise against nation, and kingdom against kingdom; [11] there will be great earthquakes, and in various places

---

What Makes Us Happy?

Luke 21:1–4 | Bishop Barron

The poor widow who gave her last penny to the temple treasury makes us consider our possessiveness. What do we tell ourselves all the time? That we're not happy because we don't have all the things that we should have or that we want to have. What follows from this is that life becomes a constant quest to get, to acquire, and to attain possessions.

Do you remember the parable of the rich fool? When his barns were filled with all his possessions, he decided to tear them down and build bigger ones. Why is he a fool? Because you have everything you need right now to be happy.

What makes you happy is always right in front of you because what makes you happy is love. Love is willing the good of the other, opening yourself to the world around you. Love is not a feeling. It's an act of the will. It is the great act of dispossession.

famines and plagues; and there will be dreadful portents and great signs from heaven.

¹² "But before all this occurs, they will arrest you and persecute you; they will hand you over to synagogues and prisons, and you will be brought before kings and governors because of my name. ¹³ This will give you an opportunity to testify. ¹⁴ So make up your minds not to prepare your

St. Francis de Sales
(1567–1622)

Introduction to the Devout Life

By Your Endurance

Luke 21:19

If our Savior himself has declared: "By your endurance you will gain your souls," should it not be a man's great happiness to possess his soul? The more perfect our patience, the more absolutely do we possess it.

Let us frequently call to mind that as our Lord has saved us by patient suffering, so we also ought to work out our salvation by sufferings and afflictions; enduring injuries and contradictions with all possible meekness.

Do not limit your patience to just some kind of injuries and afflictions, but extend it to all such afflictions that God sends you. Some people are unwilling to suffer any tribulations except those that bring honor. For example, to be wounded in battle, to be a prisoner of war, or to be persecuted for religion.

Now, these people do not love the tribulation, but the honor which accompanies it. He that is truly patient suffers tribulations indifferently, whether accompanied by ignominy or honor. To be despised, found fault with, or accused by wicked men, is pleasant to a man of good heart; but to suffer blame and ill-treatment from the virtuous, or from our friends and relatives, is the test of true patience.

defense in advance; [15] for I will give you words and a wisdom that none of your opponents will be able to withstand or contradict. [16] You will be betrayed even by parents and brothers, by relatives and friends; and they will put some of you to death. [17] You will be hated by all because of my name. [18] But not a hair of your head will perish. [19] By your endurance you will gain your souls.

THE DESTRUCTION OF JERUSALEM FORETOLD

[20] "When you see Jerusalem surrounded by armies, then know that its desolation has come near. [21] Then those in Judea must flee to the mountains, and those inside the city must leave it, and those out in the country must not enter it; [22] for these are days of vengeance, as a fulfillment of all that is written. [23] Woe to those who are pregnant and to those who are nursing infants in those days! For there will be great distress on the earth and wrath against this people; [24] they will fall by the edge of the sword and be taken away as captives among all nations; and Jerusalem will be trampled on by the Gentiles, until the times of the Gentiles are fulfilled.

THE COMING OF THE SON OF MAN

[25] "There will be signs in the sun, the moon, and the stars, and on the earth distress among nations confused by the roaring of the sea and the waves. [26] People will faint from fear and foreboding of what is coming upon the

---

No Timetables

Luke 21:34–36 | Bishop Barron

Jesus urges us to watch and pray as we await his coming again. In one sense, Christianity is a religion of fulfillment (the Lord has come), but in another sense, it is a religion of waiting, for we expect the Second Coming of Jesus in the fullness of his power.

So we wait, watch, and keep vigil, which is difficult. But what we all know is that great things take time. For example, when a woman becomes pregnant, she has to wait nine long months before the baby is ready.

"How long does this analysis take?" a woman once asked the psychiatrist Carl Jung. "Just as long as it takes," came the answer. Gestation, growth, healing—during any of these processes, the very worst thing one can do is to pick at it, to force it, to make it operate according to our private timetables.

That's why Jesus calls us to "be alert at all times, praying that you may have the strength … to stand before the Son of Man."

world, for the powers of the heavens will be shaken. ²⁷ Then they will see 'the Son of Man coming in a cloud' with power and great glory. ²⁸ Now when these things begin to take place, stand up and raise your heads, because your redemption is drawing near."

THE LESSON OF THE FIG TREE

²⁹ Then he told them a parable: "Look at the fig tree and all the trees; ³⁰ as soon as they sprout leaves you can see for yourselves and know that summer is already near. ³¹ So also, when you see these things taking place, you know that the kingdom of God is near. ³² Truly I tell you, this generation will not pass away until all things have taken place. ³³ Heaven and earth will pass away, but my words will not pass away.

EXHORTATION TO WATCH

³⁴ "Be on guard so that your hearts are not weighed down with dissipation and drunkenness and the worries of this life, and that day does not catch you unexpectedly, ³⁵ like a trap. For it will come upon all who live on the face of the whole earth. ³⁶ Be alert at all times, praying that you may have the strength to escape all these things that will take place, and to stand before the Son of Man."

³⁷ Every day he was teaching in the temple, and at night he would go out and spend the night on the Mount of Olives, as it was called. ³⁸ And all the people would get up early in the morning to listen to him in the temple.

THE PLOT TO KILL JESUS

22 Now the festival of Unleavened Bread, which is called the Passover, was near. ² The chief priests and the scribes were looking for a way to put Jesus to death, for they were afraid of the people.

³ Then Satan entered into Judas called Iscariot, who was one of the twelve; ⁴ he went away and conferred with the chief priests and officers of the temple police about how he might betray him to them. ⁵ They were greatly pleased and agreed to give him money. ⁶ So he consented and began to look for an opportunity to betray him to them when no crowd was present.

THE PREPARATION OF THE PASSOVER

⁷ Then came the day of Unleavened Bread, on which the Passover lamb had to be sacrificed. ⁸ So Jesus sent Peter and John, saying, "Go and prepare the Passover meal for us that we may eat it." ⁹ They asked him, "Where do you want us to make preparations for it?" ¹⁰ "Listen," he said to them, "when you have entered the city, a man carrying a jar of water will meet you; follow him into the house he enters ¹¹ and say to the owner of the house, 'The teacher asks you, "Where is the guest room, where I may eat the Passover with my disciples?" ' ¹² He will show you a large room upstairs, already furnished.

Make preparations for us there." ¹³ So they went and found everything as he had told them; and they prepared the Passover meal.

THE INSTITUTION OF THE LORD'S SUPPER

¹⁴ When the hour came, he took his place at the table, and the apostles with him. ¹⁵ He said to them, "I have eagerly desired to eat this Passover with you before I suffer; ¹⁶ for I tell you, I will not eat it until it is fulfilled in the kingdom of God." ¹⁷ Then he took a cup, and after giving thanks he said, "Take this and divide it among yourselves; ¹⁸ for I tell you that from now on I will not drink of the fruit of the vine until the kingdom of God comes." ¹⁹ Then he took a loaf of bread, and when he had given thanks, he broke it and gave it to them, saying, "This is my body, which is given for you. Do this in remembrance of me." ²⁰ And he did the same with the cup after supper, saying, "This cup that is poured out for you is the new covenant in my blood. ²¹ But see, the one who betrays me is with me, and his hand is on the table. ²² For the Son of Man is going as it has been determined, but woe to that one by whom he is betrayed!" ²³ Then they began to ask one another which one of them it could be who would do this.

Broken Bread, Broken Body

Luke 22:14–23 | Bishop Barron

There is a powerful link between what happened in the upper room the night before Jesus died and what happened the next day on Calvary. What Jesus did the night before he died was to anticipate sacramentally what he would do the next day.

"Then he took a loaf of bread, and when he had given thanks, he broke it and gave it to them, saying, 'This is my body, which is given for you.'" The broken bread anticipates the body broken on the cross. Jesus, as the Icon of God, is nothing but giving. He gives himself away as food, as sacrifice, as offering.

"And he did the same with the cup after supper, saying, 'This cup that is poured out for you is the new covenant in my blood.'" The cup of the Last Supper anticipates and sacramentally re-presents the blood that will be copiously poured out the next day. Jesus is love poured out, all the way to death.

What Catholics do at every Mass is to make present again, in an unbloody way, this terrible sacrifice. We offer to the Father what the Son did, for it is pleasing to the Father, and we join ourselves to it.

THIS IS MY BODY, WHICH IS GIVEN FOR YOU.

LUKE 22:19

Understanding the Last Supper

Luke 22:14–30 | Bishop Barron

LUKE TELLS US THAT, at the climactic moment of his life and ministry, Jesus "took his place at the table, and the apostles with him." At this Last Supper, Jesus, in a culminating way, embodied Yahweh's desire to sit in easy intimacy with his people, sharing his life with them. He said, "I have eagerly desired to eat this Passover with you before I suffer." Yahweh established the Passover meal as a sign of his covenant with his holy people Israel. Thus Jesus, Yahweh made flesh, gathered his community around the Passover table.

All of the familiar Passover motifs of liberation, redemption, unity, and festivity are at play here, but they are being redefined and reconfigured in relation to Jesus. The Isaian vision of the sumptuous meal on God's holy mountain is described as "eschatological," implying that it has to do with God's deepest and final desire for the world that he has made. At the commencement of the Last Supper, as he settled in with his disciples, Jesus explicitly evoked this eschatological dimension: "For I tell you, I will not eat it until it is fulfilled in the kingdom of God." And when he took the first cup of Passover wine, he reiterated the theme: "For I tell you that from now on I will not drink of the fruit of the vine until the kingdom of God comes."

It is most important to remember that this meal took place on the night before Jesus' death—which is to say, at the moment when he was summing up his life and preparing for his own Passover into the realm of the Father. Therefore, insisting that he will not eat or drink again until the kingdom arrives is tantamount to explaining that this meal has a final and unsurpassable symbolic significance, that it is his last word spoken, as it were, in the shadow of the eternal, and thus redolent of the divine order. The room of the Last Supper is Isaiah's holy mountain, and the meal that Jesus hosts is the "feast of rich food, a feast of well-aged wines" (Isa. 25:6). It is as though the longed-for future has appeared even now in time.

What stood at the heart of this event? Jesus took the unleavened bread of the Passover, the bread symbolic of Israel's hasty flight from slavery to freedom, blessed it in accord with the traditional Passover prayer of blessing, broke it, and distributed it to his disciples saying, "This is my body, which is given for you. Do this in remembrance of me." And then, after they had eaten, he took a cup of wine—traditionally called the cup of blessing—and said, "This cup that is poured out for you is the new covenant in my blood."

In order to appreciate these perhaps overly familiar words, we have to put ourselves in the thought world of Jesus' first audience. As they heard these extraordinary statements, the Apostles were undoubtedly hearing overtones and resonances from the scriptural and liturgical tradition. Jesus was using the Passover supper to give a definitive interpretation to the actions that he would take the next day, Good Friday. As this bread is broken and shared, so, he was saying, my body tomorrow will be broken and offered; as this cup is poured out, so my blood tomorrow will be poured out in sacrifice. His body, he was implying, will be like the animals offered by Abraham when God struck a covenant with him, and his blood will be like the bulls' blood sprinkled by Moses on the altar and on the people, sealing the agreement of the Torah. In his crucified body, he will be like the Passover lamb slaughtered in the temple, signifying Israel's total commitment to Yahweh and Yahweh's to Israel. Moreover, his body will be like that of Isaac as he waited for the knife of his father to fall, with the telling difference that Jesus' Father will carry through the sacrifice.

And if we attend carefully to the words over the cup, we can't help but see that his act on the cross will be the condition for the possibility of the perfect covenant of which Jeremiah dreamed. When Jesus said, "This cup that is poured out for you is the new covenant in my blood," his disciples certainly thought of the promise that one day Yahweh would effect a fully realized union with his people. And when they heard that this covenant was to be accompanied by the shedding of blood, how could they not think of the link between Jeremiah's dream and the suffering servant of Isaiah?

In sum, the words of Jesus over the bread and cup at the Last Supper effected a stunning gathering of the variety of strands of covenantal and sacrificial theology in the Hebrew Scriptures. The covenants and their accompanying sacrifices that mark the entire religious history of the Jews are being recapitulated, Jesus says, in me and my sacrifice.

But to say "body" and "blood," in the nondualist context of first-century Judaism, is to say "self." And since Jesus' word is the divine Word, it is not merely descriptive but transformative. It creates, sustains, and changes reality at the most fundamental level. Thus Jesus was also inviting his disciples to feed on his very self and thereby to draw his life into theirs, conforming themselves to him in the most intimate and complete way possible. What was foreshadowed when Mary laid the Christ child in the manger came, at this meal, to full expression.

Why did Jesus invite his disciples to consume the bread and wine that he had radically identified with the sacrifice of his body and blood? In Jeremiah's prophecy of the New Covenant, Yahweh had said, "I will put my law within them, and I will write it on their hearts" (Jer. 31:33). This means that the everlasting agreement would be written not on stone tablets, but in the flesh of the people's hearts; it would be not an oppressive law externally imposed, but a rule congruent with the deepest longing of the human soul. Jesus thus wanted them to ingest his sacrifice so as to appropriate it in the most intimate, organic way, making it bone of their bone and flesh of their flesh. Thomas Aquinas commented that the Old Law of the Torah and the various covenants had a mitigated effectiveness, precisely because they appeared as external to the human heart. But, he continued, the New Law of the Gospel is efficacious because it is realized internally, through the identification of Christ and his Body the Church. And nowhere is this identification more complete than in the Eucharist, when a disciple physically consumes the incarnate Christ, the Law par excellence.

Finally, we must never keep the account of the fall far from our minds when we consider these events. If trouble began with a bad meal (seizing at godliness on our own terms), then our salvation commences with a rightly structured meal (God offering us his life as a free gift). But it is of great moment that, immediately after this extraordinary event—this constitution of the Church around God's gift of self—Jesus speaks of treachery: "But see, the one who betrays me is with me, and his hand is on the table." In the biblical reading, God's desires have been, from the beginning, opposed. Consistently, human beings have preferred the isolation and separation of sin to the festivity of the sacred meal. Theologians have called this anomalous tendency the *mysterium iniquitatis* (the mystery of evil), for there is no rational ground for it, no reason why it should exist. But there it stubbornly is, always shadowing the good, parasitic upon that which it tries to destroy. Therefore, we should not be too surprised that, as the sacred meal comes to its richest possible expression, evil accompanies it. Judas the betrayer expresses the *mysterium iniquitatis* with particular symbolic power, for he had spent years in intimacy with Jesus, taking in the Lord's moves and thoughts at close quarters, sharing the table of fellowship with him, and yet he saw fit to turn Jesus over to his enemies and to interrupt the coinherence of the Last Supper. Those of us who regularly gather around the table of intimacy with Christ and yet engage consistently in the works of darkness are meant to see ourselves in the betrayer.

What follows is a scene that, were it not so tragic, would be funny. Having experienced at firsthand the intense act of love by which Jesus formed a new humanity around the eating of his Body and the drinking of his Blood, having sensed that the deepest meaning of this new life is self-sacrificing love, the disciples quarrel about titles and honors: "A dispute also arose among them as to which one of them was to be regarded as the greatest." In the table fellowship that he practiced throughout his ministry, Jesus consistently undermined the systems of domination and the social stratifications that marked the culture of his time. His order (God's kingdom) would be characterized by an equality and mutuality born of our shared relationship to the Creator God, who "makes his sun rise on the evil and on the good" (Matt. 5:45). Therefore, games of ambition and claims of social superiority are inimical to the community that finds its point of orientation around the table of Jesus' Body and Blood. And this is why Jesus responded so promptly and unambiguously to the disciples' childish preoccupations: "The kings of the Gentiles lord it over them; and those in authority over them are called benefactors. But not so with you; rather the greatest among you must become like the youngest, and the leader like one who serves."

If, as Feuerbach said, we are what we eat, then those who eat the Flesh of Jesus and drink his Blood must constitute a new society, grounded in love, service, nonviolence, and nondomination. Reminding them of their crucial importance as the first members of the Church, Jesus said, "I confer on you, just as my Father has conferred on me, a kingdom … and you will sit on thrones judging the twelve tribes of Israel." The order of love that obtains within God became flesh in Jesus and, through Jesus, was given to the community that he founded. That community in turn, the new Israel, would be, in accord with Isaiah's prediction, the means by which the whole world would be gathered to God. Here the story of the multiplication of the loaves and fish comes to mind. Initially, the disciples refused their mission to be the new Israel and feed the crowd, but then, in light of the miracle of grace, they became the distributors of grace. A very similar dynamic is on display in the account of the Last Supper. It is never enough simply to eat and drink the Body and Blood of Jesus; one must become a bearer of the power that one has received. The meal always conduces to the mission.

THE DISPUTE ABOUT GREATNESS

²⁴ A dispute also arose among them as to which one of them was to be regarded as the greatest. ²⁵ But he said to them, "The kings of the Gentiles lord it over them; and those in authority over them are called benefactors. ²⁶ But not so with you; rather the greatest among you must become like the youngest, and the leader like one who serves. ²⁷ For who is greater, the one who is at the table or the one who serves? Is it not the one at the table? But I am among you as one who serves.

²⁸ "You are those who have stood by me in my trials; ²⁹ and I confer on you, just as my Father has conferred on me, a kingdom, ³⁰ so that you may eat and drink at my table in my kingdom, and you will sit on thrones judging the twelve tribes of Israel.

JESUS PREDICTS PETER'S DENIAL

³¹ "Simon, Simon, listen! Satan has demanded to sift all of you like wheat, ³² but I have prayed for you that your own faith may not fail; and you, when once you have turned back, strengthen your brothers." ³³ And he said to him, "Lord, I am ready to go with you to prison and to death!" ³⁴ Jesus said, "I tell you, Peter, the cock will not crow this day, until you have denied three times that you know me."

PURSE, BAG, AND SWORD

³⁵ He said to them, "When I sent you out without a purse, bag, or sandals, did you lack anything?" They said, "No, not a thing." ³⁶ He said to them, "But now, the one who has a purse must take it, and likewise a bag. And the one who has no sword must sell his cloak and buy one. ³⁷ For I tell you, this scripture must be fulfilled in me, 'And he was counted among the lawless'; and indeed what is written about me is being fulfilled." ³⁸ They said, "Lord, look, here are two swords." He replied, "It is enough."

JESUS PRAYS ON THE MOUNT OF OLIVES

³⁹ He came out and went, as was his custom, to the Mount of Olives; and the disciples followed him. ⁴⁰ When he reached the place, he said to them, "Pray that you may not come into the time of trial." ⁴¹ Then he withdrew from them about a stone's throw, knelt down, and prayed, ⁴² "Father, if you are willing, remove this cup from me; yet, not my will but yours be done." ⁴³ Then an angel from heaven appeared to him and gave him strength. ⁴⁴ In his anguish he prayed more earnestly, and his sweat became like great drops of blood falling down on the ground. ⁴⁵ When he got up from prayer, he came to the disciples and found them sleeping because of grief, ⁴⁶ and he said to them, "Why are you sleeping? Get up and pray that you may not come into the time of trial."

The lamb's wool

The Passover lamb was required to be without blemish, and here we can see that the lamb's wool is spotless and pure. This parallels Christ's innocence in the eyes of God and his role as a pure sacrifice on behalf of sinners.

Tied feet

The lamb's feet have been tied for the slaughter, yet there is no indication of resistance or struggle. This reflects the prophecy about Christ in Isaiah 53:7:

"He was oppressed, and he was afflicted,
yet he did not open his mouth;
like a lamb that is led to the slaughter,
and like a sheep that before its shearers is silent,
so he did not open his mouth."

FRANCISCO DE ZURBARÁN | *1635–1640*

Agnus Dei

Essay by Michael Stevens

In this detailed painting by Francisco de Zurbarán, what appears to be a simple still-life painting of an ordinary lamb turns out to be one of the most complex and paradoxical symbols of Jesus.

The Hebrew custom of the Passover meal comes from the twelfth chapter of Exodus, where "the destroyer" (Exod. 12:23), or Angel of Death, passed over the households of the Jews who were captive in Egypt, allowing them to escape from slavery into freedom. Prior to their escape, God commanded the sacrificing of a spotless lamb, whose blood was then used to mark the doors of the Israelite households. The lamb was then eaten in a sacred meal that took place the night before the Hebrews fled, in anticipation of their journey ahead. That night, when the Angel of Death visited, each door that was covered by the blood of the lamb was safe from the final plague that struck the Egyptians.

Read within the context of the person of Jesus, the image of the Passover lamb powerfully foreshadows the sacrifice of Jesus on the cross, whose blood, like the paschal lamb, saves us from death and frees us from the shackles of sin. The fact that the Passover meal required the physical eating of the flesh of the lamb is of crucial significance as well: in the same way, we as Catholics eat the Flesh of Jesus in the Mass. Furthermore, Jesus' institution of the Eucharist at the Last Supper took place on the night of Passover, during this very meal. All of this helps us to see clearly that Christ is the New Lamb, whose blood and sacrifice set us free.

G.K. Chesterton
(1874–1936)

———

Orthodoxy

He Who Has No Sword Must Buy One

Luke 22:36

These are the kind of thoughts which in combination create the impression that Christianity is something weak and diseased. First, for instance, that Jesus was a gentle creature, sheepish and unworldly, a mere ineffectual appeal to the world; second, that Christianity arose and flourished in the dark ages of ignorance, and that to these the Church would drag us back; third, that the people still strongly religious or (if you will) superstitious—such people as the Irish—are weak, unpractical, and behind the times.

I only mention these ideas to affirm the same thing: that when I looked into them independently I found, not that the conclusions were unphilosophical, but simply that the facts were not facts. Instead of looking at books and pictures about the New Testament I looked at the New Testament. There I found an account, not in the least of a person with his hair parted in the middle or his hands clasped in appeal, but of an extraordinary being with lips of thunder and acts of lurid decision, flinging down tables, casting out devils, passing with the wild secrecy of the wind from mountain isolation to a sort of dreadful demagogy; a being who often acted like an angry god—and always like a god.

Christ had even a literary style of his own, not to be found, I think, elsewhere; it consists of an almost furious use of the *a fortiori*. His "how much more" is piled one upon another like castle upon castle in the clouds. The diction used about Christ has been, and perhaps wisely, sweet and submissive. But the diction used by Christ is quite curiously gigantesque; it is full of camels leaping through needles and mountains hurled into the sea.

Morally it is equally terrific; he called himself a sword of slaughter, and told men to buy swords if they sold their coats for them. That he used other even wilder words on the side of non-resistance greatly increases the mystery; but it also, if anything, rather increases the violence. We cannot even explain it by calling such a being insane; for insanity is usually along one consistent channel. The maniac is generally a monomaniac. Here we must remember the difficult definition of Christianity already given; Christianity is a superhuman paradox whereby two opposite passions may blaze beside each other. The one explanation of the Gospel language that does explain it, is that it is the survey of one who from some supernatural height beholds some more startling synthesis.

THE BETRAYAL AND ARREST OF JESUS

⁴⁷ While he was still speaking, suddenly a crowd came, and the one called Judas, one of the twelve, was leading them. He approached Jesus to kiss him; ⁴⁸ but Jesus said to him, "Judas, is it with a kiss that you are betraying the Son of Man?" ⁴⁹ When those who were around him saw what was coming, they asked, "Lord, should we strike with the sword?" ⁵⁰ Then one of them struck the slave of the high priest and cut off his right ear. ⁵¹ But Jesus said, "No more of this!" And he touched his ear and healed him. ⁵² Then Jesus said to the chief priests, the officers of the temple police, and the elders who had come for him, "Have you come out with swords and clubs as if I were a bandit? ⁵³ When I was with you day after day in the temple, you did not lay hands on me. But this is your hour, and the power of darkness!"

PETER DENIES JESUS

⁵⁴ Then they seized him and led him away, bringing him into the high priest's house. But Peter was following at a distance. ⁵⁵ When they had kindled a fire in the middle of the courtyard and sat down together, Peter sat among

them. ⁵⁶ Then a servant-girl, seeing him in the firelight, stared at him and said, "This man also was with him." ⁵⁷ But he denied it, saying, "Woman, I do not know him." ⁵⁸ A little later someone else, on seeing him, said, "You also are one of them." But Peter said, "Man, I am not!" ⁵⁹ Then about an hour later still another kept insisting, "Surely this man also was with him; for he is a Galilean." ⁶⁰ But Peter said, "Man, I do not know what you are talking about!" At that moment, while he was still speaking, the cock crowed. ⁶¹ The Lord turned and looked at Peter. Then Peter remembered the word of the Lord, how he had said to him, "Before the cock crows today, you will deny me three times." ⁶² And he went out and wept bitterly.

THE MOCKING AND BEATING OF JESUS

⁶³ Now the men who were holding Jesus began to mock him and beat him; ⁶⁴ they also blindfolded him and kept asking him, "Prophesy! Who is it that struck you?" ⁶⁵ They kept heaping many other insults on him.

JESUS BEFORE THE COUNCIL

⁶⁶ When day came, the assembly of the elders of the people, both chief priests and scribes, gathered together, and they brought him to their council. ⁶⁷ They said, "If you are the Messiah, tell us." He replied, "If I tell you, you will not believe; ⁶⁸ and if I question you, you will not answer. ⁶⁹ But from now on the Son of Man will be seated at the right hand of the power of God." ⁷⁰ All of them asked, "Are you, then, the Son of God?" He said to them, "You say that I am." ⁷¹ Then they said, "What further testimony do we need? We have heard it ourselves from his own lips!"

JESUS BEFORE PILATE

23 Then the assembly rose as a body and brought Jesus before Pilate. ² They began to accuse him, saying, "We found this man perverting our nation, forbidding us to pay taxes to the emperor, and saying that he himself is the Messiah, a king." ³ Then Pilate asked him, "Are you the king of the Jews?" He answered, "You say so." ⁴ Then Pilate said to the chief priests and the crowds, "I find no basis for an accusation against this man." ⁵ But they were insistent and said, "He stirs up the people by teaching throughout all Judea, from Galilee where he began even to this place."

JESUS BEFORE HEROD

⁶ When Pilate heard this, he asked whether the man was a Galilean. ⁷ And when he learned that he was under Herod's jurisdiction, he sent him off to Herod, who was himself in Jerusalem at that time. ⁸ When Herod saw Jesus, he was very glad, for he had been wanting to see him for a long time, because he had heard about him and was hoping to see him perform some

sign. [9] He questioned him at some length, but Jesus gave him no answer. [10] The chief priests and the scribes stood by, vehemently accusing him. [11] Even Herod with his soldiers treated him with contempt and mocked him; then he put an elegant robe on him, and sent him back to Pilate. [12] That same day Herod and Pilate became friends with each other; before this they had been enemies.

JESUS SENTENCED TO DEATH

[13] Pilate then called together the chief priests, the leaders, and the people, [14] and said to them, "You brought me this man as one who was perverting the people; and here I have examined him in your presence and have not found this man guilty of any of your charges against him. [15] Neither has Herod, for he sent him back to us. Indeed, he has done nothing to deserve death. [16] I will therefore have him flogged and release him."

[18] Then they all shouted out together, "Away with this fellow! Release Barabbas for us!" [19] (This was a man who had been put in prison for an insurrection that had taken place in the city, and for murder.) [20] Pilate,

---

St. Cyril of Alexandria
(354–430)

Commentary on Luke

Tree of Adam, Tree of Christ

Luke 23:33

Consider how the Savior and Lord of all, by whom the Father brought all things into existence, now refashions human nature, restoring it to its intended state. The first man [Adam] began in a paradise of delight … but when he spurned the lone commandment which he had been given he fell under a curse and into condemnation, eating the fruit of a forbidden tree.

Now, Christ becomes the fruit of a different tree [the cross] … that he might crown our nature with his own glory.

Is not this mystery profound? Must we not confess that this plan is more sublime than language can describe?

wanting to release Jesus, addressed them again; ²¹ but they kept shouting, "Crucify, crucify him!" ²² A third time he said to them, "Why, what evil has he done? I have found in him no ground for the sentence of death; I will therefore have him flogged and then release him." ²³ But they kept urgently demanding with loud shouts that he should be crucified; and their voices prevailed. ²⁴ So Pilate gave his verdict that their demand should be granted. ²⁵ He released the man they asked for, the one who had been put in prison for insurrection and murder, and he handed Jesus over as they wished.

THE CRUCIFIXION OF JESUS

²⁶ As they led him away, they seized a man, Simon of Cyrene, who was coming from the country, and they laid the cross on him, and made him carry it behind Jesus. ²⁷ A great number of the people followed him, and among them were women who were beating their breasts and wailing for him. ²⁸ But Jesus turned to them and said, "Daughters of Jerusalem, do not weep for me, but weep for yourselves and for your children. ²⁹ For the days are

St. Francis de Sales
(1567–1622)

Introduction to the Devout Life

Not Judging Our Neighbor

Luke 23:34

A just man, when he can no longer excuse either the action or the intention of someone who acts wrongly, nevertheless will not judge him, but puts the remembrance of it out of his mind, and leaves the judgment to God.

Thus, Jesus on the cross, not being able altogether to excuse the sin of those that crucified him, yet at least extenuated the malice of it by alleging their ignorance.

When we cannot excuse the sin, let us at least render it deserving of compassion, attributing it to the most favorable cause, such as ignorance or weakness.

But may we never then judge our neighbor? No, truly, never.

surely coming when they will say, 'Blessed are the barren, and the wombs that never bore, and the breasts that never nursed.' [30] Then they will begin to say to the mountains, 'Fall on us'; and to the hills, 'Cover us.' [31] For if they do this when the wood is green, what will happen when it is dry?"

[32] Two others also, who were criminals, were led away to be put to death with him. [33] When they came to the place that is called The Skull, they crucified Jesus there with the criminals, one on his right and one on his left. [34] Then Jesus said, "Father, forgive them; for they do not know what they are doing." And they cast lots to divide his clothing. [35] And the people stood by, watching; but the leaders scoffed at him, saying, "He saved others; let him save himself if he is the Messiah of God, his chosen one!" [36] The soldiers also mocked him, coming up and offering him sour wine, [37] and saying, "If you are the King of the Jews, save yourself!" [38] There was also an inscription over him, "This is the King of the Jews."

Drowning All the Sins of the World

Luke 23:34 | Bishop Barron

Jesus permitted the darkness of the world to envelop him. In the densely textured Passion narratives of the Gospels we see all forms of human dysfunction on display. Jesus was met by betrayal, denial, institutional corruption, violence, stupidity, deep injustice, and incomparable cruelty, but he did not respond in kind. Rather, like the scapegoat, upon whom "all the iniquities of the people of Israel" (Lev. 16:21) were symbolically placed on the Day of Atonement, Jesus took upon himself the sins of the world. As he hung from the cross, he became sin, as St. Paul would later put it, and bearing the full weight of that disorder he said, "Father, forgive them; for they do not know what they are doing."

Jesus on the cross drowned all the sins of the world in the infinite ocean of the divine mercy, and that is how he fought. We can see here how important it is to affirm the divinity of Jesus, for if he were only a human being, his death on the cross would be, at best, an inspiring example of dedication and courage. But as the Son of God, Jesus died a death that transfigured the world.

The theological tradition has said that God the Father was pleased with this sacrifice of his Son, but we should never interpret this along sadistic lines, as though the Father needed to see the suffering of his Son in order to assuage his infinite anger. The Father loved the willingness of the Son to go to the very limits of godforsakenness—all the way to the bottom of sin—in order to manifest the divine mercy.

René Girard
(1923–2015)

The Scapegoat

They Do Not Know What They Are Doing

Luke 23:34

"Father, forgive them; for they do not know what they are doing." Christians insist here on the goodness of Jesus. This would be fine were it not that their insistence eclipses the sentence's real meaning, which is scarcely ever recognized. The commentary on this sentence implies that the desire to forgive unpardonable executors forces Jesus to invent a somewhat trifling excuse for them that hardly conforms to the reality of the Passion.

Commentators who refuse to believe what this sentence says can only feel faint admiration for it, and their devotion imbues the text with the taint of their own hypocrisy. The most terrible distortion of the Gospels is our ability to project our own hypocrisy on them. In reality the Gospels never seek lame excuses; they never speak for the sake of speaking; sentimental verbiage has no place in them.

If we are to restore to this sentence its true savor we must recognize its almost technical role in the revelation of the scapegoat mechanism. It says something precise about the men gathered together by their scapegoat. They do not know what they are doing. That is why they must be pardoned. This is not dictated by a persecution complex or by the desire to remove from our sight the horror of real violence.

[39] One of the criminals who were hanged there kept deriding him and saying, "Are you not the Messiah? Save yourself and us!" [40] But the other rebuked him, saying, "Do you not fear God, since you are under the same sentence of condemnation? [41] And we indeed have been condemned justly, for we are getting what we deserve for our deeds, but this man has done nothing wrong." [42] Then he said, "Jesus, remember me when you come

into your kingdom." ⁴³ He replied, "Truly I tell you, today you will be with me in Paradise."

THE DEATH OF JESUS

⁴⁴ It was now about noon, and darkness came over the whole land until three in the afternoon, ⁴⁵ while the sun's light failed; and the curtain of the temple was torn in two. ⁴⁶ Then Jesus, crying with a loud voice, said, "Father, into your hands I commend my spirit." Having said this, he breathed his last. ⁴⁷ When the centurion saw what had taken place, he praised God and said, "Certainly this man was innocent." ⁴⁸ And when all the crowds who had gathered there for this spectacle saw what had taken place, they returned home, beating their breasts. ⁴⁹ But all his acquaintances, including the women who had followed him from Galilee, stood at a distance, watching these things.

THE BURIAL OF JESUS

⁵⁰ Now there was a good and righteous man named Joseph, who, though a member of the council, ⁵¹ had not agreed to their plan and action. He came from the Jewish town of Arimathea, and he was waiting expectantly for the kingdom of God. ⁵² This man went to Pilate and asked for the body of Jesus. ⁵³ Then he took it down, wrapped it in a linen cloth, and laid it in a rock-hewn tomb where no one had ever been laid. ⁵⁴ It was the day of Preparation, and the sabbath was beginning. ⁵⁵ The women who had come with him from Galilee followed, and they saw the tomb and how his body was laid. ⁵⁶ Then they returned, and prepared spices and ointments.

On the sabbath they rested according to the commandment.

The Way Up Is Down

Luke 23:44-49 | Bishop Barron

On the cross of Jesus, we meet our own sin, but we can't stop telling the story at this point. Dante and every other spiritual master know that the only way up is down. When we live in convenient darkness, unaware of our sins, we will never make spiritual progress. So we need the light, however painful it is. Only then can we begin to rise. Once Dante made it all the way to the center of hell, he suddenly found himself climbing out.

That's why on the cross, we also meet the divine mercy that has taken that sin upon himself in order to swallow it up. In other words, we have found, in that cross, the way up. And this is precisely why the Church celebrates the cross. We want to hold up this thing that was considered too horrible to look at. We want to embrace and kiss the very source of our pain.

Christ's skin

Christ is covered with small red spots, which look identical to the telltale symptoms of St. Anthony's Fire. By including such an explicit visual reference to the disease, Grünewald allowed the viewers to truly see themselves in the narrative of the artwork.

Christ's feet divided below the knee

One of the terrible sufferings that often came with St. Anthony's Fire was amputation of the legs. Here, the artist splits the composition of the panels just below Jesus' knee to allude to an amputation, encouraging the viewer to draw strength from the pain that Christ endured on Calvary.

Luke 23:26–49

MATTHIAS GRÜNEWALD | *1512–1516*

The Isenheim Altarpiece

Essay by Michael Stevens

This altarpiece, painted by Matthias Grünewald, is one of the most brutal depictions of Christ's Crucifixion in the history of art. Every feature of Christ's body expresses the misery of his Passion, from his gnarled, open, straining hands, to his contorted feet that buckle under his bodyweight.

The profound suffering of Jesus is echoed in the poses and expressions of the Apostle John, Mary the mother of Jesus, and Mary Magdalene, who are shown to the left of the cross weeping bitterly at the horror they are witnessing. To the right, John the Baptist is portrayed pointing at Christ, with Christ the Lamb of God at his feet.

This piece was painted for the Monastery of St. Anthony, which provided medical care for people suffering from the disease of Erysipelas, also known as St. Anthony's Fire, which was common in the medieval period. This fungal disease causes intensely painful red welts on the skin, and at the time, often required amputation.

Because Grünewald knew that the people viewing this altarpiece were often suffering the terrible symptoms of this disease, Christ himself presents its symptoms from the cross, thereby uniting the miseries of the illness to the redemptive power of his Passion. In the lower composition, the dead Christ is positioned so that his legs are split just below the knee by the separation between the left and right panels, which recalls the amputations that took place in the hospital. Again, this is meant to signify Jesus' level of empathy with our human suffering, and remind us that no matter how great our own pains, his agony on the cross—later conquered by the Resurrection—was greater still.

Pope St. John Paul II
(1920–2005)

Evangelium Vitae

Darkness Came Over the Whole Land

Luke 23:44–48

Looking at "the spectacle" of the cross we shall discover in this glorious tree the fulfillment and the complete revelation of the whole Gospel of life.

In the early afternoon of Good Friday, "darkness came over the whole land…while the sun's light failed; and the curtain of the temple was torn in two." This is the symbol of a great cosmic disturbance and a massive conflict between the forces of good and the forces of evil, between life and death. Today we too find ourselves in the midst of a dramatic conflict between the "culture of death" and the "culture of life." But the glory of the cross is not overcome by this darkness; rather, it shines forth ever more radiantly and brightly, and is revealed as the center, meaning, and goal of all history and of every human life.

THE RESURRECTION OF JESUS

24 But on the first day of the week, at early dawn, they came to the tomb, taking the spices that they had prepared. [2] They found the stone rolled away from the tomb, [3] but when they went in, they did not find the body. [4] While they were perplexed about this, suddenly two men in dazzling clothes stood beside them. [5] The women were terrified and bowed their faces to the ground, but the men said to them, "Why do you look for the living among the dead? He is not here, but has risen. [6] Remember how he told you, while he was still in Galilee, [7] that the Son of Man must be handed over to sinners, and be crucified, and on the third day rise again." [8] Then they remembered his words, [9] and returning from the tomb, they told all this to the eleven and to all the rest. [10] Now it was Mary Magdalene, Joanna, Mary the mother of James, and the other women with them who told this to the apostles. [11] But these words seemed to them an idle tale, and they did not believe them. [12] But Peter got up and ran to the tomb;

Death Doesn't Have the Final Word

Luke 24:1–12 | Bishop Barron

Notice the startling realism with which Luke depicts the Resurrection. Even in Luke's time—toward the end of the first century—there were people who wanted to explain away the Resurrection or to soften it into symbolic language. There are many who advocate this position today, of course.

In light of the Resurrection, we know that God's deepest intention for us is life, and life to the full. He wants death not to have the final word; he wants a renewal of the heavens and the earth. Therefore, we have to stop living in the intellectual and spiritual space of death.

What if we really believed, deep down, that death did not have the final word? Would we live in such fear, in such a cramped spiritual space? Or would we see that the protection of our egos is not the number one concern of our existence?

---

stooping and looking in, he saw the linen cloths by themselves; then he went home, amazed at what had happened.

THE WALK TO EMMAUS

[13] Now on that same day two of them were going to a village called Emmaus, about seven miles from Jerusalem, [14] and talking with each other about all these things that had happened. [15] While they were talking and discussing, Jesus himself came near and went with them, [16] but their eyes were kept from recognizing him. [17] And he said to them, "What are you discussing with each other while you walk along?" They stood still, looking sad. [18] Then one of them, whose name was Cleopas, answered him, "Are you the only stranger in Jerusalem who does not know the things that have taken place there in these days?" [19] He asked them, "What things?" They replied, "The things about Jesus of Nazareth, who was a prophet mighty in deed and word before God and all the people, [20] and how our chief priests and leaders handed him over to be condemned to death and crucified him. [21] But we had hoped that he was the one to redeem Israel. Yes, and besides all this, it is now the third day since these things took place. [22] Moreover, some women of our group astounded us. They were at the tomb early this morning, [23] and when they did not find his body there, they came back and told us that they had indeed seen a vision of angels who said that he was alive. [24] Some of those who were with us went to the tomb and found it just as the women had said; but they did not see him." [25] Then he said

to them, "Oh, how foolish you are, and how slow of heart to believe all that the prophets have declared! [26] Was it not necessary that the Messiah should suffer these things and then enter into his glory?" [27] Then beginning with Moses and all the prophets, he interpreted to them the things about himself in all the scriptures.

[28] As they came near the village to which they were going, he walked ahead as if he were going on. [29] But they urged him strongly, saying, "Stay with us, because it is almost evening and the day is now nearly over." So he went in to stay with them. [30] When he was at the table with them, he took bread, blessed and broke it, and gave it to them. [31] Then their eyes were opened, and they recognized him; and he vanished from their sight. [32] They said to each other, "Were not our hearts burning within us while he was talking to us on the road, while he was opening the scriptures to us?" [33] That same hour they got up and returned to Jerusalem; and they found the eleven and their companions gathered together. [34] They were saying, "The Lord has risen indeed, and he has appeared to Simon!" [35] Then they told what had happened on the road, and how he had been made known to them in the breaking of the bread.

The LORD HAS RISEN INDEED!

LUKE 24:34

The Emmaus Journey

Luke 24:13–35 | Bishop Barron

THE EMMAUS STORY opens with two people going the wrong way. The entire momentum of Luke's Gospel is in the direction of Jerusalem. It is to that city that Jesus sets his face; it is there that he cleanses the temple, celebrates his Last Supper, does battle with the enemies of Israel, rises from the dead; and it is there that he sends the Holy Spirit for the formation of the Church. Jerusalem is Mt. Zion, true pole of the earth, to which all the tribes of the Lord are called. Therefore, these two erstwhile followers of Jesus, heading away from the holy city, are going decidedly in the wrong direction, against the grain.

Jesus joins them on their journey—though we are told that they are prevented from recognizing him—and he asks them what they are talking about. Throughout his ministry, Jesus associated with sinners. He stood shoulder to shoulder in the muddy waters of the Jordan with those seeking forgiveness through the baptism of John; over and over again, he ate and drank with disreputable types, much to the chagrin of the self-righteous; and at the end of his life he was crucified between two thieves. Jesus hated sin, but he liked sinners and was consistently willing to move into their world and to engage them on their terms.

Prompted by Jesus' curious questions, one of the travelers, Cleopas by name, recounts all of the "things" concerning Jesus of Nazareth. Cleopas has all of the "facts" straight; there is not one thing he says about Jesus that is wrong. But his sadness and his flight from Jerusalem testify that he doesn't see the whole picture. He is like someone who has heard every word of a joke, but doesn't "get it" and hence can't laugh.

I love the clever and funny cartoons in the *New Yorker* magazine, but occasionally there is a cartoon I just don't understand. I've taken in all of the details; I've seen the main characters and the objects around them; I've understood the caption. Yet I don't see why it's funny. And then there comes a moment of illumination: though I haven't seen any further detail, though no new piece of the puzzle has emerged, I discern the pattern that connects them together in a meaningful way. In a word, I "get" the cartoon.

Having heard Cleopas' account, Jesus says, "Oh, how foolish you are, and how slow of heart to believe all that the prophets have declared!" And then he opens the Scriptures to them, disclosing the great biblical patterns that make sense of the "things" that they have witnessed. The still-hidden Christ applies the hermeneutic that enables his dejected disciples to understand the whole of Scripture and hence the whole of God's purpose. And that interpretive key is none other than his own suffering and death, his willingness to go to the limits of godforsakenness in order to save those who had wandered from the divine love. He demonstrated, we presume, that the narrative commencing with Adam and Eve, continuing through Abraham, Isaac, Jacob, Moses, David, Isaiah, and Jeremiah, centered around and pointed to a sacrificial love so complete that, by it, the effects of sin are undone.

Without revealing to them any new detail about himself, Jesus shows them the form, the overarching design, the meaning—and through this process they begin to "get" him: they begin to understand the Bible in its totality, and their hearts burn within them. Without these clarifying forms, human life is a hodgepodge, a blur of events, a string of meaningless happenings.

The two disciples press him to stay with them as they draw near the town of Emmaus. Jesus sits down with them, takes bread, says the blessing, breaks it, and gives it to them, and in that moment they recognize him. Though they were, through the mediation of Scripture, beginning to see, they still did not fully grasp who he was. But in the Eucharistic moment, in the breaking of the bread, their eyes are opened.

The ultimate means by which we understand Jesus Christ is not the Scriptures but the Eucharist, for the Eucharist is Christ himself, personally and actively present. The embodiment of the Paschal Mystery, the Eucharist is Jesus' love for the world unto death, his journey into godforsakenness in order to save the most desperate of sinners, his heart broken open in compassion. And this is why it is through the lens of the Eucharist that Jesus comes most fully and vividly into focus.

In fact, as many commentators have pointed out over the centuries, this narrative is a symbolic presentation of the liturgy. We come to Mass, like these two disciples, often walking in the wrong direction. This is why we beg, in the *Kyrie Eleison*, for the forgiveness of our sins. But Jesus, with infinite patience, comes to join us, opening up for us the meaning of the Scriptures, showing us once again how the Old Testament story culminates in and centers around him. This is the Liturgy of the Word. Though this illumination is necessary, it is not sufficient. We don't fully understand who Jesus is until we sit down with him at the sacred sacrificial banquet that makes present his saving cross. In the Liturgy of the Eucharist, in the breaking of the bread and the drinking of the cup, we see him in his Real Presence. Finally, having seen, we move, presumably in a more correct direction. At the close of the liturgy, we are sent: "Go forth, the Mass is ended." Hans Urs von Balthasar said that Jesus vanished immediately after being recognized by the two Emmaus disciples because he disappears into the mission of the Church. So the Eucharistic Christ becomes our mission, our work.

JESUS APPEARS TO HIS DISCIPLES

[36] While they were talking about this, Jesus himself stood among them and said to them, "Peace be with you." [37] They were startled and terrified, and thought that they were seeing a ghost. [38] He said to them, "Why are you frightened, and why do doubts arise in your hearts? [39] Look at my hands and my feet; see that it is I myself. Touch me and see; for a ghost does not have flesh and bones as you see that I have." [40] And when he had said this, he showed them his hands and his feet. [41] While in their joy they were disbelieving and still wondering, he said to them, "Have you anything here to eat?" [42] They gave him a piece of broiled fish, [43] and he took it and ate in their presence.

The hand of Christ

The hand of Christ is raised in blessing in a way that is directly modeled on the actions of the priest in the Mass. It is no coincidence that this was the moment the disciples recognized Jesus—at the moment of consecration.

The bystander

A bystander in the background appears unmoved and oblivious to the miraculous nature of the scene that is unfolding. This is meant to symbolize all nonbelievers whose eyes have not yet been opened to the person of Jesus.

The still life

The still life formed by the food on the table could easily stand alone as a painting unto itself. The level of detail and smoothness of the brushwork creates an incredibly lifelike effect—as if one could reach out and touch the dishes spread out on the tablecloth.

Luke 24:13–35

CARAVAGGIO | *1601*

The Supper at Emmaus

Essay by Michael Stevens

In Caravaggio's *Supper at Emmaus*, we see Cleopas and his companion at the moment they recognize Christ in the breaking of the bread. Cleopas' companion clutches the arms of his chair in disbelief, and leans to look closer at Jesus—as if to confirm his senses are not deceiving him. Cleophas throws out his arms in joy, reaching both forward to the viewer and backward toward Jesus. Together the two figures' reactions combine to show both the intensity of their surprise and the immediacy of their realization. Caravaggio has captured a split second of miraculous power and frozen it in time, allowing us to savor with clarity what these disciples experienced in an instant.

But Caravaggio's goal with this painting was not only to report the experience of these two disciples, but also to draw us in as viewers to become eyewitnesses at the table as well. The artist leaves an open space on the right side with room enough for another chair, representing the invitation to take a seat in the scene. Even the food, which is rendered in spectacular detail, has been pushed over to our side of the table, and draws us to the meal by engaging our appetite. The gestures of the figures pull us into the scene with their extreme foreshortening that breaks out from the picture plan into our space. Even the basket of fruit is positioned to show its bottom edge protruding from the edge of the tabletop—as if it is about to fall right out of the picture onto the gallery floor.

Why did Caravaggio devote so much energy to drawing us into this story? It is because of the all-encompassing significance of the Resurrection. We who recognize that Jesus is not dead, but alive, are never the same, and we must invite everyone—with great urgency—to come and meet him as well.

We Killed God…
and God Still Loves Us

Luke 24:36–40 | Bishop Barron

Luke tells us that, upon seeing the resurrected Jesus, his disciple "were startled and terrified." It is worthwhile dwelling on this fear. On the one hand, it is a terror born of the confrontation with the strange and unknown, that which does not fit into customary categories. But on the other hand, it is a fear derived from guilt. In accord with the plot of most ghost stories, they are terrified because the one they abandoned and betrayed and left for dead is back— undoubtedly for revenge!

As in almost all of the other accounts of the post-Resurrection appearances, Luke's risen Jesus does two things in the presence of his shocked followers. First, he says, "Shalom," or "Peace be with you." This peace, this *shalom*, is the universal well-being that had been longed for throughout the Old Testament, that had indeed been sought ever since Eden. It is the serenity that comes from participating in the very life of God.

Next, he shows them his wounds. This move is a reiteration of the judgment of the cross: don't forget, he tells them, what the world did when the Author of life appeared. A woundless Christ is embraced much more readily by his executioners, since he doesn't remind them of their crime. But the Jesus who stubbornly shows them his wounds will not permit this exculpating forgetfulness.

In this, he opens up a new spiritual world and thereby becomes our Savior. From ancient creation myths to the *Rambo* and *Dirty Harry* movies, the principle is the same: order, destroyed through violence, is restored through a righteous exercise of greater violence. Some agent of chaos is corralled and conquered by fighting him (or it) on his own terms and overpowering him. If domination is the problem (as in the ancient stories), then a counter-domination is the solution; if gun violence is the problem (as in most cop movies), then a bigger and more skillfully handled gun is the solution. And in these myths, God or the gods are customarily invoked as the sanction for the process.

And then there is Jesus. The terrible disorder of the cross (the killing of the Son of God) is addressed not through an explosion of divine vengeance but through a radiation of divine love. When Christ confronts those who contributed to his death, he speaks words not of retribution, but of reconciliation and compassion. Mind you, the awful texture of the disorder is not for a moment overlooked—that is the integrity of the judgment—but the problem is resolved through nonviolence and forgiveness.

We can begin to sense here the source of the ecstatic religious experience of the first believers: we killed God and God still loves us; we have tried, as thoroughly as possible, to distance ourselves from God, and he returns; we performed the most heinous, unthinkable act, and we are still offered peace. What appeared rhetorically in the Sermon on the Mount and more concretely on the cross now shines in all of its transfigured glory. The gods who sanctioned scapegoating and the restoration of order through violence are now revealed to be phony gods, idols, projections of a sinful consciousness, and the true God comes fully into the light.

It is in this way that Jesus "takes away the sin of the world" (John 1:29). The old schemas of handling disorder through vengeance restored a tentative and very unreliable "peace," which was really nothing but a pause between conflicts.

Evil met with evil only intensifies, just as fire met with fire only increases the heat, and an "eye for an eye," as Gandhi noted, succeeds only in eventually making everyone blind. But what takes away violence is a courageous and compassionate nonviolence, just as water, the "opposite" of fire, puts out the flames. On the cross, the Son of God took on the hatred of all of us sinners, and in his forgiving love, he took that hatred away.

By creating a way out of the net of our sinfulness, Jesus did what no mere philosopher, poet, politician, or social reformer could possibly do.

He saved us.

---

⁴⁴ Then he said to them, "These are my words that I spoke to you while I was still with you—that everything written about me in the law of Moses, the prophets, and the psalms must be fulfilled." ⁴⁵ Then he opened their minds to understand the scriptures, ⁴⁶ and he said to them, "Thus it is written, that the Messiah is to suffer and to rise from the dead on the third day, ⁴⁷ and that repentance and forgiveness of sins is to be proclaimed in his name to all nations, beginning from Jerusalem. ⁴⁸ You are witnesses of these things. ⁴⁹ And see, I am sending upon you what my Father promised; so stay here in the city until you have been clothed with power from on high."

THE ASCENSION OF JESUS

⁵⁰ Then he led them out as far as Bethany, and, lifting up his hands, he blessed them. ⁵¹ While he was blessing them, he withdrew from them and was carried up into heaven. ⁵² And they worshiped him, and returned to Jerusalem with great joy; ⁵³ and they were continually in the temple blessing God.

Not a Ghost

Luke 24:39–43 | Bishop Barron

That the Resurrection is a literary device, or a symbol that Jesus' cause goes on, is a fantasy born in the faculty lounges of Western universities over the past couple of centuries. The still-startling claim of the first witnesses is that Jesus rose bodily from death, presenting himself to his disciples to be seen, even handled.

It is a contemporary prejudice that ancient people were naïve, easily duped, willing to believe any far-fetched tale, but this is simply not the case. They knew about visions, dreams, hallucinations, and even claims to ghostly hauntings.

In fact, on St. Luke's telling, when the risen Lord appeared to his disciples in the upper room, their initial reaction was that they were seeing a specter. But Jesus himself moved quickly to allay such suspicions: "Look at my hands and my feet; see that it is I myself. Touch me and see; for a ghost does not have flesh and bones as you see that I have."

While they were, in Luke's words, "disbelieving and still wondering" in "their joy," the risen Jesus asked if there was anything to eat, and then consumed broiled fish in their presence. This has nothing to do with fantasies, abstractions, or velleities, but rather with resurrection at every level.

THE MESSIAH IS TO

SUFFER

and to RISE

FROM THE

DEAD

ON THE THIRD DAY.

LUKE 24:46

THE GOSPEL
ACCORDING
to JOHN

Introduction to the Gospel of John

Abbot Jeremy Driscoll, OSB

YOU ARE ABOUT TO OPEN UP A TREASURE: a profound and enthralling Gospel that offers access to the person of Jesus. The whole is written so that, as the author says at the end, "you may come to believe that Jesus is the Messiah, the Son of God, and that through believing you may have life in his name" (John 20:31). And in fact, that is the effect of a careful reading of this text with an open heart. The reader bends toward belief and begins to feel a new kind of life associated with encountering Jesus.

It is clear that the stories of Jesus' actions and words that the Evangelist recounts are those of someone who knew Jesus well and accompanied him through the crucial years of his ministry (John 19:35). It is also clear that considerable time has passed since the events recounted had occurred, for there is a quality of voice in the narrative indicating that all the stories and words of Jesus have been deeply digested and pondered. They are remembered in that way. I imagine myself meeting such an eyewitness, and with excitement I ask him to tell me what it was like to be with Jesus. I ask him to tell me stories, to tell me the sorts of things he said. But then the beginning of the answer surprises me. He gets a faraway look in his eyes and commences, "In the beginning was the Word, and the Word was with God, and the Word was God" (John 1:1).

Mysterious. Vast. He is going to tell me about Jesus, but the context is before time began and then the beginning of the entire cosmos and creation. The so-called "prologue" of this Gospel (John 1:1–18) is the poetic summary of the whole story, and its atmosphere is meant to permeate and interpret all that follows. It contains the astounding claim that the Word who is God and through whom all things came to be "became flesh and lived among us" (John 1:14). It also contains a summary of the dramatic encounter that shapes the whole text, an encounter that is meant to continue even now for the reader: "He came to what was his own, and his own people did not accept him. But to all who received him, who believed in his name, he gave power to become children of God" (John 1:11–12).

It is useful to think of the story as occurring in two halves. The first half, chapters 1 to 12, tells the first part of the summary: "He came to what was his own, and his own people did not accept him." Jesus works astounding signs: changing water into wine; curing a dying boy from a distance; healing a paralytic; feeding five thousand people with five loaves of bread; restoring sight to a blind man; and finally, raising a man from the dead after he was already four days in the tomb. All of these "signs"—that's the Evangelist's word for them—are meant to point to a meaning, and the meaning lies in Jesus himself. They are meant to reveal the mystery of his person and the reason for his coming among us. And so the signs are followed by discourses in which the hearers either come to faith in Jesus or move away from him and reject him. (A dramatic example is found in John 6:60–71.) They provoke a decision. Are you for or against Jesus? Do you believe in him or not?

I love reading these discourses. I never tire of going over them. I feel Jesus speaking to me through these words and revealing the mystery of his person to me as I ponder their meaning. I see that he is completely caught up in his relationship with his Father, which is his preferred name for God. He says things like "For whatever the Father does, the Son does likewise" (John 5:19); "I declare what I have seen in the Father's presence" (John 8:38); and "The Father and I are one" (John 10:30). This is an amazing and challenging revelation.

The second half (chapters 13 to 21) is arranged differently. Jesus does not work any more astounding signs, and the audience for his words is no longer those who may or may not believe in him. Instead, his words are intimate teachings (chapters 13–17) delivered to his disciples on the night before his death in the context of a supper. This part opens with the moving words: "Having loved his own who were in the world, he loved them to the end" (John 13:1). Then the second half tells the second part of the prologue's summary: "But to all who received him, who believed in his name, he gave power to become children of God." With these intimate teachings, in fact, Jesus is preparing his disciples in advance for the sign that will dominate the action of the second half of the story. The story told now is of the trial of Jesus, his death by crucifixion, and his Resurrection from the dead. And Jesus' teaching about all this in advance reveals that these events are meant to effect for us an incredible intimacy between ourselves and Jesus and his Father. That is the purpose of his death and Resurrection; it is Jesus' intention and the Father's. "No one takes [my life] from me, but I lay it down of my own accord. I have power to lay it down, and I have power to take it up again. I have received this command from my Father" (John 10:18).

Reading carefully and prayerfully these intimate teachings can have the effect of slowly penetrating the reader with a sense of an interior presence of Jesus, opening up the mystery of his person. He says, "Those who love me will keep my word, and my Father will love them, and we will come to them and make our home with them" (John 14:23). And this is what happens; this is the gift of this Gospel.

In chapter 17 we overhear Jesus praying to his Father about us, about what he is asking for from the Father as he goes to his death. This is a prayer that, in virtue of the Resurrection, never ceases to sound before the Father. It reveals Jesus established in the permanent condition of interceding for us. He prays, "The glory that you have given me I have given them, so that they may be one, as we are one, I in them and you in me, that they may become completely one, so that the world may know that you have sent me and have loved them even as you have loved me" (John 17:22–23).

With words and revelations like these, we are prepared to follow with some understanding the awful and awesome events of Jesus' arrest, trial, and Crucifixion (chapters 18–19). He moves with a quiet sovereign dignity through all that happens. Pilate means to put him on trial, but in effect Jesus puts Pilate on trial (John 18:28–38). That Jesus is crucified is, of course, dreadful in the extreme. Yet there is a level at which it can also be understood as his being "lifted up" and drawing "all people" to himself (John 8:28, 12:32). As he dies, he hands his mother over to his beloved disciple John, and him to her (John 19:26–27). And even Jesus' dead body gives life—for when the soldier's lance pierces it, blood and water flow out (John 19:34), signifying the Eucharist and Baptism; which is to say, the blood and water have never stopped flowing, and they continually give life to those who believe in Jesus.

The Resurrection stories that conclude the Gospel are peaceful and joyful. Mary Magdalene comes early in the morning to the tomb but finds that it is open and the body of Jesus is not in it. Panicked, she informs Peter and John, and they run to the tomb and enter it. The body of Jesus is not there, but strangely, the burial clothes are there neatly rolled up. What could it mean? They depart, but then the risen Jesus appears to Mary. She moves to embrace him, but he mysteriously does not allow it. Later he appears and shows himself alive to his disciples, who are in a room with locked doors; and yet Jesus is suddenly standing in their midst. This happened once on the day he rose, and it happened again a week later. On this occasion Thomas places his hand in the nail marks in the hands and in the wounded side of the crucified and now risen body of Jesus, and he exclaims what every reader is also invited to exclaim: "My Lord and my God!" (John 20:28).

The story ends there—except there is an appendix that adds yet another Resurrection appearance in Galilee. And so it ends a second time. Both times the writer says in effect, "There's a whole lot more I could tell you, but I've told you this much to help you believe." It is because Jesus is risen that the words of this Gospel still have so much power and impact. This is especially true of the intimate teachings in chapters 13–17. Though in the chronology of the story they are uttered before the death of Jesus, now in the reading one feels the risen Jesus present to the reader and saying them still. The fruits and the meaning of Jesus' death and Resurrection are continually revealed in them.

Amazing. Grace.

Abbot Jeremy Driscoll, OSB, is the leader of the Benedictine community of monks at Mount Angel Abbey in Saint Benedict, Oregon. He teaches, serves on various Vatican commissions, and conducts conferences and retreats.

THE WORD BECAME FLESH

1 In the beginning was the Word, and the Word was with God, and the Word was God. ² He was in the beginning with God. ³ All things came into being through him, and without him not one thing came into being. What has come into being ⁴ in him was life, and the life was the light of all people. ⁵ The light shines in the darkness, and the darkness did not overcome it.

⁶ There was a man sent from God, whose name was John. ⁷ He came as a witness to testify to the light, so that all might believe through him. ⁸ He himself was not the light, but he came to testify to the light. ⁹ The true light, which enlightens everyone, was coming into the world.

¹⁰ He was in the world, and the world came into being through him; yet the world did not know him. ¹¹ He came to what was his own, and his own people did not accept him. ¹² But to all who received him, who believed in his name, he gave power to become children of God, ¹³ who were born, not of blood or of the will of the flesh or of the will of man, but of God.

¹⁴ And the Word became flesh and lived among us, and we have seen his glory, the glory as of a father's only son, full of grace and truth. ¹⁵ (John testified to him and cried out, "This was he of whom I said, 'He who comes after me ranks ahead of me because he was before me.' ") ¹⁶ From

---

St. John Chrysostom
(349–407)

_____

Homilies on the Gospel of John

He Was in the Beginning with God

John 1:1–2

Just as one traveling out to sea passes cities, beaches, and ports, which fade from view as the infinite horizons of the open ocean appear, so this evangelist [John] carries us away from everything familiar, to the unlimited expanse that lies above created things....

For the intellect, rising to the phrase "the beginning" enquires, "What beginning?" and finds that the word "was" exceeds its abilities, leaving it no place to perch. Wearied, the mind turns backward to things below. For this phrase "in the beginning" is nothing else than the expression of eternal and limitless being.

The Word Became Flesh

John 1:1–18 | Bishop Barron

THE PROLOGUE TO THE GOSPEL OF JOHN is one of the most magnificent passages in the Scriptures, and indeed one of the gems of the Western literary tradition.

John commences: "In the beginning was the Word." No first-century Jew would have missed the significance of that opening phrase, for the first word of the Hebrew Scriptures, *bereshit*, means precisely "beginning." The Evangelist is signaling that the story he will unfold is the tale of a new creation, a new beginning. The Word, he tells us, was not only with God from the beginning, but indeed was God. Whenever we use words, we express something of ourselves. For example, as I type these words, I'm telling you what I know about the prologue to the Johannine Gospel; when you speak to a friend, you're telling him or her how you feel or what you're afraid of; when an umpire shouts out a call, he's communicating how he has assessed a play; etc. But God, the sheer act of being itself, the perfect Creator of the universe, is able utterly to speak himself in one great Word, a Word that does not simply contain an aspect of his being but rather the whole of his being. This is why we say in the Nicene Creed that the Word is "God from God, Light from Light, true God from true God"; and this is why St. John says that the Word was God.

Then we hear that through this Word "all things came into being." The Logos of God would necessarily contain the fullness of rationality and order, for he is nothing other than the mind of God. Hence when the Father made the universe, he "consulted" the Son, the way that an artist might consult a preliminary draft or an architect a diagram. The Word is the prototype in which all forms of reasonable structure are implicitly present. And this is precisely why the universe is not dumbly there but intelligibly there, why it is marked, in every nook and cranny, by reasonability. As I have argued elsewhere, this mystical theology of creation through the Word is one of the conditions for the possibility of the physical sciences, for every scientist must assume the intelligibility of what she investigates.

Next, we are told of "a man sent from God" whose name was John. The Baptist came, St. John tells us, "as a witness to testify to the light," for he was not, himself, the light. From time immemorial, God has sent messengers, spokespersons. Think of all of the prophets and patriarchs of Israel, indeed of every sage, philosopher, artist, or poet who has communicated something of God's truth and beauty. All of these could be characterized as witnesses to the light. The point is that the one to whom the Baptist bears witness is someone qualitatively different, not one more bearer of the Word, however impressive, but the Word himself. What is being held off here is the tendency—as prevalent today as in the ancient world—to domesticate Jesus and turn him into one more in a long line of prophets and seers.

"He was in the world, and the world came into being through him; yet the world did not know him." In that pithily crafted line, we sense the whole tragedy of sin. Human beings were made by and for the Logos and therefore they find their joy in a sort of sympathetic attunement to the Logos. Sin is the disharmony that comes when we fall out of alignment with God's reasonable purpose. But then comes the incomparably good news: "But to all who received him, who believed in his name, he gave power to become children of God." It is a basic principle of nature that nothing at a lower level of being can rise to a higher level unless it is drawn upward. A chemical can become part of a more complex structure only if it is assimilated by a plant; a plant can become ingredient in a sentient nature only if it is devoured by an animal; an animal can participate in rationality only if it is taken in by a human being. By this same principle, a human being can become something higher—not through his own efforts but only when a superior reality assimilates him. The Church Fathers consistently taught that God became human so that humans might become God—which is to say, participants in the divine nature. In a word, we can become children of God precisely because God reached down to us and became a Son of Man.

The entire prologue comes to its climax with the magnificent phrase: "And the Word became flesh and lived among us." The Gnostic temptation has tugged at the Church, on and off, for nearly the past two thousand years. This is the suggestion, common to all forms of puritanism, that the spiritual is attained through a negation of the material. But authentic Christianity, inspired by this stunning claim of

St. John, has consistently held off Gnosticism, for it knows that the Word of God took to himself a human nature and thereby elevated all of matter and made it a sacrament of the divine presence.

The Greek term behind "lived" in "lived among us," *skenoo*, is literally translated as "to tabernacle" or "to pitch a tent." No Jew of John's time would have missed the wonderful connection implied between Jesus and the temple. According to the twenty-sixth chapter of the book of Exodus, the ark of the covenant—the embodiment of Yahweh's presence—was originally housed in a tent or tabernacle. The Evangelist is telling us that now, in the flesh of Jesus, Yahweh has established his definitive Tabernacle among us.

Word Study

σκηνόω

SKĒNOŌ

Verb
To tabernacle, dwell

Medallions

From the center, the circular medallions of the window radiate outward in groups of 8, 16, 32, and 32. The entire set of medallions adds up to the number 88, forming a cohesive meditation on the number 8. The number 8 represents eternity, because it is just beyond the number 7, the number of days in the timespan of a week.

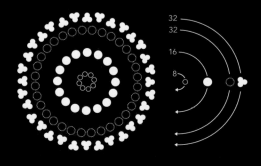

The North Rose Window

Essay by Michael Stevens

Rose windows are one of the defining features of Gothic architecture, and their mesmerizing complexity has captivated the minds of Christians everywhere for centuries. The finest rose windows ever made are those of Notre-Dame de Paris, and between its three splendid examples of this style, the North Rose Window is the largest and most complex. It was constructed around 1250, but despite its age remains almost completely original.

This symphony in stained glass perfectly exemplifies two concepts laid out in the theological prologue of John: the Identity of Jesus as the Word, or the Logos, and the identity of Jesus as the light.

The Greek word Logos in this context refers to Christ as the mind, pattern, and plan of God made incarnate. In the North Rose Window, we see an analogous example of patterning, ordering, and coherence of elements— in this case, the coordination of the materials of glass and stone. There is a sense of profound harmony and unity of elements, even within the incredible complexity of colors and shapes—a structure that holds the entire design together. If we look closely at the center, we see this unifying force is the central image of Jesus and Mary, around which these dazzling shapes are oriented and find a purposeful alignment.

In the first chapter of John we also read that Jesus is the light that shines in the darkness. The North Rose Window captures this reality with poetic grandeur as well, as the entire north transept of the cathedral basks in the powerful glow of the rose window. Everything about Notre Dame's exterior—from its massive stone facade to its impenetrable walls and imposing portals—would lead one to believe that its interior would be terrifyingly dark. Yet inside awaits an optical symphony of luminous color that seems to defy the height and weight of the cathedral's architecture. Like Jesus, the light captured by the windows of Notre Dame shines even into the depths of the darkest places, filling what would otherwise be a cavernous void with life and beauty.

his fullness we have all received, grace upon grace. ¹⁷ The law indeed was given through Moses; grace and truth came through Jesus Christ. ¹⁸ No one has ever seen God. It is God the only Son, who is close to the Father's heart, who has made him known.

THE TESTIMONY OF JOHN THE BAPTIST

¹⁹ This is the testimony given by John when the Jews sent priests and Levites from Jerusalem to ask him, "Who are you?" ²⁰ He confessed and did not deny it, but confessed, "I am not the Messiah." ²¹ And they asked him, "What then? Are you Elijah?" He said, "I am not." "Are you the prophet?" He answered, "No." ²² Then they said to him, "Who are you? Let us have an answer for those who sent us. What do you say about yourself?" ²³ He said,

> "I am the voice of one crying out in the wilderness,
>   'Make straight the way of the Lord,'"

as the prophet Isaiah said.

²⁴ Now they had been sent from the Pharisees. ²⁵ They asked him, "Why then are you baptizing if you are neither the Messiah, nor Elijah, nor the prophet?" ²⁶ John answered them, "I baptize with water. Among you stands one whom you do not know, ²⁷ the one who is coming after me; I am not

---

Look, Here Is the Lamb of God!

John 1:36 | Bishop Barron

In John's prologue, we read that the Word of God's covenantal love, which was addressed to Abraham, Moses, and David, has become flesh in Jesus of Nazareth. Jesus is the covenant in person.

But throughout Israel's history, the covenant between God and humanity is always accompanied by sacrifice. Therefore, when John the Baptist spies Jesus, he turns to two of his disciples and says, "Look, here is the Lamb of God!" This is one of the first and most important interpretive keys that John the Evangelist gives us: Jesus is the one who will play the role of the sacrificial lambs offered in the temple. Jesus, the covenant in person, will perforce be a sacrificed victim as well.

Pope Leo the Great, writing in the sixth century, gave expression to a patristic commonplace when he said, "There was no other reason for the Son of God becoming flesh than that he should be fixed to the cross." Jesus came in short to be the suffering servant who would, through a sacrifice, take away the sins of the world.

worthy to untie the thong of his sandal." ²⁸ This took place in Bethany across the Jordan where John was baptizing.

THE LAMB OF GOD

²⁹ The next day he saw Jesus coming toward him and declared, "Here is the Lamb of God who takes away the sin of the world! ³⁰ This is he of whom I said, 'After me comes a man who ranks ahead of me because he was before me.' ³¹ I myself did not know him; but I came baptizing with water for this reason, that he might be revealed to Israel." ³² And John testified, "I saw the Spirit descending from heaven like a dove, and it remained on him. ³³ I myself did not know him, but the one who sent me to baptize with water said to me, 'He on whom you see the Spirit descend and remain is the one who baptizes with the Holy Spirit.' ³⁴ And I myself have seen and have testified that this is the Son of God."

THE FIRST DISCIPLES OF JESUS

³⁵ The next day John again was standing with two of his disciples, ³⁶ and as he watched Jesus walk by, he exclaimed, "Look, here is the Lamb of God!" ³⁷ The two disciples heard him say this, and they followed Jesus. ³⁸ When Jesus turned and saw them following, he said to them, "What are you looking for?" They said to him, "Rabbi" (which translated means Teacher), "where are you staying?" ³⁹ He said to them, "Come and see." They came and saw where he was staying, and they remained with him that day. It

---

What Are You Looking For?

John 1:38 | Bishop Barron

Jesus' question to the two young men who are following him—"What are you looking for?"—is an indispensably important one. Many people go through life not really knowing what they most fundamentally want, and accordingly, they drift. The correct answer to Jesus' question is "eternal life" or "friendship with God" or "holiness." This is the simple, clear, unambiguous articulation of the end goal that any believer should have as he endeavors to lead his life.

Now, other people may know, more or less, what they want spiritually, but they lack the courage and attention to pursue that end in the face of distractions and opposition. They know that they should be growing in holiness, but the secular culture proposes sex, pleasure, power, and honor so attractively that they lose their way. Or perhaps they receive withering criticism from those who are stuck in the old, standard way of life, and they give in.

What are we looking for?

René Girard
(1923–2015)

———

The Scapegoat

Lamb... or Scapegoat?

John 1:29–36

The Gospels constantly reveal what the texts of historical persecutors, and especially mythological persecutors, hide from us: the knowledge that their victim is a scapegoat....

The expression scapegoat is not actually used, but the Gospels have a perfect substitute in *the Lamb of God*. Like "scapegoat," it implies the substitution of one victim for all the others but replaces all the distasteful and loathsome connotations of the goat with the positive associations of the lamb. It indicates more clearly the innocence of this victim, the injustice of the condemnation, and the causelessness of the hatred of which it is the object.

was about four o'clock in the afternoon. ⁴⁰ One of the two who heard John speak and followed him was Andrew, Simon Peter's brother. ⁴¹ He first found his brother Simon and said to him, "We have found the Messiah" (which is translated Anointed). ⁴² He brought Simon to Jesus, who looked at him and said, "You are Simon son of John. You are to be called Cephas" (which is translated Peter).

JESUS CALLS PHILIP AND NATHANAEL

⁴³ The next day Jesus decided to go to Galilee. He found Philip and said to him, "Follow me." ⁴⁴ Now Philip was from Bethsaida, the city of Andrew and Peter. ⁴⁵ Philip found Nathanael and said to him, "We have found him about whom Moses in the law and also the prophets wrote, Jesus son of Joseph from Nazareth." ⁴⁶ Nathanael said to him, "Can anything good come out of Nazareth?" Philip said to him, "Come and see." ⁴⁷ When Jesus saw Nathanael coming toward him, he said of him, "Here is truly an Israelite in whom there is no deceit!" ⁴⁸ Nathanael asked him, "Where did you get to know me?" Jesus answered, "I saw you under the fig tree before Philip called you." ⁴⁹ Nathanael replied, "Rabbi, you are the Son of God! You are

the King of Israel!" ⁵⁰ Jesus answered, "Do you believe because I told you that I saw you under the fig tree? You will see greater things than these." ⁵¹ And he said to him, "Very truly, I tell you, you will see heaven opened and the angels of God ascending and descending upon the Son of Man."

What's Your Center of Gravity?
John 1:43–51 | Bishop Barron

Nathanael recognizes Jesus as the Son of God and King of Israel. Like Nathaniel, once we make the decision for Jesus, once we determine that he is the supreme good, then every other claimant to supremacy must fall away. Every one of us has something or some set of values that we consider greatest. There is some center of gravity around which everything else turns.

Perhaps it is money and material things. Perhaps it is power and position. Perhaps it is the esteem of others. Perhaps it is your country or your political party or your ethnic identity. Perhaps it is your family, your kids, your wife, your husband.

None of these things are bad. However, when you place any of them in the absolute center of gravity, things go awry. When you make any of them your ultimate or final good, your spiritual life goes haywire. When you attach yourself to any of them with an absolute tenacity, you will fall apart.

THE WEDDING AT CANA

2 On the third day there was a wedding in Cana of Galilee, and the mother of Jesus was there. ² Jesus and his disciples had also been invited to the wedding. ³ When the wine gave out, the mother of Jesus said to him, "They have no wine." ⁴ And Jesus said to her, "Woman, what concern is that to you and to me? My hour has not yet come." ⁵ His mother said to the servants, "Do whatever he tells you." ⁶ Now standing there were six stone water jars for the Jewish rites of purification, each holding twenty or thirty gallons. ⁷ Jesus said to them, "Fill the jars with water." And they filled them up to the brim. ⁸ He said to them, "Now draw some out, and take it to the chief steward." So they took it. ⁹ When the steward tasted the water that had

become wine, and did not know where it came from (though the servants who had drawn the water knew), the steward called the bridegroom [10] and said to him, "Everyone serves the good wine first, and then the inferior wine after the guests have become drunk. But you have kept the good wine until now." [11] Jesus did this, the first of his signs, in Cana of Galilee, and revealed his glory; and his disciples believed in him.

[12] After this he went down to Capernaum with his mother, his brothers, and his disciples; and they remained there a few days.

St. Augustine
(354–430)

———

Harmony of the Gospels

Why Jesus Called Mary "Woman"

John 2:4

Although the Evangelist [John] himself mentions Jesus' mother by that very name [Mary], Jesus nevertheless addresses her this way: "Woman, what concern is that to you and to me?" He is not driving her away from himself with these words—she of whom he received flesh—but only means to emphasize the thought of his divinity instead, here as he is about to change water into wine. Here will stand out that divinity which made the woman, rather than the man that was made in her.

Do whatever
HE TELLS YOU.

They Have No Wine

John 2:1–12 | Bishop Barron

THROUGHOUT THE OLD TESTAMENT, the motif of the wedding is used to symbolize the marriage of God and his people as well as the good cheer that obtains when human beings come together in love. It is accordingly a particularly apt expression of the overcoming of the sundering of sin. Thus it is no accident that in the context of John's Gospel, Jesus' first public "sign" takes place at a wedding feast, for he himself is the marriage of divinity and humanity.

The narrative begins with an elegant Johannine code: "On the third day there was a wedding in Cana of Galilee." Throughout the Gospel, *te hemera te trite* (on the third day) is the expression for the day of Jesus' Resurrection from the dead. More to the point, this marriage feast takes place in Cana *of Galilee*, and Galilee, in the symbolic system of John, is the country of resurrection, that place where Jesus would meet his friends after Easter. Therefore, this story must be read through the lens of the Resurrection—which is to say, the act by which God in an unprecedented and unsurpassable way gathered humanity to himself and inaugurated the process of the universal gathering ("Christ has been raised from the dead, the first fruits of those who have died" [1 Cor. 15:20]). The wedding feast of Cana and the wedding feast of the Resurrection will stand in one another's hermeneutical light.

We hear that the disciples of Jesus—presumably at this point Andrew, Simon Peter, Philip, Nathanael, and the disciple whom Jesus loved— were invited to the wedding along with the Lord himself and his mother. The presence of both the *mathetai* (disciples) and the mother are key. In calling disciples to himself, Jesus had already inaugurated the gathering of his people (eventually the Twelve will be seen as evocative of the twelve tribes of Israel), and so their presence signals the novelty and future purpose of Jesus' ministry. Mary is a rich and multivalent symbolic figure in all of the Gospels. In Luke's infancy narrative, she emerges as the spokesperson for ancient Israel, speaking, in her Magnificat, in the words and cadences of Hannah; and as the recipient of an angelic announcement of a miraculous birth, she calls to mind not only Hannah but also Sarah and the mother of Samson as well. In Matthew's Christmas account, she is compelled to go into exile in Egypt and is then called back to her home, recapitulating thereby the journey of Israel from slavery to freedom. She is thus the symbolic embodiment of faithful and patient Israel, longing for deliverance. In John's Gospel, she is, above all, mother—the physical mother of Jesus and, through him, the mother of all who would come to new life in him. As mother of the Lord, she is, once again, Israel, that entire series of events and system of ideas from which Jesus emerged and in terms of which he becomes intelligible. Hans Urs von Balthasar comments in the same vein that Mary effectively awakened the messianic consciousness of Jesus through her recounting of the story of Israel to her son. So in the Cana narrative, Mary will speak the pain and the hope of the chosen people, scattered and longing for union.

Word Study

μαθηταὶ

M A T H Ē T A I

Noun
Disciples

We hear that in the course of the wedding celebration "the wine gave out." In an era when such parties lasted upward of several days, this was not a minor difficulty. With the wine depleted, the spirit of conviviality would dissipate, the celebration would wind down quickly, and the hosts, as well as the bride and groom, would be profoundly embarrassed. Noticing the difficulty, the mother of Jesus said to him, "They have no wine."

Let us press ahead with a symbolic reading of this iconic episode. Wine—that which changes, uplifts, and enlivens the consciousness, that which produces good feeling and good fellowship—evokes the Spirit of God, the divine life. When we are linked to that infinite source, when we partake freely of it, we are brought to personal joy and a deep sense of community connection. It is the elixir that makes of human life a communal celebration; it is the condition for the possibility of the gathering. To be in sin is nothing other than to be sundered from that source and hence to fall into a depression of the spirit, a listlessness and loneliness. When Mary quietly suggests to Jesus that the wedding party has run out of wine, she is ancient Israel speaking to its God, reminding him that the people have run out of joy, purpose, and connection to one another, that they have become dry bones with no life. She is taking up the lament of so many of the Hebrew prophets and sages: "How long, O Lord?"

What follows is the most puzzling part of the story, Jesus' seemingly cold distancing of himself from this reasonable request of his mother: "Woman, what concern is that to you and to me? My hour has not yet come." First, his addressing her as "woman" should not be construed as a mark of disrespect; rather, it should be interpreted as a densely textured symbolic act. Eve, in the Old Testament context, is the woman par excellence; Mary is presented here as the New Eve, the new representative of the human race, with whom God is seeking union. As is fitting in this Cana setting, the theme of human Bride and divine Bridegroom is being hinted at. But if she is the Woman with whom God seeks union, why the aloof and off-putting words? The best explanation, in my judgment, is that this is a narrative device that serves to highlight the importance of Jesus' "hour" and shows the relation between what he does at Cana and what will transpire in that hour. Like "the third day," "hour" is code for the Paschal Mystery, Jesus' passage through death to life. In that event, God will effect the perfect marriage between himself and the human race, for he will enter into the most intimate union with us, embracing even death itself and leading us into the bridal chamber of the divine life. Thus, the exchange with Mary brings to our attention the ultimate purpose and correct symbolic setting for the action that Jesus will perform for the humble bride and groom of Cana.

Unfazed by her son's response, Mary says to the *diakonoi* (the table servers), "Do whatever he tells you." Once again, this is Israel who is speaking. The rupture between God and humanity is irreparable from the human side and through human effort. The dysfunction into which men and women have fallen is like an addiction or an obsession: any attempt on their part to overcome the difficulty will only sink them deeper into it. Therefore the proper attitude in the presence of the saving God is obedience and acquiescence, imitating his moves, responding to his commands, doing whatever he tells us.

We come to the heart of the matter as Jesus commences his work of transformation. "Now standing there were six stone water jars for the Jewish rites of purification, each holding twenty or thirty gallons." These huge containers, used in connection with the religious life of the people, are empty, and this calls to mind the tiredness and uselessness of a religiosity unconnected to the divine Spirit.

Word Study

διακόνοις

DIAKONOIS

Noun
Assistants, ministers

In this regard, these jars play the same symbolic role as the priest and Levite in the parable of the Good Samaritan. But they are, we might say, eloquently empty, for they represent the potential for life: in relation to God, human religiosity, indeed human being, is a passive receptacle, something waiting to be filled.

Jesus now does two things—one visible and one invisible—and we must attend carefully to both. He first tells the servants to fill the jars with water, and John pointedly tells us that "they filled them up to the brim." The divine giver is now responding to the request of long-suffering Israel. The first thing he gives is the opportunity for them to contribute to the process of their vivification. Mind you, this is not in conflict with what I just specified concerning the attitude of total acquiescence, since he himself is giving, through his command, their very capacity to cooperate. So the filling of the jars to the limit is symbolic of all that human agency—through the divine prompting and power—can bring to the task of cultivating human flourishing: art, music, science, technology, politics, spirituality. All of this is obviously good, but it remains provisional and inadequate, for remember that the problem is that they are out of wine, not water. What they (Israel, the human race) require is not just the ordinary nourishment that water provides but rather intoxication, elevation, something greater.

Jesus tells them, "Now draw some out, and take it to the chief steward." When the steward tastes the water (now transformed into wine), he remarks on its extraordinary quality and undoubtedly passes on to the bride and groom the good news that they have wine in super-abundance—180 gallons! Jesus has changed the water into wine, taking something relatively insipid and making it tasty and intoxicating. He has received what they gave him and has not negated it, but rather raised it to a new pitch of intensity. Augustine's comment that Jesus simply accelerates and concentrates a natural process that occurs all the time—rainwater gives rise to grapes, which give rise to wine—is pertinent here. The water isn't cleared out in order for the divine contribution to be made; instead, the divine contribution is precisely the "perfecting" of the water. This quality of God's giving is congruent, of course, with the Christology of Chalcedon, the noncompetitive coming together of the divine and human natures: when God and a creature meet, the creature is confirmed and made more authentically itself. What is being hinted at in the Cana miracle is the elevation and expansion of human culture under the influence of the divine life. Filled with God's Spirit, architecture, art, science, politics, etc. become more completely themselves and realize their own deepest purposes. God gives our very capacity to give, and then he gives further by transfiguring our gift to our greater benefit. This miracle is hence a particularly apt iconic representation of divine-human coinherence.

Now, we mustn't forget that the purpose of this water made wine is to increase and prolong the celebration of a wedding. Because of Jesus' miracle, a large group of celebrants will continue to be gathered around a couple who have chosen to form, themselves, an intimate community for the rest of their lives. Read symbolically, this wine is the divine Spirit that alone grounds authentic human coinherence. When human solidarity is based upon something other than God's love—mutual self-interest, political considerations, shared convictions, etc.—it will inevitably shake apart and dissolve. Aristotle knew that a friendship endures only in the measure that both friends have commonly given themselves to a good that transcends them individually, and Augustine knew that people love each other most appropriately when they do so for the sake of God. What both appreciated was that without a transcendent ground or point of reference, the other-orientation of the partners would quickly devolve into self-preoccupation. When God and humanity are married, the connections between human beings intensify and deepen, vertical coinherence giving rise to horizontal coinherence. This fully developed one-in-the-otherness is on iconic display in the story of the wedding at Cana. It is a picture of the divine gatherer at work.

JESUS CLEANSES THE TEMPLE

[13] The Passover of the Jews was near, and Jesus went up to Jerusalem. [14] In the temple he found people selling cattle, sheep, and doves, and the money changers seated at their tables. [15] Making a whip of cords, he drove all of them out of the temple, both the sheep and the cattle. He also poured out the coins of the money changers and overturned their tables. [16] He told those who were selling the doves, "Take these things out of here! Stop making my Father's house a marketplace!" [17] His disciples remembered that it was written, "Zeal for your house will consume me." [18] The Jews then said to him, "What sign can you show us for doing this?" [19] Jesus answered them, "Destroy this temple, and in three days I will raise it up." [20] The Jews then said, "This temple has been under construction for forty-six years, and will you raise it up in three days?" [21] But he was speaking of the temple of his body. [22] After he was raised from the dead, his disciples remembered that he had said this; and they believed the scripture and the word that Jesus had spoken.

[23] When he was in Jerusalem during the Passover festival, many believed in his name because they saw the signs that he was doing. [24] But Jesus on his part would not entrust himself to them, because he knew all people [25] and needed no one to testify about anyone; for he himself knew what was in everyone.

Where Divinity and Humanity Meet

John 2:13–22 | Bishop Barron

We shouldn't be surprised that Jesus came into the temple and made a ruckus. He was not just being a rabble-rouser. He was rectifying the temple so as to rectify the people of Israel.

When pressed for a sign, Jesus said that he would tear the temple down and rebuild it in three days. He was talking, as John tells us, of the Temple of his body. He was saying that this old temple, which had served its purpose relatively well, would now give way to a new and definitive Temple. His own body, his own person, would be the place where divinity and humanity meet, and hence the place of right praise.

Cleansing the Temple

John 2:13–17 | Bishop Barron

Jesus is prophetic to the depth of his being, and his prophetic vocation will manifest itself in all of his speech, gestures, and actions. This entails that his confrontation with fallen powers and dysfunctional traditions will be highly focused, intense, and disruptive.

An episode recorded in all four Gospels is Jesus' paradigmatically prophetic act of cleansing the temple. Standing at the heart of the holy city of Jerusalem, the temple was the political, economic, cultural, and religious center of the nation. Turning over the tables of the money-changers and driving out the merchants, shouting in high dudgeon, and upsetting the order of that place was to strike at the most sacred institution of the culture, the unassailable embodiment of the tradition. It was to show oneself as critic in the most radical and surprising sense possible. That this act of Jesus the warrior flowed from the depth of his prophetic identity is witnessed to by the author of John's Gospel: "His disciples remembered that it was written, 'Zeal for your house will consume me.'"

Many of the historical critics of the New Testament hold that this event—shocking, unprecedented, perverse—is what finally persuaded the leaders that Jesus merited execution.

MASACCIO | *1427*

The Holy Trinity

Essay by Michael Stevens

In Masaccio's fresco of the Holy Trinity, we see the beginnings of a revolution in the medium of fresco painting. In this image lie the seeds of the High Renaissance: linear perspective, classical architecture, and geometric proportions. These elements—newly rediscovered in ancient Greek and Roman art—will later influence masterpieces such as Raphael's *School of Athens,* da Vinci's *Last Supper,* and Michelangelo's frescoes in the Sistine Chapel.

In this work, we see the Trinity, with the Father holding up the crucified Son and the dove of the Holy Spirit flying between them. This image is the visual illustration of the famous words of John 3:16: "For God so loved the world that he gave his only Son, so that everyone who believes in him may not perish but may have eternal life."

In *The Trinity,* God the Father gives his son up in a literal, physical gesture. This gesture is made more powerful and dramatic through the artist's use of deep space and convincing perspective, which causes the cross to leap forward, as if Jesus is in the same space as the viewer. Below, a *memento mori* has been painted in the form of a skeleton, to remind us of the short time we have on earth to receive the grace that God offers. We are presented with a question: Do we accept the saving power that the Father offers us in Christ, or do we remain dead in our sin?

Classical architecture

The columns, arches, and other architectural features that surround the Trinity in this fresco are lifted directly from classical Greek and Roman buildings. This classical styling became commonplace in the High Renaissance, but at the time of this fresco, it represented something very new for Christian art.

Throne of Mercy

This arrangement of figures, with the Father presenting the Son on the cross and the Spirit above, was common during this era and is known as the Throne of Mercy. This is because God's gift of his Son to redeem the world is the ultimate image of mercy.

NICODEMUS VISITS JESUS

3 Now there was a Pharisee named Nicodemus, a leader of the Jews. [2] He came to Jesus by night and said to him, "Rabbi, we know that you are a teacher who has come from God; for no one can do these signs that you do apart from the presence of God." [3] Jesus answered him, "Very truly, I tell you, no one can see the kingdom of God without being born from above." [4] Nicodemus said to him, "How can anyone be born after having grown old? Can one enter a second time into the mother's womb and be born?" [5] Jesus answered, "Very truly, I tell you, no one can enter the kingdom of God without being born of water and Spirit. [6] What is born of the flesh is flesh, and what is born of the Spirit is spirit. [7] Do not be astonished that I said to you, 'You must be born from above.' [8] The wind blows where it chooses, and you hear the sound of it, but you do not know where it comes from or where it goes. So it is with everyone who is born of the Spirit." [9] Nicodemus said to him, "How can these things be?" [10] Jesus answered him, "Are you a teacher of Israel, and yet you do not understand these things?

[11] "Very truly, I tell you, we speak of what we know and testify to what we have seen; yet you do not receive our testimony. [12] If I have told you about earthly things and you do not believe, how can you believe if I tell

---

Diamonds from the Dirt

John 3:16 | Bishop Barron

In dialogue with Nicodemus, the Logos personally delineates the nature of his mission: "For God so loved the world that he gave his only Son, so that everyone who believes in him may not perish but may have eternal life."

In his passion to set right a disjointed universe, God broke open his own heart in love. The Father sent not simply a representative, spokesman, or plenipotentiary, but his own Son into the dysfunction of the world so that he might gather that world into the bliss of the divine life. God's center—the love between the Father and the Son—is now offered as our center; God's heart breaks open so as to include even the worst and most hopeless among us. In so many spiritual traditions, the emphasis is placed on the human quest for God, but this is reversed in Christianity. Christians do not believe that God is dumbly "out there," like a mountain waiting to be climbed by various religious searchers. On the contrary, God, like the hound of heaven in Francis Thompson's poem, comes relentlessly searching after us. Because of this questing and self-emptying divine love, we become friends of God, sharers in the communion of the Trinity.

In light of the entire Gospel, we know that the momentum of this enfleshment is toward the total self-gift of the cross. There is a terrible interpretation of the cross that has, unfortunately, infected the minds of many Christians. This is the view that the bloody sacrifice of the Son on the cross was "satisfying" to the Father, an appeasement of a God infinitely angry at sinful humanity. In this reading, the crucified Jesus is like a child hurled into the fiery mouth of a pagan divinity in order to assuage its wrath. It is no wonder that many, formed by this cruel theology, find the Christian doctrine of the cross hard to accept.

What eloquently gives the lie to that awful interpretation is this passage from John's Gospel, which is often proposed as a summary of the Christian message. God the Father is not some pathetic divinity whose bruised personal honor needs to be restored; rather, God is a parent who burns with compassion for his children who have wandered into danger. It is not out of anger or vengeance or a desire for retribution that the Father sends the Son but precisely out of love. Does the Father hate sinners? No, but he hates sin. Does God harbor indignation at the unjust? No, but God despises injustice. Thus God sends his Son, not gleefully to see him suffer, but to set things right.

St. Anselm, the great medieval theologian, who is often unfairly blamed for the cruel theology of satisfaction, was eminently clear on this score. We sinners are like diamonds that have fallen into the muck; made in the image of God, we have soiled ourselves through violence and hatred. God, claimed Anselm, could have simply pronounced a word of forgiveness from heaven; but this would not have solved the problem. It would not have restored the diamonds to their original brilliance. Instead, in his passion to reestablish the beauty of creation, God came down into the muck of sin and death and brought the diamonds up and polished them off. In so doing of course, God had to get dirty. This sinking into the dirt   the divine solidarity with the lost—is the "sacrifice" that the Son makes to the infinite pleasure of the Father. It is a sacrifice expressive not of anger or vengeance but of compassion.

GOD SO LOVED THE WORLD THAT HE

GAVE HIS ONLY SON.

JOHN 3:16

St. Thomas Aquinas
(1225–1274)
———
Commentary on the
Gospel of John

Four Signs That God's Love
Is the Greatest

John 3:16

[John] shows us here, from four standpoints, that this love of God is the greatest. First, from the person of the one loving, because it is God who loves, and immeasurably. So he says, For God so loved: "O favorite among peoples, all his holy ones were in your charge" (Deut. 33:3).

Secondly, from the condition of the one who is loved, because it is man, a bodily creature of the world, i.e., existing in sin: "God proves his love for us in that while we still were sinners Christ died for us" (Rom. 5:8). Thus he says, the world.

Thirdly, from the greatness of his gifts, for love is shown by a gift; as Gregory says: "The proof of love is given by action." But God has given us the greatest of gifts, his Only Begotten Son, and so he says, that he gave his Only Begotten Son. "He who did not withhold his own Son, but gave him up for all of us" (Rom. 8:32).

He says his Son, i.e., his natural Son, consubstantial, not an adopted son, i.e., not those sons of which the Psalmist says: "I say: You are gods" (Ps. 82:6). This shows that the opinion of Arius is false: for if the Son of God were a creature, as he said, the immensity of God's love through the taking on of infinite goodness, which no creature can receive, could not have been revealed in him. He further says Only Begotten, to show that God does not have a love divided among many sons, but all of it is for that Son whom he gave to prove the immensity of his love: "The Father loves the Son and shows him all that he himself is doing" (John 5:20).

Fourthly, from the greatness of its fruit, because through him we have eternal life. Hence he says, so that whoever believes in him should not perish, but have eternal life, which he obtained for us through the death of the cross.

you about heavenly things? [13] No one has ascended into heaven except the one who descended from heaven, the Son of Man. [14] And just as Moses lifted up the serpent in the wilderness, so must the Son of Man be lifted up, [15] that whoever believes in him may have eternal life.

[16] "For God so loved the world that he gave his only Son, so that everyone who believes in him may not perish but may have eternal life.

[17] "Indeed, God did not send the Son into the world to condemn the world, but in order that the world might be saved through him. [18] Those who believe in him are not condemned; but those who do not believe are condemned already, because they have not believed in the name of the only Son of God. [19] And this is the judgment, that the light has come into the world, and people loved darkness rather than light because their deeds were evil. [20] For all who do evil hate the light and do not come to the light, so that their deeds may not be exposed. [21] But those who do what is true come to the light, so that it may be clearly seen that their deeds have been done in God."

JESUS AND JOHN THE BAPTIST

[22] After this Jesus and his disciples went into the Judean countryside, and he spent some time there with them and baptized. [23] John also was baptizing at Aenon near Salim because water was abundant there; and people kept coming and were being baptized [24] —John, of course, had not yet been thrown into prison.

[25] Now a discussion about purification arose between John's disciples and a Jew. [26] They came to John and said to him, "Rabbi, the one who was

with you across the Jordan, to whom you testified, here he is baptizing, and all are going to him." [27] John answered, "No one can receive anything except what has been given from heaven. [28] You yourselves are my witnesses that I said, 'I am not the Messiah, but I have been sent ahead of him.' [29] He who has the bride is the bridegroom. The friend of the bridegroom, who stands and hears him, rejoices greatly at the bridegroom's voice. For this reason my joy has been fulfilled. [30] He must increase, but I must decrease."

THE ONE WHO COMES FROM HEAVEN

[31] The one who comes from above is above all; the one who is of the earth belongs to the earth and speaks about earthly things. The one who comes from heaven is above all. [32] He testifies to what he has seen and heard, yet no one accepts his testimony. [33] Whoever has accepted his testimony has certified this, that God is true. [34] He whom God has sent speaks the words of God, for he gives the Spirit without measure. [35] The Father loves the Son and has placed all things in his hands. [36] Whoever believes in the Son has eternal life; whoever disobeys the Son will not see life, but must endure God's wrath.

The Great Gatherer

John 3:19 | Bishop Barron

The Israelite hope was that, in the messianic era, Israel would become a godly nation gathered around the common worship of the true God at the temple on Mount Zion, and that this united Israel would become, in turn, a beacon to the other nations of the world.

Jesus' entire preaching and ministry should be read under this rubric of the great gathering. He went out consistently to the margins of society in order to lure the lost sheep of the house of Israel, and he hosted festive suppers to which were invited both the rich and the poor, both male and female, both saints and sinners, both the righteous and the unrighteous. This open table fellowship was the concrete acting out of the kingdom prophecy of Isaiah.

But the opposition that Jesus faced throughout his ministry brings into sharp relief a basic form of human dysfunction: our preference for the patterns of exclusion, domination, division, and violence. As St. John put it, "The light has come into the world, and people loved darkness rather than light."

JESUS AND THE WOMAN OF SAMARIA

4 Now when Jesus learned that the Pharisees had heard, "Jesus is making and baptizing more disciples than John"[2] —although it was not Jesus himself but his disciples who baptized—[3] he left Judea and started back to Galilee.[4] But he had to go through Samaria.[5] So he came to a Samaritan city called Sychar, near the plot of ground that Jacob had given to his son Joseph.[6] Jacob's well was there, and Jesus, tired out by his journey, was sitting by the well. It was about noon.

[7] A Samaritan woman came to draw water, and Jesus said to her, "Give me a drink."[8] (His disciples had gone to the city to buy food.)[9] The Samaritan woman said to him, "How is it that you, a Jew, ask a drink of me, a woman of Samaria?" (Jews do not share things in common with Samaritans.) [10] Jesus answered her, "If you knew the gift of God, and who it is that is saying to you, 'Give me a drink,' you would have asked him, and he would have given you living water."[11] The woman said to him, "Sir, you have no bucket, and the well is deep. Where do you get that living water?[12] Are you greater than our ancestor Jacob, who gave us the well, and with his sons and his flocks drank from it?"[13] Jesus said to her, "Everyone who drinks of this water will be thirsty again,[14] but those who drink of the water that I will give them will never be thirsty. The water that I will give will become in them a spring of water gushing up to eternal life."[15] The woman said to

---

Tired Out by His Journey

John 4:6 | Bishop Barron

In this magnificent narrative of the woman at the well, we hear that Jesus sat down by Jacob's well, "tired out by his journey." This description is straightforward enough on the literal level: Who wouldn't be tired after a morning's march through dry country?

But as Augustine and others have reminded us, it has another sense on the mystical level. Jesus is tired from his incarnational journey into human sin and dysfunction, signified by the well. "Everyone who drinks of this water will be thirsty again," Jesus says to the woman, indicating that the well is emblematic of errant desire, her tendency to fill up her longing for God with the transient goods of creation: money, pleasure, power, honor. In order to effect a change in her, the Lamb of God had to be willing to enter into her dysfunctional world and to share the spiritual weariness of it.

him, "Sir, give me this water, so that I may never be thirsty or have to keep coming here to draw water."

¹⁶ Jesus said to her, "Go, call your husband, and come back." ¹⁷ The woman answered him, "I have no husband." Jesus said to her, "You are right in saying, 'I have no husband'; ¹⁸ for you have had five husbands, and the one you have now is not your husband. What you have said is true!" ¹⁹ The woman said to him, "Sir, I see that you are a prophet. ²⁰ Our ancestors worshiped on this mountain, but you say that the place where people must worship is in Jerusalem." ²¹ Jesus said to her, "Woman, believe me, the hour is coming when you will worship the Father neither on this mountain nor in Jerusalem. ²² You worship what you do not know; we worship what we know, for salvation is from the Jews. ²³ But the hour is coming, and is now here, when the true worshipers will worship the Father in spirit and truth, for the Father seeks such as these to worship him. ²⁴ God is spirit, and those who worship him must worship in spirit and truth." ²⁵ The woman said to him, "I know that Messiah is coming" (who is called Christ). "When he

Fulton Sheen
(1895–1979)

———

Life of Christ

The World's Broken Cisterns

John 4:13–14

Here was his philosophy of life. All the human satisfactions of the cravings of body and soul have one defect; they do not satisfy forever. They only serve to deaden the present want; but they never extinguish it. The want always revives again. The waters the world gives fall back to earth again; but the water of life which he gives is a supernatural impulse, and pushes onward even to heaven itself.

Our Blessed Lord did not attempt to dislodge the world's broken cisterns without offering something better. He did not condemn the earthly streams nor forbid them; he merely said that if she restricted herself to the wells of human happiness, she would never be completely satisfied.

The Woman at the Well

John 4:1–42 | Bishop Barron

In John's narrative, the Samaritan woman comes to the well seeking water. There she confronts Jesus, who reminds her that she has returned again and again to that well but has never been satisfied. In spiritual terms, this rhythm of drinking and becoming thirsty again is evocative of the trap of concupiscent desire. When one seeks to fill her infinite hunger for God with something finite, something corruptible, she will never be satisfied and will return to the source repeatedly but each time will be more frustrated, more weary. Jesus tells the woman at the well not to seek the center of her life in the perishable and passing things of the finite realm, but rather to seek living water, the power of the eternal. In Thomistic terms, Jesus is drawing the woman from the corruptible to the necessary.

But, as Thomas himself implies, there is the danger that one could become fixated at the level of the necessary powers without penetrating to that which is necessary through itself—namely, God. The Samaritan woman faces the same danger. Having been lured by Christ away from the well and having acknowledged that Jesus is a prophet, she asks him whether appropriate worship takes place in the Jerusalem temple, as the Jews say, or on the holy mountain, as the Samaritans have it. She is seeking the center and orientation of her life, not in the properly eternal reality of God, but rather in a particular religious tradition. She is wondering whether to anchor her life in one of those necessary powers—one of those great principalities that falls, nevertheless, short of God.

Jesus' answer to this question is magnificent: "Woman, believe me, the hour is coming when you will worship the Father neither on this mountain nor in Jerusalem. . . . God is spirit, and those who worship him must worship in spirit and truth." In other words, the divine is not a reality in this world, not something that can be caught in the categories of finitude, not "this" or "that," but is rather spirit that transcends even those necessary powers that are the great religious traditions.

Jesus shakes the Samaritan woman out of her immersion in the corruptible goods of the world, and then out of her allegiance to even those noble necessities that are religions, in order to open her mind and heart to the uncontrollable, unlimited mystery that is God.

comes, he will proclaim all things to us." ²⁶ Jesus said to her, "I am he, the one who is speaking to you."

²⁷ Just then his disciples came. They were astonished that he was speaking with a woman, but no one said, "What do you want?" or, "Why are you speaking with her?" ²⁸ Then the woman left her water jar and went back to the city. She said to the people, ²⁹ "Come and see a man who told me everything I have ever done! He cannot be the Messiah, can he?" ³⁰ They left the city and were on their way to him.

³¹ Meanwhile the disciples were urging him, "Rabbi, eat something." ³² But he said to them, "I have food to eat that you do not know about." ³³ So the disciples said to one another, "Surely no one has brought him something to eat?" ³⁴ Jesus said to them, "My food is to do the will of him who sent me and to complete his work. ³⁵ Do you not say, 'Four months more, then comes the harvest'? But I tell you, look around you, and see how the fields are ripe for harvesting. ³⁶ The reaper is already receiving wages and is gathering fruit for eternal life, so that sower and reaper may rejoice together. ³⁷ For here the saying holds true, 'One sows and another reaps.' ³⁸ I sent you to reap that for which you did not labor. Others have labored, and you have entered into their labor."

³⁹ Many Samaritans from that city believed in him because of the woman's testimony, "He told me everything I have ever done." ⁴⁰ So when the Samaritans came to him, they asked him to stay with them; and he stayed there two days. ⁴¹ And many more believed because of his word. ⁴² They said to the woman, "It is no longer because of what you said that we believe, for we have heard for ourselves, and we know that this is truly the Savior of the world."

JESUS RETURNS TO GALILEE

⁴³ When the two days were over, he went from that place to Galilee ⁴⁴ (for Jesus himself had testified that a prophet has no honor in the prophet's own country). ⁴⁵ When he came to Galilee, the Galileans welcomed him, since they had seen all that he had done in Jerusalem at the festival; for they too had gone to the festival.

JESUS HEALS AN OFFICIAL'S SON

⁴⁶ Then he came again to Cana in Galilee where he had changed the water into wine. Now there was a royal official whose son lay ill in Capernaum. ⁴⁷ When he heard that Jesus had come from Judea to Galilee, he went and begged him to come down and heal his son, for he was at the point of death. ⁴⁸ Then Jesus said to him, "Unless you see signs and wonders you will not believe." ⁴⁹ The official said to him, "Sir, come down before my little boy dies." ⁵⁰ Jesus said to him, "Go; your son will live." The man believed the word

that Jesus spoke to him and started on his way. [51] As he was going down, his slaves met him and told him that his child was alive. [52] So he asked them the hour when he began to recover, and they said to him, "Yesterday at one in the afternoon the fever left him." [53] The father realized that this was the hour when Jesus had said to him, "Your son will live." So he himself believed, along with his whole household. [54] Now this was the second sign that Jesus did after coming from Judea to Galilee.

JESUS HEALS ON THE SABBATH

5 After this there was a festival of the Jews, and Jesus went up to Jerusalem. [2] Now in Jerusalem by the Sheep Gate there is a pool, called in Hebrew Beth-zatha, which has five porticoes. [3] In these lay many invalids—blind, lame, and paralyzed. [5] One man was there who had been ill for thirty-eight years. [6] When Jesus saw him lying there and knew that he had been there a long time, he said to him, "Do you want to be made well?" [7] The sick man answered him, "Sir, I have no one to put me into the pool when the water is stirred up; and while I am making my way, someone else steps down

---

Resisting God's Work

John 5:1–16 | Bishop Barron

Jesus encounters a man who has been ill for thirty-eight years. He is lying on his mat, next to a pool, and Jesus asks, "Do you want to be made well?" The man confirms, and Jesus replies, "Stand up, take your mat and walk." Immediately, the man is healed.

Now at this point, the story really heats up, because we notice something that is frequently on display in the Gospels: the resistance to the creative work of God, the attempt to find any excuse, however lame, to deny it, to pretend it's not there, to condemn it.

One would expect that everyone around the cured man would rejoice, but just the contrary: the religious leaders are infuriated and confounded. They see the healed man and their first response is, "It is the sabbath; it is not lawful for you to carry your mat."

Why are they so reactive? Why don't they want this to be? Well, because we sinners don't like the ways of God. We find them troubling and threatening. Why? Because they undermine the games of oppression and exclusion that we rely upon in order to boost our own egos.

Let this encounter remind us that God's ways are not our ways, and that there is one even greater than the sabbath.

ahead of me." [8] Jesus said to him, "Stand up, take your mat and walk." [9] At once the man was made well, and he took up his mat and began to walk.

Now that day was a sabbath. [10] So the Jews said to the man who had been cured, "It is the sabbath; it is not lawful for you to carry your mat." [11] But he answered them, "The man who made me well said to me, 'Take up your mat and walk.'" [12] They asked him, "Who is the man who said to you, 'Take it up and walk'?" [13] Now the man who had been healed did not know who it was, for Jesus had disappeared in the crowd that was there. [14] Later Jesus found him in the temple and said to him, "See, you have been made well! Do not sin any more, so that nothing worse happens to you." [15] The man went away and told the Jews that it was Jesus who had made him well. [16] Therefore the Jews started persecuting Jesus, because he was doing such things on the sabbath. [17] But Jesus answered them, "My Father is still working, and I also am working." [18] For this reason the Jews were seeking all the more to kill him, because he was not only breaking the sabbath, but was also calling God his own Father, thereby making himself equal to God.

The Son Can Do Nothing on His Own

John 5:19 | Bishop Barron

The New Testament sense is that the suffering of the world is produced by the breaking of the loop of grace, the insistence that one's life should be one's own. When this attitude dominates, when we want the knowledge of good and evil for ourselves, when we want what is coming to us, we end up losing the little that we think we have.

Jesus saved us by the whole course of his obedience. His Savior's life was an obedient response to the will of God, a displacement of his own concerns in favor of the Father's: "The Son can do nothing on his own, but only what he sees the Father doing."

THE AUTHORITY OF THE SON

[19] Jesus said to them, "Very truly, I tell you, the Son can do nothing on his own, but only what he sees the Father doing; for whatever the Father does, the Son does likewise. [20] The Father loves the Son and shows him all that he himself is doing; and he will show him greater works than these, so that you will be astonished. [21] Indeed, just as the Father raises the dead

and gives them life, so also the Son gives life to whomever he wishes. [22] The Father judges no one but has given all judgment to the Son, [23] so that all may honor the Son just as they honor the Father. Anyone who does not honor the Son does not honor the Father who sent him. [24] Very truly, I tell you, anyone who hears my word and believes him who sent me has eternal life, and does not come under judgment, but has passed from death to life.

[25] "Very truly, I tell you, the hour is coming, and is now here, when the dead will hear the voice of the Son of God, and those who hear will live. [26] For just as the Father has life in himself, so he has granted the Son also to have life in himself; [27] and he has given him authority to execute judgment, because he is the Son of Man. [28] Do not be astonished at this; for the hour is coming when all who are in their graves will hear his voice [29] and will come out—those who have done good, to the resurrection of life, and those who have done evil, to the resurrection of condemnation.

WITNESSES TO JESUS

[30] "I can do nothing on my own. As I hear, I judge; and my judgment is just, because I seek to do not my own will but the will of him who sent me.

[31] "If I testify about myself, my testimony is not true. [32] There is another who testifies on my behalf, and I know that his testimony to me is true. [33] You sent messengers to John, and he testified to the truth. [34] Not that I accept such human testimony, but I say these things so that you may be saved. [35] He was a burning and shining lamp, and you were willing to rejoice for a while in his light. [36] But I have a testimony greater than John's. The works that the Father has given me to complete, the very works that I am doing, testify on my behalf that the Father has sent me. [37] And the Father who sent me has himself testified on my behalf. You have never heard his voice or seen his form, [38] and you do not have his word abiding in you, because you do not believe him whom he has sent.

[39] "You search the scriptures because you think that in them you have eternal life; and it is they that testify on my behalf. [40] Yet you refuse to come to me to have life. [41] I do not accept glory from human beings. [42] But I know that you do not have the love of God in you. [43] I have come in my Father's name, and you do not accept me; if another comes in his own name, you will accept him. [44] How can you believe when you accept glory from one another and do not seek the glory that comes from the one who alone is God? [45] Do not think that I will accuse you before the Father; your accuser is Moses, on whom you have set your hope. [46] If you believed Moses, you would believe me, for he wrote about me. [47] But if you do not believe what he wrote, how will you believe what I say?"

More Than a Mere Prophet

John 5:31–47 | Bishop Barron

The first hearers of Jesus were astonished by the authority of his speech. This wasn't simply because he spoke with conviction and enthusiasm; it was because he refused to play the game that every other rabbi played, tracing his authority finally back to Moses. He went, as it were, over the head of Moses.

His listeners knew they were dealing with something qualitatively different than anything else in their religious tradition or experience. They were dealing with the prophet greater than Moses, whom Israel had long expected.

And Jesus *had* to be more than a mere prophet. Why? Because we all have been wounded, indeed our entire world compromised, by a battle that took place at a more fundamental level of existence. The result is the devastation of sin, which we all know too well. Who alone could possibly take it on? A merely human figure? Hardly. What is required is the power and authority of the Creator himself, intent on remaking and saving his world, binding up its wounds and setting it right.

FEEDING THE FIVE THOUSAND

6 After this Jesus went to the other side of the Sea of Galilee, also called the Sea of Tiberias. [2] A large crowd kept following him, because they saw the signs that he was doing for the sick. [3] Jesus went up the mountain and sat down there with his disciples. [4] Now the Passover, the festival of the Jews, was near. [5] When he looked up and saw a large crowd coming toward him, Jesus said to Philip, "Where are we to buy bread for these people to eat?" [6] He said this to test him, for he himself knew what he was going to do. [7] Philip answered him, "Six months' wages would not buy enough bread for each of them to get a little." [8] One of his disciples, Andrew, Simon Peter's brother, said to him, [9] "There is a boy here who has five barley loaves and two fish. But what are they among so many people?" [10] Jesus said, "Make the people sit down." Now there was a great deal of grass in the place; so they sat down, about five thousand in all. [11] Then Jesus took the loaves, and when he had given thanks, he distributed them to those who were seated; so also the fish, as much as they wanted. [12] When they were satisfied, he told his disciples, "Gather up the fragments left over, so that nothing may be lost." [13] So they gathered them up, and from the fragments of the five barley loaves, left by those who had eaten, they filled twelve baskets.

[14] When the people saw the sign that he had done, they began to say, "This is indeed the prophet who is to come into the world."

[15] When Jesus realized that they were about to come and take him by force to make him king, he withdrew again to the mountain by himself.

Feeding of the Five Thousand

John 6:1-15 | Bishop Barron

The tone of John's intense meditation on the meaning of the Eucharist in the second half of John 6 is set with the familiar story of the feeding of the five thousand, the only miracle story mentioned in all four Gospels. This scene deeply affected the first Christians.

Jesus instructs the crowd to recline on the grass. Taking the barley loaves and dried fish, Jesus makes a meal that satisfies the enormous crowd. They are hungry, tired, worn out from their exertions, and Jesus gives them sustenance for the day.

For Thomas Aquinas, the great metaphor for the Eucharist is sustenance, food for the journey. Baptism defines us, making us sons and daughters of God; Confirmation strengthens and deepens this identity; Marriage and Holy Orders seal us in our life's vocation. These are sacraments offered once at key moments in one's life.

Then there is the Eucharist, which is daily food, nourishment to get us through the day-to-day. How effective would we be if we never ate, or ate only on special occasions and in a festive environment? Not very. So, in the spiritual life, we must eat and drink or we will not have the strength.

JESUS WALKS ON THE WATER

[16] When evening came, his disciples went down to the sea, [17] got into a boat, and started across the sea to Capernaum. It was now dark, and Jesus had not yet come to them. [18] The sea became rough because a strong wind was blowing. [19] When they had rowed about three or four miles, they saw Jesus walking on the sea and coming near the boat, and they were terrified. [20] But he said to them, "It is I; do not be afraid." [21] Then they wanted to take him into the boat, and immediately the boat reached the land toward which they were going.

Hovering Over Troubled Waters

John 6:16–21 | Bishop Barron

Water is, throughout the Scriptures, a symbol of danger and chaos. At the very beginning of time, when all was a formless waste, the Spirit of the Lord hovered over the surface of the waters. This signals God's lordship over all of the powers of darkness and disorder.

In the Old Testament, the Israelites are escaping from Egypt, and they confront the waters of the Red Sea. Through the prayer of Moses, they are able to walk through the midst of the waves.

Now in the New Testament, this same symbolism can be found. In all four of the Gospels there is a story of Jesus mastering the waves. The boat, with Peter and the other disciples, is evocative of the Church, the followers of Jesus. It moves through the waters, as the Church will move through time.

All types of storms—chaos, corruption, stupidity, danger, persecution—will inevitably arise. But Jesus comes walking on the sea. This is meant to affirm his divinity: just as the Spirit of God hovered over the waters at the beginning, so Jesus hovers over them now.

THE BREAD FROM HEAVEN

²² The next day the crowd that had stayed on the other side of the sea saw that there had been only one boat there. They also saw that Jesus had not got into the boat with his disciples, but that his disciples had gone away alone. ²³ Then some boats from Tiberias came near the place where they had eaten the bread after the Lord had given thanks. ²⁴ So when the crowd saw that neither Jesus nor his disciples were there, they themselves got into the boats and went to Capernaum looking for Jesus.

²⁵ When they found him on the other side of the sea, they said to him, "Rabbi, when did you come here?" ²⁶ Jesus answered them, "Very truly, I tell you, you are looking for me, not because you saw signs, but because you ate your fill of the loaves. ²⁷ Do not work for the food that perishes, but for the food that endures for eternal life, which the Son of Man will give you. For it is on him that God the Father has set his seal." ²⁸ Then they said to him, "What must we do to perform the works of God?" ²⁹ Jesus answered them, "This is the work of God, that you believe in him whom he has sent." ³⁰ So they said to him, "What sign are you going to give us then, so that we may see it and believe you? What work are you performing? ³¹ Our ancestors ate the manna in the wilderness; as it is written, 'He gave them bread from heaven to eat.'" ³² Then Jesus said to them, "Very truly, I tell you, it

was not Moses who gave you the bread from heaven, but it is my Father who gives you the true bread from heaven. [33] For the bread of God is that which comes down from heaven and gives life to the world." [34] They said to him, "Sir, give us this bread always."

[35] Jesus said to them, "I am the bread of life. Whoever comes to me will never be hungry, and whoever believes in me will never be thirsty. [36] But I said to you that you have seen me and yet do not believe. [37] Everything that the Father gives me will come to me, and anyone who comes to me I will never drive away; [38] for I have come down from heaven, not to do my own will, but the will of him who sent me. [39] And this is the will of him who sent me, that I should lose nothing of all that he has given me, but raise it up on the last day. [40] This is indeed the will of my Father, that all who see the Son and believe in him may have eternal life; and I will raise them up on the last day."

[41] Then the Jews began to complain about him because he said, "I am the bread that came down from heaven." [42] They were saying, "Is not this Jesus, the son of Joseph, whose father and mother we know? How can he now say, 'I have come down from heaven'?" [43] Jesus answered them, "Do not complain among yourselves. [44] No one can come to me unless drawn by the Father who sent me; and I will raise that person up on the last day. [45] It is written in the prophets, 'And they shall all be taught by God.' Everyone who has heard and learned from the Father comes to me. [46] Not that anyone has seen the Father except the one who is from God; he has seen the Father. [47] Very truly, I tell you, whoever believes has eternal life. [48] I am the bread of life. [49] Your ancestors ate the manna in the wilderness, and they died. [50] This is the bread that comes down from heaven, so that one may eat of it and not die. [51] I am the living bread that came down from heaven. Whoever eats of this bread will live forever; and the bread that I will give for the life of the world is my flesh."

[52] The Jews then disputed among themselves, saying, "How can this man give us his flesh to eat?" [53] So Jesus said to them, "Very truly, I tell you, unless you eat the flesh of the Son of Man and drink his blood, you have no life in you. [54] Those who eat my flesh and drink my blood have eternal life, and I will raise them up on the last day; [55] for my flesh is true food and my blood is true drink. [56] Those who eat my flesh and drink my blood abide in me, and I in them. [57] Just as the living Father sent me, and I live because of the Father, so whoever eats me will live because of me. [58] This is the bread that came down from heaven, not like that which your ancestors ate, and they died. But the one who eats this bread will live forever." [59] He said these things while he was teaching in the synagogue at Capernaum.

THE WORDS OF ETERNAL LIFE

⁶⁰ When many of his disciples heard it, they said, "This teaching is difficult; who can accept it?" ⁶¹ But Jesus, being aware that his disciples were complaining about it, said to them, "Does this offend you? ⁶² Then what if you were to see the Son of Man ascending to where he was before? ⁶³ It is the spirit that gives life; the flesh is useless. The words that I have spoken to you are spirit and life. ⁶⁴ But among you there are some who do not believe." For Jesus knew from the first who were the ones that did not believe, and who was the one that would betray him. ⁶⁵ And he said, "For this reason I have told you that no one can come to me unless it is granted by the Father."

⁶⁶ Because of this many of his disciples turned back and no longer went about with him. ⁶⁷ So Jesus asked the twelve, "Do you also wish to go away?" ⁶⁸ Simon Peter answered him, "Lord, to whom can we go? You have the words of eternal life. ⁶⁹ We have come to believe and know that you are the Holy One of God." ⁷⁰ Jesus answered them, "Did I not choose you, the twelve? Yet one of you is a devil." ⁷¹ He was speaking of Judas son of Simon Iscariot, for he, though one of the twelve, was going to betray him.

For my FLESH

IS TRUE FOOD

and my BLOOD IS

TRUE DRINK.

St. Ignatius of Antioch
(35–108)

———

Epistle to the Ephesians

The Medicine of Immortality
John 6:50–53

Come together in common through grace, individually, in one faith, and in Jesus Christ, who was of the seed of David according to the flesh, both the Son of man and the Son of God. In this way you will obey the bishop and the presbytery with an undivided mind, breaking one and the same bread, which is the medicine of immortality and the antidote to prevent us from dying, enabling us to live forever in Jesus Christ.

St. Justin Martyr
(100–165)

———

First Apology

Not Common Bread
John 6:55

We call this food Eucharist.... Not as common bread nor common drink do we receive these; but since Jesus Christ our Savior was made incarnate by the word of God and had both flesh and blood for our salvation, so too ... the food which has been made into the Eucharist ... is both the flesh and the blood of that incarnated Jesus.

St. Gregory of Nyssa
(335–394)

———

On the Baptism of Christ

The Body of Christ
John 6:55

The bread again is at first common bread; but when the mystery sanctifies it, it is called and actually becomes the Body of Christ.

RAPHAEL | *1509–1511*

The School of Athens and
The Disputation of the Holy Sacrament

Essay by Michael Stevens

The Raphael frescoes of the papal palace are among the greatest artistic treasures of the Vatican, rivaled only by Michelangelo's frescoes on the Sistine Ceiling. One room in particular, the *Stanza della Segnatura* (Room of the Signature) is especially beautiful and represents the culmination of all Renaissance thought in a single space. In this room, each of the four walls corresponds to a different area of intellectual life, the most famous of them being the frescoes corresponding to philosophy and theology.

Philosophy is represented by the fresco *The School of Athens*, which features all of the major ancient philosophers of the Western world. In the center of this sprawling cluster of figures are Plato (on the left, pointing upward) and Aristotle (on the right, gesturing downward). They are shown in the vast halls of the School of Athens, which was the epicenter of philosophy in ancient Greece. Plato points up to the sky to the world of forms, the abstract realm of metaphysical perfection, whereas Aristotle contradicts this by gesturing downward to earth, emphasizing the concrete world of human beings instead. The result of these conflicting gestures is a sense of tension between the material and immaterial—tension that begs for resolution.

Raphael provides the resolution to the discord in *The School of Athens* on the opposite wall, through his *Disputation of the Holy Sacrament*. Here we see the heavenly realm of God and the angels joined to the earth below by the Eucharist, which is positioned on the altar on the boundary between these domains. The Host is directly across the room from the figures of Plato and Aristotle in *The School of Athens*, and it is as if Raphael is fitting the last remaining jigsaw piece into the reasoning of the great philosophers: the person of Jesus—true God and true man—who draws together the heavenly and the material in his Body and Blood.

Jesus' Most Challenging Sermon

John 6:48–66 | Bishop Barron

THE MOST CHALLENGING SERMON that Jesus ever preached was not the Sermon on the Mount; it was the discourse he gave in the Capernaum synagogue after the miracle of multiplying the loaves and fish. The Sermon on the Mount—with its calls for love of one's enemy, the cleansing of the interior self, and nonresistance to evil—was certainly intellectually confounding. But the talk that Jesus gave at Capernaum concerning the sacrament of his Body and Blood was not only philosophically problematic; it was, quite literally, revolting. Even at a distance of two thousand years and after volumes of theological reflection, readers today can still find his words awfully hard to accept. We can tolerate easily enough the claim that Jesus is a spiritual teacher of great importance; we might even accept that his person is central in regard to our relation to God. But that his flesh is real food and his blood real drink? That the ingesting of these elements is essential to gaining eternal life? Even the most sympathetic of contemporary listeners is likely to react the same way many in Jesus' original audience reacted: with a shake of the head and perhaps even a shudder of disgust.

To understand why Jesus' own hearers would have responded in a particularly negative way to these words, we must remember the clear and repeated prohibitions in the Hebrew Scriptures against the consuming of flesh with blood. In Genesis 9:3-4, we find this: "Every moving thing that lives shall be food for you; and just as I gave you the green plants, I give you everything. Only, you shall not eat flesh with its life, that is, its blood." In Leviticus 3:17, we read, "It shall be a perpetual statute throughout your generations, in all your settlements: you must not eat any fat or any blood." And in Deuteronomy 12:23, we discover, "Only be sure that you do not eat the blood; for the blood is the life, and you shall not eat the life with the meat." Finally, the expression "to eat someone's flesh" was commonly used in Jesus' time to designate the most vicious and unwarranted kind of attack.

Therefore, when Jesus says, "I am the living bread that came down from heaven.... The bread that I will give for the life of the world is my flesh," he is implying something about as nauseating and religiously objectionable as possible. It is, accordingly, a rather remarkable understatement when John writes, "The Jews then disputed among themselves, saying, 'How can this man give us his flesh to eat?'"

So what does Jesus do when confronted with this objection? One would think that, in order to mollify his opponents, he would take the opportunity to soften his rhetoric, to offer a metaphorical or symbolic interpretation of his words, so as at least to answer the most obvious difficulties. Instead, he intensifies what he had said: "Very truly, I tell you, unless you eat the flesh of the Son of Man and drink his blood, you have no life in you." The Greek term behind "eat" here is not the usual *phagein* but rather *trogein*, a word customarily used to describe the way animals devour their food. We might render it "gnaw" or "chomp." Therefore, to those who are revolted by the realism of his language, Jesus says, essentially, "Unless you gnaw on my flesh...you have no life in you."

How do we appropriate this shocking talk? If we stand in the great Catholic tradition, we honor these unnerving words of Jesus, resisting all attempts to soften them or explain them away. We affirm what the Church has come to call the doctrine of the "Real Presence." Vatican II re-expressed the traditional Catholic belief when it taught that, though Jesus is present to us in any number of ways—in the proclamation of the Gospel, in the gathering of two or three in his name, in the person of the priest at the liturgy, in the poor and suffering—he is nevertheless present in a qualitatively different way in the Eucharist. In the consecrated elements, he is "really, truly, and substantially" present to us; that is to say, his very self—Body and Blood, Humanity and Divinity—is offered to us under the form of bread and wine. Thomas Aquinas expressed this difference as follows: though in all of the other sacraments the power of Christ is present, in the Eucharist *ipse Christus*—Christ himself—is present. And this is why, for Catholics, the Eucharist is not one sign among many, one inspiring symbol among others. It is the very soul and life of the Church, the hinge upon which the life of the Church turns. The centrality of the Eucharist to the life of the community was pithily summed up in the title of John Paul II's last encyclical, *Ecclesia de Eucharistia* (The Church Comes from the Eucharist).

But still, what prevents us from walking away from this teaching? How can our reaction to this doctrine—however ecclesially important it may be—be anything but that of the first people who heard it? Let me open up one avenue of explanation. Depending upon the circumstances and the authority of the speaker, human words can change reality. If I were to walk up to you at a party and say, "You're under arrest," you would ignore me or perhaps assume I was starting a joke. But if a uniformed and properly deputed police officer came to your door and said those same words, you would, in fact, be under arrest. Or if I, from the vantage point of my box seat, were to shout out "Safe" as a Major League baseball player slid into third base, my exclamation would have no objective effect; but if the properly designated umpire, stationed just outside of the third-base foul line, shouted "You're out" as the player slid in, the unfortunate man would be, in point of fact, out. Further, a word of praise uttered by a beloved professor can start a student on the career path that will determine his life; and a word of criticism from a parent can wound so deeply that a child never recovers emotionally. The point is this: even our puny words can, to a greater or lesser degree, change reality.

Now consider the divine word. According to the author of Genesis, God spoke and things came into being. "Then God said, 'Let there be light'; and there was light" (Gen. 1:3). And in the fifty-fifth chapter of the book of the prophet Isaiah, we find this extraordinary divine assertion: "For as the rain and the snow come down from heaven, and do not return there until they have watered the earth ... so shall my word be that goes out from my mouth; it shall not return to me empty, but it shall accomplish that which I purpose, and succeed in the thing for which I sent it" (Isa. 55:10–11). God's word, on the biblical telling, is not so much descriptive as creative. It does not express a state of affairs that already exists; it makes a state of affairs to be. God's word speaks things into existence, determining them at the deepest roots of their being. And doesn't St. John express this idea in the prologue to his Gospel? "In the beginning was the Word, and the Word was with God, and the Word was God.... All things came into being through him, and without him not one thing came into being" (John 1:1, 3).

Who is Jesus but this creative Word of God made flesh? Therefore, what Jesus says, is. If he were merely a powerful preacher or prophet, his words could affect reality only superficially, as we saw in the examples above. But he is more than a prophet, more than a teacher. On the night before he died, Jesus took bread, said the blessing, broke it, and gave it to his disciples, saying, "Take, eat; this is my body" (Matt. 26:26). In the same way, after the meal, he took the cup filled with wine. Giving thanks, he passed the cup to his friends and said, "Drink from it, all of you; for this is my blood of the covenant" (Matt. 26:27–28). Given who he is, these words bore the creative power of the Logos of God. They effected a change, therefore, not simply at the level of symbolic or metaphorical reconfiguration; instead, they pierced to the very roots of the existence of those elements and changed them into something else, into his Body and Blood. In his great treatise on the Eucharist, Thomas Aquinas appropriately compares this "substantial" change to the act of creation, since both are based upon the unique power of the divine Word.

This change, this transubstantiation, explains why the Church comes from the Eucharist, and why eternal life comes from eating the Lord's Body and drinking his Blood.

Word Study

φαγεῖν	τρώγειν
PHAGEIN	TRŌGEIN
Verb	Verb
To eat	*To gnaw, chew*

THE UNBELIEF OF JESUS' BROTHERS

7 After this Jesus went about in Galilee. He did not wish to go about in Judea because the Jews were looking for an opportunity to kill him. [2] Now the Jewish festival of Booths was near. [3] So his brothers said to him, "Leave here and go to Judea so that your disciples also may see the works you are doing; [4] for no one who wants to be widely known acts in secret. If you do these things, show yourself to the world." [5] (For not even his brothers believed in him.) [6] Jesus said to them, "My time has not yet come, but your time is always here. [7] The world cannot hate you, but it hates me because I testify against it that its works are evil. [8] Go to the festival yourselves. I am not going to this festival, for my time has not yet fully come." [9] After saying this, he remained in Galilee.

JESUS AT THE FESTIVAL OF BOOTHS

[10] But after his brothers had gone to the festival, then he also went, not publicly but as it were in secret. [11] The Jews were looking for him at the festival and saying, "Where is he?" [12] And there was considerable complaining about him among the crowds. While some were saying, "He is a good man," others were saying, "No, he is deceiving the crowd." [13] Yet no one would speak openly about him for fear of the Jews.

[14] About the middle of the festival Jesus went up into the temple and began to teach. [15] The Jews were astonished at it, saying, "How does this man have such learning, when he has never been taught?" [16] Then Jesus answered them, "My teaching is not mine but his who sent me. [17] Anyone who resolves to do the will of God will know whether the teaching is from God or whether I am speaking on my own. [18] Those who speak on their own seek their own glory; but the one who seeks the glory of him who sent him is true, and there is nothing false in him.

[19] "Did not Moses give you the law? Yet none of you keeps the law. Why are you looking for an opportunity to kill me?" [20] The crowd answered, "You have a demon! Who is trying to kill you?" [21] Jesus answered them, "I performed one work, and all of you are astonished. [22] Moses gave you circumcision (it is, of course, not from Moses, but from the patriarchs), and you circumcise a man on the sabbath. [23] If a man receives circumcision on the sabbath in order that the law of Moses may not be broken, are you angry with me because I healed a man's whole body on the sabbath? [24] Do not judge by appearances, but judge with right judgment."

IS THIS THE CHRIST?

[25] Now some of the people of Jerusalem were saying, "Is not this the man whom they are trying to kill? [26] And here he is, speaking openly, but they

Joseph Ratzinger (Pope Benedict XVI)
(1927–)

Introduction to Christianity

Where Is This Man From?

John 7:27–28

The origin of Jesus is shrouded in mystery. It is true that in St. John's Gospel the people of Jerusalem object to his messianic claim on the grounds that "we know where this man is from; but when the Messiah comes, no one will know where he is from." But Jesus' immediately following words disclose how inadequate this alleged knowledge of his origin is: "I have not come on my own. But the one who sent me is true, and you do not know him."

Certainly Jesus comes from Nazareth. But what does one know of his true origin just by being able to name the geographical spot from which he comes? St. John's Gospel emphasizes again and again that the real origin of Jesus is "the Father," that he comes from him more totally than anyone sent by God before, and in a different way.

Infinitely More Than a Teacher

John 7:28–29 | Bishop Barron

There has been a disturbing tendency in recent years to deny Jesus' divinity and to turn him into an inspiring spiritual teacher, like the Buddha or the Sufi mystics.

But if that's all he is, why bother? The Gospels are never content with such a reductive description. Though they present Jesus quite clearly as a teacher, they know that he is infinitely more than that. They affirm that something else is at stake in him and our relation to him.

Jesus plainly declares his relationship with his Father: "I have not come on my own. But the one who sent me is true, and you do not know him. I know him, because I am from him, and he sent me."

say nothing to him! Can it be that the authorities really know that this is the Messiah? [27] Yet we know where this man is from; but when the Messiah comes, no one will know where he is from." [28] Then Jesus cried out as he was teaching in the temple, "You know me, and you know where I am from. I have not come on my own. But the one who sent me is true, and you do not know him. [29] I know him, because I am from him, and he sent me." [30] Then they tried to arrest him, but no one laid hands on him, because his hour had not yet come. [31] Yet many in the crowd believed in him and were saying, "When the Messiah comes, will he do more signs than this man has done?"

OFFICERS ARE SENT TO ARREST JESUS

[32] The Pharisees heard the crowd muttering such things about him, and the chief priests and Pharisees sent temple police to arrest him. [33] Jesus then said, "I will be with you a little while longer, and then I am going to him who sent me. [34] You will search for me, but you will not find me; and where I am, you cannot come." [35] The Jews said to one another, "Where does this man intend to go that we will not find him? Does he intend to go to the Dispersion among the Greeks and teach the Greeks? [36] What does he mean by saying, 'You will search for me and you will not find me' and 'Where I am, you cannot come'?"

RIVERS OF LIVING WATER

[37] On the last day of the festival, the great day, while Jesus was standing there, he cried out, "Let anyone who is thirsty come to me, [38] and let the one who believes in me drink. As the scripture has said, 'Out of the believer's

---

Thirsting for God

John 7:37–38 | Bishop Barron

In the narrative of the woman at the well, Jesus expresses his thirst in the presence of the Samaritan woman: "Give me a drink." Mother Teresa interpreted this, along Augustinian lines, as God's thirst for our faith and friendship. But here Jesus says, "Let anyone who is thirsty come to me, and let the one who believes in me drink." All human beings are also thirsty, ultimately, for friendship with God. Accordingly, a major work of Mother Teresa's community would be to slake thirst—both of Jesus for intimacy with human souls, and of human beings for God's love.

This multivalent theological meditation on thirst would be expressed later in every house established by Mother Teresa's congregation with an image of the crucified Jesus and, next to him, the words "I thirst"—Jesus' cry from the cross.

St. Augustine
(354–430)

—

Tractates on the Gospel of John

Rivers of Living Water

John 7:37–39

The Lord, therefore, cries aloud to us to come and drink, if we are thirsty within; and he says that when we have drunk, rivers of living water will flow from our heart.... What is the river that flows from the heart of the inner man? The love of his neighbor. For if he thinks that what he drinks ought to only satisfy himself, there is no living water flowing from his heart. But if he does good to his neighbor, the stream is not dried up but flows.

heart shall flow rivers of living water.'" [39] Now he said this about the Spirit, which believers in him were to receive; for as yet there was no Spirit, because Jesus was not yet glorified.

DIVISION AMONG THE PEOPLE

[40] When they heard these words, some in the crowd said, "This is really the prophet." [41] Others said, "This is the Messiah." But some asked, "Surely the Messiah does not come from Galilee, does he? [42] Has not the scripture said that the Messiah is descended from David and comes from Bethlehem, the village where David lived?" [43] So there was a division in the crowd because of him. [44] Some of them wanted to arrest him, but no one laid hands on him.

THE UNBELIEF OF THOSE IN AUTHORITY

[45] Then the temple police went back to the chief priests and Pharisees, who asked them, "Why did you not arrest him?" [46] The police answered, "Never has anyone spoken like this!" [47] Then the Pharisees replied, "Surely you have not been deceived too, have you? [48] Has any one of the authorities or of the Pharisees believed in him? [49] But this crowd, which does not know the law—they are accursed." [50] Nicodemus, who had gone to Jesus before, and who was one of them, asked, [51] "Our law does not judge people without first giving them a hearing to find out what they are doing, does it?" [52] They replied, "Surely you are not also from Galilee, are you? Search and you will see that no prophet is to arise from Galilee."

Adjust Your Vision and Expectations

John 7:40–44 | Bishop Barron

People have mixed reactions to Jesus' message. But what does he say as he preaches? "Repent, for the kingdom of heaven has come near" (Matt. 4:17). We must not flatten this out or render it too spiritually abstract, as though he were talking only about becoming nicer people, more generous and more kind. His preaching was about more than that. It was part and parcel of his messianic vocation.

What he was saying was something like this: a new order is breaking out in Israel; the tribes are coming back together and Yahweh is going to reign. Therefore, adjust your lives, your vision, your expectations. Start living even now as members of this new kingdom.

Israelites knew that a major task of the Messiah was to engage the enemies of Israel, to deal definitively with those powers opposed to God's creative purpose. This very much included political oppressors, religious charlatans, and self-absorbed Pharisees—all of whom Jesus deals with and confronts.

THE WOMAN CAUGHT IN ADULTERY

8 [53] Then each of them went home, [1] while Jesus went to the Mount of Olives. [2] Early in the morning he came again to the temple. All the people came to him and he sat down and began to teach them. [3] The scribes and the Pharisees brought a woman who had been caught in adultery; and making her stand before all of them, [4] they said to him, "Teacher, this woman was caught in the very act of committing adultery. [5] Now in the law Moses commanded us to stone such women. Now what do you say?" [6] They said this to test him, so that they might have some charge to bring against him. Jesus bent down and wrote with his finger on the ground. [7] When they kept on questioning him, he straightened up and said to them, "Let anyone among you who is without sin be the first to throw a stone at her." [8] And once again he bent down and wrote on the ground. [9] When they heard it, they went away, one by one, beginning with the elders; and Jesus was left alone with the woman standing before him. [10] Jesus straightened up and said to her, "Woman, where are they? Has no one condemned you?" [11] She said, "No one, sir." And Jesus said, "Neither do I condemn you. Go your way, and from now on do not sin again."

The Woman Caught in Adultery

John 8:1–11 | Bishop Barron

RENÉ GIRARD HAS IDENTIFIED the scapegoating mechanism as basic to the maintenance of order in most human communities. When tensions arise among people due to mimetic and competitive desire for limited goods, scapegoats—usually outsiders, or those who are different in any way—are automatically identified, and upon them is cast the collective anxiety of the group. This dynamic is at play from the gossiping conversation circle to the academic society to the nation-state: the establishment of order through blaming and expulsion.

What Girard saw as the greatest contribution of Christianity was just this unveiling of the demonic character of the scapegoating mechanism and the consequent proposal of a new nonviolent model of social order, based not on exclusion but on forgiveness and positive mimesis. One of the clearest demonstrations of both dysfunctional social dynamics and the new form of Christian ordering is the Johannine story of the woman caught in adultery. The scribes and Pharisees bring to Jesus a woman to whose adultery they have been eyewitnesses. Where, one wonders, must they have been standing and how long must they have been waiting in order to catch this unfortunate *in flagrante*? Their eagerness to find a victim, and their willingness to go to great extremes in the process, is eloquent testimony to the common and insatiable human need for scapegoats.

Having discovered her in her sin, they rush her to a prominent religious spokesperson. Girard shows throughout his writings that the scapegoating move typically finds a religious sanction because it is appreciated as the means whereby a kind of peace is brought to a riven group. God or the gods must smile on such a process. Hence, the woman's accusers confidently quote the scriptural demand: "Now in the law Moses commanded us to stone such women. Now what do you say?" The novelty of the Gospel is revealed in Jesus' refusal to contribute to the energy of the gathering storm: "Jesus bent down and wrote with his finger on the ground." Because it creates a sense of community, however perverted, scapegoating is practically irresistible, especially to those who feel threatened by already-existing tensions and rivalries within a group. By declining to cooperate with the process, Jesus effectively breaks its momentum.

Obviously frustrated by this unexpected opposition from a representative of religion, the scribes and Pharisees press him, but they are met with one of the most devastating one-liners in the Bible, a remark that is not only rhetorically smart but spiritually revolutionary: "Let anyone among you who is without sin be the first to throw a stone at her."

Jesus thereby directs the counterproductive energy of scapegoating violence back toward the accusers, compelling them to see their own mimetic desire and to appreciate the ways that it has led to a breakdown in community. In so doing, he effectively unveils the dangerous secret that the unstable order of the society has been predicated upon a violent act of exclusion. The Church Fathers emphasized this point with a neat interpretive move: they imagined that Jesus was writing in the sand none other than the sins of those who were threatening the woman. The effect of this unveiling was to compel an identification between the accusers and the accused, so that a new community of compassion and forgiveness could be forged. Whether they knew it fully or not, the scribes and Pharisees were connected to the woman by Jesus' words.

And that healthier connection necessarily forced the breakdown of the scapegoating society: "When they heard it, they went away, one by one, beginning with the elders." Having stopped its momentum by his silence, Jesus dissolves the crowd by his speech.

Then we see, at least in seminal form, the new order: "And Jesus was left alone with the woman standing before him. Jesus straightened up and said to her, 'Woman, where are they? Has no one condemned you?' She said, 'No one, sir.' And Jesus said, 'Neither do I condemn you. Go your way, and from now on do not sin again.'" Jesus and the woman—in Augustine's magnificent phrase *misericordia et misera* (mercy with misery)—are the core of a renewed communion, for their connection is not the consequence of condemnation but rather the fruit of forgiveness offered and accepted. As giver and receiver of compassion, Jesus and the woman embody the social form that participates in the loop of grace.

The ending of this episode constitutes a reversal of the opening. The scribes and Pharisees were intensely interested in the woman's behavior, because they needed her as a scapegoat; this is why, as we saw, they had been watching her so closely. At the end of the story, Jesus lets her go. Phony communions are but collectivities of egotists, in which each member of the group is trying to draw every other into his sphere of influence. This is especially true with regard to scapegoats themselves, who are clung to possessively even as they are despised. A *communio* of love, on the other hand, is predicated upon the connection whereby each looks to the good of the other, letting the other be for his own sake. Even were she to wander hundreds of miles away, the woman caught in adultery would be inextricably connected to Jesus and he to her, precisely through an act of love proffered and taken in.

The final admonition of the Lord to sin no more is perfectly congruent with this interpretation. Sin is always a form of sundering. Even a seemingly "private" or "victimless" sin such as adultery is, in fact, divisive, and hence both participates in and contributes to the overall spirit of false *communio*. Jesus is therefore telling the woman not to return to the way of being from which he has just extricated her.

JESUS THE LIGHT OF THE WORLD

[12] Again Jesus spoke to them, saying, "I am the light of the world. Whoever follows me will never walk in darkness but will have the light of life." [13] Then the Pharisees said to him, "You are testifying on your own behalf; your testimony is not valid." [14] Jesus answered, "Even if I testify on my own behalf, my testimony is valid because I know where I have come from and where I am going, but you do not know where I come from or where I am going. [15] You judge by human standards; I judge no one. [16] Yet even if I do judge, my judgment is valid; for it is not I alone who judge, but I and the Father who sent me. [17] In your law it is written that the testimony of two witnesses is valid. [18] I testify on my own behalf, and the Father who sent me testifies on my behalf." [19] Then they said to him, "Where is your Father?" Jesus answered, "You know neither me nor my Father. If you knew me, you would know my Father also." [20] He spoke these words while he was teaching in the treasury of the temple, but no one arrested him, because his hour had not yet come.

JESUS FORETELLS HIS DEATH

[21] Again he said to them, "I am going away, and you will search for me, but you will die in your sin. Where I am going, you cannot come." [22] Then the Jews said, "Is he going to kill himself? Is that what he means by saying, 'Where I am going, you cannot come'?" [23] He said to them, "You are from below, I am from above; you are of this world, I am not of this world. [24] I told you that you would die in your sins, for you will die in your sins unless you believe that I am he." [25] They said to him, "Who are you?" Jesus said to them, "Why do I speak to you at all? [26] I have much to say about you and much to condemn; but the one who sent me is true, and I declare to the world what I have heard from him." [27] They did not understand that he was speaking to them about the Father. [28] So Jesus said, "When you have lifted up the Son of Man, then you will realize that I am he, and that I do nothing on my own, but I speak these things as the Father instructed me. [29] And the one who sent me is with me; he has not left me alone, for I always do what is pleasing to him." [30] As he was saying these things, many believed in him.

TRUE DISCIPLES

[31] Then Jesus said to the Jews who had believed in him, "If you continue in my word, you are truly my disciples; [32] and you will know the truth, and the truth will make you free." [33] They answered him, "We are descendants of Abraham and have never been slaves to anyone. What do you mean by saying, 'You will be made free'?"

Second Vatican Council
(1962–1965)

———

Gaudium et Spes

The Dramatic Struggle

John 8:34

Although he was made by God in a state of holiness, from the very onset of his history man abused his liberty, at the urging of the evil one. Man set himself against God and sought to attain his goal apart from God. Although they knew God, they did not glorify him as God, but their senseless minds were darkened and they served the creature rather than the Creator.

What divine revelation makes known to us agrees with experience. Examining his heart, man finds that he has inclinations toward evil too, and is engulfed by manifold ills which cannot come from his good Creator. Often refusing to acknowledge God as his beginning, man has disrupted also his proper relationship to his own ultimate goal as well as his whole relationship toward himself and others and all created things.

Therefore man is split within himself. As a result, all of human life, whether individual or collective, shows itself to be a dramatic struggle between good and evil, between light and darkness. Indeed, man finds that by himself he is incapable of battling the assaults of evil successfully, so that everyone feels as though he is bound by chains. But the Lord himself came to free and strengthen man, renewing him inwardly and casting out that "ruler of this world" (John 12:31) who held him in the bondage of sin. For sin has diminished man, blocking his path to fulfillment.

The call to grandeur and the depths of misery, both of which are a part of human experience, find their ultimate and simultaneous explanation in the light of this revelation.

·VIA·PVLCHRITVDINIS·

THE BUILDERS OF SAINTE-CHAPELLE | *Thirteenth century*

The Stained Glass of Sainte-Chapelle

Essay by Michael Stevens

Sainte-Chapelle, which translates as "Holy Chapel," was the royal chapel to the king of France and served as the reliquary for the crown of thorns after it was brought from the Middle East to Europe. The architecture of this chapel represents the culmination of the ideas set forth by the Gothic style: an emphasis on vertical motion toward heaven; high ceilings; and towering, curtain-like walls of stained glass designed to allow as much light into the space as possible.

This obsession with light in French church architecture ties in directly with the Gospel, where Jesus tells us that he is the light of the world. The windows of Sainte-Chapelle are not only marvelous in their own right, they also reveal and heighten the beauty of the surfaces nearby, which reflect the colors and patterns of glass—each in its own way. In this same manner, we as Christians are called to reflect the light of Jesus. The more light we can receive from him, the more distinct and luminous our own lives will become. We begin to see with greater clarity, as well as recognize the characteristic qualities that the light of Jesus impresses upon everything it comes in contact with.

Rayonnant stained glass

Sainte-Chapelle represents the principles of the Gothic church building pushed to its absolute extremes. This era, known as the Rayonnant style, was famous for its towering windows that maximized the natural light that entered the interior of the church.

Bundled colonettes

Because the windows of Sainte-Chapelle are so large, exceptionally strong columns called bundled colonettes were designed to bear the entire load of the ceiling. Because of these columns, almost none of the weight of the ceiling falls on the areas of glass.

Star-painted ceiling

Church ceilings of this time period often featured a repeating star pattern on a field of blue. This represents the dissolving of the boundary between heaven and earth during the Mass.

³⁴ Jesus answered them, "Very truly, I tell you, everyone who commits sin is a slave to sin. ³⁵ The slave does not have a permanent place in the household; the son has a place there forever. ³⁶ So if the Son makes you free, you will be free indeed. ³⁷ I know that you are descendants of Abraham; yet you look for an opportunity to kill me, because there is no place in you for my word. ³⁸ I declare what I have seen in the Father's presence; as for you, you should do what you have heard from the Father."

JESUS AND ABRAHAM

³⁹ They answered him, "Abraham is our father." Jesus said to them, "If you were Abraham's children, you would be doing what Abraham did, ⁴⁰ but now you are trying to kill me, a man who has told you the truth that I heard from God. This is not what Abraham did. ⁴¹ You are indeed doing what your father does." They said to him, "We are not illegitimate children; we have one father, God himself." ⁴² Jesus said to them, "If God were your Father, you would love me, for I came from God and now I am here. I did not come

This Mysterious Limp

John 8:34 | Bishop Barron

Jesus speaks with Jewish leaders who want to kill him, telling them they are hardened in their sin. He says, "Very truly, I tell you, everyone who commits sin is a slave to sin."

In the Christian tradition, sin is a kind of nonbeing, an illusion, if you will. To live in sin is to live stubbornly in an unreal world. Our mind becomes confused and our will disoriented. This helps explain why the devil is often referred to as "the father of lies."

Theologian Henri de Lubac gives voice to this conviction when he refers to sin as *cette claudication mystérieuse* (this mysterious limp). It is a deformation, a corruption.

All of us sinners have, to one degree or another, bought into the lie. At the heart of the lie—and we can see it in the Genesis account—is the deification of the ego. I become the center of the universe, I with my needs and my fears and my demands.

And when the puny "I" is the center of the cosmos, the tie that binds all things to one another is lost. The basic reality now becomes rivalry, competition, violence, and mistrust.

on my own, but he sent me. [43] Why do you not understand what I say? It is because you cannot accept my word. [44] You are from your father the devil, and you choose to do your father's desires. He was a murderer from the beginning and does not stand in the truth, because there is no truth in him. When he lies, he speaks according to his own nature, for he is a liar and the father of lies. [45] But because I tell the truth, you do not believe me. [46] Which of you convicts me of sin? If I tell the truth, why do you not believe me? [47] Whoever is from God hears the words of God. The reason you do not hear them is that you are not from God."

[48] The Jews answered him, "Are we not right in saying that you are a Samaritan and have a demon?" [49] Jesus answered, "I do not have a demon; but I honor my Father, and you dishonor me. [50] Yet I do not seek my own glory; there is one who seeks it and he is the judge. [51] Very truly, I tell you, whoever keeps my word will never see death." [52] The Jews said to him, "Now we know that you have a demon. Abraham died, and so did the prophets; yet you say, 'Whoever keeps my word will never taste death.' [53] Are you greater than our father Abraham, who died? The prophets also died. Who do you claim to be?" [54] Jesus answered, "If I glorify myself, my glory is nothing. It is my Father who glorifies me, he of whom you say, 'He is our God,' [55] though you do not know him. But I know him; if I would say that I do not know him, I would be a liar like you. But I do know him and I keep his word. [56] Your ancestor Abraham rejoiced that he would see my day; he saw it and was glad." [57] Then the Jews said to him, "You are not yet fifty years old, and have you seen Abraham?" [58] Jesus said to them, "Very truly, I tell you, before Abraham was, I am." [59] So they picked up stones to throw at him, but Jesus hid himself and went out of the temple.

Before A B R A H A M   W A S ,

I AM.

JOHN 8:58

G.K. Chesterton
(1874–1936)
———
The Everlasting Man

Before Abraham Was, I Am

John 8:58

What should we feel at the first whisper of a certain suggestion about a certain man? Certainly it is not for us to blame anybody who should find that first wild whisper merely impious and insane. On the contrary, stumbling on that rock of scandal is the first step. Stark incredulity is a far more loyal tribute to that truth than a modernist metaphysic that would make it out merely a matter of degree. It were better to rend our robes with a great cry against blasphemy, like Caiaphas in the judgment, or to lay hold of the man as a maniac possessed of devils like the kinsmen and the crowd, rather than to stand stupidly debating fine shades of pantheism in the presence of so catastrophic a claim.

There is more of the wisdom that is one with surprise in any simple person, full of the sensitiveness of simplicity, who should expect the grass to wither and the birds to drop dead out of the air, when a strolling carpenter's apprentice said calmly and almost carelessly, like one looking over his shoulder: "Before Abraham was, I am."

A MAN BORN BLIND RECEIVES SIGHT

9 As he walked along, he saw a man blind from birth. [2] His disciples asked him, "Rabbi, who sinned, this man or his parents, that he was born blind?" [3] Jesus answered, "Neither this man nor his parents sinned; he was born blind so that God's works might be revealed in him. [4] We must work the works of him who sent me while it is day; night is coming when no one can work. [5] As long as I am in the world, I am the light of the world." [6] When he had said this, he spat on the ground and made mud with the saliva and spread the mud on the man's eyes, [7] saying to him, "Go, wash

St. Thomas Aquinas
(1225–1274)

———

Commentary on the
Gospel of John

Mystically Understanding the Pool

John 9:6–7

Augustine gives the mystical and allegorical explanation. He says that the spittle, which is saliva that descends from the head, signifies the Word of God, who proceeds from the Father, the head of all things: "I came forth from the mouth of the Most High" (Sir. 24:3). Therefore, the Lord made clay from spittle and the earth when the Word was made flesh. He anointed the eyes of the blind man—that is, of the human race. And the eyes are the eyes of the heart, anointed by faith in the Incarnation of Christ.

But the blind man did not yet see, because the anointing produced a catechumen, who has faith but has not yet been baptized. So he sends him to the pool of Siloam to wash and receive his sight, i.e., to be baptized, and in Baptism to receive full enlightenment. Thus, according to Dionysius, Baptism is an enlightenment: "I will sprinkle clean water upon you, and you shall be clean from all your uncleannesses" (Ezek. 36:25). And so this Gospel is appropriately read in Lent, on Holy Saturday, when those about to be baptized are examined.

Nor is it without reason that the Evangelist adds the meaning of the pool, saying, "which means Sent," because whoever is baptized must be baptized in Christ, who was sent by the Father: "As many of you as were baptized into Christ have clothed yourselves with Christ" (Gal. 3:27). For if Christ had not been sent, none of us would have been freed from sin.

in the pool of Siloam" (which means Sent). Then he went and washed and came back able to see. [8] The neighbors and those who had seen him before as a beggar began to ask, "Is this not the man who used to sit and beg?" [9] Some were saying, "It is he." Others were saying, "No, but it is someone like him." He kept saying, "I am the man." [10] But they kept asking him, "Then how were your eyes opened?" [11] He answered, "The man called Jesus made mud, spread it on my eyes, and said to me, 'Go to Siloam and wash.' Then I went and washed and received my sight." [12] They said to him, "Where is he?" He said, "I do not know."

THE PHARISEES INVESTIGATE THE HEALING

[13] They brought to the Pharisees the man who had formerly been blind. [14] Now it was a sabbath day when Jesus made the mud and opened his eyes. [15] Then the Pharisees also began to ask him how he had received his sight. He said to them, "He put mud on my eyes. Then I washed, and now I see." [16] Some of the Pharisees said, "This man is not from God, for he does not observe the sabbath." But others said, "How can a man who is a sinner perform such signs?" And they were divided. [17] So they said again to the blind man, "What do you say about him? It was your eyes he opened." He said, "He is a prophet."

A Microcosm of the Spiritual Life

John 9:1–41 | Bishop Barron

The story of the man born blind is a microcosm of the spiritual life. "As [Jesus] walked along, he saw a man blind from birth." Jesus responds by doing something a little weird: he makes a mud paste and rubs it on the blind man's eyes. And then Jesus tells the man to wash in the pool of Siloam.

When the man comes back able to see, his neighbors are confused. Some say it's the same person, and others say it just looks like him. This is wonderful. Once you've put on the Lord Jesus Christ, you're changed in every aspect of your life to the point where you may seem odd and different to others.

But that wasn't the end of the story. It then takes a dramatic turn. The Pharisees interrogate the healed man. It becomes clear that Jesus healed him on a sabbath day, and so they condemn Jesus. They throw the formerly blind man out, but Jesus looks for him. He asks the man: "Do you believe in the Son of Man?" Jesus wants us to put every ounce of our trust in him—and our vision will deepen. This in many ways is the heart of the matter: de-center your ego and re-center it on Christ. And now that you see, believe!

¹⁸ The Jews did not believe that he had been blind and had received his sight until they called the parents of the man who had received his sight ¹⁹ and asked them, "Is this your son, who you say was born blind? How then does he now see?" ²⁰ His parents answered, "We know that this is our son, and that he was born blind; ²¹ but we do not know how it is that now he sees, nor do we know who opened his eyes. Ask him; he is of age. He will speak for himself." ²² His parents said this because they were afraid of the Jews; for the Jews had already agreed that anyone who confessed Jesus to be the Messiah would be put out of the synagogue. ²³ Therefore his parents said, "He is of age; ask him."

²⁴ So for the second time they called the man who had been blind, and they said to him, "Give glory to God! We know that this man is a sinner." ²⁵ He answered, "I do not know whether he is a sinner. One thing I do know, that though I was blind, now I see." ²⁶ They said to him, "What did he do to you? How did he open your eyes?" ²⁷ He answered them, "I have told you already, and you would not listen. Why do you want to hear it again? Do you also want to become his disciples?" ²⁸ Then they reviled him, saying, "You are his disciple, but we are disciples of Moses. ²⁹ We know that God has spoken to Moses, but as for this man, we do not know where he comes

---

Now I See

John 9:25 | Bishop Barron

In the strange and strikingly beautiful account of the healing of the man born blind, we find an iconic representation of Christianity as a way of *seeing*.

The crowds are amazed, but the Pharisees—consternated and skeptical—accuse the man of being naïve and the one who healed him of being a sinner. With disarming simplicity the visionary responds: "I do not know whether he is a sinner. One thing I do know, that though I was blind, now I see."

This is precisely what all Christians say when they have encountered the light of Christ. It was St. Augustine who saw in the making of the mud paste a metaphor for the Incarnation: the divine power mixing with the earth, resulting in the formation of a healing balm. When this salve of God made flesh is rubbed onto our eyes blinded by sin, we come again to see.

from." ³⁰ The man answered, "Here is an astonishing thing! You do not know where he comes from, and yet he opened my eyes. ³¹ We know that God does not listen to sinners, but he does listen to one who worships him and obeys his will. ³² Never since the world began has it been heard that anyone opened the eyes of a person born blind. ³³ If this man were not from God, he could do nothing." ³⁴ They answered him, "You were born entirely in sins, and are you trying to teach us?" And they drove him out.

SPIRITUAL BLINDNESS

³⁵ Jesus heard that they had driven him out, and when he found him, he said, "Do you believe in the Son of Man?" ³⁶ He answered, "And who is he, sir? Tell me, so that I may believe in him." ³⁷ Jesus said to him, "You have seen him, and the one speaking with you is he." ³⁸ He said, "Lord, I believe." And he worshiped him. ³⁹ Jesus said, "I came into this world for judgment so that those who do not see may see, and those who do see may become blind." ⁴⁰ Some of the Pharisees near him heard this and said to him, "Surely we are not blind, are we?" ⁴¹ Jesus said to them, "If you were blind, you would not have sin. But now that you say, 'We see,' your sin remains.

JESUS THE GOOD SHEPHERD

10 "Very truly, I tell you, anyone who does not enter the sheepfold by the gate but climbs in by another way is a thief and a bandit. ² The one who enters by the gate is the shepherd of the sheep. ³ The gatekeeper opens the gate for him, and the sheep hear his voice. He calls his own sheep by name and leads them out. ⁴ When he has brought out all his own, he goes ahead of them, and the sheep follow him because they know his voice. ⁵ They will not follow a stranger, but they will run from him because they do not know the voice of strangers." ⁶ Jesus used this figure of speech with them, but they did not understand what he was saying to them.

⁷ So again Jesus said to them, "Very truly, I tell you, I am the gate for the sheep. ⁸ All who came before me are thieves and bandits; but the sheep did not listen to them. ⁹ I am the gate. Whoever enters by me will be saved, and will come in and go out and find pasture. ¹⁰ The thief comes only to steal and kill and destroy. I came that they may have life, and have it abundantly.

¹¹ "I am the good shepherd. The good shepherd lays down his life for the sheep. ¹² The hired hand, who is not the shepherd and does not own the sheep, sees the wolf coming and leaves the sheep and runs away—and the wolf snatches them and scatters them. ¹³ The hired hand runs away because a hired hand does not care for the sheep. ¹⁴ I am the good shepherd. I know my own and my own know me, ¹⁵ just as the Father knows me and I know

the Father. And I lay down my life for the sheep. [16] I have other sheep that do not belong to this fold. I must bring them also, and they will listen to my voice. So there will be one flock, one shepherd. [17] For this reason the Father loves me, because I lay down my life in order to take it up again.

St. Augustine
(354–430)

———

Tractates on the Gospel of John

The Low Gateway

John 10:1–18

Keep hold of this: that Christ's sheepfold is the Catholic Church. Whoever would enter the sheepfold, let him enter by the door, let him preach the true Christ. Not only let him preach the true Christ, but seek Christ's glory, not his own; for many, by seeking their own glory, have scattered Christ's sheep instead of gathering them. For Christ the Lord is a low gateway: he who enters by this gateway must humble himself, so that he will not bump his head.

The Good Shepherd

John 10:11 | Bishop Barron

In the thirty-fourth chapter of the book of the prophet Ezekiel, we hear that God would one day come and shepherd Israel himself. Shepherds guarded, guided, protected, and watched over their flocks—just as God guards, guides, protects, and watches over Israel.

This image comes to a climactic expression in the words of Jesus: "I am the good shepherd." What precisely makes him good? A good shepherd lays down his life for the sheep. The good shepherd is so other-oriented, so devoted to his sheep, that he is willing to surrender his life that they might live.

Sure, a good shepherd should do all that he can to protect and guide his flock, but who among us would really expect him to give his life for them? But this is precisely what Jesus does.

Imagine the difference between human beings and sheep; and now multiply that difference infinitely. That would give you some idea of the difference between God and humanity. And yet God is willing to lay down his life for the likes of us.

[18] No one takes it from me, but I lay it down of my own accord. I have power to lay it down, and I have power to take it up again. I have received this command from my Father."

[19] Again the Jews were divided because of these words. [20] Many of them were saying, "He has a demon and is out of his mind. Why listen to him?" [21] Others were saying, "These are not the words of one who has a demon. Can a demon open the eyes of the blind?"

JESUS IS REJECTED BY THE JEWS

[22] At that time the festival of the Dedication took place in Jerusalem. It was winter, [23] and Jesus was walking in the temple, in the portico of Solomon. [24] So the Jews gathered around him and said to him, "How long will you keep us in suspense? If you are the Messiah, tell us plainly." [25] Jesus answered, "I have told you, and you do not believe. The works that I do in my Father's name testify to me; [26] but you do not believe, because you do not belong to my sheep. [27] My sheep hear my voice. I know them, and they follow me. [28] I give them eternal life, and they will never perish. No one will snatch them out of my hand. [29] What my Father has given me is greater than all else, and no one can snatch it out of the Father's hand. [30] The Father and I are one."

How to Hear Jesus' Voice

John 10:27–30 | Bishop Barron

How wonderful and strange that Christianity is not a set of ideas. It's not a philosophy or an ideology. It's a relationship with someone who has a voice. The first disciples were privileged to hear the voice of the historical Jesus, with its very particular tonality and texture.

But we can hear his voice too, in our own way, when we hear the Scriptures proclaimed at Mass. At Mass, Catholics don't just read the Bible; we *hear* the Bible.

We hear the voice of Jesus too when the bishops and the popes speak. We can also hear the voice of Jesus in our conscience, which Newman called "the aboriginal vicar of Christ in the soul."

We can hear the voice of Jesus in good spiritual friends as well, in those people who comfort us and challenge us, and keep calling us to higher ideals and encourage us when we fall. And we listen to Jesus because he is leading us to a renewed and transformed life on high with God.

³¹ The Jews took up stones again to stone him. ³² Jesus replied, "I have shown you many good works from the Father. For which of these are you going to stone me?" ³³ The Jews answered, "It is not for a good work that we are going to stone you, but for blasphemy, because you, though only a human being, are making yourself God." ³⁴ Jesus answered, "Is it not written in your law, 'I said, you are gods'? ³⁵ If those to whom the word of God came were called 'gods'—and the scripture cannot be annulled—³⁶ can you say that the one whom the Father has sanctified and sent into the world is blaspheming because I said, 'I am God's Son'? ³⁷ If I am not doing the works of my Father, then do not believe me. ³⁸ But if I do them, even though you do not believe me, believe the works, so that you may know and understand that the Father is in me and I am in the Father." ³⁹ Then they tried to arrest him again, but he escaped from their hands.

⁴⁰ He went away again across the Jordan to the place where John had been baptizing earlier, and he remained there. ⁴¹ Many came to him, and they were saying, "John performed no sign, but everything that John said about this man was true." ⁴² And many believed in him there.

I AM THE GOOD SHEPHERD. THE GOOD SHEPHERD LAYS DOWN HIS LIFE *for the* SHEEP.

JOHN 10:11

UNKNOWN ARTIST | *Second century*

Christ the Good Shepherd

Essay by Michael Stevens

In this second-century fresco, we see one of the earliest surviving images of Christ. He is shown as a shepherd, with one goat over his shoulder, and two others at his feet. The image is drawn from the tenth chapter of John, in which Jesus describes himself as the good shepherd.

This fresco is located in the Roman catacombs, the vast network of tunnels and underground burial sites where many of the earliest Christians were buried. The catacombs became a gathering place for the persecuted early Church, whose operations needed to be kept secret in many cases.

The underground nature of the Church at this time in history made it fertile ground for the development of secret symbols that were known only among Christians. These included the anchor, the fish (still common in Christian communities today), the breaking of the bread (signifying the celebration of the Mass), and images like this one, which depict Christ and other holy figures in ways that were not as obvious to hostile persecutors.

Painting style

The manner in which Christ's face and body are painted reflects the style of Roman painting that was common at the time. The visual language of pagan Rome—typically used to portray the gods of mythology—is used for a new purpose in this fresco: to tell the story of Jesus Christ.

Christ as the New David

The motif of Christ the good shepherd strongly recalls the Hebrew shepherd-king David. In this image, the implication is that Jesus not only fulfills David's role as a shepherd but as a king as well.

THE DEATH OF LAZARUS

11 Now a certain man was ill, Lazarus of Bethany, the village of Mary and her sister Martha. ² Mary was the one who anointed the Lord with perfume and wiped his feet with her hair; her brother Lazarus was ill. ³ So the sisters sent a message to Jesus, "Lord, he whom you love is ill." ⁴ But when Jesus heard it, he said, "This illness does not lead to death; rather it is for God's glory, so that the Son of God may be glorified through it." ⁵ Accordingly, though Jesus loved Martha and her sister and Lazarus, ⁶ after having heard that Lazarus was ill, he stayed two days longer in the place where he was.

⁷ Then after this he said to the disciples, "Let us go to Judea again." ⁸ The disciples said to him, "Rabbi, the Jews were just now trying to stone you, and are you going there again?" ⁹ Jesus answered, "Are there not twelve hours of daylight? Those who walk during the day do not stumble, because they see the light of this world. ¹⁰ But those who walk at night stumble, because the light is not in them." ¹¹ After saying this, he told them, "Our friend Lazarus has fallen asleep, but I am going there to awaken him." ¹² The disciples said to him, "Lord, if he has fallen asleep, he will be all right." ¹³ Jesus, however, had been speaking about his death, but they thought that he was referring merely to sleep. ¹⁴ Then Jesus told them plainly, "Lazarus

---

Facing Down Death

John 11:1–44 | Bishop Barron

Jesus came primarily as a warrior whose final enemy is death. It is easy to domesticate Jesus, presenting him as a kindly moral teacher. But that is not how the Gospels present him. He is a cosmic warrior who has come to do battle with those forces that keep us from being fully alive.

Throughout the Gospels, Jesus deals with the effects of death and a death-obsessed culture: violence, hatred, egotism, exclusion, false religion, phony community. But the final enemy he must face down is death itself. Like Frodo going into Mordor in *The Lord of the Rings*, Jesus has to go into death's domain, get into close quarters with it, and take it on.

Coming to Lazarus' tomb, Jesus feels the deepest emotions and begins to weep. This is God entering into the darkness, confusion, and agony of the death of sinners. He doesn't blithely stand above our situation, but rather takes it on and feels it at its deepest level.

St. Augustine
(354–430)

———

Tractates on the Gospel of John

A Greater Deed

John 11:1–44

Among all the miracles performed by our Lord Jesus Christ, the resurrection of Lazarus holds a foremost place in preaching. But if we consider attentively who did it, our duty is to rejoice rather than to wonder.

A man was raised up by him who made man: for he is the only One of the Father, by whom, as you know, all things were made. And if all things were made by him, what wonder is it that one was raised by him, when so many are daily brought into the world by his power?

It is a greater deed to create men than to raise them again from the dead. Yet he deigned both to create and to raise again; to create all, to resuscitate some.

is dead. ¹⁵ For your sake I am glad I was not there, so that you may believe. But let us go to him." ¹⁶ Thomas, who was called the Twin, said to his fellow disciples, "Let us also go, that we may die with him."

JESUS THE RESURRECTION AND THE LIFE

¹⁷ When Jesus arrived, he found that Lazarus had already been in the tomb four days. ¹⁸ Now Bethany was near Jerusalem, some two miles away, ¹⁹ and many of the Jews had come to Martha and Mary to console them about their brother. ²⁰ When Martha heard that Jesus was coming, she went and met him, while Mary stayed at home. ²¹ Martha said to Jesus, "Lord, if you had been here, my brother would not have died. ²² But even now I know that God will give you whatever you ask of him." ²³ Jesus said to her, "Your brother will rise again." ²⁴ Martha said to him, "I know that he will rise again in the resurrection on the last day." ²⁵ Jesus said to her, "I am the resurrection and the life. Those who believe in me, even though they die, will live, ²⁶ and everyone who lives and believes in me will never die. Do you believe this?" ²⁷ She said to him, "Yes, Lord, I believe that you are the Messiah, the Son of God, the one coming into the world."

JESUS WEEPS

[28] When she had said this, she went back and called her sister Mary, and told her privately, "The Teacher is here and is calling for you." [29] And when she heard it, she got up quickly and went to him. [30] Now Jesus had not yet come to the village, but was still at the place where Martha had met him. [31] The Jews who were with her in the house, consoling her, saw Mary get up quickly and go out. They followed her because they thought that she was going to the tomb to weep there. [32] When Mary came where Jesus was and saw him, she knelt at his feet and said to him, "Lord, if you had been here, my brother would not have died." [33] When Jesus saw her weeping, and the Jews who came with her also weeping, he was greatly disturbed in spirit and deeply moved. [34] He said, "Where have you laid him?" They said to him, "Lord, come and see." [35] Jesus began to weep. [36] So the Jews said, "See how he loved him!" [37] But some of them said, "Could not he who opened the eyes of the blind man have kept this man from dying?"

JESUS RAISES LAZARUS TO LIFE

[38] Then Jesus, again greatly disturbed, came to the tomb. It was a cave, and a stone was lying against it. [39] Jesus said, "Take away the stone." Martha, the sister of the dead man, said to him, "Lord, already there is a stench because

---

St. John Henry Newman
(1801–1890)

Parochial and Plain Sermons

Why Did Jesus Weep?

John 11:35

On first reading these words ["Jesus began to weep"] the question naturally arises in the mind—why did our Lord weep at the grave of Lazarus? He knew he had power to raise him, so why should he act the part of those who sorrow for the dead? … Jesus wept from spontaneous tenderness; from the gentleness and mercy, the encompassing loving-kindness and exuberant fostering affection of the Son of God for his own work, the race of man. Their tears touched him at once, as their miseries had brought him down from heaven. His ear was open to them, and the sound of weeping went at once to his heart.

he has been dead four days." ⁴⁰ Jesus said to her, "Did I not tell you that if you believed, you would see the glory of God?" ⁴¹ So they took away the stone. And Jesus looked upward and said, "Father, I thank you for having heard me. ⁴² I knew that you always hear me, but I have said this for the sake of the crowd standing here, so that they may believe that you sent me." ⁴³ When he had said this, he cried with a loud voice, "Lazarus, come out!" ⁴⁴ The dead man came out, his hands and feet bound with strips of cloth, and his face wrapped in a cloth. Jesus said to them, "Unbind him, and let him go."

THE PLOT TO KILL JESUS

⁴⁵ Many of the Jews therefore, who had come with Mary and had seen what Jesus did, believed in him. ⁴⁶ But some of them went to the Pharisees and told them what he had done. ⁴⁷ So the chief priests and the Pharisees called a meeting of the council, and said, "What are we to do? This man is performing many signs. ⁴⁸ If we let him go on like this, everyone will believe in him, and the Romans will come and destroy both our holy place and our nation." ⁴⁹ But one of them, Caiaphas, who was high priest that year, said to them, "You know nothing at all! ⁵⁰ You do not understand that it is better for you to have one man die for the people than to have the whole nation destroyed." ⁵¹ He did not say this on his own, but being high priest that year he prophesied that Jesus was about to die for the nation, ⁵² and not for the nation only, but to gather into one the dispersed children of God. ⁵³ So from that day on they planned to put him to death.

⁵⁴ Jesus therefore no longer walked about openly among the Jews, but went from there to a town called Ephraim in the region near the wilderness; and he remained there with the disciples.

⁵⁵ Now the Passover of the Jews was near, and many went up from the country to Jerusalem before the Passover to purify themselves. ⁵⁶ They were looking for Jesus and were asking one another as they stood in the temple, "What do you think? Surely he will not come to the festival, will he?" ⁵⁷ Now the chief priests and the Pharisees had given orders that anyone who knew where Jesus was should let them know, so that they might arrest him.

MARY ANOINTS JESUS

12 Six days before the Passover Jesus came to Bethany, the home of Lazarus, whom he had raised from the dead. ² There they gave a dinner for him. Martha served, and Lazarus was one of those at the table with him. ³ Mary took a pound of costly perfume made of pure nard, anointed Jesus' feet, and wiped them with her hair. The house was filled with the fragrance of the perfume. ⁴ But Judas Iscariot, one of his disciples (the one who was about to betray him), said, ⁵ "Why was this perfume not sold for three hundred denarii and the money given to the poor?" ⁶ (He said

this not because he cared about the poor, but because he was a thief; he kept the common purse and used to steal what was put into it.) ⁷ Jesus said, "Leave her alone. She bought it so that she might keep it for the day of my burial. ⁸ You always have the poor with you, but you do not always have me."

THE PLOT TO KILL LAZARUS

⁹ When the great crowd of the Jews learned that he was there, they came not only because of Jesus but also to see Lazarus, whom he had raised from the dead. ¹⁰ So the chief priests planned to put Lazarus to death as well, ¹¹ since it was on account of him that many of the Jews were deserting and were believing in Jesus.

JESUS' TRIUMPHAL ENTRY INTO JERUSALEM

¹² The next day the great crowd that had come to the festival heard that Jesus was coming to Jerusalem. ¹³ So they took branches of palm trees and went out to meet him, shouting,

> "Hosanna!
> Blessed is the one who comes in the name of the Lord—
> the King of Israel!"

¹⁴ Jesus found a young donkey and sat on it; as it is written:

> ¹⁵ *"Do not be afraid, daughter of Zion.*
> *Look, your king is coming,*
> *sitting on a donkey's colt!"*

¹⁶ His disciples did not understand these things at first; but when Jesus was glorified, then they remembered that these things had been written of him and had been done to him. ¹⁷ So the crowd that had been with him when he called Lazarus out of the tomb and raised him from the dead continued to testify. ¹⁸ It was also because they heard that he had performed this sign that the crowd went to meet him. ¹⁹ The Pharisees then said to one another, "You see, you can do nothing. Look, the world has gone after him!"

SOME GREEKS WISH TO SEE JESUS

²⁰ Now among those who went up to worship at the festival were some Greeks. ²¹ They came to Philip, who was from Bethsaida in Galilee, and said to him, "Sir, we wish to see Jesus." ²² Philip went and told Andrew; then Andrew and Philip went and told Jesus. ²³ Jesus answered them, "The hour has come for the Son of Man to be glorified. ²⁴ Very truly, I tell you, unless a grain of wheat falls into the earth and dies, it remains just a single grain; but if it dies, it bears much fruit. ²⁵ Those who love their life lose it, and those who hate their life in this world will keep it for eternal life. ²⁶ Whoever serves me must follow me, and where I am, there will my servant be also. Whoever serves me, the Father will honor.

St. Cyril of Alexandria
(378–444)

Commentary on the Gospel of John

Taking on Every Assault
John 12:27

Death could never have been defeated except by the death of the Savior, nor any of the other sufferings of the flesh: for unless he had felt dread, human nature could not have become free from dread; unless he had experienced grief, there could never have been any deliverance from grief; unless he had been troubled and alarmed, no escape from these feelings could have been found.

Every one of the emotions which assault human nature can be found in Christ … so that they might be thoroughly subdued by the power of the Word dwelling in the flesh, thereby changing the nature of man for the better.

JESUS SPEAKS ABOUT HIS DEATH

²⁷ "Now my soul is troubled. And what should I say—'Father, save me from this hour'? No, it is for this reason that I have come to this hour. ²⁸ Father, glorify your name." Then a voice came from heaven, "I have glorified it, and I will glorify it again." ²⁹ The crowd standing there heard it and said that it was thunder. Others said, "An angel has spoken to him." ³⁰ Jesus answered, "This voice has come for your sake, not for mine. ³¹ Now is the judgment of this world; now the ruler of this world will be driven out. ³² And I, when I am lifted up from the earth, will draw all people to myself." ³³ He said this to indicate the kind of death he was to die. ³⁴ The crowd answered him, "We have heard from the law that the Messiah remains forever. How can you say that the Son of Man must be lifted up? Who is this Son of Man?" ³⁵ Jesus said to them, "The light is with you for a little longer. Walk while you have the light, so that the darkness may not overtake you. If you walk in the darkness, you do not know where you are going. ³⁶ While you have the light, believe in the light, so that you may become children of light."

Light on the figure of Christ

In a subtle gesture of reverence, Tanner reserves the brightest highlight for Christ himself. This enhances the mysterious quality of the lighting within the tomb and underscores the power of Christ as the focal point of this Gospel account.

An autobiographical hint

The dark-skinned figure at the top left was likely included by the artist as a symbolic autobiographical detail. Tanner spent much of his life surrounded by white artists and patrons, so the placement of this person in the scene could be an illustration of Tanner's own experience in the art world.

Lighting outside the cave

Tanner provides only a sliver of sunlight from outside the tomb, but with this detail he completely changes the viewer's reading of the painting. Instead of seeing this as a nighttime scene in the open outdoors, we suddenly read this as a daytime scene in the depths of a tight, enclosed, cavernous space. Furthermore, the light from outside the tomb holds the promise of hope for Lazarus, who will soon emerge from the tomb to step out into the light of day.

John 11:38–44

HENRY OSSAWA TANNER | *1896*

The Resurrection of Lazarus

Essay by Michael Stevens

Henry Ossawa Tanner was a master painter of the late nineteenth century, famous for his lifelike portraits, coloristic landscapes, and emotionally captivating biblical scenes. He was the first black artist to secure an international reputation and came from a family that valued both faith and education—two values that helped to define Tanner's career and style. He was born in the United States but spent most of his life in Paris, which was the cultural and artistic center of the Western world.

Tanner's painting *The Resurrection of Lazarus* was a breakthrough work in his career and was widely acclaimed in the French salons where it was first exhibited. Ultimately it opened the door for Tanner to study and paint in the Holy Land, which allowed for even greater focus on the genre of biblical narrative painting.

In this scene, we see Jesus standing confidently over the tomb of Lazarus, who clasps his chest as he is brought back to life. Jesus' open hands communicate a gentle authority, contrasted by the frantic reactions of the surrounding crowd, who cover their faces and gasp in disbelief.

The entire scene is bathed in warm, inviting light, which is a defining feature of Tanner's work from this time. This light provides enough detail to see the figures and their reactions, while the scene remains dark enough to maintain a sense of focus and intrigue. The overall effect is one of comfort in the healing presence of Jesus, as well as shock at the miracle of witnessing a dead man being raised.

I Will Draw All People to Myself

John 12:32 | Bishop Barron

The biblical God is a great gathering force. In his own nature, he is a community of love, a unity in difference. This infinitely intense divine love gives rise to a universe of interconnected things, all joined to each other through their common center in God. God's preoccupation, from the beginning, is the coming together of the many as one, gathering in. That which stands opposed to God, therefore, is always a power of separation.

The early Church Father Origen of Alexandria commented "ubi divisio ibi peccatum" (where there is division, there is sin), and the English word "sin" is rooted in the German *Sunde*, which means "sundering" or "separating." In the wake of sin, God conceived a rescue operation in the form of a people Israel. He gathered in the family of Abraham and shaped them according to his own heart, giving them the laws, covenants, and rituals that would unite them in love and hence make them pleasing to God and attractive to all the nations. As is argued throughout the Bible, the distinctiveness of Israel was, therefore, not *against* the world but precisely *for* the world.

Jesus is none other than the fulfillment of Israel—the true Covenant, the embodiment of the Law, the authentic Temple—and therefore he is the supreme Gatherer: "And I, when I am lifted up from the earth, will draw all people to myself." His Body the Church is the instrument by which he continues this work up and down the centuries.

THE UNBELIEF OF THE PEOPLE

After Jesus had said this, he departed and hid from them. [37] Although he had performed so many signs in their presence, they did not believe in him. [38] This was to fulfill the word spoken by the prophet Isaiah:

> "Lord, who has believed our message,
>   and to whom has the arm of the Lord been revealed?"

[39] And so they could not believe, because Isaiah also said,

> [40] "He has blinded their eyes
>   and hardened their heart,
>   so that they might not look with their eyes,
>   and understand with their heart and turn—
>   and I would heal them."

41 Isaiah said this because he saw his glory and spoke about him.

42 Nevertheless many, even of the authorities, believed in him. But because of the Pharisees they did not confess it, for fear that they would be put out of the synagogue; 43 for they loved human glory more than the glory that comes from God.

SUMMARY OF JESUS' TEACHING

44 Then Jesus cried aloud: "Whoever believes in me believes not in me but in him who sent me. 45 And whoever sees me sees him who sent me. 46 I have come as light into the world, so that everyone who believes in me should not remain in the darkness. 47 I do not judge anyone who hears my words and does not keep them, for I came not to judge the world, but to save the world. 48 The one who rejects me and does not receive my word has a judge; on the last day the word that I have spoken will serve as judge, 49 for I have not spoken on my own, but the Father who sent me has himself given me a commandment about what to say and what to speak. 50 And I know that his commandment is eternal life. What I speak, therefore, I speak just as the Father has told me."

I HAVE COME AS LIGHT INTO THE WORLD, SO THAT EVERYONE WHO BELIEVES IN ME SHOULD NOT REMAIN IN THE DARKNESS. JOHN 12:46

**Hans Urs
von Balthasar**
(1905–1988)

———

*Explorations in
Theology, Vol. III:
Creator Spirit*

Peter's Appalling Yes

John 13:1–20

The dialogue with Peter… begins with his profoundest shock: "Lord, are you going to wash my feet?" This is utterly inappropriate, the turning upside-down of every human order of rank, and this to the fullest extent, since not even a free Israelite, let alone the "Lord and Teacher" could be given the task of washing feet, but only a slave.

Jesus' reply gives no explanation but merely confirms the incomprehensibility for the present. "You do not know now what I am doing, but later you will understand"—after the Resurrection and the sending of the Spirit who interprets this.

Peter must utter his Yes *in persona Ecclesiae* [in the person of the Church] in a state of nonunderstanding, in pure obedience, indeed, more than this, in the confusion of an elemental shrinking back in terror, a terror that is expressed in Peter's second statement: "You will never wash my feet." In other words: This is what I can never permit under any circumstances. Why? Because this means the collapse of the total religious order of values of the natural man. God is above, man is below. The saint is above, the sinner is below.…

The only thing that matters now is the *conditio sine qua non* [the necessary condition]: to let this happen in a state of terror and incomprehension. This is why Jesus compels Peter here to say Yes.

The freedom to say No is something purely abstract for the believer, i.e., for the one who loves; if what he wills is love, the fellowship with Jesus, then he must will what he himself does not want at all: the reversal of the world's order, the Lord's service as a slave. And it is worse than this, because it is after all a question of the dirt on Peter's feet: the one who is utterly pure takes the sin upon himself.

What John wants us to understand here is that this Yes, which is pressed out of Peter, is something appalling for him. Peter is so often required to leap over his own shadow, and here this happens once again in a kind of desperation of love that cannot do anything else: "Lord, not my feet only but also my hands and my head!"

JESUS WASHES THE DISCIPLES' FEET

13 Now before the festival of the Passover, Jesus knew that his hour had come to depart from this world and go to the Father. Having loved his own who were in the world, he loved them to the end. ² The devil had already put it into the heart of Judas son of Simon Iscariot to betray him. And during supper ³ Jesus, knowing that the Father had given all things into his hands, and that he had come from God and was going to God, ⁴ got up from the table, took off his outer robe, and tied a towel around himself. ⁵ Then he poured water into a basin and began to wash the disciples' feet and to wipe them with the towel that was tied around him. ⁶ He came to Simon Peter, who said to him, "Lord, are you going to wash my feet?" ⁷ Jesus answered, "You do not know now what I am doing, but later you will understand." ⁸ Peter said to him, "You will never wash my feet." Jesus answered, "Unless I wash you, you have no share with me." ⁹ Simon Peter said to him, "Lord, not my feet only but also my hands and my head!" ¹⁰ Jesus said to him, "One who has bathed does not need to wash, except for the feet, but is entirely clean. And you are clean, though not all of you." ¹¹ For he knew who was to betray him; for this reason he said, "Not all of you are clean."

¹² After he had washed their feet, had put on his robe, and had returned to the table, he said to them, "Do you know what I have done to you? ¹³ You call me Teacher and Lord—and you are right, for that is what I am. ¹⁴ So if I, your Lord and Teacher, have washed your feet, you also ought to wash one another's feet. ¹⁵ For I have set

you an example, that you also should do as I have done to you. [16] Very truly, I tell you, servants are not greater than their master, nor are messengers greater than the one who sent them. [17] If you know these things, you are blessed if you do them. [18] I am not speaking of all of you; I know whom I have chosen. But it is to fulfill the scripture, 'The one who ate my bread has lifted his heel against me.' [19] I tell you this now, before it occurs, so that when it does occur, you may believe that I am he. [20] Very truly, I tell you, whoever receives one whom I send receives me; and whoever receives me receives him who sent me."

JESUS FORETELLS HIS BETRAYAL

[21] After saying this Jesus was troubled in spirit, and declared, "Very truly, I tell you, one of you will betray me." [22] The disciples looked at one another, uncertain of whom he was speaking. [23] One of his disciples—the one whom Jesus loved—was reclining next to him; [24] Simon Peter therefore motioned to him to ask Jesus of whom he was speaking. [25] So while reclining next to Jesus, he asked him, "Lord, who is it?" [26] Jesus answered, "It is the one to whom I give this piece of bread when I have dipped it in the dish." So when he had dipped the piece of bread, he gave it to Judas son of Simon Iscariot.

Pampering the Monkey on Our Backs

John 13:16 | Bishop Barron

Jesus pointedly calls us to humble behavior. St. Catherine of Siena once heard the Lord say to her, "You are she who is not, and I Am He Who Is." And St. Paul said, "What do you have that you did not receive? And if you received it, why do you boast as if it were not a gift?" (1 Cor. 4:7).

To believe in God is to know these truths. To live them out is to live in the attitude of humility. Thomas Aquinas said that humility is truth. It is living out the deepest truth of things: God is God, and we are not.

Now, all of this sounds very clear when it's stated in this abstract manner, but we know how hard it is to live out. In our fallen world, we forget so readily that we are creatures, that we have been made from nothing. Then our egos begin to inflate: "I am; I want; I expect; I demand." The ego becomes a massive monkey on our backs, and it has to be fed and pampered constantly.

But as Jesus says, "Servants are not greater than their master, nor are messengers greater than the one who sent them."

²⁷ After he received the piece of bread, Satan entered into him. Jesus said to him, "Do quickly what you are going to do." ²⁸ Now no one at the table knew why he said this to him. ²⁹ Some thought that, because Judas had the common purse, Jesus was telling him, "Buy what we need for the festival"; or, that he should give something to the poor. ³⁰ So, after receiving the piece of bread, he immediately went out. And it was night.

THE NEW COMMANDMENT

³¹ When he had gone out, Jesus said, "Now the Son of Man has been glorified, and God has been glorified in him. ³² If God has been glorified in him, God will also glorify him in himself and will glorify him at once. ³³ Little children, I am with you only a little longer. You will look for me; and as I said to the Jews so now I say to you, 'Where I am going, you cannot come.' ³⁴ I give you a new commandment, that you love one another. Just as I have loved you, you also should love one another. ³⁵ By this everyone will know that you are my disciples, if you have love for one another."

JESUS FORETELLS PETER'S DENIAL

³⁶ Simon Peter said to him, "Lord, where are you going?" Jesus answered, "Where I am going, you cannot follow me now; but you will follow afterward." ³⁷ Peter said to him, "Lord, why can I not follow you now? I will lay down my life for you." ³⁸ Jesus answered, "Will you lay down your life for me? Very truly, I tell you, before the cock crows, you will have denied me three times.

Making Us More Adept at Love

John 13:34 | Bishop Barron

We find joy in God alone, for our souls have been wired for God. But here's the trick—and the whole of the Christian life is on display here: God is love. God is self-emptying on behalf of the other. But this means paradoxically that to have God is to be what God is—and that means giving one's life away.

Now we see the link between joy and commandments: "I give you a new commandment, that you love one another. Just as I have loved you, you also should love one another." And now we begin to understand the laws, commands, and demands of the Church. All are designed to make us more adept at love, at giving ourselves away. Don't steal; don't kill; don't covet your neighbor's goods or wife; honor your mother and father; worship God. All of these commands—positive and negative—are meant to awaken love and make it possible.

The triangular pose of Christ

Christ's body forms a triangle, which points to his divine membership in the Trinity. The triangle was a symbol of perfection in Renaissance times, with its equal sides and angles representing ideal mathematical proportion.

Geometric elements

All of the diagonal lines of perspective, called orthogonals, converge on the head of Christ. Da Vinci famously omitted the use of halos in this painting, and instead uses the underlying geometry of the composition, combined with the daylight emanating from the background window, to reveal Christ's divine nature.

Surface damage

Da Vinci attempted a variety of experimental techniques with *The Last Supper* and used a combination of oil and tempera on dry plaster instead of the traditional tempera on wet plaster. Because of this, the paint did not adhere securely to the plaster as it would have in a traditional fresco, and now—after centuries of deterioration—very little of the original survives.

LEONARDO DA VINCI | *1495–1498*

The Last Supper

Essay by Michael Stevens

Leonardo da Vinci's *Last Supper* is one of the most famous and parodied images in the history of art. Because of its iconic status, though, it can be difficult to see it with fresh eyes, and all too easy to miss the brilliant symbols that da Vinci embeds within its compositional elements.

One of the most striking aspects of this painting is da Vinci's manipulation of time. It is unclear exactly what moment in the Last Supper story has been captured. There are a few possibilities. The energy and movement of the figures suggests that they are arguing about something, so this could be the moment when Christ tells the Apostles that one of them will betray him. Based on the position of Jesus' right hand, which reaches toward a metal dish along with Judas, this could also be the moment in which Jesus identifies Judas as his betrayer. Alternatively, the way that Christ reaches toward a glass of wine and a small loaf of bread on the table suggests that this could be the moment immediately before the consecration.

All of this ambiguity regarding the timing of events in the scene points to the eternal nature of the Eucharist that all Masses everywhere participate in. Instead of a linear progression of events, we seem to be viewing the entire meal from a vantage point that defies the limitations of time.

Beyond this, da Vinci also sets up a complex geometric structure underlying the picture that reflects a deeper theological reality. Leonardo synthesizes the realms of science, mathematics, and art into a single painting that is rational, lifelike, theologically insightful, and beautiful.

JESUS THE WAY TO THE FATHER

14 "Do not let your hearts be troubled. Believe in God, believe also in me. [2] In my Father's house there are many dwelling places. If it were not so, would I have told you that I go to prepare a place for you? [3] And if I go and prepare a place for you, I will come again and will take you to myself, so that where I am, there you may be also. [4] And you know the way to the place where I am going." [5] Thomas said to him, "Lord, we do not know where you are going. How can we know the way?" [6] Jesus said to him, "I am the way, and the truth, and the life. No one comes to the Father except through me. [7] If you know me, you will know my Father also. From now on you do know him and have seen him."

[8] Philip said to him, "Lord, show us the Father, and we will be satisfied." [9] Jesus said to him, "Have I been with you all this time, Philip, and you still do not know me? Whoever has seen me has seen the Father. How can you say, 'Show us the Father'? [10] Do you not believe that I am in the Father and the Father is in me? The words that I say to you I do not speak on my own; but the Father who dwells in me does his works. [11] Believe me that

---

Jesus Compels a Choice

John 14:6 | Bishop Barron

Either Jesus is who he says he is (in which case we are obliged to give our whole lives to him, making him Lord of every aspect of our personality and every dimension of our society) or he is a madman (in which case we should be against him). What does not remain, as C.S. Lewis saw so clearly, is the bland middle position that, though he isn't divine, he is a good, kindly, and wise ethical teacher. If he isn't who he says he is, then he isn't admirable at all; instead, he is guilty of making the most insane and outrageous claims of any major figure in world history.

The classical apologetic tradition expresses this dichotomy in the pithy adage *aut Deus, aut malus homo*—either he is God or he's a bad man. Thus Jesus compels a choice, a decision, in a manner that no other religious founder does. The Buddha could claim that he had found a way that he wanted to share with his followers, but Jesus said, "I *am* the way." Mohammed could say that, through him, the final divine truth had been communicated to the world, but Jesus said, "I *am* the truth." Confucius could maintain that he had discovered a new and uplifting form of life, but Jesus said, "I *am* the life." And thus, we are either with Jesus or we are against him. No other founder forces that choice as clearly as Jesus does.

I am in the Father and the Father is in me; but if you do not, then believe me because of the works themselves. [12] Very truly, I tell you, the one who believes in me will also do the works that I do and, in fact, will do greater works than these, because I am going to the Father. [13] I will do whatever you ask in my name, so that the Father may be glorified in the Son. [14] If in my name you ask me for anything, I will do it.

THE PROMISE OF THE HOLY SPIRIT

[15] "If you love me, you will keep my commandments. [16] And I will ask the Father, and he will give you another Advocate, to be with you forever. [17] This is the Spirit of truth, whom the world cannot receive, because it neither sees him nor knows him. You know him, because he abides with you, and he will be in you.

[18] "I will not leave you orphaned; I am coming to you. [19] In a little while the world will no longer see me, but you will see me; because I live, you also will live. [20] On that day you will know that I am in my Father, and you in me, and I in you. [21] They who have my commandments and keep them are those who love me; and those who love me will be loved by my Father,

---

The Coinherence of the Father and Son

John 14:7–10 | Bishop Barron

Jesus declares his mutual indwelling with God: "Do you not believe that I am in the Father and the Father is in me?" Charles Williams, a friend of C.S. Lewis and J.R.R. Tolkien, identified this indwelling as "coinherence" and considered it the master idea of Christianity.

How do we often identify ourselves? Almost exclusively through the naming of relationships: we are sons, brothers, daughters, mothers, fathers, members of organizations, or members of the Church.

Yet, in this Gospel passage, see how Jesus identifies himself. Jesus reveals the coinherence that obtains within the very existence of God. "Lord," Philip said to him, "show us the Father, and we will be satisfied." Jesus replied, "Have I been with you all this time, Philip, and you still do not know me? Whoever has seen me has seen the Father."

How can this be true, unless the Father and the Son coinhere in each other? Though Father and Son are really distinct, they are utterly implicated in each other by a mutual act of love. As Jesus says, "The Father who dwells in me does his works."

and I will love them and reveal myself to them." ²² Judas (not Iscariot) said to him, "Lord, how is it that you will reveal yourself to us, and not to the world?" ²³ Jesus answered him, "Those who love me will keep my word, and my Father will love them, and we will come to them and make our home with them. ²⁴ Whoever does not love me does not keep my words; and the word that you hear is not mine, but is from the Father who sent me.

²⁵ "I have said these things to you while I am still with you. ²⁶ But the Advocate, the Holy Spirit, whom the Father will send in my name, will teach you everything, and remind you of all that I have said to you. ²⁷ Peace I leave with you; my peace I give to you. I do not give to you as the world gives. Do not let your hearts be troubled, and do not let them be afraid. ²⁸ You heard me say to you, 'I am going away, and I am coming to you.' If you loved me, you would rejoice that I am going to the Father, because the Father is greater than I. ²⁹ And now I have told you this before it occurs, so that when it does occur, you may believe. ³⁰ I will no longer talk much with you, for the ruler of this world is coming. He has no power over me; ³¹ but I do as the Father has commanded me, so that the world may know that I love the Father. Rise, let us be on our way.

Knowing God from Within

John 14:15–17 | Bishop Barron

Jesus promises to send us the Spirit of truth who will make us intimate friends of God. The Holy Spirit is the love shared by the Father and the Son. We have access to this holy heart of God only because the Father sent the Son into the world, into our dysfunction, even to the limits of godforsakenness—and thereby gathered all of the world into the dynamism of the divine life.

Those who live in Christ are not outside of God as petitioners or supplicants; rather, they are *in* God as friends, sharers in the Spirit. And this spiritual life is what gives us knowledge of God—a knowledge, if you will, from within.

When the great masters of the Christian way speak of knowing God, they do not use the term in its distanced, analytical sense; they use it in the biblical sense, implying knowledge by way of personal intimacy. This is why St. Bernard of Clairvaux, for one, insists that initiates in the spiritual life know God not simply through books and lectures but through experience, the way one friend knows another. That knowledge is what the Holy Spirit facilitates.

I AM
THE WAY,
AND
THE TRUTH,
AND
THE LIFE.

———

NO ONE COMES

to the FATHER EXCEPT

THROUGH ME.

JOHN 14:6

JESUS THE TRUE VINE

15 "I am the true vine, and my Father is the vinegrower. ² He removes every branch in me that bears no fruit. Every branch that bears fruit he prunes to make it bear more fruit. ³ You have already been cleansed by the word that I have spoken to you. ⁴ Abide in me as I abide in you. Just as the branch cannot bear fruit by itself unless it abides in the vine, neither can you unless you abide in me. ⁵ I am the vine, you are the branches. Those who abide in me and I in them bear much fruit, because apart from me you can do nothing. ⁶ Whoever does not abide in me is thrown away like a branch and withers; such branches are gathered, thrown into the fire, and burned. ⁷ If you abide in me, and my words abide in you, ask for whatever you wish, and it will be done for you. ⁸ My Father is glorified by this, that you bear much fruit and become my disciples. ⁹ As the Father has loved me, so I have loved you; abide in my love. ¹⁰ If you keep my commandments, you will abide in my love, just as I have kept my Father's commandments and abide in his love. ¹¹ I have said these things to you so that my joy may be in you, and that your joy may be complete.

¹² "This is my commandment, that you love one another as I have loved you. ¹³ No one has greater love than this, to lay down one's life for

---

We Live in Him, He in Us

John 15:1–8 | Bishop Barron

Jesus declares that he is the vine and we are the branches. He is the power and energy source in which we live. This image is closely related to Paul's metaphor of the Body of Christ.

The point is that we live in him and he in us. Jesus is the source of supernatural life in us, and without him, we would have none of it. If, therefore, you are separated from the vine, you will die spiritually; you will stop living a supernatural life.

What does this look like concretely, to be attached to the vine? It means a steady immersion in the prayer of the Church. It means steady communion with God, speaking to him on a regular basis. It means an immersion in the Scriptures, soaking in the truth of the Bible. It means engaging in the corporal and spiritual works of mercy.

And, of course, it means you must participate in the sacraments—especially Confession and the Eucharist. By the sacraments, we stay close to the Christ who forgives our sins and who enlivens our spirits.

We Must Look

John 15:11 | Bishop Barron

During the discourse he gave the night before he died, Jesus summed up his life and ministry in these words: "I have said these things to you so that my joy may be in you, and that your joy may be complete." And therefore Christians can begin to confidently and enthusiastically look for the joy of Christ all around us. Many of the spiritual masters have defined prayer, not as an escape from the ordinary, but as a kind of heightened attention to the depth dimension of the everyday and the commonplace. Where is the divine will displayed? For the one who has the discipline of vision, everywhere and in everything. For many, the spiritual life becomes dysfunctional precisely at this beginning stage. They don't look.

---

one's friends. ¹⁴ You are my friends if you do what I command you. ¹⁵ I do not call you servants any longer, because the servant does not know what the master is doing; but I have called you friends, because I have made known to you everything that I have heard from my Father. ¹⁶ You did not choose me but I chose you. And I appointed you to go and bear fruit, fruit that will last, so that the Father will give you whatever you ask him in my name. ¹⁷ I am giving you these commands so that you may love one another.

THE WORLD'S HATRED

¹⁸ "If the world hates you, be aware that it hated me before it hated you. ¹⁹ If you belonged to the world, the world would love you as its own. Because you do not belong to the world, but I have chosen you out of the world—therefore the world hates you. ²⁰ Remember the word that I said to you, 'Servants are not greater than their master.' If they persecuted me, they will persecute you; if they kept my word, they will keep yours also. ²¹ But they will do all these things to you on account of my name, because they do not know him who sent me. ²² If I had not come and spoken to them, they would not have sin; but now they have no excuse for their sin. ²³ Whoever hates me hates my Father also. ²⁴ If I had not done among them the works that no one else did, they would not have sin. But now they have seen and hated both me and my Father. ²⁵ It was to fulfill the word that is written in their law, 'They hated me without a cause.'

²⁶ "When the Advocate comes, whom I will send to you from the Father, the Spirit of truth who comes from the Father, he will testify on my behalf. ²⁷ You also are to testify because you have been with me from the beginning.

Positioning of figures

The figures were intentionally positioned in a manner similar to a Greek frieze: either fully frontal or in direct profile, without interaction with each other. Because of this, the work was originally criticized for its lack of narrative content, but has since become one of the most celebrated of its time.

The painting's border

Seurat believed that by adding a border around the painting between the frame and the compositional boundary of the image, the luminosity of the colors and lighting in the scene would be heightened.

Detail of stippling technique

Rather than painting a single coat of color from an even mixture of paint, Seurat's pointillist technique blends colors directly in the viewer's eye and mind through a phenomenon known as optical mixing.

See *We Must Look* (commentary on John 15:11)

GEORGES SEURAT | *1884–1886*

A Sunday Afternoon on the Island of La Grande Jatte

Essay by Michael Stevens

Georges Seurat was unique among French painters of his era. Passionately rigorous and fiercely innovative, he absorbed the stylistic language of Impressionism and developed it into a visual lexicon wholly his own. He is credited for developing the technique of pointillism as well as codifying new approaches to color theory in painting and conté crayon drawing.

Seurat wanted to develop a new way of depicting the world that incorporated the latest scientific scholarship in optics and color theory. While many of his Impressionist contemporaries embraced a more spontaneous and improvisational way of painting, Seurat was extremely methodical and meticulous, creating labor-intensive, large-scale works that he described as Neo-Impressionist.

His most famous work is *A Sunday Afternoon on the Island of La Grande Jatte,* which exemplifies his pointillist technique: the process of placing thousands of tiny dots of color immediately next to one another to create the illusion of mixing hues.

Seurat embodies the artistic impulse to find a fresh way of seeing things. But this challenge to see things through a different lens extends to the spiritual life as well. Through prayer, we are able to develop an awareness of God's presence and influence in the most ordinary scenes imaginable. When we look closely, we begin to see grace at work in the world. We realize that it is more beautiful, more carefully composed, and more saturated with God's power than we could ever fully comprehend.

I Have Called You Friends

John 15:15 | Bishop Barron

Psychologists tell us that a true friend is someone who has seen us at our worst and still loves us. If you have encountered me only on my best days, when all is going well and I am in top form, and you like me, I have no guarantee that you are my friend. But when you have dealt with me when I am most obnoxious, most self-absorbed, most afraid and unpleasant, and you still love me, then I am sure that you are my friend.

The old Gospel song says, "What a friend we have in Jesus!" This is not pious sentimentalism; it is the heart of the matter. What the first Christians saw in the dying and rising of Jesus is that we killed God, and God returned in forgiving love. We murdered the Lord of life, and he answered us not with hatred but with compassion. He saw us at our very worst, and loved us anyway. Thus they saw confirmed in flesh and blood what Jesus had said the night before he died: "I do not call you servants any longer … but I have called you friends." They realized, in the drama of the Paschal Mystery, that we have not only been shown a new way; we have been drawn into a new life, a life of friendship with God.

---

16 "I have said these things to you to keep you from stumbling. [2] They will put you out of the synagogues. Indeed, an hour is coming when those who kill you will think that by doing so they are offering worship to God. [3] And they will do this because they have not known the Father or me. [4] But I have said these things to you so that when their hour comes you may remember that I told you about them.

THE WORK OF THE SPIRIT

"I did not say these things to you from the beginning, because I was with you. [5] But now I am going to him who sent me; yet none of you asks me, 'Where are you going?' [6] But because I have said these things to you, sorrow has filled your hearts. [7] Nevertheless I tell you the truth: it is to your advantage that I go away, for if I do not go away, the Advocate will not come to you; but if I go, I will send him to you. [8] And when he comes, he will prove the world wrong about sin and righteousness and judgment: [9] about sin, because they do not believe in me; [10] about righteousness, because I am going to the Father and you will see me no longer; [11] about judgment, because the ruler of this world has been condemned.

[12] "I still have many things to say to you, but you cannot bear them now.

Ask and Ask Again

John 16:5–15 | Bishop Barron

During his final teaching, Jesus promises to send us the Holy Spirit. The Spirit is the fuel of the Church, the energy and life force of the Body of Christ. And we can't get him through heroic effort. We can only get him by asking for him. That's why for the past two thousand years, the Church has begged for the Holy Spirit, this power from on high.

Jesus told us that the Father would never refuse someone who asked for the Holy Spirit. So ask, and ask again! The one prayer that is always appropriate, whether one is experiencing success or failure, whether one is confident or afraid, whether one is young or old, is "Come, Holy Spirit!"

This is the fundamental prayer of the Church. It's why we pray it, as the first Apostles did, in the presence of Mary and with her support, for in the Hail Mary, we say, "Pray for us sinners, now and at the hour of our death." What are we asking her to pray for but the Holy Spirit?

---

¹³ When the Spirit of truth comes, he will guide you into all the truth; for he will not speak on his own, but will speak whatever he hears, and he will declare to you the things that are to come. ¹⁴ He will glorify me, because he will take what is mine and declare it to you. ¹⁵ All that the Father has is mine. For this reason I said that he will take what is mine and declare it to you.

SORROW WILL TURN INTO JOY

¹⁶ "A little while, and you will no longer see me, and again a little while, and you will see me." ¹⁷ Then some of his disciples said to one another, "What does he mean by saying to us, 'A little while, and you will no longer see me, and again a little while, and you will see me'; and 'Because I am going to the Father'?" ¹⁸ They said, "What does he mean by this 'a little while'? We do not know what he is talking about." ¹⁹ Jesus knew that they wanted to ask him, so he said to them, "Are you discussing among yourselves what I meant when I said, 'A little while, and you will no longer see me, and again a little while, and you will see me'? ²⁰ Very truly, I tell you, you will weep and mourn, but the world will rejoice; you will have pain, but your pain will turn into joy. ²¹ When a woman is in labor, she has pain, because her hour has come. But when her child is born, she no longer remembers the anguish because of the joy of having brought a human being into the world. ²² So you have pain now; but I will see you again, and your hearts will

Fulton Sheen
(1895–1979)
—

Three to Get Married

The Unbroken Succession of Truth

John 16:13–15

In this passage our Lord tells his disciples that the Holy Spirit, who is to come, will in the future reveal divine knowledge that has been communicated to him in his procession from both the Father and Son. It is that same Spirit who, in fulfillment of the promise "When the Spirit of truth comes, he will guide you into all the truth," descended on the Apostles on the day of Pentecost and became the soul of the Church. The continuous, unbroken succession of the truth communicated by Christ to his Church has survived to our own day—not because of the human organization of the Church, for that is carried on by frail vessels, but because of the profusion of the Spirit of Love and Truth over Christ's Vicar and over all who belong to Christ's Mystical Body, which is his Church.

rejoice, and no one will take your joy from you. [23] On that day you will ask nothing of me. Very truly, I tell you, if you ask anything of the Father in my name, he will give it to you. [24] Until now you have not asked for anything in my name. Ask and you will receive, so that your joy may be complete.

PEACE FOR THE DISCIPLES

25 "I have said these things to you in figures of speech. The hour is coming when I will no longer speak to you in figures, but will tell you plainly of the Father. 26 On that day you will ask in my name. I do not say to you that I will ask the Father on your behalf; 27 for the Father himself loves you, because you have loved me and have believed that I came from God. 28 I came from the Father and have come into the world; again, I am leaving the world and am going to the Father."

29 His disciples said, "Yes, now you are speaking plainly, not in any figure of speech! 30 Now we know that you know all things, and do not need to have anyone question you; by this we believe that you came from God." 31 Jesus answered them, "Do you now believe? 32 The hour is coming, indeed it has come, when you will be scattered, each one to his home, and you will leave me alone. Yet I am not alone because the Father is with me. 33 I have said this to you, so that in me you may have peace. In the world you face persecution. But take courage; I have conquered the world!"

St. Cyril of Alexandria
(378–444)

Commentary on John

Leaving and Going

John 16:28

And when Jesus says that he came into this world and again left the world and went to the Father, he does not mean that he either abandoned the Father when he became man, nor that he abandoned the race of man when in his flesh he went to the Father; for he is truly God, and with his inexpressible power fills all things, and is not far from anything that exists.

JESUS PRAYS FOR HIS DISCIPLES

17 After Jesus had spoken these words, he looked up to heaven and said, "Father, the hour has come; glorify your Son so that the Son may glorify you, ² since you have given him authority over all people, to give eternal life to all whom you have given him. ³ And this is eternal life, that they may know you, the only true God, and Jesus Christ whom you have sent. ⁴ I glorified you on earth by finishing the work that you gave me to do. ⁵ So now, Father, glorify me in your own presence with the glory that I had in your presence before the world existed.

⁶ "I have made your name known to those whom you gave me from the world. They were yours, and you gave them to me, and they have kept your word. ⁷ Now they know that everything you have given me is from you; ⁸ for the words that you gave to me I have given to them, and they have received them and know in truth that I came from you; and they have believed that you sent me. ⁹ I am asking on their behalf; I am not asking on behalf of the world, but on behalf of those whom you gave me, because they are yours. ¹⁰ All mine are yours, and yours are mine; and I have been

---

Transforming the Darkest Places

John 17:11–19 | Bishop Barron

Jesus' great prayer sums up his wonderful work as he is about to return to his Father. Jesus was, in his very person, the meeting of heaven and earth. God and humanity came together in him, and his entire ministry was the outward expression of that inward identity. Calling a scattered Israel to unity, inviting the poor to table fellowship, healing the sick in body and heart, embodying the path of forgiveness and love, Jesus was bringing God's will and purpose to earth.

Now, in his Passion and death, Jesus brought heaven all the way down. He carried the divine light into the darkest places of the human condition—hatred, cruelty, violence, corruption, stupidity, suffering, and death itself—and thereby transformed them. What proves that heaven is able to transform earth is, of course, the Resurrection of Jesus from the dead.

We now know that cruelty, hatred, violence, fear, suffering, and death are not the most powerful forces in the world. We now know that the divine love is more powerful. God's kingdom has, in principle, broken the kingdoms of the world, which thrive upon and in turn produce those very negativities.

**Joseph Ratzinger
(Pope Benedict XVI)**
(1927–)

*Jesus of Nazareth:
Holy Week*

The New High Priest

John 17:1–26

According to rabbinic theology, the idea of the covenant—the idea of establishing a holy people to be an interlocutor for God in union with him—is prior to the idea of the creation of the world and supplies its inner motive. The cosmos was created—not that there might be manifold things in heaven and earth, but that there might be a space for the "covenant," for the loving "yes" between God and his human respondent. Each year the Feast of Atonement restores this harmony, this inner meaning of the world that is constantly disrupted by sin, and it therefore marks the high point of the liturgical year.

The structure of the ritual described in Leviticus 16 is reproduced exactly in Jesus' prayer: just as the high priest makes atonement for himself, for the priestly clan, and for the whole community of Israel, so Jesus prays for himself, for the Apostles, and finally for all who will come to believe in him through their word—for the Church of all times. . . .

Jesus' prayer manifests him as the high priest of the Day of Atonement. His cross and his exaltation is the Day of Atonement for the world, in which the whole of world history—in the face of all human sin and its destructive consequences—finds its meaning and is aligned with its true purpose and destiny.

glorified in them. [11] And now I am no longer in the world, but they are in the world, and I am coming to you. Holy Father, protect them in your name that you have given me, so that they may be one, as we are one. [12] While I was with them, I protected them in your name that you have given me. I guarded them, and not one of them was lost except the one destined to be lost, so that the scripture might be fulfilled. [13] But now I am coming to you, and I speak these things in the world so that they may have my joy made complete in themselves. [14] I have given them your word, and the world has hated them because they do not belong to the world, just as I do not belong to the world. [15] I am not asking you to take them out of the world, but I ask you to protect them from the evil one. [16] They do not belong to the world, just as I do not belong to the world. [17] Sanctify them in the truth; your word is truth. [18] As you have sent me into the world, so I have sent them into the world. [19] And for their sakes I sanctify myself, so that they also may be sanctified in truth.

[20] "I ask not only on behalf of these, but also on behalf of those who will believe in me through their word, [21] that they may all be one. As you, Father, are in me and I am in you, may they also be in us, so that the world

---

About One Thing

John 17:20–21 | Bishop Barron

The Church is one because its founder is one. Jesus compels a choice precisely because he claims to speak and act in the very person of God. Jesus simply cannot be one teacher among many, and therefore those who walk in his way must be exclusively with him.

Moreover, the God whom Jesus incarnates is one. The Israelite conception of God is fiercely monotheistic and hence it excludes any diversity or syncretism at the level of basic belief.

Joseph Ratzinger (the future Pope Benedict XVI) commented that the opening line of the Nicene Creed, "I believe in one God," is a subversive statement because it automatically rules out any rival claimant to ultimate concern. To say that one accepts only the God of Israel and Jesus Christ is to say that one rejects as ultimate any human being, any culture, any political party, any artistic form, or any set of ideas.

Søren Kierkegaard said that the saint is someone whose life is about one thing; a Christian, I would argue, is someone who, at the most fundamental level of his or her being, is centered on the one God of Jesus Christ.

This helps to explain why, on the last night of his life on earth, while sitting at supper with his disciples, the core of the Church, Jesus prayed, "I ask not only on behalf of these, but also on behalf of those who will believe in me through their word, that they may all be one."

may believe that you have sent me. ²² The glory that you have given me I have given them, so that they may be one, as we are one, ²³ I in them and you in me, that they may become completely one, so that the world may know that you have sent me and have loved them even as you have loved me. ²⁴ Father, I desire that those also, whom you have given me, may be with me where I am, to see my glory, which you have given me because you loved me before the foundation of the world.

²⁵ "Righteous Father, the world does not know you, but I know you; and these know that you have sent me. ²⁶ I made your name known to them, and I will make it known, so that the love with which you have loved me may be in them, and I in them."

I ASK NOT ONLY ON
BEHALF OF THESE,
BUT ALSO ON BEHALF OF
THOSE WHO WILL BELIEVE
IN ME THROUGH THEIR
WORD, THAT THEY MAY
ALL BE ONE.

JOHN 17:20–21

THE BETRAYAL AND ARREST OF JESUS

18 After Jesus had spoken these words, he went out with his disciples across the Kidron valley to a place where there was a garden, which he and his disciples entered. ² Now Judas, who betrayed him, also knew the place, because Jesus often met there with his disciples. ³ So Judas brought a detachment of soldiers together with police from the chief priests and the Pharisees, and they came there with lanterns and torches and weapons. ⁴ Then Jesus, knowing all that was to happen to him, came forward and asked them, "Whom are you looking for?" ⁵ They answered, "Jesus of Nazareth." Jesus replied, "I am he." Judas, who betrayed him, was standing with them. ⁶ When Jesus said to them, "I am he," they stepped back and fell to the ground. ⁷ Again he asked them, "Whom are you looking for?" And they said, "Jesus of Nazareth." ⁸ Jesus answered, "I told you that I am he. So if you are looking for me, let these men go." ⁹ This was to fulfill the word that he had spoken, "I did not lose a single one of those whom you gave me." ¹⁰ Then Simon Peter, who had a sword, drew it, struck the high priest's slave, and cut off his right ear. The slave's name was Malchus. ¹¹ Jesus said to Peter, "Put your sword back into its sheath. Am I not to drink the cup that the Father has given me?"

JESUS BEFORE THE HIGH PRIEST

¹² So the soldiers, their officer, and the Jewish police arrested Jesus and bound him. ¹³ First they took him to Annas, who was the father-in-law of Caiaphas, the high priest that year. ¹⁴ Caiaphas was the one who had advised the Jews that it was better to have one person die for the people.

St. Cyril of Alexandria
(378–444)

Commentary on John

From Garden to Garden

John 18:1

The place [where Jesus was betrayed] was a garden, typifying the paradise of old. For in it, as it were, all places were recapitulated; and in this garden our return to man's ancient condition was achieved. For it was in the garden of paradise that the troubles of mankind originated, while in this garden Christ's sufferings began—those sufferings which brought deliverance from all the evils that had befallen us in times past.

Christic the King

John 18:33-38 | Bishop Barron

ONE OF THE EARLIEST and most basic forms of Christian proclamation is this: *Iesous Kyrios* (Jesus is Lord). We tend to think of this claim in "religious" terms, as an indication that Jesus is Lord in a spiritual sense, and it does indeed carry such a meaning. But when the first Christians used the phrase, it had a provocative political overtone as well. For in the ancient world, in the lands surrounding the Mediterranean, Caesar was the lord, the one to whom ultimate allegiance was owed. *Kaisar Kyrios* (Caesar is Lord) was a watchword of the time and a proof of loyalty. In saying, therefore, that Jesus is *Kyrios*, they were directly challenging Caesar and all of the powers that operated under his aegis and in his name. It should not be too surprising then that Paul spent much of his ministry in jail, and that (with the exception of John) all the Apostles were martyred, and that the Church was for three centuries periodically beset by brutal persecution. The enemies of the faith clearly understood what was entailed in the boast that someone crucified by Caesar was in fact the Lord. Ours has been, from the beginning, a troublemaking faith.

Political rulers come across in the New Testament about as well as they do in the Old Testament—which is to say, not very. In Luke's Christmas account, Caesar Augustus is implicitly compared unfavorably to the Christ child, the newborn king. Herod, the king of the Jews, is so desperate and self-absorbed that he hunts down that same child, killing innocent children in a vain attempt to stamp out his rival. Later, Herod's son, Herod Antipas, persecutes both John the Baptist and Jesus himself, and Jewish political/religious leaders are presented in all four of the Gospels as vain, corrupt, and violent. (Nicodemus and Joseph of Arimathea are rare exceptions.) And the public career of Jesus comes to a climax when the Lord confronts Caesar's local representative, the crafty and self-regarding Pontius Pilate. Despite some attempts to romanticize him as a tortured but well-meaning man, Pilate was a fairly typical Roman governor: coldly efficient, concerned with good order, and, when necessary, brutal. He once put down a rebellion by nailing hundreds of Jews to the walls of Jerusalem. And like so many of the other political rulers of that time and place, he quite correctly perceived Jesus as a threat.

In John's version of the story, when Pilate stands face to face with Jesus, he asks: "Are you the King of the Jews?" Jesus answers evasively, for he knows what Pilate means by "king": one more earthly ruler obsessed with power and all too willing to use violence to preserve it. Then he adds: "My kingdom is not from this world." We have to be careful in interpreting this observation, because there is always a double meaning to the term "world" in the Gospel of John. On the one hand, "world" designates the universe that God has created and that he sustains in love. This is the world that God loved enough to send his only Son as its Savior. On the other hand, "world" means that manner of ordering things which is out of step with God's intentions; it indicates a political and cultural realm in which selfishness, hatred, division, and violence hold sway.

What Jesus implies, therefore, is not that his kingdom is irrelevant to ordinary experience, but that his way of ordering is radically out of step with the way practiced by Caesar, Pilate, Herod, and all the other usual suspects. In short, Jesus' kingdom has everything to do with "this world" in the first sense of the term and nothing to do with it in the second. Jesus continues: "If my kingdom were from this world, my followers would be fighting to keep me from being handed over to the Jews." *The* mark of the worldly kingdom is violence and the maintenance of order through force and fear. Though it is counter-intuitive in the extreme, and unrealistic, to say the very least, Jesus' reign will eschew all such means. It will suffer injustice, but it will not perpetuate it. These dynamics of Jesus' kingdom are on full display in the events of Good Friday. Christ the King is crowned and he assumes his throne, but the crown is made of thorns, and the throne is a Roman instrument of torture.

Three and a half centuries after the New Testament period, Augustine, the Bishop of Hippo Regius on the North Africa seacoast and a man imbued with the best of Roman culture, wrote a book entitled *The City of God*. Heartbroken over the fall of Rome to northern barbaric tribes, this worthy literary successor of Cicero and Cato composed a sustained and vigorous attack on the empire he loved. From the establishment of the city to the present day, Augustine argued, Rome's power had been predicated upon violence and the oppression of the weak by the strong. Roman order was conditioned by a *libido dominandi* (a lust to dominate), which was in turn supported by the worship of violent, capricious, and deeply immoral gods. And this meant, he concluded, that the justice of Rome (trumpeted by its defenders as the very paragon of right order) was in fact a pseudo-justice, akin to the discipline and purposefulness one might find in a successful gang of robbers. Real order, Augustine continued, will come only when forgiveness, nonviolence, and the love of enemies are the regnant values—and only when these are supported by the worship of the true God who is, by his very nature, love. There is a direct line that runs from the New Testament to *The City of God*, for both present the contours of the new kingdom, and both pronounce judgment on the old.

Now, I would submit, this proclamation of the kingship of Jesus Christ poses a special challenge to us Americans. We are undoubtedly the dominant political and cultural power of the present day, and we are, still, a predominantly Christian country. This sets up a certain tension, to say the least. Even as we love our country (as Augustine surely loved Rome), we have to maintain that our loyalty to Christ is greater than our loyalty to the American political order. Reading it through the lenses provided by the Gospel, we must remain critical of the deep dysfunction of our society: the availability of abortion on demand, the growing acceptance of the legitimacy of euthanasia, the terrible violence on our city streets, the stockpiling of weapons of incomparable destructiveness, the waging of preemptive war, etc. Have we Christians accommodated ourselves too readily to the social and political structures? Have we effectively surrendered to the power of the world? One way to answer those questions is to ask two others: How many Christian martyrs are there among us? How many of us are in prison for our faith?

I have heard rather frequently over the years the suggestion that the kingship of Christ is an outmoded idea, an image alien to our democratic sensibilities, and that, consequently, we should adopt the language of, say, Christ the President or Christ the Prime Minister. But this would be counterproductive. We have enormous control over presidents and prime ministers; they must stand regularly before the electorate and can, at the whim of the people, be put out of office. They must, to a large extent, pander to the shifting desires of those who choose them as representatives. We sinners would love just that kind of relationship with Jesus. A king, on the other hand, is one to whom total allegiance is due, one who is not subject to the people but who rather commands and orders them. If the way of Jesus is to prevail over and against the enormous power of the way of the world, he must be acknowledged as King and Commander—and we must be willing to march in his army.

PETER DENIES JESUS

¹⁵ Simon Peter and another disciple followed Jesus. Since that disciple was known to the high priest, he went with Jesus into the courtyard of the high priest, ¹⁶ but Peter was standing outside at the gate. So the other disciple, who was known to the high priest, went out, spoke to the woman who guarded the gate, and brought Peter in. ¹⁷ The woman said to Peter, "You are not also one of this man's disciples, are you?" He said, "I am not." ¹⁸ Now the slaves and the police had made a charcoal fire because it was cold, and they were standing around it and warming themselves. Peter also was standing with them and warming himself.

THE HIGH PRIEST QUESTIONS JESUS

¹⁹ Then the high priest questioned Jesus about his disciples and about his teaching. ²⁰ Jesus answered, "I have spoken openly to the world; I have always taught in synagogues and in the temple, where all the Jews come together. I have said nothing in secret. ²¹ Why do you ask me? Ask those who heard what I said to them; they know what I said." ²² When he had said this, one of the police standing nearby struck Jesus on the face, saying, "Is that how you answer the high priest?" ²³ Jesus answered, "If I have spoken wrongly, testify to the wrong. But if I have spoken rightly, why do you strike me?" ²⁴ Then Annas sent him bound to Caiaphas the high priest.

PETER DENIES JESUS AGAIN

²⁵ Now Simon Peter was standing and warming himself. They asked him, "You are not also one of his disciples, are you?" He denied it and said, "I am not." ²⁶ One of the slaves of the high priest, a relative of the man whose

ear Peter had cut off, asked, "Did I not see you in the garden with him?" ²⁷ Again Peter denied it, and at that moment the cock crowed.

JESUS BEFORE PILATE

²⁸ Then they took Jesus from Caiaphas to Pilate's headquarters. It was early in the morning. They themselves did not enter the headquarters, so as to avoid ritual defilement and to be able to eat the Passover. ²⁹ So Pilate went out to them and said, "What accusation do you bring against this man?" ³⁰ They answered, "If this man were not a criminal, we would not have handed him over to you." ³¹ Pilate said to them, "Take him yourselves and judge him according to your law." The Jews replied, "We are not permitted to put anyone to death." ³² (This was to fulfill what Jesus had said when he indicated the kind of death he was to die.)

³³ Then Pilate entered the headquarters again, summoned Jesus, and asked him, "Are you the King of the Jews?" ³⁴ Jesus answered, "Do you ask this on your own, or did others tell you about me?" ³⁵ Pilate replied, "I am not a Jew, am I? Your own nation and the chief priests have handed you over to me. What have you done?" ³⁶ Jesus answered, "My kingdom is not from this world. If my kingdom were from this world, my followers would be fighting to keep me from being handed over to the Jews. But as it is, my kingdom is not from here." ³⁷ Pilate asked him, "So you are a king?" Jesus answered, "You say that I am a king. For this I was born, and for this I came into the world, to testify to the truth. Everyone who belongs to the truth listens to my voice." ³⁸ Pilate asked him, "What is truth?"

JESUS SENTENCED TO DEATH

After he had said this, he went out to the Jews again and told them, "I find no case against him. ³⁹ But you have a custom that I release someone for you at the Passover. Do you want me to release for you the King of the Jews?" ⁴⁰ They shouted in reply, "Not this man, but Barabbas!" Now Barabbas was a bandit.

G.K. Chesterton
(1874–1936)

The Everlasting Man

What Is Truth?

John 18:38

In this story of Good Friday, it is the best things in the world that are at their worst. That is what really shows us the world at its worst. It was, for instance, the priests of a true monotheism and the soldiers of an international civilization. Rome, the legend, founded upon fallen Troy and triumphant over fallen Carthage, had stood for a heroism which was the nearest that any pagan ever came to chivalry....

But in the lightning flash of this incident, we see great Rome, the imperial republic, going downward under her Lucretian doom. Scepticism has eaten away even the confident sanity of the conquerors of the world. He who is enthroned to say what is justice can only ask, "What is truth?" So in that drama which decided the whole fate of antiquity, one of the central figures is fixed in what seems the reverse of his true role. Rome was almost another name for responsibility. Yet he stands forever as a sort of rocking statue of the irresponsible. Man could do no more. Even the practical had become the impracticable. Standing between the pillars of his own judgment-seat, a Roman had washed his hands of the world.

19 Then Pilate took Jesus and had him flogged. ² And the soldiers wove a crown of thorns and put it on his head, and they dressed him in a purple robe. ³ They kept coming up to him, saying, "Hail, King of the Jews!" and striking him on the face. ⁴ Pilate went out again and said to them, "Look, I am bringing him out to you to let you know that I find no case against him." ⁵ So Jesus came out, wearing the crown of thorns and the purple robe. Pilate said to them, "Here is the man!" ⁶ When the chief priests and the police saw him, they shouted, "Crucify him! Crucify him!" Pilate said to them, "Take him yourselves and crucify him; I find no case against him." ⁷ The Jews answered him, "We have a law, and according to that law he ought to die because he has claimed to be the Son of God."

St. Augustine
(354–430)

*Tractates on the
Gospel of John*

Silent as a Sheep

John 19:9–12

In comparing the accounts of the different Gospels together, we find that this silence [of Jesus] was maintained more than once—namely, before the high priest, before Herod, and before Pilate—so that the prophecy of him, "Like a sheep that before its shearers is silent, so he did not open his mouth" (Isa. 53:7), was amply fulfilled.

To many of the questions put to him, he did indeed reply, but where he did not reply, this comparison of the sheep shows us that his was not a silence of guilt, but of innocence; not of self-condemnation, but of compassion, and willingness to suffer for the sins of others. . . .

When he was silent, he was silent not as guilty or crafty, but as a sheep: when he answered, he taught as a shepherd.

⁸ Now when Pilate heard this, he was more afraid than ever. ⁹ He entered his headquarters again and asked Jesus, "Where are you from?" But Jesus gave him no answer. ¹⁰ Pilate therefore said to him, "Do you refuse to speak to me? Do you not know that I have power to release you, and power to crucify you?" ¹¹ Jesus answered him, "You would have no power over me unless it had been given you from above; therefore the one who handed me over to you is guilty of a greater sin." ¹² From then on Pilate tried to release him, but the Jews cried out, "If you release this man, you are no friend of the emperor. Everyone who claims to be a king sets himself against the emperor."

¹³ When Pilate heard these words, he brought Jesus outside and sat on the judge's bench at a place called The Stone Pavement, or in Hebrew Gabbatha. ¹⁴ Now it was the day of Preparation for the Passover; and it

The Higher Authority

John 19:10–11 | Bishop Barron

In his treatise on law, Thomas Aquinas teaches that positive law, the concrete prescriptions by which a society is governed, is derivative from the natural law, the first principles of morality and their immediate applications. Natural law in turn is grounded in the eternal law, which is none other than the reasonability of the divine mind itself. When this nesting relationship is overlooked, positive law becomes but an expression of the will to power of the legislator, and the moral integrity of a society so governed is fatally compromised. At least a vestige of this Thomistic understanding can be discerned in the American Declaration of Independence, precisely in its affirmation of humans' rights to life, liberty, and happiness, explicitly recognized as "endowed by their Creator." The implication is that the positive laws that govern the United States must be correlated to objective moral principles, articulated as rights, which in turn are implanted in us by God.

Joseph Ratzinger proposes a reading of Jesus' conversation with Pontius Pilate that is apposite in this context. Under pressure from the restive crowd, Pilate both abdicates moral responsibility and confesses ignorance of any objective ground for moral decision-making: "What is truth?" (John 18:38). Having severed any possible link between positive law and natural law, he surrenders to the whim of the crowd, asking them to decide whether an obviously guilty man or an obviously innocent man should be released. This, Ratzinger argues, is the prototype of the moral governance by public opinion poll so prevalent in contemporary society. But what the severance of positive, moral, and eternal law inevitably results in is the ultimacy of the legislator's will to power. Thus Pilate bullyingly says to Jesus, "Do you refuse to speak to me? Do you not know that I have power to release you, and power to crucify you?" To which the one who came to testify to the Truth responds, "You would have no power over me unless it had been given you from above." Pilate's authority, the legitimacy of which Jesus does not question, is nevertheless subalternate to the higher authority of God.

---

was about noon. He said to the Jews, "Here is your King!" [15] They cried out, "Away with him! Away with him! Crucify him!" Pilate asked them, "Shall I crucify your King?" The chief priests answered, "We have no king but the emperor." [16] Then he handed him over to them to be crucified.

Jesus of Nazareth, the King of the Jews

John 19:19–20 | Bishop Barron

The author of John's Gospel was a master of irony, and one of his most delicious twists involves the sign that Pontius Pilate placed over the cross of the dying Jesus: *Iesus Nazarenus, Rex Iudaeorum* (Jesus of Nazareth, the King of the Jews). The Roman governor meant it as a taunt, but the sign—written out in the three major languages of that time and place, Hebrew, Latin, and Greek—in fact made Pilate, unwittingly, the first great evangelist.

The King of the Jews, on the Old Testament reading, was destined to be the King of the world—and that kingship is precisely what Pilate effectively announced. What commenced with David's gathering of the tribes of Israel would now reach completion in the criminal raised high on the cross, thereby drawing all people to himself. Even at Calvary, where Jesus' Church had dwindled to three members, his little community was catholic, for it was destined to embrace everyone. And he would do it not through political machinations or military conquest but through the weirdly attractive power of his death on an instrument of torture.

THE CRUCIFIXION OF JESUS

So they took Jesus; [17] and carrying the cross by himself, he went out to what is called The Place of the Skull, which in Hebrew is called Golgotha. [18] There they crucified him, and with him two others, one on either side, with Jesus between them. [19] Pilate also had an inscription written and put on the cross. It read, "Jesus of Nazareth, the King of the Jews." [20] Many of the Jews read this inscription, because the place where Jesus was crucified was near the city; and it was written in Hebrew, in Latin, and in Greek. [21] Then the chief priests of the Jews said to Pilate, "Do not write, 'The King of the Jews,' but, 'This man said, I am King of the Jews.'" [22] Pilate answered, "What I have written I have written." [23] When the soldiers had crucified Jesus, they took his clothes and divided them into four parts, one for each soldier. They also took his tunic; now the tunic was seamless, woven in one piece from the top. [24] So they said to one another, "Let us not tear it, but cast lots for it to see who will get it." This was to fulfill what the scripture says,

> "They divided my clothes among themselves,
>   and for my clothing they cast lots."

[25] And that is what the soldiers did.

Meanwhile, standing near the cross of Jesus were his mother, and his mother's sister, Mary the wife of Clopas, and Mary Magdalene. [26] When

St. Theophylact
(1050–1107)

___

*Catena Aurea of St.
Thomas Aquinas*

King of the Whole World

John 19:19–22

The title written in three languages signifies that our
Lord was King of the whole world: practical, natural,
and spiritual. The Latin denotes the practical, because
the Roman empire was the most powerful, and best
managed one; the Greek the physical, the Greeks
being the best physical philosophers; and lastly, the
Hebrew the theological, because the Jews had been
made the depositaries of religious knowledge.

Jesus saw his mother and the disciple whom he loved standing beside
her, he said to his mother, "Woman, here is your son." [27] Then he said to
the disciple, "Here is your mother." And from that hour the disciple took
her into his own home.

[28] After this, when Jesus knew that all was now finished, he said (in
order to fulfill the scripture), "I am thirsty." [29] A jar full of sour wine was
standing there. So they put a sponge full of the wine on a branch of hyssop
and held it to his mouth. [30] When Jesus had received the wine, he said, "It
is finished." Then he bowed his head and gave up his spirit.

JESUS' SIDE IS PIERCED

[31] Since it was the day of Preparation, the Jews did not want the bodies left
on the cross during the sabbath, especially because that sabbath was a day
of great solemnity. So they asked Pilate to have the legs of the crucified
men broken and the bodies removed. [32] Then the soldiers came and broke
the legs of the first and of the other who had been crucified with him. [33] But
when they came to Jesus and saw that he was already dead, they did not
break his legs. [34] Instead, one of the soldiers pierced his side with a spear,
and at once blood and water came out. [35] (He who saw this has testified
so that you also may believe. His testimony is true, and he knows that he
tells the truth.) [36] These things occurred so that the scripture might be
fulfilled, "None of his bones shall be broken." [37] And again another passage
of scripture says, "They will look on the one whom they have pierced."

Mary's Role at the Crucifixion

John 19:25–27 | Bishop Barron

Jesus entrusts care of his mother to St. John. We can see some background for this profound action in *The Passion of the Christ*, the most provocative and popular religious movie in decades.

In that film, we are compelled to see the scenes through the eyes of Mary, the mother of Jesus. Early in Luke's Gospel, we are told that when Mary hears the prophecies of the angels about her son, she "treasured all these words and pondered them in her heart" (Luke 2:19). She is the theologian par excellence, the one who understands. So when she sees Jesus being led away to his Crucifixion, she weeps and then she says "Amen."

In scene after scene, we watch her spiritual comprehension. The wonderful scene where she is marked with the blood of her son is especially evocative. But none is better than the Pietà depiction at the very end, where Mary is holding the lifeless body of Jesus. There we see Mary's role: to present the sacrifice of her son to us and for us.

THE BURIAL OF JESUS

³⁸ After these things, Joseph of Arimathea, who was a disciple of Jesus, though a secret one because of his fear of the Jews, asked Pilate to let him take away the body of Jesus. Pilate gave him permission; so he came and removed his body. ³⁹ Nicodemus, who had at first come to Jesus by night, also came, bringing a mixture of myrrh and aloes, weighing about a hundred pounds. ⁴⁰ They took the body of Jesus and wrapped it with the spices in linen cloths, according to the burial custom of the Jews. ⁴¹ Now there was a garden in the place where he was crucified, and in the garden there was a new tomb in which no one had ever been laid. ⁴² And so, because it was the Jewish day of Preparation, and the tomb was nearby, they laid Jesus there.

"WOMAN, HERE IS YOUR SON."
THEN HE SAID *to the* DISCIPLE,
"HERE IS YOUR MOTHER."   JOHN 19:26–27

John 19:16–30

HENDRICK TER BRUGGHEN | *1624–1625*

The Crucifixion with the Virgin and Saint John

Essay by Michael Stevens

Hendrick ter Brugghen was one of the leaders of the Utrecht Caravaggisti—the Netherlandish followers of Caravaggio. In this painting, we see many elements that overlap with Caravaggio's style—dramatic use of contrasting lights and darks, expressive and realistic faces—but also a rootedness in Ter Brugghen's native tradition of painting. There is a deep sensitivity to the sufferings of Jesus with a visceral, contorted depiction of the crucified Christ's anatomy.

Mary and the Apostle John stand at the foot of the cross, and their expressions—while full of grief and shock—are reverent and reflective. They are among the few who remain with Jesus through his Passion. The artist positions the two figures as intermediaries between Jesus and us. He uses them to set an example of the proper response to such deep desolation: fixing one's eyes on Jesus and staying with him to the bitter end.

"The Place of the Skull"

John 19:17 mentions that Jesus was taken to Golgotha, "The Place of the Skull." This scriptural detail is shown in artistic representations of the Crucifixion by the inclusion of a single skull at the foot of Christ's cross.

INRI inscription

John 19:19 tells us that Pilate wrote the inscription "Jesus of Nazareth, the King of the Jews" on the cross of Christ for the crowd to see. This phrase is traditionally abbreviated in art as INRI, from the Latin translation of this phrase: *Iesus Nazarenus, Rex Iudaeorum*. Other artistic depictions follow the Gospel text even more closely and write out the entire statement in the three languages mentioned in John: Hebrew, Latin, and Greek.

THE RESURRECTION OF JESUS

20

Early on the first day of the week, while it was still dark, Mary Magdalene came to the tomb and saw that the stone had been removed from the tomb. ² So she ran and went to Simon Peter and the other disciple, the one whom Jesus loved, and said to them, "They have taken the Lord out of the tomb, and we do not know where they have laid him." ³ Then Peter and the other disciple set out and went toward the tomb. ⁴ The two were running together, but the other disciple outran Peter and reached the tomb first. ⁵ He bent down to look in and saw the linen wrappings lying there, but he did not go in. ⁶ Then Simon Peter came, following him, and went into the tomb. He saw the linen wrappings lying there, ⁷ and the cloth that had been on Jesus' head, not lying with the linen wrappings but rolled up in a place by itself. ⁸ Then the other disciple, who reached the tomb first, also went in, and he saw and believed; ⁹ for as yet they did not understand the scripture, that he must rise from the dead. ¹⁰ Then the disciples returned to their homes.

JESUS APPEARS TO MARY MAGDALENE

¹¹ But Mary stood weeping outside the tomb. As she wept, she bent over to look into the tomb; ¹² and she saw two angels in white, sitting where

---

The Greatest Grave Robber

John 20:1–9 | Bishop Barron

St. John's narrative of the Resurrection opens on the morning of the first day of the week. It is still dark—just the way it was at the beginning of time before God said, "Let there be light" (Gen. 1:3). But a light is about to shine, and a new creation is about to appear.

The stone had been rolled away. That stone, blocking entrance to the tomb of Jesus, stands for the finality of death. When someone we love dies, it is as though a great stone is rolled across them, permanently blocking our access to them. And this is why we weep at death—not just in grief but in a kind of existential frustration.

But the stone had been rolled away. Undoubtedly, Mary Magdalene thought that a grave robber had been at work. The wonderful Johannine irony is that the greatest of grave robbers had indeed been at work. The Lord said to the prophet Ezekiel, "I am going to open your graves, and bring you up from your graves" (Ezek. 37:12). What was dreamed about, what endured as a hope against hope, has become a reality. God has opened the grave of his Son.

St. John Chrysostom
(349–407)

Homilies on the Gospel of John

Why the Disciples Believed

John 20:4–8

If any persons had removed the body of Jesus, would they have stripped it before doing so? Or if anyone had stolen it, would they have taken the trouble to remove the cloth, and roll it up, and lay it in a place by itself? They would have taken the body as it was.

On this account John tells us, by anticipation, that the body of Jesus was buried with much myrrh, which glues linen to the body even more firmly than lead. So when you hear that the linen wrappings lay apart, you may not endure those who say that the body of Jesus was stolen.

For a thief would not have been so foolish as to spend so much trouble on a superfluous matter. Why should he undo the clothes? And how could he have escaped detection if he had done so? He would probably have spent much time in so doing, and be found out by delaying and loitering.

But why do the clothes lie apart, while the cloth was folded together by itself? That you may learn that it was not the action of men in confusion or haste, the placing some in one place, some in another, and then wrapping them together.

From this the disciples believed in the Resurrection. On this account Christ afterwards appeared to them, when they were convinced by what they had seen.

the body of Jesus had been lying, one at the head and the other at the feet. ¹³ They said to her, "Woman, why are you weeping?" She said to them, "They have taken away my Lord, and I do not know where they have laid him." ¹⁴ When she had said this, she turned around and saw Jesus standing there, but she did not know that it was Jesus. ¹⁵ Jesus said to her, "Woman, why are you weeping? Whom are you looking for?" Supposing him to be the gardener, she said to him, "Sir, if you have carried him away, tell me where you have laid him, and I will take him away." ¹⁶ Jesus said to her, "Mary!" She turned and said to him in Hebrew, "Rabbouni!" (which means Teacher). ¹⁷ Jesus said to her, "Do not hold on to me, because I have not yet ascended

Fulton Sheen
(1895–1979)

———

Life of Christ

Jesus and Mary Magdalene

John 20:15–17

Poor Magdalen! Worn from Good Friday, wearied by Holy Saturday, with life dwindled to a shadow and strength weakened to a thread, she would "take him away." Three times did she speak of "him" without defining his name. The force of love was such as to suppose no one else could possibly be meant.

Jesus said to her: "Mary!"

That voice was more startling than a clap of thunder. She had once heard Jesus say that he called his sheep by name. And now to that One, who individualized all the sin, sorrow, and tears in the world and marked each soul with a personal, particular, and discriminating love, she turned, seeing the red livid marks on his hands and feet, she uttered but one word: "Rabbouni!" (which is Hebrew for "Teacher").

Christ had uttered "Mary" and all heaven was in it. It was only one word Mary uttered, and all earth was in it. After the mental midnight, there was this dazzle; after hours of hopelessness, this hope; after the search, this discovery; after the loss, this find. Magdalen was prepared only to shed reverential tears over the grave; what she was not prepared for was to see him walking on the wings of the morning.

Only purity and sinlessness could welcome the all holy Son of God into the world; hence, Mary Immaculate met him at the door of earth in the city of Bethlehem. But only a repentant sinner, who had herself risen from the grave of sin to the newness of life in God, could fittingly understand the triumph over sin. To the honor of womanhood it must forever be said: A woman was closest to the cross on Good Friday, and first at the tomb on Easter Morn.

to the Father. But go to my brothers and say to them, 'I am ascending to my Father and your Father, to my God and your God.'" [18] Mary Magdalene went and announced to the disciples, "I have seen the Lord"; and she told them that he had said these things to her.

JESUS APPEARS TO THE DISCIPLES

[19] When it was evening on that day, the first day of the week, and the doors of the house where the disciples had met were locked for fear of the Jews, Jesus came and stood among them and said, "Peace be with you." [20] After he said this, he showed them his hands and his side. Then the disciples rejoiced when they saw the Lord. [21] Jesus said to them again, "Peace be with you. As the Father has sent me, so I send you." [22] When he had said this, he breathed on them and said to them, "Receive the Holy Spirit. [23] If you forgive the sins of any, they are forgiven them; if you retain the sins of any, they are retained."

JESUS AND THOMAS

[24] But Thomas (who was called the Twin), one of the twelve, was not with them when Jesus came. [25] So the other disciples told him, "We have seen the Lord." But he said to them, "Unless I see the mark of the nails in his hands, and put my finger in the mark of the nails and my hand in his side, I will not believe."

The Grant of Divine Forgiveness
John 20:19–23 | Bishop Barron

There is no greater manifestation of the divine mercy than the forgiveness of sins. Jesus' disciples were waiting in the upper room, the followers who had denied, betrayed, and abandoned their master, when Jesus came and stood in their midst. When they saw him, their fear must have intensified: undoubtedly he was back for revenge.

Instead, he spoke a simple word: "Shalom" (Peace be with you). He showed them his hands and his side, lest they forget what the world (and they) did to him, but he does not follow up with blame or retribution—only a word of mercy.

And then the extraordinary commission: "Receive the Holy Spirit. If you forgive the sins of any, they are forgiven them; if you retain the sins of any, they are retained." Jesus' mercy is communicated to his disciples, who in turn are sent to communicate it to the world.

This is the foundation for the sacrament of Penance, or Confession, which has existed in the Church from that moment to the present day as the privileged vehicle of the divine mercy.

---

²⁶ A week later his disciples were again in the house, and Thomas was with them. Although the doors were shut, Jesus came and stood among them and said, "Peace be with you." ²⁷ Then he said to Thomas, "Put your finger here and see my hands. Reach out your hand and put it in my side. Do not doubt but believe." ²⁸ Thomas answered him, "My Lord and my God!" ²⁹ Jesus said to him, "Have you believed because you have seen me? Blessed are those who have not seen and yet have come to believe."

THE PURPOSE OF THIS BOOK

³⁰ Now Jesus did many other signs in the presence of his disciples, which are not written in this book. ³¹ But these are written so that you may come to believe that Jesus is the Messiah, the Son of God, and that through believing you may have life in his name.

JESUS APPEARS TO SEVEN DISCIPLES

21 After these things Jesus showed himself again to the disciples by the Sea of Tiberias; and he showed himself in this way. ² Gathered there together were Simon Peter, Thomas called the Twin, Nathanael of Cana in Galilee, the sons of Zebedee, and two others of his disciples. ³ Simon Peter said to them, "I am going fishing." They said to him, "We will go with you." They went out and got into the boat, but that night they caught nothing.

St. Gregory the Great
(540–604)

Homilies on the Gospel of John

Why Jesus Was on the Shore
John 21:4

We may ask why, after Jesus' Resurrection, he stood on the shore to receive the disciples, whereas before he walked on the sea. The sea signifies the world, which is tossed about with various causes of tumults, and the waves of this corruptible life; the shore, by its solidity, symbolizes rest.

The disciples then, inasmuch as they were still upon the waves of this mortal life, were laboring on the sea; but the Redeemer, having by his Resurrection thrown off the corruption of the flesh, stood upon the shore.

Why Did Jesus Appear Only to a Few?
John 21:1–19 | Bishop Barron

The risen Jesus appeared to seven disciples on the shore of the Sea of Tiberias. The eminently surprising and unexpected fact that Jesus rose bodily from the dead gives birth to Christianity, and to the excitement you can sense on every page of the New Testament.

But why did the risen Jesus appear only to a few? Why didn't he make himself readily apparent to anyone who wanted to see? John Henry Newman theorized that if Jesus had appeared publicly and indiscriminately to all, the lasting power of the Resurrection would have been lessened. Some would believe; others wouldn't. Some would get it; others wouldn't. Some would be fascinated, others indifferent. And that would be it.

Instead, Jesus deigned to appear to a small coterie of dedicated disciples who knew him, loved him, and understood him—confident that they would be the effective bearers of his message to the rest of the world.

⁴ Just after daybreak, Jesus stood on the beach; but the disciples did not know that it was Jesus. ⁵ Jesus said to them, "Children, you have no fish, have you?" They answered him, "No." ⁶ He said to them, "Cast the net to the right side of the boat, and you will find some." So they cast it, and now they were not able to haul it in because there were so many fish. ⁷ That disciple whom Jesus loved said to Peter, "It is the Lord!" When Simon Peter heard that it was the Lord, he put on some clothes, for he was naked, and jumped into the sea. ⁸ But the other disciples came in the boat, dragging the net full of fish, for they were not far from the land, only about a hundred yards off.

⁹ When they had gone ashore, they saw a charcoal fire there, with fish on it, and bread. ¹⁰ Jesus said to them, "Bring some of the fish that you have just caught." ¹¹ So Simon Peter went aboard and hauled the net ashore, full of large fish, a hundred fifty-three of them; and though there were so many, the net was not torn. ¹² Jesus said to them, "Come and have breakfast." Now none of the disciples dared to ask him, "Who are you?" because they knew it was the Lord. ¹³ Jesus came and took the bread and gave it to them, and did the same with the fish. ¹⁴ This was now the third time that Jesus appeared to the disciples after he was raised from the dead.

Tests of Discipleship

John 21:15–19 | Bishop Barron

Peter knows his sin—he betrayed Jesus three times. But Jesus brings him through the process of repentance and gives him the key to transformation. Three times Peter denied the Lord, and so three times Jesus asks him to reaffirm his faith: "Simon son of John, do you love me?"

Notice that Christianity is not a set of ideas or convictions or principles. It is a relationship with a person. Do you love Jesus? Has he become your friend?

When Simon says yes, Jesus tests him: "Feed my lambs. . . . Tend my sheep. . . . Feed my sheep." The test of love is action. Are we willing to do what Jesus did? Are we willing to go on mission on his behalf?

Then we hear that wonderful closing section: "When you were younger, you used to fasten your own belt and to go wherever you wished. But when you grow old, you will stretch out your hands, and someone else will fasten a belt around you and take you where you do not wish to go." The ultimate test of discipleship is our willingness to abandon our egos and be carried by a power greater than ourselves.

The Heavenly Meal

John 21:1–14 | Bishop Barron

THROUGH CERTAIN HINTS in the Old Testament, some first-century Jews had begun to cultivate the conviction that at the end of time God would bring the righteous dead back to life and restore them to a transfigured earth. In the risen Jesus, the first Christians saw this hope being realized. In Paul's language, Christ was "the first fruits" of those who had fallen asleep—that is to say, the initial instance of the general resurrection of the dead (1 Cor. 15:20). In him, they saw the dawn of the promised restoration. And thus they began to see that the sacred banquet was not simply an expression of full-flourishing in this world, not simply about justice, peace, and nonviolence here below, but also the anticipation of an elevated, transfigured, perfected world where God's will would be completely done and his kingdom completely come.

One of the most beautiful evocations of this heavenly meal is found in the beginning of this chapter of John's Gospel. The author of John's Gospel was a literary genius, and his work is marked by subtle and intricate symbolism. Therefore, we must proceed carefully as we examine this story. He tells us that the risen Christ appeared to his disciples by the Sea of Tiberias in Galilee. Throughout the Gospels, beautiful Galilee, Jesus' home country, is symbolic of the land of resurrection and new life. After the Paschal events in Jerusalem, the disciples of Jesus had returned there and taken up, it appears, their old livelihood, for John tells us that seven of them, under the leadership of Peter, were in a boat heading out to fish. But we must attend to the mystical depth of the narrative. When he appeared to them after his Resurrection, Jesus, according to John, breathed on these disciples and said, "Receive the Holy Spirit" (John 20:22) and "As the Father has sent me, so I send you" (John 20:21). Therefore, we should appreciate this fishing expedition as a symbol of the Church (the barque of Peter), across space and time, at its apostolic task of seeking souls.

At the break of dawn, they spied a mysterious figure on the distant shore, who shouted out to them, "Children, you have no fish, have you?" When they answered in the negative, he instructed them to cast the net over the right side of the ship. When they did so, they brought in a huge catch of fish. The life and work of the Church, John seems to be telling us, will be a lengthy, twilight struggle, a hard toil that will often seem to bear little or no fruit. But after the long night, the dawn of a new life and a new order will break, the transfigured world inaugurated by Jesus. The catch of fish that he makes possible is the totality of people that Christ will gather to himself; it is the new Israel, the eschatological Church. We know this through a subtle bit of symbolism. When the fish are dragged ashore, John bothers to tell us their exact number, 153, a figure commonly taken in the ancient world to signify the total number of species of fish in the sea.

After the miraculous haul, the "disciple whom Jesus loved," traditionally identified as the author of the Gospel, shouted, "It is the Lord!" St. John, the one who rested on the breast of the Lord at the Last Supper and who had the greatest intuitive feel for Jesus' intentions, represents here the mystical dimension of the Church. Up and down the centuries, there have been poets, preachers, teachers, liturgists, mystics, and saints who have an instinct for who Jesus is and what he desires. They are the ones who, typically, see the working of the Lord first, who recognize his purposes even before the leadership of the Church does. John's cry in this story anticipates their intuitions and discoveries. What the mystics and poets are ultimately sensing is the eschatological purpose of the Church, the shore toward which the barque of the Church is sailing.

When Peter hears that it is the Lord, he throws on clothes. What seems like an incidental detail is symbolically rich. After their sin, Eve and Adam made clothes for themselves, for they were ashamed. So Peter, who had three times denied Jesus, felt similarly ashamed to appear naked before the Lord. He therefore represents, in this symbolic narrative, all those sinners across the centuries who will, in their shame and penitence, seek forgiveness from Christ.

As the disciples come ashore, they see that Jesus is doing something altogether in character: he is hosting a meal for them. "They saw a charcoal fire there, with fish on it, and bread. . . . Jesus said to them,

'Come and have breakfast.'" Symbolically, they have arrived at the end of time and the end of their earthly mission, and they are, at the dawn of a new age, ushered into the definitive banquet of which the meals from Eden through the Last Supper were but anticipations. Disciples, mystics, saints, and forgiven sinners are welcome at this breakfast inaugurating the new and elevated manner of being that God had wanted to give us from the time of the Garden of Eden.

JESUS AND PETER

¹⁵ When they had finished breakfast, Jesus said to Simon Peter, "Simon son of John, do you love me more than these?" He said to him, "Yes, Lord; you know that I love you." Jesus said to him, "Feed my lambs." ¹⁶ A second time he said to him, "Simon son of John, do you love me?" He said to him, "Yes, Lord; you know that I love you." Jesus said to him, "Tend my sheep." ¹⁷ He said to him the third time, "Simon son of John, do you love me?" Peter felt hurt because he said to him the third time, "Do you love me?" And he said to him, "Lord, you know everything; you know that I love you." Jesus said to him, "Feed my sheep. ¹⁸ Very truly, I tell you, when you were younger, you used to fasten your own belt and to go wherever you wished. But when you grow old, you will stretch out your hands, and someone else will fasten a belt around you and take you where you do not wish to go." ¹⁹ (He said this to indicate the kind of death by which he would glorify God.) After this he said to him, "Follow me."

JESUS AND THE BELOVED DISCIPLE

²⁰ Peter turned and saw the disciple whom Jesus loved following them; he was the one who had reclined next to Jesus at the supper and had said, "Lord, who is it that is going to betray you?" ²¹ When Peter saw him, he said to Jesus, "Lord, what about him?" ²² Jesus said to him, "If it is my will that he remain until I come, what is that to you? Follow me!" ²³ So the rumor spread in the community that this disciple would not die. Yet Jesus did not say to him that he would not die, but, "If it is my will that he remain until I come, what is that to you?"

²⁴ This is the disciple who is testifying to these things and has written them, and we know that his testimony is true. ²⁵ But there are also many other things that Jesus did; if every one of them were written down, I suppose that the world itself could not contain the books that would be written.

St. Thomas Aquinas
(1225–1274)

———

Commentary on the Gospel of John

The World Itself Could Not Contain Enough Books

John 21:25

Now the words and deeds of Christ are also those of God. Thus, if one tried to write and tell of the nature of every one, he could not do so; indeed, the entire world could not do this. This is because even an infinite number of human words cannot equal one word of God.

From the beginning of the Church, Christ has been written about; but this is still not equal to the subject. Indeed, even if the world lasted a hundred thousand years, and books were written about Christ throughout that whole time, his words and deeds could not be completely revealed.

BUT THERE
ARE ALSO MANY
OTHER THINGS
THAT JESUS DID;
IF EVERY ONE
OF THEM WERE
WRITTEN DOWN,

THE WORLD
ITSELF COULD
NOT CONTAIN
THE BOOKS
THAT WOULD
BE WRITTEN.

JOHN 21:25

John 21:18–19

CARAVAGGIO | *1601*

The Crucifixion of Saint Peter

Essay by Michael Stevens

In the twenty-first chapter of John, we read of a moving exchange between Christ and Peter. After Jesus' Resurrection, Peter is asked three times by Christ if he loves him. He responds "Yes, Lord; you know that I love you" each time. Jesus in turn instructs Peter: "Feed my lambs," and later, "Tend my sheep." After their conversation, Jesus prophesies that Peter will die a martyr's death. In this piece by Caravaggio, we see this moment playing out, according to the words of Christ in John 21:18:

> *"Very truly, I tell you, when you were younger, you used to fasten your own belt and to go wherever you wished. But when you grow old, you will stretch out your hands, and someone else will fasten a belt around you and take you where you do not wish to go."*

As Jesus converses with Peter, Jesus asks him three times if he loves him. In this moment, Jesus is granting Peter forgiveness for each of his three denials. After this moment of reconciliation, Christ immediately commissions Peter to serve the Church, calling him to feed his lambs. Peter, the man who denied Jesus for fear of death, now embraces death rather than renounce his Lord.

The feet of foreground figure

Caravaggio was known for his unvarnished realism, and nowhere is this clearer than in details such as the dirty feet of Peter's crucifier. While these lifelike touches give Caravaggio's painting its visceral power, they were considered irreverent by some of the artist's critics—unworthy of sacred art.

Motion and energy

Art of the Baroque era was known for its sense of movement and instability. This stylistic tendency is exemplified by Caravaggio's use of precariously positioned diagonal lines, as well as the sense of strain with which the figures push against the immense weight of the cross.

All Bishop Barron commentary entries not listed below are excerpted from his unpublished homily texts.

Matthew

1:23 - Why Jesus and Not Emmanuel?
John Chrysostom, *Homilies on Matthew*, 5.3, New Advent, http://www.newadvent.org/fathers/2001.htm.

1:18–25 - God, the Cave-Man
G.K. Chesterton, *The Everlasting Man* (San Francisco: Ignatius Press, [1925] 1993), 169.

2:11 - The Three Gifts
Thomas Aquinas, *Commentary on the Gospel of St. Matthew*, trans. Paul M. Kimball (Camillus, NY: Dolorosa Press, [1270] 2012), 72.

3:13–17 - One with Sinners
Fulton J. Sheen, *Life of Christ* (Park Ridge, IL: Word on Fire, [1958] 2018), 54.

4:3–10 - The Strategy of Jesus
Robert Barron, *Eucharist* (Maryknoll, NY: Orbis Books, 2018), 81–82.

5:1–48 - Unpacking Jesus' Greatest Sermon
Robert Barron, "The Greatest Sermon Ever Preached," episode #025 from "Word on Fire Show" podcast, May 31, 2016, https://wordonfireshow.com/episode25/.

6:9 - Our Father, Not My Father
John Chrysostom, *Homilies on Matthew*, 19.6, New Advent, http://www.newadvent.org/fathers/2001.htm.

6:33 - Surrender First
Robert Barron, *Seeds of the Word: Finding God in the Culture* (Skokie, IL: Word on Fire, 2015), 147.

7:1–5 - Enlarging Your Soul
Robert Barron, *And Now I See: A Theology of Transformation* (New York: Crossroad, 1997), 214.

7:28 - They Were Astounded at His Teaching
John Chrysostom, *Homilies on Matthew*, 25.1, New Advent, http://www.newadvent.org/fathers/2001.htm.

8:1–4 - Why Does Jesus Touch the Leper?
Thomas Aquinas, *Commentary on Saint Matthew's Gospel*, trans. Paul M. Kimball (Camillus, NY: Dolorosa Press, [1270] 2012), 316–317.

9:9–13 - The Calling of Matthew
Robert Barron, *Word on Fire: Proclaiming the Power of Christ* (New York: Crossroad, 2008), 127–133.

10:34–39 - The Sword That Separates
G.K. Chesterton, *Orthodoxy* (Park Ridge, IL: Word on Fire, [1908] 2017), 133–134.

11:12 - Pushing Hard Against the Age
Flannery O'Connor, *The Habit of Being: Letters of Flannery O'Connor* (New York: Farrar, Straus and Giroux, 1979), 229.

11:12 - The Violent Bear It Away
Robert Barron, *The Strangest Way: Walking the Christian Path* (Maryknoll, NY: Orbis Books, 2002), 127–133.

11:28 - And I Will Give You Rest
John Chrysostom, *Homilies on Matthew*, 38.3, New Advent, http://www.newadvent.org/fathers/2001.htm.

12:30 - Whoever Is Not with Me Is Against Me
Robert Barron, *2 Samuel: Brazos Theological Commentary on the Bible* (Grand Rapids, MI: Brazos Press, 2015), 145.

13:44–46 - The Pearl of Great Price
Robert Barron, *The Strangest Way: Walking the Christian Path* (Maryknoll, NY: Orbis Books, 2002), 119.

14:23 - The Mother of Quiet
John Chrysostom, *Homilies on Matthew*, 50.1, New Advent, http://www.newadvent.org/fathers/2001.htm.

14:30–31 - Why Did Peter Sink?
Fulton J. Sheen, *Life of Christ* (Park Ridge, IL: Word on Fire, [1958] 2018), 161–162.

15:7–8 - Why Sincerity Is Critical to Prayer
Thomas Merton, *No Man Is an Island* (New York: Houghton Mifflin Harcourt, 1955), 204–205.

16:13–18 - Who Do You Say That I Am?
Robert Barron, *Catholicism: A Journey to the Heart of the Faith* (New York: Image, 2011), 120–122.

16:18 - Why the Church Is Indestructible
G.K. Chesterton, *Heretics*, from *The Collected Works of G.K. Chesterton, Vol. 1* (San Francisco: Ignatius Press, [1905] 1986), 37.

16:18–19 - On This Rock I Will Build My Church
Cyprian of Carthage, *Treatises*, 1.4, New Advent, http://www.newadvent.org/fathers/0507.htm.

17:1–8 - The Strange Light
Robert Barron, *Word on Fire: Proclaiming the Power of Christ* (New York: Crossroad, 2008), 76–81.

17:24–27 - Why Did Jesus Pay the Temple Tax?
Fulton J. Sheen, *Life of Christ* (Park Ridge, IL: Word on Fire, [1958] 2018), 254–255.

18:15–17 - The Right Way to Correct Someone
Robert Barron, *The Strangest Way: Walking the Christian Path* (Maryknoll, NY: Orbis Books, 2002), 108–109.

19:16–30 - Finding True Freedom
Robert Barron, *The Strangest Way: Walking the Christian Path* (Maryknoll, NY: Orbis Books, 2002), 108–109.

20:29–34 - Two Blind Men
John Chrysostom, *Homilies on Matthew*, 66.1, New Advent, http://www.newadvent.org/fathers/2001.htm.

21:5 - Riding on a Donkey
Fulton J. Sheen, *Life of Christ* (Park Ridge, IL: Word on Fire, [1958] 2018), 331–332.

22:32 - The God of Abraham, Isaac, and Jacob
Thomas Merton, *No Man Is an Island* (New York: Houghton Mifflin Harcourt, 1955), 233–234.

23:26 - Clean the Inside of Your Cup
Cyril of Jerusalem, *Catechetical Lectures*, 1, New Advent, http://www.newadvent.org/fathers/3101.htm.

24:34 - This Generation?
John Chrysostom, *Homilies on Matthew*, 77.1, New Advent, http://www.newadvent.org/fathers/2001.htm.

25:6 - Here Is the Bridegroom
Thomas Merton, *No Man Is an Island* (New York: Houghton Mifflin Harcourt, 1955), 254–255.

25:31–46 - You Did It to Me
Robert Barron, *Catholicism: A Journey to the Heart of the Faith* (New York: Image, 2011), 55–60.

26:26–28 - The Words with Power
Robert Barron, *Eucharist* (Maryknoll, NY: Orbis Books, 2018), 130.

26:50–51 - Cutting Off the Ear
Hilary of Poitiers, *On Matthew*, 32.2.20, quoted in Manlio Simonetti, ed., *Ancient Christian Commentary on Scripture: Matthew 14–28* (Downers Grove, IL: InterVarsity Press, 2002), 261.

27:46 - My God, My God, Why Have You Forsaken Me?
John Chrysostom, *Homilies on Matthew*, 88, New Advent, http://www.newadvent.org/fathers/2001.htm.

27:32–66 - Burying the Old Cultures, Rising of the New
G.K. Chesterton, *The Everlasting Man* (San Francisco: Ignatius Press, [1925] 1993), 212.

28:8–10 - Undoing Eve's Curse
Jerome, *Commentary on Matthew*, 4.28.8–9, quoted in Manlio Simonetti, ed., *Ancient Christian Commentary on Scripture: Matthew 14–28* (Downers Grove, IL: InterVarsity Press, 2002), 309.

28:11–15 - Bribery of the Guards
Fulton J. Sheen, *Life of Christ* (Park Ridge, IL: Word on Fire, [1958] 2018), 529–530.

28:19–20 - Walking the Way of Holiness
Robert Barron, *The Strangest Way: Walking the Christian Path* (Maryknoll, NY: Orbis Books, 2002), 114.

Mark

1:1 - Fighting Words
Robert Barron, *Catholicism: A Journey to the Heart of the Faith* (New York: Image, 2011), 34–35.

1:9–13 - The Paradoxes of Christ
Gregory of Nazianzus, *Orations*, 29, New Advent, http://www.newadvent.org/fathers/3102.htm.

1:14–15 - A New Way of Seeing
Robert Barron, *And Now I See: A Theology of Transformation* (New York: Crossroad, 1997), 1–7.

2:5–7 - Why Jesus Could Forgive Sin
Irenaeus, *Against Heresies*, 5.17, New Advent, http://www.newadvent.org/fathers/0103.htm.

2:7 - How Do We Truly Forgive?
Robert Barron, *The Strangest Way: Walking the Christian Path* (Maryknoll, NY: Orbis Books, 2002), 109.

3:13 - He Called Those Whom He Wanted
Robert Barron, *The Priority of Christ: Toward a Postliberal Catholicism* (Grand Rapids, MI: Brazos Press, 2007), 300.

3:13 - You Cannot Make Yourself a Disciple
Joseph Ratzinger, *Jesus of Nazareth: From the Baptism to the Transfiguration* (New York: Doubleday, 2007), 170.

3:31 - Brothers of Christ?
Augustine, *Tractates on the Gospel of John*, 10.2, New Advent, http://www.newadvent.org/fathers/1701.htm.

4:35–41 - Seeing at a Deeper Level
Robert Barron, *And Now I See: A Theology of Transformation* (New York: Crossroad, 1997), 7.

5:1–20 - Restoring the Scapegoat
Robert Barron, *And Now I See: A Theology of Transformation* (New York: Crossroad, 1997), 211–214.

6:3 - You Are My Son
Justin Martyr, *Dialogue with Trypho*, 79, New Advent, http://www.newadvent.org/fathers/0128.htm.

6:6–13 - Battling the Devil
Robert Barron, *Vibrant Paradoxes: The Both/And of Catholicism* (Skokie, IL: Word on Fire, 2016), 11.

6:30–44 - The New Moses
Fulton J. Sheen, *Life of Christ* (Park Ridge, IL: Word on Fire, [1958] 2018), 159.

7:1–23 - From Ritual to Encounter
Joseph Ratzinger, *Jesus of Nazareth: Holy Week: From the Entrance into Jerusalem to the Resurrection* (San Francisco: Ignatius Press, 2011), 57–60.

7:31–37 - Be Opened
Robert Barron, *Word on Fire: Proclaiming the Power of Christ* (New York: Crossroad, 2008), 216–221.

8:22–26 - Healing the Blind
Robert Barron, *And Now I See: A Theology of Transformation* (New York: Crossroad, 1997), 214–216.

8:22–26 - A Place Apart
Hans Urs von Balthasar, *Explorations in Theology, Vol. IV: Spirit and Institution* (San Francisco: Ignatius Press, [1974] 1995), 250–251.

9:3 - White as Snow
Augustine, *Sermons on Selected Lessons of the New Testament*, 28, New Advent, http://www.newadvent.org/fathers/1603.htm.

9:2–8 - The Dazzling and Terrifying Light
Robert Barron, *The Priority of Christ: Toward a Postliberal Catholicism* (Grand Rapids, MI: Brazos Press, 2007), 62–63.

9:22–24 - Rise to Faith
Hans Urs von Balthasar, *Explorations in Theology, Vol. IV: Spirit and Institution* (San Francisco: Ignatius Press, [1974] 1995), 252–253.

10:6–8 - Becoming One Flesh
Robert Barron, *Seeds of the Word: Finding God in the Culture* (Skokie, IL: Word on Fire, 2015), 246–247.

10:32 - Amazed and Afraid
Robert Barron, *Catholicism: A Journey to the Heart of the Faith* (New York: Image, 2011), 80.

10:46–52 - Let Me See Again
Robert Barron, *And Now I See: A Theology of Transformation* (New York: Crossroad, 1997), 9–10.

11:1 - The New Temple
Robert Barron, *Vibrant Paradoxes: The Both/And of Catholicism* (Skokie, IL: Word on Fire, 2016), 40.

12:34 - You Are Not Far from the Kingdom
John Henry Newman, *Parochial and Plain Sermons* (San Francisco: Ignatius Press, [1891] 1997), 1682.

13:13 - The End
Hilary of Poitiers, *On the Trinity*, 11.28, New Advent, http://www.newadvent.org/fathers/3302.htm.

13:33 - Watch and Pray
John Henry Newman, *Parochial and Plain Sermons* (San Francisco: Ignatius Press, [1891] 1997), 938.

14:22–25 - Not Readers, But Actors
Fulton J. Sheen, *Life of Christ* (Park Ridge, IL: Word on Fire, [1958] 2018), 355–357.

14:24 - Being For One Another
Joseph Ratzinger, *Introduction to Christianity*, 2nd edition (San Francisco: Ignatius Press, 2004), 251–252.

14:3–52 - Odd Details in the Passion Account
Robert Barron, *Word on Fire: Proclaiming the Power of Christ* (New York: Crossroad, 2008), 58–63.

14:61–15:20 - Are You the King?
Robert Barron, *2 Samuel: Brazos Theological Commentary on the Bible* (Grand Rapids, MI: Brazos Press, 2015), 81.

15:15 - The Judge on the Cross
Augustine, *Tractates on the Gospel of John*, 31.11, New Advent, http://www.newadvent.org/fathers/1701.htm.

15:39 - The One Voice Not Silenced
Robert Barron, *And Now I See: A Theology of Transformation* (New York: Crossroad, 1997), 260–261.

15:34 - When God Seemed to Be an Atheist
G.K. Chesterton, *Orthodoxy* (Park Ridge, IL: Word on Fire, [1908] 2017), 139–140.

16:1–8 - What Does the Resurrection Mean?
Robert Barron, *Word on Fire: Proclaiming the Power of Christ* (New York: Crossroad, 2008), 51–57.

Luke

1:26–38 - Mary Undoing Eve
Irenaeus, *Against Heresies*, 5.19, New Advent, http://www.newadvent.org/fathers/0103.htm.

1:36–38 - Heaven Holding Its Breath
Joseph Ratzinger, *Jesus of Nazareth: The Infancy Narratives* (New York: Image Books, 2012), 36–37.

1:46–56 - My Soul Magnifies the Lord
Robert Barron, *Catholicism: A Journey to the Heart of the Faith* (New York: Image, 2011), 113–115.

1:5–45 - Mary and the New David
Robert Barron, *2 Samuel: Brazos Theological Commentary on the Bible* (Grand Rapids, MI: Brazos Press, 2015), 65–66, 77–78.

2:7 - The House of Christmas
G.K. Chesterton, *The Collected Poems of G.K. Chesterton* (New York: Dodd, Mead, and Company, [1911] 1932), 129–130.

2:7 - No Place for Them in the Inn
Joseph Ratzinger, *Jesus of Nazareth: The Infancy Narratives* (New York: Image Books, 2012), 168–169.

2:1–14 - Jesus vs. Caesar
Robert Barron, *The Priority of Christ: Toward a Postliberal Catholicism* (Grand Rapids, MI: Brazos Press, 2007), 91–95.

3:10–17 - The Play Between Nature and Grace
Robert Barron, "Grace, Nature, and What Advent Is Finally About," Word on Fire, December 22, 2015, https://www.wordonfire.org/resources/article/grace-nature-and-what-advent-is-finally-about/5023.

4:5–8 - God, Power, and Politics
Robert Barron, *Seeds of the Word: Finding God in the Culture* (Skokie, IL: Word on Fire, 2015), 140–141.

4:16–21 - The Prophecy Fulfilled
Fulton J. Sheen, *Life of Christ* (Park Ridge, IL: Word on Fire, [1958] 2018), 259–260.

5:1–11 - Jesus Getting Into Your Boat
Robert Barron, *The Priority of Christ: Toward a Postliberal Catholicism* (Grand Rapids, MI: Brazos Press, 2007), 274–275.

5:8 - Sinners Who Know It
Robert Barron, *The Strangest Way: Walking the Christian Path* (Maryknoll, NY: Orbis Books, 2002), 67–68.

6:24 - The Danger of Riches
John Henry Newman, *Parochial and Plain Sermons* (San Francisco: Ignatius Press, [1891] 1997), 447.

6:20–26 - The Freedom of Detachment
Robert Barron, *The Strangest Way: Walking the Christian Path* (Maryknoll, NY: Orbis Books, 2002), 51–53.

7:36–50 - The Symbol of the Woman
Gregory the Great, *Homilies on the Gospels*, 2.33.5, quoted in Hans Urs von Balthasar, *Explorations in Theology, Vol. II: Spouse of the Word* (San Francisco: Ignatius Press, [1961] 1991), 225.

7:36–50 - The Pharisee and the Sinful Woman
Robert Barron, *And Now I See: A Theology of Transformation* (New York: Crossroad, 1997), 217–221.

8:26–39 - The Demons and the Pigs
Fulton J. Sheen, *Life of Christ* (Park Ridge, IL: Word on Fire, [1958] 2018), 291–292.

8:45–46 - Touching Jesus with Our Hearts
Pope Francis, *Lumen Fidei*, 31, encyclical letter, Vatican website, June 29, 2013, http://www.vatican.va/content/francesco/en/encyclicals/documents/papa-francesco_20130629_enciclica-lumen-fidei.html.

8:52 - Not Dead, But Sleeping
Cyril of Alexandria, *Commentary on Luke*, 46, Tertullian.org, http://www.tertullian.org/fathers/index.htm.

9:10–17 - The Loop of Grace
Robert Barron, *Eucharist* (Maryknoll, NY: Orbis Books, 2018), 42–44.

10:25–28 - The Greatest Commandment
Robert Barron, *Word on Fire: Proclaiming the Power of Christ* (New York: Crossroad, 2008), 22–27.

10:34–35 - The Inn of the Church
John Chrysostom, quoted in Thomas Aquinas, *Catena Aurea: Commentary on the Four Gospels, Collected out of the Works of the Fathers: St. Luke* (Oxford: John Henry Parker, 1843), 375.

11:13 - The One Gift Never Refused
Thomas Merton, *No Man Is an Island* (New York: Houghton Mifflin Harcourt, 1955), 179–180.

11:27–28 - The New Community
Robert Barron, *Catholicism: A Journey to the Heart of the Faith* (New York: Image, 2011), 17.

11:27–28 - Blessed Be the Mother
Fulton J. Sheen, *Three to Get Married* (Princeton, NJ: Scepter, [1951] 1996), 163–164.

12:13–21, 33–34 - The Truly Rich
Cyril of Alexandria, *Commentary on Luke*, 89, Tertullian.org, http://www.tertullian.org/fathers/index.htm.

12:33 - Purses That Don't Wear Out
Robert Barron, *Bridging the Great Divide: Musings of a Post-Liberal, Post-Conservative Evangelical Catholic* (Lanham, MD: Rowman & Littlefield, 2004), 118–122.

13:34 - As a Hen Gathers Her Chicks
Robert Barron, *Eucharist* (Maryknoll, NY: Orbis Books, 2018), 84.

14:28–30 - Build the Foundation of Virtue
Gregory of Nyssa, *On Virginity*, 17, New Advent, http://www.newadvent.org/fathers/2907.htm.

15:11–32 - Mercy of the Father
Pope John Paul II, *Dives in Misericordia*, 6, encyclical letter, Vatican website, November 30, 1980, http://www.vatican.va/content/john-paul-ii/en/encyclicals/documents/hf_jp-ii_enc_30111980_dives-in-misericordia.html.

15:11–32 - The Prodigal Son
Robert Barron, *The Priority of Christ: Toward a Postliberal Catholicism* (Grand Rapids, MI: Brazos Press, 2007), 76–83.

16:13 - Freed from the Shackles
Augustine, quoted in Thomas Aquinas, *Catena Aurea: Commentary on the Four Gospels, Collected out of the Works of the Fathers: St. Luke* (Oxford: John Henry Parker, 1843), 554.

17:21 - Looking for the Kingdom
G.K. Chesterton, *What I Saw in America*, from *The Collected Works of G.K. Chesterton*, Vol. 21 (San Francisco: Ignatius Press, [1922] 1990), 241–242.

18:1–8 - Unceasing Petitions
Augustine, *Our Lord's Sermon on the Mount*, 2.15, New Advent, http://www.newadvent.org/fathers/1601.htm.

18:9–14 - Yesterday a Sinner, Today a Saint
Francis de Sales, *Introduction to the Devout Life* (Dublin: M. H. Gill and Son, 1885), 185.

19:10 - To Save the Lost
Thomas Merton, *No Man Is an Island* (New York: Houghton Mifflin Harcourt, 1955), 179–180.

19:40 - The Stones Cry Out
G.K. Chesterton, *Orthodoxy* (Park Ridge, IL: Word on Fire, [1908] 2017), 101.

20:17–19 - No One Can Remain Indifferent
Fulton J. Sheen, *Life of Christ* (Park Ridge, IL: Word on Fire, [1958] 2018), 346–347.

21:19 - By Your Endurance
Francis de Sales, *Introduction to the Devout Life* (Dublin: M. H. Gill and Son, 1885), 99.

22:14–30 - Understanding the Last Supper
Robert Barron, *Eucharist* (Maryknoll, NY: Orbis Books, 2018), 44–48, 85–88.

22:36 - He Who Has No Sword Must Buy One
G.K. Chesterton, *Orthodoxy* (Park Ridge, IL: Word on Fire, [1908] 2017), 148–149.

23:33 - Tree of Adam, Tree of Christ
Cyril of Alexandria, *Commentary on Luke*, 153, Tertullian.org, http://www.tertullian.org/fathers/index.htm.

23:34 - Not Judging Our Neighbor
Francis de Sales, *Introduction to the Devout Life* (Dublin: M. H. Gill and Son, 1885), 181.

23:34 - Drowning All the Sins of the World
Robert Barron, *Catholicism: A Journey to the Heart of the Faith* (New York: Image, 2011), 31.

23:34 - They Do Not Know What They Are Doing
René Girard, *The Scapegoat* (Baltimore, MD: Johns Hopkins University Press, [1982] 1986), 110–111.

23:44–48 - Darkness Came Over the Whole Land
Pope John Paul II, *Evangelium Vitae*, 50, encyclical letter, Vatican website, March 25, 1995, http://www.vatican.va/content/john-paul-ii/en/encyclicals/documents/hf_jp-ii_enc_25031995_evangelium-vitae.html.

24:13–35 - The Emmaus Journey
Robert Barron, *Eucharist* (Maryknoll, NY: Orbis Books, 2018), 137–141.

24:36–40 - We Killed God . . . and God Still Loves Us
Robert Barron, *And Now I See: A Theology of Transformation* (New York: Crossroad, 1997), 263–265.

24:39–43 - Not a Ghost
Robert Barron, *Vibrant Paradoxes: The Both/And of Catholicism* (Skokie, IL: Word on Fire, 2016), 152.

John

1:1–2 - He Was in the Beginning with God
John Chrysostom, *Homilies on the Gospel of John*, 2.9, New Advent, http://www.newadvent.org/fathers/2401.htm.

1:1–18 - The Word Became Flesh
Robert Barron, *Vibrant Paradoxes: The Both/And of Catholicism* (Skokie, IL: Word on Fire, 2016), 132–135.

1:36 - Look, Here Is the Lamb of God!
Robert Barron, *Eucharist* (Maryknoll, NY: Orbis Books, 2018), 78–79.

1:38 - What Are You Looking For?
Robert Barron, *Seeds of the Word: Finding God in the Culture* (Skokie, IL: Word on Fire, 2015), 40–41.

1:29–36 - Lamb . . . or Scapegoat?
René Girard, *The Scapegoat* (Baltimore, MD: Johns Hopkins University Press, [1982] 1986), 117.

2:4 - Why Jesus Called Mary "Woman"
Augustine, *Harmony of the Gospels*, 4.10.11, New Advent, http://www.newadvent.org/fathers/1602.htm.

2:1–12 - They Have No Wine
Robert Barron, *The Priority of Christ: Toward a Postliberal Catholicism* (Grand Rapids, MI: Brazos Press, 2007), 72–76.

2:13–17 - Cleansing the Temple
Robert Barron, *The Priority of Christ: Toward a Postliberal Catholicism* (Grand Rapids, MI: Brazos Press, 2007), 76.

3:16 - Diamonds from the Dirt
Robert Barron, *The Strangest Way: Walking the Christian Path* (Maryknoll, NY: Orbis Books, 2002), 31–32.

3:16 - Four Signs That God's Love Is the Greatest
Thomas Aquinas, *Commentary on the Gospel of John*, trans. Fabian R. Larcher, O.P., 477, Aquinas.Institute, https://aquinas.cc/la/on/~Ioan.

3:19 - The Great Gatherer
Robert Barron, *Exploring Catholic Theology: Essays on God, Liturgy, and Evangelization* (Grand Rapids, MI: Baker Academic, 2015), 73.

4:6 - Tired Out by His Journey
Robert Barron, *Eucharist* (Maryknoll, NY: Orbis Books, 2018), 82.

4:13–14 - The World's Broken Cisterns
Fulton J. Sheen, *Life of Christ* (Park Ridge, IL: Word on Fire, [1958] 2018), 107.

4:1–42 - The Woman at the Well
Robert Barron, *Thomas Aquinas: Spiritual Master* (New York: Crossroad, 2008), 75–76.

5:19 - The Son Can Do Nothing on His Own
Robert Barron, *The Priority of Christ: Toward a Postliberal Catholicism* (Grand Rapids, MI: Brazos Press, 2007), 114.

6:50–53 - The Medicine of Immortality
Ignatius of Antioch, *Epistle to the Ephesians*, 20, adapted from New Advent, http://www.newadvent.org/fathers/0104.htm.

6:55 - Not Common Bread
Justin Martyr, *First Apology*, 66, adapted from New Advent, http://www.newadvent.org/fathers/0126.htm.

6:55 - The Body of Christ
Gregory of Nyssa, *On the Baptism of Christ*, adapted from New Advent, http://www.newadvent.org/fathers/2910.htm.

6:48–66 - Jesus' Most Challenging Sermon
Robert Barron, *Word on Fire: Proclaiming the Power of Christ* (New York: Crossroad, 2008), 169–175.

7:27–28 - Where Is This Man From?
Joseph Ratzinger, *Introduction to Christianity*, 2nd edition (San Francisco: Ignatius Press, 2004), 271.

7:37–38 - Thirsting for God
Robert Barron, *The Priority of Christ: Toward a Postliberal Catholicism* (Grand Rapids, MI: Brazos Press, 2007), 334.

7:37–39 - Rivers of Living Water
Augustine, *Tractates on the Gospel of John*, 32.4, New Advent, http://www.newadvent.org/fathers/1701.htm.

8:1–11 - The Woman Caught in Adultery
Robert Barron, *The Priority of Christ: Toward a Postliberal Catholicism* (Grand Rapids, MI: Brazos Press, 2007), 101–103.

8:34 - The Dramatic Struggle
Gaudium et Spes, 13, Vatican website, December 7, 1965, http://www.vatican.va/archive/hist_councils/ii_vatican_council/documents/vat-ii_const_19651207_gaudium-et-spes_en.html.

8:58 - Before Abraham Was, I Am
G.K. Chesterton, *The Everlasting Man* (San Francisco: Ignatius Press, [1925] 1993), 198.

9:6–7 - Mystically Understanding the Pool
Thomas Aquinas, *Commentary on the Gospel of John*, trans. Fabian R. Larcher, O.P., 1311, Aquinas.Institute, https://aquinas.cc/la/en/~Ioan.

9:25 - Now I See
Robert Barron, *And Now I See: A Theology of Transformation* (New York: Crossroad, 1997), 1–2.

10:1–18 - The Low Gateway
Augustine, *Tractates on the Gospel of John*, 45.5, New Advent, http://www.newadvent.org/fathers/1701.htm.

11:1–44 - A Greater Deed
Augustine, *Tractates on the Gospel of John*, 49.1, New Advent, http://www.newadvent.org/fathers/1701.htm.

11:35 - Why Did Jesus Weep?
John Henry Newman, *Parochial and Plain Sermons* (San Francisco: Ignatius Press, [1891] 1997), 565–568.

12:27 - Taking on Every Assault
Cyril of Alexandria, *Commentary on John*, 8, Tertullian.org, http://www.tertullian.org/fathers/index.htm.

12:32 - I Will Draw All People to Myself
Robert Barron, *Catholicism: A Journey to the Heart of the Faith* (New York: Image, 2011), 146–147.

13:1–20 - Peter's Appalling Yes
Hans Urs von Balthasar, *Explorations in Theology, Vol. III: Creator Spirit* (San Francisco: Ignatius Press, [1967] 1993), 220–221.

14:6 - Jesus Compels a Choice
Robert Barron, *Exploring Catholic Theology: Essays on God, Liturgy, and Evangelization* (Grand Rapids, MI: Baker Academic, 2015), 190–191.

15:11 - We Must Look
Robert Barron, *The Strangest Way: Walking the Christian Path* (Maryknoll, NY: Orbis Books, 2002), 145–146.

15:15 - I Have Called You Friends
Robert Barron, *The Strangest Way: Walking the Christian Path* (Maryknoll, NY: Orbis Books, 2002), 97–98.

16:13–15 - The Unbroken Succession of Truth
Fulton J. Sheen, *Three to Get Married* (Princeton, NJ: Scepter, [1951] 1996), 62.

16:28 - Leaving and Going
Cyril of Alexandria, *Commentary on John*, 11.2, Tertullian.org, http://www.tertullian.org/fathers/index.htm.

17:1–26 - The New High Priest
Joseph Ratzinger, *Jesus of Nazareth: Holy Week: From the Entrance into Jerusalem to the Resurrection* (San Francisco: Ignatius Press, 2011), 78–79.

17:20–21 - About One Thing
Robert Barron, *Catholicism: A Journey to the Heart of the Faith* (New York: Image, 2011), 156–157.

18:1 - From Garden to Garden
Cyril of Alexandria, *Commentary on John*, 11.12, Tertullian.org, http://www.tertullian.org/fathers/index.htm.

18:33–38 - Christ the King
Robert Barron, *Word on Fire: Proclaiming the Power of Christ* (New York: Crossroad, 2008), 45–50.

18:38 - What Is Truth?
G.K. Chesterton, *The Everlasting Man* (San Francisco: Ignatius Press, [1925] 1993), 210–211.

19:9–12 - Silent as a Sheep
Augustine, *Tractates on the Gospel of John*, 116.4, New Advent, http://www.newadvent.org/fathers/1701.htm.

19:10–11 - The Higher Authority
Robert Barron, *2 Samuel: Brazos Theological Commentary on the Bible* (Grand Rapids, MI: Brazos Press, 2015), 69–70.

19:19–20 - Jesus of Nazareth, the King of the Jews
Robert Barron, *2 Samuel: Brazos Theological Commentary on the Bible* (Grand Rapids, MI: Brazos Press, 2015), 81.

19:19–22 - King of the Whole World
Theophylact, quoted in Thomas Aquinas, *Catena Aurea: Commentary on the Four Gospels, Collected out of the Works of the Fathers: St. John* (Oxford: John Henry Parker, 1843), 579.

20:4–8 - Why the Disciples Believed
John Chrysostom, *Homilies on the Gospel of John*, 85.4, New Advent, http://www.newadvent.org/fathers/2401.htm.

20:15–17 - Jesus and Mary Magdalene
Fulton J. Sheen, *Life of Christ* (Park Ridge, IL: Word on Fire, [1958] 2018), 524–525.

21:4 - Why Jesus Was on the Shore
Gregory the Great, *Homilies on the Gospel of John*, 24, quoted in Thomas Aquinas, *Catena Aurea: Commentary on the Four Gospels, Collected out of the Works of the Fathers: St. John* (Oxford: John Henry Parker, 1845), 618.

21:1–14 - The Heavenly Meal
Robert Barron, *Eucharist* (Maryknoll, NY: Orbis Books, 2018), 49–52.

21:25 - The World Itself Could Not Contain Enough Books
Thomas Aquinas, *Commentary on the Gospel of John*, trans. Fabian R. Larcher, O.P., 2660, Aquinas.Institute, https://aquinas.cc/la/en/~Ioan.